D0849589

BOOK AND VERSE

Illinois Medieval Studies

*A list of books in the series appears
at the end of this book.*

Book and Verse

A GUIDE TO MIDDLE ENGLISH
BIBLICAL LITERATURE

James H. Morey

UNIVERSITY OF ILLINOIS PRESS

Urbana and Chicago

© 2000 by the Board of Trustees of the University of Illinois
Manufactured in the United States of America
⊗ This book is printed on acid-free paper.

Library of Congress Cataloging-in-Publication Data
Morey, James H., 1961–
Book and verse : a guide to Middle English biblical literature /
James H. Morey.
p.   cm. — (Illinois medieval studies)
Includes bibliographical references (p.   ) and index.
ISBN 0-252-02507-5 (alk. paper)
1. English literature—Middle English, 1100–1500—History and
criticism.   2. Bible—Criticism, interpretation, etc.—History—
Middle Ages, 600–1500.   3. Christian literature, English
(Middle)—History and criticism.   4. Christianity and literature—
England—History—To 1500.   5. Bible—In literature.   6. Literary
form.   I. Title.   II. Series.
PR275.B5M67   1999
220′.0942′0902—dc21   99-6489
CIP

C 5 4 3 2 1

For Barbara

Quhen men sekis þe wysdome in mony bukis
It stoppis his wyt, and sal neuer fynde an ende

—Ecclesiastes 12:12, in the *Wisdom of Solomon*

Contents

ABBREVIATIONS   xiii

ACKNOWLEDGMENTS   xix

Introduction   1

1. The Medieval Idea of the Bible   9

2. The Official Reception of Biblical Literature   24

3. The Place of English in Post-Conquest England   48

4. Genre, Audience, and Self-Representation   56

CONCLUSION   85

Guide to the Main Entries   87

1 Comprehensive Old and New Testament Works   91

Fall and Passion 91	FP
Trinity Poem on Biblical History 92	TP
Versions of Robert Grosseteste's *Chateau d'Amour* 95	CA
Charter of the Abbey of the Holy Ghost 98	CHG
Cursor Mundi 99	CM
English Translations of Ranulph Higden's *Polychronicon* 107	Poly

A Middle English Summary of the Bible   110   MES

The Mirour of Mans Saluacioune   112   MMS

Middle English Translation of the *Bible* of Roger
  D'Argenteuil   118   BRA

II.A   Primarily Old Testament Works, in Approximate
       Vulgate Order   121

Versions of the *Life of Adam and Eve*   121   LAE

Canticum de Creatione   124   CC

William of Shoreham's *On the Trinity, Creation, the Existence
  of Evil, Devils, Adam and Eve, etc.*   125   TCE

Wise Admonitions: Biblical Texts Paraphrased   127   WA

Old Testament Sentences   130   OTS

Historye of the Patriarks   132   HP

Genesis and Exodus   133   GE

Old Testament History   142   OTH

A Middle English Metrical Paraphrase of the Old Testament   146   POT

Caxton's *Golden Legend*   154   CGL

Iacob and Iosep   158   JJ

The Storie of Asneth   159   SA

The Fyve Wyles of King Pharao   161   KP

The Ten Commandments   162   TC

Pety Job   168   PJ

Metrical Life of Job   170   MLJ

II.B   The Psalter   172

General Note on Medieval Psalters   172

Surtees Psalter   174   SPs

Midland Prose Psalter   175   MPPs

Richard Rolle's Psalter and Commentary   175   RPs

Penitential Psalms   177

   Richard Maidstone   177   RMPs

   Thomas Brampton   180   TBPs

Primer Version of the Psalms   182   PPs

Jerome's *Abbreviated Psalter*   186   JPs

St. Bernard's *Eight-Verse Psalter*   189   BPs

Psalms Versified by John Lydgate   189   LPs

Versions of Psalm 50 ("Miserere")   191   MPs

Commentary on Psalm 90 ("Qui habitat") and   QHPs
   on Psalm 91 ("Bonum est")   193   BEPs

Stanzaic Version of Psalm 129 ("De profundis")   194   DPPs

II.C   Canticles and Hymns   195   CH

II.D   Miscellaneous Old Testament Pieces   197

Lydgate's *Epistle to Sibille*   197   ES

Wisdom of Solomon (Ecclesiastes)   197   WS

Pistel of Swete Susan (Susanna)   198   PSS

Cleanness   199   Cl

Patience   201   Pat

III.A   Primarily New Testament Works, in Approximate
   Vulgate Order   203

Childhood of Jesus   203   CJ

Estorie del Euangelie   205   EE

A Newe Lessoun off Crystys Ressurrectoun   208   CR

Pepysian Gospel Harmony   209   PGH

A Tretys That Is a Rule and a Forme of Lyvynge   215   RFL

Versions of the *Gospel of Nicodemus*   216   GNs, GNp

*The Middle English Prose Complaint of Our Lady and
   Gospel of Nicodemus*   221   PCL

The Devil's Parlament   224   DP

*The Harrowing of Hell and the Destruction of
   Jerusalem*   226   HH, DJ

The Three Kings of Cologne   226   TK

Titus and Vespasian   228   TV

Book to a Mother   231   BM

III.B   Temporale Narratives   234

The South English Nativity of Mary and Christ   235   NMC

South English Ministry and Passion   237   MP

The Southern Passion   242   SP

Long Life of Christ   247   LLC

Conception of Marie and the *Expanded Nativity*   249   ConM, EN

The Abridged Life of Christ   252   ALC

The Metrical Life of Christ   252   MLC

Stanzaic Life of Christ   256   SLC

III.C Passion Narratives   263

Passion of Our Lord   264   PL

The Northern Passion   265   NP

Meditations on the Life and Passion of Christ   268   MLP

Versions of the Charter of Christ   270   ChC

Þe Lamentacioun þat was bytwene vre lady and
    seynt Bernard   273   LLB

Meditations on the Supper of Our Lord   276   MS

A remembraunce of the passioun of our lord Jesu Criste   279   RP

Songs of Love-Longing   280   SLL

William Dunbar's Passion of Christ   281   PC

John Lydgate's Cristes Passioun   282   CP

Scottish Passion of Christ   283   SPC

Contemplations of the Dread and Love of God   283   CDL

Liber Aureus de Passione et Resurrectione Domini   284   LA

Versions of the Hours of the Cross (anonymous)   284   HC

William of Shoreham's Hours of the Cross   286   HCS

John Audelay's Biblical Paraphrases on the Passion   287   HCA

Walter Kennedy's Passion of Christ   288   HCK

Meditations for Goostely Exercise in the Tyme of the Masse   290   MTM

III.D Miscellaneous New Testament Pieces   291

Commentary on the Benedictus   291   CB

Ballad of the Twelfth Day   292   BTD

Pearl   292   Prl

A Disputison bitwene child Jhesu & Maistres of þe lawe
    of Jewus   294   DJM

Bodley Verse Pieces from the Gospels   295   BVP

Rawlinson Strophic Pieces from the Gospels   296   RSP

Euangelium in Principio   297   EP

Joseph of Arimathea   297   JA

Versions of the Beatitudes   298   Beat

Translations of Edmund of Abingdon's
    Speculum ecclesie   300   SE

Pater Noster in English 302 PN

Parable of the Laborers in the Vineyard 305 PLV

The Seven Works of Bodily Mercy 306 SWM

The Woman of Samaria 307 WomS

Resurrection and Apparitions 308 RA

Story of the Resurrection 309 SR

The Sixteen Conditions of Charity 309 SCC

Sir John Clanvowe's *The Two Ways* 310 TW

The Quatrefoil of Love 313 QL

Selected Lives from the *South English Legendary* 314 SEL

III.E Lectionaries 319

Ormulum 320 Orm

Northern Homily Cycle 323 NHC

III.F Prose Gospel Commentaries and Lives of Christ 331

The "Commentaries" on Matthew, Mark, and Luke 332 MML

Oon of Foure (Clement of Llanthony) 333 OF

Versions of Ludolphus of Saxony's *Vita Christi* 334 VC

Nicholas Love's *Mirrour of the Blessed Life of Jesu Christ*
and Other Translations of *MVC* and *MPC* 335 MBL

III.G Epistles 344

Pauline Epistles 344 PE

Prose Version of Epistles, Acts, and Matthew 346 PCE

III.H Versions of Revelation 351

Apocalips of Jesu Crist 351 AJC

BIBLIOGRAPHY 355

INDEX OF BIBLICAL CHAPTERS 383

INDEX OF BIBLICAL PEOPLE, PLACES,
AND EVENTS 395

INDEX OF MANUSCRIPTS 413

GENERAL INDEX 419

Abbreviations

MIDDLE ENGLISH WORKS

		section
AJC	*Apocalips of Jesu Crist* (Revelation)	III.H
ALC	*Abridged Life of Christ*	III.B
Beat	Versions of the Beatitudes	III.D
BEPs	Commentary on Psalm 91, "Bonum est"	II.B
BM	*Book to a Mother*	III.A
BPs	St. Bernard's *Eight-Verse Psalter*	II.B
BRA	*Bible* of Roger D'Argenteuil	I
BTD	*Ballad of the Twelfth Day*	III.D
BVP	*Bodley Verse Pieces*	III.D
CA	*Chateau d'Amour* (Grosseteste)	I
CB	*Commentary on the Benedictus*	III.D
CC	*Canticum de Creatione*	II.A
CDL	*Contemplations of the Dread and Love of God*	III.C
CGL	Caxton's *Golden Legend*	II.A
CH	Canticles and Hymns	II.C
ChC	*Charter of Christ*	III.C
CHG	*Charter of the Abbey of the Holy Ghost*	I
CJ	*Childhood of Jesus*	III.A
Cl	*Cleanness*	II.D
CM	*Cursor Mundi*	I
ConM	*Conception of Marie*	III.B
CP	*Cristes Passioun* (Lydgate)	III.C

CR	*A Newe Lessoun off Crystys Ressurrectoun*	III.A
DJ	*Destruction of Jerusalem*	III.A
DJM	*Disputison bitwene child Jesu & Maistres of þe lawe of Jewus*	III.D
DP	*Devil's Parlament*	III.A
DPPs	"De profundis," Psalm 129	II.B
EE	*Estorie del Euangelie*	III.A
EN	*Expanded Nativity*	III.B
EP	*Euangelium in Principio*	III.D
ES	*Epistle to Sibille* (Lydgate)	II.D
FP	*Fall and Passion*	I
GE	*Genesis and Exodus*	II.A
GNp	*Gospel of Nicodemus*, prose	III.A
GNs	*Gospel of Nicodemus*, stanzaic	III.A
HC	Anonymous Hours of the Cross	III.C
HCA	John Audelay's Hours of the Cross	III.C
HCK	Walter Kennedy's Hours of the Cross	III.C
HCS	William of Shoreham's Hours of the Cross	III.C
HH	*Harrowing of Hell*	III.A
HP	*Historye of the Patriarks*	II.A
JA	*Joseph of Arimathea*	III.D
JJ	*Iacob and Iosep*	II.A
JPs	Jerome's *Abbreviated Psalter*	II.B
KP	*Fyve Wyles of King Pharao*	II.A
LA	*Liber Aureus de Passione et Resurrectione Domini*	III.C
LAE	*Life of Adam and Eve*	II.A
LLB	*Lamentacioun þat was bytwene vre lady and seynt Bernard*	III.C
LLC	*Long Life of Christ*	III.B
LPs	Psalms Versified by John Lydgate	II.B
MBL	*Mirrour of the Blessed Life of Jesu Christ* (Love)	III.F
MES	Middle English Summary of the Bible	I
MLJ	*Metrical Life of Job*	II.A
MLC	*Metrical Life of Christ*	III.B
MLP	*Meditations on the Life and Passion of Christ*	III.C
MML	Commentaries on Matthew, Mark, and Luke	III.F
MMS	*Mirour of Mans Saluacioune*	I
MP	*South English Ministry and Passion*	III.B
MPs	"Miserere," Psalm 50	II.B
MPPs	*Midland Prose Psalter*	II.B

MS	*Meditations on the Supper of Our Lord*	III.C
MTM	*Meditations for Goostely Exercise in the Tyme of the*	
	Masse	III.C
NHC	*Northern Homily Cycle*	III.E
NMC	*South English Nativity of Mary and Christ*	III.B
NP	*Northern Passion*	III.C
OF	*Oon of Foure* (trans. of Clement of Llanthony's	
	Unum ex Quattuor)	III.F
Orm	*Ormulum*	III.E
OTH	*Old Testament History*	II.A
OTS	*Old Testament Sentences*	II.A
Pat	*Patience*	II.D
PC	*Passion of Christ* (Dunbar)	III.C
PCE	Pauline and Catholic Epistles (ed. Paues)	III.G
PCL	*Middle English Prose Complaint of Our Lady*	
	and Gospel of Nicodemus	III.A
PE	Pauline Epistles (ed. Powell)	III.G
PGH	*Pepysian Gospel Harmony*	III.A
PJ	*Pety Job*	II.A
PL	*Passion of Our Lord*	III.C
PLV	Parable of the Laborers in the Vineyard	III.D
PN	Pater Noster	III.D
Poly	*Polychronicon* (Higden)	I
POT	*Middle English Metrical Paraphrase of the Old*	
	Testament	II.A
PPs	Primer Version of the Psalms	II.B
Prl	*Pearl*	III.D
PSS	*Pistel of Swete Susan* (Susannah)	II.D
QHPs	Commentary on Psalm 90, "Qui habitat"	II.B
QL	*Quatrefoil of Love*	III.D
RA	*Resurrection and Apparitions*	III.D
RFL	*A Tretys That Is a Rule and a Forme of Lyvynge*	III.A
RMPs	Richard Maidstone's Penitential Psalms	II.B
RP	*A remembraunce of the Passion of our lord Jesu Criste*	III.C
RPs	Rolle's Psalter and Commentary	II.B
RSP	*Rawlinson Strophic Pieces from the Gospels*	III.D
SA	*Storie of Asneth*	II.A
SCC	Sixteen Conditions of Charity	III.D
SE	Translations of Edmund of Abingdon's *Speculum*	
	ecclesie	III.D

SEL	Selected Lives from the *South English Legendary*	III.D
SLC	*Stanzaic Life of Christ*	III.B
SLL	*Songs of Love-Longing*	III.C
SP	*Southern Passion*	III.B
SPC	*Scottish Passion of Christ*	III.C
SPs	*Surtees Psalter*	II.B
SR	*Story of the Resurrection*	III.D
SWM	*Seven Works of Bodily Mercy*	III.D
TBPs	Thomas Brampton's Penitential Psalms	II.B
TC	Ten Commandments	II.A
TCE	William of Shoreham's *On the Trinity, Creation, the Existence of Evil, Devils, Adam and Eve, etc.*	II.A
TK	*Three Kings of Cologne*	III.A
TP	*Trinity Poem on Biblical History*	I
TV	*Titus and Vespasian*	III.A
TW	*Two Ways* (Clanvowe)	III.D
VC	trans. of Ludolphus of Saxony's *Vita Christi*	III.F
WA	*Wise Admonitions: Biblical Texts Paraphrased*	II.A
WomS	*Woman of Samaria*	III.D
WS	*Wisdom of Solomon* (Ecclesiastes)	II.D

BIBLICAL BOOKS

Gen.	Genesis	Cant.	Canticle of Canticles
Ex.	Exodus	Wis.	Wisdom
Lev.	Leviticus	Ecclus.	Ecclesiasticus
Num.	Numbers	Is.	Isaias
Deut.	Deuteronomy	Jer.	Jeremias
Jos.	Josue	Lam.	Lamentations
Judg.	Judges	Bar.	Baruch
Ruth	Ruth	Ez.	Ezechiel
1-4Kg.	1-4 Kings	Dan.	Daniel
1-2Para.	1-2 Paralipomenon	Os.	Osee
1-2Esdras	1-2 Esdras	Joel	Joel
Tob.	Tobias	Amos	Amos
Judith	Judith	Ab.	Abdias
Est.	Esther	Jonah	Jonah
Job	Job	Mich.	Micheas
Ps.	Psalms	Nahum	Nahum
Prov.	Proverbs	Hab.	Habacuc
Eccles.	Ecclesiastes	Soph.	Sophonias

Agg.	Aggeus	Phil.	Philippians
Zach.	Zacharias	Col.	Colossians
Mal.	Malachias	1-2Thess.	1-2 Thessalonians
1-2Mach.	1-2 Machabees	1-2Tim.	1-2 Timothy
Matt.	Matthew	Titus	Titus
Mark	Mark	Phlm.	Philemon
Luke	Luke	Heb.	Hebrews
John	John	James	James
Acts	Acts	1-2Pet.	1-2 Peter
Rom.	Romans	1-3John	1-3 John
1-2Cor.	1-2 Corinthians	Jude	Jude
Gal.	Galatians	Rev.	Revelation
Eph.	Ephesians		

OTHER ABBREVIATIONS

Add.	Additional
Archiv	*Archiv für das Studium der neueren Sprachen und Literaturen*
BJRL	*Bulletin of the John Rylands Library*
BL	British Library, London
BN	Bibliothèque Nationale, Paris
c.	century
CCSL	Corpus Christianorum, series Latina
CSEL	Corpus scriptorum ecclesiasticorum Latinorum
EETS es	Early English Text Society, extra series
EETS os	Early English Text Society, original series
EETS ss	Early English Text Society, supplementary series
IMEV	*Index of Middle English Verse,* Brown and Robbins (1943)
IMEV/S	*Supplement to the Index of Middle English Verse,* Robbins and Cutler (1965)
IPMEP	*Index of Printed Middle English Prose,* Lewis, Blake, and Edwards (1985)
JEGP	*Journal of English and Germanic Philology*
Lib.	Library
MÆ	*Medium Ævum*
Manual	*Manual of the Writings in Middle English: 1050–1500,* Severs and Hartung (1967–)
MLN	*Modern Language Notes*
MLR	*Modern Language Review*
MP	*Modern Philology*
MPC	*Meditationes de passione Christi,* ed. Stallings (1965)

MS   manuscript
MVC   *Meditationes Vitae Christi,* ed. Peltier (1864–71)
N&Q   *Notes & Queries*
ns   new series
PL   Patrologia Latina, Migne (1844–64)
PMLA   *Publications of the Modern Language Association*
SC   *Summary Catalogue of Western Manuscripts in the Bodleian*
              Library at Oxford, Madan et al. (1895–1953)
SCH   Studies in Church History
SEL   *South English Legendary*
SHS   *Speculum Humanae Salvationis,* ed. Lutz and Perdrizet
              (1907–9)
SP   *Studies in Philology*
STC   *A Short Title Catalogue of Books Printed in England, Scotland,*
              and Ireland and of English Books Printed Abroad 1475–1640,
              Pollard and Redgrave (1926)
Univ.   University

Acknowledgments

A BOOK OVER ten years in the making could not have been written without help from numerous institutions and individuals, especially the staffs at the following libraries: Cornell University, Texas Tech University, the University of Texas, Emory University, the Huntington Library in San Marino, California, the Bodleian Library at Oxford, and the British Library in London. The National Endowment for the Humanities and the Emory University Research Committee have supported this project through several grants and research leaves. I wish to thank in particular Emory's Graduate School, especially Associate Provost Eleanor Main, for a generous publication subvention.

Permission to reprint parts of my *Speculum* article (vol. 68, 1993) has kindly been granted by the Medieval Academy.

My Cornell committee—Thomas Hill, Winthrop Wetherbee, and Alice Colby-Hall—will recognize some, but I hope not much, of my dissertation. They, and my chairman, the late and lamented R. E. Kaske, guided me early in my career, and I thank them again now. Michael Twomey—practically a fifth committee member—has been an unfailing source of advice and bibliographical acuity.

Charles Wright of the University of Illinois at Urbana-Champaign and Patricia Hollahan of the University of Illinois Press convince me that, if there is a modern equivalent to the Doctor Universalis, the Ph.D. in Old English probably comes closest. They saved me from many errors, but a book of this type is particularly susceptible to mistakes and inconsistencies, and I take responsibility for those that remain.

Finally, I thank the dedicatee for her patience, support, and love.

BOOK AND VERSE

Introduction

THE BEGINNING of the Reformation in England is conventionally dated from the appearance of the Lollards in the late fourteenth century. Their leader, John Wyclif, at least fostered, if he did not actually make, the first complete translations of the Bible (from the Latin Vulgate) into English. The Wycliffite Bible is often cited as the cornerstone of early reform in England simply because it allowed freer access to Scripture and hence the popularization of God's Word. Church reform, increased lay spirituality, and the rise of a readership of a vernacular Bible were indeed given a major impetus by the Lollards, and when one speaks of the Bible in Middle English, the Wycliffite Bible most often is meant. Before Wyclif, and indeed even as late as the sixteenth century when the Reformation was in full force, it is widely assumed that the Bible was largely unknown to lay folk because of the relentless suppression by the Catholic church of any attempt to spread the Word in the vernacular. This assumption, however, raises the curious paradox that biblical allusions and models and large-scale appropriations of biblical narratives pervade nearly every medieval genre, intended for both lay and learned audiences, at a time when, ostensibly, the Scriptures were inaccessible. It may be no exaggeration to say that a medieval plowman, like Erasmus's plowman, knew more Bible stories than most contemporary college seniors and that allusions to biblical events and characters would resonate more meaningfully in the imagination of the former than of the latter. This book therefore has two major purposes: to explode the myth that lay people had no access to the Bible before the Reformation and to provide a guide to the variety and extent of biblical literature in England, exclusive of Wyclif, from the twelfth into the fifteenth century.

    Biblical material enjoyed popularity in the vernacular from the time of
the earliest English poetry. Cædmon, for example, is said to have "made
wonder poesyes an Englysch ny3 of al þe storyes of holy wryt."[1] Whether he
actually did or not, for centuries the English believed that he did, with no
less an authority than the Venerable Bede to credit that belief. A considerable amount of biblical material does in fact exist from Anglo-Saxon times,
and any fair characterization of Old English literature by the preponderance
of prose and verse which survives must conclude that it is overwhelmingly
sacred and religious, not secular and heroic.

    The tradition of biblical paraphrase continued after the Conquest: of
the few twelfth- and thirteenth-century Middle English manuscripts to have
survived, most have biblical contents and models. Given the impetus of
the Fourth Lateran Council in 1215, which was dedicated to reforming the
clergy and increasing lay spirituality, the thirteenth and fourteenth centuries saw a proliferation of summaries of the Creation and Fall, Gospel
harmonies, Lives of Christ, Passion narratives, paraphrases of the Epistles,
and other biblically based literature which forms the subject of this book.
In this literature are numerous passages which qualify as translation. The
Wycliffite Bible thus superseded a large corpus of biblical paraphrases and
translations which had been transmitting a sense of Scripture to the lay folk
in the centuries leading up to the activities of the Lollards. This literature
anticipated and to some degree set the stage for later reformist movements
simply because it provided a precedent for the existence of biblical material
in English and because it was directed specifically toward a lay audience.
The introductions to the paraphrases often express an egalitarian desire to
spread the Word among native English who know no other tongue, and who
are as much entitled to the saving grace of Scripture as learned clerks. The
attentive reader or listener could gain a considerable acquaintance with biblical literature, especially those parts of the Bible which, because of their
importance in the liturgy or because of their memorable and picturesque
qualities, have been identified and used by the Church as the core of sacred
history and the way to salvation. The paraphrases were a medium through
which, from the late twelfth into the fifteenth century, the Bible was promulgated in the vernacular, and this corpus, I argue, constitutes the Middle
English vernacular "Bible" in the centuries before Wyclif.

    The authors of these works, in prose and verse, often take pains to achieve
some kind of completeness and coherence: the Fall of the Angels is a necessary preliminary to the Passion of Christ, a précis of Genesis and Exodus
introduces a paraphrase of Paul's Epistles, and Pentecost, not the Resurrection or Ascension, is the endpoint of many Passion narratives.[2] Caxton, in

his translation of the *Golden Legend* (**CGL**), reversed the pattern whereby the Old Testament prefaces the New by starting with a synopsis of events from the Nativity to Pentecost, leading into an extensive treatment of the Old Testament, and finally undertaking the Lives of Saints. Several of the more comprehensive paraphrases (e.g., *Cursor Mundi* [**CM**], the translation of the *Polychronicon* [**Poly**], the *Middle English Metrical Paraphrase of the Old Testament* [**POT**]) contain material from Numbers, Judges, Kings, Job, Tobias, Judith, Esdras, and Machabees. In other works, a pattern emerges wherein, after the highpoints of Genesis and Exodus, there is a quantum leap to the Incarnation, Passion, Resurrection, and Pentecost. Bede outlines a similar pattern (with another quantum leap from Acts to Revelation) in Cædmon's output: "He sang of the creation of the world, the origin of the human race, and the whole story of Genesis. He sang of Israel's exodus from Egypt, the entry into the Promised Land, and many other events of scriptural history. He sang of the Lord's Incarnation, Passion, Resurrection, and Ascension into heaven, the coming of the Holy Spirit, and the teaching of the Apostles. He also made many poems on the terrors of the Last Judgement, the horrible pains of Hell, and the joys of the Kingdom of Heaven."[3] The practice of summarizing and recapitulating is in fact biblical (e.g., Judith 5:6–23, Acts 7: 2–53, Acts 13:16–25, Heb. 11:4–40, and any number of genealogies).

Visual analogues are not hard to find, as for example in a Latin Bible produced in England in the later thirteenth century. The "I" of the "In principio" (Gen. 1:1) fills the left margin and is illuminated by scenes from the six days of Creation. The seventh scene depicts the Fall, and the last jumps to the Crucifixion.[4] The latter two scenes are nicely counterpointed: the serpent in the Tree corresponds to Christ on the Cross; Eve and Adam below the Tree correspond to Mary and John at the base of the Cross. Biblical stories, in all of their variety, tell one story when read with the right gloss. Although the Passion is the culmination and highpoint of sacred history, toward which Old Testament prophecy and typological readings have pointed, the impulse to continue through the Resurrection and into the Acts of the Apostles reflects a concern to show how the Word is spread in space and time. Middle English biblical literature shares the same apostolic impulse: one should move from the text into the world. A collection of saints' lives is a logical sequel, and in fact an important category of biblical literature—narratives known as the temporale (see below)—often prefaces the sanctorale itself. Moralizations and doctrinal messages are common, yet, as I will try to demonstrate throughout, a paraphrase read in its entirety is more than just a truncated Bible with an explanatory gloss. Though the works are highly selective and often bear little syntactic resemblance to the Vulgate, one can still derive a strong sense of the most important components of biblical history, as well as some impression of the style of the Bible itself. Each production makes its own choice of materials and pursues its own program, whether it be educational, penitential, soteriological, or recreational. The variety of the forms of biblical literature and of their possible applications are two of this study's central concerns.

Any book which takes as its subject the Bible in Middle English and which tries to situate itself within the fields of lay literacy and popular culture must proceed with caution and humility. Biblical paraphrase pervades the literature of the period, and no study can encompass all of its manifestations. I hope, however, that this book covers all of the major instances of biblical literature in Middle English, and that it may serve both as a means of access for scholars who wish to discover the extent and character of biblical material before Wyclif and as a critical study of an unjustly neglected body of Middle English literature. Nearly all of the works covered here receive only cursory, if any, mention in literary histories of the period. The most complete guides to date are the volumes in the *Manual of the Writings in Middle English,* particularly the contribution by Lawrence Muir in volume 2 (1970; "Translations and Paraphrases of the Bible, and Commentaries") and that of Robert R. Raymo in volume 7 (1986; "Works of Religious and Philosophical Instruction"). Neither of these guides, however, provides the kind of detailed breakdown of biblical contents which the entries in this book aim for, and the *Manual* volumes are becoming dated and unwieldy, though the bibliographic and manuscript resources in the *Manual* are invaluable.[5]

Deciding what to include and, especially, what to exclude, has been difficult; while the coverage tries to be as comprehensive as possible, it is by no means exhaustive. In terms of structure, the existence of some biblical narrative framework qualifies many works for inclusion; in terms of content, the sheer quantity of biblical material which is adapted qualifies others. Idiosyncratic productions, such as the *Old Testament Sentences* (**OTS**), are included because the contents, however eclectic, are almost wholly biblical, and the order of verses from Proverbs and Ecclesiastes is immaterial. The author has produced his own "Book of Wisdom." Non-narrative biblical books, such as the Psalter and Ecclesiastes, are included because full-scale paraphrases and translations exist. "Paraphrase" is the dominant modus operandi, and while the term suffers from its associations with imitative school exercises, I use it throughout to refer to the systematic appropriation and refashioning of biblical texts. Paraphrases can be loose, when key words appear in a generally familiar context, or close, when key words appear in an identifiable context with fairly close correspondence to specific biblical chapters and verses.

Either kind of paraphrase often includes various allusions to biblical and apocryphal events, ideas, and doctrines. By giving illustrative quotations, I hope to avoid quibbling overmuch about precise definitions of paraphrase. The works, as can be seen, vary widely in originality and sophistication, but have in common the intention to promulgate biblical material. Allusion to and quotation of the Bible is ubiquitous in Middle English; the emphasis here, however, falls on works that retell substantial parts of the Bible: whole books, abstracted highlights from several books, or discrete units such as the story of Joseph, the Ten Commandments, or various Canticles. Narratives are common, in prose and verse, and include both shorter lyric poems which tell biblical stories and works which structure a narrative around a cento of biblical verses. The narrative may be discontinuous in biblical/canonical terms, but a new narrative has been constructed by the author either directly from the Vulgate or from preexisting Middle English works. Full coverage of the lyric, ballad, commonplace book, and carol traditions would vastly complicate this project, though the role of these genres in the dissemination of biblical material cannot be overlooked.[6]

The drama also seeks to propagate biblical stories among lay people, but it is excluded because of the sheer size of the dramatic corpus, and because many fine studies have been devoted to it.[7] It should be noted, however, that the drama draws upon many of the same bodies of material and in some cases borrows directly from existing English paraphrases both in verse (e.g., the *Southern Passion* [**SP**]) and in prose (e.g., Nicholas Love's *Mirror* [**MBL**]). It is in any event a relatively simple matter to locate biblical material within dramatic cycles due to their chronological organization, in discrete units, from Creation to Doomsday. One would not expect, however, to find material from Acts in Passion narratives, or from Numbers in a Life of Christ (see, for example, the *Stanzaic Life of Christ* [**SLC**] or the *Ormulum* [**Orm**]), but such inclusions are routine. The liberality and originality of the adaptations are a source of continual fascination.

Versified lectionaries and homiliaries have extended biblical passages in the form of liturgical pericopes appointed to be read during the Church year. Major texts in this group are the *Ormulum* and the *Northern Homily Cycle* [**NHC**], and they appear here as works representative of their genre. The former is an admittedly idiosyncratic late twelfth-century homiliary existing in a unique manuscript, and the latter an early fourteenth-century collection existing in three recensions in twenty-one manuscripts. They are only two examples of a vast body of medieval homiletic literature which has been studied primarily in terms of its philological value and sometimes for the literary qualities of some of its exempla. My emphasis falls on the 30- to 100-

line biblical paraphrase which begins each homily and on which the exemplum draws for its imagery and authority.[8] Taken together, these introductory passages cover substantial parts of the New Testament as well as parts of the Old, and they are an unambiguously popular means of spreading the Word. Homily and sermon cycles were perhaps the most widely diffused medieval literary form, and the public perception of biblical literature derived at least as much from this medium as from the drama. That the texts are liturgically based need not imply that they were used exclusively during divine service. There are many texts, subsumed under the term "pastoralia," which assisted peripherally in the worship and instruction of the devout.[9] The organization of liturgical readings according to the Church year gives a narrative basis for the cycles themselves. The *Ormulum* has even been called a Life of Christ.

Many of the works have Latin and French sources which will be identified where possible, though one should always bear in mind that the manuscript histories of source texts are often at least as tangled, and their cultural contexts as intricate, as those of the Middle English works. All such citations simply point the way any source studies must take. One source, however, stands out for its widespread influence: the *Historia Scholastica* (composed ca. 1169–75), an encyclopedic Latin work by Peter Comestor, the "Master of Stories."[10] Comestor produced it as a biblical abridgement and gloss for students at the University of Paris, but it quickly became one of the most important resources for biblical material in the later Middle Ages; it was translated extensively into Middle English and every other major European vernacular. Comestor's reputation for storytelling derives from the emphasis in the *Historia* on coherent narrative, the explanation of textual ambiguities, and the synthesis of biblical, apocryphal, and classical history. Midrashic legend is also prominent. These characteristics made the *Historia* readily susceptible to the excision and reexpression of narrative units. Thus the *Historia* was both a source book for legends and a kind of reference tool for proverbs and recondite lore. The years of gathering and sifting material in the lecture hall and elsewhere allowed Comestor to incorporate a great deal of apocryphal, legendary, and historical material, including examples taken from pictures in churches (PL 198.1340), notes from the examination of relics (col. 1544), disagreements with Plato (cols. 1055–67) and testimony from travelers to the Holy Land. In short, Comestor sought to provide a comprehensive guide to reading Scripture even as he retold the narrative highlights. Differences between authorities were not ignored, and though Comestor presented variant readings and addressed some theological questions he was more interested in weighing than in resolving them. It can be argued that, simply because it was a set school text and was translated into vernacular languages before any full translation of the Bible, the *Historia* had a more decisive effect on clerical and lay knowledge of the Bible from the late twelfth to the late fourteenth century than the Vulgate itself. The infrequency of lay ownership of Vulgates and the widespread ignorance of Latin are often cited as factors which mitigated against any knowledge of the Bible among the general population. But because such a quantity of vernacular biblical literature exists, owning a Vulgate and knowing how to read Latin were no more necessary before the Reformation than after. In the Middle Ages, the Vulgate was the Bible, but the Bible was not necessarily the Vulgate.

The chapters proceed as follows. Chapter 1 discusses the medieval idea of the Bible as a synthesis of translation, paraphrase, and commentary wherein no one component is more authoritative than another, with the result that the whole is treated as a "canonical" text. Chapter 2 provides a historical outline of the official reception of biblical literature on the Continent (France in particular) and in England, with attention to the relationship between medieval vernacular culture and formal ecclesiastical structures. Chapter 3 concentrates on the evolution of the vernacular in England and the challenge of English translation. Chapter 4 analyzes how works of biblical literature represent themselves in their prologues and sets up a literary taxonomy. The main entries follow: the order of treatment corresponds to the order of the Vulgate canon, though the heterogeneity of contents of many of the works makes absolute classification impossible. The indexes and cross-references direct the reader to all relevant biblical verses, events, or characters, as the case may be. The guide to the entries provides more specific information on their organization.

NOTES

1. Waldron, "Trevisa's Prefaces," 292, and see Bede's *History of the English Church,* IV.24. Cf. the Anglo-Saxon biblical poetry in Oxford, Bodleian Lib. Junius 11, which preserves biblical paraphrases from ca. 1000 or earlier, the *Paris Psalter,* the glosses to the Lindisfarne and Rushworth Gospels, and these prose translations: the West Saxon Gospels, the *Heptateuch,* Ælfric's *Genesis.* See, in general, Morrell, *Manual;* Marsden, *Text of the Old Testament;* Liuzza, *Gospels;* Crawford, *Heptateuch;* Remley, *Old English Biblical Verse;* Shepherd, "English Versions."

2. See **FP, PCE,** and, for example, **PL** or **MLP.**

3. Bede, *History of the English Church,* 252. Bede, like every other medieval Christian exegete, read both Testaments as one. While scholarly practice in some disciplines uses the term "Hebrew Bible" for the pre-Christian canon, this book uses "Old Testament."

4. See Schutzner, *Medieval and Renaissance Books,* plate 2. Plate 1 reproduces a simi-

lar illumination from a slightly earlier Paris Bible, except that the Day of Rest takes the place of the Fall.

5. In 1911 Mary W. Smyth undertook to index biblical quotations in English from 1025 to 1350 (*Biblical Quotations*). Her coverage is chronologically limited, especially since she omits the numerous works of biblical literature from the latter half of the fourteenth century, when their production was most common, and there is no general index, but her work is still useful. The two books by Fowler (*Bible in Early English Literature* and *Bible in Middle English Literature*) are not as comprehensive as the titles imply; he chooses to cover in depth a few relevant works (including a chapter on the Wycliffite translations). The bibliography by Friedman and Wegmann (*Iconography*) is useful, especially the entries on biblical figures in chap. 4.

6. See Woolf, *Religious Lyric;* Gray, *Themes and Images;* Wenzel, *Preachers;* and Fowler, *Bible in Middle English Literature,* chap. 2; see E. Wilson, *Index,* for a representative commonplace book. The collections by C. Brown (*English Lyrics XIIIth Century, Religious Lyrics XIVth Century, Religious Lyrics XVth Century*) and Greene (*Early English Carols*) are the most comprehensive. Note especially several of Greene's running titles: Carols of the Advent and Nativity [Luke 2], of the Epiphany [Matt. 2], of the Passion, of the Annunciation [Luke 1], of the Trouble of Joseph [Matt. 1], and of Christ's Pleading [scourging, seven last words]. An index of biblical material, if only keyed to these collections, would be a worthy project.

7. Kolve, *Corpus Christi,* and Woolf, *Mystery Plays,* are especially good since they pay attention to the full range of vernacular biblical literatures. See also Fowler, *Bible in Middle English Literature,* chap. 1.

8. Tubach's definition is helpful: "the exemplum is an attempt to discover in each narrative event, character, situation or act a paradigmatic sign that would either substantiate religious beliefs and Church dogma or delineate social ills and human foibles" (*Index Exemplorum,* 523). Note Smetana's distinction between a homily, "a discourse that expounds or comments on a text of sacred scripture for the instruction and edification of the listeners," and a sermon, "an address on a dogmatic or moral theme" ("Paul the Deacon's Anthology," 78). See also Heffernan, "Sermon Literature," and Wenzel, "Medieval Sermons."

9. "[T]he term embraces any and every literary aid or manual which may be of help to a priest in his *cura animarum,* whether with respect to his own education or that of the people in his charge" (Boyle, "Fourth Lateran Council," 31).

10. See Morey, "Peter Comestor."

CHAPTER 1

The Medieval Idea
of the Bible

THE BOOK was an impressive and revered medieval icon, but for practical purposes, relevant as much today as in the Middle Ages, the Bible consists of those stories which have achieved familiarity through church service, selective reading, and literary treatments. One must be aware that even the canon has a canon—those parts of the Bible which constitute a commonly received tradition and which were copied and circulated in various formats from antiquity. A neatly printed and bound Bible was simply unknown within a manuscript culture. The production and possession of a biblical pandect, almost always in deluxe format, were noteworthy distinctions of a medieval scriptorium, in some ways comparable to the possession of a complete Gutenberg Bible today.

Why some parts are now more familiar than others is a complex question. Even relatively devout and educated individuals are sometimes surprised to discover what is, and is not, in the Bible: many vivid biblical stories—for example Moses's murder and secret burial of the Egyptian (Ex. 2:12) or the Lord's later attempt to kill Moses (Ex. 4:24)—rarely figure in the modern popular repertoire. On the other hand, some obscure biblical verses have accreted extensive and well-known bodies of apocryphal legend—for example the Heavenly Rebellion and Fall of the Angels (Is. 14:12–13, Luke 10:18, 2Pet. 2:4, Jude 6, Rev. 12:7–12) and, even more tenuously, the Harrowing of Hell (Matt. 27:52, 1Pet. 3:19) or the *Storie of Asneth* (**SA**; Gen. 41: 45–50). Minor apocryphal details, such as the presence of the ox and ass at Christ's Nativity, derive from a single Old Testament verse (Is. 1:3). These and other verses serve as triggers which launch or complement a "biblical" narrative, and are part of the cento tradition in which narratives are strung out between selected verses. The evolution of this selectivity and complementarity can be seen in medieval biblical literature and, of course, in their Renaissance epigones such as *Paradise Lost*.[1] Today, as we marvel at the instantaneous access provided by electronic data bases and search engines, we should remind ourselves that the Bible, with its canonical order and various traditions of textual division, has been susceptible to a similar kind of access unlike any other text in the history of Western civilization.[2]

Works of Middle English biblical literature differ widely in scope and genre, but they all played a significant role in disseminating Scripture among the "lewed" folk (see chap. 4 for a discussion of this term). While many have considerable intrinsic merit, perhaps what they do best is show how medieval scholars read texts, particularly sacred ones. Geoffrey Shepherd's observation concerning the Anglo-Saxons holds equally well for their descendants: "In our century, we have been urged to read the Bible as literature. In dealing with the early English, we must turn the phrase about: the Anglo-Saxons tended to read all literature as the Bible and judged all writing by the standards that they found implicit there."[3] The Bible was undeniably the central text which shaped the medieval idea of storytelling. On a stylistic level, the influence of biblical phraseology and narrative on individuals who probably had the Psalter memorized and who read the Bible daily must have been considerable. With regard to content, Middle English biblical paraphrasers were close readers par excellence. Nothing in Holy Writ is superfluous, and economical reading meant that everything is potentially useful. The narratives may seem free-associative, but readings are always grounded in the text: any particular turn or explanation can be traced back through a linked sequence of details. For example, in Genesis 4:23, the man whom Lamech confesses to have slain was taken to be Cain, who is mentioned in the next verse. A legend, based on these obscure verses, grew up around the episode which also accounted for the "young man" mentioned by Lamech: he is the unfortunate guide to the blind Lamech who directed him to shoot and who was then beaten to death. Likewise, in Luke 7:36–50, the woman who anoints Christ with the precious oil was identified as Mary Magdalen simply because she is the first female to be mentioned after the story is told (Luke 8:2). Since the woman is identified as a sinner, poets capitalized on the implications for Mary's character.[4] Thus, though the rationale for any given association is often less than transparent, legends sprang up from close readings of the biblical narrative.

The importance of the *lectio divina* meant that reading is the paramount activity, and that all reading is a commentary on what has been read. Context

—working with all the previously encountered information thought relevant to a question—was very important. Hence the well-known "lack of originality" in medieval works in this tradition since episodes can almost always be shown to have a source. Yet highly original and poetically sophisticated reworkings of the Bible were routine medieval phenomena. If any works can be accused of being purely derivative, they are of course the Wycliffite translations, both the exceedingly literal earlier version (attributed to Nicholas of Hereford) and the more idiomatic later version (attributed to John Purvey). Purvey follows more modern principles of textual criticism rather than informal medieval practices wherein whatever material thought to have a logical or even whimsical connection to the project at hand is adapted, with little concern about its origin.[5]

Wyclif is the heir to this vernacular tradition, but the intentions and experiences of these earlier producers of biblical literature were much different from those of the Wycliffites, not least because they often wrote in verse. Margaret Deanesly notes that "[n]o verse translations, or Bible stories, or 'moralisations,' or homilies on the gospels, could be appealed to by teachers [Purvey, etc.] in support of their doctrine, as in the case of a prose translation: and therefore no verse translation was ever condemned as heretical."[6] The question of heresy and of various other forms of official resistance will be treated in chapter 2, but a fundamental distinction between the Wycliffite project and the other forms of biblical literatures should be observed. It is not that the Wycliffites "could" not appeal to an antecedent literature, they would not. The Lollards produced a straight prose translation, devoid of commentary, while biblical paraphrasers freely adapted selected passages with frequent glosses, moralizations, and apocryphal digressions. As manuscripts were copied in the fifteenth century, Wycliffite texts often absorbed various independent biblical productions, and clear distinctions between Wycliffite and non-Wycliffite texts are often impossible. One can argue, however, that fifteenth-century readers were perhaps as indifferent to the distinctions as we are unsure how to impose them.

Translators such as Nicholas of Hereford and Purvey did not cite the many renderings of the Bible as a precedent and justification for their complete prose translation since Wyclif himself complains that preachers, and especially friars, rely overmuch on rhyme and apocryphal stories: "ut aliqui ritmisando et aliqui poemata vel fabulas predicando adulterantur multipliciter verbum Dei."[7] Wyclif goes on to complain that such "verba ficta et poemata ritmisata" are merely pretexts for loosening the purses of listeners. A description of the friars in the nonconformist "Seven Werkys of Mercy Gostly" (once attributed to Wyclif) expresses similar sentiments in English: "For þei docken Goddis word, and tateren it bi þer rimes, þat þe fowrme þat Crist ȝaf it is hidde by ypocrisie."[8] In a characteristic move these preachers are linked to the Antichrist. Wyclif expresses the long-standing bias against verse ("turned," and hence suspect) in favor of prose ("pro-versus," "turned forward," and hence true), and he objects to the existence of the accompanying commentary which preempted individual interpretation. Wyclif is also reacting against the abuses of preaching friars who, by the end of the fourteenth century, were exploiting their position for monetary gain.[9] Corruption was real, but in his wholesale and somewhat puritanical condemnation Wyclif dismissed a literature which had been the primary medium for lay knowledge of the Bible for centuries.

Despite genuine interest in how widely and in what forms the Bible was known in medieval England, too often modern critics also dismiss these works as "mere biblical paraphrase." I would speculate that *Cleanness* and *Patience,* two examples of Old Testament paraphrase produced by an acknowledged master of elegy and romance, would have received much less critical attention than they have if they did not appear in London, BL Cotton Nero A.x between *Pearl* (itself biblically based) and *Sir Gawain and the Green Knight.* Relevant chapter and verse may be cited, but how the paraphrasers shape and adapt the biblical material even as they work within a tradition is rarely appreciated fully. Poets, paraphrasers, and commentators felt compelled to reshape the biblical narrative because the bare text of the Bible does not always make sense. It demands interpretation, and there were known to exist various texts and traditions which could explain the ambiguities and aporias. In addition, they felt authorized to apply various materials because of a general respect for writing; anything that was copied into a folio format was presumably highly valued. Books, whether they be books of the Bible, of a Church father, or of a Hebrew doctor, are the repositories of truth, at least when read in the right way. When discrepancies between these authorities occur, or when no explanation whatsoever appears, the incapacity of human understanding is to blame, not the text itself.

For those unable to afford or to read books, physical representations of biblical subjects, be they manuscript illuminations, sculptural tympani, or monumental stained glass windows, constituted a "Bible of the Poor." What the illiterate could not read, it has been argued, they could learn visually. There is no doubt that artwork of various kinds had some effect on lay knowledge of Scripture; the questions are, of course, what kind of knowledge, and how complete? Art historians continue to debate the function and effect of stained glass windows in medieval society, but only rarely admit that modern scholars with binoculars and the Princeton Art Index often have great

trouble even identifying some scenes. While the average peasant or bour-
geois churchgoer may have recognized certain biblical subjects as they were
represented, I think it unlikely that they *learned* any significant amount of
the Bible from artwork, though medieval docents may have conducted tours
as instructive as those of their modern counterparts, and some artwork has
scripted captions which explain the contents of the scene (again only for
those who could read).[10] The majority of the English medieval population
probably never visited sites such as York, London, and Canterbury where
quantities of such work were to be found. Surely those who did visit were as
overwhelmed as modern tourists.

Manuscript illustrations probably had somewhat more effect, if only because books traveled widely, could be perused more easily and at greater
leisure, and had a quantity of explanatory text. There are both picture books
(i.e., a picture covers half or more of the page) and illustrated books (with
pictures anywhere on the page).[11] The *Estoire del Evangelie* (**EE**) in the Vernon manuscript is, for example, illustrated. Of course, only aristocrats and
clergy would have had access to such manuscripts, and one must remember that it is not uncommon for the illustration to have no discernible relationship to the contiguous text. Nonetheless, the quantity of illuminated
Bibles which survive testifies to some degree of influence, especially with
regard to texts associated with the *Historia Scholastica*. For example, Paris,
Bibliothèque de l'Arsenal 5211, called by Berger a "Bible abrégée" but now
called the Arsenal Bible or the Acre Bible made for St. Louis (ca. 1250),
cites "l'estoire" (i.e., the *Historia Scholastica*) as its source for Machabees.[12]
An important series of twenty frontispieces appears in the manuscript, one
for each of the Old Testament books translated. The influences are ultimately Byzantine, but some miniatures are in the "tradition of English psalter illustrations."[13] Another important illustrated manuscript, and this an
English production of the fourteenth century, is London, BL Egerton 1894,
the Egerton Genesis. It is fragmentary, but 150 scenes from Genesis appear
with "a text in Anglo-French which has some connection with the *Historia
Scholastica* of Peter Comestor."[14] Here is another medium for the circulation
of Peter's text, at least among those who could afford to own such a manuscript. Illustrations provide important clues to the circulation and relationship of works derived from the *Historia,* and to how at least one medieval
reader—the illuminator—read or was directed to read the text.[15]

The *Historia Scholastica* combines Hebrew, apocryphal, folkloristic, and
biblical material, and Comestor's synthesis of this material into an officially
approved text provided a precedent for annexing texts and traditions pertinent to biblical history. None of the Middle English works translates the

whole of the *Historia,* but the penchant for the liberal reworking of materials
is reflected in the variety and extent of the biblical literature which was produced. Choosing from Comestor's copious material requires considerable
skill, to say nothing of the work required in turning Latin prose into sometimes very distinguished—as in *Genesis and Exodus* (**GE**)—English verse. The
sheer length of other poems—for example the 1,531 twelve-line stanzas of
the *Middle English Metrical Paraphrase of the Old Testament* (**POT**)—testifies to
their comprehensiveness and to the labor involved. Orm's dogged persever-
ance through 20,000 lines (one-eighth of the planned work) of a lectionary
for lay folk or the *Cursor Mundi* (**CM**) poet's 30,000-line counterblast to the
popularity of secular romance testifies not only to their faith in God but also
to the comprehensiveness of their literary enterprises. Sacred and secular
subjects sometimes do conflict, as for example in the prologue to the *Cursor
Mundi* or the introduction to the Middle English translation of Robert of
Gretham's *Miroir,* a Gospel lectionary which describes itself as "a litel tretiʒ
of diuinite to turn man from romances and gestes, wherein he lesiþ mychel
of his tyme þat so setteþ his hert from god, and to give him instead þing þat
is profitable boþe to lyf & to soule."[16] Even in reactions against the popularity of secular romance, authors often prefer to exploit the continuities
between the sacred and the secular to sustain their educational or doctrinal venture. The willingness of medieval readers to understand the Old and
New Testaments as one story—governed, of course, by typological exegesis—extended to their predilection to read all literature, if not as a sacred
text, at least as a text which has something to contribute to religious understanding. Because God speaks in parables, interpretation and explanation
are necessary; imaginative authors and readers met their needs by writing
and reading a wide range of sacred and secular materials. Authors of any
age are inevitably readers (or at least listeners) before they are writers, but
in the Middle Ages the hermeneutic imperative was especially strong.

   An important biblical verse which demonstrates the centrality of writing
in the teleology of salvation is Romans 15:4: "Quaecumque enim scripta
sunt, ad nostram doctrinam scripta sunt: ut per patientiam, et consolatio-
nem scripturarum, spem habeamus." As A. J. Minnis points out, the " 'all'
[quaecumque] came to mean 'almost anything', writing of all kinds." Writings may not necessarily be inerrant, but the "discriminating reader" may
interpret the corpus of sacred and secular writings so as to serve his or
her own "doctrine."[17] Hence not only all of Scripture but anything written
has, when properly applied, doctrinal and salvific significance. Chaucer cites
Romans 15:4 in conjunction with the famous fruit and chaff image at the
end of the *Nun's Priest's Tale:* "For seint Paul seith that al that writen is, / To

oure doctrine it is ywrite, ywis; / Taketh the fruyt, and lat the chaf be stille" (4631–33). Chaucer's "Retraction" reinvokes the verse: "For oure book seith, 'Al that is writen is writen for our doctrine,' and that is myn entente." Caxton cites the verse ("but al is wryton for our doctryne") in the preface to his edition of Malory as the last of many reasons why his Arthurian enterprise is worth reading.[18] The Franciscan who in the early fourteenth century based his own allegorical narrative on Ovid's *Metamorphoses* begins his work with a citation of Romans 15:4 as a kind of scriptural license for the pagan contents:

> Se l'escripture ne me ment,
> Tout est pour nostre enseignement
> Quandu'il a es livres escript,
> Soient bon ou mal li escript.[19]

Chaucer appropriates many texts; the author of the *Ovide moralisé* adapts a classical text and Comestor primarily biblical ones; yet each appeals to and appropriates earlier authorities in order to justify current productions and to make them doctrinally relevant.

The Vernon manuscript (ca. 1390), which weighs in at nearly fifty pounds and which (with its sister text the Simeon manuscript) is one of the most comprehensive and important anthologies of Middle English prose and verse, reflects in its organization and contents the doctrinal relevance of a variety of texts, and therefore reflects the spirit of Romans 15:4.[20] In Vernon one can find the *South English Legendary* (**SEL**), the *Pistel of Swete Susan* (**PSS**), an A-text of *Piers Plowman*, the *Northern Homily Cycle* (**NHC**), several "homiletic romances," the *Old Testament History* (**OTH**), the *Estoire del Evangelie* (**EE**), among many other texts.[21] A glance at the entry for Oxford, Bodleian Lib. Eng. poet. a.1 in the manuscript index reveals how many examples of biblical literature Vernon contains. Biblically based instruction is closely linked to the salvation of the audience: the manuscript's own index calls itself *Salus anime* or *Sowlehele*. Although Vernon is certainly a distinguished and rare production, the contents and organization demonstrate how a variety of texts can be used for doctrinal purposes, and how indeed the manuscript has some pretensions as a "Bible." Vernon is divided into five major parts; the first two each begin with a major instance of biblical literature, part one with the *Old Testament History,* and part two with the *Estoire del Evangelie.* Both derive from the *Historia Scholastica* and, as the titles indicate, follow a biblical model from the history of the Jews to the story of salvation. It may also be significant that the very last item in the manuscript, a twenty-four-line poem on the Trinity, mentions the Bible in the final four lines:

> I may sei wiþ-outen bost
> Þe holy Book leyh neuere.
> ffader and Sone and holygost
> Beo wiþ us nou and euere! [22]

The use of the first person in the context of the "holy Book" gives the impression of an author or compiler looking back with pride over the entire project. Thus the Vernon manuscript reflects the impulse, inaugurated by Comestor in the twelfth century, that promoted the wide doctrinal applicability of texts and that profited from the variety and power of writing. Texts, even Hebrew, classical, and pagan ones, are not to be argued down but read in the right way: do not disarm the text, arm the reader. My point is that those who produced biblical literature took remarkable liberties in their adaptations of Scripture and in large measure established and legitimated the practice of textual appropriation. God's word is a code which must be broken. Indeed, Scripture was regarded as a set of puzzles which the Jews and other nonbelievers could not solve, and it was thus the job of exegetes to provide keys for the faithful. The *Historia* and its successors are in broad terms just such attempts. Their didacticism cannot be ignored, but it is didacticism geared directly to salvation.

The salvific power of understanding the text is expressed parabolically in the story of the man without a wedding garment and its aphoristic ending "multi sunt enim vocati, pauci autem electi" (Matt. 22:14). This verse, like Romans 15:4, is widespread in biblical literature (it enunciates, for example, the guiding principle of *Cleanness* [Cl]) and it illustrates how Bible stories functioned. One of the most striking uses of the verse is when "Scripture" herself preaches a sermon on Matthew 22:14 to the dreamer in *Piers Plowman:*

> "A saith soth," quod Scripture tho, and skypte an heyh, and prechede;
> Ac be matere þat she meuede, if lewede men hit knewe,
> The lasse, as Y leue, louyon þei wolde
> The bileue of Oure Lord þat lettred men techeth.
> Of here teme and here tales Y took ful good hede;
> Heo saide in here sarmon selcouthe wordes:
> "*Multi* to a mangerye and to þe mete were sompned;
> And whan þe peple was plenere ycome, þe porter vnpynnede þe gate,
> And plihte in *Pauci* priueiliche and lette þe remenaunt go rome." [23]

If the "lewede" folk really knew what Scripture was saying, "the less would they love" (line 44) the faith which promises supposedly easy salvation. In short, as Christ explains elswhere (Matt. 13:9–14, citing Is. 6:9), the proper understanding of Scripture is only for those with the ears to hear. All of

Scripture acts parabolically, and parables themselves are stylistically escha-tological. Many are called, but few are chosen; that is, just as the elect are separated from the damned on Doomsday, those with the knowledge to in-terpret Scripture correctly are separated from those who can not.[24] Acts of literary criticism, proper or improper, are thus the Last Judgment in micro-cosm.

The sometimes freewheeling use of sources raises the question of *auc-toritas* and recalls the extraordinary twelfth-century division by Hugh of St. Victor of the New Testament into "the Gospel, the Apostles, and the Fathers."[25] The early exegetes (Hugh would be referring primarily to Je-rome, Augustine, Ambrose, and Gregory) thus achieve a status which places them beyond mere scoliasts. Even as Hugh recognizes the difference be-tween Scripture and commentary, the margins become blurred, and works which synthesize biblical, apocryphal, and patristic material are invested with an authority little short of that of Scripture itself. Another twelfth-century scholar, Alain de Lille, attributes literal, tropological, and allegori-cal significances to his own work, the *Anticlaudianus*. Only those suitably trained should read it, "lest the pearl, trampled under the feet of swine, be lost."[26] While Alain was far from claiming to have written another Bible, his use of specialized terminology and value-laden imagery, especially the in-vocation of Matthew 7:6, problematizes the question of medieval attitudes toward authorship. The source of *auctoritas* is very complex; in many cases attempts to differentiate an "auctor" from an "expositor" or a "compilator" result in distinctions without a difference. Beryl Smalley insists that none of the Paris masters confused the *authentica* (of the Fathers) with *magistralia* (of later teachers), and Comestor is often careful to identify sources, but I wish to argue for a kind of continuum from Scripture through the Fathers to these twelfth-century productions.[27] Later readers and translators of the *His-toria* treated the whole with respect.[28] Thus the more liberal attitude toward the status of commentary extended to "modern" texts like the *Historia* and later vernacular texts which synthesized biblical narrative and commentary.

The avoidance of allegorical interpretation in the works is consistent with the Victorine emphasis on the literal exegesis of Scripture and with what Grabmann calls the "biblical-moral school" of twelfth-century Paris.[29] Smalley attributes the Victorine (and also fraternal) emphasis on literal ex-planation to the newly discovered works of Aristotle with their doctrine "that substance could only be known through its sensible manifestations."[30] Early exegetes such as Augustine justified the necessity of allegory and the use of tropes because "an awareness of them is necessary to a solution of the ambi-guities of the Scriptures, for when the sense is absurd if it is taken verbally, it is to be inquired whether or not what is said is expressed in this or that trope which we do not know; and in this way are many hidden things discovered."[31] Augustine spends the whole of book 3 of the *De doctrina Christiana* on those ambiguous signs in Scripture which are "absurd" unless given a transliteral interpretation. The twelfth-century "literalist" school was largely a reaction against the overly allegorical interpretations of commentators who had applied Augustine's advice extravagantly. Comestor and the Victorines do not deny that the Bible requires interpretation, but they do insist that more objective and literal means be used. One of the more striking examples of a scene which seems to require explanation is in Exodus 32, where Aaron himself fabricates the golden calf. In order to rationalize the disturbing complicity of an otherwise holy man in an idolatrous act, Comestor posits the prior resistance and subsequent death of Hur: "Sed indignatus populus, spuens in faciem, ut traditur, eum suffocavit" (PL 198.1189). Aaron, fearing a similar fate, acquiesces. Hur, however, appears only in Exodus 17 and 24, and is not even mentioned in connection with the golden calf. Beyond the quaint character of the legend is the larger point that the biblical narrative is supplemented by logical effective causes to explain apparent inconsistencies.[32]

The Word of God is the base text, and the main points of the biblical stories are faithfully reproduced, but extraordinary in these works are the highly imaginative commentaries, moralizations, and figures used to illumine the biblical significances. Priests are threatened with death if the bell is not rung before mass (a metaphor for the preaching of the Gospel which must "ring" from the pulpit [cf. Is. 58:1]), a bishop appears as a rapist, an abbess as a whore, and Caiphas adjures Christ "In þe name of þe Trinite" to declare whether he is the son of God or not.[33] These works preserve a long tradition of what W. A. Pantin calls "orthodox clerical criticism" by clerics themselves.[34] Bold and farsighted Chaucer is often credited with exposing religious fraud, which indeed he does with rare skill, but there was a long antecedent tradition of anticlerical literature. Given the vast corpus of twelfth-, thirteenth-, and fourteenth-century literature which contains such criticism, one is apt to wonder wherein lie the innovations of the reformers.[35] In a discussion of how medieval Latin Passion narratives reshape the biblical text, Thomas Bestul cites a remarkable passage from the *Meditationes Vitae Christi* (*MVC*) to argue that "In their innovative re-narrations of the incidents of the life of Christ and their lively invention of non-biblical details, the Passion narratives present a rewritten, reformulated, highly variable, and decidedly non-canonical biblical text, which was self-consciously made and occasionally theoretically defended."[36] This is to touch lightly on very complex issues which later chapters will discuss in greater depth, but I wish to point out the oversimplifications from which the medieval Church and its literature have suffered. Here lies the central problem of trying to assess the variety of biblical literature: given the religious motivations of the poets and their doctrinal intentions, how does one account for the liberal treatment of the Word of God? One explanation for their willingness to adapt biblical narrative and to apply diverse materials is that one text's appeal to another has biblical precedent. The typological reading of the Old Testament in the New was the medieval version of intertextuality; as I have suggested earlier, intertextual readings were extended to whatever writings of doctrinal significance were to hand.

The motives for paraphrasing, versifying, and otherwise refashioning the Scriptures go well beyond the banal observations that rhyme serves as a mnemonic device for traveling minstrels or as a diversion for an otherwise bored audience. There is a larger aesthetic and moral principle at work, well stated by Umberto Eco in a discussion of the eleventh-century *Schedula Diversarum Artium* by the clerk Theophilus. Eco writes that "since man is created in the image of God, he has the power to give life to forms. He discovers his need for beauty both by chance and by reflection on his own soul, and by practice and endeavour he develops his artistic powers. He finds in the Scriptures a divine commandment on art where David sings, 'Lord, I have loved the beauty of Thy house.' "[37] By mixing their own artistry with the Word of God, the paraphrasers sought to bridge the gap between the human and the divine. Such an attitude is fundamentally opposed to Wyclif's objections to versification, or to Edmund of Abingdon's, who in his *Speculum Ecclesie* (**SE**) objects to rhymed versions of the Pater Noster "for God him-self made hit; and therefor he doth gret schome and gret vnreurrence to God that taketh him to rymede wordes and queynts, and leueth the wordes and the preyere that he vs tauhte."[38] We have what could be called a split between conservative and liberal; the monolithic view of the Middle Ages which prevails in popular conception and in much scholarship has emphasized the conservative, whereas the evidence of much biblical literature reveals a neglected but much more interesting liberalism. A significant milestone in the movement from latitudinarianism to puritanism is the 1408 Oxford *Constitutions,* promulgated by Archbishop Arundel, against the Wycliffite translations. Interestingly, the Wycliffites had passed a similar milestone even before 1408 in their rejection of biblical paraphrases, and even though conformists and nonconformists were bitter rivals, it is the nature of most religious controversies that each side could be said to defend a conservative position as each claimed to represent the true practice and faith. Wyclif and Arundel will be discussed in chapter 2, but here one should note that, in the centuries prior to the *Constitutions*, biblical paraphrasers worked in a tolerant atmosphere with considerable autonomy, and that their projects were marked by a liberalism rejected by Wyclif.

The willingness to read the Bible discontinuously and to apply extrabiblical material demonstrates how, for these authors, the larger history of Christian salvation subsumes the history of both Testaments and of the world. One rule with wide application to biblical literature is that the Vulgate and the *Historia Scholastica* are picked apart and used almost at random. At any given point, the authors may refer to another event in sacred or secular history, and many recapitulate history from Creation to Doomsday (sometimes more than once in the same work) noting the highlights. The view of history is the traditionally linear biblical one, a progression from the first to the last days, but the attitude to the history of their own time is that it is virtually at a standstill. We are in the sixth, and last, Age of the World. The Apocalypse is imminent, and thus comprehensive retrospectives give the impression of history at its end (see especially the *Polychronicon*). Now is the time to sum up, spread the Word, and save as many souls—especially English souls—as possible. It is sometimes disconcerting, and an indication of the poet's considerable command of his sources, to see how freely materials are adapted. But given the use of *florilegia* and other abstracted material (including collections of exempla, aids to preaching, liturgical reading, or recollections from a sermon) authors could range among texts without knowing complete ones.[39] The body of medieval commonplaces so often transmitted by learned works and, in turn, by sermons and biblical paraphrases should be regarded as a repertoire of popular culture. This is one reason why the *Historia* and the works which derive from it are so seminal: because Peter Comestor had access to a wide variety of texts his work was a watershed which collected and then disseminated an eclectic range of material, both biblical and extrabiblical.

A larger debate, which will be the subject of chapter 4, concerns the role of this material in the life of that oft-cited abstraction, the medieval audience. Because the extant corpus of biblical literature preserves vast amounts of biblical, exegetical, and legendary material, this literature was the medium through which nonuniversity graduates achieved book learning. Here the Middle English audience went to school, and the study of popular religious literature can make the medieval audience less abstract. Here also are the subtexts which both supplied the significances to authors writing other texts and allowed those authors to incorporate allusions which their audiences understood.

NOTES

1. Earlier traditions of biblical paraphrase are discussed by Kartschoke (*Bibeldichtung*) and by Roberts (*Biblical Epic*), who notes that the primary motive for late classical paraphrasers was to "improve" (108) the Bible, at least in stylistic terms, by imitating the classics. Medieval paraphrasers were much more concerned with making the salvific power of the Bible as widely available as possible. Bottigheimer (*Bible for Children*) covers the post-Reformation tradition of Bible paraphrases for children.

2. Various reference systems have been imposed on the text of the Bible throughout its history (notably the Eusebian Canons), and differences still exist, especially between Catholic and Protestant Bibles. Chapter numbers as we know them were imposed by Stephen Langton, archbishop of Canterbury, in the early thirteenth century; verses were designated by the Parisian printer Robert Estienne ("Stephanus") in the 1560s as a marketing ploy to sell his editions of the Bible. See the Note on Psalter Numbering (p. 173).

3. Shepherd, "English Versions," 365.

4. For the poet of **NHC** Mary had used the oil to anoint her own body "quil scho haunted hir folye" (Small, *Metrical Homilies*, 15).

5. Note Purvey's concern in the prologue to the later version of the Old Testament with excluding the spurious and with ascertaining the "true" Latin text to be translated: "First, this symple creature hadde myche trauaile, with diuerse felawis and helpcris, to gedere manie elde biblis, and otherc doctouris, and comune glosis, and to make oo Latyn bible sumdel trewe" (Forshall and Madden, *Holy Bible*, 1:57).

6. Deanesly, *Lollard Bible*, 146.

7. Wyclif, *Opera Minora*, 331.

8. Wyclif, *Select Works*, 3:180.

9. See Owst for other reactions against the friars (*Preaching*, 80–88), and cf. Chaucer's Parson: "Thou getest fable noon ytoold for me; / For Paul, that writeth unto Thymothee, / Repreveth hem that weyven soothfastnesse, / And tellcn fables and swich wrecchednesse" (*Parson's Prologue*, X.31–34, citing 1Tim. 1:4, 4:7; 2Tim. 4:4).

10. See Fowler's discussion of the biblical program of the windows in a church in Fairford, Gloucestershirc (*Bible in Early English Literature*, 27–39) and Caviness, who reviews the scholarship on the question. She points out that stained glass windows "were created well before the manuscript recension that has come to be known as the *Biblia Pauperum* or the Bible of the Poor was invented" ("Biblical Stories in Windows," 103). In quoting from a variety of medieval sources which promote pictures as lay Bibles, Caviness cautions that the "effects on the populace are hoped for, though not actually observed" (105).

11. Important picture Bibles are the *Biblia Pauperum* (facsimile ed. by Henry), the *Speculum Humanae Salvationis* (*SHS;* see **MMS**), the *Bible moralisée* (see Wormald, "Bible Illustration," 332–33) and the *Holkham Bible Picture Book* (Hassall), which has 231 pictures from both Testaments accompanied by Anglo-Norman prose, and sometimes verse, captions. The speech of the Shepherds on Christmas Eve is, however, in English. All four are thirteenth- or early fourteenth-century and provide a brief text with the illumination. The *Biblia Pauperum* and the *SHS* emphasize typological relationships between the Testaments while the *Bible moralisée* emphasizes the moral application of the stories.

12. Berger, *Bible française*, 100.

13. Buchthal, *Miniature Painting*, 55 and plates 62–81. *Stjórn*, the Old Norse translation of the *Historia*, also contains illuminations influenced by English psalters. See Selma Jónsdóttir, *Illumination*, 33–42.

14. Wormald, "Bible Illustration," 320. For the facsimile edition see James, *Illustrations*.

15. See Andersson-Schmitt ("Verwendung," 19–26) and Morgan ("Illustration") for observations concerning the illustrations in historiated Bibles connected with Comestor.

16. Quoted by Goates, *Pepysian Harmony*, xi (the *Mirror* appears with **PGH** and with **PCE**). The relevant *Cursor Mundi* lines are 1–28, 85–88.

17. Minnis, *Medieval Theory*, 205. Minnis cites the views expressed by Isidore of Seville, Ranulph Higden, Boccaccio, William Caxton, and others in support of this interpretive strategy. Cf. 2Tim. 3:16.

18. Crotch, *William Caxton*, 95.

19. *Ovide moralisé*, vol. 1, book 1, lines 1–4. Cf. lines 2139–40: "La devine page et la fable / Sont en ce, ce samble, acordable." Robertson discusses these and related texts (*Preface to Chaucer*, 337–65).

20. See the facsimile by Doyle (*Vernon Manuscript*), the important collection of essays edited by Pearsall (*Vernon Manuscript*), and Hanna's introduction to Handlist 12 of the *Index of Middle English Prose*.

21. The term "homiletic romance" is Lawton's (*Joseph of Arimathea*, xiii).

22. Furnivall, *Minor Poems*, 740.

23. Langland, *Piers Plowman*, C.xii.42–50.

24. See Kelly and Irwin, "Meaning of *Cleanness*." Christopher argues for a similar principle of the *verbum reale* in a discussion of Milton and Luther: "God's words, it was presumed, were never spoken without effect, since they always left the metaphysical status of the hearer changed: either he was unresponsive, and so damned, or he was granted grace in the 'hearing.' There was no such thing as casual reading of Scripture or casual attendance at a sermon. This principle obtained beyond the initial access of grace; with subsequent hearing, one's heart was hardened more or grew in grace and understanding" (*Milton*, 108–9).

25. "The books in each Testament are divided into three groups. The Old Testament contains the Law, the Prophets, and the Hagiographers; the New contains the Gospel, the Apostles, and the Fathers" (Hugh of St. Victor, *Didascalicon*, 103).

26. Alain de Lille, *Anticlaudianus*, 40–41. The work was written between 1181 and 1184. Alain's rhetoric is reminiscent of Walter Map's and Pope Innocent III's reaction against the biblical translations of the Waldensians. Two of the four books in Alain's *De Fide Catholica contra Haereticos* were directed against the Albigensians and the Waldensians.

27. Smalley, *Study of the Bible*, 225–26. See also Baldwin, "Masters at Paris," 138–72, especially Baldwin's citation of Peter the Chanter's "dental image" wherein the apostles are the front teeth, the expositors of Scripture are the canines, and the modern masters are the molars (161).

28. See **POT**, where a scribe in one of the manuscripts has noted deviations from both the Bible and the *Historia*.

29. Grabmann, *Scholastischen Methode*, 2:476.

30. Smalley, *Study of the Bible*, 292.

31. Augustine, *On Christian Doctrine*, 104, book III.29. Cf. Hugh of St. Victor: "Even so the Divine Page, in its literal sense, . . . [seems] to impart something which smacks of the absurd . . . [but] the spiritual meaning admits no opposition" (*Didascalicon*, 140). See also Pépin, "Histoire de l'exégèse allégorique."

32. See **MMS** lines 120, 2166; and for a remarkable fifteenth-century woodcut of Hur's suffocation in the *SHS* presented as an antitype to Christ's "first derision" (Matt. 26:67), see Wilson and Wilson, *Medieval Mirror,* 178.

33. See **Orm** line 900 ff.; **NHC** pp. 80–82; **MLC** line 2359.

34. Pantin, *English Church,* 211. Pantin's history is especially sensitive to literary questions.

35. See Owst, *Literature and Pulpit,* chaps. 5 and 6, and see Besserman, *Chaucer's Biblical Poetics,* where many of these same questions are addressed vis à vis Chaucer's use of biblical materials.

36. Bestul, *Texts of the Passion,* 17, where he quotes from Peltier, *MVC,* 12:511 and the translation by Ragusa and Green, *Meditations,* 5.

37. Eco, *Art and Beauty,* 100, quoting Ps. 25:8.

38. Horstmann, *Yorkshire Writers,* 1:251.

39. For an excellent analysis of thirteenth-century preaching tools, see Rouse and Rouse, *Preachers,* 3–90.

CHAPTER 2

The Official Reception of Biblical Literature

A COMMON misconception about post-Conquest England is that, until the late fourteenth century, English was the silenced language — at least in literary terms — of the dispossessed masses. Latin, French, and Anglo-Norman surely held sway for legal and political, as well as literary, purposes, but the evidence of the extant documents demonstrates that English continued to serve as an important language of social, commercial, and religious discourse throughout the period. Another, related misconception is that, throughout Christendom, the Catholic church relentlessly suppressed any attempt to make Scripture accessible to lay folk. Central to both misconceptions are attitudes toward language: English versus French, English versus Latin, and the wider question of the languages of the commons versus the languages of authority. This chapter reviews a variety of ecclesiastical, legal, and historical documents from the Norman Conquest to the early fifteenth century in order to investigate what place English had with regard to the other languages, and how the Church did and did not accommodate lay spirituality in England and, for purposes of comparison, on the Continent. Depending on the language in which Scripture, and indeed any formal learning, was expressed, depending on whether that expression was oral or written, and finally depending on who was doing the expressing, it is possible to demonstrate a complex symbiosis of languages and learning, particularly when it involved the expression of Holy Writ. As Siegfried Wenzel has demonstrated in *Macaronic Sermons,* such sermons reveal how languages, particularly Latin and English, work in tandem to achieve doctrinal purposes. Although Wenzel works primarily with Latin sermons containing short English inserts (in prose and verse), a corresponding principle obtains for Middle English biblical works with short Latin inserts. Such a symbiosis simultaneously invests the work with authority and contributes to a certain degree of leveling between the languages. The Latin phrases are, in addition, often geared to the English translations and genuinely functional (unlike the intimidation tactics of Chaucer's Summoner [I.637–47] or the "saffroned" speech of the Pardoner [VI.344–45]). Studious listeners and readers would indeed be able to learn some Latin as they heard or read the work. Examples of the interplay of Latin and English can be seen in the *Estoire del Evangelie* (**EE**), the first of the Trinity manuscript poems (**WA**), most Psalter treatments, the Commentary on the Benedictus (**CB**), the Pauline Epistles (**PE**), the *Mirour of Mans Saluacioune* (**MMS**), and many other works.

Even today, one may debate what counts as literacy and how widespread it is in the United States, or anyplace else. The character and extent of medieval lay literacy present an even more difficult set of questions. Wenzel's book is only one of many that have addressed the subject: books by Brian Stock, M. T. Clanchy, Anne Hudson, Eamon Duffy, and H. Leith Spencer represent some of the more recent, and valuable, work in the field.[1] While it is impossible to reduce such comprehensive and sometimes divergent works to a common conclusion, they can (especially Clanchy's and Duffy's) be seen to demonstrate that a wide cross section of the population in England from the twelfth through the fourteenth centuries participated in social, commercial, and religious discourses which required considerable intellectual and imaginative engagement, and which took a variety of forms well beyond the traditional model of individuals reading books. In part 1 of his book, "The Structures of Traditional Religion," Duffy documents the extent to which "traditional" religion (a term he prefers to "popular" [3]) pervaded the lives of the English in the late Middle Ages. Nicholas Watson discusses a similar phenomenon, which he calls "vernacular theology."[2] I wish to extend these arguments and demonstrate how this same population was not obstructed in its access to Scripture. The best evidence for this access is the production in England of biblical translations, paraphrases, and a huge homiletic corpus before and after the major linguistic and cultural upheaval of the Norman Conquest. Official resistance to vernacular Scripture hardened gradually over time, and became most intolerant in the suppression of the Lollards. The crucial turning point came in the early fifteenth century, when the Lollard controversy came to a head with Arundel's *Constitutions*. But before Wyclif, vernacular treatments of Scripture were not considered unorthodox, much less heretical. Even after Wyclif's posthumous declaration as a heretic in 1415, works of biblical literature continued to be produced through the fifteenth century, with only some minor disquiet expressed by a few of the authors. The critical difference lay precisely between translating Scripture verbatim, with no glosses, and selectively paraphrasing and rearranging Scripture, usually, but not always, with traditional exegesis and apocryphal additions.

The most numerous witnesses to the corpus of biblical literature, as with most extant Middle English works, are, in fact, fifteenth-century manuscripts. Given the vagaries of manuscript survival, however, one should be cautious about extrapolating from the relative abundance or dearth of manuscripts in any given century to the literary tastes or intellectual climate of that century. Watson warns against the "unconscious acknowlegment of the axiom that 'fifteenth-century' equals 'inferior.' "[3] Scholars hold up mirrors to the evidence, and they report and interpret what they see. Where there is much evidence, much can be done; a lack of evidence, especially of manuscripts, imposes silence and necessitates speculation. Both Spencer's and Wenzel's books include the words "Late Middle Ages" or "Late-Medieval" in their titles, and Duffy uses primarily late fourteenth- and fifteenth-century evidence. I wish to use, however, the evidence that does exist from the twelfth and thirteenth centuries to argue for the continuity and strength of the tradition of biblical literature and for the accessibility of major portions of the Bible in English. The wealth of fifteenth-century manuscripts is the culmination, and reflection, of an English medieval tradition, and not an exclusively late medieval phenomenon.

The Official Reception on the Continent

The contrast between England and the Continent was often stark. The following is perhaps the most extreme example of hierarchical dominance if not paranoia:

> Qui custodit linguam suam sapiens est. Ille est vituperandus qui loquitur latinum circa romançum, maxime coram laicis, ita quod ipsi met intelligunt totum; et ille est laudandus qui semper loquitur latinum obscure, ita quod nullus intelligat eum nisi clerici; et ita debent omnes clerici loqui latinum suum obscure in quantum possunt et non circa romançium.[4]

> He who guards his tongue is wise. One who speaks Latin in the presence of Romance-speakers, and above all in front of lay-folk, so that they understand everything, is to be excoriated; and one who always speaks Latin obscurely, so that no one understands him except clerks, is to be praised; and so all clerks ought to speak their Latin as obscurely as they are able, and not in the presence of romance-speakers.

In other words, do not speak your Latin with a Romance accent. Here Latin is the secret and mysterious language used to ensure the dominance of the clique, but more remarkable is the fear that lay people could conceivably learn to understand, especially those speaking romance vernaculars less different from Latin than the languages spoken today. Clearly pronounced Latin, like macaronics, could conceivably allow studious listeners and readers to pick up some of the language. Thus learning Latin (and thereby acquiring access to the world of learning, including Scripture) is inhibited and discouraged because it threatens the position of the literate elite.

A better-documented and pertinent case of official resistance involves the Waldensians of France, who were responsible for the production of the first major body of biblical vernacular literature in Europe. Circa 1173, Pierre Valdus (alias Peter Waldo), a merchant from Lyons who underwent a conversion on the order of Saul's, directed two priests to translate parts of the Bible into Provençal. The result was the so-called "Bible des Pauvres" which became a source book for recitations to the illiterate.[5] One of the other numerous productions associated with the Waldensians is the *Evangéliaire des laïques de Metz*.[6] It dates circa 1200 and is a vernacular lectionary combining a close paraphrase of the Gospel (and also parts of the Pauline epistles) with commentary meant not for scholastic disputation but for the edification of the illiterate faithful. The *Ormulum*, written in Lincoln, dates from nearly the same time and is similar in form and purpose. Orm, an Augustinian canon, may well have been working in isolation, but his work should be seen in the larger context of lectionaries such as this one which, in addition to providing materials for the service, had a populist agenda. Orm's work is the nearest English counterpart to several of the continental paraphrases and homily cycles which encountered official resistance, and his work provides a perspective on the situation in England. English paraphrasers of the twelfth, thirteenth, and fourteenth century met nothing like the opposition met by some paraphrasers on the Continent.

By producing versions of the Scriptures, and by preaching to lay folk without authorization, the Waldensians were acting like candidates in theology, and they were usurping (much like the friars) the office of preaching traditionally reserved to the secular clergy.[7] In gauging the reasons for the Church's resistance, it is useful to note the description by Peter the Chanter (d. 1197) of the study of Scripture at university: "In tribus igitur consistit exercitium sacrae scripturae: circa lectionem, disputationem, et praedicationem."[8] All three practices overlap and describe the conduct of the Waldensians as well as of university lecturers. Another quite remarkable perspective can be found in John Trevisa's *Dialogus inter Dominum et Clericum* which was often prefixed to Trevisa's translation of Higden's *Polychronicon*. Though the "Dialogue" is later (ca. 1387?) and Trevisa was associated with the Oxford translation debates concerning the Lollards, this brief work illustrates an attitude toward the act of preaching which reflects that of Peter the Chanter. The lord, who may represent Trevisa's patron, Lord Thomas of Berkeley, argues the case for the necessity of lay instruction, and cites Jerome, King Alfred, Cædmon, and Bede as orthodox exemplars of the propriety of translating the Bible. He goes on to say that "Also þe gospel and prophecy and þe ryȝt [fey] of holy churche mot be tauȝt and ypreched to Englyschmen þat conneþ no Latyn. . . . and þat ys noȝt ydo bote by Englysch translacion. Vor such Englysch prechyng ys verrey Englysch translacion, and such Englysch prechyng ys good and neodful; þanne Englysch translacion ys good and neodfol."[9] Here again is the simple and striking symbiosis of preaching and translation. The *Myroure of Oure Lady*, a guide to worship for the sisters at the Brigittine convent at Syon in the south of England, makes a similar point: "for redyng is a maner of spekynge."[10]

Spencer discusses a variety of sermon collections meant for lay reading in fourteenth-century England and concludes that "The distinction between reading and preaching, *lectio* and *prædicatio*, had always been thinly drawn and, by the late Middle Ages and early modern period, the two were evidently perceived as complementary practices."[11] To carry a text from one language to another is to carry the text from one people to another (note how Old English *þeod* and *geþeode* denote, respectively, a people and a language). From twelfth-century Paris to late fourteenth-century England, these scholastic practices constituted a set of closely related activities. The idea begins to emerge that any Bible study, be it reading, preaching, or translating, was closely allied to reproducing the text itself. All such studies are biblically based, and none lends itself to easy categorization as "oral" or "literate." Thus the cleric compiling a homily book or lectionary does essentially the same kind of work as someone preaching in the pulpit or actually translating Scripture. Today we recognize significant differences, but the medieval perspective was more flexible. The question here is one of attitude, and strict equivalences are not possible, but even some idea of this unity of endeavor suggests how high these translators and preachers thought their calling to be, and why the church reacted with increasing displeasure.

The Waldensian translations are notable not only for their intended audience but also because an Englishman, Walter Map, was deputed by Pope Alexander III at the third Lateran council in 1179 to argue against the Waldensian sect. Map's account of the debate appears in his famous *De Nugis Curialium*, and although the work survives only in a single manuscript, and

although its pervasive sarcasm and irony significantly complicate its interpretation, his reaction to the Waldensians defines the central issue: biblical
hermeneutics is not for dilettantes.

Vidimus in concilio Romano sub Alexandro papa tertio celebrato
Valdesios, homines ydiotas, illiteratos, a primate ipsorum Valde dictos,
qui fuerat ciuis Lugduni super Rodanum, qui librum domino pape
presentauerunt lingua conscriptum Gallica, in quo textus et glosa
Psalterii plurimorumque legis utriusque librorum continebantur. Hii
multa petebant instancia predicacionis auctoritatem sibi confirmari,
quia periti sibi uidebantur, cum uix essent scioli. Moris etenim est ut
aues, que subtiles non uident laqueos aut rete, liberos ubique credant
meatus. Nonne qui capciosis exercitantur tota uita sermonibus, qui
capere et capi uix possunt, profunde rimatores abissus, nonne hii
timentes offensam reuerenter omnia de Deo proferunt, cuius tam celsa
dignitas ut nulle possint ad eam laudes uel oracionum uirtutes
ascendere nisi misericordia traxerit illas? In singulis diuine pagine
apicibus tot uolitant pennis uirtutum sentencie, tot sapiencie
accumulantur opes, ut de pleno possit haurire cui[cun]que Deus
donauerit in quo. Nunquid ergo margarita porcis, uerbum dabitur
ydiotis, quos ineptos scimus illud suscipere, nedum dare quod
acceperunt? Absit hoc, et euellatur. A capite descendat unguentum in
barbam, et hinc in uestimentum; a fonte deriuentur aque, non a plateis
paludes.

At the Roman Council under Pope Alexander III, I saw some
Waldensians, simple illiterate men, called after their leader Waldo
(Valdès), who was a citizen of Lyons on the Rhône. They offered the
pope a book written in the French tongue, in which was contained the
text, with a gloss, of the Psalter and many of the books of the two
Testaments. They pressed very earnestly that the right of preaching
should be confirmed to them; for in their own eyes they were learned,
though in reality hardly beginners. It is the common case that birds
which do not see fine snares or nets think that there is a free passage
everywhere. Do we not see that those who practise themselves all their
days in subtle discourse, who hardly can either entrap others or be
entrapped, the explorers of the deepest depths—are not they, fearing
offence, always cautious in their utterance about God, whose state is so
high that neither praise nor the strength of prayer can mount to him
unless his mercy draws it? In every letter of the divine page there flit on
the wings of virtues so many sayings, there is heaped up such wealth of
wisdom, that any to whom the Lord has given the means can draw from
its fulness. Shall then the pearl be cast before swine, the word be given
to the ignorant, whom we know to be unfit to take it in, much less to
give out what they have received? Away with such a thought, uproot it!
From the head let ointment go down to the beard and thence to the

clothing; from the spring let the water be led, not puddles out of the streets.[12]

Map's similes are unflattering and his tone condescending, but it is important to note that the most complex of his similes deprecates the interpretive powers of even his most learned peers, the "profunde rimatores abissus." The central bird simile delineates Map's most serious objection; the two "nonne" clauses rhetorically contrast university-trained scholars with the rude Waldensians. Thus the point is not that these neophytes have dared to produce a Bible, but that they have presumed to offer interpretations in matters properly addressed only by those qualified to do so, and only by those to whom God has given the ability. The Waldensians specifically request the right to preach, not to produce or possess biblical translations, which is a fait accompli. Map's appeal to divine authority is self-serving, but it illustrates how seriously he views the infraction. The two biblical echoes at the end of the passage shed some light on Map's attitude. The first (Matt. 7:6) shows clearly enough that Scripture will be wasted on those who have no capacity to appreciate it: "Nolite dare sanctum canibus: neque mittatis margaritas vestras ante porcos, ne forte conculcent eas pedibus suis, et conversi dirumpant vos" ("Give not that which is holy to dogs; neither cast ye your pearls before swine, lest perhaps they trample them under their feet, and turning upon you, they tear you"). The last clause of this verse is rarely cited along with the pearl/swine imagery, but it can hardly have been far from Map's consciousness; these pearls of wisdom can be turned back against the proper custodians. Casting them abroad is more than just a profanation, it is a threat to the status quo. The second echo builds on this idea of a threat. Here Map paraphrases Psalm 132, verses 1–2: "Ecce quam bonum et quam decorum habitare fratres in uno sicut unguentum optimum in capite quod descendit in barbam, barbam Aaron, quod descendit super oram vestimentorum eius" ("Behold how good and how pleasant it is for brethren to dwell together in unity, like the precious ointment on the head, that ran down upon the beard, the beard of Aaron, which ran down to the skirt of his garment"). The psalm celebrates the fraternity of the priestly caste—the Levites—and Map is outraged by the efforts of the interlopers. He seems to take the rather odd oil image as a sign of the homogeneity and uniformity of priests in a kind of oleaginous apostolic succession. The figure extends into the water image, with the suggestion that oil and water do not mix: the pure waters of biblical interpretation are derived only from proper sources, not from the mud of public ways.

If one were to read Map sympathetically, he argues for the necessity of proper qualifications. In an unsympathetic reading, especially as the biblical echoes imply, Map arrogates to a dominant clique any possibility of biblical study. In the same chapter Map says as much (again echoing Matt.7:6): "quos si admiserimus, expellemur" ("if we let them in, we shall be turned out").[13] Later in the *De Nugis Curialium* Map expresses contempt for the vernacular itself and the "school of mummers" who write in it:

> Cesar en Lucani, Eneas Maronis, multis uiuunt in laudibus, plurimum suis meritis et non minimum uigilancia poetarum. Nobis diuinam Karolorum et Pepinorum nobilitatem uulgaribus ritmis sçola mimorum concelebrat; presentes uero Cesares nemo loquitur.

> Caesar lives in the mighty praises of Lucan, Aeneas in those of Maro, largely by their own merits, and yet not the least by the alertness of the poets. For us the troupe of buffoons keeps alive the divine fame of the Charlemagnes and Pepins in popular ballads, but of our modern Caesars no one tells.[14]

One wonders to what "vulgar rhymes" Map refers—obviously it is to some portion of the Matter of France and not to any biblical translation—but he makes it clear that Latin is to be preferred for past and present poetry.

The problems associated with vernacular translations persisted with Pope Alexander's successor, Innocent III, who is a central figure in the question of the official toleration of vernacular translation and the question of lay piety. Overall, it seems as if he tried to accommodate some of the sects as much as possible, going so far as to establish a kind of pseudo-monastic rule under which members of one sect of lay religious in thirteenth-century Lombardy —the Humiliati—lived communally and preached to one another, though not on doctrinal points.[15] Innocent recognized the piety of these simple folk and tried to ensure that they be innocent of heresy. One of his bulls, dated July 12, 1199, responds to concerns expressed by the archbishop of Metz about translations of the Gospels, the Pauline epistles, and other books done by lay people in his diocese; presumably the bishop wants punitive action authorized or confirmed. Exactly what the bishop requested is unclear, and unfortunately his letter as well as several others in the exchange do not survive. Innocent's letter, however, has become a locus classicus for whether or not the medieval church banned vernacular Bible reading as early as the end of the twelfth century.

> Sane significavit nobis venerabilis frater noster . . . Metensis episcopus per litteras suas, quod tam in diocesi quam urbe Metensi laicorum et mulierum multitudo non modica tracta quodammodo desiderio Scripturarum Euangelia, epistolas Pauli, Psalterium, Moralia Iob et plures alios libros sibi fecit in Gallico sermone transferri, translationi huiusmodi adeo libenter—utinam autem et prudenter—intendens, ut

secretis conventionibus talia inter se laici et mulieres eructare
presumant et sibi invicem predicare. . . . Licet autem desiderium
intelligendi divinas scripturas et secundum eas studium adhortandi
reprehendendum non sit, sed potius comendandum: in eo tamen
apparent merito arguendi, quod tales occulta conventicula celebrant,
officium sibi predicationis usurpant, sacerdotum simplicitatem eludunt
et eorum consortium aspernantur, qui talibus non inherent. . . . Porro, si
quis obiciat, quod iuxta preceptum Dominicum non est sanctum
dandum canibus ned margarite mittende sunt ante porcos [Matt. 7:6],
cum et Christus ipse non omnibus quidem sed solis apostolis dixerit:
"Vobis datum est nosse misterium regni Dei, ceteris autem in parabolis"
[Matt. 13:11, Luke 8:10]; intelligat canes et porcos non eos esse, qui
sanctum gratanter accipiunt et margaritas libenter acceptant, sed illos
qui sanctum dilacerant et margaritas contempnunt . . . Propter quod
simplicioribus inquit apostolus: "Quasi parvulis in Christo lac potum
dedi vobis, non escam" [1Cor. 3:1–2]. . . . Tanta est enim divine scripture
profunditas, ut non solum simplices et illiterati, sed etiam prudentes et
docti non plene sufficiant ad ipsius intelligentiam indagandam; propter
quod dicit Scriptura: "Quia multi defecerunt scrutantes scrutinio"
[Ps. 63:7]. Unde recte fuit olim in lege divina statutum, ut bestia, que
montem tetigerit, lapidetur [Ex. 19:13].[16]

The bishop of Metz has signified to us that both in his city and in his
diocese a multitude of laymen and women, led to a large extent by a
desire of understanding the scriptures, have had translated for
themselves the gospels, epistles of S. Paul, the psalter, the moralisation
on Job, and many other books in the French tongue. They intend that
with this translation, made thus at their own discretion (would that it
had been made with prudence as well), laymen and women shall
presume to hold forth on such matters, and to preach to each other. . . .
Now although the desire of understanding holy scriptures, and zeal for
exhorting in accordance with them, is not to be reprehended but rather
commended, yet in this matter certain laymen appear to be justly
accused: because they hold secret conventicles, usurp to themselves the
office of preaching, elude the simplicity of priests, and scorn the
company of those who cling not to these things. . . . Furthermore, if
someone object, that according to the divine precept that the holy not
be given to dogs nor pearls be cast before swine [Matt. 7:6], just as
Christ himself not to everyone but only to the apostles said: "to you it is
given to know the mystery of the kingdom of God, to the rest in
parables" [Matt. 13:11, Luke 8:10]; let him understand that the dogs
and swine are not those who thankfully receive the holy and cheerfully
accept the pearls, but those who tear apart the holy and despise the
pearls. . . . for what says the apostle to simple people?: "Even as babes in
Christ I have fed you with milk and not with meat" [1Cor. 3:1–2]. . . . For
such is the depth of divine scripture, that not only the simple and

illiterate, but even the prudent and learned, are not fully sufficient to
try to understand it. *For many seek and fail in their search* [Ps. 63:7],
whence it was of old rightly written in the divine law, that *the beast which
touched the mount should be stoned* [Ex. 19:13].[17]

Innocent invokes, as did Map before him, the image of casting pearls before swine; his direction that any beast touching the sacred mountain (i.e.,
Holy Writ) be stoned is from Heb. 12:20, an echo of Ex. 19:13.[18] Immediately before this echo of the Mosaic law Innocent quotes Ps. 63:7, which
reinforces the idea that amateur exegesis promotes heterodoxy; only those
in the "consortium" of priests, not the "conventicula" of usurpers, should be
allowed to interpret. The quotations, and some of the rhetoric, contribute
to the increasingly negative tone of the letter, but I quote it at this length
to indicate how subtle and measured Innocent's approach is as he considers
the question from multiple viewpoints.

In response to Margaret Deanesly's discussion of Innocent's policy,
Leonard E. Boyle reconsiders Innocent's letter of 1199 and another in which
he appoints three abbots to investigate the matter.[19] Boyle's principal objection is that Deanesly confuses the *narracio,* wherein Innocent simply re-
capitulates the archbishop's objections, with the *dispositio,* wherein Innocent
makes his own position clear. But however tolerant Innocent himself was,
Deanesly is not alone in confusing (if that is indeed the case) the *narracio* and
the *dispositio:* what powerful individuals are thought to have said is always
more important than what they may have intended. As Innocent's letter was
cited through the centuries, it conveyed at the very least the impression
that the translations were indeed forbidden by the pope. Boyle also emphasizes the words "in eo tamen apparent merito arguendi." Here he rejects
Deanesly's translation of "in this matter certain laymen appear to be justly
accused" in favor of "they appear indeed worthy of being taken to task—
argued with—on this account."[20] Boyle concludes that the pope, who com-
mends the desire to understand Scripture, was not prohibiting vernacular
translation but censuring those who "usurp the office of preaching" reserved
for priests alone.[21] Innocent's objection is thus very similar to Map's, except
that the bull had more far-reaching consequences. What the preaching in
question consisted of, however, and the extent of literacy within the sects,
are open questions. There is some evidence that Waldo himself and others
with no formal schooling simply memorized and recited gospel passages and
that this was their "preaching."[22] Alexander Patschovsky, on the other hand,
argues for a considerable degree of literacy among both the "organisational
elite of the community" and the preacher in the field.[23] The *Constitutiones* of
the Fourth Lateran Council in 1215 threaten with excommunication those

who appropriate preaching duties but mention neither the production nor suppression of vernacular Scripture.[24] Preaching was itself divided between doctrinal preaching and penitential preaching (e.g., by friars). The former was strictly regulated, while hearing confession appears to have been more informal. In any event, neither the Waldensians nor the members of other suspect groups were ordained or professed.

One would suppose that a Church founded upon a Scripture at least two removes (Septuagint and Vulgate, with the added complication of the Vetus Latina translations) from the original would be sympathetic to any orthodox treatment. One of Christ's final injunctions—"Go ye into the whole world, and preach the gospel to every creature" (Mark 16:15)—and Pentecost itself attest that the work of spreading the Word in multiple tongues was the germinal principle and sine qua non of the Church. The *Constitutiones* of Lateran 1215 are themselves almost Pentecostal in their provision of an official framework for lay instruction. This council marked the culmination of Innocent III's papacy, during which the Church began to show much greater interest in lay spirituality and education. For example, constitution 21 required yearly confession and communion from everyone:

> Omnis utriusque sexus fidelis, postquam ad annos discretionis pervenerit, omnia sua solus peccata confiteatur fideliter, saltem semel in anno proprio sacerdoti, et iniunctam sibi poenitentiam studeat pro viribus adimplere, suscipiens reverenter ad minus in pascha eucharistiae sacramentum . . .

> All the faithful of either sex, after they have reached the age of discernment, should individually confess all their sins in a faithful manner to their own priest at least once a year, and let them take care to do what they can to do the penance imposed on them. Let them reverently receive the sacrament of the eucharist at least at Easter . . .[25]

The understaffed and sometimes poorly educated clergy were not equal to this task; hence the rise of the friars and the explosion of instructional materials teaching the proper modes of confession. Archbishop Pecham's Lambeth *Constitutions* of 1281 were the formal English response to Lateran IV; they were the model for Archbishop Thoresby of York's instructions for clergy, produced in English in 1357 by John Gaytryge as the *Lay Folks Catechism*. These "pastoralia" contain, and are often coordinated with, various biblical works, especially with regard to fundamental points of instruction such as the Psalter, the Ten Commandments, and the Pater Noster.[26]

Constitution 9 bears even more closely on the question of lay instruction:

> Quoniam in plerisque partibus intra eandem civitatem atque dioecesim permixti sunt populi diversarum linguarum, habentes sub una fide

varios ritus et mores, districte praecipimus ut pontifices huiusmodi
civitatum sive dioecesum, provideant viros idoneos, qui secundum
diversitates rituum et linguarum divina officia illis celebrent et
ecclesiastica sacramenta ministrent, instruendo eos verbo pariter et
exemplo.

Since in many places peoples of different languages live within the same
city or diocese, having one faith but different rites and customs, we
therefore strictly order bishops of such cities and dioceses to provide
suitable men who will do the following in the various rites and
languages: celebrate the divine services for them, administer the
church's sacrament, and instruct them by word and example.[27]

The "officia," which presumably refer to preaching duties and of course not
to the Mass itself, were to be in the vernacular, and I would place special emphasis on the "suitable men" who were qualified by their language skills to
preach "by word and example" in the appropriately accessible language.[28]
When it came to lay instruction, there was no "official" language.

The case of the Waldensians demonstrates, however, that vernacular
translations of Scripture by lay people were prima facie evidence of heresy
and could be so treated. Very soon after Innocent's letters translators had
much to fear, at least on the Continent. Evidence of outright suppression
appears in Alberic's account for the year 1200 of the resolution of the difficulties at Metz:

Item in urbe Metensi pullulante secta, que dicitur Valdensium, directi
sunt ad predicandum quidam abbates, qui quosdam libros de Latino in
Romanum versos combusserunt et predictam sectam extirpaverunt.[29]

Likewise in the city of Metz a sect was swarming, the Waldensians, and
certain abbots were sent to preach, who burnt certain books translated
from Latin into Romance, and they extirpated the aforementioned sect.

The intricacies of Map's similes and the hypothesized intentions of Innocent's bull thus achieve a certain irrelevance in the face of political realities,
but the distinctions they draw contribute to a better understanding of what
exactly was perceived as a threat.

Despite the more liberal attitudes promulgated at Lateran IV, preaching
or translating became a dangerous enterprise. Boyle concludes his discussion of Innocent's treatment of vernacular Scripture as follows: "Perhaps,
in conclusion, one is making too much of all this. I do not think so. The
plain fact is that while everyone admits, as the *Cambridge History of the Bible*
does, that 'no universal and absolute prohibition of the translation of the
Scriptures into the vernacular nor of the use of such translations by clergy
or laity was ever issued by any council of the Church or any pope,' these

three letters of Innocent III are repeatedly adduced, as they are by this same *Cambridge History,* as letters 'which could reasonably be taken to represent condemnation of translation.'"[30]

But such a prohibition does exist in the register of the Council of Toulouse which took place in 1229, under Innocent's successor, Gregory IX, and under the specific auspices of the papal legate Cardinal Romain Frangipani. Its general heading is "de inquirendis haereticis, deque aliis ecclesiasticae disciplinae capitibus celebratum."[31] The introduction notes that it was well attended by archbishops, bishops, and secular authorities of the Languedoc region, where the Cathars and Waldensians were particularly virulent. The relevant decree is capitulum xiv:

> *Ne laici habeant libros Scripturae, praeter psalterium, & Divinum officium: at eos libros ne habeant in vulgari lingua.* Prohibemus etiam, ne libros veteris testamenti aut novi, laici permittantur habere: nisi forte psalterium, vel breviarium pro Divinis officiis, aut horas beatae Mariae aliquis ex devotione habere velit. Sed ne praemissos libros habeant in vulgari translatos, arctissime inhibemus.[32]

> *Lay people shall not have books of scripture, except the psalter and the divine office: and they shall not have these books in the vulgar tongue.* Moreover we prohibit that lay people should be permitted to have books of the Old or New Testament, except perchance any should wish from devotion to have a psalter, or a breviary for the divine office, or the hours of the blessed Virgin: but we most strictly prohibit their having even the aforesaid books translated into the vulgar tongue.[33]

This was evidently a minor council and not ecumenical as the Fourth Lateran Council had been fourteen years earlier; perhaps it was merely an ad hoc response to a local problem. But other capitula from the Toulouse register are obviously patterned on Lateran 1215, and it is reasonable to assume that attendance must have overlapped. The immediately preceding capitulum (xiii), like constitution 21 of Lateran 1215, requires regular confession and communion, but Toulouse requires thrice-yearly compliance as opposed to Lateran's annual requirement.[34] The first fourteen capitula, in fact, have to do with the discovery and punishment of heretics, and are largely based on Lateran's constitution 3 ("De haereticis").[35] Also noteworthy are similar territorial prohibitions issued at Tarragona (northeast Spain) in 1234, at Bologna in 1242 (at the Dominican general chapter), and at Béziers (southern France) in 1246.[36] Thus there were official prohibitions, by councils, of vernacular Scripture as early as 1229. A series of ad hoc responses could have a cumulatively repressive effect, as did the English restrictions some 150 years later. In 1688 the Reformation historian and polemicist Edward Stillingfleet still recalls the Tolouse decree with some vehemence in his reaction to the Council of Trent (1545–63).[37] The cumulative effect of the papal letters and conciliar decrees must surely have inhibited lay access to biblical material.

Deanesly's book, especially chapter 2, "The Prohibitions of Vernacular Bible Reading in France, Italy and Spain," remains a comprehensive indictment of how the Church on the Continent tightened its control of lay knowledge of Scripture from the tenth through the fourteenth century. One final example extends the threat of official sanction from Scripture itself to biblically based works. Jacob van Maerlant, a Fleming, translated the *Historia Scholastica* into Dutch circa 1271; he omits all biblical quotation in his subsequent translation of Vincent of Beauvais's *Speculum Historiale*. Objections must have been raised to his work since he states in the prologue to his *Speculum* translation that "the papacy might take it amiss . . . because I have made known to the lay people secret things out of the Bible."[38] He almost certainly refers to those biblical passages which he translated from the *Historia*. Maerlant was summoned to Rome for having done so, and the case achieved such notoriety that one vernacular partisan (he who counts sixty Latin heretics in Latin—see below, p. 53) apparently cites Maerlant as the Fleming who "translatid al þe Bibel in-to Flemyche, for wiche dede he was somoned before þe Pope of grete enmyte & þe boke was taken to examynacion & truely aproued; it was deliuered to hym aȝene in conf[u]cioun to his enemyes."[39] Neither the *Historia* nor the *Speculum* qualify as a Bible, but even biblical quotation and paraphrase raised objections. The authorities at Rome either accepted the translation of the *Historia,* the orthodoxy of which was never questioned, or simply declined to prosecute, but Maerlant had learned his lesson when the time came for the *Speculum* translation.

The Official Reception in England

One could construe the preceding documents negatively and conclude that England lagged behind the Continent in official legislation against vernacular Scripture, as it lagged behind in other cultural phenomena. More positively, one could conclude that England enjoyed a much more liberal atmosphere with regard to vernacular Scripture up to, and even through, the fifteenth century. But given the sacral character of the Bible and the insistence that only the Church speak on doctrinal points, the vernacular movement was bound to conflict, over time, with Latin, one of the *linguae sacrae.* A vernacular translation can easily be regarded as an abasement, and the question of the status of a language is bound up with cultural and political considerations. The conflict in England came to a head in the early fifteenth century, at the height of the Lollard controversy and when copies of the Wycliffite translations were circulating.

In 1384, the year of Wyclif's death, one can see the increasingly vigorous reaction against unauthorized preaching: "Power (as hertofore granted to the archbishop of Canterbury) for Alexander, archbishop of York, and his suffragans in their dioceses, to arrest and imprison all maintainers or preachers of conclusions contrary to sound doctrine and subversive of the Catholic faith, which have been condemned by Holy Church, some as heresies, others as errors . . ." [40] Similar powers were extended to secular authorities four years later, except now books are the object of enforcement: "Appointment of John Godard and John Hothom, knights, William de Risseby and the sheriff of York, upon credible information that Master Nicholas Hereford and the late Master John Wyclif caused certain books, booklets, schedules, and quires (*quaternos*) to be written and published containing divers heresies and errors . . . to investigate, arrest, take and with all speed bring before the Council all such books." [41]

Another official reaction is the famous statute *De haeretico comburendo* of 1401. This was the first imposition by the secular authorities in England of the death penalty for heresy, yet the rhetoric is reminiscent of earlier papal restrictions. Speaking of the nonconformists,

> praedicant & docent hiis diebus publice et occulte . . . conventiculas & confederationes illicitas faciunt, scolas tenent & exercent, libros conficiunt atque scribunt, populum nequiter instruunt & informant . . . [42]

> they preach & teach these days publicly and secretly . . . they make illicit conventicles and confederations, they hold and conduct schools, they manufacture and write books, they nefariously instruct and inform the people . . .

The statute ends with the disturbing prescription that those found guilty "coram [populo] in eminenti loco comburi faciant" ("be burned before the people in a prominent place"). [43] Although the Bible is not mentioned, it is probable that the subject matter of the preaching, teaching, and writing was biblical. The Lollards were making their presence felt. [44]

The culmination of the official restrictions is article 7 of Arundel's 1408 *Constitutions*, which prohibited the translating or even the reading of vernacular Scripture unless by license of the bishop; it is the first outright ban on such activity in England. After referring to Jerome's warning that any translation may deform the true scriptural significance, the article continues

> statuimus igitur atque ordinamus, ut nemo deinceps aliquem textum sacrae scripturae auctoritate sua in linguam Anglicanam, vel aliam

transferat, per viam libri, libelli, aut tractatus, nec legatur aliquis huismodi liber, libellus, aut tractatus jam noviter tempore dicti Johannis Wyclif, sive citra, compositus, aut in posterum componendus, in parte vel in toto, publice, vel occulte, sub majoris excommunicationis poena, quosque per loci dioecesanum, seu, si res exigerit, per concilium provinciale ipsa translatio fuerit approbata: qui contra fecerit, ut fautor haeresis et erroris similiter puniatur.[45]

We therefore constitute and ordain, that no one henceforth translate into the English tongue or any other by his own authority any text of sacred scripture, by way of books, booklets, or tracts, nor that he read any such book, booklet, or tract composed either recently by the said John Wyclif, or since, or yet to be composed, in part or in whole, publicly, or in secret, under the pain of excommunication, in every place of the diocese, unless, if circumstance requires, the translation be approved by the provincial council: he who does otherwise, let the perpetrator be punished in the same manner for heresy and error.

Arundel's ban made the Wycliffites well-known—indeed infamous—but at the same time made use of their translations dangerous. The specific reference to "libelli" makes it clear that portable copies of the Scriptures (in more than one language, as the phrase "vel aliam" implies) were in existence and that copies in a variety of forms were proliferating rapidly. The official restrictions progress from the archbishops' ban on preaching (1384) to the bans in the patent letters and in the statute on making books (1388 and 1401) to Arundel's specific prohibition of vernacular Scriptures (1408). Watson sums up the change in climate succinctly: "here Pecham's *minimum* necessary for the laity to know if they are to be saved has been redefined as the *maximum* they may hear, read, or even discuss."[46] Many writers at the turn of the century were aware of the debate and of the dangers.

An illustration of the turmoil of the times is the following excerpt from the *Myroure of Oure Ladye,* written for the sisters at the Brigittine convent at Syon, which reflects one spiritual adviser's apprehension over Archbishop Arundel's ban and the new atmosphere of intolerance: "And for as moche as yt is forboden vnder payne of cursynge, that no man shulde haue ne drawe eny texte of holy scrypture in to englysshe wythout lycense of the bysshop dyocesan. And in dyuerse places of youre seruyce ar suche textes of scrypture; therefore I asked & haue lysence of oure bysshop to drawe suche thinges in to englysshe to your gostly comforte and profyt."[47]

Scribal additions and deletions in fifteenth-century manuscripts also indicate the change in climate. The following addition to the *Myroure* by a fifteenth-century reviser shows how officials became less tolerant of the use of vernacular materials in service: "This lokeynge on the englyshe whyle the

latyn ys redde. ys to be vnderstonde of them that haue sayde theyre mat-
tyns or redde theyr legende before. For else I wolde not counsell them to
leue the herynge of the latyn for entendaunce of the englysshe."[48] Deletions
tell their own story. The earliest manuscript of the *Estoire del Evangelie* (**EE**)
(London, Dulwich College XXII, ca. 1300) reads as follows:

> Sum þng of þe [Jesus] write ant rede
> Þare þoureau of þe to winne mede
> [a]nt þei þat hit schal here
> Of þe godspelle may sum þing lere
> Þat writin is þare-inne of þe
> On english tunge þoreu swink of me.[49]

A fifteenth-century copy of the poem in Oxford, Bodleian Lib. Add. C.38
omits not only this passage but also nearly all of the Latin quotations, primarily from Scripture, which Dulwich included. The scribe is evidently
aware of the current controversy over vernacular Scripture, and he wishes
to downplay his role as an English evangelizer. Likewise, the manuscript histories of sermon and homily cycles reveal the rising pressure against vernacular translations. Later manuscripts of the *Northern Homily Cycle* (**NHC**)
include less and less biblical material, in Latin or in English, and some manuscripts copy only the exempla, omitting the Gospel passages entirely.[50]

More overt unease is expressed in a Middle English translation of Robert
of Gretham's Anglo-Norman gospel lectionary, the *Miroir* or *Les Evangiles des
Domnées* (ca. 1280). In that collection Robert had expressed the utility of the
collection in terms of supplementing his patroness's rich diet of romances.[51]
The Middle English adapter takes a different tack when he offers his own
opinions on translation. After insisting that everything he has translated
has its basis in Holy Writ he writes: "Latin ne wil I sette non ther inne, for
it semeth as it were a prid for to telle another that he ne vnderstondeth
nouȝt. And so it is a gret folie for to speke Latin to lewed men. For iche
man schal ben vndernommen at the dai of dome efter his own langage."[52]
The last sentence is especially comforting to those of us who lack facility
with languages. The author has a more mundane and pressing concern, however: "Mi name ne wil I nouȝt nemni, for the enemis that miȝht heren it. . . .
For it is the maner of the enemis for to ben grucchand and noious, and
wil blethelich coniecten the wordes of holy writ, and wil tellen it on hir
maner."[53] He obviously feels some apprehension over having provided such
a close English translation, and fears reprisal. His egalitarian attitude is ad-
mirable, though perhaps the most interesting feature here is his accusation
that his enemies, presumably traditional churchmen, "coniect"—reconstrue

or misconstrue—Scripture on their own. This is exactly the accusation which the Church had used against earlier vernacular translators.

The most dramatic unease over the propriety of biblical translation appears in the late fourteenth-century *Prose Version of Epistles, Acts, and Matthew* (**PCE**). After a brief summary of Genesis through the Flood, a debate ensues between a learned brother and two less-learned interlocutors—a brother and a sister—concerning the duty of the learned to teach those who are "lewed & vnkunnynge . . . þinges þat beþ nedeful to þe hele of oure soules; þat is to seye, what þing is plesynge to God, & what displeseþ hym also."[54] The learned brother acknowledges his responsibility but refuses, since "we beþ now so fer y-fallen a-wey from Cristis lawe, þat ȝif y wolde answere to þyn axynges y moste vnderfonge þe deþ."[55] The petitioners persist, and back up their argument with quotations from the Old Testament and the example of Christ.[56] Their biblical acumen belies their professed ignorance, and the sly use of *praetereo* combined with *occultatio* provides another means of injecting some of the material which is the object of their request. They finally threaten to ask someone else for instruction, and they imply the damnation of the learned brother by stating that the person who does comply with their wishes will be judged according to what is right at Doomsday. He responds: "Broþer, þou hast agast me sumwhat wiþ þyn argumentys. For þouȝ þou ne hafe noȝt y-ben a-mong clerkes at scole, þi skelis þat þou makest beþ y-founded in loue þat is a-bote resoun þat clerkes useþ in scole."[57] Though unschooled, the brother can produce arguments and reasons inspired by love. Such powers, it appears, are innate and exceed the endowments of formal learning. The learned brother resumes with a précis of Exodus and Leviticus, but his initial reluctance and fear of death are puzzling. Because the Catholic and Pauline epistles were traditionally the domain of scholastic debate in theology, perhaps he is reluctant to tread on the territory of the dialecticians and therefore hedges.[58] The five manuscripts of **PCE** all date from circa 1400 and the superior may well be sensitive to the growing opposition to vernacular translation inspired by the Lollards, but considerations other than official condemnation seem to operate here. Given the context of the original request for instruction (immediately after the destruction of humankind in the Flood because of its hopelessly sinful nature), the learned brother's fear seems to be based not on the possibility of secular punishment but on some kind of divine retribution resulting from the disclosure of the means of penance; the world is once again so far gone that any eleventh-hour measures to find out what is "pleasing" to God are inappropriate. Significantly, the petitioners secure his assent by invoking exactly what he fears most—the Last Judgment. From this prologue, and from the placement of the debate in the sequence of biblical material, several conclusions may be drawn.

First, the threat of Doomsday is the motivating force for the presentation of the biblical material. The petitioners never ask for a translation, and the word "Bible" is not once mentioned in the prologue. Instead, they ask for "þinges þat beþ nedeful to þe hele of oure soules." One might expect a selection of works from the Vernon manuscript (which calls itself "Sowlehele") or a *summa* on confession such as Robert Mannyng's *Handlyng Synne*.[59] Instead one gets a close translation of some biblical books. The means of salvation are closely connected to lay acquaintance with Scripture. Second, what is primarily a translation of New Testament epistles requires a prologue abstracted from Genesis, Exodus, and Leviticus, with a liberal sprinkling of quotations from other books. Acts and part of Matthew follow, and the whole text, by virtue of its inclusiveness, has some pretensions to being a complete Bible. These summaries and quotations appear without qualm and almost as a matter of course, and the author takes great pains to introduce and contextualize his translation of the Epistles with the essential material from the Old Testament. He thus reflects a hierarchy of biblical material which can be seen in other major works.[60]

Lastly, the tone of the debate is far removed from the continental controversies involving the Waldensians or Jacob van Maerlant. The emphasis is wholly on humanity's relationship to God, Scripture, the Last Judgment, and the means of personal salvation. The learned brother does not refuse because he fears punishment; he refuses because he will not transgress a body of principle. Even in a set of manuscripts copied in the midst of Wycliffite activity, the official sanction or condemnation of the translation is not an issue. The petitioners get their translation because they are innately worthy, and because the learned have a moral obligation to teach both men and women (see the discussions of **LLB, MML,** and **MBL**).

The social class of the audience is an issue, however. The brother and sister are novitiates who have not been to school, and thus may be seen to be impinging on the prerogatives of the educated upper classes. Some insight into the access to Scripture by a member of the aristocracy is provided by the author of an anonymous Lollard tract who refers to a sermon eulogizing Anne of Bohemia (wife of Richard II, d. August 4, 1394) delivered by Thomas Arundel himself: "in his comendynges of hir, he seide: it was more joie of his þan of any woman þat euere he knewe ffor, not-wiþstanding þat sche was an alien borne, sche hadde on Engliche al þe foure Gospeleris wiþ þe doctoris vpon hem. And he seide sche hadde sent hem vn-to him, and he seide þei weren goode and trewe and comended hir in þat sche was so grete a lady, & also an alien, & wolde so lowliche studiee in so vertuous bokis." [61] The author of this tract, as is obvious from the rest of the text, is a vernacular partisan, and he may intentionally overdo the account of Arundel's commendation, but Arundel apparently approved of the translations nonetheless and granted a license as was required. There was, apparently, nothing illicit about the ownership and use of vernacular Scripture, at least by a member of the royal house, at the end of the fourteenth century, if the text was accompanied by a traditional gloss. The form taken by the biblical text was far more important than the biblical contents per se. Arundel also approved the production and circulation of Nicholas Love's *Mirror* (**MBL**) as a kind of conservative antidote to the Wycliffite translations. [62] Love's work was nonthreatening because it conformed with the tradition of biblical paraphrase accompanied by orthodox exegesis.

Most importantly, the quantity of biblical literature which exists in fifteenth-century manuscripts demonstrates that the transmission and possession of the Bible in various forms was not seriously inhibited and that these fifteenth-century texts derived from a vigorous antecedent tradition. Watson's observation is again helpful: "[T]o a remarkable extent these texts dated from what had clearly been canonized as a theological golden age, an age of vernacular *auctores,* not from the age of brass in which fifteenth-century readers were now living. It was evidently an inadvertent side effect of the *Constitutions* to help precipitate this creation of a canon of theological writing by simply sealing it up, making it so hard for later writers to contribute further to this literature that it is fair to say that original theological writing in English was, for a century, almost extinct." [63] The production of new works clearly slowed down even as the copying of existing works sped up.

Finally, Anne Hudson, who has worked on the subject of vernacular English Scriptures extensively, characterizes the intellectual climate at the turn of the century as follows:

> questions raised by Wyclif could still be debated openly in the early
> years of the fifteenth century in Oxford, with the implication that the
> hardening of attitudes, and definition of the bounds of authority, took
> place, not at the departure of Wyclif for Lutterworth in 1382, but nearly
> twenty-five years later under the zeal of Arundel. In 1401 the question of
> biblical translation could be debated openly, without accusations of
> heresy being levelled against defenders of the view, and without
> identification of the proponents of translations as *Wycliffistes.* [64]

The decisive break came in the early fifteenth century; prior attitudes toward the Bible were formed in a more tolerant atmosphere and fostered the production of a wide variety of biblical literatures. The minor disquiet expressed by the author of the *Myroure* or by the learned brother in **PCE** is almost the only evidence of possible official suppression before the Lollard controversy exploded. There is, on the contrary, abundant evidence that many authors of biblical literature in English were impelled by nationalistic motives, and by what could be called a kind of religious egalitarianism.

NOTES

1. Stock, *Implications;* Clanchy, *Memory to Written Record;* Hudson, *Premature Reformation;* Duffy, *Stripping of the Altars;* Spencer, *Preaching.* Chaytor's *Script to Print* is dated but remains valuable. See also Parkes, "Literacy"; Coleman, *Medieval Readers,* esp. chap. 2; Orme, *Education and Society;* Richter, "Socio-linguistic Approach"; and Bäuml, "Varieties and Consequences."

2. Watson, "Censorship," 823.

3. Ibid.

4. Richter, "Latina Lingua," 19. The quotation is some advice given by Virgilius, the philosopher of Cordoba, ca. 1290. Cf. Prov. 12:18 and 21:23, and the advice given in the letter of James, especially chap. 3, to guard one's "lingua." Richter attempts to determine when Latin would have ceased to be understood in Italy. The existence of thirteenth-century vernacular Italian translations argues for extensive enough differences by that time; the vernacular in Gaul was clearly distinct from Latin by the ninth century (21).

5. For the Waldensians, see Thouzellier, *Catharisme,* and Patschovsky, "Literacy of Waldensianism." Moore (*Popular Heresy*) and Peters (*Heresy and Authority*) translate some source documents. For bibliography on this and other heresies, see Berkhout and Russell (*Medieval Heresies,* 53–61).

6. Paris, Bibliothèque de l'Arsenal 2083. See Berger, *Bible française,* 40–46, 365. For other biblical materials in French, see Bonnard (*Traductions de la Bible*) and Smeets ("Traductions").

7. Rouse and Rouse provide a very good discussion, centered on Lateran IV, of how the Church promoted and inhibited various kinds of preaching in the thirteenth century (*Preachers,* 47–64). A Canterbury statute of 1213 or 1214 prohibited unlicensed preaching; see canon 51 in Whitelock et al., *Councils and Synods,* vol. 2, part 1, 33–34. The standard work on the subject is Charland, *Artes praedicandi.* Also important is Owst, *Preaching,* now largely superseded by Spencer, *Preaching.*

8. Peter the Chanter, *Verbum Abbreviatum,* PL 205.25.

9. Waldron, "Trevisa's Prefaces," 292–93, lines 146–53, and see Hanna, "Thomas Berkeley," 894–95.

10. Blunt, *Myroure,* 66. In *Vineyard* Illich provides a good discussion of somatic effects as "reading" progressed from an active, oral recitation to a silent, private pursuit.

11. Spencer, *Preaching,* 38.

12. James et al., *De Nugis Curialium,* distinc. I.xxxi, p. 124.

13. Ibid., 127.

14. Ibid., distinc. V.i, p. 404. Cf. Map's scornful reference to "Marlborough French" (distinc. V.6, p. 496). On two occasions Map quotes English: once to refer to a *ghild-*

hus (guild hall [distinc. II.xii, p. 154]) and again to quote the English proverb "Haue hund to godsib, ant stenc in þir oþer hond, quod est: Canem suscipe compatrem, et altera manu baculum" (distinc. V.iiii, p. 422).

15. See Bolton, who points out in "Innocent III's Treatment of the *Humiliati*" that licenses were required for any preaching, but that bishops were ordered to grant them routinely to such groups.

16. Hageneder et al., *Register Innocenz' III.*, 271–73. This letter also appears in PL 214.695–96. It was codified as the " 'Cum ex injuncto,' De haereticis," in Innocent's *Decretals*, collected by the monk Rainerius (PL 216.1210–14) and promulgated by Pope Gregory IX (Innocent's nephew) in 1234. While Innocent may not have so intended, the letter has been repeatedly adduced as the standard authority for suppressing lay reading.

17. Deanesly's translation (*Lollard Bible*, 31), with my translation of the lines concerning Matt. 7:6, 13:11, and Luke 8:10, which Deanesly omits.

18. The connection of Holy Writ to a mountain appears in the preface to Gregory's *Expositio in Canticis Canticorum* (CCSL 144, p. 7 [caput 5]): "Bestia enim tangit montem, quando irrationabilibus motibus dediti scripturae sacrae celistudini propinquant." While Gregory refers to the spirit in which one is properly to approach the interpretation of Scripture (cf. *Moralia*, CCSL 143, p. 329 [book 6, caput 58]), Innocent seems to refer to the status of the interpreters themselves. Wenzel notes similar imagery in a sermon in Oxford, Bodleian Lib. Bodley 649, fol. 80v (early fifteenth c.): "And so you [priests] who are prefigured by Moses, give yourselves up to your cure of souls, engage in devout prayers and the understanding and contemplation of God. And you who belong to the laity, take your Our Father and your Creed and do not climb any higher" (*Macaronic Sermons*, 79).

19. Boyle, "Innocent III." The other letter is in Innocent's *Register* (Hageneder et al., *Register Innocenz' III.*, 432–34 [PL 214.793–95]).

20. Boyle, "Innocent III," 101.

21. Ibid.

22. Deanesly, *Lollard Bible*, 27, 39, 62. "Lollard" may derive from the Middle Dutch *lullen*, 'to mumble', and is apparently related to this practice of the Waldenses, Beghards, and others of reciting the Scripture they have memorized. For other suggestions concerning what a Lollard is or does see Gradon, "Langland," 195–97. Cf. Chaucer's use of the term in the epilogue to the *Man of Law's Tale* (II.1173, 1177).

23. Patschovsky, "Literacy of Waldensianism," 134.

24. Boyle makes this point ("Innocent III," 106). See Tanner, *Decrees*, 1:234–35, constitution 3.

25. Text and translation from Tanner, *Decrees*, 1:245.

26. Blake prints Gaytryge's sermon (*Religious Prose*, 72–87). For other commentary and bibliography on this enormous field, see *Manual*, 7:2270 [20]; S. Powell, "Transmission and Circulation"; Boyle, "Fourth Lateran Council"; Hughes, *Pastors and Visionaries;* Gillespie, "*Doctrina* and *Predicatio*"; and Simmons and Nolloth, *Lay Folks Catechism.* The *Lay Folks Catechism* survives in twelve manuscripts, including Cambridge, Sidney Sussex College 55; Cambridge, Trinity College 305; Lincoln, Cathedral Lib. 91; London, Lambeth Palace 408; Oxford, Bodleian Lib. Bodley 789.

27. Text and translation from Tanner, *Decrees*, 1:239.

28. The phrase "verbo pariter et exemplo" may mean "by word and example," as

Tanner translates it, and thus enunciate the principle that deeds should substantiate words, but given the context of preaching, the "verbum" may be the "Word," and the "exemplum" the narrative exposition. The emphasis thus falls on what the priest does in the pulpit as opposed to what he does in his life. For a discussion of this phrase, see Illich, *Vineyard*, 78–79.

29. Scheffer-Boichorst, *Chronica*, 878. Boyle accuses Deanesly of "not playing fair with the facts" by assuming that these "certain abbots" were acting under Innocent's authority, yet he concedes that "[p]erhaps the Cistercian abbots did burn the translations" ("Innocent III," 105). Innocent's letter to the abbots asking them to look into the matter appears in his *Register* (Hageneder et al., *Register Innocenz' III.*, 432–34 [PL 214.793–95]).

30. Boyle, "Innocent III," 107, quoting Hargreaves, "Wycliffite Versions," 391.

31. Mansi, *Collectio*, vol. 23, col. 191. For a summary, in French, of the capitula of this council, and for extensive notes, see Hefele, *Histoire*, vol. 5, part 2, pp. 1494–1501. For a general treatment, see Mundy, *Repression of Catharism.*

32. Mansi, *Collectio*, vol. 23, col. 197. Both Lortsch (*Histoire de la Bible*, 12–16) and Rost (*Bibel im Mittelalter*, 76–78) cite this capitulum in their discussions of vernacular Bibles.

33. Deanesly's translation (*Lollard Bible*, 36–37). Boyle does not address this decree in "Innocent III."

34. Mansi, *Collectio*, vol. 23, col. 197; Tanner, *Decrees*, 1:245. Toulouse adds that anyone who does not comply shall be "suspectus de haeresi habeatur."

35. Mansi, *Collectio*, vol. 23, cols. 192–97; Tanner, *Decrees*, 1:233–35.

36. See Deanesly, *Lollard Bible*, 36–38; Rost, *Bibel im Mittelalter*, 76–78; and Lortsch, *Histoire de la Bible*, 12–16.

37. Edward Stillingfleet, *Council of Trent*, with "An Appendix . . . concerning the Prohibition of Scripture in Vulgar Languages by the Council of Trent" (149–63). Stillingfleet calls the Toulouse Council an "Order of the Inquisition" (58). He also mentions Pope Gregory VII's ban in 1079 on the translation of the Office into Slavonic because portions of Scripture would necessarily be translated (PL 148.155); see Deanesly, *Lollard Bible*, 24.

38. Deanesly, *Lollard Bible*, 72.

39. Bühler, "Lollard Tract," 173–74, lines 126–30.

40. Lyte and Morris, *Calendar, 1381–1385*, 487. This excerpt is dated Dec. 8, 1384. See also Deanesly, *Lollard Bible*, 235–37, and Hudson, "Lollard Book Production."

41. Lyte and Morris, *Calendar, 1385–1389*, 427. This entry is dated Apr. 16, 1388; see pp. 430, 448, 468, etc., for similar appointments.

42. Tomlins et al., *Statutes*, 2:126.

43. Ibid., 2:128.

44. Hudson states that "Suspicion of the vernacular was evidently known in Wyclif's own lifetime [ca. 1330–1384]" (*Premature Reformation*, 30). On pp. 166–68 she documents fifteenth-century persecutions based on owning vernacular books.

45. Wilkins, *Concilia*, 3:317.

46. Watson, "Censorship," 828. This article provides a very good discussion of the "Oxford Translation Debate" and of Arundel's *Constitutions.*

47. Blunt, *Myroure*, 71. Earlier the author writes "Of psalmes I haue drawen but fewe, for ye may haue them of Rycharde hampoules drawynge, and out of Englysshe

bibles if ye haue lysence therto" (3). Rolle's Psalter (**RPs**) did not require a special license.

48. Blunt, *Myroure,* 71, and see Hargreaves, *Mirror,* 277–80.

49. Campbell, *"Evangelie,"* lines 35–40.

50. See Nevanlinna, *Northern Homily Cycle,* 1:105, 126. A similar impulse to drop the biblical passages in favor of the exposition and exempla may be observed in the two surviving manuscripts of an independent sermon cycle (see introduction to section III.E below). Cambridge, Univ. Lib. Kk.6.28 copies the biblical text, while Kk.6.2 does not. See also the example of the *Lay Folks Mass Book.*

51. For the Anglo-Norman text of Robert's prologue, see Meyer ("Manuscrits Français," 296–303) and for an edition of eight dominicals see Robert of Gretham, *Miroir.* For the English version, see Duncan (*"Mirror* and Its Manuscripts") and Hudson (*Premature Reformation,* 414–15). One of the manuscripts, Oxford, Bodleian Lib. Holkham misc. 40, also contains **PCE.** The cycle precedes the epistles. Hudson notes that Holkham has "extra material that has no counterpart in the French original" (415).

52. Forshall and Madden, *Holy Bible,* 1:xx, n. f, where they print parts of London, BL Harley 5085.

53. Ibid.

54. Paues, *English Biblical Version* (1904), 4.

55. Ibid., 4–5.

56. They invoke Ezekiel, Jeremias, and Job, among others. The parable of the talents (Matt. 25:14–30) is interpreted (ibid., 6–7) so that the talents represent the "tresoure" (i.e., knowledge) of God which ought not to be hidden but be increased through teaching.

57. Ibid., 8.

58. See Smalley, *Study of the Bible,* 363.

59. Mannyng, *Handlyng Synne.*

60. For example, Alfred prefaces his Anglo-Saxon laws with some Mosaic laws from Ex. 22–23, and Nicholas Trevet begins his *Chronicle* (which was translated into Middle English, see *Manual,* 8.2666 [35]) with a summary of biblical history from the Creation to the Crucifixion.

61. Bühler, "Lollard Tract," 178, lines 294–301. Deanesly (*Lollard Bible*) prints a version of this treatise as appendix 2, no. 3, but she misattributes it to John Purvey. Hudson shows that it is a Lollard adaptation of a Latin treatise by Richard Ullerston in 1401 ("Debate," 9 ff.). Bühler notes that "wherever Biblical quotations are used, these are not taken from the Wycliffite Bible, but are independent translations" (169).

62. For a sympathetic account of Arundel's dealings with nonconformists see Aston, *Thomas Arundel,* chap. 11, "Arundel and Heresy, 1382–97," pp. 320–25. See also Watson, "Censorship," 852–59.

63. Watson, "Censorship," 835.

64. Hudson, "Debate," 16–17.

❖ CHAPTER 3

The Place of English in Post-Conquest England

THE PREVIOUS chapter outlined the nature of official resistance to biblical literature; this chapter attempts to give some sense of how biblical literature was in fact accommodated within official practice and daily life. Given the considerable body of texts which the main entries document, it is important to determine who in England produced and used them, and under what circumstances. No one model suffices in all cases. There were multifarious ways of spreading the Word, from public preaching, to smaller-scale group instruction, to private reading and scribal glossing. Numerous ecclesiastical and historical documents, and several English texts which reflect on the vernacular literary enterprise, give some perspective on the intended purpose and use of biblical literature in English life.

In 1187, Jocelin of Brakelond described Samson, abbot of the Benedictine monastery of Bury St. Edmunds, as follows:

> Homo erat eloquens, Gallice et Latine, magis ratione dicendorum quam ornatui verborum innitens. Scripturam Anglice scriptam legere nouit elegantissime et Anglice sermocinari solebat populo, set secundum linguam Norfolchie, ubi natus et nutritus erat, unde et pulpitum iussit fieri in ecclesia et ad utilitatem audiencium et ad decorum ecclesiae.[1]

> There was a man eloquent in French and Latin, who dazzled more because of his speaking than the ornateness of his words. He knew how to read written compositions in English most elegantly, and he was accustomed to preach to the people in English, but in the tongue of Norfolk, where he was born and raised; thus he ordered a pulpit to be made in the church both for the benefit of the audience and for the decoration of the church.

I have translated the infinitive *legere* as simply "to read," but the verb may indeed connote its primary meanings of 'to gather, collect, select'.[2] Thus Samson may not be passively transmitting the copy set before him but actively editing it. He was apparently skilled at preaching extemporaneously in English while reading a presumably Latin, though possibly English, text. The syntax of the passage is unclear, that is, as to whether he preached in English from Latin texts or whether the texts were in English to begin with. Whatever the language, Samson's expertise is a particularly vivid example of the symbiosis of reading and preaching discussed in chapter 2 and of how concerned some individuals were to accommodate particular needs of the audience by preaching in the local dialect. Even the pulpit, while part of the decoration of the church, serves first a utilitarian purpose: the congregation needs to see and to hear. Vernacular preaching did of course continue after the Conquest, and those who did it well, and who enjoyed a particular rapport with their congregation, were recognized and praised. The following record, from the Acts of the second Provisional Chapter of St. Augustine's, Canterbury (Sept. 11–15, 1340), also highlights the importance of vernacular preaching:

> Ordinati sunt eciam ad predicandum in capitulo futuro proximo celebrando . . . dominus prior de Wigornia in latinis, die vero processionis quo contigerit, prior de Salopia vel dominus Iohannes de Marry monachus Norwicensis in lingua materna, si ipsum priorem contigerit predpediri.[3]

> Those designated to preach in the next chapter meeting to be celebrated are . . . the Prior of Worcester in Latin, and on the following day of procession, the Prior of Shrewsbury or John de Marry, Monk of Norwich, in the mother tongue, if it happens that the Prior is impeded.

Latin sermons are appropriate for the chapter, and English for the public "procession." It is notable that vernacular preaching was so important that the act designates a backup. Later in these acts and statutes a "letter of the presidents" describes the closing ceremonies of a chapter meeting; a sermon "ad populum in lingua vulgari" is the last piece of business.[4] An account of the miracles of Mary in the Lincoln Thornton manuscript (mid-fifteenth century) describes how a friar preaches in Latin and English back to back: "And first he prechide gud latyne, / And sythyne Inglysche gud & fyne."[5] The story concerns the friar's attempt to exorcise a demon from a knight sitting in a church; despite the fabulous quality of the story, such multilingual preaching did take place. Perhaps the English sermon followed the Latin in toto, but it I think it more likely that some kind of simultaneous translation took place. These first two snapshots of daily religious life come from the be-

ginning (1186) and end (1340) of the "dark" period in post-Conquest English
history, at least in terms of the survival of manuscripts; the last comes from
the high point of late medieval manuscript production (ca. 1450). There is
no question that vernacular preaching continued throughout the period,
but I wish to emphasize how the use of English in the religious life of the
community was an accepted, sanctioned, and relatively continuous part of
that life.

There is good evidence, though not as much, that vernacular writing continued as well. The survival of dialects of Old English and their metamorpho-
sis into the various dialects of Middle English have been well documented
through the use of English in the transmission of biblical texts. Versions
of the Creation and the Fall from Genesis, or of the Pater Noster, appear
in nearly every textbook history of the English language. The single most
studied, glossed, translated, and paraphrased biblical book throughout the
history of English is certainly Psalms. William of Malmesbury reports that
Alfred, shortly before his death in 899, had begun a translation that almost
certainly survives as the first fifty prose Psalms in the Paris Psalter (Paris, BN
Fonds Latin 8824, mid-eleventh c.). A metrical version of Psalms 51–150 follows, and both prose and verse are accompanied by the Latin text (on the
left) in parallel columns of equal size.[6]

In the mid-twelfth century, Lanfranc produced the so-called Canterbury
or Eadwine Psalter (Cambridge, Trinity College R.17.1, ca. 1155–60). Here
all three Latin versions appear in three-column format: the Hebrew version with an Anglo-Norman gloss, the Roman version with an Old English
gloss, and the Gallican with commentary from the *Glossa Ordinaria*.[7] The
magnificent illustrations are patterned after those in the famous Utrecht
Psalter; the Old English gloss is the last of thirteen surviving continuous
Old English Psalter glosses.[8] That Old English would again appear on some
kind of equal footing in a deluxe manuscript with the language of the ruling
class and with one of the *linguae sacrae* is an endorsement of English itself,
and the format makes the manuscript a kind of Rosetta stone of language
hierarchies. While it simply may be the case that each text happened to
travel with its particular gloss, a certain logic does seem to govern the as-
signments: Jerome's last and "best" version gets the Anglo-Norman gloss;
the most common (Gallican-Vulgate) version gets the most common Latin
commentary; and the earliest (least familiar or prestigious?) version gets the
Old English gloss. Augustine brought the Roman version to England in 597;
it was replaced in liturgical use by the Gallican version during the course
of the Benedictine reform of the late tenth century. In the Eadwine Psalter,
the Gallican version with its glosses and scholia takes up over two-thirds of

each page and therefore clearly takes pride of place. The Old English gloss is compressed into the central column and shows signs of modernization into Middle English, primarily through a weakening of the inflectional system and other "errors" in Old English. O'Neill concludes that "the copying of the English gloss was a project bungled in both planning and execution," partly because of some odd interpolations into the gloss from the Old English *Paris Psalter*.[9] The point here is that, nearly a century after the Conquest, in southern England, English served as an aid to understanding a biblical book. There is also evidence that later Middle English versions of the Psalter (**SPs** and **RPs**) were influenced by this tradition of Old English glosses, and approximately twenty manuscripts containing Old English homilies and other religious texts from Worcester Cathedral Library contain Middle English and Latin glosses in the so-called Tremulous Hand of a thirteenth-century scribe.[10] It may also be mentioned that the *Anglo-Saxon Chronicle* continued to be written through 1154 in Peterborough, and that copying and translation of various Old English chronicles and charters testifies to the continued understanding and use of Old English in the centuries after the Conquest.[11]

More testimony is provided by two twelfth- or thirteenth-century manuscripts of the West Saxon Gospels: Oxford, Bodleian Lib. Hatton 38 and the closely related London, BL Royal 1.A.xiv (there are four complete, and two fragmentary, eleventh-century manuscripts).[12] Like the Eadwine Old English gloss, the texts show signs of modernization in the form of orthographical variation and a weakening of the inflectional system. W. W. Skeat cautions that "perhaps *not* many of the copies have perished, that they may *never* have been very numerous, and that there is at present not the faintest trace of any other version," though there is the tradition that, at the end of his life, Bede was translating the Gospel of John.[13] More recently, Roy Liuzza's work on the Yale fragments of the Gospels suggests that they may have existed in a wider variety of forms and in greater numbers than Skeat thought; in his 1994 edition Liuzza concludes that "the text of the Old English version of the Gospels was the object of close study and could be read with comprehension, copied with care, and corrected with accuracy even half a century after the date usually regarded as the end of the Old English period."[14] The Anglo-Saxon tradition of biblical translation was thus well established, it persisted into the Middle English period, and it was known to sixteenth-century Protestant reformers. The first printed edition of the West Saxon Gospels appeared in 1571, and the existence of these Old English biblical versions was cited by Elizabethan Protestants as justification and precedent for their own projects of biblical translation.[15]

The challenge posed by Anglo-Norman to the indigenous Anglo-Saxon culture generated a considerable reaction among English writers. Pride in their early literature, pressured by Norman culture, promoted a nostalgic defense of and interest in Old English. The Worcester "Tremulous Hand" describes how Ælfric translated "Genesis, Exodus, Vtronomius, Numerus, Leuiticus," through which books the people were taught in English. After a nostalgic litany of great Anglo-Saxons he continues:

> Þeos læ[rden] ure leodan on Englisc,
> Næs deorc heore liht, ac hit fæire glod.
> [Nu is] þeo leore forleten, and þet folc is forloren.
> Nu beoþ oþre leoden þeo læ[reþ] ure folc,
> And feole of þen lorþeines losiæþ and þet folc forþ mid.[16]

Ingulph's Chronicle, a thirteenth- or fourteenth-century fabrication of events following the Norman invasion, records how duplicate Anglo-Saxon charters had been saved from a fire at Croyland Abbey and used "to instruct the juniors in a knowledge of the Saxon characters." [17] His stated purposes were to rescue Anglo-Saxon from the neglect suffered under the Normans and to enable the abbey to support the antiquity of its claims against adversaries. Even though, or perhaps because, the *Chronicle* purports to be earlier than it in fact is, it testifies to the perceived authority and importance of Old English. Even as late as the fifteenth century, Englishmen cited the achievements of their Anglo-Saxon forebears as a kind of golden age of English letters. Perhaps precisely because of the native language's esoteric quality and venerable associations it was included in the Eadwine Psalter.

Not everyone, however, was so enthusiastic about the capacity of English to render Scripture. The author of *The Chastising of God's Children* writes:

> Many men repreuen it to haue þe matyns or þe sautir or þe gospels or
> þe bible in englisshe, bicause þei mowe nat be translated into vulgare,
> word bi worde as it stondiþ, wiþoute grete circumlocucion, aftir þe
> feelynge / of þe first writers, þe whiche translatid þat into latyn bi
> techyng of þe holi goost. Naþeles, I wil nat repreue suche translacion,
> ne I repreue nat to haue hem on englisshe, ne torede on hem where þei
> mowen stire ʒou more to deuocion and to þe loue of god; but uttirli to
> usen hem in englisshe and leue þe latin, I holde it nat commendable,
> and namly in hem þat bien bounden to seien her sautir or her matyns of
> oure lady.[18]

The author's primary concern here is with how non-Latinate religious are to meet their devotional obligations. He balances his tolerance for English vernacular materials with his concern for proper form and the spiritual welfare of his audience. One suspects that the words "circumlocucion" and "feelynge" imply a great deal: the divine inspiration of Scripture is presumably the meaning of the latter term, and "circumlocucion" would indicate that English cannot convey the grammatical subtlety of Latin. The impoverishment of English in terms of grammar and vocabulary made it incapable of reproducing even the literal level, let alone the higher exegetical levels based on the literal.[19] Thus English was hopelessly handicapped. An effective riposte to such criticisms, and one which marvelously fuses the ontological categories of language, faith, and history, is part of the Lollard tract discussed in chapter 2: "And to hem þat seien þat þe Gospel on En[g]liche wolde make men to erre, wyte wel þat we fynden in Latyne mo heretikes þan of all oþer langagis, ffor þe decres rehersiþ sixti Latyn eretikes."[20]

The issue of translation from one language to another is extremely complex; that the Bible is the text being translated charges the issue even more. As seen in the previous chapter, the Church's objections to translations are at least fourfold. First, even a "literal" translation deforms the text.[21] A translator with the best intentions is inevitably an interpreter, not just a clear medium. Second, reworking the Bible makes possible the inclusion of nonorthodox material. Third, a vernacular translation allows unqualified people to expound upon the Bible and transmit dangerous opinions. Fourth, and perhaps most objectionable, the new breed of lay religious who were taking orders and who were founding their own religious movements were usurping ecclesiastical authority. The threat to authority, no matter what was actually preached, was at least as objectionable as any corruption of doctrine.

It is difficult to document how successfully English competed with Latin and Anglo-Norman from the twelfth into the thirteenth and fourteenth centuries. As is the case with most historical phenomena, no clear progression exists. English was widely accepted as a medium of lay piety, but whenever there were threats to the status quo—particularly to the position and prerogatives of the learned—and whenever people presumed to transmit in English authorized texts which they could cite in arguments with their betters, the vernacular was threatened and sometimes suppressed. In general terms the attitudes toward the vernacular varied considerably from the twelfth to the early fourteenth centuries given the purpose of the work, the time or place of composition, the status of the author, and especially the context of religious controversy. The official clergy's perception of a threat and their willingness to be tolerant were inversely proportional.

NOTES

1. Jocelin, *Chronicle,* 40. Franzen cites other examples of vernacular preaching in the thirteenth century (*Tremulous Hand,* 185) and discusses the knowledge and use of Old English after the mid-twelfth century (103–10).

2. Illich discusses the practice of monastic *lectio* (*Vineyard*, 57–58).

3. Pantin, *Documents*, 2:15.

4. Ibid., 2:61. This letter dates from 1343. In *Macaronic Sermons,* Wenzel discusses similar instances of mixed preaching, esp. chap. 6, "Bilingualism in Action."

5. Horstmann, *Altenglische Legenden Neue Folge,* 503. Lincoln, Cathedral Lib. 91, fol. 147b (facsimile by Brewer and Owen, *Thornton Manuscript*).

6. "He [Alfred] began to translate the Psalter, but reached the end of his life when he had barely completed the first part" (William of Malmesbury, *Gesta Regum Anglorum* (ca. 1120), 193 (book 2.123). For Alfred's authorship, see Bately, "Lexical Evidence."

7. Jerome's three translations of the Psalter into Latin are the Roman version (based on the Septuagint and perhaps on some Old Latin translations); the Gallican (based on Origen's Hexaplaric text, a recension of the Septuagint with the Hebrew—this version appears in the Vulgate); and the Hebrew (Jerome's last version "iuxta Hebraeos"). Harsley, *Canterbury Psalter,* edits the Old English gloss. Facsimile by James, *Canterbury Psalter.* See esp. O'Neill, "English Version," and Sisam and Sisam, *Salisbury Psalter.*

8. O'Neill, "English Version," 124.

9. Ibid., 133, and see O'Neill, "Another Fragment": the interpolations indicate that these Old English metrical psalms "were still read and appreciated at Christ Church Canterbury as late as the mid twelfth century" (436).

10. See Franzen, *Tremulous Hand,* and W. Collier, " 'Englishness.' " Collier notes how "A particular feature of the Hand's annotations is the vast number of biblical passages, written in Old English in the text, which he extracts into Latin in the margin" (37).

11. See O'Neill, "English Version," 136, C. Clark, "People and Languages," and her edition of the *Peterborough Chronicle.* See esp. Oxford, Bodleian Lib. Laud misc. 636, a *Chronicle* manuscript in which "The occasional marginalia (in Latin) and *notas* of s. xiii/xiv (e.g. on f. 18) show that the OE text was read and to some extent understood at this date" (Ker, *Catalogue,* entry 346). Bodleian Lib. Laud misc. 509, a copy of the Old English *Hexateuch,* has marginalia from the late thirteenth or early fourteenth century. See Ker, *Catalogue,* entries 344 and 142, and Crawford, "Late Old English Notes."

12. For the dating and description of the manuscripts, see Liuzza, *Gospels,* and the entries in Ker, *Catalogue,* where fol. 80r of Hatton 38 appears as plate 7.

13. Skeat, *Four Gospels,* here the Luke vol. (1874) xi. Skeat prints Hatton in full. For the translation by Bede, see below, p. 59.

14. Liuzza, *Gospels,* lxxiii, and "Yale Fragments."

15. Liuzza, *Gospels,* xiii–xiv.

16. "A Worcester Fragment," in Dickins and Wilson, *Early Middle English Texts,* 1–2, lines 15–19 (see *Manual,* 5:1435 [79], and W. Collier, " 'Englishness' "). The author refers to the Old English *Hexateuch,* presumed to be by Ælfric. See the introduction to the facsimile ed. by Dodwell and Clemoes, *Hexateuch.* "They [our forebears] taught our people in English, their light was not dark, but it glowed fairly. Now is their learning forgotten, and that folk is lost. Now other people teach our folk, and many of the [English] teachers perish, and the folk with them."

17. Riley, *Ingulph's Chronicle.* The *Chronicle,* in Latin, purports to contain a contemporary account of the fire in 1091.

18. Bazire and Colledge, *Chastising*, 221.

19. Cf. "Palmer's Determination" (Deanesly, *Lollard Bible,* appendix 2, no. 2): "dictiones Angliae sunt monosillabae, sicut *ston, bon, non, don, gon, man, that, math, rat.* Igitur in istis monosillabis non habent locum tales figurae grammaticales, ncc possunt orationes et propositiones ab incongruitate et falsitate per eas salvari" (427). On p. 428 English is compared to the grunting of pigs. Hudson questions the authorship and suggests a date ca. 1407 ("Debate," 16).

20. Bühler, "Lollard Tract," 176, lines 206–10.

21. Earlier translators, such as Jerome, Boethius, and Ælfric struggled with this age-old question. While Jerome and Ælfric recognize the impossibility of a literal translation and opt for a more idiomatic treatment which preserves the sense, Boethius adopts the principle of *fidus interpres*—word for word translation. See Ælfric's preface to Genesis (Crawford, *Heptateuch*); Schwarz, *Principles and Problems;* and Copeland, "Fortunes of 'non verbo pro verbo.'"

❖ CHAPTER 4

Genre, Audience, and Self-Representation

THE TAXONOMIC impulse is as strong in the criticism of medieval literature as it is in the literary history of any period, but for the medievalist the assignation of categories and the definitions of genre are complicated by a number of factors. First, the sheer chronological range — usually several centuries — in question; second, a similarly vast geographical expanse; and third, the amount of anonymous literature. The medievalist often has fewer chronological, geographical, and biographical parameters than are available to critics of later periods. The healthy effect of these factors, however, is a reliance on what the texts say, along with whatever paleographical information the manuscripts may yield. Here I wish to examine what the introductory material to works of biblical literature reveals about why and for whom they were produced. Biblical literature and other works of lay instruction share with other genres, such as romance, a rationale of production: they present themselves as broadly conceived works of popular literature for the entertainment, edification, and salvation of the Anglophone audience.

In the preface to a collection of essays devoted to the study of popular literature, Thomas J. Heffernan notes that "terms such as 'catechesis,' 'non-literate,' 'didactic,' 'courtly,' and 'popular' remain misunderstood and poorly defined."[1] He goes on to point out that the principle of "virtuosity" governs our perceptions of poetic merit: many works of religious instruction remain in an "aesthetic limbo" because, according to empiric measures (usually the volume of criticism), they have not generated much interest, and because they do not meet traditional belle-lettristic standards.[2] These two factors obviously are related, but at the risk of setting up a tendentious comparison, the attention devoted to Chaucer (as the extreme example) is well out of proportion to the attention devoted to Middle English religious literature. As Nicholas Watson points out, "In terms not only of quantity but of innovation the period 1340–1410 has as much right to be considered a 'golden age' of religious as it is of secular writing."[3] By no means should the Chaucer, Langland, and *Pearl*-poet triumvirate be denied the attention and scholarly resources (editions, critical studies, conferences) their genius deserves, but that very genius makes them, in important ways, uncharacteristic of the age. We run the risk of a top-down taxonomy, as opposed to a sense of literary taste from the grassroots, and it is important to remember that for every one person who read *Pearl*, some hundreds (at least) would have read a work such as Nicholas Love's *Mirror.* A more genuine and representative sense of Middle English literature can only be generated by studying the more common and popular, if also perhaps more pedestrian, literary works. Another comparison is helpful in demonstrating the unreliability, or at least the protean nature, of critical taste: if one were to choose the most "important" Chaucerian works, compelling arguments could be made for the *Boece* and the *Romaunt of the Rose,* two works which have received comparatively little scholarly attention and which even Chaucerians rarely read. Eustache Deschamps was probably not alone among Chaucer's contemporaries in thinking of him as a "grant translateur" who worked within well-defined medieval traditions, just as Chaucer himself is aware of how new corn must come out of the old fields of old books (*Parliament of Fowls,* lines 22–25). The Bible is, of course, one of the oldest fields of all.

Anne Middleton addresses the questions of the medieval audience and of the authorial voice in an interesting discussion of a slightly altered fourteenth-century triumvirate, that of Gower, Langland, and Chaucer. She posits the idea of "common speech" to argue that "Their poetry, and Ricardian public poetry generally, speaks 'as if' to the entire community—as a whole, and all at once rather than severally—rather than 'as if' to a coterie or patron. By its mode of address and diction it implies that the community is heterogeneous, diverse, made up of many having separate 'singular' interests."[4] The heterogeneity of the implied audience is reflected by the heterogeneity of the literatures produced to entertain and instruct it. Even though terms such as "didactic" and "popular" overlap, and even if the tone of many Ricardian poems "implies" a broader audience, works of religious and biblical instruction have a clearly defined purpose and audience. They are popular because they say so themselves. So many of these works begin with an appeal to the "lewed" folk—the term most often used to characterize the audience—that such an appeal amounts to a convention. Just as an allusion to the Troy story or to a springtime setting (*Natureingang*) aligns a work within a certain genre and raises expectations, so is an appeal to the "commun" or "lewed" folk a conventional means of beginning a popular work of instruction. This is not to say that any work which does not so begin was not popular, but that the presence of such an appeal is one empiric standard. The following quotations present some examples of such introductions. I believe that nothing better shows the character and intended purpose of these works.

The first 270 lines of the *Cursor Mundi* are an extended explanation of why, how, and for whom the poem was produced. After having listed many of the romances in "Inglis, frankys, and latine" (line 24) which, to the poet's displeasure, have found such wide acceptance, he continues:

> Þis ilk bok is es translate   232
> In to Inglis tong to rede
> For the loue of Inglis lede,
> Inglis lede of Ingland,   235
> For the commun at understand.
> Frankis rimes here I redd,
> Communlik in ilka sted,
> Mast es it wroght for frankis man:
> Quat is for him na frankis kan?   240
> Of Ingland the nacion,
> Es Inglis man þar in commun;
> Þe speche þat man wit mast may spede
> Mast þar-wit to speke war nede.
> Selden was for ani chance   245
> Praised Inglis tong in france;
> Giue we ilkan þare langage,
> Me think we do þam non outrage.
> To laud and Inglis man i spell
> Þat understandis þat i tell.[5]   250

The nationalistic and egalitarian motives here are obvious, and have been illuminatingly discussed by John J. Thompson and, in a larger context, Thorlac Turville-Petre.[6] The repetition of "Inglis," "Ingland," "frankis," and "france" illustrates how English was reasserting itself against the Anglo-Norman culture which had dominated at least literary production on the island since the Conquest. The use of two words deserves special note: *commun* and *lede*. The *commun*, of course, refers to the unlearned masses for whose edification this work was composed. Lines 236 and 238, however, indicate that there were two "communs"—those whose native language was

English and those who understood French. The poet complains that the Francophones already have a widely disseminated vernacular literature; for this reason he wishes to promote a national identity through a vernacular English literature. Feelings, if not of cultural inferiority, at least of competition and local pride, generated a great deal of thirteenth- and fourteenth-century literature.[7] Pride in one's native heritage was not an exclusive characteristic of English speakers, of course. The prologue to the Anglo-Norman *Merlin's Prophecies* attests to similar feelings among the French commons:

> Kar tote gent ne entendunt mye
> Lettre en Latyn ne clergie,
> Et pur ço l'ai jo feet en romaunz,
> Ke tut entendunt, petiz et grauns.[8]

> For all people hardly understand
> Writing in Latin or learned matters,
> And for this reason I have made it into French,
> So all may understand, young and old.

During the Wycliffite controversy it was very common to justify English translations by appealing to works, especially biblical ones, known to exist in other languages. A proponent of vernacular translation in a Lollard tract circa 1407 first cites translations in "Spaynesche tunge, Frensche tunge & Almayne," and then notes how the venerable Bede "translatid þe Bibel or a grete parte of þe Bibile, [in-to Englyshe] wos originals ben in many abbeis in Englond" and how "a man of Lonndon, his name was Wyring, hadde a Bible in Englische of norþen speche, wiche was seen of many men and it semed too hundred ʒeer olde."[9] The same tract describes John of Gaunt's reaction when a bill was introduced in Parliament in 1395 by two archbishops and various clergy to "anulle" (line 281) English Bible translations: "[he] answered þer-to scharpely, seying þis sentence: we wel not be þe refuse of alle men, for siþen oþer naciouns han Goddis lawe, wiche is lawe of oure byleue, in þer owne modir langage, we wolone haue oure in Engliche wo þat eure it bigrucche; and þis he affermede with a grete oþe."[10]

We need not guess in which language the duke of Lancaster swore. Thus the author appeals not only to the enlightened practice of contemporary cultures but also to a golden age of English letters before the cultural upheaval of the Conquest.[11] As demonstrated in chapter 3 above, Anglo-Saxon manuscripts were being read and copied at least as late as the thirteenth century. Even the perception that such an extensive corpus once existed led both the *Cursor Mundi* poet at the beginning of the fourteenth century and John of Gaunt at the end to express the need for a vernacular literature in specifically nationalistic terms. The impulse continued into the fifteenth

century, with an emphasis on the classics, as for example with the commis-
sion by Henry V of John Lydgate to translate the Troy story:

> By-cause he wolde that to hyӡe and lowe
> The noble story openly wer knowe
> In oure tonge, aboute in every age,
> And y-writen as wel in oure langage
> As in latyn and frensche it is.[12]

Henry V thus continues the tradition of royal patronage for English translations inaugurated by Alfred.

The second word of special note from the *Cursor Mundi* passage appears
in lines 234 and 235. *Lede,* like *commun,* refers to a body of people, but it
is of interest because of its possible relationship to *lewed,* the word used
most often to describe the audience of biblical and most popular literature.
Lede derives from Anglo-Saxon *leode* ("people," "nation") from which the adjective *lewed* may also derive. The standard etymological tools do not offer
much help. The *Middle English Dictionary* goes no further than to cite Anglo-
Saxon *læwede* as the root for *lewed.* In his *Wörterbuch,* Ferdinand Holthausen,
under *læwede,* says simply "unbekannte Herkunft." The *Oxford English Dictionary* concedes that *lewd* is "of difficult etymology" and cites two unlikely
derivations—one from Latin *laicus* and the other from Old English *læwan* (to
betray). C. M. Lotspeich argues for a derivation from Old English *læw* 'in-
jury' or 'mutilation', but I would suggest that Anglo-Saxon *leode* is another
possible source.[13] The Indo-European derivation of *leode* is well documented.
Bosworth and Toller's *Anglo-Saxon Dictionary* cites Old Saxon *liud,* Old Frisian
liod, and Icelandic *ljóð.* The problem, however, is to discern some etymological connection between *læwede* and this tradition—in particular how to
account for the "w" in *læwede.* Those who are interested in the technical
aspects of the derivation may refer to the note.[14] The etymology is important since the meaning of "lewed" is of critical importance in understanding how these works represent themselves. The central idea is the people,
and "lewed" literature is simply literature meant for the general population,
just as "popular" derives from *populus* and "vulgar" from *vulgus.* There are
no negative connotations in this context—certainly not in the *Cursor Mundi*
passage where service to this community is a matter of pride.[15] Its only negative sense in these prologues is "unlettered" but even in this sense it bears
the positive connotation "therefore in need of instruction." The semantic
evolution of "lewed" is not without interest. For Langland, it can be a term
of reproach: " 'Lewed lorel!' quod Piers 'litel lokestow on þe Bible' " (*Piers
Plowman,* B.vii.137); for Chaucer, with his typical self-deprecation but also
with some warmth, the term implies a chummy intimacy between himself

and the Eagle in the *House of Fame:* " 'A ha!' quod he, 'lo, so I can / Lewedly to a lewed man / Speke' " (865–66). In the *Middle English Dictionary, lewed* runs the gamut from the nonpejorative "untutored" or "non-clerical" to "stupid," "uncouth," and "evil," and culminates in the wholly negative Modern English "lewd."

Someone with no pretensions to any education would be "lewed," and so would a man or woman who had some rudimentary reading and writing skills, and perhaps knew some Latin prayers by heart. The *Lay Folks Mass Book,* a northern English translation (ca. 1300) of a mid-twelfth-century French original, provides this marvelous bit of liturgical coaching for those struggling through a church service:

> Loke pater-noster þou be prayande,   480
> Ay to þou here þo preste be sayande
> per omnia secula al on hight,
> Þen I wold þou stode vp-right,
> for he wil saie with hegh steuen
> pater noster to god of heuen;   485
> herken him with gode wille,
> and whils he saies, hold þe stille,
> bot answere at temptacionem
> set libera nos a malo, amen.
> hit were no nede þe þis to ken,   490
> for who con not þis are lewed men.
> when þis is done, saye priuely
> other prayer none þer-by.
> pater noster first in laten,
> and sithen in englishe als here is wryten.[16]   495

The Pater Noster does follow in English, and here is an example of both languages being used in tandem. One need know just enough Latin to follow along as best one can, and make the appropriate responses. However, not being able to recognize key points in the Latin service, or to recite the Lord's prayer in Latin, qualifies one as "lewed" (491). The author (named "Jeremy" in line 18) clearly expects the congregation to be able to recite the Pater Noster in Latin ("there is no need to teach you this" [490]), whether the members understand it or not, but he does not expect them to know the Lord's Prayer in English since he supplies a translation immediately after line 495. He may also be exercising some caution in that, whereas the Latin text is fixed by rote memorization, the English text may be improvised upon by his listeners too freely. The Pater Noster does in fact exist in numerous Middle English versions (see **PN**). In the section on confession, Jeremy follows the same practice: "many saien confiteor; / were als gode saie þis þer-for." The confession in English follows; it is "as good" as the Latin; the Apostles' Creed also appears in English.[17] The gospel itself must have been read in Latin, but translation here would be unnecessary since the sermon, which immediately follows the gospel reading, customarily paraphrased it. Referring to the reading of the gospel, Jeremy concedes that "Clerkes heren on a manere, / bot lewed men bos anoþer lere" (lines 173–74: "Clerks hear in one manner; it behooves lewed men to learn another"). The *Lay Folks Mass Book* thus describes an essentially bilingual service among "lered & lewed" (line 50) wherein the significance and potency of the prayers and the preaching are the same for all, but concessions are made to the individual capacities of listeners.[18]

Two other examples of the use of "lewed" which reflect both the positive and negative semantic alternatives appear in the *Meditations on the Supper of our Lord* (**MS**) (ca. 1315–30), a versification of the Passion story. After Jesus washes the feet of the disciples, the poet comments:

> Ensample of mekenes to þe he lete,
> Whan he wysshe hys dyscyples fete;
> A grete ensample of mekenes loke [behold],
> Whan he hys flesshe to þy fode toke.
> A feyre monasshyng hys sermoun shewed,
> Þat þe lered men shulde teche þe lewed.[19]

Three examples of Christ's humility and ministry, feet washing, the institution of the Eucharist, and preaching, culminate in the last line—which has no counterpart in the Latin *Meditaciones* (*MPC*)—in which "lewed" denotes relative differences in degree more than absolute differences in kind. In the immediate context of the poem, Christ is meek but also learned; the disciples are "lewed" but will be, in their turn, learned when they go forth to preach the gospel to the "lewed" population. By extension, this very poem, in which the more learned poet teaches his audience, emulates the same pattern. Later in the *Meditations*, the word "lewed" appears in a very different context. Christ is before Pilate:

> Nat onely a mysdoer now he ys holde
> But as a lewed fole he ys eke tolde:
> Þey cryed on hym, as foules on owle,
> With wete and eke dung þey hym defoule.[20]

Thus we see that in the same early fourteenth-century poem "lewed" can span the semantic range from "unlettered" to "despicable." The word is multivalent, and must always be read in context.

Some "lewed" folk desired to pursue their educations by taking orders. These lay religious—brothers and sisters in minor orders, associated with a house but in less than full command of Latin—were one of the primary audiences for English biblical literature, and they represented a wide cross section of medieval society, from the exceptionally talented son of a cowherd (Cædmon) to the daughters of a nobleman (the sisters for whom the *Ancrene Riwle* was produced).[21] They constituted a middle ground between professed or ordained *clerici* and the "lewed" folk, and this intermediary position allowed them first to consume, and then perhaps in their own turn to produce, the rapidly proliferating works of religious instruction. Their academic and linguistic deficiencies raised the problem of how they were to fulfill their devotional duties.

The orders formulated various solutions, having mostly to do with the memorization of essential Latin prayers and responses such as the confession, the litany, and important psalms. A fourteenth-century *Customary* from St. Augustine's, Canterbury, entitled "De disciplina fratrum laicorum, et qualiter instrui debeant," requires memorization of these texts "pro more laycali." Eric Colledge rightly remarks that this phrase "may not unjustly be interpreted as 'whether they understand them or not,' " just as Jeremy's congregation simply followed along.[22] Earlier in the *Customary* the novitiates may declare their intention to become professed in Latin, French, or English.[23] That such unschooled people could enter religious life at all doubtless encouraged the production of vernacular works meant to integrate them into the life of their order. Lay literacy admitted of considerable degree, ranging from complete written and spoken knowledge of the Office, to some knowledge (with or without understanding the meaning) of basic prayers in Latin, to the knowledge of those same prayers in the vernacular. It is important to note how liberal an attitude the Church had toward the indoctrination of novitiates. Structures existed within social and ecclesiastical organizations to accommodate those with varying levels of ability, and regardless of sex. The Northern Metrical Version of the Benedictine rule is directed specifically to non-Latinate women:

> Monkes & als all leryd men
> In latyn may it lyghtly ken,
> And wytt þarby how þay sall wyrk
> To sarue God and haly kyrk.
> Bott tyll women to mak it couth,
> Þat leris no latyn in þar ȝouth,
> In ingles is it ordand here,
> So þat þay may it lyghtly lere.[24]

A work which provides an unusually intimate look into the lives of female lay religious is the early thirteenth-century *Ancrene Riwle,* written by a male

superior as an instructional manual for the religious life of four ancho-
resses.[25] The first of its eight sections, on daily devotional practice, is per-
meated with biblical quotation, particularly of Psalms. The sisters clearly
knew substantial portions of the Bible by heart, though the degree of their
Latinity is not clear. Most of the scriptural quotations are translated into
English, and perhaps this feature is part of their ongoing instruction. Indeed, they seem to have progressed beyond their "lewed brethren" who are
not familiar with the Latin office:

> Vre leawede breþren siggeð þus hore vres. vor vhtsong ine werkedawes
> heihte 7 twenti <pater nosteres> . . . 7 þenne schal siggen hwo se con.
> domine labia mea aperies. deus in adiutorium meum intende. . . . ʒif ei
> of ou wule don þus heo voleweð her ase in oþre obseruaunces muchel of
> vre ordre. 7 wel ich hit reade.[26]

> Our lewed brethren say thus their hours: before dawn during the week
> twenty-eight Pater Nosters . . . then shall say whoever is able "Lord open
> thus my lips, Lord rise up to help me" . . . If any of you will do thus you
> follow here as in other observances much of our order, and I advise it
> strongly.

All who were able ("hwo se con") were to recite what they knew as best they
could, and there are numerous concessions to various levels of ability, such
as the option to repeat one prayer over and over rather than tackle the whole
repertoire. The sisters are also able to write: "Euerich on sigge hire vres
also heo haueð iwriten ham" ("Let everyone say her hours as she has written them").[27] Such a stipulation certainly implies some literacy, and at least
some knowledge of Latin since the instructor often directs that the hours
be said in Latin. The following quotations give some further insight into the
linguistic capacities of the sisters:

> Al þet ʒe euer siggeð of swuche oðer bonen. ase of pater nosteres 7 of
> auez on ower owene wise. psalmes 7 v-reisuns. al ich am wel ipaied.
> euerichon sigge þet hire best bereð on heorte. verslunge of hire sautere.
> redinge of en-glichs oðer of freinchs.[28]

> All that you ever say of such other prayers—Pater Nosters and Aves in
> your own manner, Psalms and orisons—I am well pleased if everyone
> says those that she knows best by heart, verses from her Psalter, reading
> in English or in French.

Not only did they have access to English and French psalters, but also they
were free to choose which Psalms to read as their heart moved them, and
to pray in their "owene wise." Shortly afterwards, however, he directs that
"touward te preostes tiðen herkneð se wel se ʒe muwen. auh mid him ne
schule ʒe nouðer uerslen ne singen þat he hit muwe iheren." In other words,

follow the priest's prayers as best you can, but do not let him hear you pray-
ing by yourself.

The sisters for whom the *Ancrene Riwle* was written were a specialized audience, though probably characteristic of the middle-level *conversi* for whom
much biblical literature was produced. Equally important constituents of
the audience were the more broadly based "lewed" folk for whom a variety of
literatures were produced, including romances such as *Richard the Lionheart*,
the prologue of which reads in part:

> In Frenssche bookys þis rym is wrouȝt,
> Lewede men ne knowe it nouȝt—
> Lewede men cune Ffrensch non,
> Among an hondryd vnneþis on—;
> Neuerþeles, wiþ glad chere,
> Ffele of hem þat wolde here
> Noble iestes, j vndyrstonde,
> Off douȝty knyȝtes off Yngelonde.
> Þerfore now j wolde ȝow rede
> Off a kyng, douȝty in dede.[29]

Speaking of children set to books which contain "Miche of Godes priuete,"
the preface to *Of Arthour and of Merlin* runs in part thus:

> Auauntages þai hauen þare
> Freynsch and Latin eueraywhare.
> Of Freynsch no Latin nil y tel more
> Ac on I[n]glisch ichil tel perfore:
> Riȝt is þat I[n]glische vnderstond
> Þat was born in Inglond.
> Freynsche vse þis gentilman,
> Ac euerich Inglische Inglische can;
> Mani noble ich haue yseiȝe,
> Þat no Freynsche couþe seye.[30]

Both of these romances appear in the Auchinleck manuscript (ca. 1330–40),
which contains several works of biblical literature, and which is remarkable
in that it is written almost exclusively in English.[31] The above prologues make
it clear that knowledge of French was becoming rare in the early to mid-
fourteenth century even among the nobility, and that if romances—or any
stories whatsoever—were to be read or recited they had to be in English.
It does seem somewhat inconsistent, however, that romances, albeit about
noble and pious English heroes, follow these prologues, not religious tracts.
Either the authors of these prologues express straightforward nationalistic
sentiments or, as is more likely, they genuinely feel that their tales qualify
as moral reading. The prologues recuperate the "geste" or "tale" into the

body of doctrinal literature. The prologue to *Of Arthour and of Merlin* notes the difference between French and Latin Sunday school reading and a good English story, yet again it is unclear whether it is meant as Saturday night entertainment, independent of any religious agenda, or whether the English romance serves the same doctrinal purposes as the French and Latin material, only in a different language. I would favor the latter alternative, since the poets obviously think that their stories, if read in the right spirit, serve a moral purpose.[32]

Some examples from works with a specifically religious agenda broaden the perspective on how these literatures share a rationale of production. There are, first of all, the explicit programs of such works as the *Lay Folks Mass Book* and the *Lay Folks Catechism*. Another example comes from the *Pricke of Conscience* which, if the number of surviving manuscripts means anything (117—more than any other Middle English poem), surely merits the designation "popular":[33]

> Þarfor þis buke es on Ynglese drawen,
> Of sere maters, þat er unknawen
> Til laude men þat er unkunnand,
> Þat can na latyn understand,
> To make þam þam-self first knaw
> And fra syn and vanytese þam draw,
> And for to stir þam til right drede,
> When þai þis tretisce here or rede,
> Þat sal prikke þair conscience with-yn.[34]

Here the English production is the doctrinal equivalent and linguistic counterpart to the Latin, and the motivations are primarily didactic and penitential; the conventional appeal to "laude men" once again appears. The poet repeats this appeal toward the end of the poem where nationalistic sentiments surface:

> In þir seven er sere materes drawen
> Of sere bukes, of whilk som er unknawen,
> Namly til lewed men of England,
> Þat can noght bot Inglise undirstand;
> Þarfor þis tretice drawe I wald
> In Inglise tung þat may be cald
> Prik of Conscience als men may fele.[35]

Gospel lectionaries express the same appeal to the lewed folk and provide another example of how remarkably unified the rationale of literary composition was across genres. The prologue to the original version of the *Northern Homily Cycle* (**NHC**), for example, is more extensive than either of the prologues in the two revisions, and here its populist rationale finds fullest expression. The homilist explains that it is the duty of all Christians to serve God as they are able: the "lewed" with "rihtwis fare" (righteous living) and the "lered" with "rihtwis lare" (righteous learning/teaching). He continues

> Forthi wil I of my pouert,
> Schau sum thing that Ik haf in hert,
> On Ingelis tong that alle may
> Understand quat I wil say,
> For laued men hauis mar mister,
> Godes word for to her,
> Than klerkes that thair mirour lokes,
> And sees hou thai sal lif on bokes,
> And bathe klerk and laued man
> Englis understand kan,
> That was born in Ingeland,
> And lang haues ben thar in wonand.
> Bot al men can noht, I wis,
> Understand Latin and Frankis,
> Forthi me think almous it isse,
> To wirke sum god thing on Inglisse
> That mai ken lered and laued bathe,
> Hou thai mai yem thaim fra schathe.[36]

Nationalistic and egalitarian feelings are again evident here, especially given the bias in favor of the "laued" who, even though both "lered and laued" were to derive some benefit, have "more" need than clerks to hear God's Word. These lines explain the personal motivation for having undertaken an English production, but the raison d'être of the work is the power of the Word to save man from damnation:

> Forthi tha godspells that always
> Er red in kirc on Sundays,
> Opon Inglis wil Ic undo,
> Yef God wil gif me grace tharto,
> For namlic on the Sunnenday,
> Comes lawed men thair bede to say
> To the kirc, an for to lere
> Gastlic lare that thar thai here,
> For als gret mister haf thay,
> To wit quat the godspel wil say
> Als lered men, for bathe er bouht
> Wit Cristes blod, and sal be broht
> Til heuenis blis ful menskelie. (5)[37]

There is a persistent concern in this collection with "buying" mankind from hell; Christ's sacrifice pertains to both the learned and unlearned, and the heavenly reward is equal for all believers. The imagery of "buying" man out of hell corresponds to the "ransom theory" of redemption, associated with Gregory of Nyssa, by which Christ compensates for humankind's sinfulness with his death. The homilist uses the word "ranceoun" (8), and his frequent references to Christ's historical Harrowing of Hell assume personal application as the redemption of each Christian soul from the power of the devil. For other Christian thinkers (e.g., Abelard) the ransom theory was theologically unacceptable; Christ did not owe the devil anything and thus the Passion is an act of perfect love (cf. John 15:13).[38] The homilist's social views intersect with his theological ones: Christ's sacrifice applies to every individual, high and low, learned and lewed, and if believers are to understand the significance of Christ's sacrifice, it must be explained in English.

That the unlearned and underprivileged have indeed appropriated the Gospels and made them their own is demonstrated by an extraordinary change the homilist makes in one of his gospel texts. In the paraphrase of the lection for the third Sunday in Advent (Matt. 11:2–5), in response to John's question "quither it war he / That suld cum mannes bote to be" (34), Christ invites the disciples to draw their own conclusions:

> I gif the blind, he said, thair siht,
> I ger the halt men ga riht,
> I mac unhale men al hale,
> And def men I bet of bale,
> I rais men fra ded to life,
> And pouer men mas me ful rife.(35)

The last proof, that "the poor have the Gospel preached to them" (Matt. 11:5), is rewritten as "And pouer men mas me ful rife."[39] The homilist, in an otherwise close paraphrase of the lection, exactly reverses the meaning of this verse. The poor are not being preached to but themselves are preaching, either literally or by emulating Christ through their conduct. Here is subtle but significant evidence of how the homilist recognized the transforming and empowering effect of vernacular texts.

The most important feature of lectionaries like the *Northern Homily Cycle* as narratives is how each homily synthesizes its components—pericope, paraphrase, exposition, and exemplum—and how the cycle itself is written with a program.[40] Old and New Testament stories in the paraphrase are united by thematic and typological correspondences, which in turn are mapped onto the expository and exemplary material. For example, in telling how Christ cleanses the leper in Matthew 8:1–4, the homilist recalls the cleansing by Elias of the Syrian warrior Naaman in 4Kings 5 (130–32). In that story, Naaman travels to Israel in order to be cleansed by the great prophet. After Elias does so, having refused all reward, Elias's servant Giezi runs after Naaman to obtain some payment by a subterfuge. Elias then strikes Giezi with leprosy for his greed. The homilist briefly summarizes Naaman's healing and then tells at greater length Giezi's machinations, adding the observation that Giezi "was unhale thoru symonye, / That mikel spilles nou clergye" (130). The homilist frankly admits contemporary clerical corruption, and makes other class-conscious comments such as how the poor suffer most in wars and how the rich eat what the poor earn (23, 136). Leprosy is metaphorically extended as a "gastlye" representation of Original Sin ("Mankind of Adam leper haued smitte" [132]); we are all lepers (i.e., sinners) and the homily reinforces the universality of the condition by citing a story from each Testament in which upper- and lower-class individuals suffer.

The *narracio* for the last homily, "In purificationem Beate Marie" (164–71), in the fragmentary Edinburgh manuscript, best reveals the universality of application and the popular tenor of the whole cycle. An abbess, after having raised a foundling to become a nun at her abbey, is tempted by the devil and conceives a child by the butcher. She confides her sin to the young nun, who promises to kill the child as soon as it is born; no one will hear the "squeling" (167). But, as the homilist moralizes, no one can trust a foundling, and the nun does her own bit of squealing by telling the bishop what has happened; the matter becomes public and many nuns are happy to hear of their superior's downfall. The abbess, in turn, prays to Mary, who miraculously delivers the child so that, upon examination, the abbess is proven a virgin. The young nun is now sentenced to be burned for slander, but the abbess tells the whole story to the bishop, who remits the sentence. The baby grows up in a hermitage and becomes a bishop later in life. As in the account of Namaan and Giezi, the principle of *antimetabole* governs—reciprocal punishments and reprieves. The plot comes full circle as another foundling enters religious life and presumably generates stories very much like the one just told. The larger point of the exemplum, however, is not just that Mary can remedy all despair and sin but that all of the members of the abbey (except the paternal, stable bishop) are sinful, from the abbess and the foundling down to the butcher and the envious nuns. All were guilty of varying degrees of sin, but all were forgiven.

What I have been calling the common rationale of production for works of biblical literature appears again in one of the longest and most comprehensive biblical paraphrases (over 18,000 lines), the *Middle English Metrical Paraphrase of the Old Testament* (**POT**). After invoking the Trinity in the first stanza (compare the opening to **GE**), the poet cites his sources and names his audience in stanza 2:

This buke is of grett degre,
    Os all wettys that ben wyse,
ffor of the bybyll sall yt be
    The poyntes that ar mad most in price,
Als maysters of dyuinite
    and on, the maystur of storyse,
ffor sympyll men soyn [soon] forto se,
    settes yt þus in this schort assyse;
And in moyr schort maner
    is my mynd forto make yt,
That men may lyghtly leyre
    to tell and vnder take yt.[41]

No specific appeal to "lewed" men appears here; only toward the end of the poem (stanza 1479 of 1531) does the reference appear in the poet's prayer that "god graunt hym hele þat hath turned yt / in ynglysch lawd men forto lere." Here then is the same egalitarian appeal common to many Middle English poems, but in the second stanza the poet varies the convention somewhat and directs the poem to "sympyll men" as a digest of biblical material. By "sympyll men" I would hazard the guess that the poet means those lay novitiates in a monastery who were ignorant of Latin. Only such an audience, and not lay people generally, would require such a massive production. Thus this poem is a means for the *conversi* to acquaint themselves with a text—the *Historia Scholastica*—which formed an important part of what can be called the monastic core curriculum. The prologue also demonstrates how the poet thought of biblical paraphrase in terms of a continuum from the "bybyll" itself, through the "maystur of stories," to his own "buke." Peter Comestor set the material in "schort assyse," and the poet will now retell the same material "in moyr schort maner"; he simply continues a well-attested practice and assumes a considerable sense of authorship by referring to "my mynd." The poet elaborates on his rationale for making the poem in stanza 3:

This boke that is the bybyll cald,
    and all that owtt of yt is drawn,
ffor holy wrytt we sall yt hald
    and honour yt euer os our awn;
All patriarkes and prophettes yt told,
    so [e]uer þer saynges sekerly ar knawn,
And all wer fygurs fayr to fald [set forth?]
    how coymmyng of crist miȝt be kawn [meditated on?].
God graunt vs crist to knaw
    All our form faders crauyd

> And so to lere is law
> that our sawlis may be sauyd.[42]

First, "all" that is drawn out of the Bible is "holy wrytt," including, as the parallelism from "This buke" of stanza 2 to "This boke" of stanza 3 makes clear, the *Historia* and this very poem. Second, the poet puts himself in the tradition of Bible tellers and has a very proprietary sense of Scripture. Holy Writ is "our awn"; since individuals cannot own what they cannot read the poet envisions his project as kind of empowerment. Third, the poem is a means to save souls.

All of these prologues demonstrate that appealing to a lower-class vernacular audience was conventional across a wide range of works, from romances and pastoral works to biblical paraphrases and homily cycles. They envisage the same audience and direct their efforts along largely the same lines. Middle English authors were acutely aware of their audience's need for moral and spiritual guidance, and they were aware of a parallel literature for the commons in French which already met these needs. Writing poetry in English and contributing to the spiritual welfare of the English people were part of the same project.

Comparable to the *Middle English Metrical Paraphrase* in scope and intention is the late twelfth-century *Ormulum,* which has been described as a text with no literary influence, and indeed minimal influence of any kind. It can serve, however, as a significant example of how the Word was spread among the "lewed" folk in the late twelfth century—the time when we know very little about English religious and literary culture. The work was edited in the nineteenth century, and since then it has been studied almost exclusively from paleographical and philological standpoints.[43]

Many brief tags throughout the work, such as "Swa summ þe Goddspell kiþeþþ" (660—"As the Gospel makes known") and "Þatt stanndeþþ o þe Goddspellboc / Þatt þwerrt út nohht ne leȝheþþ" (315–16—"That stands in the Gospel book / Which flat out does not lie"), acknowledge the principal authority. "Þwerrt út," by the way, is Orm's favorite intensifier. At one point, late in the collection, Orm refers to a "soþ boc" (19941) which is not the Bible. The piece of information in question is the name of the castle— "Macheronnte"—where John was imprisoned. Josephus may be the ultimate source of this detail, though it is also found in Ælfric. Orm's debt to Ælfric and to the Old English homiletic tradition is considerable.[44] The *Ormulum* also anticipates encyclopedic compilations like the *Cursor Mundi* in the attention devoted to natural history and science. For example, John the Baptist precedes Christ just as the "reord" ("voice") anticipates "spæche" and culminates in the "word" (9563–70). Augustine makes the same point in demonstrating how the continuum from the physical sound to the meaningful word was exactly reversed when the Word was made flesh.[45] The cosmic and mystical significance of each letter in holy names (e.g., Iesus—line 4302 ff., with numerological significance assigned to each letter; Adam—line 16390 ff., derived from the four points of the compass) and the frequent enumeration of sins and their corresponding virtues also show Orm's concern with teaching his congregation about the world and universe around them.

Each of the thirty-two homilies in the collection begins with some eighty to two hundred lines of paraphrase, or approximately 20 percent of the total number of lines. Any ratios are potentially misleading since Orm often repeats material and incorporates paraphrase throughout any given homily. Orm thus follows the "ancient" model of homily composition which begins with a substantial preface of biblical material; a "modern" homily (the distinction begins to operate in the fourteenth century) states a biblical verse—the theme—and devotes the bulk of the homily to exposition.[46] The latter form is characterized by a meticulous organization starting from the theme and then continuing with related verses (pro-themes) to develop a sometimes subtle theological point. The scriptural verses serve as springboards to dialectic and doctrinal argument. The ancient form begins with a large chunk of biblical text followed by moralizations and illustrative stories. Clearly, the ancient form is more suited for the instruction of a lay audience unfamiliar with the biblical story itself. Orm usually separates the biblical matter from the accompanying illustrative material by the formula

> Her endenn twa Goddspelless þuss,
> 7 uss birrþ hemm þurrhsekenn,
> To lokenn whatt teȝȝ læren uss
> Off ure sawle nede. (241–44)

> Here end two Gospel [readings] thus,
> And we ought to search them through,
> To see what they teach us
> Of our souls' need.

Orm often combines *two* gospel texts and presents as one homily what a lectionary presents as two separate homilies, each on one of the gospel texts—here Luke 1:5 and Luke 1:18. This combination of material contributes to the unusual length of many of Orm's homilies, and it demonstrates how the presentation of larger chunks of biblical material was a priority. Orm provides contextualized and narratively coherent stories rather than a single verse (the theme) from which, as a starting point, a preacher would launch into the exposition and exemplum.

The following sample gives some idea of the character of Orm's paraphrase, particularly his amplificatory style. The theme—Luke 3:4–6—has inspired many poets and musicians over the ages. Orm's paraphrase is perhaps the earliest poetic treatment of these famous verses in English.

Affterr þatt itt iss writenn þuss	9195
Onn Ysayȝess lare;	
Þe rowwst iss herrd off ænne mann	
Þatt epeþþ þuss i wesste	
Till illkess kinness follc, gaþ till,	
7 ȝarrkeþþ Godess weȝȝe,	9200
Gaþ till, 7 rihhteþþ swiþe wel	
Drihhtiness narrwe stiȝhess;	
Nu skét shall illc an dale beon	
All heȝhedd upp 7 filledd,	
7 illc an lawe 7 illc an hill	9205
Shall niþþredd beon 7 laȝhedd;	
And all þatt ohht iss wrang 7 crumb	
Shall effnedd beon 7 rihhtedd.	
7 whærse iss all unnsmeþe gét	
Þurrh bannkess 7 þurrh græfess,	9210
7 sharrp, 7 ruhh, 7 gatelæs	
Þurrh þorrness 7 þurrh breress,	
Þær shulenn beon ridinngess nu,	
7 effne 7 smeþe weȝȝess.	
7 all mannkinn shall seon full skét	9215
Crist, Godess Sune, onn eorþe.	

After that it is written thus	9195
According to Isaias;	
The voice is heard of one man	
Who cries thus in the waste	
To each kind of folk, go to it,	
And prepare God's ways,	9200
Go to it, and make as straight as possible	
The Lord's narrow paths;	
Now quickly shall each dale be	
All raised up and filled,	
And each mound and each hill	9205
Shall be made low and leveled;	
And all that is in any way wrong and crooked	
Shall be made even and straight,	
And wherever is an unsmooth way	

Through banks and through ditches,   9210
And sharp, and rough, and pathless,
Through thorns and through briars,
There shall be ridings now,
And even and smooth ways,
And all mankind shall quickly see   9215
Christ, God's Son, on earth.

The evocation of the Northumbrian landscape and the promise of "nith-ered" hills and smooth roads must have been especially appealing to Orm's audience. Orm takes great pains to make his listeners feel at home in his poetry and to engage them personally. The phrase "gaþ till" in lines 9199 and 9201 is more than just a metrical filler; it seems to mean something like "go to it" and, like "þwerrt út," is one of the more vivid signs of the preacher's colloquial enthusiasm.

Yet taking, as Orm does here, twenty-two lines to paraphrase three bib-lical verses has led to repeated censures of his undue repetitiveness. Such repetition takes place not only within homilies by means of doublets and simple restatements of the subject but also by wholesale lifting which some-times extends over thousands of lines. For example, lines 3830–43 closely reproduce lines 668–80. His eccentric system of phonetic spelling has also tried the patience of modern readers. Lines 95–100 in the dedication enjoin future scribes to copy the spelling and rhymes with scrupulous care. Crit-ics cite as proof of Orm's wistful incompetence that no copies were made (or survive), and hence that the *Ormulum* is a text with no literary influence. Orm, however, certainly envisaged a wider audience, nonextant copies may indeed have been made, and if survival in a unique manuscript disqualifies a poem from due consideration, more than a few English poems, earlier and later, would be consigned to oblivion.

As can be seen in the above sample, repetition is not so much the rule as variation by means of rhetorical *expolitio*.[47] More importantly, both the aural and orthographical features demonstrate how Orm wished to accommodate his listeners. Repetition and variation are characteristic of oral delivery, and a consistent phonetic spelling would allow individuals with minimal educa-tion to read the poem aloud, or perhaps even to allow priests who were un-familiar with the Northumbrian dialect to read the homilies and be under-stood by the congregation. Two of Orm's personal touches support the latter possiblity: he twice names himself as the author (dedication line 324, pref-ace line 2) and "broþerr Wallterr" (dedication line 1) as the recipient of the book. As a piece of pure speculation, it may be the case that Orm, a native of Northumbria (Orm is a Norse name and he lived at a time and place in

England where Scandinavian influence was clearly present), produced the book for Walter (a Norman?) who had been sent to preach in this unfamiliar territory.

The pride Orm takes in himself as author and in his work as a valuable contribution to society is greater than that of nearly any other Middle English poet and indeed greater, at least in terms of its actually having been expressed, than nearly any other medieval poet. Authorial anonymity is one convention which Orm did not choose to observe. The *Ormulum* shares, however, several characteristics with other biblical paraphrases. First, Old Testament stories are synthesized with those from the New, as for example (lines 8611–710) when in the homily on Matthew 2:19–20 (entry to heaven based on following the commandments) Orm conflates the story of Elias and the Widow of Sarephta (3Kg. 17) with Elias's rapture to heaven in a fiery chariot (4Kg. 2). Second, references to Doomsday (e.g., 8535, 10494, 18610) are linked to the preaching of the apostles or to the Harrowing of Hell as a single theological unit. The salvific event—be it preaching or Christ's dramatic intervention—in the face of hell and damnation at the end of history focuses the attention of the narrative and makes the Harrowing (at the midpoint of history) into a metaphor for the salvation of each Christian soul. Third, Orm's prefatory material parallels other prologues to works of biblical literature in that the translation of biblical texts makes possible the salvation of the "English folk." Addressing Walter, Orm writes in the dedication:

> Icc hafe wennd inntill Ennglissh
> Goddspelless hallȝhe lare,
> Affterr þatt littlc witt þatt me   15
> Min Drihhtin hafeþþ lenedd.
> Þu þohhtesst tatt itt mihhte wel
> Till mikell frame turrnenn,
> ȝiff Ennglissh follc, forr lufc off Crist,
> Itt wollde ȝerne lernenn,   20
> 7 follȝhenn itt, 7 fillenn itt
> Wiþþ þohht, wiþþ word, wiþþ dede.
> . . .
> Icc hafe sammnedd o þiss boc
> Þa Goddspelless neh alle,   30
> Þatt sinndenn o þe messeboc
> Inn all þe ȝer att messe.
> 7 aȝȝ affterr þe Goddspell stannt
> Þatt tatt te Goddspell meneþþ,
> Þatt man birrþ spellenn to þe follc   35
> Off þeȝȝre sawle nede.

I have turned into English
[The] Gospels' holy learning,
According to the little wit that to me   15
My Lord has loaned.
You thought that it might well
Result in great profit,
If English folk, for the love of Christ,
It would eagerly learn,   20
And follow it, and fulfill it,
With thought, with word, with deed.

. . .

I have collected in this book
The Gospels nigh all,   30
That are in the massbook
In all the year at mass [i.e., for the liturgical year].
And always after the Gospel stands
That which the Gospel means,
That one ought to tell to the folk   35
Concerning the needs of their souls.

Despite the humility topos in lines 15–16, Orm recognizes the inevitability
and importance of his personal mediation:

Forr whase mót to læwedd follc
Larspell off Goddspell tellenn,
He mót wel ekenn maniȝ word
Amang Goddspelless wordess. (55–58)

For whoever would to lewed folk
Learning from the Gospels tell,
He must add many words
Among the Gospels' words.

Since so many of the homilist's own words appear amidst the sacred text, reproducing and interpreting biblical verses is a "Heh wikenn" (line 66 of the
dedication—a "high calling"). Like the author of the *Middle English Metrical
Paraphrase of the Old Testament*, Orm places himself in the middle of the production of a paraphrase and recognizes that there is no such thing as a clear
medium for the transmission of texts. Scripture is full of "deope diȝhell-
nesse" (5500), and each component in its dissemination—the preacher, the
audience, and the means and sources of interpretation—is a persistent object of inquiry. In the relationship between preacher and congregation, for
example, Orm insists on the power of the preacher and on the duty of the
congregation to obey him:

7 te birrþ lufenn wel þin preost
7 lutenn himm 7 lefftenn,
ʒét forrþenn þohh he nohht ne beo
Swa god mann summ himm birrde. (6140–43)

And it behooves you well to love your priest
And to obey him and praise him,
Even if he is however not
As good a man as he ought to be.

The efficacy of preaching did not depend on the moral status of the preacher. Christ, Orm assures us, will drag to hell all priests who do not act as they ought. The verb used by Orm to express obligation—"birrþ" ('to behoove')—appears on almost every page of the *Ormulum* and is another indication of Orm's sense of duty and of the poem's exhortative and prescriptivist qualities.[48] Orm's authoritarian and didactic tone persists even though his audience must have been socially mixed. On four occasions Orm addresses his listeners as "laferrdinngess" ("lordings"—lines 918, 11679, 16328, 18611), a term more often used by romance narrators when addressing their listeners.

Conspicuously absent from the modes of address is the formula "lered and lewed" which is so common in biblical and other literatures from later centuries. Mentions of the "læredd" are often scornful and almost always refer to the Jews. In a particularly vehement outburst where the "lered and lewed" are juxtaposed, Orm describes how an important purpose of the coming of the Magi was to contradict the "laþe lærede follc" (7452) who were corrupting the faith of the "lawedd" (7442). The explanations of how the Jews and their traditions fit into Orm's own time are some of the most interesting features of the collection, not least since the *Ormulum* predates Edward the First's expulsion of the Jews from England in 1290. The Jews were, in Beryl Smalley's memorable phrase, "a kind of telephone line to the Old Testament," yet Orm rarely misses an opportunity to challenge their exegetical expertise.[49] For example, there are lengthy and detailed treatments of the ranks of priests (based on Levitical traditions from the Old Testament [461 ff.]) and of the significance of Jewish sacrificial (962 ff.) and ceremonial (1668 ff.) practices. These treatments function first of all as simple expositions of the Bible according to the Old Law. Then, not surprisingly, Orm reads the Jewish practices typologically in the superior light of Christian revelation: Christ's sacrifice surpasses in value any of the Jewish ones, the animals sacrificed have tropological significance (be as meek as the lamb, as faithful as the monogamous turtledove), the ark of the covenant is the body of the church, and so on.

A more interesting issue is how Orm regards the Jews as his principal rivals in biblical interpretation. He considers it ironic that the Jews, whom he rightly regards as the people of the Book and the guardians of Scripture, do not know how to interpret it properly. The Jews, like the devil at the Crucifixion, have allowed themselves to be fooled; the former, even though they "læredd wass o boke" (12100) did not recognize Christ's divinity in much the same way that the latter believed Christ to be only a man, thus falling victim to the *pia fraus* (12001 ff.) and thereby enabling the Harrowing. Satan, according to apocryphal traditions stemming from Matthew 27:19, never would have allowed the Crucifixion to occur had he known of Christ's divinity and of the consequences to his hold on damned souls. The dream of Pilate's wife (Matt. 27:19), after which she urges her husband to disassociate himself from Jesus, was supposed to have been inspired by Satan in order to prevent the Crucifixion. Lumping the Jews and the devil together is clearly invidious, but the comparison makes a significant epistemological point. Whether or not one can obtain and control knowledge determines the validity of interpretation, especially scriptural interpretation, and hence determines the possibility of personal salvation.

The Pharisees provide another example. They also are described as "læredd o boke" (14277), though their learning is bound in a purely "flæshlike" or "stafflike" (i.e., literal) means of interpretation. The achievement of Christ's teaching, and therefore of the New Testament, is that the "bokess flæshliȝ witt / Till gatliȝ witt wass wharrfedd" (14286–287). As demonstrated by his typological readings, Orm gets considerable moral mileage out of his "fleshly-ghostly" hermeneutic engine, but the point is not just that Christ outwitted the devil, or worked more miracles, or saved more souls, but that he was a better critic.

As a final example, the devil's own attempt at biblical exegesis shows how the devil (like the Jews) can quote Scripture but not apply it properly.[50] After having taken Christ to the pinnacle of the temple during the temptation in the desert (Matt. 4:6–7) the devil quotes Psalm 90:11–12:

> et dixit ei: Si filius Dei es, mitte te deorsum. Scriptum est enim: Quia angelis suis mandavit de te, et in manibus tollent te, ne forte offendas ad lapidem pedem tuum. Ait illi Iesus: Rursum scriptum est: Non tentabis dominum Deum tuum.

> and [the devil] said to him: If thou be the Son of God, cast thyself down, for it is written: That he hath given his angels charge over thee, and in their hands shall they bear thee up, lest perhaps thou dash thy foot against a stone. Jesus said to him: It is written again: Thou shalt not tempt the Lord thy God.

Orm comments as follows:

> he toc biforenn Crist
> All wrang þe bokess lare,
> Forr þatt wass seʒʒed off Cristess þeoww
> Þurrh Daviþ þe proféte,
> Þatt he droh forþ all alls itt off
> Crist sellfenn writenn wære.
> Forr Drihhtin hafeþþ seʒʒed 7 sett
> Onn engleþeod tatt wikenn,
> To ʒemenn 7 to frofrenn her
> Þe laferrd Cristess þeowwess. (11925–934)

> he took before Christ
> All wrong the book's learning,
> For that was said of Christ's servant
> Through David the prophet,
> That [which] he brought forth as if it
> Were written of Christ himself.
> For the Lord has decreed and set
> On the company of angels that duty,
> To protect and comfort here
> The Lord Christ's servants.

The word play (11932) on "angel-nation" and "Angle-nation" (reminiscent of Pope Gregory's pun in his anonymous biography and repeated in Bede's *History of the English Church,* II.i) suggests the contemporary application Orm wished his words to have (cf. the previous injunction to obey and praise one's priest); the duty of the English people was indeed to protect and comfort God's servants. On another level Orm pointedly denies the devil the privilege of a typological reading. For Orm, David meant to refer in his psalm only to temptations suffered by Christ's servants, and thus it is improper to see those temptations as an antitype of Christ's own temptations. Christ himself refutes the devil by quoting another text—"thou shalt not tempt the Lord thy God" (Deut. 6:16)—but the devil's real error lies in not having quoted the psalm verse (90:13) which immediately follows the ones he does cite:

> 7 nollde nohht te laþe gast
> Þær draʒhenn forþ, ne mælenn
> Off þatt tæraffterr sone iss seʒʒd
> 7 writenn off himm sellfenn;
> Forr þær iss sett an oþerr ferrs
> Þatt spekeþþ off þe deofell,
> Þatt Godess þeowwess gan onn himm
> 7 tredenn himm wiþþ fote. (11939–946)

> And the loathly spirit would not
> There draw forth, nor speak
> Of that [which] immediately thereafter is said
> And written of himself.
> For there is set another verse
> That speaks of the devil,
> That God's servants [should] go to him
> And tread him underfoot.

For Orm, as for so many other biblical scholars and paraphrasers, both Testaments are linked in subtle yet significant ways. That the full context of the devil's citation refers to the suppression of creatures seen to represent the devil is an eloquent refutation of his own argument. The devil in the New Testament quotes the Old only selectively (deliberately, it seems; cf. the use of "nollde" in line 11939) and thus damns himself out of his own mouth. In paraphrasing this exchange, Orm teaches simultaneously the importance of knowing both Testaments and of quoting in context—something he is always careful to do in his own homilies. Even as he paraphrases Scripture for his audience Orm demonstrates the power of understanding it properly.

Attentive listeners in Orm's parish would become familiar with a considerable amount of the Bible as well as with basic exegetical principles. One can only speculate on how many other zealous twelfth- and thirteenth-century preachers composed their own biblical paraphrases for the edification of the "lewed." In making these points I am not arguing for Orm's theological distinction or for his poetic virtuosity, but in writing the *Ormulum* so as to engage and teach the lowest common denominator of his audience Orm extended the possibility of biblical knowledge and hence of personal salvation as comprehensively as he was able. Individuals like Orm produced the corpus of biblical literature in English from the "dark" days of post-Conquest England into the fifteenth century. As idiosyncratic as the *Ormulum* is, it stands as an important and, I would claim, representative example of the many works dedicated to spreading the Word among the English.

NOTES

1. Heffernan, *Popular Literature,* ix.
2. Ibid., x–xi.
3. Watson, "Censorship," 823.
4. Middleton, "Idea of Public Poetry," 98. "Common speech" is discussed on p. 100 and following. Illich speaks of "a universal call to learning" pertaining to lay and learned populations, as early as the twelfth century (*Vineyard,* 77).
5. Morris, *Cursor Mundi.* Quotations are from London, BL Cotton Vespasian A.iii.
6. J. Thompson, "Popular Reading Tastes," *"Cursor Mundi,"* and *Cursor Mundi: Poem;* Turville-Petre, *England the Nation,* esp. 1–70.

7. Cf. the *Cursor Mundi* poet's concern, late in the poem, that even dialectal impediments be overcome. He prefaces his adaptation of the story of Mary's death and assumption, which he attributes to Edmund of Abingdon, with the following: "In suthrin englis was it draun, / And i hauc turned it till vr aun / Langage of the norþren lede, / Þat can nan oþer englis rede" (lines 20061–20064).

8. Quoted from M. Legge, *Anglo-Norman Literature*, 288.

9. Bühler, "Lollard Tract," 173–74, lines 113–14, 131–33, 140–43. Who "Wyring" was and what kind of a Bible he owned are unknown.

10. Ibid., 178, lines 285–90. For a description of this parliament, see Deanesly, *Lollard Bible*, 282.

11. Cf. Trevisa's "Dialogus inter dominum et clericum" (Waldron, "Trevisa's Prefaces"), where the lord explains how Alfred translated the Psalter, how Cædmon "made wonder poesyes an Englysch nyʒ of al þe storyes of holy wryt," and how Bede "translatede Seint Iohn hys gospel out of Latyn ynto Englysch" (292, lines 136–44). The works of Cædmon and Bede's translation of John have not survived, if they indeed ever existed. The *Polychronicon* also notes how Bede "tornede Seynt Iohn his gospel into Englisshe" (Higden, 6:224).

12. Lines 111–15 of the prologue to *Troy Book*, cited by Pearsall in *Lydgate*, 125.

13. "In prehistorical OE the word probably meant 'physically mutilated,' 'weak,' and the regular OE meaning of 'unlearned' is due to a figurative usage by the priests, who found it a convenient alliterating contrast to *gelæred*" (Lotspeich, "Etymologies," 3). "Lewed" was often glossed as "laicus" (e.g., Herrtage and Wheatley, *Catholicon Anglicum*, 215), but this hardly counts as an etymology. The transparency of any etymology to a medieval reader and writer is less important than the words with which *lewed* was associated.

14. To my knowledge, the only two authorities who have suggested a connection are Toller, who in his *Supplement* entry for *læwed* (noun, 'a layman') prints "see *leod*," and John Small in a note to the prologue of **NHC**: "*laued* from AS. leode, léud, the people" (*Metrical Homilies* 175). I would suggest two possibilities to account for the "w." The first and less likely is that the "w" appears before inflexional endings, on analogy to accusative singular *beadwe* from the noun *beadu* ('battle') or the genitive singular *gearwes* from the adjective *gearu* ('ready'). On this principle *læwede* would mean something like "of the leode," especially since final "e" does indicate an inflected form. *Beadu*, being a wo-stem, has the "w" in the root. *Leode*, however, being an i-stem, has no such resource for intrusive "w." Thus the second and more likely possibility is that the "w" is an orthographical variant to the "u" in attested spellings of *leode* such as *leud;* indeed, *laud* is a variant spelling of *lewed* in line 249 of the *Cursor Mundi* passage.

15. It is worth noting how, in the first line of his *Brut*, Lagamon styles himself as a priest "on leoden" (Laʒamon, *Laʒamon: Brut*). Here he does not just name himself as a secular priest; he situates himself among the people and sets himself the task of gathering foreign language books and of translating them into English (lines 14–28). Once again linguistic and nationalistic concerns intersect.

16. Simmons, *Lay Folks Mass Book* (*Manual*, 7.2350 [195]). The *Mass Book* is not a translation of the missal, and there is no treatment of the eucharist, though "rubrics and devotions are provided for the whole of the mass" (xxviii).

17. Simmons, *Lay Folks Mass Book*, lines 63–64. It may be worth noting that the words "als gode" appear in the earliest manuscript of the *Mass Book*, London, BL

Royal 17.B.xvii (ca. 1375), and not in the two manuscripts representing later revisions. This is one of many signs of the progressively less liberal attitude toward English as the Reformation approached.

18. In "Medium and Message," Minnis makes a similar point in a discussion of Henry of Ghent (a late thirteenth-century Parisian master): "The well-prepared exegete has to discriminate not only between different expositions, but also between different types of auditor. This issue is addressed directly in *quaestiones* which consider the intellectual and moral capabilities of the receivers of exposition" (227). And later: "The *modus* of Holy Scripture is singular, but the needs of human beings are diverse—and hence stylistic diversity and pluralism in the Bible, and exegetical diversity and pluralism on the part of Bible commentators, is fully justified" (234). I would extend Minnis's points to the question of the language in which the Bible and its exegesis appear.

19. Cowper, *Meditations,* lines 165–70.

20. Ibid., lines 503–6.

21. A very good discussion of lay religious is Eric Colledge's introduction to Bazire and Colledge, *Chastising,* 1–90.

22. Ibid., 66, quoting from E. Thompson, *Customary,* 1:280.

23. E. Thompson, *Customary,* 1:276. The companion rule for novitiates of St. Peter's preferred French over English and even Latin: "In qua quidem scola, sicut nec alibi in claustro, debet Anglico ydiomate aliquid proferri; sed neque Latino, nisi prior aut idem magister vel aliquis strenuus frater, docendi aut exortandi gracia, Latine aliquid velit exprimere; sed Gallice jugiter, sicut et in capitulo, ab omnibus et a singulis in claustro est loquendum" (2:164). R. M. Wilson, "English and French," provides many other instances in which languages interface.

24. Kock, *Rule of St. Benet,* 48 (lines 9–16 from London, BL Cotton Vespasian A.xxv, earlier fifteenth c.).

25. The work exists in seventeen manuscripts: nine in Middle English, four in a French translation, and four in a Latin translation. A comparison of the differences among these versions would provide a good perspective on changing religious practices in terms of both time and place.

26. Day, *Ancrene Riwle,* 10–11, from London, Cotton Nero A.xiv (second quarter of the thirteenth c.), quoting Pss. 50:17 and 34:2.

27. Ibid., 8.

28. Ibid., 18–19.

29. Brunner, *Versroman über Richard Löwenherz,* lines 21–30.

30. Macrae-Gibson, *Of Arthour and of Merlin,* lines 17–26.

31. Facsimile edition by Pearsall and Cunningham, *Auchinleck Manuscript.* Folios 46r–48r cover lines 947–1004 of the *Speculum Gy de Warewyke,* ed. Morrill, which paraphrase the story of Elias and the Widow of Sarephta (3Kg. 17:9–16). Folios 66r–69v cover lines 1–274 of **NMC.** See the index entry for Edinburgh, National Lib. of Scotland Advocates 19.2.1, and Turville-Petre, *England the Nation,* chap. 4, "Englishness in the Auchinleck Manuscript" (108–41). Though nearly all the contents have French or Anglo-Norman sources only the *Sayings of the Four Philosophers* contains some Anglo-Norman macaronics; *Kyng Alisaunder, Speculum Gy de Warewyke,* and a few of the religious poems have some Latin insertions (see Pearsall and Cunningham, viii).

32. Cf. "Es darf daher angenommen werden, dass sich diese englischen Gedichte

an ein sehr viel breiteres Publikum richteten als vielfach geglaubt wurde, und bei weitem nicht allein dem Unterhaltungsbedürfnis der breiten Masse dienten" (Mehl, *Romanzen*, 14).

33. See appendix D, "Preservation of Texts," *IMEV/S*, 521. The *Canterbury Tales* rank second (among poems) with sixty-four manuscripts. Kennedy notes that the prose *Brut* is in "at least 172" manuscripts and that the Wycliffite Bible is in "about 200" manuscripts (Review of *Popular Literature*, 181).

34. Morris, *Pricke of Conscience*, lines 336–44. Cf. Mannyng, *Handlyng Synne:* "For lewed men y vndyr toke / On englyssh tonge to make þys boke" (lines 43–44).

35. Morris, *Pricke of Conscience*, lines 9545–51.

36. Small, *Metrical Homilies*, 2–4. Cited hereafter by page number in the text.

37. Cf. the second degree of contemplation in Edmund of Abingdon's *Speculum Ecclesie* (**SE**): "Bot nowe may þou say to me: 'I þat knawes na letters, how may I euer-mare com to contemplacyone of haly writte?' Now, my dere frende, vndirstande me swetely and I sall say perchance to þe: all þat es wretene may be tald. If þou kane noghte vndirstand haly writt, here gladly þe gud þat mene saise þe; and whene þou heres haly wryte owþer in sermone or in preue collacyone, take kepe als-tyte if þou here oghte þat may availe þe till edyfycacyone" (Horstmann, *Yorkshire Writers*, 1:223–24). The tenor of the passage is reminiscent of Romans 15:4, esp. the phrase "all þat es wretene may be tald."

38. Cf. Langland, *Piers Plowman*, B.xviii.351 ff.; *Paradise Lost* III.297 and XII.424; and see Turner, *"Descendit ad Inferos,"* 182. Marx, *Devil's Rights*, provides a good discussion of the various theories of redemption.

39. A variant reading in Cambridge, Univ. Lib. Gg.5.31 is "mak my name ryf." Either way, the verse means something like "poor men make me (my name) known widely."

40. For a study of these components in a homily from the **NHC** on John 1:19–28, see Morey, "Legal and Spiritual Sanctuary."

41. Kalén, *Middle English Metrical Paraphrase*, 3.

42. Ibid., 4.

43. In 1878, Holt revised White's edition of 1852. Burchfield, "*Ormulum* Manuscript," announces an edition in progress. Quotations from Holt's text do not reproduce all of his diacritical marks.

44. Morrison, "Orm's English Sources." Morrison sees Orm's particular debts to lie not so much in content as in vocabulary and phrasing.

45. Augustine, *On Christian Doctrine*, 14 (book I.xiii).

46. See Ross, *Sermons*, xliii–lv.

47. Defined in the *Rhetorica ad Herennium* as "dwelling on the same topic and yet seeming to say something ever new" (365).

48. Cf. lines 173–74 of the *Lay Folks Mass Book* (see above, p. 62). *Birþ* is from Old Norse *byrja* 'to bear', as in to bear on someone to do something. Cf. "pertinet ad me."

49. Smalley, *Study of the Bible*, 362.

50. St. Bernard's *Eight-Verse Psalter* (**BPs**) contains a remarkable instance of the Devil not just quoting, but teaching, the Psalter.

Conclusion

ONCE AWARE of the number, variety, and extent of vernacular materials which transmitted a sense of biblical literature to lay audiences from the twelfth into the fifteenth century in England, one is tempted to ask facetiously "who needed Wyclif?" Obviously, the production of the Lollard Bible was both a necessary step in the systematic dissemination of vernacular Scripture and an important precedent for the work of William Tyndale and his heirs. Ironically, the shadow cast by the Wycliffite Bible over Middle English biblical paraphrase is comparable to the eclipse of Wyclif himself by Reformation translators and even the eclipse of Tyndale by the Authorized Version. Translators, like prophets, are without honor in their own countries, and rarely in or after their own times.

Nevertheless, these works of biblical literature played an important role in the life of both the English commons and the aristocracy. Those responsible for their production, though working independently at many different times and places, did as much, if not more, to spread the Word in medieval England as did Wyclif and his circle. Indeed, in late fourteenth- and early fifteenth-century England, as the manuscripts testify, the copying and reading of the Lollard translations and biblical paraphrases were parallel enterprises. Manuscript copying and notation demonstrate an unbroken tradition of the reading and writing of biblical literature in English from Anglo-Saxon times.

These works of biblical literature were also responsible for shaping the narratives, verses, and set pieces that, even today, people carry around in their heads as a kind of provisional "Bible." The eclectic choice of biblical stories and the liberal synthesis of those stories with legend and apocrypha formed a memorable, accessible, and popular body of biblical material. Chapters 2, 3, and 4 describe some of the social and political dynamics that governed the accessibility, and the popularity. The presentation of biblical material "coram laycis" was, due to a more liberal church, demonstrably more egalitarian and democratic in England than on the Continent. An anecdotal but instructive example of the contrast between the Continent and England is the use of the phrase "coram laycis" itself in Spain by Virgilius, the hypervigilant guardian of the Latin tongue (see chapter 2) and in the *Northern Homily Cycle*. In the earliest manuscript of that cycle (mid-fourteenth-century), after a Latin poem on the Fifteen Last Signs, a rubric states "Isti versus omittantur a lectore quando legit Anglicum coram laycis." Suppression of content is not the issue, since two English translations of the Signs precede the Latin verses. The rubric demonstrates sensitivity to the audience, not jealous paranoia. The rubric also reveals that this manuscript is not a fund of material preachers consulted when preparing sermons but something close to the verbatim substance of what was preached, week by week, to English congregations.

In light of the quantity of biblical literature which does exist, one can conclude that when English authors incorporated biblical material in their works, either through brief allusions or more comprehensive adaptations, audiences could be presumed to have an informed sense of what lay behind such treatments. As modern scholars continue to evaluate the biblical poetics of major authors such as Chaucer, Langland, and Rolle and of many other minor, mostly anonymous, authors, consultation must always be made not only of the Vulgate and of other Latin biblical materials and commentaries but also of Middle English biblical literature which, because of its accessibility and familiarity, was the primary biblical resource of the English Middle Ages.

❖ Guide to the Main Entries

THE ENTRIES provide answers to the following questions: how much of what parts of the Bible appear in Middle English, and where can this biblical material be found? Answers to these questions have been facilitated most by the *Manual of the Writings in Middle English* (*Manual*, Severs and Hartung [1967–]), the *Index of Middle English Verse* (*IMEV*, Brown and Robbins [1943]), its *Supplement* (*IMEV/S*, Robbins and Cutler [1965]), the *Index of Printed Middle English Prose* (*IPMEP*, Lewis et al. [1985]), and the volumes in the *Index of Middle English Prose*, especially Handlist VIII (Ogilvie-Thomson, *Index* [1991]). The entries update and render more accessible, as well as extend, the invaluable information provided by these works. The labor of those who have edited the texts, particularly those published by the Early English Text Society (EETS), has also been of critical importance. Although a great deal of material remains in manuscript, a surprising amount has been printed, often in nineteenth- and early twentieth-century scholarship, and usually with the advantage of being single text editions, not editorial reconstructions.

I have tried to strike a balance between ease of use and comprehensiveness of coverage, but a caveat is in order: medieval manuscripts and their contents are always more complicated than any brief description can convey.

The entries follow a standard format:

Title (with variant titles)

Standard References (where available): *IMEV* number or *IPMEP* number, and
    citation of entry in the *Manual* by volume, page, and item number.

List of Manuscripts, with shelf mark, foliation, date, and other pertinent information such as the number of lines and rhyme scheme. The listing is, in most cases, complete, though for some works existing in more than ten manuscripts it is not, and is so noted.

Editions, where they exist, of the various manuscripts. The list of editions is usually complete, though for some frequently edited poems (such as those by the *Pearl*-poet) it is not. Excerpts in anthologies and readers are, for the most part, not cited.

Facsimiles, where available, of complete manuscripts or works. Facsimilies of individual leaves are, in general, not cited.

Studies which bear on the biblical contents and/or character of the work are sometimes cited, especially if they are recent, but the entries are not intended to be bibliographies of scholarship on the works. The editions, the information in the *Manual,* and other standard bibliographies readily provide this information.

Discussion of how the poem qualifies as biblical literature, of the narrative or dramatic setting of the piece, and citation of its sources, sometimes with illustrative quotations.

Summary of Contents (by line or page; events, names, and illustrative quotations; biblical citations):

Line or page references are to the edition cited, and are arranged by breaks in the narratives and/or subject matter.

The events, names, and illustrative quotations are as complete as practicable, with a concentration on biblical material, though also with some (non-systematic) attention to apocryphal and other contents. Complete attention to material beyond the biblical contents would require concording the corpus of Middle English biblical literature; as desirable as such a concordance would be, it is not the goal of this work. The biblical citations are nevertheless helpful in this regard since certain biblical verses are often associated with the same apocryphal stories (see above, p. 9).

Biblical citations are always to the Vulgate. In some cases, such as with citations from the Gospels, specific chapters and verses are cited, and one can expect to find fairly complete correspondence between the Middle English work and the Vulgate. Users should be alert to the synoptic "problem" in that Matthew, Mark, and Luke, and indeed also

John, share many stories. I have tried to cite the Gospel or Gospels most close to the Middle English, but corresponding passages in other Gospels should always be checked. Since the Bible often quotes itself, similar caution should be exercised when dealing with all of the citations. In other cases, only a biblical chapter will be cited, and users should therefore *not* assume that the entire chapter appears in Middle English. Exact correspondence is not always possible and would be cumbersome if attempted. The citation of a biblical chapter simply means that some material from that chapter (often, but not always, identified under the "Event" heading) appears in Middle English.

Consultation of the indexes should, in most cases, guide the user to the Middle English work or works most likely to contain the biblical material of interest. *It has not been possible, however, to list or index every biblical verse or every detail of each text.* Some accounts of the Flood or Passion, for example, are more detailed than others, and often the entries and the index can do little more than indicate where particular material is likely to be found. It follows that shorter works are covered in more detail, and longer works in less detail. Cross references are given where appropriate, but users should exercise their own ingenuity and be persistent.

❖ I Comprehensive Old and New Testament Works

Fall and Passion **FP**

IMEV 3366
Manual, 2:392 [29]

1. London, BL Harley 913 (29v–31r), early 14th c., 216 lines rhyming abab.

Editions: Furnivall, *Early English Poems,* 12–15; Mätzner, *Altenglische Sprachproben,* vol. 1, part 1, 124–28; Heuser, *Kildare-Gedichte,* 106–12.

FP (ca. 1275–1325) is one of the so-called Kildare-Gedichte, a collection of religious poems in Harley 913 which was almost certainly written in Ireland and which thus preserves the earliest extant remains of the English language in Ireland. Friar Michael of Kildare is credited with at least one of the poems, his "Hymn." See Turville-Petre, *England the Nation,* for a discussion of the other contents, including the well-known *Land of Cockaygne* (156–75).

FP runs from the Fall of the Angels to Christ's Ascension, and has been characterized by Seymour as "a *Paradise Lost* and a *Paradise Regained*" (*Anglo-Irish Literature,* 63). The parallel is apt since the psychological manipulation of Eve by the devil, and of Adam by Eve, is stressed, as well as theological points such as the mystery of the Incarnation. A minor numerological pattern may also be present: line 100 tells of Christ's entry into the world ("þe doʒtir ber þe fader") and line 200 his departure from it ("Holi boke telliþ is uprising"). In such a short poem the Passion is necessarily brief, though there is room for the unique detail (line 164) that Mary wept exactly four tears of blood.

Line references are to Heuser's edition:

Lines	Event	Bible
1–16	Introductory prayer	
9–32	Fall of the Angels for seven days and nights (see Morey, "Fall in Particulate")	Is. 14:13–14
33–48	Creation of Man, prohibition of Tree	Gen. 1:26; 2:15–16
49–84	Temptation and Fall of Man	Gen. 3:1, 4–5, 17, 24
85–92	Coming of the Prophets, Moses	
93–104	Annunciation	Luke 1:26
105–124	Judas betrays Christ, Scourging	Matt. 26:14, 67–68
125–140	Christ before Pilate, Crucifixion	John 19:4, 34
141–152	Joseph of Arimathea, Deposition, Burial	John 19:38–42
153–180	Sorrows of Mary; raising the Temple in three days; Barabbas; Resurrection	John 20:11; Matt. 26:61; 27:21
181–196	Harrowing of Hell	
197–216	Resurrection, commissions Disciples, Ascension	Mark 16:15, 19

Trinity Poem on Biblical History TP

IMEV 1946
Manual, 2:401 [50]

> 1. Cambridge, Trinity College 323 (B.14.39) (36r–42r), mid.-13th c., 349 lines.

Editions: Reichl, *Religiöse Dichtung,* 391–404; Brunner, "Mittelenglische Marienstunden," 231–43.

The last of three biblical paraphrases in Trinity 323 (the previous two are **WA** and **BTD**), **TP** condenses biblical history from the Fall of the Angels to martyrdoms of apostles and saints. Apocryphal detail is prominent, notably two mentions of the Heavenly Rebellion (lines 9–16, 25–36, quoting Is. 14:13) before and after the creation of Adam and Eve, and two mentions of the Harrowing (165–68, 293–97). The fall of Lucifer is especially vivid: "At nose ant mouþe is bret wes so brent brunston, / Asse me hit fint in þe pokalips of þe louer Sein Johon" (Reichl, *Religiöse Dichtung,* lines 27–28).

Imagery from the end of time is used to describe an event which must have taken place somewhere near the beginning.

Apocryphal details include the common motif of how Cain slew Abel with "one asse chehec" (86) and the odd touches that Lucifer looked over his left shoulder to see Michael and Gabriel ready to throw him down (33), that "iesus crist" appeared to Cain to ask him "Wer is þi broþer, þu fule heuelinke?" (90 [Where is your brother, you foul heathen?]) and that Adam languished in Hell for 4004 years (135).[1]

A larger structural concern is how a poet can get from one end of biblical history to the other in just 349 lines. In order to sum up the many descendants of Adam and Eve the poet resorts to *praetereo:* "Wose hedde þen Genesi ant couþe loke þeron, / He miste of heire childeren nemmen moni on" (109–10). For the rest of the Old Testament the poet employs a series of "I think on . . ." phrases (see below, lines 109–36). A subsequent mention of the suffering of Joseph recalls the suffering of the king "on þe treo" in line 129. The poem then moves into Gabriel's annunciation to Mary and thence into the life and work of Christ. Perhaps taking a hint from the use of genealogies in the Bible, the poet uses names and brief references to historical events to advance his narrative rapidly into new material. It is also conceivable that, like the *scop* in *Deor,* the poet lists subjects in his repertoire. Curious listeners may have been tempted to ask for a story about Jacob and Esau, or Samson and Dalila.

Despite the narrative compression and the rapid shifts of time and place, the poem is not marked by incongruities. The poet takes the premise of the unity of biblical history very seriously, and he even extends it to the liturgical calendar. After a litany of martyred saints, the poet ends the whole poem with a four-line formula to find the date of Easter:

> Ate feste of Seint Benedist
> Þenne is þe dai euene wid þe nist
> Nim þenne mone of foutennist
> Þe necste sunedai þerhefter paske rist. (346–49)

Biblical history, the sanctorale, and the liturgical year are all reflected in the organic structure of a single poem.

From Reichl, *Religiöse Dichtung:*

---

1. Cf. the 4604 years in *St. Patrick's Purgatory* (Kölbing, "Zwei Bearbeitungen von St. Patriks Purgatorium," line 583) and the "seuene thousand wynter" in Langland, *Piers Plowman,* C.xx.309.

Lines	Event	Bible
1–40	Creation, Fall of the Angels	Gen. 1–2
41–64	Fall of Man, God's curses	Gen. 3
65–96	Cain and Abel	Gen. 4:1–12
97–108	Seth, Lamech, Henoch	Gen. 5
109–136	Summary of Old Testament:	

Hic þenche on Adam ure feder ant on Abel þe
   gode,
So i do of Noe ant of þe stronke flode;
Wu Moyses tog Godis lawe in von beit
   wordes gode;
Ant of þe prophetis þat in Godis laue stoden.
So i do of Abraham ant of Sarra þe briste;
Of Ysaac ant of Rebecca, þe holi nede vuste;
Of Jacob ant of Esau, so faire here fader
   hem diste;
Josepes breþeren tuelue hine solden vid vnriste.
I þenche on Dalida þat Samsun ablende,
Wid hire suikedomes fule heo hine scende;
Wu David Urien is sonit to is deþe sende,
Wor Bersabe is wiue; Salomon a kende. (113–24)

Lines	Event	Bible
137–156	Annunciation	Luke 1:26–38
157–172	Joseph doubts Mary, reassured by angel	Matt. 1:18–25
173–224	Magi, Herod; allusions to Balaam's prophecy at 183 and the rod of Jesse at 194	Matt. 2:1–12; Num. 24:17; Is. 11:10
225–256	Flight to Egypt, Slaughter of Innocents, Archelaus	Matt. 2:13–23
257–268	Christ's baptism by John the Baptist	Matt. 3:13–17
269–280	Synopsis of Christ's miracles, preaching, calling of the Disciples	
281–292	Judas, betrayal, Scourging, Crucifixion	Matt. 26; 27
293–296	Harrowing of Hell	
297–312	Post-Resurrection appearances to Mary Magdalen, Thomas	John 20
313–320	Ascension; commission of Disciples	Matt. 28
321–345	Pentecost; acts and fates of various apostles and saints	
346–349	Formula for finding the date of Easter	

Versions of Robert Grosseteste's *Chateau d'Amour* **CA**

Manual, 7:2337 [182]

This text became widely influential in the medieval allegorical tradition, especially the allegory of the Four Daughters of God (based on Ps. 84:11) and the allegory of the Castle of Love (see Cornelius, "Figurative Castle"). Raymo's *Manual* entry gives a comprehensive treatment. The following concentrates on the biblical contents.

There are four Middle English versions, plus a series of passages integrated into **CM,** notably at lines 9375–10122 (Four Daughters of God and Castle of Love and Grace) and lines 18661–750 (Doubting Thomas). See J. Thompson, *Cursor Mundi: Poem,* 147. All are based on Grosseteste's Anglo-Norman production. Grosseteste died in 1253.

Version A, the Castle of Love
IMEV 3270

1. Oxford, Bodleian Lib. English poet. a.1 (Vernon) (293r col. c–296v col. a), ca. 1390, 1,862 lines in octosyllabic couplets.
2. London, BL Add. 22283 (Simeon) (84v col. b–87v col. a), ca. 1400.
3. Oxford, Bodleian Lib. Add. B.107 (*SC* 29560) (1r–45v), 15th c.

Editions: 1 and 3—Sajavaara, *Chateau d'Amour,* 260–319.

1—Horstmann, *Minor Poems,* 355–94.

See *Manual* for many other editions.

Facsimile: 1—Doyle, *Vernon Manuscript.*

Lines	Event	Bible
57–65	Isaias's prophecy, "Prince of Pes"	Is. 9:6
83–187	Six-day Creation, Sabbath, Fall of Angels, Adam and Eve, Prohibition	Gen. 1; 2
188–208	Fall of Man, expulsion from Eden	Gen. 3
262–67	Three Laws: Natural and Positive for Adam; Law given to Moses on Sinai	Ex. 19
275–566	Allegory of the King and Four Daughters	Ps. 84:11
595–614	Prophets of Christ: Moses, Jonas, Habacuc, Elias, Daniel, Jeremias, David, Isaias, Eliseus, Samuel	
655–670	Incarnation in "þe castel of alle flour" (669 [i.e., Mary])	
959–960	"Mi ȝok is softe . . ."	Matt. 11:30
1036–1046	Temptation of Christ: "Go awei, Sathan, go!"	Matt. 4:7–10

Lines	Event	Bible
1265–1290	Miracle at Cana; feeds five thousand; Lazarus	John 2:1–11; Matt. 14:17–21; John 11:39–43
1415–1460	Doubting Thomas; Jesus commissions Disciples	John 20:19–29
1652–1678	"When I was hongry, ȝe ȝeue me mete"	Matt. 25:35–41

Version B, Myrour of Lewed Men
IMEV/S 145

> 1. London, BL Egerton 927 (1r–28r), early 15th c., 1,250 lines in couplets.

Editions: Sajavaara, *Chateau d'Amour,* 320–53; Horstmann, *Minor Poems,* 407–42; Hupe, "Grosseteste's *Chasteau d'Amour,*" 427–55.

> From Sajavaara's edition:

Lines	Event	Bible
Prose prologue: "her is no thing sayd bot as haly writ says and grete doctours" (p. 320)		
15–72	Creation; Adam and Eve, Temptation, Fall, Expulsion: " 'Of all the trees,' quod Eue, 'that thar is, we may ete at our liking, / Out-tan on that is forbod paraunter for dred of deyng' " (55–56)	Gen. 1; 2; 3
73–146	Ten Commandments	Ex. 20:1–17
343–350	"Prince of pece"	Is. 9:6
545–563	Temptation in the Desert: "If thou be Goddes sone . . . make of stones brede!"	Matt. 4:1–10
605–672	Passion; recollection of the Circumcision	Matt. 27; Luke 2:21
691–726	Miracle at Cana; feeds five thousand; Lazarus	John 2:1–11; Matt. 14:17–21; John 11:39–43
785–800	Harrowing of Hell	
813–830	Doubting Thomas; Jesus commissions Disciples	John 20:19–29; Mark 16:15–16
853–854	Pentecost	Acts 2:1–4
1053–1070	Seven Works of Bodily Mercy	Matt. 25:35–41

Version C, King and Four Daughters, what Horstmann calls "De principio Creationis mundi"
IMEV 1677

1. Oxford, Bodleian Lib. Ashmole 61 (*SC* 6922) (78v–83r), late 15th c., 440 octosyllabic couplets.

Editions: Sajavaara, *Chateau d'Amour*, 354–65; Horstmann, *Altenglische Legenden Neue Folge*, 349–54.

The 22-line prologue cites the "romance" which "Grostyd" translated into French from Latin; the English poet seeks to replicate the exercise for "men of Ingelond" who likewise do not "know latyn, ebrew & grew."

A synopsis of the six-day Creation notes that the sun was seven times brighter before the fall than it is now (44); likewise the moon was as bright as the sun is now (Is. 30:26). The creations of Adam ("In þe veyll of Ebron of cley gente [73]) and Eve (from a "rybe-bone" [87]) are narrated; their union is glossed as the institution of "wedloke" (94).

Two laws apply in paradise (122): the natural (obedience to God), and the positive (the prohibition of the tree in Gen. 3).

> "Bot a tre I the forbyde.
> Ete þou not þerof for non nede!
> Iff þou ete þer of, I þe sey,
> Sone þer after þou schall dey." (129–32)

Adam breaks the positive law "fore lufe of hys wyfe" (150) (anticipating Milton).

A general lament concerning the effects of Original Sin and the degeneracy of the times follows to line 222. An allegorical exposition of the Four Daughters of God (based on the four cardinal virtues: mercy, truth, justice, peace) takes up the rest of the poem, with only a brief mention of the rescue of Noah, his wife, his three sons, and their wives from the Flood (355–60). A Latin quotation of Ps. 84:11 ends the poem, as an epigraph to the reconciliation of the Daughters of God by the Son, Wisdom.

Version D, Foure Doughters
IMEV/S 879

1. London, BL Cotton Appendix VII (1r–2v), later 14th c., 192 lines in stanzas rhyming aabccb, atelous.

Edition: Sajavaara, *Chateau d'Amour*, 366–71.

The allegory of the daughters and son take up nearly the whole of this fragment. There are no biblical contents except for a recollection of Noah, his sons, and their wives in lines 160–65.

Charter of the Abbey of the Holy Ghost CHG

IPMEP 590
Manual, 7:2341 [186]
Jolliffe, *Check-List,* H.9

24 MSS, including:

1. Oxford, Bodleian Lib. Laud misc. 210 (*SC* 1292) (136r–146v), early
   15th c.
2. Oxford, Bodleian Lib. Eng. poet. a.1 (Vernon) (360v–363r),
   ca. 1390.
3. Maidstone Museum 6 (41r–58v), early 15th c.

Edition: 1 and 2 — Horstmann, *Yorkshire Writers,* 1:337–62.

There are three printings by Wynkyn de Worde in 1496, 1497, and 1521.
See Jenkinson, *Abbaye,* for a facsimile of the 1496 printing.

CHG appears in some manuscripts, including manuscripts 1 and 2, with
the *Abbey of the Holy Ghost* (*Manual,* 7:2340 [184]); in other manuscripts and
in the de Worde printing the pieces are conflated. Like the versions of **ChC,**
this work presents itself as a legal document whereby mankind is enfeoffed,
disinherited of, and then reinvested with the allegorical "Abbey of the Holy
Ghost" — here a metaphor for Creation. Christ's calling of the disciples, for
example, is his reassembly of the inmates of the Convent (Reason, Shrift,
Predication, etc.). Raymo notes in the *Manual* that "[s]ome of the Biblical
material has been taken from a Middle English Devotional work, *The Life
of the Virgin Mary and Christ,* extant in Trinity College, Dublin, MS 423. . . .
Their common source is the pseudo-Bonaventuran *Meditationes vitae Christi*"
(7:2341–42).

From Horstmann's edition:

Page	Event	Bible
339	God grants Adam and Eve lordship over the earth	Gen. 1:28
341–344	Temptation: "what tyme þat ȝe eten þerof ȝe schul ben as goddis knowand good & wicked" (341); God's curses	Gen. 3:1–24
345	Anticipation of the Harrowing of Hell after 4,600 years	
346–348	Lamentations of David, Solomon, Isaias, and Jeremias	Ps. 68:4; 143:5; Cant. 3:2; 5:6; 6:12; 4:9; 3:1;

Page	Event	Bible
		5:8; Wis. 9:10; Is. 64:1; Jer. 45:3; Lam. 2:2; 1:18, 21, 16; Jer. 9:1; Lam. 2:13; 5:16
349–352	Intercession by the Four Daughters of God	Ps. 84:11
352–354	Incarnation; Nativity; Jesus disputes with the doctors in the Temple; Temptation in the Desert: "fy on þe, satanas" (354)	Luke 2:41–51; Matt. 4:1–10
354–355	Calling of Peter, Andrew, James and John, sons of Zebedee; Peter's question	Matt. 4:17–22; 19:27–29
355–356	Woman taken in adultery; tribute to Caesar	John 8:1–11; Matt. 22:15–21
356–357	Last Supper, washes Disciples' feet; Agony in Gethsemani	John 13:1–5; Matt. 26:36–45
358–360	Arrest, Malchus's ear; Christ before Caiphas Scourging; Crucifixion	Matt. 26:47–57, 67; 27:27–31
361–362	Last Words; Harrowing of Hell	John 19:28–30

Cursor Mundi CM

IMEV 2153
Manual, 7:2276 [31]

1. Oxford, Bodleian Lib. Laud misc. 416 (*SC* 1479) (65r–181v), 15th c.
2. Oxford, Bodleian Lib. Fairfax 14 (*SC* 3894) (4v–125), late 14th c.
3. Cambridge, Trinity College 588 (R.3.8) (1v–144), ca. 1400.
4. London, BL Cotton Vespasian A.iii (2v–163), ca. 1340. Parts of the Passion section taken from **SP**. Sce J. Thompson, *Cursor Mundi: Poem,* 75–79.
5. London, BL Add. 31042 (London Thornton), verses 10630–14914 and verses 17111–17188 on 3r–32v, mid-15th c. Accompanies **NP, CP, MPs, CJ**, *Proverbs of Solomon* (*Manual,* 9.2975 [45]).
6. London, BL Add. 36983 (1v–174), 1442. Omits verses 14916–17288 (replaced by lines 1–1140 of **MS**); omits verses 22005–23898 (replaced by lines 4085–6407 of the *Pricke of Conscience,* ed. Morris).
7. London, Arundel College of Arms LVII (1v–132), ca. 1400. Omits verses 1–152.
8. Edinburgh, College of Physicians (37r–50v contain verses 18989–23944, 1r–15v contain lines 22418–24968, missing seven folios, misbound), ca. 1325. Accompanies **NHC**.

9. Göttingen, Niedersächsische Staats- und Universitätsbibliothek
Theol. 107r (1r–169), 14th c. Illustrated; see Horrall, "Man
Yhernes Rimes."
10. Montreal, McGill Univ. Lib. 142 (four leaves), verses 20129–20314,
actually a fragment from the *Southern Assumption* (*IMEV/S* 165). See
Sargent, "McGill 'Southern Assumption.' "

Editions: 1—Morris, *Cursor Mundi* (EETS os 59, pp. 536–666, lines 9325–
11621; EETS os 62, pp. 926–1060, lines 16227–18512; EETS os 68, pp.
1651–1662, lines 1–270).
2—Morris, *Legends of the Holy Rood,* 108–21 [extracts].
2, 3, 4, 9—Morris, *Cursor Mundi.*
5—Horrall et al., *Southern Version,* 2:151–92, lines 10630–12712 and 3:
165–210, lines 12713–17187.
6—Morris, *Cursor Mundi* (EETS os 68, pp. 1651–67, lines 1–270,
9517–9752).
7—Morris, *Cursor Mundi* (EETS os 68, pp. 1657–63, lines 153–270; pp.
1587–1637, lines 18989–23644); Horrall et al., *Southern Version* (the base
text of the Ottawa edition, with variants from 1, 3, and 6).
8—Morris, *Cursor Mundi* (EETS os 68, pp. 1587–1637).
10—Sargent, "McGill 'Southern Assumption.' "
Studies: J. Thompson, *Cursor Mundi: Poem;* Fowler, *Bible in Early English
Literature,* 165–93; Horrall, "For the Commun."

Most of the poem is in short couplets. Some sections, such as the Passion,
are in long-line septenaries.

The *Cursor Mundi,* much like the *South English Legendary,* is a comprehensive, and unwieldly, collection of Middle English verse consisting largely of
biblical paraphrase. Of the many works of biblical literature, **CM** is the most
likely to be mentioned in English literary histories, but it rarely makes anything more than a cameo appearance.

Its length in the extant manuscripts ranges from twenty-four thousand
to thirty thousand lines. Manuscript 8, in a northern dialect, is closest to
the earliest version it is possible to postulate (Horrall, "Manuscripts," 72).
Although a single poet (ca. 1300?) may have taken the initiative to translate and compile the various sections of the work, it seems likely that the
divergent contents and organization of the manuscripts indicate the role of
various ad hoc compilers. **CM** is, in fact, an " 'open' compilation" (J. Thompson, review of *Southern Version,* 120) into which separate poems were dropped
and spliced (see, e.g., *IMEV* 1786, 3208, and J. Thompson, "Textual Interpolations," "Textual Instability"). A comprehensive study of the poem's con-

tents would indeed acquaint one with the diversity and variety of medieval popular culture.

This kind of encyclopedic collection makes it a true *omnium-gatherum*. Thompson identifies it as an "anecdotal literary-didactic" work (*"Cursor Mundi,"* 101); lines 267–68 describe how "Cursor o werld man aght it call / For almast it ouer-rennes all." In such productions it is inevitable that the narrative is somewhat fractured and that discontinuities would appear as material is derived variously from the Bible, the Fathers, the apocrypha, mythology, the *Historia Scholastica,* and French texts such as *La Bible de Herman de Valenciennes,* Robert Grosseteste's *Chateau d'Amour,* and the *Traduction anonyme de la Bible entière.* Two general principles can be seen to govern the work. First, knowledge of biblical literature contributes to the general religious education of the faithful and thereby enhances their chances for salvation. Second, knowledge of apocrypha, myth, and legend contributes to an understanding of natural history and of the physical world. Doctrinal messages are downplayed in favor of explaining the mechanics of the narrative on a literal level. The story line is important, and the treatment of sacred history amounts to a unified whole, but because the biblical text seems not to make sense it demands an interpretation. Hence the poet is determined to provide efficient causes for those biblical stories which appear to have weak narrative links. Like all historiated Bibles, **CM** thrives off a paradox: in its zeal to unify and render coherent the Bible story, it fractures the Bible itself with explanations which sometimes lead a poem into seemingly bizarre extrabiblical material. The goal is to facilitate the understanding of the Bible. Along the way, and with no qualms of heterodoxy, such texts become, for practical purposes, vernacular Bibles.

It would be otiose to catalog in detail the biblical contents of **CM.** Suffice it to say that the poem is organized around the seven ages of the world, and that the tables of contents in volumes 66 and 68 of Morris's EETS edition and the outlines in the frontmatter to the volumes in Horrall's Ottawa project provide useful guides. The poet provides his own summary of contents in lines 115–220, from Creation through the Old and New Laws, to Doomsday, finishing with the Conception of the Virgin Mary (only manuscript 8 actually stops here, at line 24968). The annotations by Horrall et al., and the comprehensive study by J. Thompson (*Cursor Mundi: Poem*), are invaluable.

The outline below provides a complementary guide to relevant biblical chapters. Citation of a biblical chapter does not, in most cases, indicate that the entire chapter is paraphrased. Apocryphal material frequently intervenes: for example, the Fall of the Angels, Seth's quest for the oil of mercy (see Quinn, *Quest*), the Wonders of Solomon, Infancy narratives, the Harrowing of Hell, dialogues between Christ and Man, the Inventio Crucis, the Fifteen Signs before Doomsday (see Heist, *Fifteen Signs*). As noted above, these poems are often independent productions which have been patched into the **CM** narrative.

From manuscript 4, edited by Morris, *Cursor Mundi:*

Lines	Event	Bible
FIRST AGE		
27–410	Creation	Gen. 1–2
411–510	Creation and Fall of the Angels	
585–974	Adam and Eve, Eden, the Fall	Gen. 3
1045–1412	Cain, Abel, Seth	Gen. 4–5
1413–1552	Genealogy of Adam	
[there are parallels throughout to **LAE**]		
SECOND AGE		
1553–2000	Noah, the Flood	Gen. 6
2001–2080	Rainbow; drunkenness of Noah	Gen. 9
2081–2194	Sem, Cham, Japheth; Melchisedech; their descendants	Gen. 9–10
2195–2314	Nemrod, Tower of Babylon	Gen. 11
THIRD AGE		
2315–3116	Abraham, Sara, Lot; Agar, Ismael; Sodom and Gomorrha; Lot's wife and daughters; Abimelech	Gen. 12–21
3117–3208	Sacrifice of Isaac	Gen. 22
3209–3408	Rebecca, Cetura	Gen. 23–25
3409–4036	Jacob, Esau; Rachel, Laban, Lia	Gen. 25–33
4037–4238	Joseph and his brothers	Gen. 37
4239–4428	Putiphar's wife	Gen. 39
4429–4668	Joseph's dreams	Gen. 40–41
4669–5494	Joseph's hegemony in Egypt; Benjamin; death of Jacob	Gen. 42–50
5494–6300	Moses; Burning Bush; plagues; Red Sea crossing	Ex. 1–14
6301–6486	Wandering in Sinai; Ten Commandments	Ex. 15–20
6487–6666	Golden calf; "horned" Moses; Ark of the Tabernacle	Ex. 32–37
6667–6880	Laws of Moses	Ex. 21–23
6881–6922	Death of Moses	Deut. 34
6923–6992	Josue, entry into Israel	Jos. 1–3
6993–7082	Judges of Israel (with references to contemporaneous events and persons such as Hercules and Troy):	

Lines	Event	Bible
	Caleb, Othoniel, Aod	Judg. 3
	Samgar, Barac, Debbora	Judg. 4
	Gedeon	Judg. 6
	Thola, Jair	Judg. 10
	Jephte	Judg. 11
	Abesan, Ahialon, Abdon	Judg. 12
7083–7262	Samson (and Dalila)	Judg. 13–16
7263–7286	Heli and his sons (Ophni and Phinees)	1Kg. 4:10–18
7287–7438	Samuel, Saul, Jesse, David	1Kg. 8–16
7439–7592	David and Goliath	1Kg. 17
7593–7836	Saul's jealousy of David; Jonathan; reports of Saul's death	1Kg. 18–31 2Kg. 1

FOURTH AGE

7837–7972	David, Bethsabee, Urias, Nathan	2Kg. 11–12
8353–8434	Solomon's accession	3Kg. 1
8459–8482	Solomon's authorship of Ecclesiastes, Proverbs, and Canticles	
8539–8756	Solomon's wisdom	3Kg. 3
8757–8889	Building of the Temple	3Kg. 5
8979–9132	Solomon's excesses and death	3Kg. 11

[apocryphal wonders associated with Solomon intervene throughout]

9133–9222	Solomon's successors:	
	Roboam, Abiam, Asa,	3Kg. 14–15;
	Josaphat, Joram, Elias,	18; 22; 4Kg. 2;
	Eliseus, Azarias, Joatham, Achaz,	15–16; 18–22;
	Ezechias, Manasses, Amon, Josias, Joachin,	24–25
	Sedecias, Nabuchodonosor	

[Sketchy catalog of rulers and events of their reigns. Lines 9165–68 list the Minor Prophets in Azarias's time: Isaias, Joel, Osee, Abdias, Amos, Jonas, Micheas]

FIFTH AGE

9229–9264	Genealogies of Joseph and Mary	Matt. 1:11–17
9264–9374	Isaias's prophecy of Christ	Is. 11:1; 7: 14–15; 9:6
9375–9516	Recapitulation of Creation, Adam; the natural and positive laws; Christ as the New Man; brightness of the sun and moon	Gen. 1–3; Is. 30:26
9517–9816	Four Daughters of God from **CA**	Ps. 84:11
9817–9876	Excursus on Isaias's names of God	Is. 9:6
9877–10093	Parable of the Castle of Love and Grace	
10094–10122	Prayer to Mary; sun through glass analogy	

Lines	Event	Bible
	(see J. Thompson, *Cursor Mundi: Poem*, 142–43; **CJ,** stanzaic version line 433; and **DJM,** 130–32)	
10123–10574	Conception of Mary; Joachim, Anne, Elizabeth (derives from Wace's *Fête de la conception Notre Dame*. See J. Thompson, *Cursor Mundi: Poem*, 152)	Luke 1
10574–10816	Childhood, marriage of Mary; Joseph's flowering rod	Is. 11:1
10817–11176	Annunciation; Zachary; John the Baptist; Joseph's doubts	Luke 1; Matt. 1
11177–11594	Nativity of Christ; Simeon; Magi (Jasper, Melchior, Baltassar/Attropa); Herod, Slaughter of the Innocents	Luke 2; Matt. 2
11595–12576	Infancy of Christ; travels in Egypt (parallels Gospel of Ps. Matthew)	
12577–12658	Disputes with Temple doctors	Luke 2:41–52
12659–12751	Anne's husbands and their progeny	

SIXTH AGE

12752–12915	John the Baptist, Christ's baptism	Matt. 3
12916–13001	Temptation in the Desert	Matt. 4
13002–13241	Death of John the Baptist (prophesies in Hell)	Matt. 14
13242–13359	Christ's ministry	Matt. 4:18–25
13360–13451	Miracle at Cana	John 2
13452–13519	Feeding the five thousand	John 6
13520–13685	Healing the blind man on Sabbath	John 9
13686–13759	Woman taken in adultery	John 8:1–11
13760–13961	Healing the lame man on Sabbath	John 5
13962–14383	Raising of Lazarus; Martha, Mary, Simon	John 11–12
14384–14720	Unbelief of the Jews despite Christ's preaching and miracles	
14721–14775	Jesus cleanses Temple; raising the Temple in three days	John 2:13–22
14776–14936	More Jewish resistance	

[for treatments of the Passion in MSS 4, 5, 6, and 9 see J. Thompson, *Thornton*, 49–51, and *Cursor Mundi: Poem*, 66]

14937–15160	Mt. Olivet; entry into Jerusalem	Matt. 21:1–11
15161–15272	Last Supper	Luke 22:7–23
15273–15384	Jesus washes Disciples' feet	John 13:1–30
15385–15822	Gethsemani, Betrayal by Judas	Matt. 26:36–56
15823–16016	Buffeting; Peter's denial	Matt. 26:65–74

Lines	Event	Bible
16017–16450	Trial, Pilate, Herod, Barabbas, Scourging	Matt. 27:11–31
16451–16542	Judas repents, boiled cock comes back to life (cf. Elliott, *Apocryphal New Testament*, 672), hangs himself, bursts, potter's field	Matt. 27:1–10; Acts 1:18–19
16543–17100	Crucifixion; Joseph of Arimathea	John 19; Matt. 27
17101–17270	Dialogue between Christ and Man (also in MS 9 and two other MSS. See J. Thompson, *Thornton*, 51; *Manual*, 3.679 [2])	
	Resurrection (an independent 466-line poem only in MS 4)	Matt. 28; John 20–21
17271–17832	Fate of Joseph of Arimathea	
17833–18512	Account of Carius and Lucius	
18513–18638	Pilate's letter to Rome	
18661–18706	Doubting Thomas	John 20:19–29
18863–19044	Pentecost	Acts 1–2
19045–19114	Peter heals a cripple	Acts 3
19115–19214	Arrest of the apostles	Acts 4
19215–19286	Ananias and Saphira	Acts 5:1–11
19287–19380	Apostles freed by an angel	Acts 5:12–42
19381–19476	Stoning of Stephen	Acts 6, 7
19477–19600	Philip, Simon Magus	Acts 8
19601–19748	Saul's conversion; Ananias	Acts 9:1–31
19749–19802	Peter heals Eneas and Dorcas	Acts 9:32–43
19803–20010	Cornelius; Peter's vision	Acts 10
20065–20108	Christ's charge to John and Mary (see *IMEV* 3976, 2165, and *Manual*, 2:450 [318]	John 19:26–27
20109–20848	Assumption of Mary [see *IMEV* 3976, 2165]	
20849–21236	Fates of the apostles	
21237–21346	The four Evangelists	
21347–21846	Inventio Crucis legend	

SEVENTH AGE

[Major sources in this section include the *Elucidarium* of Honorius Augustodunensis, the *De ortu et tempore antichristi* of Adso Dervensis, and anonymous Old French versions of the "Fifteen Signs before Doomsday" (see J. Thompson, *Cursor Mundi: Poem*, 171, and Heist, *Fifteen Signs*).]

21847–21974	Doomsday	
21975–22426	Antichrist	
22013–22022	Dan	Gen. 49:16–17
22052–22064	Satan bound for one thousand years [see Emmerson, *Antichrist,* 160]	Rev. 20:1–7
22427–22710	Fifteen Signs before Doomsday	Rev. 8

Lines	Event	Bible
22711–23194	How the dead shall be raised	
22963–22991	Vale of Josaphat	Joel 3:2–12
23195–23350	Nine Pains of Hell	
23351–23652	Fourteen Joys of Heaven	
23653–23704	The world after Doomsday	
23705–23944	Exhortatory prayer	
[Lines 23945–24730 correspond to **LLB**]		
23945–24658	Lamentation of Mary at the Cross [six-line stanzas, aabccb]	
24299	Christ's charge to John	John 19:25–30
24397	Gall and Vinegar, earthquake	Matt. 27:51–52
24481	Joseph and Nicodemus	John 19:38–39
24659–24730	Apostrophe to John	
24731–24968	Story of Elsey (from Wace's *Fête de la conception Notre Dame,* ca. 1150 [*IMEV* 1885]), Festival of the Conception [in couplets: the story of the abbot who negotiates peace between William the Bastard and the king of Denmark; his rescue at sea on the Feast of Mary's Conception] [MS 8 ends here]	
24969–25102	Apostles' Creed and exposition	
25103–25402	Pater Noster and exposition (*IMEV* 788)	Matt. 6:9–13
25403–25486	Prayer to the Trinity [six-line stanzas, aabccb]	
25487–25618	Matins of the Passion (Hours of the Cross)	
25619–25683	Five Joys of Mary [five-line stanzas, aaabb, *IMEV* 1029]	
[Lines 25684–29547 constitute the so-called Book of Penance]		
25684–25931	Prayer to God the Father; miscellaneous exempla concerning David and Urias, the Good Thief, Zacheus, Adam, Judas, Cain, et al.	
25932–27147	Three means of penance	
27148–29547	The office of a priest; excursus on the Seven Deadly Sins	

Morris prints the following Appendices:

I. Acts of the Apostles from MS 8, corresponding to lines 18989–23933

II. Assumption of Mary, corresponding to lines 20011–820 [*IMEV* 3976]

III. Version of the Prologue, lines 1-270 from MS 1

IV. Cato's Morals [*Manual*, 9:2973 [35]]

In EETS os 99 Morris provides notes (pp. xxxi–lx), a glossary (pp. 1677–1793), and an index of names (pp. 1795–1820).

English Translations of Ranulph Higden's
Polychronicon Poly

John Trevisa's translation:
IPMEP 605
Manual, 8:2656 [21]

1. Cambridge, St. John's College 204 (19r–280r), ca. 1400. Thirteen other MSS, four fragments, and early prints.

Anonymous translation:
IPMEP 35
Manual 8:2661 [22]

2. London, BL Harley 2261 (1r–445r), later 15th c.

Anonymous translation taken from Trevisa:
Manual, 8:2662 [26]

3. Oxford, Trinity College 29 (1r–226v), 15th c.

Edition: 1 and 2 in parallel, with Higden's Latin—Higden, *Polychronicon*, vols. 2, 3, and 4.
Study: Fowler, *Bible in Early English Literature*, 194–246.

There are numerous universal histories in Middle English, well outlined by the entries in Kennedy's volume of the *Manual* (vol. 8, the only volume in the series dedicated to a single genre). Many begin with a synopsis of biblical history from Creation to the Acts of the Apostles. Though large-scale repetition is common among chronicles—history repeats itself, and historians repeat each other—the inclusion of biblical material is unpredictable depending on the work, and indeed the manuscript. Any systematic search would need to work through Kennedy's entries. See also Gransden, *Historical Writing c. 550* and *Historical Writing c. 1307*.

The *Polychronicon* is one of the most comprehensive, and influential, universal prose histories, covering events from the Creation to the fourteenth century. Produced by the Benedictine Ranulph Higden (d. ca. 1360), it exists in various Latin recensions. John Trevisa made his translation by 1387, and it is on the whole more complete than the anonymous fifteenth-century translation in manuscript 2. The text in manuscript 3 awaits an edition.

The history is in seven books, corresponding to the seven days of creation and the seven ages of the world. Only books 2, 3, and 4 contain biblical history (book 1 concerns world geography). Classical history and mythology constitute the bulk of the text, with frequent digressions and quotations of Josephus, Peter Comestor, and others. The amount of biblical material is in fact spare, often amounting to no more than a mention of a name, though it does include some brief narrative vignettes. There is a concentration on the historical books of the Bible, as one would expect from a monastic chronicler, and a surprising taste for prophecy, as in the excerpts from Daniel. The eclectic choice of the biblical material which does appear makes this biblical paraphrase unique and unpredictable.

The summaries of contents to the volumes in the Rolls Series are very helpful. The following outline is keyed to Trevisa's translation.

Page	Event	Bible
Higden's Book 2, vol. 2		
FIRST AGE		
219–231	General Creation; Adam and Eve; Prohibition, Temptation, Fall, Curses, Expulsion; Cain and Abel; Seth, Henoch et al.; Lamech and his descendants; brief notices on the ages of the Patriarchs	Gen. 1; 2; 3; 4; 5
231–237	Noah, the Ark, the Flood	Gen. 6; 7
SECOND AGE		
239–251	Rainbow; descendants of Noah; Nemrod, Tower of Babel	Gen. 8; 9; 10; 11
285–293	Abraham; Pentapolis; Melchisedech; Agar, Ismael; Lot and his daughters	Gen. 12; 13; 14; 16; 17; 19
295–297	Isaac; death of Sarah; Rebecca	Gen. 21; 23; 24
303–307	Jacob, Rachel, Laban; Joseph; Putiphar; Pharaoh's dreams; Jacob enters Egypt; death of Jacob; death of Joseph	Gen. 30; 37; 41; 46; 49; 50
315–333	Oppression of the Hebrews; Teremuth rescues Moses; Moses spurns Pharaoh's crown, trial by coals; murder of the Egyptian; Moses marries Sephora; Moses, Aaron, and the plagues; Joseph's bones; Red Sea crossing; Manna; Moses on Sinai; Twelve Spies survey the land	Ex. 1; 2; 4; 13; 14; 16; 17; 19; Num. 13; 14
337–339	Death of Moses; Josue leads Israel into the Promised Land	Deut. 34; Jos. 1; 3; 5
349–353	Israel under Chusan, Othoniel, Eglon, Aod (the left-handed), Samgar	Judg. 3

Page	Event	Bible
379–381	Debbora and Barac; Gedeon	Judg. 4; 6
389–395	Abimelech; Thola and Jair	Judg. 9; 10
399	Jephthe	Judg. 11
407, 418	Abesan, Ahialon, Abdon	Judg. 12
439	Samson	Judg. 16
441–451	Heli, Samuel, Saul	1 Kg. 4; 10

[vol. 3]

FOURTH AGE

3–15	David the musician; Solomon's judgment; the Temple; Queen of Saba	3 Kg. 3; 6; 10
17–29	Roboam; Jeroboam's idolatry; Abiam; rapture; Jehu kills Joram and Jezabel; Joas protected within the Temple	3 Kg. 12; 14; 16; 4 Kg. 2; 9; 11
29–33	Amasias; Jeroboam II; leprosy of Azarias	4 Kg. 14; 15
45–47	Sellum slays Zacharias; Manahem	4 Kg. 15
53, 69	Sennacherib slain by sons; Ezechias receives gifts from Babylon	4 Kg. 19; 20
75, 83–85	Manasses, Amon; Josias's Book of the Law; his death in battle; visions of Jeremias	4 Kg. 21; 22; 23; Jer. 1
89–97, 101–103	Nabuchodonosor besieges Jerusalem, destroys Temple; Captivity begins	4 Kg. 25

Higden's Book 3

FIFTH AGE

107	Death of Godolias; Jeremias in captivity; fate of the Ark of the Covenant (cf. pp. 187, 259)	4 Kg. 25; Jer. 43; 2 Mach. 2
113	Daniel interprets Nabuchodonosor's dreams	Dan. 3, 4
119	Evilmerodach releases Joachin	4 Kg. 25
121	Susanna	Dan. 13
123	Daniel's visions	Dan. 7
129	Baltassar, the handwriting on the wall	Dan. 5
133, 137	Daniel in the lions' den; Gabriel explicates the seventy weeks; the Man in Linen	Dan. 6; 9; 10
147	Isaias's prophecy concerning Cyrus	Is. 45:1
151	End of the Captivity; Temple rebuilt	1 Esdras 4, 5
173	Judith slays Holofernes	Judith 13
181	Darius; Zorobabel; Aggeus and Zacharias	1 Esdras 4; 5
235	Artaxerxes; Esdras and Nehemias	1 Esdras 7
249	Esdras reads the law to the people	2 Esdras 8
257	Nehemias rebuilds walls of Jerusalem	2 Esdras 2; 4
263	"Hiderto þe ordre of þe holy storie is i-take of þe bookes of Hebrewes . . . but what dedes and doynges foloweþ after þis beeþ i-take of	

Page	Event	Bible
	Iosephus Affrican and of þe bookes of Machabeis."	
413 [vol. 4]	Alexander defeats Darius	1 Mach. 1:1–8
31–39	A history of the translations of the Old Testament	
105	Death of Heliodorus	2 Mach. 3:25
113–121	Wickedness of Jason; Antiochus defiles Temple; martyrdom of the seven brethren and their mother; Judas Machabeus; death of Antiochus; Temple purified	2 Mach. 5; 6; 7; 8; 9; 10
121–123	Judas defeats Demetrius and Nicanor	2 Mach. 14; 15
123–136	Jonathan; Alexander; Demetrius; Tryphon; Simon; John Hyrcanus	1 Mach. 10; 11; 12; 13; 14; 15; 16
247–251	Isachar, Anna, Joachim, Mary; Elizabeth, John the Baptist	Luke 1

Higden's Book 4

SIXTH AGE

Page	Event	Bible
265–269	Joseph's doubts; decree from Augustus; Egypt; Slaughter of the Innocents	Matt. 1:19–20; 2 Luke 2
291	Christ disputes with Temple doctors	Luke 2:46
335–339	John baptizes Christ; Miracle at Cana; feeds five thousand; Temptation in the Desert; cleanses Temple; calls Disciples	Luke 3:21; John 2:1–16; Matt. 14:17–21; Luke 4:2
341	John the Baptist beheaded	Matt. 14:10
345–347	Crucifixion and associated miracles	Matt. 27:51
351	Matthias chosen	Acts 1:23
353–357	Apocryphal history of Judas Iscariot	
357	Stephen stoned	Acts 7:58
359	Conversion of Paul, Ananias	Acts 9:17

A Middle English Summary of the Bible MES

Manual, 2:401 [51]

1. Oxford, Trinity College 93 (1r–200r), ca. 1400.

Edition: Reilly, "Summary of the Bible."

This text is, in the words of its editor, "the only extant summary of the whole Bible" in Middle English (iv). Every book is represented except for 2 Machabees, Revelation, and the Catholic Epistles, and it seems likely that even these books appeared on leaves now missing from the manuscript. The entire work is in prose.

It has some connection with the Wycliffite Bible since it shares some of the same glosses, but according to Neil Ker "quotations agree sometimes with the earlier Wycliffite version and sometimes with the later Wycliffite version and sometimes with neither."[2] It includes 4 Esdras, whereas the Wycliffite Bible does not. The style and structure are most interesting for a study of biblical paraphrase. Simply put, it is hard to imagine a suitable purpose for such an extensive summary—502 pages of text in Reilly's edition. Some examples may help to illustrate the problem. Gen. 3:14–24 is rendered simply as "How þe serpent, þe man and þe woman were ponysched." Gen. 9:8–29 appears as follows: "God ordeyned þat þe reynbow shold be a token of þe covenant þat he made with Noe, which covenant was þat þe world shold no more generally be destroyed with water. Noe tilled vyne. He drank wyne and was dronken. He slepyng, his pryue members were naked; þis sawe Cham and told his ij breþer. Þey went bakward and couerd his pryue members. Noe cursed Chanaan, þe issu of Cham, and blessed Sem. Noe liued nyne hondred and fifty ȝere and dyed" (Reilly, "Summary of the Bible," 2–3).

Reilly proposes that the manuscript was intended as some kind of reference tool for the production of the later Wycliffite version, or that they both derive from some lost source. But if the early version was already done, as is almost certain from the date of Trinity 93, why did someone go to all the trouble to produce and copy such a summary when a fairly literal, and certainly more complete, translation already existed? Such a summary, obviously enough, is useful only to someone who knows the particulars already, and it could conceivably serve to refresh memories or to facilitate an answer to questions such as "what does the rainbow mean?" or "who saw Noah drunk and naked?" It may also be another attempt to produce a more easily accessible digest of main points, like the one in **PCE** or like the fifteen-chapter prologue to the later Wycliffite version of the Old Testament.[3] Trinity 93 shares at least one aspect with other comprehensive Old and New Testament summaries: the desire to embrace, control, and digest the main points of the Bible.

---

2. Ker, "Summary," 116. This article was the first twentieth-century notice of the manuscript. Ker prints the summaries of Ruth, 4 Esdras 15–16 ("IV Ezra is not common in Latin Bibles and most of the manuscripts in which it occurs are of English origin" [116]), Ps. 34, and the brief comment on the common gloss and on Nicholas of Lyra which follows the summary of Ps. 150.

3. Forshall and Madden, *Holy Bible*, 1:1–60. This prologue, which briefly summarizes each book and notes its applicability to daily life, is in itself a prose paraphrase and summary of the Old Testament.

The Mirour of Mans Saluacioune MMS

IMEV/S 511.5
Manual, 2:450 [316]

    1. Beeleigh Abbey, Maldon, Essex, Christina Foyle (1r–63v), 1429,
    5,132 lines in couplets.

Edition: Mirour, ed. Henry.

    MMS translates the *Speculum Humanae Salvationis* (*SHS,* ed. Lutz and Per-
drizet, and see Wilson and Wilson, *Medieval Mirror*), which is of unknown
authorship or provenance; manuscript evidence suggests, however, a date
between 1310 and 1324. Avril Henry, the editor of the unique Middle English
version, counts 394 manuscripts from the fourteenth and fifteenth centuries
which contain translations of *SHS* into various vernaculars. The Middle English version is written on a paper manuscript with an Italian watermark
of 1429.

    Its sources include the Vulgate, the *Historia Scholastica,* the *Legenda Aurea,*
and Aquinas's *Summa Theologica.* The work is governed by a strict typological
structure. Each of the first forty-two chapters is, in Henry's words, "composed of four events and four associated illustrations. In the most general
sense, *SHS* is an outline of the major events in history which bear on salvation."[4] The emphasis is on the life of Christ, but the typological connections
to the Old Testament turn the work into a compendium of biblical and apocryphal material. The poem qualifies as the most comprehensive and learned
typological work in Middle English. Chapters 43–45, which are 208 lines
each as opposed to the 100 lines each of the first forty-two, are a series of tales
told by an anchorite, a friar, and a priest, covering respectively the Hours
of the Passion, the Seven Sorrows of the Virgin Mary, and her Seven Joys.

    The following outline covers only the more extended biblical passages
and the more prominent allusions. Henry's index and notes provide a more
complete breakdown.

---

    4. *Mirour,* 12. Manuscripts of the *SHS* and of its translations are usually illustrated;
the Foyle manuscript, however, is not. Henry reproduces illustrations from a fifteenth-
century German manuscript in her edition.

Lines	Event	Bible
1–306	Prohemium, summary of contents	
307–428	Fall of the Angels; creation of Adam and Eve; Temptation, Fall: "God wham hym lest indures, of wham hym lest has mercy" (404); Expulsion	Gen. 1; 2; 3; Rom. 9:18
429–545	Kiss of Judas; importance of charity; the Good Samaritan; Immaculate Conception	Matt. 26:48; Dan. 4:24; Tob. 4:9; Luke 10:30–36
546–606	Dream of Astiages; Cyrus delivers the Jews from captivity; Mary as an enclosed garden; Balaam prophesies a star out of Jacob (581)	Dan. 14; 1Esdras 1; Cant. 4:12; Num. 24:17
607–704	"Of Jesse rote a ʒerd in tyme to come sall springe" (609); Ezekiel's closed gate; Mary as the Temple	Is. 11:1; Ez. 44:2; 3Kg. 6
705–804	Presentation of Mary at the Temple (the Temple of the Sun); Jepthe sacrifices his daughter; the queen of Persia's hanging garden; Mary's virtuous youth: "I slepe and myne hert wakes" (786)	Judg. 11:31–39; Cant. 5:2
805–904	Marriage of Mary and Joseph; Sara and Tobias; Asmodeus; Mary as David's tower	Matt. 1:18; Tob. 6;16–22; Cant. 4:4
905–958	Gabriel's Annunciation; Mary contrasted with Dina, Thamar, Sarah, Judith; "A mayden shalle conceyue" (934); Joseph's doubts compared to John the Baptist's, the Centurion's, Peter's, the Sunamite Woman's	Luke 1:26–27; Matt. 1:19–20; Is. 7:14; Matt. 3:14; 8:8; Luke 5:8; 4Kg. 4:4Kg. 4:8–10
959–1004	Burning Bush and Gedeon's fleece as types of Mary's Conception; Eliezer and Rebecca as types of Gabriel and Mary	Ex. 3:2–14; Judg. 6:36–40; Gen. 24:45–47
1005–1068	The dream of Pharaoh's butler; the "vignes of Engaddy" (1063)	Gen. 40:1–15; Cant. 1:14
1069–1105	Aaron's flowering rod; Sibyl's prophecy	Num. 17:8
1106–1204	Star in the East, Epiphany; water for King David; Habacuc; throne of Solomon; gifts from the queen of Saba	Matt. 2:1–12; 2Kg. 23:15–17; Dan.14:35; 3Kg. 10:2, 18–20
1205–1260	Presentation in the Temple; the Ark of the Covenant; the Ten Commandments	Luke 2:22; Ex. 20:3–17; 25:10–16
1261–1304	The menorah with seven flames; the Seven Works of Bodily Mercy; the Presentation of Samuel; Simeon	Ex. 25:31–32; Matt. 25:34–46; 1Kg. 1:19–28;

Lines	Event	Bible
	prophesies a "swerde . . . thorgh hire sawle" (1302)	Luke 2:35
1305–1368	Flight into Egypt, fall of the idols; Teremuth and Moses; Moses rejects Pharaoh's crown; Slaughter of the Innocents	Matt. 2:13–15; Is. 19:1; Ex. 2:1–10; Matt. 2:16
1369–1404	Nabuchodonosor's dream: "The feete some parte of erth" (1375)	Dan. 2:31–35
1405–1504	Baptism of Jesus; the Sea of Brass in the Temple; Naaman cured of leprosy; the crossing of the Jordan	Matt. 3:7,13; 3Kg. 7:23–25; 4Kg. 5:1–14; Jos. 3:14–17; 4:8
1505–1604	Temptation in the Desert; Daniel destroys Bel; David slays Goliath, the bear and lion	Matt. 4:1–11; Dan. 14:1–27; 1Kg. 17:34–51
1605–1654	Exorcism of Mary Magdalen; "the regne of heven is negh commyng" (1612); Prayer of Manasseh	Luke 8:2; Matt. 4:17; 2Par. 33:1–19
1655–1704	The Prodigal Son; Nathan forgives David; list of those forgiven by God	Luke 15:11–32; 2Kg.12:13
1705–1754	Palm Sunday; Christ weeps over Jerusalem; Jeremias's lament; David acclaimed: "Saul a thozand has slayne and Dauid ten thouzande" (1730)	Luke 19:38, 41; Lam. 1; 1Kg. 18:6–7
1755–1804	Temple cleansed; Heliodorus beaten in the Temple	John 2:14–16; 2Mach. 3:7, 25–27
1805–1854	Last Supper; manna from Heaven	Matt. 26:26–30; Ex. 16:15–16
1855–1904	The Paschal Lamb; Melchisedech	Ex. 12:3–6; Gen. 14:18
1905–2064	Jesus fells his arrestors; Dathan and Abiron; Lot's wife; Sennacherib's host; Her and Onan; Sara's seven husbands [a missing folio presumably continued this list of God's victories; Henry translates eighty-two lines from the *SHS*, including deeds by Samson, Samgar, and David; also Judas's betrayal linked to Joab and Amasa]	John 18:1–6; Num. 16:30–31; Gen. 19:26; 4Kg. 19:35–36; Gen. 38:7–10; Tob. 6:14; [Judg. 15:15–17; 3:31; 2Kg. 23:8; Matt. 26:46–49; 2Kg. 20:8–10; Ex. 21:24]
2065–2104	Judas as Saul (plotting David's death) and Cain (killing Abel)	1Kg. 19:9–10; Gen. 4:1–11

Lines	Event	Bible
2105–2160	Malchus; Christ before Annas and Caiphas "bide hym thyne othere cheke" (2128)	John 18:10–24; Luke 6:29
2161–2204	Mockeries of Hur (Golden Calf episode), Noah (by Cham), and Samson, "O cursyd wyghts, gos to eternale fyre!" (2201)	Ex. 32; Gen. 9:22–25; Judg. 16:20–30; Matt. 25:41, 34
2205–2252	Christ before Pilate and Herod	John 18:29–36; Luke 23:11–14
2253–2304	Scourging of Achior, Lamech (by Ada and Sella), Job (by the Devil and his wife)	Judith 6:7–13; Gen. 4:19; Job 2
2305–2360	Crucifixion, Crown of Thorns, purple robe	Matt. 27:27–30; John 19:2–3
2361–2404	Mockeries of Darius (by Apame), David (by Semei), David's messenger (by Hanon)	3Esdras 4:29; 2Kg. 16:5–10; 10:4
2405–2470	Barabbas; Pilate's wife; Christ bears the Cross as Isaac carried the wood	Matt. 27:15–24; Gen. 22:9,13
2471–2504	Parable of the Vineyard; the grape cluster from the Promised Land	Matt. 21:33–39; Num. 13:23–27
2505–2562	Simon of Cyrene; the Crucifixion; "thai noumbred al my bones" (2522); "Fadere, forgif to thaym" (2545); Jubal and Tubalcain discover music	Matt. 27:32, 34; Ps. 21:17–18; Luke 23:34; Gen. 4:21–22
2563–2604	Martyrdom of Isaias; king of Moab sacrifices his son	4Kg. 3:26–27
2605–2664	Nabuchodonosor's dream of a tree	Dan. 4:10–15
2665–2704	Codrus sacrifices himself; Eleazer and the elephant	1Mach. 6:43–46
2705–2754	Michol scorns David; Last Words on the Cross; death of Absalom; Evilmerodach butchers his father (apocryphal)	2Kg. 6:14–20; Luke 23:43, 46; John 19:26–30; 2Kg. 18:9–15
2755–2870	Sorrow of Mary, of Jacob for Joseph, of Adam and Eve for Abel	Luke 2:35; Gen. 37:23–34
2871–2904	Mary as Noemi	Ruth 1:5, 20
2905–2970	Deposition and Burial; Mary mourns Christ as David mourns Abner: "the grettest prince in Israel haf fallen today" (2944); marvels at Christ's death	John 19:38–42; 2Kg. 3:31–38; Matt. 27:51–53
2971–3004	Joseph in the well; Jonas in the whale	Gen. 37:24; Jonas 1:17
3005–3104	Harrowing of Hell; the Three Children in	Dan. 3:19–25;

Lines	Event	Bible
	the furnace; Daniel in the lions' den; Habacuc	14:29–33
3105–3152	Christ conquers the Devil as Banaias slays the lion; "Thi ȝerde and staffe, tha thinges ere grete comfort to me (3122)	2Kg. 23:20; Ps. 22:4
3153–3204	Christ as Samson and Aod	Judg. 14:5–6; 15:1–8; 3:17–22
3205–3280	Mary as Judith; recapitulation of the Jesus to the suicide of Judas; Mary triumphs over Satan	Judith 12:15; Ps. 90:13; Gen. 3:15
3281–3304	Jahal kills Sisara with a nail; Thamar slays Cyrus	Judg. 4:17–22
3305–3358	Jesus frees the patriarchs as Moses leads the Hebrews from Egypt to Sinai; cento of verses on deliverance, the Burning Bush, the Passover Lamb	Ps. 69:1; 143:5, 7, 21–22; Is. 16:1; 9:2; Ecclus. 36:18; Ex. 3:2; 12:3
3359–3404	Abraham rescued from the Chaldeans; Lot escapes from Sodom; Lot's wife	Gen. 15:7; 19:15, 24–26
3405–6340	Resurrection; the Jews bribe the guards; saints rise; Samson breaks down the gates of Gaza	Matt. 28:2–4, 11–15; 27:52; Judg. 16:3
3461–3504	Jonas cast overboard, swallowed, vomited up; "The stone whilk the biggers reproved in the heved is made angulere" (3496)	Jonah 1:15–17; 2:10; Matt. 21:42
3505–3604	Ascension; Jacob's ladder; the lost sheep; Translation of Elias; "in the name of Jhesu alle manere knee it bowe" (3579)	Mark 16:19; Acts 1:9–11; Gen. 28:10–16; Matt. 18:11–14; 4Kg. 2:11; Phil. 2:9–11
3605–3704	Cento of verses on Christ's coming again: "my Fadere of heven is vignour and eke tilman" (3624; John 15:1); Pentecost: "thas herde the disciples diuerse langeges speking" (3659); Joel's prophecy; Tower of Babel; the widow's jar of oil	John 16:16; 14:2–3; Luke 22:30; John 15:1–8; 16:20–22, 6–7, 13; Acts 1:4, 12–14; 2:1–16; Joel 2:28; Gen. 11:6–9; 4Kg. 4:2–7
3705–3754	Recapitulation of Christ's life, from the Nativity to the Burial; Mary as Anna, lamenting Tobias's absence	Tob. 5:23; 10:4
3755–3804	The lost coin; Michol betrothed to Phaltiel	Luke 15:8–9; 2Kg. 3:15–16

Lines	Event	Bible
3805–3904	Mary's Assumption; Mary as the Ark of the Covenant, before which David danced; Mary as the Woman clothed in the Sun; Mary as Solomon's mother	2Kg. 6:14–15; Rev. 12:1; 3Kg. 2: 19–20
3905–4004	Mary as mediator, as Abigail, the Woman of Thekua, and the Woman of Abela	1Kg. 25:23–25; 2Kg. 13:29; 14:12–14; 20: 21–22
4005–4059	Tharbis infatuated with Moses; Mary as defender against various biblical evildoers	Num. 12:1
4060–4104	Abimelech killed by a millstone; Michol lowers David from a window	Judg. 9:50–54; 1Kg. 19:11–12
4105–4204	Christ as knight; Assuerus hangs Aman at Esther's request: "Ask me whatevre thow wilt" (4189)	Est. 7:2–10
4205–4304	Parable of the Talents: "For the austere juge wille repe in place whare he noght sewe" (4225); the Wise and Foolish Virgins; Baltassar's warning	Matt. 25:14–30, 1–13; Dan. 5:5, 24–38
4305–4404	The state of bodies at the Resurrection; fates of martyrs; David conquers Rabbath; Gedeon conquers Soccoth; Pharaoh drowns in the Red Sea	2Kg. 12:31; Judg. 8:13–17; Ex. 14:23
4405–4504	The joys of Heaven, like Saba at the court of Solomon and the feasts of Assuerus and Job	3Kg. 10:6–9; Est. 1:3–5; Job 1:4
[The Hours of the Passion]		
4505–4556	Evensong: Jesus washes Disciples' feet	John 13:5
4557–4582	Compline: Arrest of Jesus	Mark 14:50; John 18:3
4583–4608	Matins: Caiphas, the Buffeting	Luke 22:63–65
4609–4634	Prime: Pilate and Herod	Luke 23:7–9
4635–4660	Terce: Scourging	Matt. 27:27–31
4661–4686	Sext: Pilate washes hands; Crucifixion	Matt. 27:24, 38
4687–4718	None: Last Words, side pierced	Matt. 27:46, 51–52; John 19: 28–30, 34
4719–4920	Seven Sorrows of the Virgin Mary, with recapitulations of events from the Passion [some text missing]	Luke 2:35
4921–5132	Seven Joys of the Virgin Mary (connected to many Old Testament types mentioned previously in the poem):	

Lines	Event	Bible
	Annunciation	Luke 1:26–38
	Visitation of Elizabeth, Magnificat	Luke 1:39–46
	Birth of Christ	Luke 1:57
	Epiphany	Matt. 2:1–12
	Presentation in the Temple, Simeon and Anna	Luke 2:22–38
	Christ disputes with Temple doctors	Luke 2:41–48
	Coronation	

Middle English Translation of the *Bible* of Roger D'Argenteuil BRA

IPMEP 167

    1. Cleveland, Public Lib. W q091.92-C468 (77r–99v), later 15th c.

Edition: Moe, *Roger D'Argenteuil's Bible.*

    BRA translates chapters 5–23 of a thirteenth-century French prose *Bible* attributed to Roger D'Argenteuil. The French work is based on the Vulgate, Latin compendia (the editor favors Vincent of Beauvais's *Speculum Historiale*) and a Passion narrative. Moe describes the *Bible* as a " 'livre de sapience' written to instruct a literate laity in sacred history and the essentials of Christian doctrine" (8). The French text was known to the late fourteenth-century English poet of the alliterative *Siege of Jerusalem* (9).

    The English translator "whether by choice or by reason of an incomplete French text, omitted the expository chapters and translated only the biblical and legendary narratives [the story of Adam and Eve, the Legend of the Cross, the *Legend of Veronica,* and the *Vindicta Salvatoris*]" (9). The English translation thus becomes, for the most part, a review of Christ's life and work, but three chapters covering the Creation, the Fall of Adam and Eve, and the Flood precede the New Testament material. This same organization—a body of New Testament material prefaced by a synopsis of important Old Testament events—appears in **PCE.** Occasional Latin verses passim are translated.

Chap.	Event	Bible
5	"Make we man to oure liknesse" (44); the Prohibition, Temptation, Fall: "Wotist thou nat why that God hath defendid that ye shuld not ete of thees apples of this appultree?" (45); origin of the Adam's apple.	Gen. 1:26–27; 2:7–9, 15–17; 3:1–7

Chap.	Event	Bible
6	"Sir, this made me to do Eue my felow" (46); the Curses, Expulsion; Cain and Abel; "aftir thei were corrupt by diuerse synnes of lecherie and lay by her doughtirs" (47)	Gen. 3:8–24; 4:1–16; 6:4
7	Destruction of Pentapolis; Noah and the Flood; Abraham, Isaac, and Jacob mentioned; Moses and the Commandments; summary of the Prophets Jeremias, Isaias, Daniel, Ezekiel, David, Solomon; captivity under Nabuchodonosor; Esther	Gen. 14:8–9; 19:24–25; 6:5–14; Ex. 20:1–17; Matt. 22:37–39
8	Annunciation: "Hough mai this be sith I neuer knew man?" (50); Herald Angel: "peas and good wille be so among men in erth" (51); Magi	Luke 1:28, 34–38; 2:14; Matt. 1:20, 2:11
9	Slaughter of the Innocents; Christ disputes with Temple doctors; calls Disciples; is baptized: "Who that bileueth in me & is baptizid, he shal be saued" (52); general preaching and healing; feeds five thousand	Matt. 2:16; Luke 2:46–47; Matt. 3:16–17; 14:17–20; 15:34–38; Mark 16:16
10	Palm Sunday; raises Lazarus; betrayal, arrest; Jesus before Caiphas; Peter's denials; washes Disciples' feet	Matt. 21:9; John 11:43; 18:2–11; Matt. 26:47–75; John 13:5
11	Christ before Caiphas and Pilate	John 11:50; Luke 23:1–5
12	Pilate's wife's dream; washes hands; Barabbas: "the blood . . . be upon us and upon oure children" (60)	Matt. 27:11, 19–26; John 19:11–12, 15
13	Scourging; the Wood of the Cross; Veronica	Matt. 27:27–31
14	Crucifixion; Pilate's inscription: "That as I haue writen is writen" (63); Mary entrusted to John; Last Words; marvels at Christ's death; precautions of the Jews	John 19:18–30; Matt. 27:40–43, 46, 51–53, 62–66; John 10:11
15	Joseph of Arimathea and Nicodemus "the smyth" (65); Longinus	John 19:34, 38–42; 10:11
16	Two angels appear to the Marys; bribery of the guards; appearances to Mary and the Disciples; breaks bread; charges Disciples; Ascension	Matt. 28:1–15; John 20:19; Mark 16:15–16, 19; Luke 24:13, 30
17	Pentecost; Vespasian and Veronica	Acts 2:3–4
18–23	Healing of Vespasian; Destruction of Jerusalem; death of Caiphas	

Primarily Old Testament Works, in Approximate Vulgate Order

Versions of the *Life of Adam and Eve* **LAE**

This text is one of the most important sources for stories of the Creation, Fall of the Angels, Temptation and Fall of Man, and postlapsarian life. Its influence is seen in temporale narratives, mystery plays, homily cycles, **CC, CM, SLC,** through to *Paradise Lost* (J. M. Evans, *Paradise Lost*). The story often accompanies legends of the Cross (*Manual*, 2:443–46 [302–10]. The proximate source is the Latin *Vita Adae et Evae,* which has ultimately Greek and Midrashic sources (Charlesworth, *Old Testament Pseudepigrapha*, 2:249–95).

Dialogue between Adam and Eve, Cain and Abel, humans and God, and humans and angels is prominent. The narrative ends with Solomon reading the pillars (or tables) of clay and stone created by Seth; the information thus gained was further adapted into Solomonic dialogues and catechisms (*Manual*, 3:736–42 [68–72]).

The manuscripts vary widely, but one sign of the influence of this text is that some form of it appears in Vernon, Wheatley, and Auchinleck. Its inclusion in the *SEL* ensured its wide dissemination.

Standard Version, *Tretys of Adam and Eve*
IPMEP 25
Manual, 2:442 [300]

> 1. Oxford, Bodleian Lib. Bodley 596 (*SC* 2376) (1r–12v), early 15th c.
> 2. Cambridge, Trinity College 601 (R.3.21) (249r–256v), later 15th c.

Edition: 1—Horstmann, "Nachträge" (1885), 345–53.

Page	Event	Bible
345	General account of the Creation of Heaven and Earth	Gen. 1
346	Problem of food supply, Adam wishes to die; repents in the Jordan, which ceases flowing; fish and animals sorrow with him	
347	Eve, also lamenting, is beguiled by the Devil to leave the river Tigris; her flesh is "greene as gresse, for colde of the water"; Devil explains his enmity because he was cast out from heaven	
348	Eve bears Cain and Abel; Cain slays Abel	Gen. 4
349	Seth is born; Adam recounts to Seth how the Archangel Michael led Adam back to Paradise with a "ʒerde" on an ice-bridge and revealed the future	Gen. 4:25
350	Adam tells Seth of the Temptation and Fall, emphasizing how the Devil took advantage of the temporary absence of two guardian angels; God inflicts seventy diverse wounds and sufferings on Adam	Gen. 3
351	Seth's quest for the Oil of Mercy (see Quinn, *Quest*); Michael prophesies Christ's coming	
352	Adam and Abel buried in Paradise	
353	Seth, the first to "make the shappe of lettres," fashions two tablets, one of stone and the other of clay, on which Seth writes the Creation story; the tablet of stone would survive any future floods, the one of clay would survive destruction by fire; Solomon reads them with the inspiration of an angel	

Expanded version as part of the Middle English *Legendea Aurea* (the anonymous 1438 translation known as the *Gilte Legend*) *Manual*, 2:442 [301]

1. London, BL Harley 4775 (258v–264r), 15th c.
2. London, BL Harley 1704 (18r–26v), 15th c. Prefixes Genesis 1:1–2:3 from the later Wycliffite translation.
3. London, BL Harley 2388 (20r–35v), 15th c.
4. London, BL Egerton 876 (321r– [incomplete]), 15th c.
5. Oxford, Bodleian Lib. Douce 15 (*SC* 21589) (8v–77r), 15th c. Prefixes Genesis 1:1–2:3 from the later Wycliffite translation.
6. Oxford, Bodleian Lib. Douce 372 (*SC* 21947) (158r–161v), 1438.
7. Oxford, Bodleian Lib. Ashmole 802 (*SC* 6909) (19r–48r), late 16th c.
8. London, Lambeth Palace 72 (423v–431r), 15th c.
9. London, BL Add. 39574 (Wheatley) (59v–88r), early 15th c.
10. London, BL Add. 35298 (162r–165r), 15th c.
11. Oxford, Bodleian Lib. Ashmole 244 (*SC* 7419) (187 r–v), early 17th c.

Editions: 1—Horstmann, "Nachträge" (1885), 353–65.
9—Day, *Wheatley Manuscript,* 76–99. On pp. xxii–xxxii Day describes
the very intricate relationships of these manuscripts.

The following outline is taken from Horstmann:

Page	Event	Bible
353	Creation of Adam and Eve	Gen. 1
354	Adam's constituent elements, naming; Eden, the Tree, the Prohibition	Gen. 2:8–17
355	Eve created from Adam's rib; the Serpent, Fall; divine curses	Gen. 2:18–22; 3
356	God makes coats of leather for Adam and Eve	Gen. 3:21
356–358	Problem of food supply; river penances, Jordan stops flowing, Eve's green flesh	
359	Cain murders Abel; birth of Seth; Adam and Eve have thirty-three sons and thirty-two daughters	Gen. 4
360	Adam recounts to Seth his rapture to Paradise in a fiery chariot	
361	Michael's revelation of the future, concentrating on the Last Judgment.	
362	Adam recounts the Fall to Seth; Seth starts his quest	Gen. 3
363	Michael prophesies the Harrowing of Hell	
364	Adam "in tormentis in to the last daie of dispensacioun"; he is buried "in the vale of Ebronne, as the maister of stories tellith"; the tables of stone and clay read by Solomon	

Prose Version of the *Life and Adam and Eve* in the Vernon Manuscript
IPMEP 53
Manual, 2:442 [299]

1. Oxford, Bodl. Engl. poet. a.1 (Vernon) (393r–394v), ca. 1390.

Editions: Blake, *Religious Prose,* 103–18; Horstmann, *Sammlung,* 220–27.
Facsimile: Doyle, *Vernon Manuscript.*

Vernon adds the detail that the angels fell "as thikke as the drift of the
snouh" (Blake, *Religious Prose,* 106) (see Morey, "Fall in Particulate").

Version in *South English Legendary*
IMEV 43
IMEV/S 1873.5
Manual, 2:441 [297]

1. Edinburgh, National Lib. of Scotland Advocates 19.2.1 (Auchinleck) (14r–16v), ca. 1330–40, acephalous fragment, 780 lines in couplets.

Editions: D. Laing, *Penni Worth,* 49–75; Horstmann, *Sammlung,* 139–47. *Facsimile:* Pearsall and Cunningham, *Auchinleck Manuscript.*

Canticum de Creatione CC

IMEV 1676
Manual, 2:442 [298]

1. Oxford, Trinity College 57 (157v–164v), late 14th c., 1,200 lines in stanzas rhyming aabccb.

Edition: Horstmann, "Canticum de Creatione" and *Sammlung,* 124–38. *Study:* Dunstan, "Middle English *Canticum.*"

Like **LAE,** this text transmitted many of the same Midrashic legends and apocryphal events connected with the early history of the world. **CC** is noteworthy for its comprehensiveness, its penchant for detail, and its interest in connecting historical events widely separated in time.

Quotations from Horstmann, *Sammlung:*

Lines	Event	Bible
1–18	Prologue promising pardon and protection to the listeners	
19–48	Creation, Temptation, Fall, Expulsion: "eteth an appel tyth, / And beþ as wyse as god almyth" (31–32)	Gen. 1–3
49–414	Noteworthy events and motifs: the problem of procuring enough food; Eve's request to Adam that he kill her; their respective river penances, with mention of Eve's hair floating on the surface, commiserating beasts, and the arrested flow of the river; Eve's grass-green body; the reasons for the Devil's envy (237); an angel's admonition to tithe as a "spyt and repref" (338) for the tenth order of angels that fell; Eve exiles herself, takes a veil for shame (380), and thus even today women cover their heads	
415–493	Adam answers Eve's call for help in delivering Cain; Cain gathers flowers as a present for his mother; Eve's prophetic dream that Abel will be slain	Gen. 4
494–589	Adam and Eve remain chaste for one hundred years in sorrow; Seth is born; thirty more sons and thirty-two daughters follow; Adam gathers children at his deathbed and recounts the story of the Fall; two	Gen. 3

Lines	Event	Bible
	guardian angels were responsible for northeast and southwest	
590–798	God inflicts sixty-two punishments; no grass grew in the footsteps of Adam and Eve on their track from Eden; Michael establishes a 5,500-year "term" for Adam (lines 711–12); Seth's quest for the oil of mercy (Quinn, *Quest*), has a vision of the Tree of Good and Evil with a serpent in it and a child at the top; one root reaches to Abel in Hell	
799–1106	Michael gives Seth three kernels, which are placed in Adam's mouth; the tablets of stone and clay; the kernels grow into three green rods with which Moses performs miracles; David plants them by a cistern, then composes the Psalms; once the rods grow into trees, Solomon uses them as beams in the Temple; the undercut beam miraculously assumes the correct length	
1107–1048	Maximille, a woman, becomes the first Christian martyr; the beam is discarded in a ditch; the Sibyl worships it	
1149–1187	The poem names the time periods in the history of the world, and dates itself to 1375 (lines 1186–87)	
1188–1190	The Hebrew original and Latin translations are cited	
1191–1200	Concluding prayer	

William of Shoreham's *On the Trinity, Creation, the Existence of Evil, Devils, Adam and Eve, etc.* **TCE**

IMEV 1495 (see also *IMEV* 3681)
Manual, 7:2274 [28]

1. London, BL Add. 17376 (206r–220v), mid-14th c., 894 verse fragment in six-line stanzas rhyming aabaab.

Editions: William of Shoreham, *Religious Poems*, ed. Wright, 135–68; William of Shoreham, *Poems*, ed. Konrath, 130–60.

Shoreham was vicar of Chart-Sutton in Kent from 1320. The discussion of the nature of the Trinity (lines 1–222) is prefaced by a quotation of Ps. 13:1 (Ps. 52:1): "Þat fol in hys herte sede: / 'Þer nys no gode' " (lines 4–5). Shoreham integrates sections of the Athanasian Creed, which he calls a "song," in his discussion (lines 109–92).

A capsule account of the Creation follows:

Ine daȝes sixe he made hyt Ryȝt:
Heuene and erthe and wolkne bryȝt,
Þet water te-dyȝt,
Tren and gras and erþe dreȝe,
Sonne and mone and sterren greyȝe,
Þat beþ so bryȝt;

Foȝeles, fischles ine þe depe,
Bestes, wormes for to crepe,
And a last, man;
So þat hyt was god and sad,
Al þys world, þat was ymad
Of hym þat can. (Konrath, lines 289–300)

This account prefaces a long discussion of the necessity of evil and the
Fall of the Angels, with a reference to Is. 14:13–14 in lines 394–95. The tenor
of the discussion is the standard *felix culpa* argument that evil intensifies the
glory of goodness and makes the coming of Christ necessary.

Next is a paraphrase of Gen. 3, with frequent direct quotation, of the
Temptation and Fall of Man, the covering of their bodies with leaves, and
God's respective curses on the Serpent, Eve, and Adam (lines 601–744).

"Leue dame, say me now,
Wy heþ god for-bode hyt ȝow
Þet ȝe ne mote
Eten of al þat frut þat hys
Here growynde in paradys?
To ȝoure bote?"

"We eteþ y-nou," quaþ eue, "y-wys,
Of alle þe trowes of paradys,
And beþ wel gled;
Bote þys trow mote we nauȝt take,
For boþe me and mynne make
God hyt for-bede,

And seyde, ȝef we þer-of ete,
We scholde deye, and lyf forlete
And alle blysse." (Konrath, lines 655–69)

The poem ends (imperfectly) with a prefiguration of the salvation
through the "Tree" of Christ and the necessity of Baptism to erase Original
Sin. Shoreham confuses the Tree of Life with the Tree of the Knowledge of
Good and Evil (line 788).

The poem as a whole is more of a doctrinal exposition than a biblical
paraphrase, but the sections on the Creation and the Temptation qualify

as direct paraphrases of those accounts from Genesis. The poem is also set throughout in a biblical-historical context.

Wise Admonitions: Biblical Texts Paraphrased WA

IMEV 1405

1. Cambridge, Trinity College 323 (B.14.39) (26r–27r), mid-13th c., 134 lines in octosyllabic couplets, excluding Latin quotations.

Editions: Reichl, *Religiöse Dichtung*, 303–9; Brunner, "Zwei Gedichte," 225–30; C. Brown, "Early Mention of a St. Nicholas Play."

This manuscript contains three biblical paraphrases: this one, **BTD,** and **TP.** Seven miscellaneous verse pieces intercede between the first and second, including poems on the Annunciation and Resurrection, and the second immediately precedes the third. See C. Brown's *Register,* 1:236–37, and for an outline of the contents of Trinity 323, see M. Laing, *Catalogue of Sources,* 34–7.

Like the other paraphrases in the manuscript, **WA** has no specific source but the opening lines are reminiscent of a ballad. It is hard to detect any logical continuity, and narrative is absent except for references to a St. Nicholas play in lines 33–44, quoted below.

The appeal to lay and learned listeners appears almost immediately. The first forty-four lines give some idea of the tone and affect of the poem. They contain a very interesting mix of English and Latin and some response seems to be required from the listeners. The Latin verses are often identified by book and chapter, though the quotations are often inexact.

Quoted from Brunner's edition:

Justum deduxit dominus per uias rectas & ostendit illi regnum dei [Wis. 10:10]
yc ou rede ye sitten stille
& herknet wel wid gode wille
of godes wordes ant is werkes
boþe þis lewede ant þis clerkes
for godes children wollet scechen   5
euer to heren of godes spechen
qui ex deo est verba dei audit [John 8:47]
alle þat leued on god almi[c]te
godes word hit scal hem li[c]te
ant bringen hem to heuenric blisse
þer he sculen haue ioye ant lisse   10
launterne hit is to monnes fote
ant of sunnes hit deyd bote

lucerna pedibus meiis verbum tuum et lumen [Ps. 118:105]
ant yet ic wille ou sigge more
alle þat heret godes lore
ant witet hit wel in stable þout   15
he wort him leyf þat al hat wrout
ant edi scal euere boe
ase me may in þe boc ysoe
beati qui audiunt uerbum dei & custodiunt illud [Luke 11:28]
euerhuych mon þat hauet his munde
godes worde he clepet his cuynde   20
for so þe bred fed fleys ant blod
also his word is soule fod
Non in solo pane viuit homo sed in omni
uerbo quod procedit de ore dei & cetera [Matt. 4:4]
huyc mon þat is godes foster
þerto sigge a pater noster
ant an aue marie þerto   25
þat ic is wordes inowe scewe so
þat hit boe god almycte iqueme
ant þe deuel henne to fleme

pater noster

Justum deduxit dominus per vias rectas [Wis. 10:10]
þe mon þa wole ric[t] wis boe
sittit stille and he may soe . . .   30
wou god wole for þe gode do
þat gode hope hauet him to
it was a king bi olde dawene
þat wel leuede on godes lawe
him he louede suyþe wel   35
þat he yeld him huyc a del
þat he bad he dede him some
ant þorou senicholas bone
yf ye wollet stille ben
in þis pleye ye mowen isen   40
þis mon hauede lond & lede
Ant alle þe men þat heueden nede
at him hoe mictin habbe froure
ne hatede noþing godes poure

Other verses which are paraphrased:

line   51   Ps.75:6
       55   Eccles. 5:9
       59   Ps. 38:7

65   Jer. 46:20
73   Ecclus. 23:22; Job 18:9
79   Ps. 75:7
85   Luke 12:34; Matt. 6:21
89   Ps. 30:13
93   "quoniam sompnus est retraccio spiritus a membris organicis
      ad interna" (untraced: not in Vulgate)
101   Ps. 113B:7
105   Prov. 4:16
109   Ps. 36:16
115   Luke 12:33
119   "quoniam in pauperibus habitat Christus" (untraced: not in
      Vulgate)
121   Luke 6:38
123   2Cor. 9:6

The manner of address qualifies the poem as a verse sermon, but in substance it is nothing but a paraphrase of biblical verses conjoined with apro-
pos English proverbs. The style is almost incantatory, and the audience was
obviously expected to say the Pater Noster after line 28. The preacher then
repeats his main theme ("Justum deduxit") and begins the poem anew. The
scriptural quotations punctuate the whole of the poem, but as a rule their
paraphrase precedes them: in lines 5–6, for example, "godes children" and
"godes spechen" anticipate the "qui" and the "verba dei" in the verse from
John, and the "bred" in line 21 obviously refers to the "pane" from Matt. 4:4.
One can imagine the preacher reading from his "boc" (line 18) after having
paraphrased its contents. The book is obviously not a Vulgate: it may be some
kind of preaching aid based on a verbal concordance. These concordances,
which were one of the many preaching aids produced (by the Victorines and
others) in response to Lateran 1215, compiled scriptural verses based on
how the words in a verse suggest the same or related words in other quotations and hence other contexts and ideas. The same principle of organization seems to apply here. C. Brown ("Early Mention of a St. Nicholas Play")
demonstrates that the first verse comes from the antiphon to the feast of St.
Nicholas as found in the York, Sarum, and Hereford breviaries. The poem
thus exhibits a remarkable intersection of liturgy, drama, sermon literature,
and biblical paraphrase.

The poem is unlike other biblical literature in Middle English, though
it can only be called a biblical paraphrase. Its closest analogue is perhaps
Piers Plowman because of the alternation of Latin and English. John Alford

has discussed how the Latin quotations in *Piers* are its structuring principle, and he points out that verbal concordances were as useful to sermonizers as evidently they were for Langland.[1] That principles of sermon construction were used by Langland has been repeatedly proposed.[2] As Alford points out, much of *Piers Plowman* is nothing but a paraphrase of a scriptural verse and its associated ideas, and the question which Alford answers in his article can be posed again for the Trinity poem: did the poet *begin* with the quotations or were they invoked later as they came to mind in support of the ideas already expressed in the poem? Given how free-associative this method could be, the process was almost certainly bilateral. Words suggested other words and ideas regardless of what language they happened to be in. Alford's analysis does much to elucidate the paraphrastic method of *Piers Plowman,* but I would quibble with the first observation in his article. He says that *Piers* "doesn't *look* like any other medieval poem he [a modern first-time reader] is likely to have read" (80). That may be, but **WA,** like other biblical paraphrases such as **EE** and numerous psalter treatments, have proportionally at least as many Latin quotations around which the poem is built. Readers of biblical literature may well have been familiar with this kind of poem, and Langland had ample precedent for his own methodology of poetic composition.

Old Testament Sentences OTS

Version 1

 1. Oxford, Trinity College 86 (38v–41r), later 15th c.

Version 2

 2. Oxford, Bodleian Lib. Hatton 111 (11r–13v), late 14th c.
 3. London, BL Add. 60577 (111v–113v), ca. 1500.

Pending examination

 4. London, BL Lansdowne 388 (369r–370v), later 15th c.

---

1. Alford, "Role of the Quotations," where he argues that Langland "has begun with a set of quotations, related to one another by theme and by verbal similarities, and then elaborated upon their significance by means of dramatization, paraphrase, *exempla,* and so forth" (88–89).

2. E.g., Owst, *Literature and Pulpit,* chap. 9, "A Literary Echo of the Social Gospel"; Robertson and Huppé, *Scriptural Tradition,* 2; Spearing, *Criticism,* chap. 5, "The Art of Preaching and *Piers Plowman.*" Spearing notes (111) how several passages in Langland's poem are presented as sermons (e.g., C.iii.121, C.xii.42).

Edition: In progress by Morey.
Facsimile: 3—Wilson and Fenlon, *Winchester Anthology.*

This collection of Old, and some New, Testament verses appears in the context of catechetical material such as **Beat** and **SWM.** Manuscript 1 ends with "For the loue of god lernyth thys lesson for yt wool be prophytable for vs at the day of doome" (41r).

Manuscript 1 contains the following verses:
Prov. 11:2, 21:13, 17:5, 14:21
Wis. 1:11
Rev. 21:8
Wis. 1:4
Ecclus. 14:5
Prov. 14:29, 28:9
Ps. 118:130
Dan. 12:3
Ps. 118:2
Luke 11:28
1Cor. 14:38
John 6:64, 69, 14:21, 15:10
Matt. 16:26

Manuscripts 2 and 3 contain the following verses:
2Mach. 8:5
Wis. 1:4
Ecclus. 14:5
Prov. 26:28, 21:23, 10:19
Wis. 1:11
Is. 24:2
Jer. 48:10, 9:23–24
Prov. 21:13, 17:5, 22:16, 23:13–14[3]
Ecclus. 16:3–4
Prov. 14:21, 29:15–17, 14:29
Ecclus. 3:20, 4:35
Prov. 28:27, 28:9, 28:24
Jer. 17:5, 7

---

3. Also Ecclus. 30:1–2. For other, independent occurrences of this sentiment, "he that sparethe the ȝerde fro the childe hatethe his sone" (manuscript 3, 112v), see Wenzel, *Verses in Sermons,* 146.

Ecclus. 23:12
Prov. 18:13
Ecclus. 11:7
Is. 10:1, 5:8
Tob. 4:16
Prov. 29:3
Eccles. 2:13
Ecclus. 28:21
Prov. 15:1
Lev. 19:37
Ex. 23:22
2Cor. 4:3
Ecclus. 7:19
John 14:21
Is. 47:10
John 14:15–17
Mark 11:25–26
Matt. 7:2

Historye of the Patriarks HP

Manual, 2:383 [5]

1. Cambridge, St. John's College 198 (G.31), 111 folios, 15th c.

Edition: Daly, "Historye."

Despite the importance and widespread availability, in Latin and French, of Peter Comestor's *Historia Scholastica,* **HP** is the only known English translation, in prose, of a substantial portion of Comestor's work. **HP** covers the Book of Genesis, from the Creation to the death of Jacob. The manuscript is missing the last few pages, and breaks off at Gen. 50:7.

Based upon similarities in content and phrasing, Daly favors the possibility that the translator worked from a copy of Guyart Desmoulins's translation of the *Historia,* the *Bible historiale:* "[**HP**] includes sections of Genesis which do not appear in the Latin *Historia Scholastica.* It is perhaps more likely that the translator worked from Guyart than that he combined Comestor's work with the Vulgate" (xxxiv). The final words of the preface remark only that "my processe [is] growndid / uppon Genesis and uppon Scolastica Historia" (fol. 1v–2r).

The work is primarily a literal prose translation of Genesis, with short passages of commentary interspersed. Quotations are from Daly's dissertation:

"Abraham, I shall blisse and multiplie thy sede as thike as the sterris of hevene or þe gravell of the grounde or sande of the see. Forthermore thy sede shall possesse and haue dominacion of his enemyes, and in thy sede all the poeple of erth shal be blissid, forwhi thow haviste obeyeid my conmaundment" (Gen. 22:17–18, fol. 43r).

"And the angle enquirid his name, to whom Iacob answered and seid, 'I am callid Iacob.' Then seid þe angle to hym ayene thus, 'Sothly thy name shal not be Iacob; but Israel þou shal be named, that is to say, "a man seynge God" ' " (Gen. 32:27–28, fol. 71v).

Genesis and Exodus GE

IMEV/S 2072
Manual, 2:381 [1]

1. Cambridge, Corpus Christi College 444 (1r–81r), early 14th c., 4,162 lines in octosyllabic couplets.

Editions: Arngart, *Genesis and Exodus;* Morris, *Story of Genesis and Exodus.*
Study: Buehler, *Middle English Genesis and Exodus.*

The earliest and perhaps the best paraphrase of the *Historia Scholastica* to survive in Middle English is **GE**. In the corpus of Middle English biblical literature, this poem has one of the highest percentages of material deriving directly from the *Historia*.[4]

The title is misleading since it includes parts of Numbers and ends with the death of Moses (Deut. 34). Leviticus is omitted except for the briefest of summaries in lines 3629–38. The date of original composition has been set ca. 1250, though the manuscript is written in a hand ca. 1300–25 and in what is perhaps an East Midland dialect. Because of its early date it has been studied primarily from a philological perspective; its vocabulary and spelling resemble that of the Middle English *Bestiary*, Laȝamon, and Orm. Arngart argues that the scribe (a Norman?) was unfamiliar with the language since eth appears initially and thorn never appears: nevertheless the vocabulary is almost 85 percent English and alliteration is common (*Genesis and Exodus,* 13, 43).

---

4. Morris was the first to edit the poem. His notes and glossary are a triumph of scholarship and informed judgment since he did not know at the time of either of his editions that the work follows the *Historia* closely. Bernhard ten Brink was the first to recognize the indebtedness (*Geschichte,* 1:247). Morris's line divisions in his edition (xiv) are helpful: prologue (lines 1–34), Gen. (lines 35–2536), Ex. (lines 2537–3628), Lev. (lines 3629–35), Num. (lines 3635–4118), Deut. (lines 4119–54), conclusion (lines 4155–62).

The poem's primary source is the *Historia Scholastica,* though independent consultation seems to have been made of the Vulgate itself and at one
point (lines 269–332, the temptation of Eve) the poet drew on St. Avitus's
work in Latin hexameters *Poematum de Mosaicae historiae gestis libri quinque.*[5]
The spellings of some names leads Buehler to suggest that the poet followed a version of the *Historia* which contained more of Josephus's *Antiquities* than does Migne's edition.[6] The *Genesis and Exodus* poet mentions Josephus by name only once, in line 1281 ("If iosephus ne legeð me"). Here he
echoes one of Comestor's numerous "ut dicit Josephus" tags and, in a typi-
cally medieval way of citing sources, his immediate source (Comestor) is
glossed over in favor of the prior one. Methodius is also mentioned (lines
517 ff., taken from the citations in the *Historia* PL 198:1076, 1081), though
the poet's description, "He wrot a boc ðat manige witen, / Manige tiðing
ðor-on is writen" (lines 523–24), perhaps indicates a firsthand acquaintance
with the Methodian *Revelations,* as D'Evelyn suggests ("Methodius," 146). On
the whole, however, the poet follows the *Historia* very closely.

The first eighteen lines are highly rhetorical and include the conventions
characteristic of the prologues to any number of vernacular romances, penitential manuals, and biblical paraphrases: the appeal to the "lewed" (often
with nationalistic overtones), the language dichotomy (here English versus
Latin), and the offer of moral edification—even the promise of salvation:

> Man og to luuen ðat rimes-ren   1
> Ðe wisseð wel ðe logede men
> Hu man may him wel loken
> Ðog he be lered on no boken,
> Luuen god and seruen him ay,   5
> For he it h[i]m wel gelden may,
> And to alle cristenei men
> Beren pais and luue bi-twen.
> Ðan sal him almigtin luuen
> Her bi-neðen and ðund abuuen,   10
> And giuen him blisse and soules reste
> Ðat him sal earuermor lesten.
> Ut of latin ðis song is dragen
> On engleis speche on soðe-sagen;

5. Arngart, "St. Avitus." Alcimus Avitus was bishop of Vienne ca. 500; the *Poematum* appears in PL 59:323–82. Fritzsche notes that initial capitals in the poem frequently correspond to the chapters of the *Historia* ("'Story,'" 47–48; see the table on 88–90). Fritzsche
answers the question posed by the title of his article affirmatively.

6. Buehler, *Middle English Genesis and Exodus,* 36. Manuscripts of the *Historia,* not surprisingly, varied in their contents.

Cristene men ogen ben so fagen   15
So fueles arn quan he it sen dagen,
Ðan man hem telleð soðe tale
Wið londes speche and wordes smale.[7]

One ought to love that run of rhymes   1
Which well teaches lewed men
How one may look after himself
Even if he is not learned in books;
[One ought] to love God and serve him always,   5
For he may well reward him for it;
And to all Christian men
[One ought] to bear peace and love;
Then the Almighty shall love him,
Here beneath and beyond above,   10
And give him bliss and soul's rest
That shall last him evermore.
Out of Latin this song is drawn
Into English speech, as a true story;
Christian men ought to be as delighted   15
As birds are when they see day dawn,
When one tells them a true tale
In native speech and words plain.

The prologue is carefully structured: it is built on four parallel infinitives (in lines 1, 5, and 8), each of which is governed by the first two words, "one ought." One ought to love the poem, God, and one's neighbor. The syntactic compression and elided parts of speech may be a metrical expedient or a sign of colloquial usage; any reading aloud of this prologue would require considerable variation in intonation to make itself understood. Another instance of conscious patterning is that the opening thirty-six lines appear as six interlocking six-line stanzas; after line 36 the poet continues his "run of rhymes" in couplets.[8]

At some points the poem is so close to the *Historia* that sense can be made of the Middle English only in consultation with the Latin. Of course native speakers would have less trouble than we do, but the lines referring to the first Sunday, "Ðis dai was forð in reste wrogt; / Ilc kinde newes ear was brog[t]" (lines 249–50), must at least have given a contemporary reader pause. The Latin is "Vel complevit, id est completum ostendit, cum nihil novum in eo fecerit, et tunc requievit ab operum generibus novis" (PL 198:

---

7. All quotations are from Arngart's edition. The translation is my own.
8. Including the missing line 21, the rhyme scheme is aaaabb, aaaacc, aaaadd, ddddee, eeeeff, ffffgg.

1065). In many cases it would seem that the syntactic compression is due to the poet's attempts to retain the meaning of the Latin while still writing verse.

Lines 29–60 synthesize a paraphrase of the creation with a larger doctrinal point:

Fader god of alle ðhinge,
Almigtin louerd, hegest kinge,   30
Ðu giue me seli timinge
To thaunen ðis werdes bigininge,
Ðe, leuerd god, to wurðinge,
Queðer-so hic rede or singe!
Wit and wisdam and luue godd,   35
And fer ear biðohte al in his modd.
In his wisdom was al biðogt
Ear ðanne it was on werlde brogt.
In firme bigini[n]g of nogt
Was heuene and erðe samen wrogt.   40
Ðo bad god wurðen stund and stede,
Ðis middes-wereld ðor-inine he dede.
Al was ðat firme ðhrosing in nigt,
Til he wit hise word made ligt.
Of his word ðu wislike mune,   45
Hise word, ðat is hise wise sune,
Ðe was of hin fer ear bi-foren
Or ani werldes time boren;
And of hem two ðat leue luuen
Ðe welden al her and abuuen,   50
Ðat heli luue, ða[t] wise wil,
Ðat weldet alle ðinge wit rigt & [s]kil
Migt bat wit word wurðen ligt,
Hali froure welt oc ðat migt,
For ðhre persones and on reed,   55
On migt and on godfulhed.
Ðo so wurð ligt, so god it bad,
Fro ðisternesse o-sunde[r] sad.
Ðat was ðe firme morgen-tid
Ðat euere sprong in werld wid.   60

Father, God of all things,
Almighty Lord, highest King,   30
Give thou me blessed success
To show this world's beginning,
To you, Lord God, in praise,
Whether I read or sing!
Wit and wisdom and love [is] God   35

And [he] long ago contemplated all in his mind.
In his wisdom was all considered,
Before it was brought into the world.
At the first beginning, of nothing
Was heaven and earth together wrought.   40
Then God ordered the creation of time and space,
This middle-world therein he made.
All was that first tumult in night,
Til he with his word made light.
Of his word [may] you wisely know   45
His word, that is his wise Son,
Who was of him long ago,
Before any world's time, born.
And of those two [was] that dear love [born]
Who rule all here and above,   50
That holy love, that wise will,
That rules all with right and skill.
Might ordered with word [that] light be made
Holy Spirit wields also that might,
For three Persons and one purpose,   55
One might and one Godhead.
Then so became light, as God ordered it,
From darkness divided asunder.
That was the first morning
That ever sprang in the wide world.   60

Lines 55–56 make explicit the presence of the Trinity, but a medieval audience which understood this passage at all would recognize the presence of the Trinity throughout. By supplying the suppressed copula in line 35 ("Wit and wisdom and love *is* God"), and by recognizing "luuen" (49) and "Hali froure" (54) as epithets for the Holy Spirit, the whole passage becomes much more than a paraphrase of the Creation: it is a meditation on the Trinity. The Genesis section of the *Historia* opens (PL 198.1055) with a conflation of Gen. 1:1 with John 1:1 ("In principio erat Verbum, et Verbum erat principium, in quo, et per quod Pater creavit mundum"), and thus the Middle English poet was presented with the division of God's powers. He extends the division to include the Third Person, even as he conflates the first verses of Genesis and John.

In other cases the paraphrase can be quite close. Compare the following accounts from **GE** and the *Historia* of God's work on the second day:

Đo god bad ben ðe firmament   95
Al abuten ðis walkne sent.
Of watres froren, of yses wal,
Đis middel-werld it luket al.

May no fir get melten ðat ys,

He ðe it made is migtful and wis.   100

Fecit ergo ea die *Deus firmamentum in medio aquarum,* id est quamdam
exteriorem mundi superficiem ex aquis congelatis . . . et sunt sicut et
ipsum congelatae, ut crystallus, ne igni solvi possunt. (PL 198.1058,
quoting Gen. 1:6)

When Abraham entertains the three angels (Gen. 18), a question presented itself concerning the consumption of food by ethereal beings. The
poet renders Comestor's clinical explanation, "De cibo quem sumpserunt,
potest dici quod in masticando exinanitus sit, sicut aqua calore ignis" (PL
198:1099), with no little grace as "So malt ðat mete in hem to nogt, / So a
watres drope in a fier brogt" (lines 1117–18).

The poet occasionally interjects his own voice, as for example when he
comments on the overly proud nature of women of his own time ("Wimmen
ðo nomen of here erf kep; / Pride ne cuðe bi ðat dai / Nogt so michel so
it nu mai") and when, at the end of the Genesis portion, he prays for his
own salvation in his capacity as translator ("God schilde hise sowle fro helle
bale, / Ðe made it ðus on engel-tale").[9] At the very end the poet speaks in
the first person plural and extends his benediction (lines 4155–62) to include his listeners. Remarkable throughout is the poet's clear focus on how
biblical knowledge is necessary to personal salvation.

Lines	Event	Bible
1–34	Prologue; capsule summary of the Fall, Incarnation, Harrowing	
35–212	Almanac of six-day Creation with relevant lore: "Al was ðat firme ðhrosing in niʒt, / Til he wit hise word made liʒt" (43–44); Fall of the Angels	Gen. 1
213–268	Divine Prohibition; Naming of the animals Creation of Eve; Institution of the Sabbath	Gen. 2
269–388	Fall of Lucifer: " 'Min fliʒt,' he seide, 'ic wile up-taken, / Min sete norð on heuene maken' " (277–78); Temptation, Fall, Curses, Expulsion	Is. 14:13; Gen. 4
389–502	Descendants of Adam and Eve: "Mo ðan of telleð ðe genesis" (414); Cain and Abel, Henoch, Irad, Maviael, Mathusala;	Gen. 4

9. Lines 2746–48: "Women then took care of their cattle; / Pride they knew not in that
day, / Not so much as it now is." Lines 2525–26: "God shield his soul from hell torment, /
Who made it thus in English speech."

Lines	Event	Bible
	Lamech's bigamy with Ada and Sella; Jubal, Tubalcain; Lamech slays Cain; Seth, Enos	
503–538	Henoch and Antichrist; Birth of Noah	Gen. 5
539–565	"Giants" born; Sem, Cham, and Japheth; the Ark	Gen. 6
566–658	Flood, Raven and Dove, Rainbow	Gen. 7; 8; 9
659–735	Nemrod, Babel; idolatry of Baal; Arphaxad, Sale, Heber, Phaleg, Reu, Sarug, Nachor, Thare, Aran, Abram, Lot, Sara, Melsha	Gen. 11
736–796	Abraham and Sara in Egypt	Gen. 12
797–836	Abraham and Lot in Mambre	Gen. 13
837–924	Pentapolis, capture of Lot, victory of Abraham; Melchisedech	Gen. 14
925–962	God's promise; Abraham's sacrifice	Gen. 15
963–986	Sara, Agar, Ismael	Gen. 16
987–1004	Circumcision of Abraham, names changed: "His name ðo wurð a lettre mor, His wiues lesse ðan it was or. For ðo wurð abram abraham, And sarray sarra bi-cam" (993–96)	Gen. 17
1005–1048	Angels visit Abraham and prophesy Isaac's birth; Abraham debates with God	Gen. 18
1049–1158	Lot entertains angels; destruction of Sodom; Lot's wife turned to "ston" (1120); incest with daughters; Moab and Ammon	Gen. 19
1159–1194	Sara and Abimelech	Gen. 20
1195–1280	Birth of Isaac; expulsion of Agar and Ismael; oath with Abimelech	Gen. 21
1281–1354	"Tac ðin sune ysaac in hond" (1287); Sons of Nachor	Gen. 22
1355–1358	Death of Sara	Gen. 23:1–2
1359–1444	Eliezer woos Rebecca for Isaac	Gen. 24
1445–1512	Cetura: "Get men [seið] ðat abraham / siðen calde agar ceturam" (1445–46); Jacob and Esau	Gen. 25
1513–1526	Isaac swears peace with Abimelech	Gen. 26:1–13
1527–1596	Jacob obtains Isaac's blessing, flees to Laban	Gen. 27
1597–1634	Jacob dreams of "A leddre stonden, and ðor-on / Angeles dun cumen and up gon" (1607–8); Bethel	Gen. 28
1635–1696	Laban; Lia and Rachel; birth of Reuben, Simeon, Levi, Juda	Gen. 29
1697–1734	Bala, Dan, Nephtali, Zelpha, Gad, Aser,	Gen. 30

Lines	*Event*	*Bible*
	Zabulon, Dina, Joseph; Jacob enriches himself	
1735–1784	Laban pursues Jacob	Gen. 31
1785–1822	Jacob wrestles with angel, is renamed Israel	Gen. 32
1823–1846	Jacob reconciled with Esau, raises Soccoth	Gen. 33
1847–1862	Dina raped by Sichem, avenged by Simeon and Levi	Gen. 34
1863–1898	Birth of Benjamin; death of Rachel and Isaac	Gen. 35
1899–1902	Esau in Edom	Gen. 36:1
1903–1990	Joseph dreams, is sold into slavery [Juda and Thamar omitted]	Gen. 37
1991–2040	Joseph in the house of Putiphar	Gen. 39
2041–2094	Joseph interprets dreams in prison	Gen. 40
2095–2156	Pharaoh's dreams; Joseph made ruler of Egypt; Manasses and Ephraim; Famine	Gen. 41
2157–2236	Joseph confronts brothers, demands to see Benjamin, returns silver	Gen. 42
2237–2304	Brothers entertained	Gen. 43
2305–2338	Silver cup; Juda's supplication	Gen. 44
2339–2390	Joseph reveals identity, sends for Jacob	Gen. 45
2391–2435	Pharaoh's question:	Gen. 47
	" 'Fader der[e],' quað pharaon,	
	'Hu fele ger be ðe on?'	
	'An hundred ger and .xxx. mo	
	Haue ic her drogen in werlde wo.	
	Ðog ðinkeð me ðor-often fo,	
	Ðog ic is haue drogen in wo,	
	Siðen ic gan on werlde ben,	
	Her vten-erd, man-kin bi-twen' "	
	(2399–2410)	
	Burial preparations for Jacob [Jacob's blessings and curses omitted]	
2436–2536	Funeral of Jacob; brothers ask forgiveness; death of Joseph	Gen. 50
2537–2586	Oppression of the Hebrews by Pharaoh	Ex. 1
2587–2632	Jochabed; Teremuth rescues Moses coals; war with Ethiopians, love of Tharbis, rings of remembering and forgetting	Ex. 2:1–10
2709–2772	Kills Egyptian; marries Sephora, birth of Gersam and Eliezer	Ex. 2:11–25
2773–2800	Burning Bush	Ex. 3:1–10
2801–2860	Moses's signs: rod to snake, leprous hand, water to blood; speech impediment;	Ex. 4

Lines	Event	Bible
	appointment of Aaron; Moses threatened with death	
2861–2896	Increased oppression	Ex. 5
2897–2909	"Adonay," the God of Abraham	Ex. 6:1–3
2910–2962	Contest with Iannes and Mambres	Ex. 7:9–22
2963–3014	Plagues of frogs, gnats ("smale to sen and sarp on bite" [2989]), flies: "And pharaon wroð herte on hard, / And vn-dede hem dat forward" (3013–14)	Ex. 8
3015–3062	Plague on cattle, of boils, hail	Ex. 9
3063–3120	Plague of grasshoppers, darkness	Ex. 10
3121–3178	Plague on firstborn; Passover; Egyptians despoiled	Ex. 11; 12
3179–3212	Joseph's bones	Ex. 13:19–20
3213–3280	Red Sea Crossing, Egyptians drowned	Ex. 14
3281–3290	"Moyses ðor made a newe song" (3285)	Ex. 15:1
3291–3294	Pillars of fire and cloud	Ex. 13:21–22
3295–3308	Waters of Mara	Ex. 15:23–27
3309–3350	Manna from heaven: "loc her nu: bread!" (3331)	Ex. 16
3351–3398	Water from a rock; Moses overcomes Amalec. "Amalech fleg, and israel / Hadde hegere hond and timede wel"	Ex. 17
3399–3436	Jethro's advice on choosing leaders	Ex. 18
3437–3492	Moses on Sinai; brief recapitulation of Old Testament highpoints: Adam, Noah, Abraham, Sarah, Isaac, Joseph	Ex. 19
3493–3526	Ten Commandments, with the addition of "Help the needy" (3507)	Ex. 20
3527–3536	The Two Tables of the Law: "God hem bad bodes manige on"; the Tabernacle)	Ex. 31:18
3537–3628	Golden Calf; wrath of the Levites: "Ðo woren on liue sumdel les" (3595)	Ex. 32
3629–3638	"God it tagte al ear moysen Wislike hu it wrogt sulde ben, Quilc srud, quat offrende, quilc lage, And quat for luue and quat for age Aaron bissop oðere of ðat kin Sette he, hem for to seruen ðor-in" (3629–34)	summary of Leviticus; Lev. 8:12–13
3639–3686	Further complaints by the Hebrews; fowls from heaven, "brenninge he cald ðat stede"; Appointment of the Seventy	Num. 10:33– 11:34
3687–3694	Mary smitten with leprosy	Num. 12:10–15

Lines	Event	Bible
3695–3716	Twelve Spies survey the land	Num. 13
3717–3746	Josue and Caleb quell discontent	Num. 14:1–9
3747–3806	Contest with Dathan and Abiron; schism of Core: "Alle he sunken ðe erðe wið-in" (3775)	Num. 16
3807–3844	Aaron's flowering rod; election of the Levites	Num. 17:1–10
3845–3892	Deaths of Mary and Aaron; water from a rock at Cades	Num. 20
3893–3918	Moses's "wirme of bras" (3898); conquest of Basan	Num. 21
3919–3994	Balaam and his ass: "Qui betes ðu me ðis ðridde siðe?"	Num. 22
3995–4042	Balaam resists Balac, refuses to curse Israel	Num. 23
4043–4084	Whoredom of Israel; zeal of Phinees	Num. 25
4085–4098	Numbering of the Tribes	Num. 26:1–4
4099–4118	Appointment of Josue	Num. 27:12–23
4119–4154	Moses blesses Tribes of Israel; Phasga sight of Promised Land; death of Moses	Deut. 33:1; 34
4155–4162	Concluding prayer	

Old Testament History OTH

IMEV/S 3973
Manual, 2:404 [54]

1. Oxford, Bodleian Lib. Laud misc. 622 (*SC* 1414) (65r–71r) ca. 1400, acephalous.
2. Oxford, Bodleian Lib. Eng. Poet. a.1 (Vernon) (1r–6r), ca. 1390, 1,812 lines in couplets.
3. Oxford, Bodleian Lib. Add. C.220 (*SC* 29430) (31r–32v) (stops after Noah).
4. Cambridge, St. John's College 28 (1r–21v) (see Pickering, *South English Ministry and Passion,* 61–69).
5. Cambridge, Trinity College 605 (R.3.25) (1r–6r), early 15th c.
6. London, BL Cotton Vespasian B.xvi (1r) (Adam and Eve section).
7. London, BL Egerton 1993 (1r–27r), late 14th c.
8. London, BL Stowe 949 (155r–158r) (Life of Moses section).
9. London, Lambeth Palace 223 (5r–30v).
10. Winchester College, Warden and Fellows' Library 33a (1r–12r), 15th c.

Editions: 1—partial by Furnivall, *Adam Davy's 5 Dreams,* 82–90, 96–98

(portions from 69r–70v covering the Ecclesiasticus paraphrase through to Habacuc and the Coronation and Judgment of Solomon.)

2—in progress by Morey

Facsimile: 2—Doyle, *Vernon Manuscript.*

In manuscripts 1, 2, 5, and 7 this poem precedes portions of **ConM** from the *SEL* and is thus a temporale narrative. **OTH** extends from Creation to the end of Daniel, with few apocryphal digressions (e.g., Moses and the crown of Pharaoh). In manuscripts 2, 4, and 7 the poem extends to approximately eighteen hundred lines.

Noteworthy features are its inclusion of Levitical laws and one of the most complete paraphrases of Ecclesiasticus in Middle English. The primary source for **OTH** is the *Historia Scholastica.*

The following is taken from my transcription of the facsimile of manuscript 2 (punctuation added):

Folio	Event	Bible
1r col.a	Creation of Angels, heavens, earth, Adam and Eve; Prohibition of Tree; "Ure lord caste sleep him on, a rib he dude out take"	Gen. 1; 2
1r col.b	Temptation, Fall, Curses, Expulsion: "Þo herde Adam ur lord come byfore þe heiȝe noone." "Þe eorþe he dalfe . . . And his wyf spon"	Gen. 3
1v col.a	Cain and Abel: " 'Not ich neuere,' seide Caym, 'where my broþur be, / Nam i nout his wardeyn.' " Seth; death of Adam; Giants on the earth	Gen. 4:1–17, 25; 5:3–5; 6:1–7
1v col.b	Noah, Ark, Flood, Raven and Dove, Rainbow	Gen. 6:8–15, 19; 7; 8; 9:1–17
2r col.a	Tower of Babel; Call of Abraham; Sara; angel appears to Agar, Ismael; Covenant of Circumcision; Abraham entertains three angels; Sodom and Gomorrha	Gen. 11:1–9; 12:1–5; 16:1–15; 17; 18; 19:15–26
2r col.b	Lot and his daughters; Moab and Ammon; Expulsion of Agar and Ismael; Sacrifice of Isaac; death of Sara; Isaac weds Rebecca; Abraham weds for third time, dies; Jacob and Esau	Gen. 19:30–38; 21:9–14; 22:1–14; 23:2; 24:67; 25:1–8, 21–28
2v col.a	Jacob beguiles Isaac; dreams of the ladder; serves Laban for Rachel; outwits Laban; wrestles with angel; reconciles	Gen. 27; 28:11–22; 29:15–30; 31:1–18; 32:24–25, 32; 33:1–4;

Folio	Event	Bible
	with Esau; death of Rachel; birth of Benjamin	35:18–19
2v col.b	Death of Isaac; Joseph dreams of the sheaves, is sold into slavery; accused by his lord's wife, imprisoned; interprets dreams	Gen. 35:27–29; 37:5–36; 39; 40; 41
3r col.a	Birth of Manasses and Ephraim; famine; Joseph tests his brothers	Gen. 42; 43; 44
3r col.b	"In Beniamines sac þe coupe was þo ifounde"; Israel enters Egypt; death of Jacob; Joseph's burial instructions; every male Hebrew child drowned; Pharaoh's daughter discovers Moses	Gen. 45:1–20; 47:1–6; 49:33; 50:24–26; Ex. 1; 2:1–10
3v col.a	Moses spurns Pharaoh's crown; slays Egyptian; Burning Bush; rod transforms into snake; Aaron; signs before Pharaoh; Plagues of blood, frogs, gnats, cattle, boils, hail, "worms," darkness	Ex. 2:11–12; 3:1–6; 4:1–5, 13–14; 7:10, 20–21; 8:6, 14, 17; 9:6, 10, 23; 10:13, 19, 22
3v col.b	Passover, Slaughter of Firstborn; Red Sea crossing; manna; water from a stone; Moses on Sinai, Ten Commandments; laws on slaves, lex talionis, goring ox, seducing a virgin, sabbatical year: "seþ no þing in his moodur milk"	Ex. 12:22, 29; 14:10–18; 16:14–15; 17:6; 19:18; 20:1–20; 21:1–6, 24, 28–29; 22:11, 16, 19
4r col.a	Tabernacle directions; Golden Calf; wrath of the Levites; Covenant renewed; "Horned" Moses; clean and unclean animals; purification of women, laws on bestiality, gleaning, tithes, marriage	Ex. 24:18; 32; 34:1, 29–30; Lev. 11:1–4; 12:1–5; 18:23; 19:9; 27:32; Deut. 7:3
4r col.b	Balaam and his ass; star out of Jacob; death of Moses; appointment of Josue	Num. 22:1–6, 20–35; 24:17; Deut. 34:1–9
4v col.a	Gedeon's fleece; Samson slays lion, ties brands to foxes' tails, slays Philistines with cheekbone of an ass; deceived by Dalila; collapses pillars	Judg. 6:36–40; 14:5–14; 15:4–8, 14–19; 16:1–6, 17–30
4v col.b	Saul; Samuel anoints David; David and Goliath; love of Jonathan; David weds Michol	1Kg. 16:10–13; 17:38–51; 18:1–21
5r col.a	Saul seeks to kill David with a spear; Michol tells David to flee; deaths of Jonathan and Saul: "Smyt of mid myn owne swerd myn hed"; David slays Saul's executioner; David made king	1Kg. 19:11–12, 18; 31:1–7; 2Kg. 1:1–17; 2:4

Folio	Event	Bible
5r col.b	Urias, Bethsabee, Nathan: "Þou art þulke mon of whom now ich telle"; death of child, birth of Solomon; Amnon rapes Thamar; vengeance of Absalom; Absalom flees, rebels, dies at Joab's hand	2Kg. 11:4–5, 15–17; 12:1–7, 15–16, 24; 13:1–14, 28, 34; 18:6–15, 33
5v col.a	Complaints of David's men; David numbers Israel; his choices of calamities; encounters angel; Bethsabee's jealousy of Adonias; Solomon made king; Solomon slays Adonias, builds Temple, marries Pharaoh's daughter	2Kg. 19:5–6; 24:2, 12–17; 3Kg. 1:5–21, 43; 2:10, 25; 3:1, 12–28
5v col.b	Wisdom, Judgment of Solomon; his riches and knowledge [excerpts from Ecclesiasticus begin:]	3Kg. 4:22, 33; Ecclus. 1:1, 2
6r col.a	"A riche werk wiþ þe mon þat is dronkeleuh selde is ifounde, / ffor tauerne and lecherie mony men bringeþ to grounde" (19:1–2); "Þe mon þat techeþ his child wel he sorsaweþ al his fo" (30:3); Death of Solomon; accession of Roboam, his oppressions: "In þe leste fynger þat ich habbe strengþe þer is more / Þen in my fader scholdre was for al his wyse lore."	4:4, 8, 28; 8:1, 5; 7:6; 6:6–17; 7:25–27, 29–30, 39–40; 8:2; 22:14; 37:7; 9:2–3, 7; 16:4; 19:1–2; 12:10–12; 20:3; 21:17, 25–27; 14:1; 30:3; 3Kg. 11:43; 12:3–11
6r col.b	Revolt of Israel; Jeroboam; division of kingdom; Achab becomes king; Elias fed by ravens; the Widow of Sarephta; Elias raises her son "Jonas"; calls Eliseus: "He fond Elyse gon ate plouh, mid him forþ he him nom." Elias calls down fire from heaven, his rapture: "A fuiri hors and a Cart"; recollection of Henoch; Elias purifies well; Widow's jar of oil; Daniel in the lions' den; Habacuc's impromptu journey	3Kg. 12:18–20; 16:29; 17:6–10, 19–22; 19:19–20; 4Kg. 1:7–10, 17; 2:11; Gen. 5:24; 4Kg. 2:19–22; 4:1–7; Dan. 6:16, 22–24; 14:32–42

In Vernon, there follow 110 lines recounting the voyage of the abbot of Romsey to placate the king of Denmark with gifts from William the Conqueror. During a storm on the return voyage, an angel appears and instructs the abbot concerning the proper date and observance of the feast of the Conception of Mary (7r col.a)

A *Middle English Metrical Paraphrase of the Old Testament* POT

IMEV/S 944
Manual, 2:382 [2]

1. Oxford, Bodleian Lib. Selden Supra 52 (*SC* 3440) (2r–168r), mid-15th c.
2. Longleat, Marquess of Bath 257 (119r–212r), mid-15th c.

Editions: 1—Kalén, *Middle English Metrical Paraphrase,* and Ohlander, *Middle English Metrical Paraphrase,* vols. 2–5; Heuser, "Die alttestamentlichen dichtungen des ms. Seld. Supra 52," (2Mach. 6; 7; 9); Peck, *Heroic Women,* 109–53 (Gen. 3; Judg. 11; Judith).
2—Horstmann, "Nachträge" (1887), 447–54 (2Mach. 6; 7; 9).

This poem, like **GE,** owes the bulk of its material to the *Historia Scholastica.* The poem's ponderous title befits its scale: 18,372 lines in twelve-line stanzas rhyming ababababcdcd. Longleat is missing Genesis and several other leaves throughout; its inclusion of a copy of Lydgate's *Siege of Thebes* dates the manuscript after 1420. Neither manuscript is the original, nor does one copy the other, although they share a common source to which Selden seems to be the closer. An interesting feature of Longleat is that a corrector has noted in the margin deviations from the Bible *and* the *Historia:* for example, at stanza 1249 the corrector writes "Nota Digreditur ab historia," and at stanza 1255 "Caueat lector quia hic errat translator ut in plerisque alijs" (see Kalén's edition, ix). At least one fifteenth-century reader was sensitive to the integrity of not only the Bible but also the *Historia.*

Selden has retained all of its leaves; it selectively retells the Old Testament from Genesis through 4Kings (omitting, as is common in biblical literature, Leviticus, even though the marginal notation "leuiticus" on folio 17r would lead one to believe that it is really there). Job, Tobias, Esther, and Judith also appear (Job does not appear in the *Historia Scholastica*).[10] Next are two grisly stories from 2Machabees, "De matre cum VII filiis" and "De

---

10. Kalén (cxcii) notes some debts in the Job section to **PJ,** and only here in the paraphrase do Latin headings occur, with translation. The forgiveness of the good thief (Luke 23:43) is mentioned in Job's lament (line 14989), following a comparison of Job to Lazarus raised from the dead (John 11, line 14977). Other material from the New Testament includes the Dives and Lazarus (Luke 16.19–31 at line 14715), Judas as a sign of wanhope (lines 13093 and 13121), frequent prophecies of Christ, and the assurance—quoting Rom. 15:4—that much learning may be derived from Old Testament examples (lines 11913–16). See Kalén, cxciii.

Anthioco," which tell how the pagan King Antiochus torments the mother and her sons and then executes all eight for refusing to renounce their faith. Thirty-four verse tales of saints and monks (not included in the Gothenburg edition) finish the manuscript.[11] Brief moralizing passages follow most of the books.

Kalén proposes a date of composition ca. 1400, but this date is somewhat late. Kalén assumed that this poem borrowed from the York plays since they share the same rhyme scheme and numerous lines. The York plays exist in a single manuscript (London, BL Add. 35290, ca. 1430–40), though all of the drama cycles took form throughout the fourteenth century. Given their uncertain (and in fact almost nonexistent) manuscript tradition and the likelihood that the dramatic scripts were fluid over time, it is more likely that the plays borrowed from the paraphrase rather than vice versa. This relationship would be in keeping with the dependence of the drama on **NP** and **SLC,** works which are themselves indebted to the *Historia*.[12] Thus the mystery plays, surely the most public medium for biblical material, are what might be called the end of the line of a complex literary tradition which began with Comestor's Paris lectures.

Lines	Event	Bible
[vol. 1]		
37–144	Six days of Creation	Gen. 1; 2
145–228	Prohibition, Temptation, Fall, Expulsion	Gen. 3
229–276	Cain and Abel; Tubalcain and Jubal; Seth; Mathusala; Noah, Sem, Cham, Japheth	Gen. 4; 5
277–348	Flood	Gen. 6–9:19
349–360	Drunkenness of Noah	Gen. 9:20–27
361–372	Babel	Gen. 11:1–11:9

11. Some omissions and transpositions correspond to an Old French versification, largely unprinted, studied by Ohlander in a separate article ("Old French Parallels"). The Old French poem (London, BL Egerton 2710, among others; see Smeets, "Traductions" vol. 6, part 2, entry 1808) is some 17,400 verses and has many elements from the *chanson de geste* tradition not reproduced in the Middle English. Both poems share stories from the *Historia*, such as the infant Moses averting his face from the breasts of Egyptian women, and perhaps most significantly both poems at times agree against the *Historia*. Ohlander states in the introduction to volume 3 of his edition that "It is an open question whether the English poet was influenced by the OFr. poem or whether both poets followed the same source" (5).

12. See Beadle, "Abraham's Preamble." **NP** is a source for the York, Wakefield (Towneley), and Coventry cycles. See Foster, *Northern Passion: French Text,* 81–101. The Chester cycle relies on **SLC** (Foster, *Stanzaic Life of Christ*), which repeatedly names the *Historia* as a source (via Higden's *Polychronicon*). A sporadic but helpful treatment of Comestor's contribution to English drama appears in Woolf, *Mystery Plays,* 115, 125, 135, 151, 159, 209, 228, 333, 390, 393, 399, 408.

Lines	Event	Bible
373–420	Sem's descendants; Call of Abraham	Gen. 11:10–12:3
421–480	Lot, Pentapolis; Melchisedech	Gen. 14:1–21
481–552	Ismael; Sara; Agar	Gen. 15; 16; 17
553–612	Angels visit Abraham; Sodom; Lot's wife	Gen. 18–19:26
613–636	Lot and his daughters; Moab	Gen. 19:30–38
637–660	Isaac, Sara, Agar	Gen. 21:1–21
661–728	Sacrifice of Isaac	Gen. 22
729–768	Death of Sara; Cetura; Rebecca; death of Abraham	Gen. 23–25:11
769–900	Jacob and Esau	Gen. 25: 19–28:9
901–936	Jacob's ladder	Gen. 28:10–22
937–996	Laban, Rachel, Lia; Jacob's sons	Gen. 29; 30
997–1008	"Israel" wrestles with an angel	Gen. 32:22–28
1009–1176	Juda, Her, Onan, Shelah, Thamar, Phares, Zara	Gen. 38
1177–1284	Joseph's dreams; Putiphar's wife; Joseph's stewardship	Gen. 37; 39; 40; 41
1285–1404	Joseph's test of brothers; Benjamin	Gen. 42; 43; 44; 45
1405–1440	Deaths of Jacob and Joseph	Gen. 50
1441–1468	Oppressions by Pharaoh	Ex. 1
1469–1524	Birth, discovery, rearing of Moses	Ex. 2:1–10
1525–1596	Rejection of crown, test by hot coals	apocryphal
1597–1632	Murder of Egyptian; Raguel, Sephora	Ex. 2:11–22
1633–1668	Burning Bush	Ex. 3:1–10
1669–1692	Rod of serpent; leprous hand; Aaron	Ex. 4:1–20
1693–1716	More oppression; signs before Pharaoh	Ex. 5; 7
1717–1788	Plagues	Ex. 7–11
1789–1848	Flight from Egypt; Red Sea crossing	Ex. 14
1849–1860	Song of praise	Ex. 15:1–2
1861–1920	Bitter waters of Mara; manna; water from a rock	Ex. 15; 16; 17
1921–1944	Josue; victory over Amalec	Ex. 17; 18
1945–1992	Golden Calf; wrath of the Levites	Ex. 32
1993–2016	Ark of the Covenant; Tabernacle	Ex. 37:1–3; 40

[Leviticus is wholly omitted]

Lines	Event	Bible
2017–2040	Numbering the Israelites	Num. 1
2041–2064	Mary's leprosy	Num. 12
2065–2136	Twelve Spies sent to Canaan	Num. 13
2137–2196	Unrest; Moses prays for Israel; Josue and Caleb favored	Num. 14

Lines	Event	Bible
2197–2280	Schism of Core; Dathan and Abiron	Num. 16

[The MS rubric reads "Deuteronomy," but the material continues from
Numbers with frequent uses of the *Historia Scholastica*]

Lines	Event	Bible
2281–2328	Aaron's flowering rod	Num. 17
2329–2352	Water from a rock at Cades; deaths of Mary and Aaron; appointment of Eleazer	Num. 20
2353–2394	Fiery serpents, brazen serpent	Num. 21:1–9
2395–2424	Victory over Sehon and Og	Num. 21:10–35
2425–2472	Balac; Balaam and his ass	Num. 22
2473–2520	Balaam blesses Israel	Num. 23; 24
2521–2568	Apostasy among Moabite women; zeal of Phinees	Num. 25
2569–2580	Census of Israel	Num. 26
2581–2598	Victory over Moabites; death of Balaam	Num. 31
2599–2652	Cities of Reuben and Gad; Moses's final commands	Num. 32
2653–2676	Death of Moses	Deut. 34
2677–2748	Spies to Jericho; Rahab	Jos. 2
2749–2820	Jordan stops flowing; Jericho destroyed; Rahab spared	Jos. 3; 4; 5; 6
2821–2856	Achan's theft, execution	Jos. 7
2857–2904	Ambush, sack of Hai	Jos. 8
2905–2964	Deception by the Gibeonites	Jos. 9
2965–3012	Sun stands still; conquest of five kings	Jos. 10
3013–3060	Jabin's resistance; general conquest	Jos. 11; 12
3061–3096	Division of Israel among twelve tribes	Jos. 13–21
3097–3156	Josue's final exhortation, death	Jos. 23–24

[The MS rubric reads "Judicum," but material continues from Josue]

Lines	Event	Bible
3157–3204	Phinees conquers Canaanites	Jos. 22
3205–3312	Lapse, defeat of the Benjaminites	Judg. 19; 20
3313–3360	Cenez, Eglon, Aod, Samgar	Judg. 3
3361–3384	Jabin; Debbora and Barac; famine	Judg. 4:1–6; 6:1–6
3385–3420	Gedeon and the angel; the fleece	Judg. 6:7–40
3421–3456	Gedeon defeats the Midianites	Judg. 7
3457–3480	Abimelech	Judg. 9
3481–3588	Jephte and his daughter	Judg. 11
3589–3600	Abesan, Ahialon, Abdon	Judg. 12
3601–3672	Manue and his wife	Judg. 13
3673–4440	Samson and Dalila	Judg. 14; 15; 16
4441–4633	Ruth, Noemi, Booz; genealogy of Christ	Ruth 1; 2; 3; 4
4634–4716	Elcana, Anna, Heli, Samuel	1Kg. 1
4717–4752	Heli's sons, Phinees and Ophni	1Kg. 2

Lines	Event	Bible
4753–4800	Call of Samuel	1Kg. 3
4801–4932	War with Philistines; the Ark	1Kg. 4; 5; 6
4933–5016	Eleazar; Samuel made king	1Kg. 7; 8
5017–5184	Cis; Samuel anoints Saul	1Kg. 9; 10
5185–5340	Saul rescues Jabes-Galaad from Naas	1Kg. 11
5341–5676	Saul and Jonathan defeat the Philistines	1Kg. 12; 13; 14
5677–5868	Saul spares Agag	1Kg. 15
5869–6000	Samuel anoints David; David harps for Saul	1Kg. 16
[vol. 2]		
6001–6132	David and Goliath	1Kg. 17
6133–6336	Saul envies David; Michol's love	1Kg. 18; 19
6337–6432	Jonathan intercedes for David	1Kg. 20
6433–6480	David flees to Bishop Achimelech	1Kg. 21

[Narrative interlude: "how all was to endyng broyȝt, / þe bybyll bers
wyttenese þerby. / yt ware long tyme to tell how he hys cowrse kest /
And what ferlys be fell / or he was broyȝt to rest" (6487–6492)]

Lines	Event	Bible
6481–6624	David at Ceila, Ziph, Engedi	1Kg. 23
6625–6708	Doeg informs on David, slays Achimelech	1Kg. 22
6709–6792	David spares Saul	1Kg. 24
6793–6936	David, Nabal, Abigail	1Kg. 25
6937–7020	David, Abisai, Abner; David spares Saul	1Kg. 26
7021–7140	Achis; Saul and the "wyche" of Endor	1Kg. 27; 28
7141–7224	Amalecites sack Siceleg	1Kg. 29; 30
7225–7320	Death of Saul	1Kg. 31
7321–7404	David laments Saul's death	2Kg. 1
7405–7496	David becomes king; Abner kills Asael	2Kg. 2
7497–7620	David asks for Michol; Joab kills Abner	2Kg. 3
7621–7668	Rechab and Baana kill Isboseth	2Kg. 4
7669–7896	David defeats Jebusites and Philistines	2Kg. 5
7897–7968	Ark (Michol not mentioned); the Temple	2Kg. 6; 7
7969–7992	Siba and the lame Miphiboseth	2Kg. 9
7993–8064	Hanon; war with Ammonites	2Kg. 10
8065–8160	David, Bethsabee, Urias	2Kg. 11
8161–8292	Nathan's reproach; birth of Solomon	2Kg. 12
8293–8436	Amnon rapes Thamar; vengeance of Absalom	2Kg. 13
8437–8508	Joab reconciles David to Absalom	2Kg. 14
8509–8688	Absalom consolidates power; Semei	2Kg. 15; 16
8689–8892	Chusai; Achitophel; death of Absalom	2Kg. 17; 18
8893–9024	David mourns, returns to Jerusalem	2Kg. 19
9025–9168	Revolt of Saba; Joab kills Amasa	2Kg. 20
9169–9336	Famine; "Diligam te, domine" (cf. Ps. 18); Census, Gad	2Kg. 21; 22; 24

Lines	Event	Bible

[David builds an altar on the future site of the Temple and of Calvary:
"fforther who likes to loke / how all þat werke was wroyȝt, / Go to
þe bybyll boke; / þor may þei see vn soght" (9333–36)]

Lines	Event	Bible
9337–9468	Abisag; revolt of Adonijah	3Kg. 1
9469–9624	Death of David	3Kg. 2
[vol. 3]		
9625–9720	Deaths of Adonias, Joab, Semei	3Kg. 2
9721–9840	Solomon's marriage, prayer for wisdom, judgment over the baby	3Kg. 3
9841–9864	Solomon appoints officials; credited with Canticles, Ecclesiastes, Proverbs	3Kg. 4
9865–9984	Construction of Temple; other houses	3Kg. 5; 6; 7; 8; 9
9985–10164	Solomon's concubines and adversaries; Ahias's prophecy; Solomon's death	3Kg. 10; 11
10165–10308	Revolt against Roboam; Jeroboam	3Kg. 12; 2Para. 10
10309–10452	Reign of Roboam; invasion of Sesac	3Kg. 14; 2Para. 11; 12
10453–10656	Jeroboam's apostasy; anonymous prophet	3Kg. 13
10657–10728	War between Jeroboam and Abiam	2Para. 13
10729 10848	Crimes, apostasy of Basa	3Kg. 14; 15, 2Para. 14; 15; 16
10849–10896	Ela, Zambri, Amri, Achab	3Kg. 16
10897–10956	Reign of Josaphat	2Para. 17
10957–11100	Jezabel; Elias and the Widow of Sarephta	3Kg. 16; 17
11101–11292	Elias and Abdias; contest on Mt. Carmel	3Kg. 18
11293–11376	Elias calls Eliseus	3Kg. 19
11377–11448	Naboth's vineyard	3Kg. 21
11449–11588	War between Achab and Benadad	3Kg. 20
11589–11832	Micheas's prophecies; death of Achab	3Kg. 22; 2Para. 18
11833–11904	Josaphat defeats Moabites	2Para. 20

["ffor as lerned men may loke, / sant Paule telles old and ȝyng: / All þat is
wryttyn in boke / is lefed for our lernyg" (Rom. 15:4 [lines 11913–16])]

Lines	Event	Bible
11917–12048	Ochozias's illness; Elias's resistance	4Kg. 1
12049–12060	Ascension of Elias [omitting boys and bears]	4Kg. 2
12061–12146	Defeat of Moabites	4Kg. 3
12147–12348	Eliseus provides for widow; raises dead son; relieves famine	4Kg. 4
12349–12624	Eliseus cures Naaman; Giezi's avarice	4Kg. 5

Lines	Event	Bible
12625–12948	Recovers lost ax; strikes Syrians blind; Samarian women cannibalize children	4Kg. 6
12949–13080	Four lepers rout Syrian army	4Kg. 7
13081–13128	Moralization on despair of Judas Iscariot	Matt. 27:5
13129–13428	Hazael becomes king of Syrians; deaths of Joram, Ochozias and Jezabel; letter from Elias	4Kg. 8; 9; 2Para. 21
13429–13512	Jehu slays Achab's sons and Baal worshipers	4Kg. 10
13513–13596	Joas becomes king	4Kg. 11; 2Para. 22
13597–13740	War with Hazael; Joas, Zacharias; death of Eliseus	4Kg. 12; 13; 2Para. 23; 24
13741–13836	Amasias, Azarias, Jeroboam	4Kg. 14; 2Para. 25

[The mention of Jonas in line 13829 (4Kg. 14:25) launches the poem into the Book of Jonas]

13837–13896	Disobedience, the storm, the whale	Jonas 1
13897–13968	Repentance of Ninive	Jonas 3
13969–14004	Jonas's bitterness	Jonas 4
14005–14088	Azarias profanes altar	2Para. 26; 4Kg. 15

[vol. 4]

14089–14292	"Iob was a full gentyll jew / . . . in þe land of vs he had no pere"	Job 1
14293–14412	Job's leprosy; three comforters	Job 2
14413–14424	Curses day of birth	Job 3
14425–14448	Eliphaz rebukes Job	Job 4; 5
14449–14508	Job questions divine justice	Job 6; 7
14509–14616	Baldad; Job insists on righteousness	Job 8; 9; 10
14617–14700	Sophar; Job asks why the just suffer	Job 11–14
14701–14760	Eliphaz adduces story of Dives and Lazarus; Job's complaints	Job 15; 16; 17; Luke 16:19–31
14761–14880	Baldad; Job asks for justice	Job 18; 19
14881–15048	Further debate; Job invokes Lazarus and the Good Thief, proclaims innocence	Job 20–32; John 11:38–44; Luke 23:43

[Speeches of Elihu omitted, Job 33–37]

15049–15216	God's response; Job restored	Job 38–42

[Tobias follows in non-Vulgate order (like Job, another man tried by God)]

15217–15384	Tobias, wife Anna, son Tobias, loan to Gabelus [details from *Historia Scholastica* and *Catholicon* of John Balbus (see	Tob. 1

Lines	Event	Bible
	Liljegren, review of *Middle English Metrical Paraphrase*, ed. Kalén)]	
15385–15480	Buries dead body; becomes blind	Tob. 2
15481–15540	Sends Tobias to collect from Gabelus	Tob. 4
15541–15696	Tobias interviews Raphael/Azarias	Tob. 5
15697–15806	Anna's Kid; Sara possessed by Asmodeus	Tob. 2; 3
15807–15960	Tobias catches fish, learns of its use	Tob. 6
15961–16116	Tobias marries Sara, exorcises Asmodeus	Tob. 7; 8
16117–16188	Money recovered	Tob. 9; 10
16189–16380	Tobias's dog; return to Ninive; Raphael reveals himself	Tob. 11; 12
16381–16452	Tobias healed; gives final counsel; happiness of Tobias and Sara	Tob. 14
16453–16572	Feast of Assuerus; deposition of Vasthi	Est. 1
16573–16632	Mardochai; elevation of Esther	Est. 2
16633–16680	Aman persecutes the Jews	Est. 3
16681–16788	Esther makes plans; Aman builds gallows	Est. 4; 5
16789–16932	Mardochai honored; Aman hanged	Est. 6; 7
16933–16956	Mardochai and the Jews prevail	Est. 8
[chapters 9–16 omitted]		
16957–17036	Nabuchodonosor appoints Holofernes	Judith 1; 2; 3
17037 17100	Jews prepare to resist	Judith 4
[chapters 5 and 6, the warnings of Achior, omitted]		
17101–17172	Holofernes cuts off water; Ozias counsels patience	Judith 7
17173–17256	Judith takes command; prays to God	Judith 8; 9
17257–17520	Judith deceives Holofernes	Judith 10; 11; 12
17521–17700	Judith beheads Holofernes; plans attack; confusion and defeat of the Assyrians	Judith 13; 14; 15
17701–17748	Her charitable life as a widow	Judith 16:18–25
["Þus endes þe boke of Iudyth, / als clerkes may knaw by clergy clere. / God graunt hym hele þat hath turned yt / in ynglysch lawd men forto lere!" (17741–44)]		
17749–18252	"De matre cum vii filiis," presented as a martyrology of a mother and her seven sons who died for the law of Moses (17759); paralleled with the Slaughter of the Innocents (18246)	2Mach. 7; Matt. 2.16
18253–18288	"De Anthioco": the martyrdom of Eleazar and the circumcised babies	2Mach. 6
18289–18372	Death of Antiochus	2Mach. 9

Caxton's *Golden Legend* (1483) CGL

IPMEP 682
Manual, 2:436 [7]

> No manuscripts: earliest printing by Caxton at Westminster in 1483 (*STC* 24873).

No edition.
Modernization: Jacobus de Voragine, *Golden Legend,* ed. F. S. Ellis, vols. 1 and 2.
Study: Horrall, "William Caxton's Biblical Translation."

Caxton explains his project as follows: "But forasmuch as I had by me a legend in French, another in Latin, and the third in English, which varied in many and divers places, and also many histories were comprised in the other two books which were not in the English book, and therefore I have written one out of the said three books" (Jacobus, *Golden Legend,* 1:2).

The three books are an unidentified Latin text of Jacobus de Voragine's *Legenda Aurea* (ca. 1260), the *Légende dorée,* a French translation by Jehan de Vignai (ca. 1333), and the English *Gilte Legend* (1438; see *Manual,* 2:432 [6]). None of the three contain the substantial biblical paraphrase preceding the sanctorale, which begins on p. 94 of vol. 2 (with St. Andrew).

Blake ("Biblical Additions") proposes a (nonextant) English temporale as a source for Caxton's biblical introduction. But this introduction is unlike any surviving English temporale (as, e.g., in Cambridge, St John's College 28), not least because it is prose, not verse, and because at many points Caxton's paraphrase is so close that it becomes a translation.

It may well be that Caxton and/or an associate should be credited with the creation of one of the most interesting and complete prose biblical paraphrases to be produced in the fourteenth century. While it does not qualify as the English Bible which Caxton notably never printed, it nevertheless shows him working in the tradition of Middle English biblical literature.

The New Testament section (to p. 168) is a treasury of traditional exegesis and lore wherein Caxton inserts quotations from both Testaments and the Fathers, moralizations, and extensive enumerated significances. Throughout, rubrics designate the various stories for reading according to the liturgical year.

Pages	Event	Bible
[vol. 1]		
25–41	Nativity and associated portents; shepherds; Circumcision, excursus on the Name of Jesus, Ages of the World	Luke 2
41–52	Epiphany, Baptism by John	Matt. 2; Luke 3
52–66	Liturgical significances of Septuagesima, Sexagesima, Quinquagesima, Quadragesima, Ember Days	
66–86	Passion, including abbreviated life of Pilate, Veronica's veil	Matt. 27; John 19
87–101	Resurrection; Appearances to Carpus (cf. 2 Tim. 4:13), Mary Magdalen, Peter, et al.; Harrowing; Seth's Quest	Matt. 28; John 20
101–108	Greater and Lesser Litanies	
108–122	Ascension; "Leaps" of Christ	Mark 16; Luke 24
122–141	Pentecost	Acts 2
141–149	Institution of the Eucharist	Matt. 26:26–29
149–168	Dedication of the Temple of the Church; synopsis of the Hours of the Cross (154–55)	
169–176	Creation, Prohibition, Temptation, Fall, Curses, Expulsion	Gen. 1; 2; 3
176–181	Cain and Abel: "am I keeper of my brother?" (177); Henoch; Lamech; Jubal's pillars; death of Cain; Seth and his descendants; Seth's Quest (see Quinn, *Quest*)	Gen. 4; 5
181–187	Noah; Sem, Cham, Japheth; Flood, Raven and Dove, Rainbow; Noah's drunkenness; threefold division of the world	Gen 6; 7; 8; 9
187–191	Babel; Abraham, Sara; Lot, Wars of the Kings; Melchisedech	Gen. 11; 12; 13; 14
191–194	Agar, Ismael; Covenant of Circumcision	Gen. 15; 16; 17
194–198	Abraham and Lot entertain the angels; destruction of Sodom and Gomorrha; Lot's incest with daughters; Moab and Ammon	Gen. 18; 19
198–201	Sara and Abimelech; birth of Isaac; expulsion of Agar; oath with Abimelech	Gen. 20; 21
201–207	Sacrifice of Isaac; death of Sara; Rebecca	Gen. 22; 23; 24
207–214	Jacob and Esau; deception of Isaac; Jacob's ladder	Gen. 25; 27; 28
214–222	Lia and Rachel; Jacob's prosperity; Laban's household gods	Gen. 29; 30; 31

Pages	Event	Bible
222–225	Reconciliation with Esau; Jacob wrestles with an angel	Gen. 32; 33
225–228	Sichem rapes Dina; vengeance of Simeon and Levi; Bethel; deaths of Rachel and Isaac	Gen. 34; 35
228–231	Joseph dreams, is sold into slavery	Gen. 37
231–237	Putiphar's wife; Joseph interprets dreams; marries Aseneth	Gen. 39; 40; 41
237–249	Famine; embassy of Joseph's brothers; Benjamin; Jacob enters Egypt; names of the sons of Israel	Gen. 42; 43; 44; 45; 46
249–255	Death of Jacob; blessing of Ephraim and Manasses; death of Joseph	Gen. 47; 48; 49; 50
256–259	Oppression of the Hebrews; Teremuth finds Moses; Moses kills Egyptian; marries Sephora	Ex. 1; 2
260–267	Burning Bush; empowering miracles; Aaron; oppression	Ex. 3; 4; 5; 6
267–271	Signs before Pharaoh; Plagues; Passover	Ex. 7–12
271–277	Red Sea Crossing; new song; waters of Mara; manna; water from a rock; Amalec overcome	Ex. 14; 15; 16; 17
277–288	Jethro's counsel; Moses on Sinai; Ten Commandments	Ex. 18; 19; 20; 24:12–18
288–290	Golden Calf; wrath of the Levites	Ex. 32
290–295	Aaron's flowering rod; curlews from heaven; Mary's leprosy; land surveyed; Josue and Caleb quell discontent; water from a rock; brazen serpent	Num. 17; 10; 12; 13; 14; 20; 21
295–296	Phasga sight of Promised Land; death of Moses	Deut. 34
[vol. 2]		
1–2	Josue, sun stands still, hailstones	Jos. 10:11–13
2–4	Elcana, Anna, Phenenna; birth of Samuel; Canticle of Anna; sins of Ophni and Phinees	1Kg. 1; 2
4–8	Fourfold call of Samuel; Ark captured; death of Heli; Dagon overthrown	1Kg. 3; 4; 5; 6
8–12	Joel and Abia; the people demand a king; Saul ordained; Saul spares Agag	1Kg. 8; 10; 15
12–17	Samuel anoints David; David harps before Saul; David and Goliath; love of Jonathan; envy of Saul; Michol	1Kg. 16; 17; 18
18–22	Attempts on David's life; Saul and David reconciled; death of Samuel; Nabal and Abigail	1Kg. 19; 24; 25
22–26	David spares Saul; flees to Achis; Witch of Endor; suicide of Saul	1Kg. 26; 27; 28; 31

Pages	Event	Bible
26–30	David rescues wives; slays Saul's armorbearer; Joab slays Abner; Baana and Rechab slay Isboseth	1Kg. 30; 2Kg. 1; 2; 3; 4
30–34	David king in Jerusalem with the Ark; Bethsabee; death of Urias; Nathan: "Thou art the same man" (32); David composes Ps. 50; birth of Solomon [Caxton inserts a personal reminiscence of David's penance heard "beyond the sea riding in the company of a noble knight named Sir John Capons" (33)]	2Kg. 5; 6; 11; 12
34–38	Amnon and Thamar; Absalom and Joab: "Who shall grant to me that I may die for thee, my son Absalom, Absalom my son!" (37)	2Kg. 13; 14; 15; 16; 18; 19
38–40	Saba's rebellion; Joab numbers Israel; choices of Gad; Bethsabee intervenes for Solomon over Adonias; death of David	2Kg. 20; 24; 3Kg. 1
40–46	Death of Joab; Solomon's choice of wisdom; judgment between the harlots; Solomon's dominions; the Temple and its accessories: "it passeth my cunning to express and English them" (45)	3Kg. 2; 3; 4; 5
46–51	God appears to Solomon; Hiram's displeasure; Queen of Saba; Solomon's concubines; his death	3Kg. 9; 10; 11
51–52	Roboam: "Is not my finger greater than the back of my father?" (51); idolatry of Jeroboam	3Kg. 12
52–56	Job in Hus; Satan's question: "Doth Job dread God idly?" (53); Job's wife: "forsake thy God and bless him no more, and go die" (55) [Caxton mentions Eliphaz, Baldad, and Sophar (as well as Gregory's *Moralia*) but otherwise skips Job 3–41]	Job 1; 2
56–57	Rebuke of the Comforters; restoration of Job	Job 42
57–60	Tobias's piety; loan to Gabelus; blindness	Tob. 1; 2
60–69	Asmodeus; Raphael serves as guide; Tobias's "hound"; Sara and Tobias; the "great fish" (65); the exorcism	Tob. 3; 4; 5; 6; 7; 8
69–77	Loan repaid; Tobias healed; Raphael reveals himself; prayers; prophecy; death of Tobias	Tob. 9; 10; 11; 12; 13; 14
77–82	Conquests of Nabuchodonosor and Holofernes; resistance of Israel; Achior's summary of Jewish history, his expulsion	Judith 1; 2; 3; 4; 5; 6
82–88	Siege of Bethulia; Judith's stratagem	Judith 7; 8; 9; 10; 11; 12

Pages	Event	Bible
88–93	The feast; Judith beheads Holofernes; victory of the Hebrews; Judith's canticle	Judith 13; 14; 15; 16
94–	The sanctorale begins with Andrew	

Iacob and Iosep JJ

IMEV/S 4172
Manual, 2:382 [3]

1. Oxford, Bodleian Lib. Bodley 652 (*SC* 2306) (1r–10v), later 13th c., 538 lines in couplets. Missing a leaf between folios 6 and 7.
2. Tokyo, Takamiya 32 (3r), mid-15th c., 44-line fragment.

Editions: 1—Napier, *Iacob and Iosep.*
2—Heuser, "Josephlied."
Study: Faverty, "Joseph in Old and Middle English."

The poem is in the ballad tradition, with a conventional narrative situation of a minstrel addressing a riotous audience in order to edify morally.[13] The sin of gluttony is a leitmotif throughout, contrasting a well-regulated golden age from biblical times with the depraved present.

The narrative concentrates on events in the lives of Jacob and Joseph from Gen. 37 (the dream of the sheaves) to Gen. 47 (settlement in Egypt), with additions from Midrashic traditions, probably via Old French versions, notably *La Bible des septs états du monde* and the Bibles of Herman de Valenciennes and Jehan Malkaraume. Episodes are shared with **CM,** the most prominent being how Jacob sees chaff floating down the Nile and thus surmises that food is to be had in Egypt (**CM** lines 4749–92). Napier proposes that this story appeared on the missing leaf from manuscript 1.

Page	Event	Bible
1–20	Noah's flood as a punishment for gluttony	Gen. 6; 7
21–58	Sons of Jacob; Joseph's dream of the sheaves: "ich 7 þi moder 7 þine breþren ek / Moten for fine nede comen to þine fet" (57–58)	Gen. 29; 30; 37:1–10
59–166	Envy of the brothers: "Her comeþ þe metere" (88); Reuben's intervention; Joseph's "kurtel";	Gen. 37: 11–28, 36

13. A later, and more extensive, ballad concerning Isaac, Rebecca, Jacob, Esau, Laban, Rachel, Lia, Joseph, et al., is "The History of Jacob and his Twelue Sonnes," printed by Wynkyn de Worde and John Allde but surviving in no extant manuscript (see J. Collier, *Illustrations of Popular Literature,* vol. 1, selection 3).

Page	Event	Bible
	Joseph sold to two "chapmen" and then to Putiphar	
167–86	The bloody coat: "Euere seide Iacob, 'Iosep is islawe, / Oþer summe luþere deres habbeþ him todrawe' " (179–80)	Gen. 37: 31–35
187–243	Seduction by the Queen of Egypt: "þis Ebrewisse þef, / Of me he wende stille to habben his gome" (227–28)	Gen. 39:1–20
244–277	Dreams of the Butler and the Baker	Gen. 40
278–324	Pharaoh's dream of the fat and lean kine	Gen 41:1–31
[leaf missing]		
325–399	Famine; the brothers journey to Egypt: Joseph recognizes and entertains his brothers: "He goþ into þe boure 7 wepeþ for blisse" (388)	Gen. 42:1–6, 24; 43:16, 24
400–	The golden cup; Joseph demands to see	Gen. 44:1–5;
480	Benjamin; Jacob's lament; Joseph and Benjamin reunited	42:7–15, 36; 43:29
481–538	" 'Ich am,' he seide, 'Iosep, into Egipte þat ȝe solde' " (482); Israel moves to Egypt	Gen. 45:1–28; 46:5–6; 47:6

The Storie of Asneth SA

IMEV/S 367
Manual, 2:383 [4]

1. San Marino, Huntington Lib. EL.26.A.13 (121r–132r), earlier 15th c, 933 lines: prologue of four eight-line stanzas and the remainder in rhyme royal.

Editions: Peck, *Heroic Women,* 1–67; MacCracken, "Storie of Asneth."

The poem uses Gen. 41:45–50, which simply report Joseph's marriage to Aseneth, daughter of Putiphar, as trigger verses upon which to base the apocryphal romance of Aseneth's love for Joseph at first sight, her conversion to Judaism, and her rescue by Benjamin, Simeon and Levi when Pharaoh's sons try to abduct her. The ultimate source is part of the *Old Testament Pseudepigrapha* (see edition by Charlesworth [2:177–247]).

Aseneth's prior scorn of love makes her into a medieval Atalanta and then into an Echo when Joseph does not reciprocate her feelings. Her lament over her past behavior recalls the self-recrimination of Troilus (see lines 236–516). When in fact she "converts" to the religion of love, she also converts to Judaism. The consolation of Aseneth by the angel (lines 412–516)

recalls the Annunciation to Mary by Gabriel. Lydgate in fact compares Mary
to "Assenek off Egypt, of beute pereles" in his poem "To Mary, Queen of
Heaven" (see MacCracken, "Storie of Asneth," 264). Both, of course, are
virgins who marry Josephs.

MacCracken quotes at the bottom of the pages of his edition corresponding passages from Vincent of Beauvais's *Speculum Historiale* book 6, chapters
118–24. Vincent in turn often quotes from Peter Comestor.

The prologue advances the dramatic situation of a *chanson d'aventure,*
wherein the male narrator meets his lady in the countryside and seeks to
serve her by translating the Latin into English.

From Peck, *Heroic Women:*

Lines	Event	Bible
1–32	The narrator's initial reluctance, and eventual willingness, to translate the story at the request of a lady: "As I on hilly halkes logged me late, Beside ny of a Ladi sone was I war; La Bele me desired in Englysh to translate The Latyn of that lady, Asneth Putifar. And I answered, 'Ma Bele, langage I lakke To parforme youre plesir, for yt ys ful straunge That broken tuskes shold wel harde nuttis crakke, And kerve out the kernelis, to glade with yowre graunge; For lame and unlusty now age hath me left; Mi spiritis are spended, I lakke sapience, Dulled I am with dotage, my reson ys me reft, Prived and departed from al eloquence'" (1–12)	
33–51	Pharaoh charges Joseph with the wheat supply	Gen. 41: 46–49
52–104	Effictio of Aseneth; her fortified tower	
105–151	Putiphar arranges a betrothal feast	
152–158	Aseneth balks, recalls Joseph's dubious reputation as a former prisoner and "dreme redere" (157)	Gen. 40; 41
159–209	Aseneth smitten by the sight of Joseph	
210–235	Joseph recalls past trouble with seductive women	Gen. 39:7–9
236–516	Joseph rejects Aseneth, who does penance, is consoled by an angel in the likeness of Joseph (424), and converts to Judaism	
517–593	Honeycomb of Paradise	
594–716	Marriage of Joseph and Aseneth; birth of Manasses and Ephraim	Gen. 41:45, 50–52
717–748	Famine; Jacob and his sons enter Egypt	Gen. 42:1–3

Lines	Event	Bible
749–877	Pharaoh's jealous son conspires against Joseph with Gad and Dan to abduct Aseneth; Benjamin, Simeon, and Levi intervene	Gen. 49:5, 17, 19, 22–23, 27
878–884	Death of Joseph after a forty-eight-year reign; succeeded by Pharaoh's younger son	
885–933	Epilogue on the rapacity of death; eulogy of the narrator's lady	

The Fyve Wyles of King Pharao KP

Manual, 7:2365 [222]
Jolliffe K.7.(a)(b)

1. Oxford, Bodleian Lib. Douce 15 (*SC* 21589) (77v–141r), early 15th c.
2. Oxford, Bodleian Lib. Douce 372 (*SC* 21947) (160v–163v; missing one leaf after 162v), early 15th c.
3. Cambridge, Univ. Lib. Ff.6.33 (67v–88r), mid-15th c.
4. Cambridge, Univ. Lib. Gg.6.26 (104r–105r), ca. 1500, atelous.
5. London, BL Add. 35298 (165r–167r), later 15th c.
6. London, BL Harley 1197 (75r–76v), early 15th c., atelous.
7. London, BL Harley 2388 (7v–20r), later 15th c.
8. London, BL Harley 4775 (262r–v), mid-15th c., atelous.
9. London, Lambeth Palace 72 (431r–437r), later 15th c.
10. London, BL Egerton 876 (320r–v), atelous, very faded.

Raymo provides a summary in his *Manual* entry. Edition in progress by Morey.

This work appears in manuscript anthologies, most often with **LAE** and with the English prose translation known as the *Gilte Legend* (1483) linked to Jehan de Vignai's *Légende dorée* (ca. 1333). General temptations by the Devil of mankind to sin are each connected to the conditions imposed by Pharaoh on the Israelites and his subsequent refusals to honor those conditions. There is extensive moralizing throughout.

The following verses from Exodus appear (from the prologue in manuscript 7, fols. 7v–8v):

This ys þe first he granted þat goddis peple shuld go do sacrefice to here god but to dwelle still in þe londe of egypte (Ex. 8:25)

The secunde wyle ys þat king pharao graunted goddis peple to go oute of his londe 7 make sacrefice to god so þey ȝedon not fer oute þerof. (Ex. 9:27–28)

The thrid wyle ys that kyng pharao granted to goddis peple to go fer
oute of his lond 7 do sacrefice to her gode so that þey lefton her
children in þe lond of egipt (Ex. 10:9–11)

The fourþe wyle þat king pharao graunted goddis peple to go fer oute
of Egypt 7 make sacrefice to her god 7 take her childeren wiþ hem. So
þat þey leften her shepe 7 alle her bestis in þat lond of Egypte (Ex.
10:24–26)

The fifthe wyle ys þat king pharao grauntede þat goddis peple shuld go
fer oute of Egipte 7 do sacrefice to her god 7 take wiþ hem her children
7 her bestes so þat þey spaken good of him 7 of his lond (Ex. 12:31–32)

The Ten Commandments: Ex. 20:1–17, Deut. 5:1–22 TC

The Ten Commandments are ubiquitous in Middle English literature,
in independent versions, various historiated bibles, lectionaries, commentaries, primers, confession manuals, and catechisms (e.g., *Handlyng Synne,
Ayenbite of Inwyt, Lay Folks Catechism*). See *Manual,* 7:2258 [4], 7:2273 [24]
and 7:2300 [88].

The number of manuscripts and versions is prodigious. The following list
covers only those treatments which appear in print; nevertheless it is surely
incomplete and a thorough study is needed. Kellogg and Talbert ("Wyclifite
Pater Noster") and A. Martin ("Middle English Versions") provide a general
orientation. Versions which appear in other works of biblical literature are
noted in their respective contexts, and can be located through the index.

Verse Versions
Manual, 7:2284 [42]
IMEV 176
Five couplets as lines 147–56 of the 168-line "Proverbs of Wisdom"

1. Oxford, Bodleian Lib. Rawlinson poet. f.32 (*SC* 14526) (55r).

Edition: 1—Zupitza, "Prouerbis," 247.

Audelay's "Song of the Decalogue"
IMEV 304

1. Oxford, Bodleian Lib. Douce 302 (*SC* 21876) (27v, col. 2), twenty-five
lines with refrain.

Editions: Audelay, *Poems,* 181; Greene, *Early English Carols,* #324.

IMEV 744

1. London, BL Harley 665 (90r), forty-six lines in quatrains, abab.
2. London, Lambeth Palace 853 (p. 47).

Editions: 1—Zupitza, "Zwei Umschreibungen der Zehn Gebote," 45–46.
2—Furnivall, *Hymns to the Virgin,* 104–5. See *IMEV* 1379 for the 104-line exposition which follows this version, also printed by Furnivall.

Versions in the *Speculum Christiani* (14th c.)
IMEV 1111
IMEV/S 3687
IMEV/S 1491

Forty-two MSS, including:

1. Oxford, Bodleian Lib. Ashmole 61 (*SC* 6922) (16v–17r, 22v), fifty-six lines in quatrains abab, with unique opening stanza and three final stanzas.
2. Oxford, Bodleian Lib. Bodley 89 (*SC* 1886) (3r–6v) missing two stanzas.
3. London, BL Harley 6580 (6r–12v) with extensive patristic commentary.
4. London, BL Lansdowne 344 (4v).

Editions: 1—Zupitza, "Zwei Umschreibungen der Zehn Gebote," 46–48.
2—C. Brown, "Towneley."
3 and 4—Holmstedt, *Speculum Christiani,* 16–38.
Facsimile: 1—Boffey and Thompson, "Anthologies and Miscellanies," 229 (16v–17r).

IMEV/S 1129
These versions, independent of each other, range in length from ten to sixteen lines, in couplets:

1. Oxford, New College 88 (490v), 13th c.
2. Cambridge, Emmanuel College 27 (111v), 13th c. [listed separately at *IMEV* 2694]
3. Cambridge, Trinity College 323 (B.14.39) (29r), 13th c.
4. London, BL Harley 1704 (48v–49r), 15th c.
5. London, BL Harley 2391 (134r), 15th c.
6. London, BL Royal 8.F.vii (45v), 15th c.
7. Edinburgh, National Lib. of Scotland Advocates 18.7.21 (128v), ca. 1375.
8. Oxford, Bodleian Lib.Bodley 841 (*SC* 8714) (ii v), 15th c.

Editions: 1 through 8—Reichl, *Religiöse Dichtung,* 334–37.
   1 and 3—C. Brown, *English Lyrics XIIIth Century,* 181–82, 33.
   4—Horstmann, *Yorkshire Writers,* 1:111
   7—E. Wilson, *Index,* 56.

IMEV/S 1379
104 lines in eight-line stanzas, ababbcbc

   1. Oxford, Bodleian Lib., Eng. poet. a.1 (Vernon) (408v col.b), ca. 1390.
   2. Cambridge, Magdalene College Pepys 1584 (104v–105r), 15th c.
   3. London, BL Harley 78 (86r), missing lines 1–7, also atelous.
   4. London, BL Add. 22283 (Simeon) (103r, col. 1), ca. 1400.
   5. London, Lambeth Palace 853 (p. 49).
   6. Windsor, St. George's Chapel E.I.I (29r).

Editions: 1—Furnivall, *Minor Poems,* 680–83, C. Brown, *Religious Lyrics XIVth Century,* 148–51.
   1 and 5—Furnivall, *Hymns to the Virgin,* 106–13.
Facsimile: 1—Doyle, *Vernon Manuscript.*

IMEV 1602
Fourteen couplets

   1. Oxford, Bodleian Lib., Eng. poet. a.1 (Vernon) (116r, col. 1), ca. 1390
   2. London, BL Add. 37787 (159r–160r)

Editions: 1—Horstmann, *Minor Poems,* 36.
   2—Baugh, *Worcestershire Miscellany,* 148.
Facsimile: 1—Doyle, *Vernon Manuscript.*

IMEV 2286

   1. Cambridge, Trinity College 43 (B.1.45) (42r), five couplets.

Editions: Förster, "Kleine Mitteilungen," 302–3; C. Brown, *English Lyrics XIIIth Century,* 129.

IMEV 2291

   1. Cambridge, Emmanuel College 27 (162r, col. 2), six couplets.

Edition: C. Brown, *English Lyrics XIIIth Century,* 129.

"Homily on the Ten Commandments"
IMEV 2344

1. London, BL Harley 913 (31v), twenty quatrains abab. Lines 17–40 enumerate the commandments themselves.

Editions: Furnivall, *Political, Religious, and Love Poems,* 15–16; Mätzner, *Altenglische Sprachproben,* 1:128; Heuser, *Kildare-Gedichte,* 114–16.

IMEV/S 3254
As part of the *Fasciculus Morum.* Ten lines in couplets.

Eleven MSS, including:

1. Oxford, Bodleian Lib. Bodley 410 (*SC* 2305) (21v).
2. Worcester, Cathedral Lib. F.19 (175r).
3. London, Gray's Inn 15 (72v), 15th c.
4. Oxford, Bodleian Lib. Rawlinson C.670 (*SC* 12514) (39r).

Editions: 1—Little, *Studies in English Franciscan History,* 150.
2—J. Wilson, "Worcester," 263–64.
4—Wenzel, *Verses in Sermons,* 155–57 (text similar to manuscript 3).

This version omits the second commandment (graven images), and splits the tenth.

William of Shoreham's version
IMEV 3417

1. London, BL Add. 17376 (185v), forty-three eight-line stanzas xaxaxaxa.

Editions: William of Shoreham, *Poems,* ed. Konrath, 86–97; William of Shoreham, *Religious Poems,* ed. Wright, 90–101.

"A Confession of Breaking the Ten Commandments"
IMEV 3483

1. Oxford, Bodleian Lib. Rawlinson liturg. e.7 (*SC* 15839) (14r), seven quatrains, abab

Edition: C. Brown, *Religious Lyrics XVth Century,* 211–12.

IMEV 3684
Five couplets.

1. Oxford, Univ. College 96 (109v).
2. Cambridge, Univ. Lib. Ff.6.15 (21r).

Editions: 1—C. Brown, *English Lyrics XIIIth Century,* 219–20.
2—Morris, *Old English Miscellany,* 200.

IMEV/S 3685
Twenty-four lines in couplets.
Ten MSS, including:

1. Cambridge, Univ. Lib. Ff.2.38 (32r).
2. Cambridge, Sidney Sussex College 55 (3v).
3. London, BL Harley 1706 (205r).

Editions: 2—Holmstedt, *Speculum Christiani,* lxxiv–lxxv.
   3—Maskell, *Monumenta,* 3:2541; Heuser, *Kildare-Gedichte,* 205
Facsimile: 1—McSparran and Robinson, *Cambridge University Library MS Ff.
   2.38.*

IMEV 37311

1. Salisbury, Cathedral Lib. 126 (5r), five couplets.

Edition: E. Thompson, "Scraps" (the seven deadly sins precede and the
   Creed follows; Thompson also prints a **PN** from Salisbury, Cathedral
   Lib. 82 [271v]).

Other versions, to my knowledge unprinted: *IMEV* 804, 1393, 2000, 2692,
3254, 3345, 3686, 3689, and *IMEV/S* 1856.5, 3254, 3686, 3689.5
   See also *IMEV/S* 2695.5 for a ten-line version in a copy of Caxton's *Royal
Book* (1486), written in a sixteenth-century hand.

Prose Versions
Exposition in *Dives et Pauper*
IPMEP 156
Manual, 7:2287 [45]

Twelve MSS and three early prints, including:

1. Glasgow, Univ. Lib. Hunterian 270 (11r–270v), mid-15th c.

Edition: Barnum, *Dives and Pauper.*

Expositions in *Book of Vices and Virtues* and *Ayenbite of Inwyt* (both translations
of the *Somme le Roi*)
IPMEP 48, 55, 668, 824
Manual, 7:2284 [43]

1. London, BL Add. 22283 (Simeon) (92r–93r), ca. 1400.
2. San Marino, Huntington Lib. HM 147 (1r–3r).
3. Edinburgh, Univ. Lib. 93 (4r–10v).
4. London, BL Arundel 57 (1r–2v), 1340.

Editions: 1—Francis, *Book of Vices and Virtues,* 316–33.
  2—Francis, *Book of Vices and Virtues,* 1–6.
  3—C. Martin, "Edinburgh University Library Manuscript 93."
  4—Morris, *Dan Michel's Ayenbite,* 5–11.

These texts are linked to the Wycliffite version printed by Arnold in Wyclif, *Select Works,* 3:82–92 (*IPMEP* 49). There is frequent quotation of other biblical verses beyond the Ten Commandments.

IPMEP 49

  1. York Minster XVI.L.12, 15th c.
  2. London, Lambeth Palace 408 (6v–12r), 15th c. (version in *Lay Folks Catechism*).
  3. New York, Pierpont Morgan Lib. 861 (1r–3v), mid-15th c.
  4. Manchester, John Rylands Lib. English 85 (2v–9r).
  5. Oxford, Bodleian Lib. Bodley 789 (*SC* 2643) (108r), 15th c.

Editions: 1 and 2—Simmons and Nolloth, *Lay Folks Catechism,* 33–57 (odd pages only), manuscript 2 with variants from manuscript 1.
  3—Bühler, "Middle English Texts of Morgan 861," 688–92.
  4—Kellogg and Talbert, "Wyclifite *Pater Noster,*" 371–76.
  5—Wyclif, *Select Works,* 3:82–92.

IPMEP 280

  1. Cambridge, Univ. Lib. Hh.3.13 (119r), later 15th c.

Edition: Zupitza, "Was jedermann wissen."

John Lacy's Treatise on the Ten Commandments
IPMEP 650
Manual, 7:2286 [44]

  1. Oxford, St John's College 94 (119r–126r), earlier 15th c.

Edition: Royster, "Middle English Treatise," 9–35.

Richard Rolle's Treatise on the Ten Commandments
IPMEP 667

  1. Lincoln, Cathedral Lib. 91 (Lincoln Thornton) (195v–196r).
  2. Oxford, Bodleian Lib. Hatton 12 (*SC* 4127) (209v–211v), late 14th c.

Editions: 1—Rolle, *English Prose Treatises,* 10–12; Mätzner, *Altengische Sprachproben,* 1:part 2, 128–30; Horstmann, *Yorkshire Writers,* 1:195–96.
Facsimile: 1—Brewer and Owen, *Thornton Manuscript.*

Pety Job (*Lessons of the Dirige*) **PJ**

There are three "Pety Jobs" ("little Jobs") in Middle English: one in prose and two in verse. They were used in the Office of the Dead (Dirige, so called from the first word in the antiphon [Ps. 5:9]) which consists of nine lessons from the book of Job: (1) 7:16–21, (2) 10:1–7, (3) 10:8–12, (4) 13:23–28, (5) 14:1–6, (6) 14:13–16, (7) 17:1–3, 11–15, (8) 19:20–27, (9) 10:18–22. Each version contains these verses.

The Dirige also appeared in Middle English primers (see Littlehales, *Prymer or Lay Folks Prayer Book*), though many primer readings resemble the later Wycliffite version.

These "Pety Jobs" and the primers were the primary medium for transmitting at least part of the Job story to a lay audience. The following quotation, from a collection of English guild ordinances, provides a perspective on the use of this material whenever a guild member died: "Ande at ye Dirige, euery brother and sister yat is letterede shul seyn, for ye soule of ye dede, placebo and dirige, in ye place whar he shul comen to-geder; and euery brother and sister yat bene nought letterede, shul seyn for ye soule of ye dede, xx. sythes, ye pater noster, wᵗ Aue maria."[14] This instance is particularly remarkable since this was not a craft but a social guild with no particular religious program and since it was obviously not considered unusual for either a male or female member to know at least the Placebo (Ps. 114:9) and Dirige.

One would assume that the graphic narrative in the book of Job, especially the folktale frame at the beginning and end, as well as the universal appeal of the suffering individual, would be well-suited to dramatization. God's wager with the Devil and the debate with the three comforters are always left out, however, presumably because of the troubling implications for God's character and the density of the debate. Guyart Desmoulins, who in his *Bible Historiale* translated the *Historia Scholastica* into French and who was a very important popularizer of vernacular biblical materials, simply inserts a "Pety Job" into his narrative (Comestor completely omits the story). Guyart's appropriation is especially interesting for the reasons he gives for omitting Job's debate with the three comforters: "Et ces parolles quil dirent les vns auz autres sont de sy fort latin et plaines de sy grant mistere que nulz nen peut le mistere entendre sil nest trop grans clers de diunite [/] Et pour ce les trespasseray Iou chy. Car nulz ne les deuroit oser translater [/] Car laie gent y pourroient errer" ("And these words which the ones speak to the

---

14. Smith and Smith, *English Gilds,* 20. This is the ordinance presented in 1389 to Richard II by the Guild of St. Katherine, Norwich.

others are of such difficult Latin and full of such great mystery that no one is able to understand the mystery unless he is a very learned clerk of divinity. And for that reason I omit them here. For no one ought to dare to translate them for here lay folk may err") (McGerr, "Guyart Desmoulins," 217). Guyart, like the authors of "Pety Jobs" who dealt with the book before him, feared committing some theological error and leading the "laie gent" astray. The story was more important than theological disputation, which obviously was shunned.

The association of these Job lessons with the Last Judgment versicles and the Office of the Dead seems to derive from Jerome's citation of Job 19:25, "Scio enim quod Redemptor meus vivit," and his comment: "Quid hac prophetia manifestius? Nullus tam aperte post Christum, quam iste ante Christum de resurrectione loquitur. Vult verba sua in perpetuum durare" ("What is more clear than this prophecy? Nothing is spoken concerning the resurrection so plainly after Christ as this before Christ. He wishes his words to last forever") (*Contra Johannem Hierosolymitanum*, PL 23.382). Apparently the hope of resurrection, appearing in the midst of Job's suffering, was considered to be particularly appropriate in the context of individual bereavement. The Last Judgment versicles, which end with the Canticle on the Harrowing of Hell, convey the hope of general resurrection. Over time this network of texts became the Office for the Dead, and they have indeed proven to be durable.

For the Job legend in the Middle Ages, see Besserman, *Legend of Job*, especially 56–65. For the Latin text of the Dirige see Procter and Wordsworth, *Breviarium*, 2:271–79.

IPMEP 532
Manual, 2:384 [8]

1. London, BL Add. 39574 (Wheatley) (45r–51r), early 15th c.

Edition: Day, *Wheatley Manuscript*, 59–64.

This text uses the later Wycliffite version in consultation with the Latin. It served as the basis for what Kail (*"Petty Job"*) prints as his first versification (see below), and both incorporate the responsories, versicles, and Canticle of the Last Judgment (as does Sarum).

Page	Illustrative quotations	Bible
59	"How long sparist þou not me, ne suffrist þat I swolewe my spotil?"	Job 7:19
60	"Ne hast þou softid me as mylk and cruddist me as chese?"	Job 10:10
63	"I woot forsoþe þat myn aȝenbier lyueþ"	Job 19:25

IMEV 251
Manual, 2:384 [7]

    1. Oxford, Bodleian Lib. Digby 102 (*SC* 1703) (124v–27v), 15th c., 418
    lines in stanzas rhyming abababab. Based on the prose version.

Edition: Kail, *"Petty Job,"* 107–20.

Lines	Illustrative quotations	Bible
49–50	"Wheþer þyn eyȝen ben fleschlye, / Or þou seest as man shal see?"	Job 10:4
177, 182	"Man geth out as don floures . . . / And fleeþ as shadow"	Job 14:2

IMEV/S 1854
Manual, 2:383 [6]

    1. Oxford, Bodleian Lib. Douce 322 (*SC* 21896) (10r–15r), 15th c., 684
    lines in stanzas rhyming abababbcbc. The rhyme scheme and
    meter resemble those in *Pearl* (see Gordon's edition, p. 87).
    2. Cambridge, Univ. Lib. Ff.2.38 (6r–10r), late 15th c.
    3. Cambridge, Magdalene College Pepys 1584 (48r–62r), 15th c.
    4. Cambridge, Trinity College 601 (38r–50v), 15th c.
    5. London, BL Harley 1706 (11r–15v), late 15th c.

Editions: 1—Kail, *"Petty Job,"* 120–43; Fein, *Moral Love Songs,* 289–359.
    5—Horstmann, *Yorkshire Writers,* 2:380–9, with variants from 1 and 2.
Facsimile: 2—McSparran and Robinson, *Cambridge University Library MS
    Ff.2.38.*

Lines	Illustrative quotation	Bible
505–508	"To roten erthe, ryght thus sayde I, / 'Thou are my fader of whom I cam,' / And vnto wormes sekurly, / 'Thow art my moder, thy son I am' "	Job 17:14

Metrical Life of Job **MLJ**

IMEV/S 2208
Manual, 2:384 [9]

    MLJ is not in the Pety Job tradition and covers only the "folktale frame"
of the story (chapters 1, 2, and 42). It is an independent production with
some apocryphal accretions.

    1. San Marino, Huntington Lib. HM 140 (93v–96v), 15th c., 182 lines in
    stanzas rhyming ababbcc.

Editions: Garmonsway and Raymo, "Metrical Life of Job"; MacCracken, "Lydgatiana I."

Illustrations may have once accompanied the text: "Here, lo, holy Iob his children doth sanctifie" (15); "Lo, here, the envy of this serpent and devyll Sathan" (29), and cf. lines 26, 36, 113, 162.

From Garmonsway and Raymo:

Lines	Events	Bible
1–84	Job in Hus: "God axed of hym or he had considered His man / And servant Iob" (31–32; Job 1:8) Persecution of Job; his patience: "Nakyd owte of the wombe of my moder I entrid, / Nakyd unto the erthe I shall be revertid" (75–76; Job 1:21)	Job 1
85–112	Job's wife: "Corse thi God and dye than!" (94; Job 2:9) The "frendes of Iob" (106)	Job 2
113–182	God rebukes the comforters, restores Job: "And, by processe of yeres and succession, / X children he had by his wyfe agayne" (169–70; Job 42:13)	Job 42

 **II.B** *The Psalter*

General Note on Medieval Psalters

The Psalter in the Middle Ages was the single most important and influential biblical book for the following reasons:

First, it served as a digest of biblical themes, moralizations, and stories, especially when read typologically. As Richard Rolle writes in the prologue to **RPs,** "it is perfeccioun of dyuyne pagyne, for it contenys all that other bokes draghes langly, that is, the lare of the ald testament & of the new" (Bramley, *Psalter of David,* 4).

Second, given the Davidic narrative voice and dramatic situation of a sinner before God, the Psalms assumed important functions in the penitential program of individuals. Apocalyptic preoccupations, and the fear of sudden death, led to a virtual industry revolving around the confessional. The primary activity of the clergy, as sermon and other biblical literatures testify, was ensuring the salvation of the communicant at his or her end. John Mirk's *Instructions for Parish Priests,* in the only direct injunction to read the Bible, explicitly links reading the Psalter and the Last Judgment: "ȝerne thow moste thy sawtere rede, / And of the day of dome haue drede" (Mirk, *Instructions,* lines 53–54).

Third, sections 9 through 18 of the Benedictine rule require memorization and weekly recitation. The Northern Metrical Version of the Rule compresses this regimen into a remarkable three lines: "Mor how þai sal serues do, / Nedes not her to tel þam to; / Þai know þer salmes & ilka verse" (Kock, *Rule of St. Benet,* 79, lines 1137–39).

The Psalter in Middle English takes a variety of forms:

Three complete versions, one in verse (**SPs**) and two in prose (**MPPs**
   and **RPs**).
The seven Penitential Psalms (in their usual order of appearance,
   Psalms 31, 129, 101, 142, 6, 37, and 50). See **RMPs** and **TBPs.**
The fifteen gradual psalms (119, 122, 127, 129, 130, 133, 132, 125, 121,
   120, 131, 126, 123, 124, and 128).
Psalms found in Primers (**PPs**).
Abbreviated Psalters (**JPs** and **BPs**).
Paraphrases and translations of individual psalms, notably Psalm 50
   (**MPs**) and those by John Lydgate (**LPs**).

For helpful studies of the Psalms in the Middle Ages and Renaissance, see
van Deusen, *Place of the Psalms,* and Zim, *English Metrical Psalms.*

NOTE ON LATIN PSALTER VERSIONS

The Psalter exists in four distinct Latin versions:

The Vetus Latina (Old Latin): translated from the Septuagint.
The Roman: traditionally linked to Jerome, from the Septuagint. This
   version was used by the church in Rome and Italy until the sixteenth
   century.
The Gallican: by Jerome (ca. 392), another revision based on the
   Septuagint, in use primarily in Gaul. This is the version commonly
   found in Vulgates.
The Hebraicum: Jerome's final version (ca. 400), from Hebrew. Not
   used in divine service, though often printed with the other
   Hieronymian versions.

The so-called *Our Lady's Psalter* does not, in fact, contain any psalm verses.
It was "prescribed for use by illiterate persons [and] consisted of a rosary
of fifty *Aves* and five *Pater Nosters* interspersed, and one *Credo*" (Wordsworth
and Littlehales, *Service-Books,* 255). See also "How Our Lady's Psalter Was
Founded," in Whiteford, *Myracles,* 74–75.

NOTE ON PSALTER NUMBERING

All Psalm numbers refer to the Vulgate, which differs from the numbering in the Authorized Version since the former is based on the Septuagint
(Greek) and the latter is based on the Massoretic text (Hebrew). Psalms 1–8
and 148–50 correspond in both versions, but elsewhere numbering differs:

Vulgate 9 = AV 9–10 (breaking at verse 20); Vulgate 10–112 = AV 11–113; Vulgate 113 = AV 114–15 (breaking at verse 8); Vulgate 114–15 (breaking at verse 9) = AV 116; Vulgate 116–45 = AV 117–46; Vulgate 146–7 (breaking at verse 11) = AV 147.

There are also minor differences in the numeration of the verses, notably in Psalms 9 and 113.

Chapter numbers were assigned to the Bible by Stephen Langton in the early thirteenth century; verses were not designated until the Parisian printer Robert Estienne ("Stephanus") did so in the 1560s.

Some medieval psalters exhibit a threefold division, marked by elaborate initials for Psalms 1, 51, and 101. More common is an eightfold division, again marked by initials. Each subset is known as a "nocturn"; there are, of course, many variations in recitation depending on the propers and ordinaries of particular services. See Wordsworth and Littlehales, *Service-Books,* 78–79, 108–16.

Psalms	Initialized verse	Read on
1–25	"Beatus vir"	Sundays
26–37	"Dominus illuminatio"	Mondays
38–51	"Dixi, custodiam"	Tuesdays
52–67	"Dixit insipiens"	Wednesdays
68–79	"Salvum me fac"	Thursdays
80–96	"Exultate Deo"	Fridays
97–108	"Cantate Domino"	Saturdays
109–50	"Dixit Dominus"	Spread over days of the week at Evensong

Complete Translations

Surtees Psalter **SPs**

IMEV 3103
Manual, 2:385 [10]

1. Oxford, Bodleian Lib. Bodley 425 (*SC* 2325) (1r–66r, 72r–93r), mid-14th c., missing Psalms 1–15.
2. Oxford, Bodleian Lib. Bodley 921 (*SC* 3027) (1r–101r), mid-14th c., **BVP** follows.
3. Cambridge, Corpus Christi College 278 (1r–90r), early 14th c.
4. London, BL Cotton Vespasian D.vii (1r–104r), late 13th c.
5. London, BL Egerton 614 (2r–99r), late 13th c.
6. London, BL Harley 1770 (158r–241r), late 13th c.

Editions: 4—J. Stevenson, *Psalter;* Horstmann, *Yorkshire Writers,* 2:129–273. Both editions include variants from 5 and 6.

This anonymous translation of the Psalms (ca. 1250–1300), in couplets and some quatrains (abab), may derive, like Rolle's translation, from an earlier English gloss on a Latin Psalter (see Everett, "Prose Psalter," 337, and Allen, *Writings Ascribed,* 1). It is so called because it first appeared in the publications of the Surtees Society.

Midland Prose Psalter MPPs

IPMEP 114
Manual, 2:385 [11]

1. Cambridge, Magdalene College Pepys 2498 (pp. 263–370), ca. 1400.
2. London, BL Add. 17376 (1r–149r), ca. 1350.
3. Dublin, Trinity College 69 (A.4.4) (1r–55r), ca. 1400

Edition: 2—Bülbring, *Prose Psalter,* with variants from 3.

This anonymous Psalter may not be the earliest complete English prose Psalter, as Bülbring's title claims, since it is contemporaneous with **RPs**. It is a complete translation, with glosses translated from a French glossed version of the Psalter.

An "Hours of the Cross" by William of Shoreham (**HCS**) appears in manuscript 2, though Bülbring (viii) rejects his authorship of **MPPs**.

Richard Rolle's Psalter and Commentary RPs

IPMEP 271
IMEV/S 3576
Manual, 2:386 [12] and 9:3055 [2]

38 MSS, including:

1. Oxford, Univ. College 64 (6r–137v), 15th c.
2. Oxford, Bodleian Lib. Laud Misc. 286 (*SC* 1151) (1r–163v), 15th c. Contains 120-line verse prologue.
3. Cambridge, Sidney Sussex College 89 (1r–186v), 15th c.

Edition: 1—Rolle, *Psalter of David,* collated with 2 and 3.
Modernization: Rolle, *Penitential Psalms,* penitential psalms only (Ps. 6, 31, 37, 50, 101, 129, 142).

Studies: Alford, "Biblical *Imitatio*" and "Rolle's English Psalter"; Everett, "Prose Psalter," where she prints extracts from **RPs, MPPs,** and **SPs.**

For a discussion of the manuscripts, see Allen, *Writings Ascribed,* 171–76. Classifying the manuscripts is difficult because of the appropriation of Rolle's work by the Lollards, called by Kuczynski a "scandal" (*Prophetic Song,* 12–17, 165–88). See also Hudson, *Premature Reformation,* 27–29.

Richard Rolle (d. 1349) produced his English Psalter ca. 1340 for his friend Margaret Kirkby, who later became an anchoress:

> But for the Psalms ben full darke in many a place who wol take hede,
> And the sentence is full merke—who so wol rede,
> It needeth exposicyon written wel with cunning honde
> To strive toward devocyon & hit the better understonde.
> Therfore a worthy holy man called Rychard Hampole
> Whome the Lord that all can lered lelely on his scole,
> Gloȝed the sauter that sues here in English tong sykerly,
> At a worthy recluse prayer call'd Dame Marget Kirkby.
> (from manuscript 2, in Rolle, *English Prose Treatises,* vii)

Rolle includes the Latin text, from a Gallican Psalter with some Old Latin readings (see Allen, *English Writings,* 122), and supplements the translation with an extensive commentary taken from Peter Lombard's "great gloss" on the Psalter (*Magna Glossatura;* also known as his schoolroom *catena*). Allen suggests that a "partially modernized form of the Old English glosses" (1) may have been used by Rolle and by the author of **SPs.**

The introduction emphasizes how much spiritual comfort and instruction may be derived from reading the Psalms, and how a translation thus serves the needs of the devout who do not know Latin: "In þis werk I seke no straunge Inglis, bot lightest and comunest and swilke þat es mast like vnto þe Latin, so þat þei þat knawes noght Latyn, be þe Inglis may cum tille many Latyn wordes. In þe translacioun I folow þe letter als mekil als I may, and þare I fynde na propir Inglys I folow þe witte of þe worde" (Allen, *English Writings,* 7). Here Rolle encounters the first hurdle of any translator—whether to translate according to the letter or to the sense. Rolle takes a middle road; later Rolle comments on Ps. 17:13 that "Her may we see that nan sould be swa hardy to translate or expound haly writ bot if he felid the haly gast in him. that is makere of haly writ. for soen sall he erre that is noght led with him" (Rolle, *Psalter of David,* 61).

Rolle also suggests that this translation is to be used as a trot for the Latin. The devout student will by close study "cum tille" at least some Latin vocabulary. Vernacular materials were acceptable for devotional purposes, but they were not to supplant the Latin itself. Latin and vernacular religious practice coexisted happily into the fifteenth century, when English manuscript production was at a high point. Rolle's Psalter—especially given the number of extant manuscripts—is a particularly significant example of how vigorous vernacular bibical literature could be in England.

Penitential Psalms

Two names are associated with these Psalms: Richard Maidstone and Thomas Brampton. Their Psalters are independent of each other, and Brampton's work exists in two versions. Both devote eight lines of paraphrase to each psalm verse, with alliteration and rhyme, in the manner of theme and variations. This format allows room for moralizations and for the addition of New Testament material, such as explanations of the relevance of Christ's sacrifice and of the Last Judgment.

An extensive English commentary from French on these Psalms made by Dame Eleanor Hull in the mid-fifteenth century (*Manual*, 2:389 [20]) contains numerous Latin quotations with translations. See Barratt, *Seven Psalms* for an edition of the unique manuscript, Cambridge, Univ. Lib. Kk.1.6 (2r–147r), especially the index of biblical references on pp. 321–26. The manuscript contains Lydgate's *Cristes Passioun* (**CP**), along with several other meditations on the Passion.

Order of the Penitential Psalms: 6 (anger), 31 (pride), 37 (gluttony), 50 (lust), 101 (covetousness), 129 (envy), 142 (sloth).

Richard Maidstone's *Penitential Psalms* **RMPs**

IMEV/S 1961, 3755
Manual, 2:388 [18]

27 MSS (see Maidstone, *Penitential Psalms*, for descriptions and analysis) including:

1. Oxford, Bodleian Lib. Rawlinson A.389 (*SC* 11272) (13r–20v), late 14th c., 952 lines.
2. London, BL Add. 39574 (Wheatley) (15v–45r), early 15th c., 936 lines (missing lines 1–8, 289–96).
3. New York, Pierpont Morgan Lib. 99 (92r–132r), mid-15th c.
4. Oxford, Bodleian Lib. Digby 18 (*SC* 1619) (38r–64v), mid-15th c.
5. Oxford, Bodleian Lib. Digby 102 (*SC* 1703) (128r–135r), early 15th c.
6. London, BL Royal 17.C.xvii (83r–90r), early 15th c.

IMEV/S 2157, Psalm 50 only

7. Oxford, Bodleian Lib. Eng. poet. a. 1 (Vernon) (114r), ca. 1390, the last 137 lines of Psalm 50 (lines 407–544 in Edden's ed. of Maidstone).
8. London, BL Add. 10036 (96v–100r), early 15th c., 160 lines.
9. Oxford, Bodleian Lib. Douce 141 (*SC* 21715) (145v–148r), early 15th c., 160 lines.
10. Cambridge, Univ. Lib. Dd.1.1 (226r–228r), ca. 1400.

Editions: 1—Maidstone, *Penitential Psalms.*
2—Day, *Wheatley Manuscript,* 19–59.
3—F. S. Ellis, *Psalmi Penitentiales.*
4—Adler and Kaluza, "Studien," who misattribute the poem to Rolle (see Allen, *Writings Ascribed,* 371).
7—Horstmann, *Minor Poems,* 12–16.
8—Furnivall, *Political, Religious, and Love Poems,* (1866) 251–56, (1903) 279–85.
9—Kreuzer, "Richard Maidstone's Version"; Rogers, "Richard Maidstone's Version," 107–12.
Facsimile: 7—Doyle, *Vernon Manuscript.*
Studies: Edden, "Richard Maidstone's *Penitential Psalms*"; Kuczynski, *Prophetic Song,* 124–35.

Maidstone (d. 1396) was a Carmelite friar and the confessor of John of Gaunt. His Penitential Psalms usually take the form of eight-line stanzas ryhming abababab, with a pause after line four. The Latin psalm verse precedes the eight-line paraphrase and meditation, with roughly one stanza for each verse, though some verses are split between two stanzas. The proportion of Latin verses to English stanzas in manuscript 2 is typical of the collection. The whole of each Psalm is paraphrased (excluding the introductory verse identifying the theme or occasion of the Psalm).

stanzas 1–11	Ps. 6:2–11
stanzas 12–25	Ps. 31:1–11
stanzas 26–48	Ps. 37:2–23
stanzas 49–68	Ps. 50:3–21
stanzas 69–97	Ps. 101:2–29
stanzas 98–105	Ps. 129:1–8
stanzas 106–19	Ps. 142:1–12

In Vernon (manuscript 7), the previous eight leaves are missing. They must have contained the end of **EE** and the beginning of Psalm 50. Several manuscripts (see *IMEV* 3755) begin with the following prologue:

To Goddes worsheppe þat [dere vs] bouȝte
To whom we owen to make oure moon
Of oure synnes þat we haue wrouȝte
In ȝouþe and elde, wel many oon;
Þe seuen salmes are þourȝe souȝte
In shame of alle oure goostly foon,
And in Englisshe þei ben brouȝte
[For synne in man to be fordon].

Maidstone, *Penitential Psalms*, 47

The characteristic feature of Maidstone's paraphrase is the connection of various Psalm verses to the life of Christ, especially the Passion.

Stanza	Quotations/Events	Bible
5	"For fowle with fether ne fysch with fynne / Is noon vnstedfaster þanne I"	
9	"curteys Kyng, to the I calle, / Be noght vengeable, put vp thy swerde! / In heuen when thow holdist halle, / Lat me noght be ther-oute sperde!"	Ps. 6:2–6
11	Enemies of mankind: "The world, the feend, the flesch"	1John 2:16
15–16	Passion imagery: "thornes"; "When blood oute of thy hert[e] sprong"	
30	Recollection of the raising of Lazarus, "The brothir of Marthe and Mary"	Ps. 37:6; John 11
41	Intercession of Mary	Ps. 37:16
45	Prayer to "Goddys Lombe, þat Iudas solde / For thritty pens vnrightfully"	Ps. 37:20
54	"Byholde, in synne I was conceyued / Of my moder, as men ere [a]lle; / . . . Bot sithen thy flesch, Lord, was perceyued, / Where it was leyd ful streyt in stall, / Was ther noon synful man deceyued, / That wolde on[to] thi mercy calle"	Ps. 50:7; Luke 2:7
55	Mystery of the Incarnation: "Two kyndes been to-gedir knytte: / [Thral is fre and knave is knyght], / God is man, as gospel writte"	
67	The walls of Jerusalem are, "as saith seint Ion," "Holy Chirche," and like the two testaments, they are "cordyng in oon" with Christ as the "corner stoon"	Matt. 21:42; Ps. 117:22
72–74	Passion imagery of dryness, thirst, thorns, blood; shift to first person: "[Y say my cosyn Jon morn-ynge], / I say my modir in swownynge synk; / I herde a theef me scoornynge; / Galle and eisel was my drynk"	Luke 23:39, 36
75	Christ compares himself to the pelican; the "nicticorax" appears as a "nyȝt-crowe"	Ps. 101:7

Stanza	Quotations/Events	Bible
80	"Centurio seyde, 'We doon vnriȝt, / For truly Goddis Sone this was'"	Luke 23:47
83	The stones of Sion have Christ as the cornerstone and the apostles have "a dongeoun dikide / In Syon" to which sinners may flee for refuge	Ps. 101:15
94–95	Capsule Creation and Doomsday	Ps.101:26, 27
102	"Þere I am roten, rubbe of þe rust, / Or I be brouȝt to schippis bord, / To sayle in-to þe dale of dust"	Ezek. 37
110	How Judas sold "Hym þat þis world with hondis wrouȝt"	Matt. 26:15

Thomas Brampton's *Penitential Psalms* TBPs

Manual, 2:388 [19]
IMEV/S 355 (variant version)

1. Cambridge, Univ. Lib. Ff.2.38 (28r–31v), 15th c., 549 lines (missing first 443 lines).
2. Cambridge, Magdalene College Pepys 1584 (28r–36v), 15th c., 992 lines.
3. Cambridge, Trinity College 600 (pp. 197–232), 15th c., 992 lines.

IMEV/S 1591 (normal version)

4. Cambridge, Magdalene College Pepys 2030 (1v–18r), 16th c. (missing first 54 lines and last 32).
5. London, BL Harley 1704 (13r–17v), 15th c. (missing first 488 lines and last 64).
6. London, BL Sloane 1853 (3r–30r), 15th c., 992 lines.

Editions: 1 and 2—Kreuzer, "Brampton's Paraphrase," with variant readings from 3–6.
    6—Black, *Paraphrase on the Psalms,* 1–47, with emendations from 5.
Facsimile: 1—McSparran and Robinson, *Cambridge University Library MS Ff.2.38.*
Study: Kuczynski, *Prophetic Song,* 124–35.

The two versions are distinct, but they "unquestionably stem from the same original" (Kreuzer, "Brampton's Paraphrase," 359). The version in manuscript 2 consists of 124 eight-line stanzas in iambic tetrameter, rhyming ababbcbc. The c-rhyme is governed by the refrain in line 8, "Ne reminiscaris, Domine," part of the antiphon which in medieval breviaries appeared at the end of the Penitential Psalms and before the Litany (Kreuzer, "Brampton's Paraphrase," 366). The antiphon combines Tob. 3:3, a verse from the hymn (Te Deum) of Ambrose and Augustine, and Ps. 85:5.

Depending on the length of the quoted Latin verse, two or three lines of each stanza are a close paraphrase, bordering on translation. The other lines elaborate, and the last line repeats the refrain "Ne reminiscaris domine."

Both Kreuzer and Black discuss the long-standing misattribution (beginning with John Bale) of this paraphrase to John Alcock. A mid-sixteenth-century hand in manuscript 6 names Thomas Brampton as the author and 1414 as the date of composition.

The first six stanzas recount the penitent's midwinter midnight distress concerning his sins, followed by an injunction from his confessor to repeat the Psalms in order to be forgiven. The characteristic feature of Brampton's paraphrase is his emphasis on personal sin and salvation.

stanzas 7–16	Ps. 6:2–11
stanzas 17–30	Ps. 31:1–11
stanzas 31–53	Ps. 37:2–23
stanzas 54–73	Ps. 50:3–21
stanzas 74–102	Ps. 101:2–29
stanzas 103–10	Ps. 129:1–8
stanzas 111–24	Ps. 142:1–12.

From Kreuzer, "Brampton's Paraphrase":

Stanza	Quotation/Event	Bible
9	"My soule begynnyth to trembill and quake"	Ps. 6:4
14	Doomsday recollection of the Vale of Josaphat	Joel 3:2, 12
20	"The prik of concience"	
35	"My woundis be Rotyn and festirith wt in"	Ps. 37:6
59	"Of my moder y was conseyuede / In synne so was euery chyldc [Brampton notes the two exceptions: Christ and Mary]	Ps. 50:7
80	The "nicticorax" is a "back, þat fleyth be nyght"	Ps. 101:7
87	Sion is "dauyches toure, / Hyt sygnyfyeth þe ordre of knyght"	Ps. 101:14
88	"Every knȝyt is callyd a ston / Of Syon"	Ps. 101:15
90	"Syon a merour is, to say, / That God hath bygged and sett ful hye"	Ps. 101:17
92	David and Ezekiel as exemplars of meek kings and virtuous livers	
95	Jerusalem, "the cyté of pes"	Ps. 75:2
99–100	Capsule Creation and Doomsday	Ps. 101:26, 27
119	"Syth truthe and mercy were freendys and kyst"	Ps. 84:11
120	"Teche me, lord, þe redy weye, / That y may my	Ps. 142:8;

Stanza	Quotation/Event	Bible
	soule saue; / If the gospell trewly seye / Me þar nomore but aske and haue"	Matt. 7:7

Primer Version of the Psalms PPs

Manual, 2:388 [17] and 7:2367 [225]

16 MSS and a fragment, including:

1. Cambridge, St. John's College 192 (G.24) (9r–95v), ca. 1400.
2. Cambridge, Univ. Lib. Dd.11.82 (1r–98v), early 15th c.
3. London, BL Add. 17010 (1r–77r), early 15th c.
4. London, BL Add. 27592 (12r–41v), early 15th c.

Editions: 1—Littlehales, *Prymer or Prayer-Book,* vol. 1.
2—Littlehales, *Prymer or Lay Folks Prayer Book.*
3—Maskell, *Monumenta,* 3:1–183
Facsimile: 4—Littlehales, *Pages in Facsimile.*
Studies: Bishop, *Prymer;* Butterworth, *English Primers (1529–1545),* 5, 100; Duffy, *Stripping of the Altars,* 68–77, 220–27. Littlehales summarizes the contents of thirteen manuscripts (*Prymer or Prayer-Book,* 2:2–10). Wordsworth and Littlehales provide a helpful guide, with extensive quotations and facsimiles, to the variety of materials used in medieval English prayerbooks and primers (*Service-Books,* 248–55).

In the context of psalm translations, the role of "prymers"—vernacular prayer books for private devotion—cannot be ignored. Contents vary; the fullest versions include the Hours of the Blessed Virgin Mary, Evensong, Compline, the seven Penitential Psalms, the fifteen Gradual Psalms, Canticles, the Litany, the Placebo and Dirige, the Psalms of Commendation, the Pater Noster, the Ave Maria, the Creed, the Ten Commandments, and the Seven Deadly Sins. The bulk of the material consists of various Psalms, usually numbering about fifty, translated in full. Such works in Latin are known as "Horae" or "Hours of the Virgin." The dreamer in *Piers Plowman,* speaking as a cleric in "longe clothes," describes the tools ("lomes") of his trade as follows:

> The lomes þat Y labore with and lyflode deserue
> Is *Pater-noster* and my prymer, *Placebo* and *Dirige,*
> And my Sauter som tyme and my seuene psalmes.[1]

---

1. Langland, *Piers Plowman,* C.v.45–47, and see iii.463–64. A "prymer" was central to the religious education of the "litel clergeoun" in the *Prioress's Tale* (VII.517, 541).

The contents of primers are extremely diverse, and not susceptible to easy categorization. The contents of manuscripts 2 and 3 may be compared by the following outlines.

From Littlehales, *Prymer or Lay Folks Prayer-Book,* manuscript 2 (an Hours of the Cross sequence and the nine lessons of the Dirige are interspersed throughout):

Pages	Bible
1–2	Ps. 94
2–3	Ps. 8
3–4	Ps. 18
4	Ps. 23
5	Pater Noster (Matt. 6:9–13)
5	Ave Maria (Luke 1:28)
8	Ps. 92
8	Ps. 99
8–9	Ps. 62
9	Ps. 66
9–10	Benedicite, Song of the Three Children (Dan. 3:57–90)
10–11	Ps. 148
11	Ps. 149
12	Ps. 150
12–13	Benedictus (Luke 1:68–79)
16	Ps. 53
16	Ps. 116
17–18	Ps. 117
20	Ps. 119
20–21	Ps. 120
21	Ps. 121
23	Ps. 122
23–24	Ps. 123
24	Ps. 124
26	Ps. 125
26–27	Ps. 126
27	Ps. 127
29–30	Magnificat (Luke 1:46–55)
31	Ps. 12
32	Ps. 42
32	Ps. 128
32	Ps. 130
33	Nunc dimittis (Luke 2:29–32)
35	Ps. 129

[seven Penitential Psalms]

37	Ps. 6
37–38	Ps. 31

Pages	Bible
38–39	Ps. 37
39–40	Ps. 50
41–42	Ps. 101
42	Ps. 129
42–43	Ps. 142

[fifteen Gradual Psalms, abridged]

44–45	Ps. 131
45	Ps. 132
46	Ps. 133
52	Ps. 114
52–53	Ps. 119
53	Ps. 120
53	Ps. 129
53–54	Ps. 137
54	Magnificat (Luke 1:46–55)
55	Ps. 145
56–57	Ps. 5
57–58	Ps. 6
58–59	Ps. 7
59–60	Job 7:16–21; 10:1–12
60–61	Ps. 22
61–62	Ps. 24
62–63	Ps. 26
63–65	Job 13:23–28; 14:1–6, 13–16
65–66	Ps. 39
66–67	Ps. 40
67–68	Ps. 41
68–70	Job 17:1–3, 11–15; 19:20–27; 10:18–22
70–71	Ps. 50
71–72	Ps. 64
72–73	Ps. 62
73	Ps. 66
73–74	Song of Ezekiel (Is. 38:10–20)
74–75	Ps. 148
75	Ps. 149
75	Ps. 150
75–76	Benedictus (Luke 1:68–79)
76–77	Ps. 29

[psalms of commendation]

79–88	Ps. 118
88–89	Ps. 138

From Maskell, *Monumenta,* manuscript 3 (an Hours of the Cross sequence and the nine lessons of the Dirige [pp. 132–51] are interspersed throughout):

Pages	Bible
5–6	Ps. 104 (does not appear in MS 2)
8–9	Ps. 8
9–10	Ps. 18
10–11	Ps. 23
18	Ps. 92
18–19	Ps. 99
19–20	Ps. 62
20–21	Ps. 66
21–23	Benedicite, The Song of the Three Children (Dan. 3:57–90)
24–25	Ps. 148
25–26	Ps. 149
26	Ps. 150
28	Benedictus (Luke 1:68–79)
43	Ps. 53
43–44	Ps. 116
44–46	Ps. 117
49	Ps. 119
49–50	Ps. 120
50	Ps. 121
54	Ps. 122
54–55	Ps. 123
55	Ps. 124
58	Ps. 125
59	Ps. 126
59–60	Ps. 127
64–65	Magnificat (Luke 1:46–55)
68	Ps. 12
69	Ps. 42
69–70	Ps. 128
70	Ps. 130
72	Nunc dimittis (Luke 2:29–32)
78–79	Ps. 129

[seven Penitential Psalms]

81–83	Ps. 6
84–85	Ps. 31
85–87	Ps. 37
87–90	Ps. 50
90–92	Ps. 101
92–93	Ps. 129
93–94	Ps. 142

Pages	*Bible*

[fifteen Gradual Psalms]
97–98	Ps. 131
98	Ps. 132
98–99	Ps. 133
119	Ps. 114
121	Ps. 137
122–23	Ps. 145
128–29	Ps. 5
130–32	Ps. 7
136	Ps. 22
137–38	Ps. 24
138–40	Ps. 26
143–45	Ps. 39
145–46	Ps. 40
146–47	Ps. 41
153–54	Ps. 64
154–56	Song of Ezekiel (Is. 38:10–20)
157–58	Ps. 29

[psalms of commendation]
| 162–76 | Ps. 118 |
| 177–78 | Ps. 138 |

[on 77v–79r]
180–81	Pater Noster (Matt. 6:9–13)
181	Ave Maria (Luke 1:28)
182	Ten Commandments (Ex. 20:1–17)

Jerome's *Abbreviated Psalter* (in prose) **JPs**

Manual, 2:387 [15]

Version A

    1. Oxford, Bodleian Lib. Bodley 416 (*SC* 2315) (144r–151r), ca. 1400.
    2. Oxford, Bodleian Lib. Hatton 111 (*SC* 4050) (2r–8v), late 14th c.

Version B

    3. San Marino, Huntington Lib. HM 501 (117r–121v), 15th c.

Pending Examination

    4. Glasgow, Univ. Lib. Hunterian 496 (V.7.23) (1r–9v), late 14th c.
    5. New Haven, Yale Univ. Lib. 360 (176v–185v), early 15th c.

6. Oxford, Univ. College 179 (84v–90v), an alternate Latin/English version.

Edition: In progress by Morey.
Paues, *English Biblical Version* (1904), lxiii–lxiv (short extracts from 1 and 2).

Versions of the Latin source text appear in Wordsworth, *Horae Eboracensis*, 116–22, and in Horstmann, *Yorkshire Writers*, 1:392–98, from Lincoln, Cathedral Lib. 91 (258v) (Lincoln Thornton).

The introductions to the York (1517) and Sarum (1535–36) *Horae* offer the abbreviated psalter to those who because of business or illness cannot recite a whole psalter. Another substitute Psalter, for the illiterate, was "Our Lady's Psalter" (see above p. 173).

The English versions begin and end with a general prayer to God, Mary, and the saints for the salvation of the author, his kin, friends, enemies, and all Christians. Manuscript 3 differs slightly from the Latin text in the Thornton manuscript.

From my transcription of manuscript 3:

Folio	Quotation	Psalm
117r	"Lord receyue þou my wordis wt þin eeris"	5:2–3
	"hele me for alle my bones ben disturblid"	6:3–5
117v	"liȝtne þou myn iȝen"	12:4
	"kepe þou me as þe appil of þin iȝe"	16:5–9
		18:13
	"saue me for þe mouþ of þe lioun 7 myn mekenes fro þe hornes of vnycornes"	21:20–22
		24:4–7, 11, 18
		25:9
		26:7, 9
118r	"putte þou to me a lawe in þi wey"	26:11–12
	"I rere up myn hondis to þin holy temple"	27:1–3
		27:9
	"Into þin hondis I bitake my spreit"	30:1–6
		30:16–18
		32:22
	"Take þou wepens 7 scheeld 7 rise up"	34:1–3
		34:23–24
118v	"þe foot of pride come not to me"	35:11–12
	"Forgeue þou to me þt I be refreischid"	38:13–14
		39:12, 14–18
		40:5

Folio	Quotation	Psalm
	"Lord arise up whi slepist þou"	43:23–24
		43:26
		50:3–4
	"make newe a riȝtful spirit in my bowels"	50:11–14
	"Lord þou schalt opene my lippis"	50:17
		53:3–4
119r	"my soule tristiþ in þee"	54:2
		58:2–3
	"Ne drenche þe tempest of watir me neiþir depnes of watir swolewe me neiþir pit constreyne his mouþ on me"	68:14–19
		69:2–3, 5–6
	"make þou me sauf in to þe hous of refuyȝte"	70:1–3
		70:8–9
	"Take þou not awey beestis soulis knowlechinge to þee"	73:19–20
119v		78:9
		79:3–4
	"bee þou not wrooþ wiþouten eende to us fro kynrede in to kinrede"	84:5–7
		85:1–4
	"ȝeue lordschip to þi child 7 make saaf þe sone of þin hondmaide"	85:15–17
		87:2–3
	"Lord where ben þin oolde mercies as þou hast swore to daviþ"	88:50–51
120r	"dresse þou þe werk of oure hondis"	89:13, 17
		101:2–3, 25
		108:21–22, 26
	"I am maad a dweller in erþe"	118:17–19
		118:29
	"bowe þou myn herte in to þe witnessis and not into auarise"	118:35–38
		118:66, 68, 76–77, 80, 107–9, 116–17, 124–25, 132–35, 153–54
	"I haue errid as a scheep"	118:169–76
121r		122:3
		124:4
	"Lord turne oure þraldom as þe rennynge water in þe souþ"	125:4
	"I haue cried to þee fro depnessis of watris"	129:1–2
		137:3

Folio	Quotation	Psalm
	"putte þou kepinge to my mouþ and a dore of circumstaunce to my lippis"	140:3–4
		141:7–8
	"eueriman lyuynge schal not be iustified in þi siȝt"	142:1–2
121v	"þou schalt disparple myne enemyes"	142:7–12

St. Bernard's *Eight-Verse Psalter* BPs

IMEV 908
Manual, 2:387 [16]

1. London, BL Royal 17.A.xxvii (86v–88v), early 15th c. Eight eight-line stanzas rhyming abababab, with abbreviated Latin verses.
2. London, BL Add. 37787 (81v), partial text of prologue.

Editions: 1—Black, *Paraphrase on the Psalms,* 51–54.
2—Baugh, *Worcestershire Miscellany.*

On pp. 49–51 Black prints a Latin version from London, BL Harley 1845 (15r–16r). The Latin also appears in BL Add. 33381 (161r). A twelve-verse version appears in the *Speculum Spiritualium* (Paris, 1510), 208b.

This Psalter treatment makes **JPs** look prolix. A short prose prologue (in the Latin and English versions) tells how the Devil claims to know, but refuses to reveal, eight Psalter verses that will save a man from damnation. St. Bernard counters that he will simply recite the whole Psalter each day; faced with this prospect, the Devil capitulates and recites the poem.

Stanza	Quotations (from MS 1)	Psalm
1	"ȝyf liȝt unto myn eȝe siȝt"	12:4–5
2	"In to þi hondus I be take my gost"	30:6
3	"I have spokyn with my tunge"	38:5
4	"And sene the numbre of dayis myne"	38:5
5	"Þow hast to broke, Lord, in two / Cloos imade my hondis alle"	115:16
6	"Fro me hath fliȝte perischid and failid"	141:5
7	"I cride and sayde 'þow art my trist'"	141:6
8	"Do with me sum token in gode"	85:17

Psalms Versified by John Lydgate LPs (and see DPPs)

Psalm 42: "Iudica me, Deus"
IMEV/S 4246
Manual, 6:1856 [87]

10 MSS, including:

1. Cambridge, Trinity College 601 (R.3.21) (205v–214r), mid-15th c., 664 lines in eight-line stanzas, ababbcbc.
2. London, BL Add. 31042 (London Thornton) (103r–110r), mid-15th c., lacks lines 1–57.

Edition: 1—Lydgate, *Minor Poems,* ed. MacCracken, 87–115.
Facsimile: 2—J. Thompson, *Thornton,* plates 21b, 22a, 22b.

The Psalm paraphrase is lines 89–144 (seven stanzas) of Lydgate's *Interpretacio Misse* (*The Virtues of the Mass*), a general exposition of the practice and moral significance of the Mass written for Alice de la Pole, countess of Suffolk, the daughter of Thomas Chaucer (Pearsall, *Lydgate,* 258). Cf. **MTM.**

> Verse 3: Sende downe thy lyght, sende downe thy ryghtwysnesse,
>   Thy lyght of grace for consolacioun,
>   Thy ryghtwysnesse my passage for to dresse,
>   By parfyte prayer and deuocioun,
>   To reste in quyete, lord, sende thy grace downe,
>   Me to conuey that ther be noon obstacle,
>   Toward the hygh hilles of Sioun,
>   Withyn thyne holy celestiall tabernacle. (lines 105–112)

Psalm 53: "Deus in nomine tuo" ("God in thy name make me safe and sounde")
IMEV 951
Manual, 6:1827 [33]

1. Oxford, Bodleian Lib. Ashmole 59 (*SC* 6943) (69v–70r, 134v), mid-15th c.
2. London, BL Cotton Caligula A.ii (64v–65r), earlier 15th c.
3. London, BL Harley 116 (127r), 15th c.
4. London, BL Harley 2255 (146v–148r), mid-15th c.

Editions: 2—Lydgate, *Minor Poems,* ed. MacCracken, 10–12, with variants from others; Patterson, *Penitential Lyric,* 72–74.

Nine eight-line stanzas rhyming ababcbcb, with paraphrases of various Latin prayers. See Pearsall, *Lydgate,* 259.

Psalm 88: "Misericordias Domini"
IMEV 178
Manual, 6:1876 [117]

1. Cambridge, Jesus College 56 (41r–44r), 15th c.

2. Cambridge, Trinity College 601 (193v–196r), later 15th c.
3. London, BL Harley 2255 (17r–21r), mid-15th c.

Edition: 3 — Lydgate, *Minor Poems,* ed. MacCracken, 71–77.

Twenty-four eight-line stanzas rhyming ababbcbc consisting of variations
on the first verse of the Psalm, "Eternally thy mercies I shal syng." The paraphrase alludes to David and Goliath, Debbora, Anna, Moses, the Three Children, Judith and Holofernes, Isaias, Ezechias, Habacuc, the Magnificat, and
mythological examples of "songs" and their singers. Pearsall calls it "a Biblical concordance to 'song' " (*Lydgate,* 260).

Psalm 102, "Benedic anima mea Domino" ("O þou my soule gyf laude vn-to
þe lord")
IMEV 2572
Manual, 6:1893 [159]

1. Cambridge, Trinity College 600 (pp. 19–25, 165–70), mid-15th c.
2. London, BL Harley 2251 (236r–238v), later 15th c.
3. London, BL Add. 34360 (53v–55r), later 15th c.

Edition: 1 — Lydgate, *Minor Poems,* ed. MacCracken, 1–7, with variants from
others.

Twenty-two eight-line stanzas rhyming ababbcbc, consisting of a loose
paraphrase of the Psalm in the context of a prayer for repentance and salvation. See Pearsall, *Lydgate,* 31, 259.

Versions of Psalm 50 ("Miserere") MPs

Version 1
IMEV 1956
Manual, 2:389 [21]

1. Edinburgh, National Lib. of Scotland Advocates 19.2.1 (280r–v)
   (Auchinleck), 1320–40.

Editions: Kölbing, "Kleine Publicationen," 49–50; D. Laing, *Penni Worth,*
   76–80.
Facsimile: Pearsall and Cunningham, *Auchinleck Manuscript.*

Psalm 50 is one of the penitential psalms, and was frequently excerpted
and commented upon both in Latin and English. Each of the twenty-one
Latin verses is followed by a four-line paraphrase rhyming aabb; three stan-

zas are six lines (aabbcc). There are ninety-six lines of English, including a short concluding prayer. Twelve lines are illegible.

> Verse 17:   "Lord, mi lippes þou vndo!
> Graunt me, lord, þat it be so!
> Wiþ praiers ichil honour þe,
> Þi godhed and ek þi dignete." (lines 67–70)

Version 2
IMEV 990
Manual, 2:389 [22]

> 1. London, BL Add. 31042 (London Thornton) (102r–v), 15th c., atelous.

Editions: J. Thompson, "Literary Associations," 52–55; Fein, *"Haue Mercy,"* 236–41.
Facsimile: J. Thompson, *Thornton,* plates 20b and 21a.

This fragmentary text covers only the first thirteen of the twenty-one verses in the Psalm. The paraphrase takes the form of twelve-line alliterating stanzas (resembling those in *Pearl*) for each verse, rhyming ababababcdcd, totaling 134 lines.

Version 3
IMEV/S 1123.8
Manual, 7:2369 [230]

> 1. Salisbury, Cathedral Lib. 152 (159v), 15th c.
> 2. London, BL Add. 32427 (141r), 15th c. [a Sarum Breviary].

Editions: 1—Kingdon, "Vernacular Service"; Maskell, *Monumenta,* 1:ccxl–ccxli; Wordsworth and Littlehales, *Service-Books,* 51. 2—transcribed below.
Facsimile: 1—Kingdon, "Vernacular Service."

Only the first verse of Psalm 50 appears, in the context of a vernacular *aspersio* (service of the sprinking of holy water). Kingdon discusses how the text serves as an important example of the vernacularization of church services in England.

Transcription from manuscript 2: "Haue mercy uppon me O god After thy great mercy [antiphon] And acordyng to the multytude of thy mercys: Do awey my wyckydnes [antiphon]."

Commentary on Psalm 90 ("Qui habitat") and Psalm 91 ("Bonum est") QHPs and BEPs

IPMEP 554, 115.5
Manual, 2:389 [23] and 9:3079 [33][34]

1. Oxford, Bodleian Lib. Eng. poet. a.1 (Vernon) (338v–343r), ca. 1390.
2. Cambridge, Univ. Lib. Dd.1.1 (228r–240r), 15th c.
3. Cambridge, Univ. Lib. Hh.1.11 (69r–99r), later 15th c.
4. London, Lambeth Palace 472 (223v–252v), early 15th c.
5. London, BL Harley 2397 (85v–94r), ca. 1400 [Ps. 91 only].
6. London, Westminster Abbey Treasury 4 (1r–35v), ca. 1500.
7. Tokyo, Takamiya 15, 15th c.
8. London, Sion College [non-extant]. See Allen, *Writings Ascribed,* 196.

Edition: 1—Wallner, *Exposition,* with variants from other manuscripts, notes and glossary (93–118).
Modernizations: 4—Jones, *Minor Works,* 115–213.
   6—Walsh and Colledge, *Knowledge,* 1–22.
Facsimile: 1—Doyle, *Vernon Manuscript.*
Discussions: Paues, *English Biblical Version* (1902) llv; Allen, *Writings Ascribed,* 196–97; Ekwall, "Manuscript Collections," 30–31.

Each verse (sixteen in each Psalm) is quoted in Latin, translated into English, and followed by a lengthy prose exposition (a total of ninety-two pages in Wallner's edition). The general themes of temptation, sin, and forgiveness through Christ and the sacraments are expressed with frequent metaphors (sin as a swamp or a snare, devils as hunters, God as a house of refuge, contemplation as armor, etc.).

Both works have been attributed to Walter Hilton, Augustinian canon at Thurgarton, Nottinghamshire (d. 1395 or 1396), though doubts have been expressed concerning his authorship of the "Bonum est." The Northern or North Midland dialect is consistent with Hilton's other works and with works associated with Rolle. Wallner provides comprehensive information on the manuscripts and dialect; Jones suggests several sources: *Cloud of Unknowing,* Ps.-Dionysius the Areopagite, Augustine (*Minor Works,* xl–xli). Lagorio and Sargent note in *Manual,* 9:3079, without claiming any specific indebtedness, Bernard of Clairvaux's *On the Psalm "Qui Habitat,"* and suggest that the "Bonum est" draws upon Peter Lombard's *Magna Glossatura.*

The comment on Ps. 90:4 highlights the value of reading Scripture:

Vre lord with his schuldres schal al bi-schaduwe þe: And vnder his feþures þou schalt hopen.

Þe feþeres of vre lord are wordes of þe holy writ, endyted bi þe holi gost in comfort of chosen soules, trauaylinge in þesternes of þis lyf, þe wuche wordes, ʒif þei beo treweliche festned in a meke soule, þei beren vp þe soule from al eorþlich fulþe in-to heuenly conuersacion as feþeres beren vp fro þe eorþe in-to þe eir þe bodi of a brid. (Wallner, *Exposition*, 12)

Stanzaic Version of Psalm 129 ("De profundis") **DPPs**

IMEV 2522
Manual, 2:389 [24]

> 1. London, BL Harley 2252 (23r–24v), 16th c., eleven twelve-line stanzas, abababbcbc.

Edition: Besserman, Gilman, and Weinblatt, "Commonplace-Book of John Colyns."

Psalm 129 is a penitential and a gradual psalm. The context of the paraphrase is a prayer for souls in Purgatory, with frequent recollections of Christ's Passion and Old Testament figures such as Jonas, Daniel, Joseph, Moses, Abraham, and Samuel.

The final two stanzas are Kyrie Eleison and Inclina, Domine, aurem tuam.

> ffrom dalys depe to the have I sayd
> lorde lorde here the voyce of me.
> (Ps. 129:1–2, lines 13–14)

See also Lydgate's "On De Profundis" (*IMEV* 1130, *Manual*, 6:1825 [30]), edited by MacCracken in Lydgate, *Minor Poems*, 77–84. See Pearsall, *Lydgate*, 31, 259 and Deanesly, *Lollard Bible*, 320–21, 336.

Canticles and Hymns

Canticles and Hymns **CH**

At the end of many Psalters and Primers the following Canticles and Hymns appear:

The Song of Isaias, "Confiteor tibi" (Is. 12:1–6)
The Song of Ezechias, "Ego dixi" (Is. 38:10–20)
The Song of Anna, "Exultavit" (1Kg. 2:1–10)
The First Song of Moses, "Cantemus domino" (Ex. 15:1–19)
The Prayer of Habacuc, "Domine, audivi" (Hab. 3:2–19)
The Second Song of Moses, "Audite, celi" (Deut. 32:1–43)
The Song of the Three Children, Benedicite (Dan. 3:57–88)
The Magnificat (Luke 1:46–55)
The Benedictus (Luke 1:68–79)
The Nunc dimittis (Luke 2:29–32)

Canticles in Rolle's Psalter and Commentary **RPs**

IPMEP 134
Manual, 2:386 [13]

   1. Oxford, Univ. College 64
   2. Oxford, Bodleian Lib. Bodley 288 (*SC* 2438)
For other manuscripts, see Everett, "Prose Psalter."

Editions: 1—Rolle, *Psalter of David*, 494–526, from Oxford, Univ. College 64
   (to verse 61 of second song of Moses) and from Oxford, Bodleian Laud

misc. 286 (after verse 61, to the end, omitting the Benedicite, the Benedictus, and the Nunc dimittis, which other manuscripts include). 2—Wyclif, *Select Works,* 3:3–81.

Canticles in the Midland Prose Psalter MPPs

Manual 2:387 [14]
3 MSS, including:

    1. London, BL Add. 17376, ca. 1350.

Edition: Bülbring, *Prose Psalter,* 179–96

Medieval Primers also often contained these canticles and hymns:

    1. Oxford, Bodleian Lib. Douce 275 (9v, 26r, 29r), ca. 1400 (Benedicite, Magnificat, and Nunc dimittis).
    2. London, BL Harley 2343 (2r) (Magnificat).
    3. Oxford, Bodleian Lib. Douce 246 (23r), 1446 (Benedictus).

Edition: 1, 2, 3—Maskell, *Monumenta,* 3:243–47.

These biblical passages became standard components of the liturgy, and their association with versions of the Psalter and with Primers ensured wide dissemination. They often appear with other liturgical texts such as the Te Deum and the Athanasian Creed. Once again, attention to the full contents and context of biblical paraphrases yields some surprises. A medieval reader would, for example, be most likely to encounter excerpts from Habacuc in the context of a Psalter or a Primer. Rolle's comment on a verse from the Prayer of Habacuc (3:9) reveals the populist agenda which must have been on his mind: "*Suscitans suscitabis arcum tuum: iuramenta tribubus que locutus es.* Raysand thou sall rayse thi bow: athis til kynredyns the whilke thou spake. That is, thou sall rayse haly writ. that lay slepand whils men vndirestode it noght" (Rolle, *Psalter of David,* 509). A comment such as this indicates that the whole text—Psalter and canticles—was not just a service book but a viable means of popularizing Scripture.

❖ II.D   *Miscellaneous Old Testament Pieces*

Lydgate's *Epistle to Sibille* ES

IMEV/S 3321
Manual, 6:1833 [43]

> 1. Oxford, Bodleian Lib. Ashmole 59 (*SC* 6943) (59v–62r), mid-15th c.,
> twenty rhyme royal stanzas, ababbcc.

Edition: Lydgate, *Minor Poems,* ed. MacCracken, 14–18.

This paraphrase of Prov. 31:10–31 is the longest sustained Middle English paraphrase of verses from Proverbs, a book which lends itself to selective quotation and rearrangement. Lydgate wrote the poem for Lady Sibille Boys of Holm Hale in Norfolk (Pearsall, *Lydgate,* 169). After an invocation of Martha and Mary, the poem outlines the qualities of a virtuous woman.

> Sheo resembleþe a shippe of marchandyse,
> From ful fare providing hir victayle (lines 43–44; Prov. 31:14).

Wisdom of Solomon ("Dicta Salomonis") WS

IPMEP 427
Manual, 2:390 [25]

> 1. Cambridge, Univ. Lib. Kk.1.5 (5r–12r), mid-15th c.

Editions: Lumby, *Ratis Raving,* 11–25; Girvan, *Ratis Raving,* 177–92.

The only paraphrase of Ecclesiastes in Middle English (apart from the Wycliffite versions) is **WS**, in a Lowland Scottish dialect. Girvan dates the handwriting to the second half of the fifteenth century (xi). Errors and some (minor) unintelligibility may suggest that it is a translation from French. Overall it is a very close prose paraphrase presented as a sequence of "Item he sais . . ." clauses.

Line references are to Lumby's edition:

Lines	Quotations	Eccles.
342–375	"vanite of vaniteʒ"	1:1–11
376–393	"I was kyng in Jerusalem"	1:12–18
394–441	"now wyll I pas and flow in all welthfulness"	2:1–13
442–497	"baith the wisman & the full deis"	2:14–26
498–527	"al thing has a tyme in this warld"	3:1–18
528–539	"the lyf of man and a best in this warld is bot all ane"	3:19–22
540–563	"he louit mare the ded man na the levande"	4:1–12
564–569	"It is better a pur wyss barne na an auld fule kinge"	4:13–17
570–586	"a man suld nocht be our hasty of speech"	5:1–10
587–605	"efter gret trawall the slep is swet"	5:11–19
606–632	"he has gevyne til oþire al haboundans of warldis gudis"	6:1–11
633–693	"it is better a gud name na mekil riches"	7:1–26
694–706	"I fand the woman mar bitter na the ded"	7:27–30
707–738	"þe wisdome of a wysman schawis by his contenanas"	8:1–17
731	"the dreid of god is the begynynge of wysdome"	[Prov. 1:7; 9:10, or Ps. 110:10]
739–747	"a levand dog is better na a ded lyone"	9:1–11
748–757	"as fisch ar tan with hukis, and foul with lyme wandis, so is synaris tane be-for thare tyme"	9:12–18
758–769	"the visdome of the wysman is in his rycht hand"	10:1–10
770–789	"a bakbytar may be lyknit till a neddyr"	10:11–20
790–811	"deill thi met to the trawelouris and pilgrymys"	11:1–10
812–840	"the sone, the mone, and the sternis sal al twrne agan"	12:1–11
841–849	"quhen men sekis þe wysdome in mony bukis, It stoppis his wyt, and sal neuer fynde an ende"	12:12–14

The *Pistel of Swete Susan* (Susanna) PSS

IMEV/S 3553
Manual, 2:390 [26]

1. Oxford, Bodleian Lib. Eng. poet. a.1 (Vernon) (317r–v), ca. 1390.

2. London, BL Cotton Caligula A.ii (3r–5r), late 15th c., missing first eight stanzas.

3. London, BL Add. 22283 (Simeon) (125v–126r), ca. 1400.

4. San Marino, Huntington Lib. HM 114 (184v–191v), ca. 1400.

5. New York, Pierpont Morgan Lib. M.818 (1r–5r), 15th c.

Editions: 1—Horstmann, "Legenden von Celestin und Susanna," 85–101; Furnivall, *Minor Poems,* 626–36; Peck, *Heroic Women,* 73–108.

2 and 4—Miskimin, *Susannah,* with variants from others.

2—Horstmann, "Nachträge" (1879), (with variants from 3).

4—Horstmann, "Nachträge" (1885), 339–44.

Facsimile: 1—Doyle, *Vernon Manuscript.*

The poem paraphrases Daniel, chapter 13 (sixty verses), in 364 lines in twenty-eight thirteen-line stanzas rhyming abababababcdddc, with bob and wheel. The story of Susanna's being falsely accused of fornication by the judges, and her exculpation by the young Daniel, is well known, though this chapter now forms part of the Protestant Apocrypha. In the Sarum use, Dan. 13 is the first lesson for the third Saturday in Lent.

Quotations from Miskimin:

Lines	Quotations	Bible
162–63	"Thow hast gamyd with a gome to þy goddys greue And leyn wiþ þy lemman in avowtry"	Dan. 13:37
240–43	"I am sakless of synne sche sayde in hyr sawen Grete god of þy grace þese gomes forgyfe Thatt don me delfully be ded & don out of dawen."	Dan. 13:43
335–38	"Say now so mote þu the / Vndyr what kynnes tre / Semely Sussann þu se / Do þys derne dede"	Dan. 13:58

Cleanness (*Clannesse, Purity*) Cl

IMEV 635
Manual, 2:350 [4]

1. London, BL Cotton Nero A.x (61r–86r), late 14th c., 1812 alliterative lines.

Editions: Anderson, *Cleanness;* Anderson, *Sir Gawain,* 47–137; Menner, *Purity,* and others.

Facsimile: Gollancz, *Pearl.*

Study: Fowler, *Bible in Middle English Literature,* 171–86.

Cleanness is the second of the four poems in the manuscript. Approximately four-fifths of the lines are biblically based, and although it is best known for its account of Baltassar's Feast from Daniel, a variety of other biblical books are represented. Unlike *Pearl* and *Patience* it includes several apocryphal details (that the Ark's raven eats carrion [459], that Lot's wife served salt to the angels and was thus turned to salt [984], that Christ was adored by a host of angels, ox and ass at the Nativity [1081, 1086; cf. Is. 1:3], that Christ breaks bread as if with a knife [1105]).

The poet's enthusiasm in versifying the stories and the picturesque qualities of the narrative combine to produce a very skillful and entertaining paraphrase.

Quotations from Anderson, *Sir Gawain:*

Lines	Events	Bible
1–32	Discourse on unclean priests: "The hathel clene of his hert hapenes ful fayre / For he schal loke on oure Lorde with a loue chere" (27–28)	Matt. 5:8
33–168	Parable of the Wedding Feast: "Say me, frende . . . / Hou wan thou into this won in wedes so fowle?" (139–40); "Byndes byhynde at his bak bothe two his handes, And felle fetteres to his fete festenes bylyve" (155–56)	Matt. 22: 1–14; Luke 14: 16–24
169–204	Varieties of uncleanness	
205–234	Fall of Lucifer: "I schal telde up my trone in the tramountayne, / And by lyke to that Lorde that the lyft made" (211–12)	Is. 14:3
235–264	Adam and Eve, Prohibition, Temptation, Fall; synopsis of the generations of Adam	Gen. 3; 5
265–434	The Flood: " 'sore hit me rwes / That ever I made hem myself' " (290–91); Noah, his wife, Sem, Cham, Japheth; the Ark	Gen. 6; 7
435–580	Mount Ararat, "the raven so ronk, that rebel was ever" (455), the dove; Noah's sacrifice; "Al is the mynde of the man to malyce enclyned" (518); the covenant	Gen. 8; 9: 1–11
581–600	"bythenk the sumtyme / Whether he that stykked uche a stare in uche steppe yye, / Yif hymself be bore blynde, hit is a brod wonder" (582–84)	Ps. 93:8–9
601–766	Abraham entertains the angels; Sara's laughter: "May thou traw for tykle that thou teme moghtes?" (655); Abraham debates with God: "If ten trysty in toune be tan in thi werkkes, / Wylt thou mese thy mode and menddyng abyde?" (763–64)	Gen. 18

Lines	Events	Bible
767–1014	Lot's hospitality, assault of the Sodomites; destruction of Sodom and Gomorrha; Lot's wife: "Also salt as ani se" (984)	Gen. 19: 1–28
1015–1064	Properties of the Dead Sea; allusion to *Le Roman de la Rose*	
1065–1144	Christ's birth; healing powers; properties of the Pearl	Matt. 13: 45–46
1145–1300	Sedecias's idolatry; siege and destruction of Jerusalem by Nabuchodonosor and Nabuzardan: "The kynges sunnes in his syght he slow everuchone, / And holkked ouat his auen yyen heterly bothe" (1221–22); Israel led into captivity; vessels of the Temple despoiled: "the chef chaundeler, charged with the lyght, / That ber the lamp upon loft that lemed evermore" (1272–73)	Jer. 52:1–27; 2Para. 36:11–20; Lev. 24:2
1301–1332	Daniel, Ananias, Misael, Azarias at Nabuchodonosor's court; Daniel interprets dreams; demise of Nabuchodonosor	Dan. 1: 17,19
1333–1804	Baltassar's idolatry, his feast: "Ther apered a paume, with poyntel in fyngres, That was grysly and gret, and grymly he wrytes; Non other forme bot a fust faylande the wryste Pared on the parget, purtrayed lettres" (1533–36); Daniel succeeds where the Chaldeans failed; Nabuchodonosor's madness; "Mane, Techal, Phares, merked in thrynne, / That thretes the of thyn unthryfte upon thre wyse" (1727–28); "Thenne sone was Danyel dubbed in ful dere porpor, / And a coler of cler golde kest umbe his swyre" (1743–44); a much elaborated death of Baltassar at the hands of Darius	Dan. 5:1–30; 4: 25, 34
1805–1812	How Cleanness is beloved of the Lord	

Patience Pat

IMEV 2739
Manual, 2:348 [3]

1. London, BL Cotton Nero A.x (87r–94r), late 14th c., 531 alliterative lines.

Editions: Anderson, *Sir Gawain*, 139–65; Anderson, *Patience*, and others.
Facsimile: Gollancz, *Pearl*.

Study: Fowler, *Bible in Middle English Literature*, 186–94.

Patience, the third poem in the manuscript, is based almost exclusively on the Beatitudes from Matthew and on the Book of Jonas. Like **Cl**, the poem follows a homiletic format with the statement of a biblical theme, expansion through paraphrase, and illustration by exemplum.

Once again, the energy and skill of the poet distinguish this paraphrase. Quotations from Anderson, *Sir Gawain:*

Lines	Event	Bible
1–60	The virtue of Patience; the Beatitudes: "Thay arn happen that han in hert poverté, For hores is the hevenryche to holde for ever" (13–14); "Thay ar happen also that halden her pese, For thay the gracious Godes sunes schal godly be called" (25–26)	Matt. 5:3–10
61–250	The story of Jonas, "as Holy Wryt telles" (60): " 'Rys radly,' he says, 'and rayke forth even; Nym the way to Nynyve' " (65–66); "Hope ye that he heres not that eres alle made?" (123); storm at sea; "A wylde walterande whal, as wyrde then schaped, / . . . swyftely swendged hym to swepe and his swolw opened" (247, 250)	Jonas 1; Ps. 93:8–9
251–344	Jonas in the belly of the whale: "Lorde, to the haf I cleped in cares ful stronge; / Out of the hole thou me herde of hellen wombe" (305–6); "The whal wendes at his wylle and a warthe fyndes, / And ther he brakes up the buyrne as bede hym oure Lorde" (339–40)	Jonas 2
345–408	Jonas in Ninive: " 'Yet schal forty dayes fully fare to an ende, / And thenne schal Ninive be nomen and to noght worthe' " (359–60); penance and conversion	Jonas 3
409–531	"Muche sorwe thenne satteled upon segge Jonas; / He wex as wroth as the wynde towarde oure Lorde" (409–10); "Ther he busked hym a bour, the best that he myght, / Of hay and of everferne and erbes a fewe" (436–37); "Whil God wayned a worme that wrot upe the rote, / And wyddered was the wodbynde bi that the wyye wakned" (467–68); " 'Why art thou so waymot, wyye, for so lyttel?' / 'Hit is not lyttel,' quoth the lede" (492–93); "ther ben doumbe bestes in the burgh mony, / That may not synne in no syt hemselven to greve" (516–17)	Jonas 4

Primarily New Testament Works, in Approximate Vulgate Order

Childhood of Jesus (*Ypokrephum; Kindheit Jesu*) **CJ**

Two versions: couplet and stanzaic
Couplet Version
IMEV 1550
Manual, 2:447 [311]

> 1. Oxford, Bodleian Lib. Laud misc. 108 (*SC* 1486) (11r–23v), late
> 13th c., 1,854 lines in octosyllabic couplets. This is an important *SEL*
> manuscript. **LLC** precedes.

Edition: Horstmann, *Altenglische Legenden* (1875), 1–61.

The proximate source is *Évangiles de l'Enfance*. See Holthausen, "Kindheit Jesu." The ultimate source is *The Infancy Gospel of St. Thomas* and *The Gospel of Ps-Matthew*. See Elliott, *Apocryphal New Testament,* 68–99.

The poem opens with the conventional account of the manger scene, the worshipping ox and ass (Is. 1:3), the presentation to Simeon in the Temple, the Magi, and Herod's Slaughter of the Innocents (Luke 2; Matt. 2:16). Indeed, the poet assumes that the story is so well known that "Inouȝh ȝe habbez þarof i heord telle: / Ne kepe ich more of heom spelle" (27–28).

Most of the narrative is apocryphal, and not strictly biblical. Noteworthy themes and motifs include:

While in the wilderness on the Flight to Egypt, not only the usual repertoire of wild beasts (citing Is. 11:6) but also the "Þe Dragouns of grete fliȝte" (69; cf. Ps. 148:7) worship Jesus. The tree bows to supply its fruit, and then its waters, to Mary (107ff.; a replay of Eden is evident here, as well as a prefiguration of the Eucharist: fruit and water = body and blood). Christ commands an angel to take the tree to paradise (185–208), miraculously shortens the distance of their journey to Egypt, and causes the Egyptian idols to fall upon his arrival (209–58; cf. Is. 19:1).

At age five, Christ performs miracles among his playmates (involving building and breaking dams, vivifying clay birds) which lead to their deaths, the recriminations of the Jews, and the subsequent resurrection of the playmates (301–478).

How Christ overcomes his schoolmaster Zachary (479–556), poses questions Zachary cannot answer, claims that Abraham is a personal friend.

Leaps from hill to hill; his friends try to imitate the feat with predictable results (557–638).

Hangs water–pitchers from a sun-beam (639–78).

Extricates through a narrow hole a playmate imprisoned by his father (679–750).

Explicates his "ABC" and puts his teacher to shame (751–870).

Sows and reaps a miraculous harvest of oats (985–96).

Metamorphoses Jewish children hidden in an oven into swine (997–1050). Thus the Jewish dietary restriction of pork.

Sits on a sunbeam; playmates imitate him unsuccessfully (1051–1115).

Joseph apprentices Christ to a dyer (1156–1263), in whose service Christ dyes three cloths different colors in the same cauldron.

Christ's adventures in the wilderness (1264–1361).

Remedies Joseph's mistakes in carpentry by lengthening undercut boards (1365–1431).

Miracle at Cana (1708–1800; John 2:1–11); groom named Archetriclin, a confusion with Vulgate *architriclinus* 'chief servant'.

The poet wishes to say no more "in prose ne in rime" (1826) and ends with a prayer for salvation.

Stanzaic Version, "Romance of the childhode of Ihesu Criste þat clerkes callys Ypokrephum"
(designation in manuscript 3)
IMEV 250
Manual, 2:447 [311]

1. London, BL Harley 2399 (47v–60v), 15th c., 842 lines.
2. London, BL Harley 3954 (begins 70r), ca. 1420, 694 lines. Lines 189–325 part of **DJM.**
3. London, BL Add. 31042 (163v–168v) (London Thornton), 15th c., 925 lines in eight- and twelve-line stanzas, abababbabcdcd.

Editions: 1 and 2—Horstmann, *Sammlung,* 101–23.
3—Horstmann, "Nachträge" (1885), 327–39.

Though less than half as long as the couplet version, this text recounts many of the same stories. Noteworthy material which does appear includes the attempted robbery by Barabbas and Dismas (the future good thief at the Crucifixion) on the Flight into Egypt (43–64); Pharaoh is named "Froudeus" (false god?—especially since at this point the Egyptian idols collapse; cf. Is. 19:1); Christ prophesies Judas's treachery and argues with Caiphas (190–267); Mary conceives Christ as sunshine passes through a glass (433; see **CM** line 10094); "Sydrake" and "Melchy" try to betroth their daughters to Jesus (585); Christ meets John the Baptist at the Jordan (906).

Estorie del Euangelie EE

(title derives from the Anglo-French introduction to the poem in manuscript 1)
IMEV/S 3194
Manual, 2:391 [28]

1. Oxford, Bodleian Lib. Eng. poet. a.1 (Vernon) (105r–v), ca. 1390, 396 lines, atelous, illustrated.
2. Oxford, Bodleian Lib. Add. C.38 (*SC* 30236) (71v–82r), early 15th c., 1,703 lines.
3. London, Dulwich College XXII (81v–85v), ca. 1300, 519 lines, atelous.
4. London, Univ. Lib. V.17 (Clopton) (97v–111v), early 15th c., 1,764 lines.
5. Oxford, Bodleian Lib. Rawlinson C.655 (*SC* 15481), mid-14th c., 192-line preface to **NP** [see Foster, *Northern Passion: French Text,* 10].

As adapted in **CR** (see next entry)
IMEV/S 1189

6. London, BL Royal 17.C.xvii (152v–155r), early 15th c. See **CR.** Also contains Mirk's *Instructions for Parish Priests* and **RMPs.**

IMEV 262

7. London, BL Lansdowne 388 (373r–380v), 15th c., 550-line excerpt as a Resurrection and Judgment poem, with a 54-line prologue describing the Crucifixion and Harrowing. Based on the *Southern Resurrection* (*IMEV/S* 1546 and 2105), part of the *SEL.* See also the insertion in **CM** (*IMEV* 2685), ed. Morris, *Cursor Mundi,* 62:985–91.

Editions: 1–7—Millward, *Estorie.*

 1—Horstmann, *Minor Poems,* 1–11 and Horstmann, "Mittheilungen,"
 254–59.

 2 and 3—Campbell, *"Evangelie."*

 6—Bowers, *Three Religious Poems,* 19–32.

Facsimile: 1—Doyle, *Vernon Manuscript.*

Studies: Turville-Petre, "Relationship of Vernon and Clopton
 Manuscripts"; McIntosh, "Middle English *Estoire del Euangelie*";
 Pickering, *"Newe Lessoun."*

Sources are the *Historia Scholastica* and perhaps Clement of Llanthony's gospel harmony or Victor of Capua's [d. 554] *Codex Fuldensis.*

EE, in mono-ryhming quatrains, has been studied primarily as a linguistic landmark midway between the *Ormulum* (**Orm**) and late fourteenth-century materials. It is a prayer of thanks and devotion addressed directly to Jesus. Passionate delivery and sometimes graphic imagery ("me longeth sore þi woundes to kisse" [line 10]) are two of its most distinguishing features. Meditation on the Passion can both forgive past sins and protect one from future sin; the whole poem has a penitential program. It is based on a gospel harmony, although incidents from Comestor, patristic homiletic passages, and bestiary material are combined.[1]

The oldest manuscript, 3, is a fragment of only 519 lines, but its date circa 1300 makes it at least ninety years older than the version in the Vernon manuscript (also fragmentary), which is illustrated by seven miniatures. Turville-Petre notes that "the remaining leaves were no doubt removed because of their miniatures" ("Relationship of Vernon and Clopton Manuscripts," 29; the initial capital has also been excised), and he estimates that, in their complete forms, Clopton had some 2,230 lines, and Vernon 2250 (35). Space has been left in Clopton for thirty-three miniatures; "the only text in Clopton that has a direct relationship with Vernon is the *Euangelie*" (41). **EE** extends to some 2,440 lines if the various extracts in the manuscripts are spliced.

EE begins part 2 of Vernon (at fol. 105). Thus an Old Testament poem,

---

1. The exempla of a hart, adder, and eagle (line 66 ff.) may derive from the Middle English *Bestiary* (Morris, *Old English Miscellany,* 1–25). Debts to the *Historia* include Herod's trip to Rome and the burning of the ships at Cilicia (lines 753–61; PL 198.1543), the downfall of idols at Jesus's coming into Egypt (774–83; col. 1543; cf. Is. 19:1), and the devil's presence at the crucifixion (1584–87; col. 1630). Turville-Petre cites col. 1628 for "28 lines [in manuscript 4] after [line] 1386, explaining that the dream of Pilate's wife was a device of Satan, working as usual through a woman, to thwart the Redemption" ("Relationship of Vernon and Clopton Manuscripts," 34).

OTH, and this New Testament poem, both indebted to the *Historia Scholastica,* begin the first two parts (out of five) of the most important compendium of Middle English poetry and prose.

From manuscript 2, as edited by Campbell, *"Evangelie":*

Lines	Events	Bible
1–40	Introductory prayer to Jesus	
41–179	Excursus on pagan worship of "stones & tree" (46); bestiary lore on the adder and eagle (only in MS 3).	
180–220	Old Testament prophecies of Christ	Ps. 79:3; Is. 7:14
221–284	Annunciation; Conception of Elizabeth; sun through glass analogy (only in MS 3)	Luke 1:26–38
285–336	Visitation of Elizabeth: "þe childe in my wombe makith glee as sone as i harde þe steuen of þe" (293–94); Magnificat	Luke 1:39–56
337–445	Zachary and the angel; birth of John the Baptist: "In þat tablet he wrote on-one, þe childes name shal be Iohn" (414–15); Benedictus; "Wildernesse sone he sohte / In penaunce þare his lif to lede" (437–38)	Luke 1:6–25, 57–80
446–503	Joseph's doubts calmed by the angel	Matt. 1:18–25
504–545	Decree of Caesar Augustus; Nativity in Bethlehem; ox and ass	Luke 2:1–7; Is. 1:3
546–591	Shepherds: "in þe cuntree þere bisyde Heerdes waked in a faire meede" (547–48); Circumcision	Luke 2:8–21
592–681	Magi; Herod; the star; gifts	Matt. 2:1–12
682–727	Presentation in the Temple; Simeon and Anna; Nunc dimittis	Luke 2:22–38
728–821	Slaughter of the Innocents; Flight into Egypt, Archelaus	Matt. 2:13–23
822–868	John the Baptist: "I am not worþi þer-for / to lese þe thwonge of his sho" (833–34); Baptism of Jesus: "þis is my son" (867)	Matt. 3:1, 11–17
869–946	Temptation: "Make þise stones turne to breed" (881)	Matt. 4:1–11
947–990	John imprisoned; Christ preaches and heals in Galilee; Calling of Peter, Andrew, James, John	Matt. 4:12, 18–23
991–1028	Beatitudes: "Blessed be þe poore in wille" (995)	Matt. 5:1–12
1029–1056	Palm Sunday	Matt. 21:8–11
1057–1090	Predicts betrayal and Peter's denials	Matt. 26: 20–22, 31–35

Lines	Events	Bible
1091–1140	Agony in Gethsemani: "ffadir if it þi wille be, / turne þis passion from me" (1095–96); arrest	Luke 22:39–48, 52–53
1141–1168	Peter's denials: "þan gan ihc petir biholde, / & petirs hert bigan to colde" (1163–64)	Luke 22:54–62
1169–1260	Christ before Caiphas and Pilate	Matt. 26:57–68; John 18:33–37
1261–1304	Judas returns silver, bursts; Judas compared to Peter, Mary Magdalen, David	Matt. 27:3–5; Acts 1:18
1305–1382	Christ before Herod and Pilate; Barabbas: "þerfore i wil aftir my wille / him chastise & lat him go stille" (1353–54)	Luke 23:6–25
1383–1455	Pilate's wife's warning; washes hands; road to Calvary	Matt. 27:19–31
1456–1471	Jesus addresses daughters of Jerusalem: "Blessed be wele and mylde, / þe wombe þat neuer was with childe" (1468–69)	Luke 23:27–29
1472–1583	Crucifixion; Last Words; forgives Good Thief; Longinus	Luke 23:32–46; John 19:28–29, 34
1584–1628	Joseph of Arimathea and Nicodemus; precautions of the Jews	Matt. 27:57–66; John 19:38–39
1629–1701	Resurrection, the Marys at the tomb: "Woman, whi wepestou so sore?" (1685)	Matt. 28:1–10; John 20:1–18
1702–1750	Doubting Thomas: "þi fyngyr Thomas put nou here" (1735)	John 20:19–29
1751–1788	Ascension; choosing of Matthias; Pentecost; St. Denis, altar to an unknown god (only in MSS 4 and 5)	Acts 1:6–14, 26; 2:1–15; 17
1789–1879	Seven Works of Bodily Mercy: "ȝee cursed gostes hennys ȝee wende, / in-to þe fyre þat hath none ende" (1827–28); concluding reflections on the life of Jesus	Matt. 25:35–46

A Newe Lessoun off Crystys Ressurrectoun CR

IMEV/S 1189

1. London, BL Royal 17.c.xvii (152v–155v), early 15th c., 501 lines in octosyllabic couplets (the tercet in lines 351–53 accounts for the extra line).

Edition: Bowers, *Three Religious Poems,* 19–32.
Study: Pickering, *"Newe Lessoun."*

The poem is related to **EE.** It may be acephalous since it begins "All this before Ihesu tham sayde / Or handys on Hym thai layde." The amount of biblical narrative is greatly reduced in the last third of the poem, where penitential and Doomsday themes predominate.

Lines	Events	Bible
1–52	Marys at the tomb, the angels: "Therfor be ye not in drede, / Seke Hym not emang the dede (43–44)	Mark 16:1–7; Luke 24:1–9
53–102	Jesus appears to Mary Magdalen as a "gardynere" (62): "Ihesu bad hyre ... toche hym not" (77–78); recollection of the "sewen devles" cast out from Mary	John 20:11–18; Luke 8:2
103–188	Post-resurrection appearances to Peter, Cleophas and Luke; Doubting Thomas: "Tomas ansuerd wyt drere chere 'My God, My Lord, Thu hert here!' / Ihesu hym sayd, 'For thu me se, / Tomas, wyt thi fleschely hee; / Thu it lewes wele for–thi. / Bot thai be blyssyd & celi / That of me saw reght noght / & lewes it wele wyt stedfast toght'" (175–82)	John 20:8; Luke 24:13; John 20:19–29
189–198	No one, not even Abraham, Isaac, or John the Baptist, entered Heaven before Christ prepared the way	
199–238	Ascension; Appointment of Matthias	Acts 1: 10–13, 26
239–290	Pentecost: "Summe sayd that thai drunkynd were" (268); "the mone in blode" (286)	Acts 2:1–21
291–314	Synopsis of the Creed, citing Augustine	
315–409	Seven Works of Bodily Mercy: "That ye dyd sekyre be / To any of myne ye dyd to Me" (368–69)	Matt. 25: 42–46
410–441	Seven Deadly Sins, with the odd reference that "Wrath makys man to af sore hond" (424)	
442–479	Intercessions of Mary as told by St. Bernard	
480–501	Blisses of heaven	

Pepysian Gospel Harmony **PGH**

IPMEP 530
Manual, 2:393 [31]

1. Cambridge, Magdalene College Pepys 2498 (1r–43r), ca. 1400.

Edition—Goates, *Pepysian Harmony.*

The contents of the manuscript make it an impressive biblical compendium. Following **PGH** are a "treatise" to turn attention from romances (actually the introduction to a Middle English translation of Robert of Gretham's *Miroir*), an exposition of the Ten Commandments (**TC**), **AJC, MPPs,** a version of the *Ancrene Riwle,* and **PCL.**

Mistakes and idiosyncrasies in translation strongly suggest a nonextant French source. Some parables are summarized so radically that they resemble the bare outlines in **MES.** For example, after the queries by the rich man and the disciples concerning who may be saved, the Parable of the Vineyard (Matt. 20:1–16) becomes simply: "And þanne tolde Jesus hem an ensaumple of a man þat brouȝth werk men in to his vyner. And he paied hem þat comen late raþer, & als mykel ȝaf hem as hem þat comen first" (Goates, *Pepysian Harmony,* 69). But this is unusually brief. The major points of most parables and events are paraphrased with care.

Goates finds only two apocryphal traditions in the *Harmony:* that Christ shared the manger with an ox and an ass (Is. 1:3; see also the *Gospel of Ps-Matthew* [Elliot, *Apocryphal New Testament,* 94]) and that Judas hanged himself from an elder tree.[2] Terms like "Pharisee" and "centurion" are explained by definition, numerous short phrases are added for emphasis, and "homely parallels" (xlvi) abound. The Pharisees are "þe folk of religioun in þat tyme" and John eats not locusts and wild honey (Matt. 3:4) but "ramesones and wilde-napes" (garlic and bryony) (9).

The work is clearly devotional: chapters 88 and 95, parts of the Passion narrative, bear the heading "meditacioun," and other headings follow the canonical hours. The colophon refers to "þe Gospels an Hundreþ and sex, outnomen þe Passioun of Crist," thus indicating that the seven Passion chapters (95–101) function as an independent unit.

The "Analytical Summary" on pages 114–22 of Goates's edition is more detailed than the following, which notes the principal biblical contents in each of the manuscript's 113 divisions. Nearly all of these divisions begin with a "Hou þat Jhesus . . ." formula.

---

2. See her notes on 123–24 and 132–33. The elder tree tradition was strongest in England: cf. Langland, *Piers Plowman,* A.i.66, B.i.68, C.i.64, and **NP** (lines 819–904).

MS§	Events	Bible
1	Christ's divinity and humanity	John 1:1–18
2	Zachary; Elizabeth; the Annunciation; Visitation; Joseph reassured; John's naming	Luke 1:5–68, 80; Matt. 1:18–21, 24
3	Nativity; shepherds; the ox and ass; Circumcision; Magi	Luke 2:1–21; Matt. 2:1–12; Is. 1:3
4	Simeon, Anna, Nunc dimittis	Luke 2:22–39
5	Flight into Egypt; Slaughter of Innocents	Matt. 2:13–23; Luke 2:40
6	Jesus disputes with Temple Doctors: "wharfore souȝth ȝe me? Ne wite ȝe nouȝth wel þat j moste be in my fader nedes?"	Luke 2:41–52
7	John the Baptist prophesies; baptizes Jesus	Matt. 3:1–17; John 1:19–28
8	Temptation by the Devil	Matt. 4:1–11
9	Calling of Andrew, Peter, Philip, Nathanael: "Loo, whare geþ Goddes lombe!"	John 1:29–51
10	Miracle at Cana, water into wine	John 2:1–11
11	Cleanses Temple [cf.§82]; Nicodemus born again	John 2:12–3:21
12	John's witness: "Jesus was as þe spouse & he riȝth as is frende"	John 3:22–36
13	John imprisoned; Woman of Samaria; "euerych prophete is werst honoured in his owene cuntre" [cf. §46]	John 4:1–45
14	Christ heals "prouostes son" at Capharnaum	John 4:46–54
15	Miraculous draft of fish; call of James and John	Luke 5:1–11
16	Jesus preaches in Nazareth; recalls widow of Sarephta; Namaan the Syrian	Luke 4:16–30
17	Call of "Simondes fader" (?), Andrew, James and John [repeats synoptic episode told at §15; Simon's father is not mentioned in the Gospels]	Matt. 4:13–22
18	Expels demon at Capharnaum; heals Simon's wife's mother; preaches in Galilee	Mark 1:21–39; Luke 4:33–44
19	Anonymous calls to Discipleship; asleep in boat, calms storm; Gerasene swine: "þe fendes . . . seiden þat hij weren a legioun. (þat amounted sex þousende and sex hundreþ and sexti and sex.)"	Luke 9:57–62; Matt. 8:18–27; Luke 8:26–40
20	Heals paralytic; call of Matthew-Levi; answers reproaches of the Pharisees	Matt. 9:2–17; Mark 2:1–22; Luke 5:17–39
21	Heals Jairus's daughter, woman with issue of blood, and "prince's" daughter	Mark 5:21–43

MS§	Events	Bible
22	Heals two blind men, one dumb man	Matt. 9:27–34
23	Jesus without honor in his own country	Mark 6:1–5
24	Calling of twelve Disciples, Boanerges; Beatitudes, the "ten Comaundementȝ of þe newe lawe"	Mark 3:13–19; Matt. 5:1–10
25	Sermon on the "faire playne"	Luke 6:17, 31–35, 48–49
26	Heals a leper	Luke 5:12–16
27	Heals centurion's servant	Luke 7:1–10
28	Commissions twelve Apostles: "And he badde hem be wyse as Seint Petre and symple as a douue" [Goates takes "Seint Petre" as a mistranslation of a MS abbreviation]	Matt. 10:1–16
29	Widow's daughter [sic] raised at Nain	Luke 7:11–18
30	Answers John's messengers	Luke 7:19–34
31	Anointing at Simon the Pharisee's house	Luke 7:36–8:3
32	Commissions seventy-two Disciples	Luke 10:1–16
33	Disciples report on mission; "ich seiȝ Sathan als dust falle from heuene" [see Morey, "Fall in Particulate"]	Luke 10:17–24
34	The greatest commandment [cf.§88]; Good Samaritan	Luke 10:25–37
35	Mary and Martha	Luke 10:38–42
36	Pater Noster; midnight request for a loaf of bread	Luke 11:1–13
37	Plucking corn: "ich am lord of þe sabat"	Matt. 12:1–8
38	Healing on the Sabbath	Matt. 12:9–13
39	Jesus admonishes followers	Mark 3:6–12
40	Casts out devil; Pharisees seek a sign; Jonas, Queen of Saba; "Yblissed be þe wombe þat þe bare"	Matt. 12:22–50; Luke 11:14–32
41	Rebukes Pharisees	Luke 11:37–51
42	Warnings against avarice; Signs of the Time	Luke 12:1, 13–59
43	Pilate and the Galileans; tower of Siloe; Parable of Fig Tree	Luke 13:1–9
44	Heals "bocched" woman on the Sabbath	Luke 13:10–17
45	Parables of the Sower, Mustard Seed, Leaven, Pearl of Great Price	Matt. 13:1–8, 24–34, 44–46, 52
46	Prophet without honor in own country [cf. §13]	Matt. 13:53–58
47	Heals man with a 38-year sickness	John 5:1–17
48	Dance of Salome; John beheaded; Christ enters desert	Matt. 14:6–13
49	Feeds five thousand; walks on water; the Bread of Life; discontent among followers; Judas Iscariot	Matt. 14:14–33; John 6:4–71
50	Heals in Genesar	Matt. 14:34–36

MS§	Events	Bible
51	Causes of defilement	Matt. 15:1–20
52	Heals Canaanite Woman's daughter	Matt. 15:21–28
53	Heals deaf and dumb man with spittle	Mark 7:31–37
54	Feeds four thousand	Matt. 15:32–39
55	Pharisees ask for a sign	Matt. 16:1–4
56	Disciples forget to take bread	Matt. 16:5–12
57	Heals blind man who sees trees	Mark 8:22–26
58	Herod's fear of Jesus	Matt. 14:1–2
59	Feast of Tabernacles ("loges"); Woman taken in adultery; heals blind man at Siloe	John 7:1–8:11; 9: 1–16, 34–41
60	"þou art Petre on wham j schal founde my my chirche"; foretells Passion	Matt. 16:13–28
61	Transfiguration; cures possessed boy: "Sir, ich bileue wel, ac helpeþ me misbileuande"	Mark 9:2–28
62	Predicts Death and Resurrection	Mark 9:29–31
63	Jesus pays "trewage"; teaches humility, forgiveness	Matt. 17:23–26; 18:15–35; Mark 9: 32–41
64	Samaritans refuse Jesus; Jesus rebukes James and John; first last, last first	Luke 9:51–56; 13: 22–23, 27–33
65	Heals dropsical man; Parable of the Bridal Feast	Luke 14:1–24
66	Renounce everything to follow Christ	Luke 14:25–33
67	Parables of the Lost Sheep, Coin, Prodigal Son	Luke 15:1–11, 32
68	Unjust Steward; Lazarus and Dives	Luke 16:1–25
69	Flee slander, forgive brother, do your duty	Luke 17:1–10
70	Heals ten lepers	Luke 17:12–19
71	Second Coming; Parables of the Unrighteous Judge and of the Pharisee and the Publican	Luke 17:20–22; 18:1–14
72	On divorce and marriage	Matt. 19:3–12
73	Blesses the children	Matt. 19:13–15
74	Young prince: "who so hym affieþ in his richesse ne may nomore entren wiþ inne þe blisse of heuene þan a camel may þorouȝ a nedel hole"; brief summary of Parable of the Vineyard	Matt. 19:16–30; 20:1, 9–10
75	Predicts Death and Resurrection; request of James and John	Matt. 20:17–28
76	Heals blind man of Jericho	Luke 18:35–43
77	Zacheus; Parable of the Ten Pounds	Luke 19:1–14, 26
78	Heals two blind men of Jericho	Matt. 20:29–34
79	"my fader & ich aren al on"	John 10:22–42
80	Raising of Lazarus	John 11:1–56
81	Mary anoints Jesus; Judas objects; Palm Sunday	John 12:2–11; Luke 19:28–44
82	Cleanses Temple [cf. §11]	Matt. 21:12–17

MS§	Events	Bible
83	Curses fig tree	Matt. 21:18–21
84	Christ's authority questioned	Matt. 21:23–27
85	Parables of the Sons, the Evil Husbandman, the Cornerstone, the Marriage Feast	Matt. 21:28–22:6
86	Tribute to Caesar	Matt. 22:15–22
87	Wife with seven husbands	Matt. 22:23–32
88	The greatest commandments [cf.§34]	Matt. 22:34–40
89	Christ's genealogy from David	Matt. 22:41–46
90	Hypocrisy of Pharisees; Lament over Jerusalem: "hij weren liche þe graues þat ben daubed and made faire wiþouten, and stunken wiþinne"	Matt. 23:3, 13–14, 27, 33–39
91	Widow's farthing	Mark 12:41–44
92	Voice from Heaven; Christ predicts Passion	John 12:20–35, 42–47
93	Synoptic Apocalypse; Parables of Ten Virgins and of the Talents	Matt. 25:1–4, 14–46
94	The thirty pence	Matt. 26:1–5, 14–16
95	Last Supper; predicts Peter's denials; washes Disciples' feet; gives sop to Judas; comforts Disciples.	Matt. 26:17–28; Luke 22:24–38; John 13:4–15, 21–38; with summary of John 14; 15; 16; 17
96	Agony in Gethsemani; Kiss of Judas; soldiers collapse; Malchus's ear; Man in linen cloth; Peter's denials; Annas; the Buffeting	Matt. 26:30–75; John 18:6; Mark 14:51–52

[An abridged Hours of the Cross template is imposed on the Passion]
Undern

| 97 | Caiphas; Pilate; suicide of Judas | Matt. 27:1–10; Acts 1:18 |

Midday

| 98 | Trial before Pilate and Herod; Barabbas; Scourging; Pilate's wife's dream; Pilate washes hands; Simon of Cyrene (called "leprous") | Matt. 27:11–32; Luke 23:8–12; John 19:14 |

None

| 99 | Crucifixion; Pilate's inscription; Casting of Lots; Mary entrusted to John; salvation of Good Thief | Matt. 27:33–45; John 19:19–27; Luke 23:39–45 |

Evensong

| 100 | Last Words; earthquake; Centurion's witness | Matt. 27:46–56; |

MS§	Events	Bible
		Luke 23:46–48; John 19:28–30
101	Side pierced; Joseph of Arimathea; ointment prepared; precautions of the Jews	Matt. 27:57–66; John 19:31–42; Luke 23:55–56
102	Angel opens tomb	Matt. 28:1–4
103	Peter and John investigate; Christ appears to Mary Magdalen	John 20:1–17
104	Christ appears to other women	Matt. 28:9–10
105	Guards bribed	Matt. 28:11–15
106	Disciples doubt reports	Luke 24:9–11
107	Appears to Peter	Luke 24:12, 34
108	Appears to Cleophas and Lucas	Luke 24:13–35
109	Appears to Disciples	Luke 24:36–49
110	Appears to Thomas, the Five Hundred	John 20:26–30; 1Cor. 15:6
111	Jesus commissions Disciples at Galilee	Matt. 28:16–20
112	Appears to Disciples at Tiberias	John 21:1–23
113	Exhorts Disciples; Ascension; Pentecost	Mark 16:14–20; Acts 1:3–14; 2: 2–4

A Tretys That Is a Rule and a Forme of Lyvynge Perteynyng to a Recluse RFL

(title derives from manuscript 2)
IPMEP 478, 607.5

> 1. Oxford, Bodleian Lib. Eng. poet. a.1 (Vernon) (iii verso–viii recto), ca. 1390.
> 2. Oxford, Bodleian Lib. Bodley 423 (*SC* 2322) (178r–192r), 15th c.

Editions: 1—Aelred of Rievaulx, *De Institutione Inclusarum,* 26–60;
  Horstmann, "Informacio Alredi Abbatis."
  2—Aelred of Rievaulx, *De Institutione Inclusarum,* 1–25.
Facsimile: Doyle, *Vernon Manuscript.*

The two manuscripts preserve independent translations of the *De Institutione Inclusarum* by the Cistercian Aelred of Rievaulx (d. 1167). Among other Latin works, he is the author of *The Chastising of God's Children,* which was also translated into English (Bazire and Colledge, *Chastising*); his work was known to the author of the *Ancrene Riwle,* another major exposition of female anchoritic life produced in England. As such, the **RFL** pertains mostly to matters of conduct, prayer, and the ascetic virtues, but sections of both translations counterpoint events of Christ's life with meditations wherein the individual imaginatively reconstructs the events.

Biblical quotation pervades the work, but the following outlines only those sections treating Christ's life (chapters 14–17 in manuscript 1, chapter 14 in manuscript 2).

From manuscript 1, Aelred of Rievaulx, *De Institutione Inclusarum:*

Pages	Events	Bible
39	Martha and Mary as exemplars of the active and contemplative lives; Annunciation and Incarnation	Luke 10:38–42; 1:28
40	Visitation of Elizabeth; Nativity; angel appears to the shepherds	Luke 1:39–41; 2:7, 14; Is. 9:6
41	Magi; Robbery during the Flight into Egypt by the Good Thief; Christ disputes with Temple Doctors	Matt. 2:11, 13; Luke 23:40–43; 2:41–48
42	Baptism; Temptation in the Desert; Woman taken in adultery; Anointing by Mary Magdalen	Matt. 3:16–17; 4:1–2; John 8:3–11; 12:1–3
43	Paralytic lowered through roof	Mark 2:2–7
44	Anointing at Bethany; Judas objects: "sche had ydoo a good dede in me"	John 12:1–5; Matt. 26:10
45	Enters Jerusalem; washes Disciples' feet	Matt. 21:9; John 13:5
46	As John reclined at Jesus's breast, "ren þu, suster, to þe pappys of his manhede, and þerof suk out melke"; Agony in Gethsemani: "Miȝtest þu not wake on houre wit me?"; Arrest; Malchus's ear	John 13:23; Matt. 26:36–40, 47; John 18:10
47	Peter's denials; Scourging; Jesus before Pilate	Matt. 26:75; John 19:1–5
48	Casting of lots for Christ's clothes; Crucifixion; "Fader, forȝif hem"; John and Mary entrusted to each other:	John 19:24; Matt. 27:51; Luke 23:34
49	"Wumman, lo þer þy sone"; spear of Longinus; Deposition by Joseph of Arimathea	John 19:26, 34, 38
50	Mary at the tomb: "Rabi, Maister!" "Touche me not, com not neiȝ me!"	John 20:11–18

Versions of the *Gospel of Nicodemus* GNs and GNp

This narrative was widespread in medieval Europe in a variety of forms, and is best known for its account of Christ's Harrowing of Hell, part 2 in the traditional division of the text. The bulk of the narrative, however, is biblically based since part 1 (called the "Commentaries of Nicodemus," the "Acta Pilati," or the "Gesta Pilati") concerns Christ's arrest, trial, scourging, Passion, and Deposition. As the titles imply, Pilate and Nicodemus (a supposed disciple mentioned in John 3:1–10, 7:50, and 19:39), with Joseph of Arimathea, are principal figures in the first part. See Elliott, *Apocryphal New Testament,* 164–85.

Part 2, the "Descensus Christi ad Inferos," represents itself as the account of Carius and Lucius (see below lines 1093–1248), two eyewitnesses to the Harrowing who arose at the Crucifixion (Matt. 27:52–53) and entered Jerusalem. Prophets, notably David, Isaias (Is. 9:2, cf. Matt. 4:16), Simeon (Luke 2:29–35), and John the Baptist, are quoted as they anticipate and describe Christ's entry into hell in the same terms used to describe his Incarnation on earth. See Elliott, *Apocryphal New Testament,* 185–204.

An independent 250-line translation of part 2 (*Manual,* 2:449 [313a]; *IMEV* 185, 1258, *IMEV/S* 1850.5, the "Short Couplet Harrowing") is edited by Hulme (*Harrowing,* 2–22) and is extant in three manuscripts, all available in facsimile: Oxford, Bodleian Lib. Digby 86 (*SC* 1687) 119r–120v, ca. 1275 (Tschann and Parkes, *Digby 86*); London, BL Harley 2253, 55v–56v, ca. 1310 (Ker, *Harley 2253*); Edinburgh, National Lib. of Scotland Advocates 19.2.1 (36r–37r), ca. 1340, acephalous and atelous (Pearsall and Cunningham, *Auchinleck Manuscript*). For the "Septenary Harrowing" (*Manual,* 2:449 [313b]) see below **HH** and **DJ.**

For the Old English versions, and for the relationships to the Greek and Latin sources, see Morey, *Gospel of Nicodemus.* The earliest Old English translation of the *Gospel of Nicodemus* follows translations of the four Gospels in Cambridge, Univ. Lib. Ii.2.11, giving the impression that *Nicodemus* qualified as a "fifth" gospel.

Hulme (*Harrowing*) asserts the independence of the Middle English versions from the Old French translations (xvii), notes that that the York plays on the Passion borrow from the Middle English versions (xix–xxi), and surmises that the first poetic version of the *Gospel* in Middle English was made in the early fourteenth century.

Stanzaic version **GNs**

IMEV 512
Manual, 2:448 [312a]

1. London, BL Cotton Galba E.ix (57v–66v), 15th c., 1,764 lines in twelve-line stanzas: abababababcdcd.

2. London, BL Harley 4196 (206r–215r), 15th c., 1,764 lines as above (also contains **NHC**).
3. London, BL Add. 32578 (116v–140v), 15th c., 1,812 lines as above.
4. London, Sion Coll. Arc.L.40.2 / E.25 (13r–39v), 15th c., 1,752 lines as above.

Editions: 1, 2, 3, 4 in parallel—Hulme, *Harrowing,* 22–136.
2—Horstmann, "Evangelium Nicodemi."
4—Horstmann, "Nachträge (Schluss)" (1882).

See Hulme (xxii–xxxii) for descriptions of the manuscripts.

Couplet version
IMEV 130
Manual, 2:448 [312b]

1. London, BL Add. 39996 (52v–54r), late 15th c., early 16th c.

No edition.

Quoted from manuscript 4, lines 5–12:

> þis stori wrate Nechodemus
> in Ebru for grette daynte;
> Sythen þe emperoure theodosius
> gert itte al translated bee;
> and sithen fra hande to hande,
> ffor þere vnletterede ledes
> a clerk of Inglande
> in his rymaly þus redes.

From manuscript 3, ed. Hulme, *Harrowing:*

Lines	Events	Bible
1–192	Christ before Pilate	Matt. 26:59–60
193–200	Pilate's wife Procula warns husband	Matt. 27:19
227–236	Jewish accusers recall Slaughter of Innocents; Flight into Egypt	Matt. 1:16–21
325–416	Christ before Pilate: "Pilate asked hym eft: / 'What es suthefastnes?'" (357–58); "hys blode mot vs falle / And on our childer bathe" (375–76)	Matt. 27:11–14, 22–25; Luke 23: 13–14; John 19: 33–38
433–456	Nicodemus recalls false signs of Iannes and Mambres	Ex. 7:9–11
473–492	Ten lepers, blind man, infirm man testify how Christ healed them: "Tite ta þi bedde and ga!" (484)	Luke 17:11–19; Mark 8:22–26; John 5:1–9; 9: 1–7

Lines	Events	Bible
517–528	Barabbas	Matt. 27:15–22
541–588	Pilate confutes Jews by recalling Exodus, miracles in the Sinai, Visit of Magi, Slaughter of Innocents; washes hands	Matt. 27:24
589–628	Scourging; Crown of Thorns; Longinus	John 19:1–2, 34
629–672	Pilate's inscription; Dismas and Gestas: "I hete þe forto be þis day / with me in paradyse" (655–56); "in þi hend, / my fader of mightes mast, / my saul now sall I send" (669–71)	John 19:18–22; Luke 23:39–46
673–712	Centurion, eclipse, veil torn, earthquake; dead rise	Luke 23:44–48; Matt. 27:51–54
713–724	Joseph of Arimathea, Deposition, Burial	John 19:38–42
725–792	Nicodemus warns Jews; Joseph imprisoned	
793–828	Angel appears to the two Marys	Matt. 28:1–7
853–864	Jews pay soldiers to keep silent	Matt. 28:11–15
865–888	Three priests testify to Christ's appearance to Disciples on Mt. Olivet; Ascension	Matt. 28:16–19; Luke 24:51
889–1092	Joseph and others recount how Christ appeared to them	
1093–1248	"Caryn and Lentin" recount testimony of Isaias, Simeon, John the Baptist	Matt. 27:52–53; Is. 9:2; Luke 2: 29–35
1249–1284	Adam recalls Seth's quest for the Oil of Mercy (Quinn, *Quest*)	
1285–1632	The Harrowing of Hell	
1633–1812	Pilate makes further inquiries and writes his letter to Emperor Claudius reporting that Christ died and rose again	

Prose *Gospel of Nicodemus* GNp

IPMEP 395 (see also *IPMEP* 397)
Manual, 2:448 [312c]

1. Oxford, Bodleian Lib. Bodley 207 (*SC* 2021) (120v–124r), 15th c.
2. Cambridge, Univ. Lib. Mm.1.29 (8r–16r), late 15th c.
3. London, BL Egerton 2658 (15v–18r), mid-15th c.
4. London, BL Harley 149 (255r–276r), late 15th c.
5. London, BL Add. 16165 (94v–114v), 15th c.
6. Salisbury, Cathedral Lib. 39 (129v–147r), 15th c.
7. Worcester, Cathedral Lib. F.172 (4r–12r), late 15th c.
8. Stonyhurst College B.xliii (83r–96r), 15th c.

9. Winchester College, Warden and Fellows' Lib. 33 (74r–93v).

10. Manchester, John Rylands Lib. English 895 (111r–25r).

11. Washington, Lib. of Congress pre-AC 4 (37v–63v), early 15th c.

Editions: 4—Lindström, *Gospel of Nicodemus,* in parallel with two French source texts.

1, 3, 8, 10—Holden, *Gospel of Nicodemus.*

11—Hill, *"Gospel of Nicodemus."*

See *Manual,* 2:641 [312c] for University Microfilms of early printed editions.

Hill notes that manuscript 11 is in the Harley 149 tradition (manuscript 4), though it contains, as Harley 149 does not, Simon of Cyrene (Matt. 27:32). Harley 149 contains some passages which appear in neither of the French versions (Lindström, 16–19).

From manuscript 4, ed. Lindström, *Gospel of Nicodemus:*

Pages [capitula]	Events	Bible
44–45 [1–2]	Judas and others accuse Jesus before Pilate: "thorough þe prynce Belȝebub cast oute the deuelles of folkes" (p. 45)	Matt. 12:24; 26:59–60
46–50 [3–4]	Beedle recalls entry into Jerusalem; idols bow in Jesus's presence (cf. Is. 19:1)	Matt. 21:8–9
51–52 [5]	Procula warns Pilate in a dream	Matt. 27:19
52–55 [6–7]	Jews recall Slaughter of Innocents, Flight into Egypt; debate legitimacy of Christ's birth	Matt. 2:16, 21
55–57 [8]	"Y can fynde no blame yn thys man" (55) "My reeme ys not of thys worlde" (56)	Luke 23:1–5; John 18:33–38
57–60 [9]	"Hys bloode be vppon vs and on oure chyldren" (58)	Matt. 27:25
60–63 [10]	Nicodemus parallels Christ with Moses	
63–66 [11–13]	How Christ healed "Melga," "Mossy," "Mysael" the leper; Veronica; how Christ raised Lazarus	Matt. 9:2–6, 27–30; 8:2–4; 9:20–22; John 11:44
66–69 [14–16]	"Leve vs Barabbas" (66); Pilate recalls deliverance from Egypt and miracles in the desert; washes hands; Jews recall gifts of the Magi; Christ before Herod	Matt. 27:21–27; Ex. 14:22; Matt. 2:11; Luke 23:6–12
70–71 [17]	Scourging; Crucifixion between Dismas and Gestas; "Ffadyr, forgeue these peple" (71)	Matt. 27:28–32, 34, 38; Luke 23:34
71–72 [18]	Mary entrusted to John; garments divided;	John 19:26–27;

Pages [capitula]	Events	Bible
	Christ mocked on the Cross	Matt. 27:35, 40, 42
73–74 [19]	Pilate's inscription; salvation of Dismas; wonders at Christ's death	John 19:19–22; Luke 24:39–46
74–75 [20]	Words of the Centurion; Longinus; Judas returns silver: "Y haue synned yn betrayenge of the ryghtwys bloode" (75)	Matt. 27:54, 3–4; John 19:34
[capitula numeration ceases]		
76–84	Bodies rise; Joseph of Arimathea; the Deposition and Burial; Joseph imprisoned; Jews appoint four knights to guard the tomb: "Mossy," Danyel," "Aaron," "Samuel"; their account of the angel and the Resurrection; they are bribed	Matt. 27:52–53; John 19:38–42; Matt. 28:2–8, 12–13
84–89	Jesus charges Disciples; ascends to Heaven as Elias was "rauyssched yn-to hevene" (88)	Mark 16:15–16, 19; 3Kg. 2:11
89–97	Joseph decribes how Jesus freed him from prison; that Carius and Lucius, sons of Simeon, witnessed the Harrowing	
97–125	Their account of the Harrowing of Hell, with the testimonies of the prophets and patriarchs	
126–129	Pilate's inquiries regarding Christ's divinity; the body of Christ as the Ark of the Testament	Ex. 25:10

The Middle English Prose Complaint of Our Lady and Gospel of Nicodemus PCL

1. Cambridge, Magdalene College Pepys 2498 (449r–463v), mid-14th c.
2. Leeds, Univ. Lib. Brotherton 501 (109v, 108r–v, 115r), early 15th c.
3. San Marino, Huntington Lib. HM 144 (21r–54v), late 15th c.

Editions: 1—Marx and Drennan, *Prose Complaint,* 73–136, with variants from 2, in parallel with a French version from London, BL MS Royal 20.B.v.
3—Marx and Drennan, *Prose Complaint,* 173–203.

Their edition is exemplary, with extensive commentary, a glossary, and a table of biblical sources (for the *Complaint* section only).

Manuscript 1 contains **PGH, MPPs, AJC,** the prose *Complaint of Our Lady* (**PCL**), and the earliest known Middle English prose version of the *Gospel of*

Nicodemus. The editors claim that the pairing of the last two works was inten-
tional: "Our main hypothesis is that the evidence of the manuscripts argues
that the two texts form a loose narrative sequence and that this was recognized by later manuscript compilers, redactors, and a translator."[3] Thus the
works form an organic treatment of the Death and Resurrection of Christ.
Marx and Drennan use the evidence provided by manuscript contents and
sequences to develop some sense of how medievals themselves thought of
and read these works.

The *Complaint* (pp. 73–118) derives from the Ps.-Bernard *Quis Dabit* (*Liber
de Passione Christi et Doloribus et Planctibus Matris Ejus*), Mary's "eyewitness"
account of the events leading up to, and including, the Burial and Deposition. For the sorrows of Mary tradition, see *Manual,* 3:684–87, 841–43, and
Bestul, *Texts of the Passion,* 52. For *Nicodemus* (pp. 118–36), see above, **GNs**
and **GNp.**

On pages 55–70 Marx and Drennan explain how manuscript 3 was revised to include Latin verses and to make it closer to the biblical text. The
Complaint section was revised most. There are various sententious phrases
throughout, such as "sorer owen þe lered to ben adradde þan þe lewed for
he wot what he doþe" (p. 77, lines 13–14), which are often connected to a
biblical verse (here Luke 23:34, "Father, forgive them, for they know not
what they do").

The following outline follows manuscript 1, since it is "the best representative of the early ME version of the sequence" (70). The table of biblical
sources on pages 27–30 is more detailed than the following, but it covers
only the *Complaint* section, whereas both the *Complaint* and *Nicodemus* are
covered here.

Page	Events	Bible
74	Christ prophesies death; Palm Sunday	Matt. 20:17–19; 21:7–9
75	Raising of Lazarus; plots of Caiphas	John 11:39, 45–53
76	Judas's thirty pence; Last Supper	Matt. 26:14–28
77	Identity of the Traitor; Satan enters Judas	John 13:18–27
78	Christ prophesies Peter's denial	Matt. 26:31–35
79	Washes Disciples' feet; "suffre þat þis anguisch passe fro me"	John 13:5; Luke 22:42
80	Sweats blood; comforted by angel; reproaches Disciples	Luke 22:43–46; Matt. 26:40–46

3. Marx and Drennan, *Prose Complaint,* 7. These texts are paired in five surviving manuscripts, two Anglo-Norman and three Middle English.

Page	Events	Bible
81–82	Kiss of Judas; arresting party collapses; Malchus's ear	Matt. 26:47–48; John 18:7–12
83	Peter's first denial; Christ before Annas	John 18:13–24
84	Peter's second and third denials; cock's crow	John 18:25–27; Luke 22:61–62
85–86	Christ before Caiphas; Buffeting	Luke 22:63–71
87	Christ before Pilate	Luke 23:1–7
88–89	Christ before Herod and Pilate	Luke 23:8–15
90–93	Barabbas; Pilate washes hands	Luke 23:16–25; Matt. 28:24–25
94	Good and Bad Thieves; Pilate's inscription	John 19:18–22
95–98	Simon of Cyrene; prophecy to women of Jerusalem (Veronica)	Luke 23:26–31
99	Christ's seamless garment, woven by Mary, in Pilate's possession from one of the knights	[see Marx and Drennan's note]
100–102	Nailing Christ to the Cross, with many apocryphal and legendary details	[see ibid.]
103	Christ mocked on the Cross; salvation of Good Thief	Luke 23:34–43
104	Mary entrusted to John, with the warning (from Augustine) that the example of the Good Thief should not lead to overconfidence in God's grace	John 19:26–27
105–106	Last Words; earthquake; words of the Centurion	Matt. 27:46–54; John 19:28–30
107–108	Thieves' legs broken; Longinus	John 19:31–34
109–112	Joseph of Arimathea, Nicodemus, Deposition and Burial	John 19:38–42
113	Pilate places guards	Matt. 27:62–66
114–115	Joseph of Arimathea imprisoned	
116	Christ appears to Virgin Mary; mentions Harrowing of Hell	
117	Frees Joseph by lifting "al þe hous heiȝe into þe eyre" (line 8)	
118	Appearances to the Marys and the Disciples briefly mentioned	

[*Complaint* ends; "a litel book þat he [Nicodemus] made of þe passioun & of his vparisyng" begins (118 line 16–119 line 1)]:

120	Appearance of the angel to the two Marys	Matt. 28:1–7
122	Soldiers paid to keep silent	Matt. 28:11–15
123	Christ charges Disciples on Mt. Olivet; "Egias, Fynees & Addas" witness the Resurrection	Mark 16:15–16; Matt. 28:16–19
124	Ascension	Luke 24:51

Page	Events	Bible
125–131	Nicodemus and Joseph confute the Sanhedrin	
132–136	"Carcius & Leucinus," sons of Simeon, recount the Harrowing	Matt. 27:52–53

The Devil's Parlament DP

IMEV/S 3992
Manual, 2:449 [314]

1. London, BL Add. 37492 (83r–90v), later 15th c., "A" version, 442 lines in eight-line stanzas, abababab.
2. London, Lambeth Palace 853 (pp. 157–82), ca. 1450, "B" version, 504 lines, same stanza form.
3. London, BL Add. 15225 (48r–55v), early 17th c., "B" version, 490 lines, same stanza form.

Editions: 1 and 2 in parallel—Marx, *Devil's Parlament,* 50–89, with variants from 3 and three sixteenth-century printings (90–94).
2—Furnivall, *Hymns to the Virgin,* 41–57.
3—Rollins, *Old English Ballads,* 384–404.

Marx provides the most comprehensive discussion of the manuscripts, the early printings, the "A" and "B" versions, and the language and literary context of the poem, which he describes as "a verse sermon or Lent reading" (35). The penultimate stanza in the "B" version reads

> Þis song þat Y haue sunge ȝou heere
> Is clepid Þe Deuelis Perlament;
> Þerof is red in tyme of ȝeere
> On þe first Sunday of Clene Lent.
> Whoso wole haue heuen to his hire
> Kepe he him from þe deuelis combirment;
> In heuene his soule may þere be sure
> Wiþ aungilis to pleie verament. (489–96)

The principal sources are the Vulgate and the *Gospel of Nicodemus.* Intermediary versions, analogous vernacular poems and plays, and texts such as the *Historia Scholastica* and the *Legenda Aurea* may also contribute, though precise debts cannot be ascertained. The dramatic situation of the poem is two Parliaments in Hell wherein the devils describe and debate the life and works of Christ. A Harrowing episode appears.

References are to the "A" version of Marx, *Devil's Parlament:*

Lines	Events	Bible
1–24	Annunciation; wonders associated with Christ's birth: "An Angell to shephurdys '*Gloria*' gan tell 'In erthe to man pes & rest'" (15–16)	Luke 1:26; 2:13–14
25–48	Magi; Christ disputes with the Temple Doctors; Slaughter of the Innocents	Matt. 2:1–12, 16; Luke 2:46
49–88	The devils debate the identity of Christ, quoting Scripture	John 3:14; Ps. 84:11
89–176	Temptation in the Desert: "Ihesus seyde, 'Sothly bred / Is nouȝt only mannys leuynge / But euery word of the godhed / To body & soule ys comfortyng'" (113–16); "Go fowle Sathan" (171)	Matt. 4:1–11
177–200	Synopsis of miracles: heals cripples, lepers, the deaf and dumb, expels demons, water into wine at Cana, feeds five thousand, raises Lazarus; Woman taken in adultery	Luke 8:30; John 2:1–11; Luke 9:14–17; John 11:44; 8:3
201–216	Transfiguration; "The tempyl he wolde ouerdrowe / And reysen hyt aȝen the thrydde day" (215–16)	Matt. 17:1–8; John 2:19
217–256	Betrayal of Judas; Crucifixion; dream of Pilate's wife	John 13:26–27; Matt. 27:19, 45, 51–53
257–384	Debate between Christ and the Devil; speeches of the saints; recapitulation of the Fall of the Angels and of Man, Harrowing of Hell	Is. 14:12–14
385–416	Resurrection; appears to the Five Hundred; "Maryc, nc touche mc nouȝt" (396); Doubting Thomas	1Cor. 15:6; John 20:17–20, 24–29
417–432	Christ commissions Disciples; Pentecost; "Fendys schulle flen for my name, / Venym and addrys from ȝow stelle; / Thouȝ ȝe drynke poyson it schal nouȝt tame / To greuen with neyther boch ne beel" (425–32)	Mark 16:15–18; Acts 2:4
433–442	Ascension; concluding prayer	Mark 16:19

The "B" version continues:

457–504	"Of alle þe children þat euere were borun / Saue oonli Crist himsilf aloone / Was noon so holi here biforn / As was þis holi child seynt Iohun" (465–68); Death of John the Baptist; Coronation of the Virgin; concluding prayer	Matt. 11:11; 14:10

The Harrowing of Hell and the Destruction of Jerusalem
HH and DJ

IMEV 3706
Manual, 2:449 [313b]

> 1. Cambridge, St. John's College 28 (73r–79r), 1425–50. The 320-line
> "septenary Harrowing" and the 222-line *Destruction of Jerusalem* in
> couplets.

Edition: Marx, *Devil's Parlament,* 133–47.

This pairing of stories can be found in Latin and Old English manuscripts
(see Marx, 124). The St. John's College manuscript seems to have been intended as a collection of temporale narratives associated with the *SEL.* It
also includes **OTH, NMC,** and **MP.**

Likely sources are the *Gospel of Nicodemus* (see above at **GNs** and **GNp**),
chapters 45, 53, and 67 of the *Legenda Aurea* (primarily the Life of James),
and possibly the *Speculum Historiale* (see Marx, 121–26).

Marx (127–31) and Pickering (*"Southern Passion,"* 38–40) discuss passages
shared with other *SEL* texts.

Lines	Events	Bible
1–38	Joseph of Arimathea deposes body, is imprisoned; Resurrection; the angel at the tomb	Luke 23:50–53; 24:4–6
39–46	Jewish leaders bribe guards to deceive Jews	Matt. 28:11–15
47–196	The Harrowing as recounted by "Lentyk and Kareyn"; Zachary's prophecy; Seth's Quest for Oil of Mercy (Quinn, *Quest*); Devils debate Christ's identity	Matt. 27:52–53; Luke 1:67–79
197–210	Pilate's wife warned in a dream	Matt. 27:19
211–320	Gates broken; Enoch, Elias, the Good Thief	Luke 23:42–43
321–542	Joseph of Arimathea immured; martyrdom of St. James; signs of impending destruction; Pilate's embassy to Vespasian; siege and destruction of Jerusalem by Titus; Joseph freed; threefold failure to rebuild the city	

The Three Kings of Cologne TK

Prose version
IPMEP 290
Manual, 2:630 [277]

23 MSS, including:
1. London, BL Harley 1704 (49v–76v), 15th c.
2. Cambridge, Univ. Lib. Ee.4.32 (1r–23v), 15th c.
3. London, BL Royal 18 A.x (87r–119r), early 15th c.
4. London, BL Add. 36983 (179r–215v), 1442.

Editions: 1—Wright, *Chester Plays,* 1:266–304.
2—Horstmann, *Three Kings,* 2–156 (even pages).
3—Horstmann, *Three Kings,* 3–157 (odd pages).

Rhyme Royal Version attributed to Lydgate
IMEV *31
IMEV/S 854.3,
Manual, 6:1862 [98]

1. London, BL Add. 31042 (London Thornton) (111r–119v), 15th c.,
859 lines, acephalous.

Edition: MacCracken, "Lydgatiana III."
Partial facsimile: J. Thompson, *Thornton.*

The Three Kings are of course the Magi, whose bodies were miraculously translated to Milan and then enshrined at Cologne by Frederick Barbarossa in the twelfth century. The prose version is based on John of Hildesheim's *Historia Trium Regium* (ca. 1400, printed by Horstmann on pp. 206–312), a legendary narrative with extensive pseudo-historical episodes and information concerning the Magi and the lore of the Far East. There are numerous patristic and miscellaneous biblical quotations. John claims Hebrew and Chaldaic books, translated into French, as his sources (p. 10 in Horstmann, manuscript 2). The following biblical verses structure the main narrative in the prose version. The narrative in the poetic version is very similar, though it omits the Psalter allusions, Habacuc, Simeon and Anna, the Flight to Egypt, and the thirty pennies.

From Horstmann's ed. of manuscript 2:

Pages	Events	Bible
4	Balaam's prophecy: "a sterre shall springe of Iacob"	Num. 24:17
12	"a mayde schal conceyue and bere a childe"	Is. 7:14
20	Decree from Augustus; Nativity; angel appears to the shepherds	Luke 2:1–14
32	"the sceptre of Iuda schal noȝt be bore aweye"	Gen. 49:10
34–38	The star; the Magi begin their journey	Matt. 2:2, 9
46	"kynges of thaars and of þe yle schul offre ȝiftes"	Ps. 71:10

Pages	Events	Bible
52	Translation of Habacuc	Dan. 14:35
58	"all men schul come fro Saba, bryngyng gold and encense"	Is. 60:6
60	Herod sends the Magi	Matt. 2:1–8
68	Magi offer gifts	Matt. 2:11
80–84	Magi return by another way; Herod destroys ships at Tharsis	Matt. 2:12; Ps. 47:8
90	Simeon and Anna; Flight into Egypt	Luke 2:29, 38; Matt. 2:13
94–100	History of the thirty gilt pennies, culminating in Judas's suicide	Matt. 27:3–8
100	Return to Nazareth	Matt. 2:23
102–112	St. Thomas preaches the Gospel	
116	Prester John	
124–140	St. Helen, the various translations of the bodies of the Three Kings	
142	Baptism of Jesus	Matt. 3:13
144–156	How various Christian sects worship the Three Kings.	

Titus and Vespasian TV

IMEV/S 1881
Manual, 1:160 [107]

"Long version"
1. Oxford, Bodleian Lib. Laud 622 (*SC* 1414) (71v–72v, 1r–21r), ca. 1400, 5,166 lines.
2. Oxford, Bodleian Lib. Digby 230 (*SC* 1831) (195r–223v), mid-15th c., 5,166 lines.
3. Oxford, Bodleian Lib. Douce 78 (*SC* 21652) (19r–75v), later 15th c., 2,390 lines (imperfect).
4. Oxford, Bodleian Lib. Douce 126 (*SC* 21700) (69r–83r), earlier 15th c., 1,889 lines (imperfect).
5. London, BL Harley 4733 (40v–127r), mid-15th c., 5,600 lines.
6. London, BL Add. 36523 (1r–71r), earlier 15th c., 5,182 lines.
7. London, BL Add. 36983 (Bedford) (216r–255r), 1442, 5,154 lines.
8. New Haven, Yale Univ., Beinecke Lib. Osborn a11 (1r–38v), 15th c., atelous.

"Short version"
9. London, BL Add. 10036 (2r–61v), earlier 15th c., 2,904 lines, acephalous (beginning at line 1345).

10. New York, Pierpont Morgan Lib. M 898 (1r–100r), 15th c., 3,851 lines, acephalous.

11. Cambridge, Magdalene College Pepys 2014 (23r–35v), earlier 15th c., 3,114 lines, acephalous.

Editions: 6—Herbert, *Titus and Vespasian,* with variants from 1, 2, 5, 9, collation of 4 other manuscripts.
11—Fischer, "Vindicta Salvatoris."

This romance, in octosyllabic couplets, covers much the same ground as the alliterative *Siege of Jerusalem* (*IMEV* 1583). Although the Destruction of Jerusalem and the Cure of Vespasian (connected to the Veronica legend [Matt. 9:20, see Elliott, *Apocryphal New Testament,* 213–16]) are principal concerns of both stories, the Life, Passion, and Miracles of Christ figure prominently as a sacred prologue, especially in *Titus.* There are frequent summaries of Old and New Testament events as various Roman emperors inquire into Christ's life and teaching. A similar organization of material appears in **BRA.**

Principal sources for *Titus* are the Gospels, the *Gospel of Nicodemus,* the *Legenda Aurea,* Josephus's *Jewish War* (or the Christianized Latin version *Hegesippus*), and the *Vindicta Salvatoris;* the French *La venjance de Nostre Seigneur,* or its Latin source, may also contribute (see Herbert, xvi–xviii). The prologue identifies its sources as follows:

> The Gospelles I drawe to witenesse
> Of þis matere more and lesse;
> And the passioun of Nichodeme,
> If þat ȝe take þereto good ȝeme;
> And of the geestes of emperoures
> That tellen of þese aventures:
> How Jhesu Crist was doon to deed
> Thurgh þe Jewes false reed.
> (Herbert, *Titus and Vespasian,* 7–14; cf. lines 5160–67)

From Herbert's edition, with corresponding passages from Fischer in brackets:

Lines	Events	Bible
97–112	Tribute to Caesar: "ȝelde Cesar his right, / And þat is Goddes to God almight" (109–10)	Matt. 22:15–22
113–140	Woman taken in adultery: "Whosoo withouten synne now is, / And casteth on hir þe firste stoon" (126–27)	John 8:3–11
181–184	"I come the lawes to fulfille, / Not oon poynt þerof to spille" (181–82)	Matt. 5:17–18

Lines	Events	Bible
185–208	Raising the Temple in three days [1271–86, including a description of the Scourging]	John 2:19–22
209–224	Recovering a lost beast on the Sabbath	Matt. 12:10–11
301–387	Conspiracies against Christ: "The Romaynes and oþur shul come us on, / And all oure lawes þei wil fordoon" (309–10); Caiphas's prophecy; Jesus withdraws to Ephrem	John 11:46–54
388–444	Jesus's Twelve Defenders, plus Nicodemus and Joseph of Arimathea	
445–479	Crucifixion; words of the Centurion; Longinus; wonders at Christ's death [590–656]	Matt. 27:51–54; John 19:34
480–500	Witnesses to the Resurrection: "Aggeus, Fines, and Astadas" (485); Carius and Lucius	
501–544	Joseph of Arimathea imprisoned and released by Christ	
545–590	The guards and the angel at the tomb	Matt. 28:2–7, 11–15
633–638	Ascension	Mark 16:19
699–762	Jesus laments over Jerusalem; Synoptic Apocalypse: "Heven and erthe shall passen both, / All but my wordes, þat ben soth" (761–62)	Matt. 23: 37–24:35
763–796	Cleanses Temple	Luke 19:45–48
797–810	Judas and the company of soldiers collapse	John 18:3, 6
829–914	Synopsis of Jewish history: flight from Egypt, wandering in Sinai, Babylonian captivity, destruction of Jerusalem (citing Josephus [891]) [23–82]	
915–1162	Ten warnings to the Jews, beginning with the martyrdom of St. James the Less [103–298].	
1163–2742	The story of Vespasian's cure; Tiberius; Titus; Nathan (Jewish Ambassador to Rome); life of Pilate, legend of Veronica, and destruction of Jerusalem, with occasional recapitulations of Christ's preaching and miracles [349–784, including raising of Lazarus, Pentecost, Resurrection, dream of Pilate's wife]	Matt. 9:20
2743–4348	Sieges of Acre, Jaffa, Jerusalem [1877–2957]	
4349–4486	Fate of Pilate	
4487–4864	Life of Judas Iscariot; Anointing at Bethany, thirty pence: "Loketh ȝoure monee. / I have synnede, soo dede ȝe" (4841–42); suicide [853–71, 1571–88]	John 12:3–6; Matt. 26:15; 27: 3–6; Acts 1:18

Lines	Events	Bible
4865–4884	Choosing of Matthias: "Þei kesten loot by and by, / Allweyes it fell on seynt Mathey" (4879–80)	Acts 1:15, 23–26
4885–5182	Vespasian returns to Rome; the Jews are frustrated in their attempts to rebuild Jerusalem	

Book to a Mother BM

IPMEP 767, Jolliffe A.5.(a)(b)
Manual, 7:2267 [16]

1. Oxford, Bodleian Lib. Bodley 416 (*SC* 2315) (1r–105r), ca. 1400, acephalous.
2. Oxford, Bodleian Lib. Laud misc. 210 (*SC* 1292) (20r–93v), early 15th c.
3. London, BL Add. 30897 (78r–137v), early 15th c., imperfect.
4. London, BL Egerton 826 (1r–55v), early 15th c.

Edition: 1—McCarthy, *Book to a Mother,* with variants from 2 and 3.

BM is a devotional treatise, addressed to the anonymous author's widowed mother, in homiletic form with extensive quotations from Scripture. The primary theme is Matt. 12:50 ("he þat doþ his Fader wille is his broþer, suster and moder" [McCarthy, p. 1]). There are frequent citations of the Fathers, the *Legenda Aurea,* the *Ancrene Riwle,* and the *Meditationes Vitae Christi.* The metaphor of Christ as a "Book" for all to read, as in the versions of **ChC,** is prominent, and notably the Pearl of Great Price becomes a "boc" (p. 21).

The following outline cites only longer scriptural passages and clusters; many individual verses—from Genesis through to Revelation—occur passim. Noteworthy are the synopsis of Tobias (pp. 65–69, 82–84), and the excerpts from Deuteronomy (pp. 81, 199–203) and the Epistles (pp. 157–90). From McCarthy's edition:

Pages	Events	Bible
1	Pater Noster and Ave Maria	Matt. 6:9–13; Luke 1:28
2–3	Ten Commandments	Ex. 20:1–17
3–4	Necessity of Poverty	Mark 10:21
5–7	Seven Works of Bodily Mercy	Matt. 25:34–41
9–10	Beatitudes	Matt. 5:1–12
11–12	Verses from Canticles	Cant. 1:15–16; 2:1–6; 3:10–12

Pages	Events	Bible
20	Martha and Mary	Luke 10:41–42
20–21	Parable of the Marriage Feast	Matt. 22:9–13
21	Pearl [here a "boc"] of Great Price	Matt. 13:44–46
23	Expulsions of Lucifer from Heaven, Adam and Eve from Paradise	Rev. 12:7–8; Gen. 3:24
24	Verses from Baruch	Bar. 4:1; 3:36–38
24–25	Vision of the Throne of God	Rev. 5:1–14; 22:7
26	"And I eet þis bok, and he was made in my mouth as swete as hony"	Ezek. 2:8–9; 3:1–3
28–29	David exorcises Saul; dances before the Ark	1Kg. 16:23; 2Kg. 6:14–16, 20–22
33	Visitation of Elizabeth	Luke 1:39–44
34	Flight into Egypt	Matt. 2:13–15
35–36	Mardochai, Aman, and the gallows	Est. 13:12–14; 5:9–14; 7:1–10
36	"Who loweþ him schal be hiȝed, and who hiȝeþ him schal be lowed"	Matt. 23:5–12
48	Angel appears to the shepherds	Luke 2:8–15
51–52	Magi; Candlemass; Simeon and Anna; Christ disputes in the Temple	Matt. 2:11; Luke 2:22–38
54	Baptism of Christ	Matt. 3:13–15
54–55	Temptation in the Desert	Matt. 4:1–11
60	Arrest of John	Mark 1:14–15
61	Calling of Peter, Andrew, James, and John	Matt. 4:18–22
62	Miracle at Cana	John 2:1–11
64	Woman of Samaria	John 4:16–18
64–65	Verses from Psalm 77	Ps. 77:1–8, 21, 31–37, 49
65–69	Synopsis of Tobias	Tob. 1:4–2:18; 3:8–25; 6:13–22; 8:1–10
78	Perils of having children	Luke 16:28; Matt. 24:19; Gal. 4:27; Ecclus. 16:1; Tob. 6:14–17
80–81	Verses from Psalm 5	Ps. 5:5–7, 10–11
81	Wrath of God	Deut. 32:20–23, 32–33, 37–38, 40–42
82	Evils of the Last Days	2Tim. 3:1–5; 4:3–4
82–84	Exhortation of Tobias	Tob. 12:10; 13:1–23; 14:5, 10–11
96–97	Christ expels legion of devils; Gerasene Swine	Mark 5:1–13
99–100	Prodigal Son: "ledeþ hidere a fat calf and sleiþ it"	Luke 15:11–24
103	"My ȝok is smoþe"	Matt. 11:28–30

Pages	Events	Bible
105–106	Reward of the Just	Wis. 4:18–20; 5:1–18, 21
118	Dives and Lazarus	Luke 16:19–27
126	Christ considered mad	Mark 3:20–21
126–127	Christ prays in the desert	Mark 1:35–38
133	Raising the ruler's daughter, the widow's son of Nain, Lazarus	Matt. 9:25; Luke 7:15; John 11:44
134	Anointing at Simon's house	Luke 7:36–49
144	Washes Disciples' feet	John 13:4–17
147–148	Arrest; Scourging; Christ before Caiphas; Crucifixion	Matt. 26:47–27:42
150–152	Christ teaches Disciples: "soþnesse schal deliuere ȝou"	John 8:31–32; 13:34–35; 14:12–27
153–154	"I am a uerrei uyne, and my Fadur is an erþetiliere"	John 15:1–27
154–156	"I am not of þe world"	John 16:1–4, 8–11, 20, 32–33; 17:1, 11, 14–21, 24–26; 12:39–43
157–165	Verses from 1John	1John 1:1–7; 2:3–6, 9–11, 15–29; 3:1–24; 4:1–21; 5:1–21
166–168	Verses from 2John and Jude	2John 1:6–11; Jude 1:1–23
169 174	Verses from James	James 1:1–27; 2:1–20; 3:1, 14–18; 4:1–17; 5:1–20
175–176	Verses from 1Peter	1Pet. 1:1; 2:11, 20–23; 3:1–14; 4:3, 7–11, 18–19; 5:5–8
177–179	Verses from 2Peter	2Pet. 2:1–22; 3:3–4, 10, 17–18
180–182	Verses from 1Thessalonians	1Thess. 2:1–13; 4:1–8, 11; 5:2–3, 15–18
182–183	Verses from 2Thessalonians	2Thess. 1:3–8; 2:1–2, 7, 10–11; 3:6, 14
184–189	Verses from Paul	1Tim. 2:6–10; 5:4–7, 18; 1Cor. 3:16–21; 4:9–16; 5:6, 9–11; 6:9–15; 12:12, 31; 13:1–8; 2Cor. 4:3–4; 6:14–18; 1Tim. 6:3–10, 17
190	Verses from Hebrews	Heb. 6:1, 4–8; 10:26–31
195–196	Herod commissions Magi; slaughters Innocents; slays John the Baptist	Matt. 2:8, 12, 16; Mark 6:27
199–203	Commandments and curses	Deut. 27:9–19; 25:26; 28:1–8, 13–19; 6:5–9

Temporale Narratives

Temporale Narratives
Manual, 2:403 [53]

Temporale narratives are probably the most overlooked and complicated category of biblical literature. They are most often associated with manuscripts of the thirteenth-century collection of saints' lives known as the *South English Legendary.* Only a few *SEL* manuscripts have this material, which usually appears as a scriptural preface to the sanctorale, though sometimes it is distributed throughout the collection according to the church year (see Görlach, *Textual Tradition*). Speaking of the "extensive vernacular poetic activity in the monasteries of the Southwest Midlands," and referring in particular to the hagiographies in the *SEL,* Derek Pearsall favors monastic production ("Origins of the Alliterative Revival"). As he points out, history and chronicle were the proper domains of monks, and their interests extended to the biblical historical narratives of which so much biblical literature consists. Annie Samson (*"South English Legendary"*) argues that modern distinctions between secular and religious works were less recognized in thirteenth-century England and that the *SEL* must have had extra-liturgical applications. A similar combination of temporale and sanctorale appears in works associated with the *Scottish Legendary* (see *Manual,* 2:419 [2]).

Pickering's 1973 article ("*Temporale* Narratives") provides a valuable guide to the temporale: "In practice, the term is usually understood to encompass everything non-hagiological from the Creation to Doomsday" (427). Pickering reviews twelve biblical paraphrases, amounting to some thirteen thousand lines, which probably circulated independently before their inclusion in *SEL* manuscripts. He is the authority on the subject. His conclusions in this article should be compared with the modification of some of his views on pages 32–45 of his edition of **MP** (*South English Ministry and Passion*) and elsewhere in subsequent articles.

The complex filiations of manuscripts of this group of poems (for example, the first 274 lines of **NMC** appear in the Auchinleck manuscript, known primarily as an anthology of romances) obscure how much biblical literature they contain.

The South English Nativity of Mary and Christ **NMC**

("Prologue to the *Long Life of Christ*" [*IMEV* 3452] in the *SEL*)
IMEV/S 3997

1. London, BL Stowe 949 (88v–100v), 814 lines, "A" version.
2. Edinburgh, National Lib. of Scotland, Advocates 19.2.1 (Auchinleck) (66r–69v), "C" version extract.
3. Oxford, Bodleian Lib. Bodley 779 (*SC* 2567) (255r–57v), "C" version extract.
4. Oxford, Bodleian Lib. Add. C.220 (*SC* 29430) (19r–20v), "A" version fragment.
5. Oxford, Bodleian Lib. Rawlinson poetry f.225 (*SC* 14716) (24r–34r).
6. London, Lambeth Palace 223 (33r–43r), "C" version.
7. Cambridge, St. John's College 28 (25r–35r) (**MP** follows on 35r–69v), early 15th c., "B" version.
8. London, BL Add. 10626 (9v–11v), "A" version fragment.
9. Cambridge, Trinity College 605 (179r–83r), "C" version extract.
10. Tokyo, Takamiya 54 (1r–9v), early 15th c. An "A" version, with omissions and additions (the Circumcision and Epiphany found in the *SEL* [D'Evelyn and Mill, *South English Legendary*, 1:3–5]). See Pickering and Görlach, "Newly Discovered Manuscript," 112 and Pickering, *South English Nativity of Mary and Christ*, 29.

Editions: 1—Pickering, *South English Nativity of Mary and Christ*.
    2—Turnbull, *Legendae*, 125–64 (Joachim and Anne).
Facsimile: 2—Pearsall and Cunningham, *Auchinleck Manuscript*.

Sources include the Bible, *Legenda Aurea, Gospel of Ps.-Matthew* (see Pickering, *South English Nativity of Mary and Christ*, 34–35). The proportion of apocryphal material is very high, and is treated in detail in Pickering's notes.

NMC and MP constitute what was formerly called the "Long Life of Christ" (LLC). NMC was revised into ConM (ed. Horstmann, *Altenglische Legenden* [1875], 64–80), the EN (ed. Horstmann *Altenglische Legenden* [1875], 81–109), and (with MP) the ALC. See Pickering, "Outspoken South English Legendary Poet," 22.

From Pickering, *South English Nativity of Mary and Christ:*

Lines	Events	Bible
1–12	Genealogy of Holy Family: Anne—Mary—Jesus / Isachar < / Ismerye—Elizabeth—John the Baptist	
13–94	Anne marries Joachim; their struggles to beget a child	
95–124	Mary's youth, piety, skill at weaving	
125–196	Joseph's flowering rod (cf. Is. 11:1); marriage to Mary, who enjoys all three degrees of female blessedness: "Heo was mayde and wyf and wydewe" (191)	
197–220	Mary's five friends: Rebecka, Abygee, Sephar, Susanne, Sael (201–2); their work sewing the Temple veil	
221–244	Annunciation, on the same day that Cain slew Abel, Abraham offered Isaac, Herod beheaded John the Baptist, and Christ crucified	Luke 1:26–28
245–278	Joseph's doubts dispelled by angel	Matt. 1:18–20
279–324	Joseph and Mary undergo trial by holy water to prove the divine origin of the child	
325–350	Decree of Caesar Augustus: "Þerafter þe emperour of Rome (as we fyndeþ iwryte) / A certeyn noumbre of alle þe world he seide he wolde ywrite" (325–26) [the poet adds in an aside that the emperor does so for the love of pennies, not to know the number of men (333–34)]	Luke 2:1–5
351–378	No room at the inn; Nativity	Luke 2:6–7
379–404	The midwives Tebel and Salome confirm Mary's virginity; the ox and ass worship Christ	Is. 1:3
405–440	Pagan temples fall, water turns to oil, trees flower, sun divides in three	
441–456	Octavian and the Sibyl behold a mother and child in the sun	
457–464	All Sodomites die	
465–472	A star appears according to Balaam's prophecy	Num. 24:17
473–566	Magi: Jasper, Melchior, Baltassar; Joseph is	Matt. 2:1–12

Lines	Events	Bible
	pointedly excluded lest they suspect he is the father (556–57)	
567–620	Presentation to Simeon: " 'Lord,' he seide, 'þou wult nou þi seruaunt in pes byleue, / For myn eyȝen habbeþ yseye þat bote þat þou ȝeue '" (597–98); "By oure leuedy he seide also þat hire sone swerd [wel] kene / Þorout here soule passi scholde—wel was þat [suþþe] ysene" (611–12)	Luke 2:21–35
621	Brief mention of the shepherds	Luke 2:8–20
623–646	Herod's quarrel with his sons; destruction of ships at Tharsis	Ps. 47:5–8
647–676	Slaughter of Innocents; Flight into Egypt	Matt. 2:13–18
677–744	Miracles in Egypt; Christ placates wild beasts; idols fall	Ps. 148:7; Is. 11:6–9; 65:25; 19:1
745–762	Return to Nazareth	Matt. 2:19–23
763–796	Christ disputes with the Temple Doctors	Luke 2:41–52
797–814	Enmity of Herod and Pilate	Luke 23:12

Manuscript 1, Pickering's copy text, is apparently incomplete. In three other manuscripts a narrative of John the Baptist follows. See Pickering, *South English Ministry and Passion.*

In *South English Nativity of Mary and Christ,* Pickering discusses the "B" and "C" versions which add passages from **ALC** (8–19). The B version (at line 244 of manuscript 1) adds thirty-two lines on Zachary, Elizabeth, and the birth of John the Baptist (Luke 1:5–25), and (at line 622) six lines on the shepherds and the Circumcision (Luke 2:8–14, 21). The C version adds (at line 647) an 82-line account of the Slaughter of the Innocents and the Flight into Egypt (Matt. 2:13–18).

South English Ministry and Passion **MP**

1. Cambridge, St. John's College 28 (35r–69v) early 15th c., 3,044 lines. Contains mostly temporale material. **NMC** precedes on 25r–35r.
2. Oxford, Bodleian Lib. Laud misc. 108 (*SC* 1486) (1r–10v), late 13th c., 901-line fragment [part of *IMEV* 3452, the **LLC** from the *SEL*].
3. Cambridge, Trinity College 605 (270r–v), ca. 1400, fifty-two lines on the Pater Noster from the Sermon on the Mount (lines 427–74 of manuscript 1, with four added lines after line 473).

Editions: 1—Pickering, *South English Ministry and Passion.*
    2—Horstmann, *Leben Jesu,* 29–69.

This poem, another of the temporale poems from the *SEL,* extends from the preaching of John the Baptist to early Acts of the Apostles. It constitutes a kind of sequel to **NMC,** and it was revised into **SP,** which added episodes from Christ's ministry (see Pickering, "Outspoken South English Legendary Poet," 22).

MP and **NMC** were revised into **ALC** (see Pickering, *South English Ministry and Passion,* 36–37, and 61–69 for descriptions and dating of the manuscripts).

Peter Comestor provides frequent parallels with the order of the narrative and with apocryphal details. The poem is remarkable for the amount of the biblical material paraphrased. The following table should be compared with Pickering's more detailed breakdown on pages 13–17 of his edition.

References are to Pickering, *South English Ministry and Passion:*

Lines	Events	Bible
1–46	John the Baptist preaches; baptizes Christ	Matt. 3:1–17
47–120	Temptation in the Desert; "'With bred allone,' oure lord seyde, 'man lyuyth nouȝt'" (95)	Matt. 4:1–11
121–152	Call of Peter and Andrew: "Lo, here Goddys lomb þat synnys doþ awey" (126)	John 1:35–51
153–184	Miracle at Cana	John 2:1–11
185–226	Dance of Salome; decollation of John the Baptist	Matt. 14:3–12
227–260	Prophecy of Isaias; Call of Peter, Andrew, James and John: "'Comyth,' he seyde, 'after me, and I wil ȝow make / Manfyscherys'" (251–52)	Is. 9:1–2; Matt. 4:12–22
261–272	Call of Matthew (the "tollere")	Matt. 9:9–13
273–296	Casts out unclean spirit; heals sick	Luke 4:31–37, 40–41
297–322	Visits Nazareth: "Þer is no man prophete in his own countre" (312)	Luke 4:16–24, 28–29
323–342	Heals leper, Peter's "noryȝe" [nurse]	Matt. 8:1–3, 14–15
343–360	Sermon on the Mount; the Beatitudes	Matt. 5:1–12
361–426	Twelve Apostles; Sermon on the Mount: "Þe worldis lyȝt ȝe / beþ" (369); "I come not þe lawe for to ondo, / But I come it to fulfille" (383–84); "Do so þin almesse þat þi left	Luke 6:13–16; Matt. 5:14–6:6

Lines	Events	Bible
	hand knowe not qwat þi ryȝt hand deþ" (421)	
427–472	Pater Noster	Matt. 6:9–15
473–554	Treasures in Heaven; " 'Ne iugge ȝe,' he seyde, 'no man, & ȝe schul not iugged be' " (507); stone for a fish; broad and narrow gates; know a tree by its fruit	Matt. 6:16–7:27; Luke 6:17–26
555–564	Sermon on the Plain	Luke 6:17–26, 39, 47
565–576	Heals paralytic	Matt. 9:2–8
577–590	Heals withered hand on the Sabbath	Luke 6:6–11
591–662	Heals Centurion's servant; storm at sea; Gerasene swine; "suffre hem þat dedlych ben þat þei berye þe ded" (618)	Matt. 8:5–13, 18–34
663–692	Jairus's daughter; Woman with an issue of blood	Luke 8:41–56
693–732	Commissions apostles: "Beeþ as queynte as edders . . . / As symple as culuerys" (718–19)	Matt. 9:36–8; 10:6–37
733–744	Parable of the Watchful Servant; hairs on the head; careless words	Matt. 24:43–47; 10:30; 12:36
745–780	Christ's mother and brethren; Parable of the Sower	Matt. 12:46–13:9
781–828	Feeds five thousand; walks on water	Matt. 14:13–33
829–848	"I am þe bred þat fro heuene alyȝt þat lastyn schal euere" (836)	John 6:25–54
849–878	The Woman of Canaan; heals deaf man	Mark 7:25–35
879–912	Feeds four thousand, leaven of the Pharisees, heals blind man at Bethsaida; " 'ȝa, lord,' he seyde, 'I se a man as þowȝ it were a tre' " (910)	Mark 8:1–25
913–962	Power to bind in earth and in heaven; Transfiguration	Matt. 16:13–17:9
963–1018	"Bot ȝe be meke as þis child is ȝe schul neuere to heuene wende" (966); Parables of the Lost Sheep, Unforgiving Servant	Matt. 18:1–4, 12–35
1019–1072	Marriage and divorce; blesses the little children; "For lyȝtlyere may þe camayle wende þorwȝ a nedelys eyȝe / þan ony ryche man comyn to heuene" (1063–64)	Matt. 19:1–30
1073–1088	Request of Mother of James and John	Matt. 20:20–8
1089–1124	Resurrects Widow's son at Nain; Christ anointed at Simon the Pharisee's house	Luke 7:11–16, 36–50
1125–1140	Samaritans refuse Christ; " 'He is not wurþi,' oure lorde seyde, 'to my kyngdam to	Luke 9:51–56, 61–62

Lines	Events	Bible
	wende / Þat settiþ his hand to the plouȝ & lokiþ abac at þe ende' " (1135–36)	
1141–1178	Good Samaritan; Martha and Mary	Luke 10:25–42
1179–1196	"Sekiþ and ȝe schul fynde" (1191); "Blessid be þe wombe þat þe bar & þe brestys þat þou sok also" (1195)	Luke 11:5–9, 27–28
1197–1210	Rich fool: "Ete & drynk and make þe glad" (1205)	Luke 12:15–21
1211–1238	Heals infirm woman; heals at Bethsaida, " 'ȝa, take þi cowche,' oure lord seide, 'and go forþ hol anon' " (1230)	Luke 13:10–17; John 5:2–16
1239–1254	Parable of the Bridal Feast	Luke 14:7–14
1255–1292	Parable of the Prodigal Son	Luke 15:11–32
1293–1332	Dives and Lazarus	Luke 16:19–31
1333–1346	Parable of the Pharisee and the Publican	Luke 18:10–14
1347–1364	Zacheus	Luke 19:1–10
1365–1386	Heals possessed boy	Mark 9:14–29
1387–1428	Parable of the Evil Husbandmen	Matt. 21:33–41
1429–1446	Nicodemus and being born again	John 3:1–6
1447–1526	Woman of Samaria; heals man's sick son	John 4:1–40, 46–53
1527–1556	Tribute to Caesar: "ȝelde Cesar þat Cesaris was & God þat was his also" (1538); no marriage in heaven	Matt. 22:15–30
1557–1570	Rebukes Pharisees: "Qwitlymed prowȝys [coffins]" (1567–68)	Matt. 23:1–4, 27–28
1571–1578	Herod the "fox"	Luke 13:31–32
1579–1592	Lament over Jerusalem	Matt. 23:34–39
1593–1604	Widow's "ferþing"	Mark 12:41–44
1605–1664	Woman taken in adultery: " 'My iugement is,' seide oure lord, 'þat qweche of ȝow ecchon / Is clene withoutte synne, þrow at hire þe ferste ston' " (1611–12); Abraham's descendants; "I was . . . or euere Abraham were" (1661)	John 8:3–11, 21–59
1665–1706	Jesus the Good Shepherd	John 10:1–40
1707–1722	Christ the grain of wheat; voice from heaven	John 12:24–29
1723–1768	Philip's request; "I am . . . a ryȝt trewe vyne, and my fader tylyere is"; "A litil tyme þer is to come þat ȝe schul me sen nouȝt, / & a litil after ȝe schul me se qwan I am to lyue brouȝt" (1755–56)	John 14:8–16:33
1769–1822	Parables of the Wise and Foolish Virgins, Talents	Matt. 25:1–30

Lines	Events	Bible
1823–1968	Lazarus raised; Anointing at Bethany; Palm Sunday	John 11:1–12:8
1969–1974	Synoptic Apocalypse	Matt. 24:6–7, 29
1975–1986	Destruction of Jerusalem by Titus and Vespasian	Luke 19:41–44
1987–1996	Curses fig tree	Matt. 21:18–21
1997–2032	Cleanses Temple; "Bryngyn þe temple . . . ʒif ʒe wil al to grounde, / & I wil aʒen in þe þridde day arere it in a stounde" (2011–12)	John 2:14–22; 7: 12–26
2033–2054	Judas sells Christ for thirty pence	Matt. 21:3–5, 14–16; Luke 22: 3–6
2055–2108	Prepares for Last Supper; institutes Eucharist; predicts betrayer. "Þis is my blood of þe newe lay, / Þat for oþere and ʒow schal be sched tomorwyn in þe day" (2091–92)	Matt. 26:17–29
2109–2122	Washes Disciples' feet	John 13:4–15
2123–2128	Judas designates the kiss as signal	Matt. 26:48
2129–2214	Predicts Peter's denials; Agony in Geth- semani; Betrayal and Arrest; Malchus's ear; "John" flees naked	Matt. 26:30–56; John 18:3–11; Mark 14:51–52
2215–2228	Christ before Annas	John 18:12–13, 19–24
2229–2276	Christ before Caiphas; Buffeting; Peter's denials; Pilate's wife's warning	Matt. 26:57–75; 27:19
2277–2362	Christ before Pilate and Herod; Barabbas; "He wesche his handis & seyde, 'I am giltles of his blood'" (2361)	Matt. 27:1–2, 11–12, 19; Luke 23:4–19; John 19:7–15
2363–2388	Suicide of Judas: "For þo þat he hanged was, and in þe depis stounde, / His wombe brak into þe mydde & his gottys fel doun to grounde" (2373–74)	Matt. 27:3–5; Acts 1:18
2389–2430	Scourging; "Wepiþ not for me, women . . . / But wepith for ʒoureself & for ʒoure children" (2420–21); Simon of Cyrene	Matt. 27:27–32; Luke 23:26–30
2431–2468	Crucifixion; the two Thieves: "With me . . . in paradyse schalt þou be þis day" (2467)	Luke 23:33–34, 39–43; Matt. 27: 38–40
2469–2514	Lots cast; Mary entrusted to John; gall and vinegar; "Nowʒ it is al do" (2514)	John 19:23–30
2515–2562	Eclipse, earthquake, veil torn; Baptism of St. Denis (Dionysius the Areopagite); words of the Centurion and Christ's Last Words	Matt. 27:45–46; 51–54; Luke 23: 44–46

Lines	Events	Bible
2563–2636	Spear of Longinus; excursus on Christ's blood; Deposition and Burial	John 19:31–34, 38–42; Luke 23: 50–56
2637–2672	Precautions of the Jews; Resurrection: "As hool was his tombe þo he aros as it was before; / So was his moderys wombe þo he was here bore" (2659–60)	Matt. 27:62–66; 28:1–4, 11–15
2673–2744	The Marys, Peter, and John at the tomb	Mark 16:1–7; John 20:1–17; Matt. 28:8–10
2745–2792	Appearances to Peter, Luke, and Cleophas	Luke 24:13–35; 1Cor. 15:5
2793–2824	Appearance in upper room; Doubting Thomas: "But I se his woundys þat þorwȝ hym were brouȝt / And put my fyngerys þerinne, I wil beleue it nouȝt" (2811–12)	John 20:19–29
2825–2902	Appearances at Sea of Tiberias and Galilee; "Deuelis þei schul in my name out caste & dryue iwis; / With newe tunge þei schul speke; serpentis þei schul remeue" (2896–97)	John 21:1–17; Matt. 28:16–20; Mark 16:14–18
2903–2934	Ascension	Luke 24:49–51; Acts 1:4–11
2935–2966	Choosing of Matthias	Acts 1:12–26
2967–2998	Pentecost: "þese men be drunke; þei kan not here tunge hold" (2982)	Acts 2:1–47
2999–3014	Peter and John heal lame man	Acts 3:1–16
3015–3036	Arrest of Peter and John	Acts 4:1–21
3037–3048	Preaching and Martyrdom of Apostles, Stephen	Mark 16:20; Acts 4:34–351

The Southern Passion SP

IMEV/S 483
Manual, 2:406 [58]

1. Oxford, Bodleian Lib. Laud misc. 463 (*SC* 1596) (26r–35v), early 15th c.
2. Oxford, Bodleian Lib. Bodley 779 (*SC* 2567)(25v–40r, 171r–172v), 15th c., omits 2169–2378.
3. Oxford, Bodleian Lib. English poet. a.1 (Vernon) (19v, col. 1–27r, col. 1), ca. 1390.
4. Oxford, Bodleian Lib. Tanner 17 (*SC* 9837) (48v–80r), early 15th c.

5. Oxford, Bodleian Lib. Add. C.38 (*SC* 30236) (84v–95v), ca. 1410, omits 1783–2366.
6. Oxford, Trinity College 57 (7r–22r), late 14th c.
7. Cambridge, Univ. Lib. Ff.5.48 (87v–95r), mid-15th c. Many textual variations; the only manuscript to include both **SP** and **NP.**
8. Cambridge, King's College 13, part 2 (3r–31v), mid-14th c.
9. Cambridge, Magdalene College Pepys 2344, pp. 183–237, early 14th c. (vv. 2546).
10. London, BL Egerton 2891 (40r–57v), early 14th c., ends at 2366.
11. London, BL Harley 2277 (4r–26r), ca. 1300, missing lines 595–1502 between fols. 11–12.
12. London, BL Cotton Vesp. A.iii (92r, col. 1–93r, col. 2), inserted in text of **CM** line 16749 ff. and line 16814 ff. See J. Thompson, *Cursor Mundi: Poem,* 75–79.
13. Tokyo, Takamiya 54 (42v–72r), early 15th c. Some omissions and a unique ordering of items. See Pickering and Görlach, "Newly Discovered Manuscript," 112–15.

See B. Brown, *Southern Passion,* xvii–xxx, for descriptions and relations of manuscripts 1–11.

Editions: 7—Downing, "Critical Edition," 238–48.
   9—B. Brown, *Southern Passion,* with variants from 4 and 11.
   11—C. Brown, *"Cursor Mundi,"* 149 lines on fols. 12r–14r corresponding to the insertion in manuscript 12.
   12—Morris (*Cursor Mundi;* vol. 62) 149-line insertion starting at line 16749 (Passion narrative, and a 72-line insertion at line 16814 (on Longinus and the Deposition).
Facsimile: 3—Doyle, *Vernon Manuscript.*

Like other temporale narratives, **SP** appears in numerous manuscripts of the *South English Legendary.* The *SEL,* like **CM,** accreted material over time and its manuscript versions vary widely, but **SP** is an early (1275–1285) component of that work. **NMC** and **MP** are closely related: **SP** is in fact a "careful revision" of the latter poem (Pickering, *"Southern Passion,"* 33) so as to include even more biblical material. It is remarkable both for its early date and for its very close adherence to the Vulgate. A few apocryphal stories do appear, such as some Judas legends and the miraculous conversions of Longinus and Denis (Dionysius the Areopagite, based on Paul's discourse on an "Unknown God" in Acts 17:13–34), but the poet avoids the highly affective and elaborated style which became the vogue in the fifteenth century with Passion narratives deriving from the *Meditationes Vitae Christi* (*MVC*). Where, for example, these accounts include a conventional *Planctus Mariae,* **SP** reports only that "We ne ffyndeþ nouȝt y-write þat oure lady in al hure sore / Spak ouȝt bot made deol y-now, ne miȝte no womman more" (lines 1515–16). Brown concludes that "The portions of the poem which are based upon New Testament material constitute, in short, a metrical translation, rather than a paraphrase."[1] In her introduction Brown takes considerable pains to argue that **SP** resembles the *MVC* in spirit and purpose and the *Historia Scholastica* in structure and detail. **SP** shares with the *MVC* and with **MS** both Peter's threat to tear Judas asunder with his teeth and the insistence upon the "upright Crucifixion"—that Christ was nailed by means of ladders to an already standing Cross.[2] The extent of the poet's direct reliance upon the *MVC* has been questioned by Pickering ("Devotional Elements," 156–61). The poet's debt to the *Historia,* however, is demonstrable: Brown lists forty-two instances in which details or the ordering of events derive from Petrus. This kind of thoroughgoing adaptation in a poem of 2,546 lines nearly qualifies it as a paraphrase of the *Historia*'s New Testament section.[3]

Brown puts **SP** in the larger context of popular religious literature: "For the sermon, like the drama, is a highly social expression; and in noting sources, we are really noting certain specific materials from the literature of the church which became transmuted into popular religious thought. Thus the recognition of our author's fidelity to the Vulgate text makes clear the somewhat important fact that an accurate vernacular harmony of considerable portions of the gospels was put into early circulation."[4]

---

1. B. Brown, *Southern Passion,* xii. Cf. Pickering's description of the method in **MP,** the poem which **SP** revises: "The author's method is not that of faithful translation but rather of selective paraphrase, often involving the combination of material from different gospel versions of the same episode" (*South English Ministry and Passion,* 11). Thus **SP** consciously attempts a closer biblical rendering. Elsewhere, Pickering notes how the revisers of **MP** and **NMC** make "an earlier poem more canonical by introducing new gospel translations" (*"Southern Passion,"* 50).

2. See lines 1459–61, *MPC* (the Passion section of *MVC*) chapter 6, and **MS** lines 627–58. The "upright Crucifixion" retains its hold upon the popular imagination though in practice the victim was nailed to a recumbent cross which was then raised.

3. B. Brown, *Southern Passion,* lxii–lxxviii. Four of the parallels deal with liturgical influences from the *Historia:* lines 11–16, PL 198.1598, why the Pope is absent at Palm Sunday services; lines 189–90, col. 1603, why the host is made of wheat; lines 481–82, col. 1611, why Christ is ignorant of the day of Doomsday; lines 1691–94, col. 1634, why the host should be wrapped in linen.

4. B. Brown, *Southern Passion,* xiv. Brown also considers the influence of works by Bernard of Clairvaux and Hugh of St. Victor. The poet was not wholly unoriginal, however. In lines 1899–1990 the poet criticizes the double standard which applies to male and female promiscuity and reacts against antifeminist attacks. See Pickering, " 'Defence of Women.' "

Pickering suggests that the audience of the *SEL* had "access to, or at least close familiarity with, the Gospels," and that these temporale poems were composed to provide gospel material for a "wider audience" and to "take the place of the Bible" (*South English Nativity of Mary and Christ*, 41–42). These poems represent the first and primary means of lay acquaintance with Scripture, and they were meant to educate their audience in the matter of biblical history and thereby enhance its understanding of other religious literatures.

The Ministry, Passion, Resurrection, and Ascension of Christ terminate with Stephen protomartyr, and thus introduce the sanctorale. The following synopsis of events corresponds roughly to large initials in manuscript 9 as edited by B. Brown, *Southern Passion*. Each synopsis is often connected to a liturgical practice or a moralization.

Lines	Events	Bible
1–44	Anointing at Bethany	Matt. 26:6–16; John 12:1–8
45–90	Palm Sunday	Matt. 21:1–11; Luke 19:28–40
91–138	Lament over Jerusalem (linked to future destruction by Titus and Vespasian)	Luke 19:41–47
139–162	Jesus curses the fig tree	Matt. 21:18–22
163–178	The Widow's farthing	Luke 21:1–4
179–232	Grain of wheat; "A voys þer com ffram heuene" (203); "þe while ʒe habbeþ liʒt, and mowe liʒt yseo, / By-leoueþ on liʒt þat ʒe mowe, children of liʒt beo" (225–26)	John 12:24–36
233–282	Parable of the Evil Husbandmen	Luke 20:9–19
283–344	Parable of the Marriage Feast	Matt. 22:1–14
345–390	Hidden treasure; Pearl of Great Price; the fish net	Matt. 13:44–50
391–530	Synoptic Apocalypse	Matt. 24:1–44
531–610	Parable of the Wise and Foolish Virgins	Matt. 25:1–13
611–748	Parable of the Talents (five besants are the five wits); the Great Judgment	Matt. 25:14–46
749–866	Judas and the thirty pence; Institution of the Eucharist	Matt. 26:14–29
867–914	Christ washes Disciples' feet	John 13:1–15
915–1016	Predicts Peter's betrayal; questions from Philip and Thomas	John 13: 38–14:31
1017–1076	"Byddeþ and ʒe shulleþ afonge" (1020); continues to comfort Disciples	John 16:23– 17:26
1077–1120	Prays on Mount Olivet: "red blod he gan to swete" (1107)	Luke 22:39–46
1121–1172	Arrest; Malchus's ear; "John" flees naked	Matt. 26:47–56;

Lines	Events	Bible
		Mark 14:51; John 18:1–11
1173–1274	Peter's denials; Christ before Annas and Caiphas; dream of Pilate's wife	John 18:12–27; Matt. 27:19
1275–1412	Christ before Pilate and Herod; anti-Semitic outburst (1381–86); Judas repents; Pilate washes hands: "What is soþnesse?" (1339)	Matt. 27:1–26; John 18:28–40
1413–1454	Scourging; Simon of Cyrene	John 19:1–5; Luke 23:26–30
1455–1602	Crucifixion; forgiveness of Good Thief; Mary entrusted to John; Last Words	Luke 23:32–46; Matt. 27:45–53; John 19:25–28
1603–1680	General moralizations; Longinus	John 19:34
1681–1908	Deposition; Marys at the tomb; appearance of angels; Peter and John	John 19:38– 20:18; Mark 16:3–4
1909–1990	"Defense of Women" (see Pickering, " 'Defence of Women' ")	
1991–2088	Post-Resurrection appearances	Matt. 28:8–10; Luke 24:13–35
2089–2168	Appears in upper room; Doubting Thomas	John 20:19–29
2169–2310	Appears at Sea of Tiberias; fate of John: "Þulke sulue disciple, þat bereþ witnesse of al þis, / Seint Ion þe Ewangelist, þat made þis gospel" (2298–99)	John 21:1–24
2311–2326	Appears on Mount Thabor to the eleven: "ich am and wole beo, myd ʒow in alle þinge / Alle þe dayes lo, to þe wordles endynge" (2323–24)	Matt. 28:16–20
2327–2366	"Deuelen hi shulleþ in my name, out caste and dryue; / Myd nywe tounges hi shulleþ speke, addren hi shulleþ remue; / And ʒif hi drinkeþ dedlich þing, hit ne shal ham nouʒt anuye" (2336–38)	Mark 16:14–18
2367–2398	Ascension	Luke 24:44–51
2399–2416	Ascension to right hand of God; two angels: "he shal come aʒen, at þe wordles ende" (2410)	Mark 16:19; Acts 1:9–11
2417–2466	Choosing of Matthias	Acts 1:12–26
2467–2492	Pentecost	Acts 2:1–13, 41
2493–2512	Peter and John heal a lame man at the Beautiful Gate	Acts 3:1–16
2513–2540	Apostles imprisoned by Annas and Caiphas	Acts 4:1–20
2541–2546	Martyrdom of Stephen and others	Acts 8:1–2

Long Life of Christ from the *South English Legendary* **LLC**

IMEV *15
IMEV/S 3452
Manual, 2:405 [53] and 2:413 [1]

This poem appears in various fragments, with and without a prologue (*IMEV* 213, 3997), and extends to approximately thirty-nine hundred lines in its most complete form. For other recensions, see **NMC.**

1. Oxford, Bodleian Lib. Laud misc. 108 (*SC* 1486) (1r–10v), late 13th c., 901 lines in septenary couplets, missing beginning and end and one leaf after line 90. The 141 lines following line 761 follow **SP. CJ** follows on 11r.
2. Oxford, Bodleian Lib. Bodley 779 (*SC* 2567) (254v), verses 249–517.
3. Oxford, Bodleian Lib. Rawlinson poetry f.225 (*SC* 14716) (24r), verses 1–629.
4. Oxford, Bodleian Lib. Add. C.220 (*SC* 29430) (19r), verses 470–608.
5. Cambridge, St. John's College 28 (25r). The only complete text.
6. Cambridge, Trinity College 605 (three fragments at 22r, 179r, 270r).
7. London, BL Stowe 949 (88v), verses 6–847.
8. London, BL Add. 10626 (10r), verses 60–150.
9. London, Lambeth Palace 223 (33v), verses 6–649.
10. Edinburgh, National Lib. of Scotland Advocates 19.1.2 (66r), (Auchinleck) verses 1–309.

Editions: 1—Horstmann, *Leben Jesu,* 29–69.
   10—Turnbull, *Legendae,* 125–64 (Joachim and Anne).
Facsimile: 10—Pearsall and Cunningham, *Auchinleck Manuscript.*

A glance at Horstmann's notes at the foot of each page reveals how much material from all four Gospels appears in the poem. The choice of material has no discernible rationale except that material from John appears more frequently as the Crucifixion approaches. Like the other temporale poems with which it shares material, **LLC** is an exceptionally full and close paraphrase:

> "ȝwat is it ane manne to biȝite : al þe worldes pruyte,
> And apeiri is selie soule?" (66–67, Matt. 16:26)

> ȝwane men arisez a domus dai, no wif ne schulle heo lede;
> Þare ne worth no rikeningue of mannes wif, : of seuene ne of þre,
> Ne no wilninge to fleschliche dede, : bote ase aungeles ȝe schullen be.
> (408–10, Matt. 22:30)

Turnbull's edition (printed without lineation) covers the following major episodes (many derive ultimately from the second-century *Protoevangelium of James*):

Genealogy of Holy Family: Isachar's daughters Anne (mother of Mary) and Ismerie (mother of Elizabeth, mother of John the Baptist); Joachim marries Anne, they pray for a child, Mary is born.

Wonders of her childhood, espousal to Joseph (Joseph's flowering rod; cf. Is. 11:1), his resolution that "mi sone" (p. 148) should wed Mary after him to ensure that the line persevere. Mary becomes a seamstress with five maidens — Rebecca, Abigera, Sefor, Sussanne, and Saele (p. 151); Mary sews the veil of the Temple.

Gabriel's Annunciation (Luke 1:26–30, pp. 154–55) on the same day that Adam sinned, Cain slew Abel, Abraham drew sword against Isaac, John the Baptist was beheaded, and Christ was crucified (p. 156). Zachary is struck dumb, John the Baptist born (Luke 1:8–14, pp. 158–60), Joseph doubts Mary (Matt. 1:18–20, pp. 161–64), though before the angel reassures Joseph Mary's five companions attest to her chastity.

In manuscript 1, the poem begins (imperfectly) with Christ's healing of the deaf and dumb with his spittle (Mark 7:32) — a prefiguration how some priests make the sign of the cross with spittle at Baptism — and ends (imperfectly) with Judas's betrayal.

The following is taken from Horstmann, *Leben Jesu:*

Lines	Events	Bible
6–33	Feeding of the four thousand, except here there are "six þousend" (18); recollection of other miraculous feedings	Mark 8:1; Matt.15:32; 16:5
34–39	Healing, with spittle, the blind man who sees trees	Mark 8:22
40–69	Peter's commission and rebuke	Matt. 16:13–26
70–90	Transfiguration	Matt. 17:1–9
91–109	Rescuing an ass on the Sabbath; Parable of the Bridal Feast	Luke 14:5, 8–14
110–147	Parable of the Prodigal Son	Luke 15:11–32
148–187	Dives and Lazarus	Luke 16:19–31
188–201	Parable of the Pharisee and the Publican	Luke 18:11–14
202–219	Zacheus	Luke 19:1–10
220–241	Healing the epileptic boy	Matt. 17:14–21; Mark 9:16–29
242–263	Parable of the Evil Husbandmen, but instead of paraphrasing the "rejected building stone" verses, the poet connects the treatment of the	Matt. 21:33–41

Lines	Events	Bible
	servant to the dispossession of the Jews by Titus and Vespasian	
264–301	Nicodemus and being born again	John 3:1–6
302–365	Woman of Samaria	John 4:1–40
366–379	Healing the son of the sick official	John 4:46–54
380–396	Tribute to Caesar	Matt. 22:15–21
397–410	Wife with seven husbands	Matt. 22:23–30
411–424	Rebuke of the hypocritical, "painted" Pharisees	Matt. 23:6–28
425–446	Christ's message for the "fox" Herod, followed by another warning of the destruction of Jerusalem by Titus and Vespasian	Luke 13:31–34; Matt. 23:34–39; 24:1–2
447–458	Widow's offering of her "ring"	Luke 21:1–4
459–474	Woman taken in adultery	John 8:3–11
475–518	Debate and preaching within the temple: "Ech man, quath ore louerd, þat sunne doth, sunne he seruez also"	John 8
519–560	Christ "þe dore," the "guod schepherde"	John 10
561–576	Christ the "corn of ȝwete [wheat]"; the voice from heaven	John 12:24–30
577–608	Christ the "riȝt soth vine" (excerpts)	John 14; 15; 16
609–622	Christ warns of his Death and Resurrection	John 16:16–28
623–644	Parable of the Wise and Foolish "Maidcnes"	Matt. 25:1–13
645–676	Parable of the five "wittes" [talents]	Matt 25:14–30
677–760	Raising of Lazarus of Bethany, with the notation, citing Augustine, that Lazarus told "Much of the priuete of helle" (740) after being raised	John 11
761–792	Anointing at Bethany; Judas's objection (Horstmann inserts a similar narrative from MS 1 which appears in the Life of Mary Magdalen; see **SEL**)	John 12:1–11
793–862	Enters Jerusalem; curses fig tree; cleanses Temple	Matt. 21:1–22
863–875	Rebuilding the Temple in three days	John 2:20–21
876–901	Questioning of Christ's authority; Satan enters Judas	Luke 22:3; John 13:27

Conception of Marie and the Expanded Nativity
ConM and EN

(Part of the *Long Life of Christ* in the *South English Legendary*)
IMEV/S 38, 574, 2632

Manual, 2:406 [57] and 2:413 [1]

1. Oxford, Bodleian Lib. Bodley 779 (*SC* 2567), mid-15th c. Verses
   495–648, extract from **EN** (22r–23v); verses 153–274, extract from
   ConM (271v–272v).
2. Oxford, Bodleian Lib. Ashmole 43 (*SC* 6924) (208v–212r),
   mid-14th c. Verses 1–378 of **ConM,** in couplets.
3. Cambridge, Magdalene College Pepys 2344 (pp. 353–58), early
   14th c. **ConM.**
4. London, BL Egerton 1993 (27r–40r), later 14th c. Verses 1–1173 in
   couplets of **ConM** and **EN,** atelous.
5. Oxford, Bodleian Lib. Laud misc. 622 (*SC* 1414) (71r–v), ca. 1400.
   Prologue only.
6. Oxford, Bodleian Lib. Rawlinson poetry f.225 (*SC* 14716) (28r). Birth
   of John the Baptist only.
7. Cambridge, Trinity College 605 (R.3.25) (261v–268v), earlier 15th c.
   Independent version.

Editions: 2 — Horstmann, *Altenglische Legenden* (1875), 64–80 (even pages).
4 — Horstmann, *Altenglische Legenden* (1875), 65–109 (odd pages, to
p. 81).
5 — Furnivall, *Adam Davy's 5 Dreams,* 93–96.

Horstmann prints **ConM** and **EN** as a continuous 1173-line poem under
the title "Geburt Jesu." The poems combine apocryphal material concerning the Nativity of Christ with fairly complete paraphrases of Luke chapters
1 and 2 and Matthew chapter 2. After the 84-line prologue, lines 85–280
(**ConM**) correspond closely to lines 7–192 of **NMC;** lines 281–1173 expand
lines 193–814 of **NMC.** See Pickering, "Three Nativity Poems," where he pos-
tulates separate authors for each poem.

The following outline is from Horstmann's edition of manuscript 4, the
only one which includes both poems.

Lines	*Events*	*Bible*
52–60	Simeon in the Temple	Luke 2:25
81–163	Christ's genealogy: Isachar, Anne, Mary,	
	Elizabeth, John the Baptist, Joachim	
164–276	Miracles associated with Mary's infancy;	Is. 11:1
	flowering rod of Joseph, marriage	
277–322	Zachary and Elizabeth; birth of John the	Luke 1:5–23
	Baptist	
323–387	Annunciation to Mary: "Vor þow schalt in þine	Luke 1:26–44
	wombe. conceiue wiþ oute blame, / And a sone	

Lines	Events	Bible
	ibore of þe,. þat ihc schal be his name" (343–44)	
387–414	Magnificat of Mary	Luke 1:46–56
415–468	Birth of John the Baptist; his naming; Benedictus of Zachary	Luke 1:57–79
469–494	Joseph's doubts reassured by the angel	Matt. 1:18–25
495–526	Bethlehem, the shepherds, the Nativity: "Þo douteden þe schepherdes & in gret drede weren ibrouȝt / Þo seide þe angel to hem: . ne dredeþ ow riȝt nouȝt! / Vor lo ic bringe ou tidinge . grete ioie and blis, / Þat schal beo to vch volk, . vor ibore he is iwis / To ow to day, þe saueour, . þat crist lord is" (515–19)	Luke 2:1–14
527–648	Apocryphal details associated with the Nativity: that Saint Helen takes the manger hay to Rome as a relic (604); the kneeling ox and ass (605); Tebel and Salome, midwives who examine Mary's "priutetes" (620) and confirm her virginity	Is. 1:3
649–664	Adoration of the shepherds	Luke 2:15–20
665–688	Christ's eighth-day circumcision, glossed as the first shedding of his blood for mankind, adding the death of all Sodomites: "Alle men þat on erþe wrouȝten . þe sunne of sodomie / Deiȝeden ek, þo god was bore . of his moder marie, / At otime þorw al þe world . at odeþ vchon" (681–83)	Luke 2:21
689–826	The Magi (Jasper, Melchior, Baltassar); Herod's machinations; the significations of the gifts: gold—kingship; incense—Holy Church; myrrh—Christ's bitter death	Matt. 2:1–12
827–942	Purification of Mary (Candlemass); Simeon and Anna	Luke 2:22–40
943–1022	Burning the ships of Tharsis; Slaughter of the Innocents; other recriminations by Herod	Ps. 47:5–8; Matt. 2:13–18
1023–1066	Flight into Egypt with the commonly associated motifs: bowing tree, falling idols, Mary's work as a seamstress	Is. 19:1
1067–1110	Death of Herod; accession of Archelaus; return to Nazareth	Matt. 2:19–23
1111–1148	Christ disputes with the Temple Doctors: "Sone, quaþ oure ledi, . what hastow vs ido? / Wel sori we þe habbeþ isouȝt, . þi fader and ic also. / What is þat, quaþ þis oþer, . þat ȝe me	Luke 2:41–52

Lines	Events	Bible
	habbeþ isouȝt? / Neste ȝe þ[a]t in mi fader þing . i moste nede be brouȝt." (1125–28)	
1149–1173	Pilate's attempts to deprive Herod the Tetrarch of the kingdom	Luke 23:12

The Abridged Life of Christ ALC

1. Cambridge, Trinity College 605 (22r–24r and 183r–188v). Complete text of approximately 750 lines.
2. London, BL Egerton 1993 (21r–26v). Ends in the middle of the Crucifixion.
3. Oxford, Bodleian Lib. Laud misc. 622 (*SC* 1414) (70v–71r).
4. London, Lambeth Palace 223 (30v–31v).
5. Tokyo, Takamiya 54 (39r–v).

Manuscripts 1 and 2 are the main texts which abridge and combine **NMC** and **MP** (mostly the latter). Manuscripts 3, 4, and 5 preserve only the Fifteen Signs before Doomsday (see Heist, *Fifteen Signs*) with which manuscripts 1 and 2 end. See Pickering, *South English Ministry and Passion,* 36–37, 238–39; *South English Nativity of Mary and Christ,* 31–33; "*Temporale* Narratives," 446–48.

Edition: 3—Furnivall, *Adam Davy's 5 Dreams,* 89–93.

The following is based on Pickering's summary (*South English Ministry and Passion,* 36–37) of the contents of manuscript 1.

Lines	Event	Bible
1–142	Nativity	Luke 2
143–158	Christ's baptism; fasting	Matt. 3:13–4:2
159–166	Temptation in the Desert; Miracle at Cana	Matt. 4:3–11; John 2:1–11
167–198	Decollation of John the Baptist	Matt. 14:3–12
199–210	Synopsis of Christ's ministry	
211–750	Conspiracy of the Jews; Passion; Resurrection; Ascension; Fifteen Signs before Doomsday	

The Metrical Life of Christ MLC

IMEV 72, 2365, 1579
IMEV/S 3845.3 (reckoned as three separate poems: an Infancy, a Passion, and a Resurrection narrative)

Manual, 2:393 [32]

　　1. London, BL Add. 39996 (1r–51v), mid 15th c., 5,519 lines in
　　couplets, acephalous, and missing some 320 lines after line 803.

Edition: Sauer, *Metrical Life.*

　　This temporale narrative extends from the visit of the Magi through the
Assumption of Mary. The events of the Passion are based on the canonical
Hours. Sauer maintains that given the emphasis on miracles and the omission of many important biblical stories (such as the Sermon on the Mount
and the parables) the poem was composed by a single author as "popular
religious entertainment" (19). The usual range of sources seems to have been
consulted, in particular the *Legenda Aurea,* but Sauer finds no substantial indebtedness to other Latin or vernacular Passion narratives (such as **SP** or
NP) and he pointedly denies the influence of the *Historia Scholastica* (p. 20,
n. 33).

　　There are a number of unusual motifs, such as Herod's killing of his own
son in the Slaughter of the Innocents, that angels as thick as rain accompanied Christ in the Harrowing of Hell (see Morey, "Fall in Particulate"), that
the unnamed traveler on the road to Emmaus is Saint Simon (3455), and
that Matthias and Barsabas argue over the right to replace Judas.

Lines	Events	Bible
1–176	Decree of Caesar Augustus; Nativity; the midwives "Sibil" (Tebel) and "Salome"	Luke 2:1–7
177–306	The star; shepherds; miracles at the Nativity	Matt. 2:1–2; Luke 2:8–15
307–332	Circumcision; Simeon	Luke 2:21, 25
333–502	Magi; Herod; the Adoration: "[They] wenten by anoþer way, / As þai in þe gospel sayn" (500–501)	Matt. 2:3–12
503–587	Candlemass, the two turtledoves	Luke 2:22, 24, 34, 39
588–675	Flight into Egypt; recapitulation of Miracles at the Nativity	Matt. 2:13–15
676–741	Slaughter of the Innocents, including Herod's own son	Matt. 2:16
742–787	Return from Egypt; Archelaus	Matt. 2:19–23
787–803	Jesus among the Temple Doctors	Luke 2:41–42
804–825	Jesus's Baptism: "he segh þe Holy Gost, / Þat was ful of myghtes moste, / In a dowve likenesse right" (820–22)	Matt. 3:16
826–973	Call of the Disciples: Peter, Andrew: "ʒe	Matt. 4:18–22;

Lines	Events	Bible
	schal fisshe euer ech a day, / And take men to ʒoure pray" (844–45); John and James, Simon, Jude, James the Less, Thomas of India, Matthew, Philip, Bartholomew, Judas	10:1–3; Luke 5:27; John 1:43
974–1011	Miracle at Cana	John 2:1–8
1012–1043	Christ heals the leper and the Centurion's "son"	Matt. 8:2–10
1044–1071	Christ heals dumb demoniac	Matt. 9:32–33
1072–1099	Christ heals blind man of Jericho	Luke 18:35–43
1100–1187	The Woman taken in adultery: "to smyte he schal bigynne / Which of ʒow dide neuer synne" (1158–59)	John 8:1–11
1188–1243	Cleanses Temple: "Þe Iewes asked in þat caas / Who þat his fader was" (1222–23)	Matt. 21:12–16; John 8:18–19
1244–1297	Heals the paralytic at the Sheep Gate	John 5:2–9
1298–1329	Walks on water	John 6:16–21
1330–1351	Heals various infirmities	Matt. 14:34–36; 15:29–31
1352–1377	Raises prince's daughter	Matt. 9:18, 23–26
1378–1431	Transfiguration: "He bicome þen ful right / Proprely an angel bright" (1386–87)	Matt. 17:1–9
1432–1465	Keys of the Kingdom: "Heuene keyes þou schalt haue, / Who þou wilt þou schalt saue" (1462–63)	Matt. 16:13–19
1466–1493	Raises the Widow of Nain's son	Luke 7:11–15
1494–1541	Heals demoniac boy: "Þou fende, I comaunde þee / Fro þe child þat þou fle" (1522–23)	Mark 9:17–27
1542–1585	Feeds five thousand	John 6:5–14
1586–1763	Raises Lazarus: "haddestow ben here, / My brother hade ben hole & fere" (1670–71)	John 11:1–44
1764–1821	The Jews plot against Jesus	John 11:45–54
1822–1901	Enters Jerusalem: "When ʒe comen to þe ʒate, / An asse ʒe schal fynde þerate" (1840–41)	Matt. 21:1–11
1902–1935	Judas betrays Jesus for thirty pence	Matt. 26:4–5, 14–16, 48
1936–2111	Anointing by Mary Magdalen; washes Disciples' feet; reveals traitor: "Lord, am I he / Þat to þe Iewes haþ solde þee? / Crist answerde hym þo, / He saide, Iudas, þou saist so" (2016–19); institutes Eucharist; foretells Peter's denials; "Sire, quoþ Petre,	Matt. 26:6–35; Luke 22:24–26; John 13:5–15; Luke 22:36–39

Lines	Events	Bible
	swerdes two / We haue redy & no moo. / Crist spake þen derkely, / Þese suffisen fully" (2098–2101)	
2112–2193	Agony in Gethsemani: "Lete þis heete passe me fro, / I drede sore to hit to go. / Neuerþeles not at my wille, / What þou wolt, I wole fulfille" (2166–69)	Matt. 26:36–45
2194–2264	Arrest of Christ; Malchus's ear	John 18:3–11; Matt. 26:48–56; Luke 22:51
2265–2381	Christ before Caiphas; Peter's denials; Buffeting	John 18:12–27; Luke 22:63; Matt. 26:57–75
2382–2409	Judas hangs himself	Matt. 27:3–5
2410–2657	Christ before Pilate: "wost þat I haue siche poeste / To dampne þee or to lette be?" (2450–51); "My reme is not in þis cuntre" (2471); Christ before Herod; Barabbas; Pilate's wife; "He wesshe his hondes bifore hem alle" (2625)	Matt. 27:11–31; John 18:36–38; Luke 23:5–11
2658–2915	Simon of Cyrene; Crucifixion; Dismas and Gestas, "A litel lyne þen made a Iewe / In Latyn wordes, Ebrue & Grue" (2736–37); "Þis ilke day I graunte þee / Þou schalt to paradys come with me" (2792–93); gall and vinegar; earthquake; "Wel I wote þat he is / Goddes Sone rightwis" (2842–43); spear of Longinus	Matt. 27:32–54; Luke 23:45; John 19:20, 31–34
2916–3087	Joseph of Arimathea; the Marys; Nicodemus; Deposition and Burial; precautions of the Jews	John 19:38–42; Matt. 27:57–66
3088–3153	Resurrection; the Marys try to anoint the body; the angel at the tomb	Matt. 28:1–8
3154–3299	Appears to Mary Magdalen: "sche wende þat he were / Of þat ȝorde þe gardynere" (3174–75); "Þou may not ȝett touche me" (3185); Peter and John at the tomb; the Jews bribe the guards	John 20:1–18; Matt. 28:11–15
3300–3449	Harrowing of Hell "With angels hym euer folewinge, / Þicker þen þe rayn raynynge" (3368–69); Carius and Lucius	Matt. 27:52–53
3450–3547	Appears to Cleophas and "Seynt Symond" (3455) on the road to Emmaus	Luke 24:13–35
3548–3603	Jesus appears to Disciples; eats a "rosted fisshe" and a "honycombe" (3578–79)	Luke 24:36–47

Lines	Events	Bible
3604–3651	Miraculous draft of fishes	John 21:1–14
3652–3727	Appears to the Disciples behind closed doors; Doubting Thomas: "putt þi fynger in my hert, / Þere þe spere smote so smert" (3706–7)	John 20:19–29
3728–3797	Miracle of the Vernicle; Vespasian	
3798–3887	Jesus commissions Disciples; Ascension from Mt. Olivet	Matt. 28:18–20; Acts 1:9–12
3888–3935	Election of Matthias, who argues with Barsabas	Acts 1:21–26
3936–4057	Pentecost: "In þat gleme þai myght se / Þe schappe of tonges grete plentee" (3946–47); "Þai saide of þe newe wyn, / Þat was boþe gode & fyne, / Þai were fordronken of her witte" (3994–96)	Acts 2:1–41
4058–4137	The Creed; the Apostles disperse	
4138–4307	Vicissitudes of Joseph of Arimathea in prison	
4308–4706	Tiberius healed of leprosy; death of Pilate; Vespasian cured of wasps; destruction of Jerusalem	
4707–4827	Joseph of Arimathea discovered immured in Jerusalem	
4828–5511	Assumption of Mary	
5512–5519	Closing prayer	

Stanzaic Life of Christ SLC

IMEV/S 1755
Manual, 2:392 [30]

1. London, BL Harley 3909 (1r–151v), later 15th c., 10,840 octosyllabic lines in stanzas rhyming abab, missing lines 1–66, atelous.
2. London, BL Harley 2250 (1r–47v), 15th c. Missing lines 1–623, omitting lines 693–1172, with several other minor omissions.
3. London, BL Add. 38666 (5r–173v), mid-15th c., atelous.

Edition: 1—Foster, *Stanzaic Life of Christ,* supplying lines 1–66 from manuscript 3.

SLC is a fourteenth-century compilation made at Chester from books 1 through 4 of Ranulph Higden's *Polychronicon* and from parts of the *Legenda Aurea* relevant to Christ's life. Like the *Polychronicon,* the poem is structured around the Ages of the World and it contains considerable amounts of historical, pseudo-scientific, and mythological digression. It extends from the Incarnation through Pentecost. Harley 2250 includes a rare mention of "Þo thrid boke leuetecy" (line 4239, see Foster, xiii) concerning the sacrifice of a lamb.

The cited authorities correspond for the most part with those named in the two Latin texts mentioned above, although the poet never names them. At numerous points Jerome, Isidore, Augustine, and Gregory are cited, as well as the *Historia Scholastica,* as would obviously be the case since the *Historia* is an acknowledged source of both the *Legenda* and the *Polychronicon.* The poet's confidence in these extra-biblical sources is reflected in the history of Melchisedech:

> Ierom 7 Isodre also
> And Petre in þe stories als,
> hor witnessyng 7 oþer mo
> I may not leue my3t wel be fals (2465–68)

Stanzas are grouped under Latin headings, often translated, which name the authority followed or present a biblical verse (these citations are often incorrect). At points, especially later in the poem in the Pentecost section, the verses do not advance a narrative but constitute a cento of biblical verses and commentary from Augustine and Gregory.

The provenance of Chester is strongly suggested by the reliance of the Chester dramatic cycle on **SLC.** As she had done previously with **NP,** Foster studies the relationship of the drama to the poem and concludes as follows: "The connexion between the plays and the English poem does, however, emphasize the necessity of studying vernacular literature for an understanding of the cycles. Instead of Tatian's *Gospel Harmony,* Peter Comestor's *Historia Scholastica,* and Josephus, English poems based on these may be what the dramatists knew best" (*Stanzaic Life of Christ,* xliii; see also Robert H. Wilson, "Chester Plays").

The English poems referred to by Foster are the primary medium for transmitting a sense of biblical literature not only to the dramatists but also to anyone who could read such a poem for him- or herself or who heard the poem read aloud at some church-related activity or by an itinerant friar. The poet of **SLC** seems to have a private reader in mind when writing the prologue (lines 9–16):

> A worthy wyght wylned at me
> Sertayn þyngus for to showe,
> Þat in Latyn wrytun saw he,
> In Englissh tonge, for to knowe
> Of Ihesu Cristes Natiuite
> And his werkus on a rowe,

To the whiche by good Auctorite
He myghte triste 7 fully knowe.

Nevertheless the following reference to the interface of English and Latin is one of several that could be chosen to demonstrate not only the poet's sensitivity to language difficulties but also the more public character of his audience (lines 5565–68):

ffor write Latyn may I not spar [refrain]
to sich as han vnderstondyng,
but after þe Latyn I wil declar
In Englisch, lewide to haue likyng.

Lines	Events	Bible
1–56	"There-fore now ys my by-gynnynge Atte Cristes incarnacioun" (17–18); end of the Fifth Age	Luke 1:24, 31
57–208	Excursus on the Ages of the World and on Mt. Olympus	
209–308	Visitation of Elizabeth; Magnificat; Joseph's doubts	Luke 1:39–57; Matt. 1:18–25
309–416	Decree of Caesar Augustus; Nativity; kneeling ox and ass (line 1018)	Luke 2; Is. 1:3
445–480	Tebel and Salome confirm Mary's virginity	
729–756	Isaias's prophecy of Emmanuel; Aaron's flowering rod; Ezekiel's vision of a door	Is. 7:14; Num. 17:8; Ezek. 44:1–2
1077–1092	Magi	Matt. 2:1–2
1093–1116	Annunciation to the shepherds	Luke 2
1173–1348	Circumcision; excursus on Christ's names in his capacities as Harrower of Hell, Healer, Savior; "He sais þat at te bygynnyng / Goddes sone, þat is saueour, / was with God in hym beyng, / And he God als in full honour" (1293–96)	Luke 2:21; John 1:1–2
1349–1412	Christ's fivefold shedding of blood connected to events of the Passion	Matt. 27
1413–1420	Covenant of Circumcision with Abraham	Gen. 17
1513–1600	Epiphany; Christ's Baptism: "my louede son is her" (1558); Miracle at Cana; feeding of the five thousand	Matt. 2; Luke 3:22; John 2:1–16; Matt. 14:17–21
1601–1680	Balac and Balaam: "But wen the aungel was commyng, the asse þat Balaam rode opon set ffete on spar, hym withdrawyng	Num. 22

Lines	Events	Bible
	to honour the aungel as he con" (1657–60)	
1681–1716	Balaam makes sacrifices, blesses Israel	Num. 23
1716–1812	Prophecy of the star of Jacob, connected to the star of the Magi	Num. 24
1833–1852	Jacob's prophecy to Juda	Gen. 49:8–10
1853–2028	Herod's misgivings; the Magi and the star: "Peple that was in thesternesse seghen grete light to hor likyng" (1997–98)	Matt. 2; Is. 9:2
2029–2140	Gifts of the Magi: "home a-nother way thay went" (2128)	Matt.2
2141–2264	Candlemass, rites of purification	
2297–2308	Presentation at the Temple	Luke 2:22–24
2329–2344	Offerings of Cain and Abel	Gen. 4:2–6
2345–2420	Abraham and Melchisedech	Gen. 14:14–20
2421–2496	History of Melchisedech, identified with Sem: "ffor text of Bible witerly / of his fadir spekys no thyng" (2425–26)	Heb. 7:3
2497–2536	Jacob and Esau; Noah's sacrifices; Abraham and Isaac; Covenant of Circumcision	Gen. 25:29–34; 27; 8:20; 22:2, 17
2665–2816	Presentation at the Temple; Simeon and Anna	Luke 2:22–36
2817–3164	Candlemass; miracles of the Virgin	
3164–3612	Slaughter of the Innocents; Herod and his sons; Flight into Egypt; burning of the ships at Tharsis	Matt. 2:13–16; Ps. 47:8
3613–3624	Christ disputes with the Temple Doctors	Luke 2:46
3665–3896	Septuagesima; Babylonian Captivity	
3897–4104	Sexagesima and its significances	
4105–4396	Quinquagesima: "Paule says thagh he had that grace / to speke as aungel and as mon, / and charite failet in that caas, / vertu fynd he ne con, / Saue as metal that wer sounyng / that turnet no more profyt to" (4261–66); "lo now we gone to that cite, / fulfyllet sal be althing / of prophetes spoken before of me" (4286–88); heals blind man: "thi beleue has sauet the" (4315)	1Cor. 13:1–2; Luke 18:31–33, 35–42
4397–4644	Quadragesima: "Matheu in his euangely / from Abraham til Crist comen was / Generacions euen fourty / He settes, as book mynd maas" (4453–56)	Matt. 1

Lines	Events	Bible
4645–4676	How Josue [mistake for Moses] led Israel from Egypt; the return from Babylonian Captivity, as told in "Ester" [mistake for Esdras]	Ex. 14; 1Esdras 1
4817–4892	Joseph sold into slavery; rules Egypt; famine; Israel dwells in Egypt; Plagues and Passover; Red Sea crossing	Gen. 39; 41; 42; Ex. 14; 15
4893–4948	Pentecost linked to the giving of the Old Law: "Ihesu Crist our heuen kyng / sende his gost doun to his her / In fourme of fuyr on hym to myng, / As to Moyses in al maner" (4921–24)	Acts 2; Ex. 19
4949–4996	Forty years in the desert; Manna; Feast of Tents; Feast of the Dedication of the Temple (cf. John 10:22–23)	Ex. 16
5229–5332	John baptizes Christ; Temptation in the Desert	Matt. 3:13–4:11
5333–5384	Cleanses Temple; calls Disciples; Miracle at Cana; John imprisoned and beheaded; feeding of the five thousand	Matt. 21:12; 10:2; Mark 3:13–18; John 2:1–16; 3:20; Matt. 14:10, 15–21
5385–5628	Passion; earthquake; Good and Bad Thieves; "Frendes 7 neghburs in gret nede / Aȝayn me stoden ful stifly" (5553–54)	Matt. 27; Luke 23:32, 43; Job 19:19
5629–5656	Woe to Jerusalem	Luke 19:41–44
5689–5748	"he was way to wayue our wo, / sothnes, and lif all thre in fer" (5691–92); Christ before Pilate: "in hym cause fynde I none"(5713); that Christ cures by the power of demons; that Christ cannot save himself; his captors fall at the sound of his voice	John 14:6; Luke 23:15; Matt. 12:24; 27:42; John 18:6
5781–5800	Further accusations of the Jews against Jesus	John 9:16, 24; Luke 23:5
5801–6032	"I am thirsty" (5822); vinegar and gall; Crown of Thorns; Scourging; the Crucifixion; Christ before Annas and Pilate	John 18; 19
6085–6092	"In sacrifyce his wille to sewe, / that swetly sauouret" (6087–88)	Eph. 5:2
6205–6336	Healing by contraries; "he meket hymself	Phil. 2:8;

Lines	Events	Bible
	that lorde of might / maad buxum to the deth that day" (6279–80); "the hegh keng of blisse / his owen sone ne sparet noght" (6329–30)	Rom. 8:32
6337–6424	Christ as bait, Cross as hook; Eve's "charter" with the Devil (6378)	Job 41:1
6425–6816	Life of Pilate; Veronica	
6817–7052	Life of Judas: keeper of the purse, objects to Anointing, sells Jesus for thirty pence, hangs himself	John 12:3–6; Matt. 26:15; 27:5
7213–7264	Resurrection: "when I am hauset . . . / from the erthe gostely that day, / all thing I wil dragh with me" (7249–51); Jesus as a lion	John 2:19–22; Matt. 26:32; John 12:32; Jer. 4:7
7293–7432	Signs of the risen Christ: the angel; Christ's eating; appearances to Thomas; Carpus (cf. 2Tim. 4:13); Death's dominion; "that holy body so bright / Schal no corrupcioun com ner" (7431–32)	John 20:12, 19–29; Luke 24:43; Rom. 6:9; Ps. 48:11
7433–7500	Various Epistles on the Resurrection	1Cor. 15:14; Rom. 4:25; 6:4; 1Pet. 1:3; 1Cor. 15:20–21
7501–7708	Appearances to Mary Magdalen, the Marys, Peter, Cleophas, the Disciples, Doubting Thomas, the Fishermen, on Mt. Tabor, the Disciples at table, on Mt. Olivet; the Ascension	Mark 16:9; Matt. 28:9; Luke 24:15, 36; John 20:26; 21:4; Matt. 28:16; Mark 16:14; Luke 24:50–51
7709–7800	Apocryphal post-Resurrection appearances to James, Nicodemus, Mary: "al-thagh mon may not fynde ne se / writen in none euangely, / Euel semes hit sich a son as he / shuld for-ʒete his moder in ny" (7783–86)	
7801–8108	Harrowing of Hell, with the prophets, Seth, Henoch and Elias, the Good Thief, etc.	Matt. 27:52–53
8109–8664	The Greater and Lesser Litanies	
8665–8740	The Ascension	Luke 24:50–51; Mark 16:14
9277–9312	Leaps of Christ	Cant. 2:8

Lines	Events	Bible
9337–9340	"yff ʒe louet me tenderly, / ʒe schuld haue tho mor likyng / That I go to my fader in hye, / that in heuen is heghest keng"	John 14:28
9414–9416	"a gode vocate han we / to the fader of heuen"	1John 2:1
9453–9480	The angel reproves the prostrated John	Rev. 19:10
9485–9492	"a grete bischop haue we, / Ihesu, Goddes son dere, / that percet heuen thurgh his pouste" (9486–88)	Heb. 4:14
9523–9524	"God saide he stegh vp this day / to ordayne our place whit his"	John 14:2
9613–9620	Various gifts of the Spirit	1Cor. 12:8–10
9661–9684	Manifestations of the Spirit: the Dove, the Transfiguration, the Insufflation, Pentecost	Luke 3:22; Matt. 17:5; John 20:22; Acts 2:4
9685–10004	Various verses on the Descent of the Spirit: "I come . . . to erthe her / ffor to put fir þer-in" (9821–22); "Send þi gost, lord, to þi men / 7 made so in A new maner" (9866–67); "ffor quer-so Goddes gost shall go, / þer is ffrensship þat will not faile" (9977–78)	Is. 59:11; Cant. 2:13–14; Luke 1:35; John 7:38; Luke 12:49; Ps. 103:30; Rom. 8:14; 2Cor. 3:17; Matt. 7:22
10031–10032	"haue ʒe / þo Holy Gost, syn to relese"	John 20:22–23
10081–10092	Pentecost	Acts 2:2–3
10117–10118	"an ox . . . / will not lowe quen cracche is fulle"	Job 6:5
10157–10160	"nothyng propre haden þai, / of all þat euer hom geuen was / In comune dalt was day for day, / none calles his of þat he has"	Acts 4:32
10423–10426	"he [Solomon] Askes heuenly God almyght / To knaw his wytte, what way schyn we, / Bot only ʒif he send vs doun / ffrom heuen his gost þurgh his grace"	Wis. 9:17
10545–10556	The power of the Tongue	James 3:7–9
10657–10660	"þai weren in vnite / . . . And in one place to-geder dyʒt"	Acts 2:1
10698–10700	"God wold aske his fader of gras / An-oþer counselour to Crist / to ʒyue his meyne in solas"	John 14:16
10732	"pese to ʒow All here"	John 20:21
10826–10829	"the Holy Gost þat sothefast is, / þe quyche his fader heuen flour / ffrom heghest see wold send I-wis / Shulden tech hom all maner thyng"	John 14:26

❖ III.C   *Passion Narratives*

As a glance at the biblical index in this volume indicates, those gospel chapters which cover the Passion of Christ, notably Matthew 27, are cited more often than any other chapters in any other biblical book. In the following survey, the principal passion narratives in English have been covered, but the list of works which qualify as passion narratives, meditations, or treatments—such as the one in *Piers Plowman*, passus 18 (in the B text)—is almost endless.

Two books provide helpful guides to the Passion story: for the prose Latin treatises which often underlie the English texts, Bestul, *Texts of the Passion;* for the development of Christ as a literary figure in English, from the *Dream of the Rood* to George Eliot, Bennett, *Poetry of the Passion*. Speaking of thirteenth-century poetry of the Passion Bennett remarks, "Beside this phenomenon the emergence of 'courtly love,' so called, is a mere ripple on the surface of literature, though . . . the two developments are not entirely unrelated" (32).

For all their popularity, the Gospels provide relatively little information concerning the physical circumstances of the Crucifixion. Christ's words in Luke 24:44, however ("all things must needs be fulfilled, which are written in the law of Moses, and in the prophets, and in the psalms, concerning me"), licensed the use of numerous Old Testament verses which were taken to prefigure the Passion, especially: Ps. 21:18–19; Is. 1:6; 50:6; 53:2–7; 63:1–3; Lam. 1:12 (see Wenzel, *Verses in Sermons*, 165–66, for various individual appearances of this verse); Mic. 4:8; Zach. 13:7.

Passion of Our Lord PL

IMEV 1441
Manual, 2:393 [33]

1. Oxford, Jesus College 29, part 2 (144r–55r), ca. 1300, 706 lines in
   rhyming couplets.

Edition: Morris, *Old English Miscellany,* 37–57.

The poem is in the ballad tradition (lines 1–4):

> Ihereþ nv one lutele tale. þat ich eu wille telle.
> As we vyndeþ hit iwrite. in þe godspelle.
> Nis hit nouht of karlemeyne ne of þe Duzeper.
> Ac of cristes þruwinge. þet he þolede her.

The Passion has been extended at both ends: lines 21 through 88 tell of
Christ's temptation in the desert and his early preaching and healing; lines
553 to the end (which appear to be a later addition) include an account of
Pentecost from Acts 1. The Gospel of John is the most prominent source,
not least since John is recognized as an eyewitness: "Þe ilke þat hit iseyh. he
wrot þis god-spel" (line 501; John 19:34). The inclusion of the most picturesque details from all four Gospels qualify the poem as a harmony of Passion
narratives.

Two of the few details which have no gospel authority are the reference
to the Harrowing in line 536 and Judas's fatuous warning to the Roman soldiers: "ledeþ hyne warlyche. he con wondres monye" (line 123). The poet
adds prayers for himself and his audience at the beginning and end, and
there is one brief moralization: "wel ouhte we beon aferd. if we wyse were. /
And vre sunnes bete. þe hwile we beoþ here" (lines 153–54, perhaps an echo
of Ecclus. 7:25). Overall the poem is distinguished by direct dialogue and
vivid action.

Lines	Events	Bible
1–20	Prologue	
21–40	Baptism; Temptation in the Desert	Matt. 3:13; 4:1–11
41–88	General preaching, healing; envy of Jews; Palm Sunday; cleanses Temple	Matt. 13:55; 21: 12–13; John 12:13
89–125	Judas receives thirty pence; Last Supper; traitor revealed	Mark 14:21; Matt. 26:14–16, 20–25
126–176	Predicts Peter's denials; Agony in Gethsemani; sweats blood	Matt. 26:30–46; Luke 22:39–46

Lines	Events	Bible
177–320	Kiss of Judas; Malchus's ear; Christ before Caiphas; "John" flees naked; Scourging; Peter's denials	John 18:10, 15–27; Luke 22:47–53; Matt. 26:57–75; Mark 14:51–52
321–430	Christ before Pilate; Barabbas; " 'Do a rode do a rode,' hi seyden, 'hyne a-non' " (396)	Matt. 27:11–31; John 18:29–19:16
431–502	Crucifixion; casting lots; "To day in paradyse. þu schalt beo myd me" (466); Pilate's inscription, "þet ich wrot beo iwryte. ne may hit nomon vn-do" (476); Longinus	John 19:17–24, 31–37; Luke 23: 32–47
503–535	Joseph of Arimathea; Burial; precautions of the Jews	Matt. 27:57–66
536–618	Harrowing of Hell: "to-brek he helle dure and ouercom heore king" (536); Resurrection; appearance to Mary Magdalen and Disciples; eats bread and a "huny-comb" (616)	John 20:1–20; Luke 24:36–43
619–656	Commissions Disciples; Ascension	Luke 24:44–53; Matt. 28:16–20; Acts 1:6–11
657–688	Pentecost: "þe holy gost heom com vp-on. in fury tunge" (660); early evangelism and persecutions by Nero and Dacian	Acts 2:1–8
689–706	Prayer for salvation of poet and readers	

The Northern Passion NP

IMEV/S 1907
Manual, 2:444 [303] (concerns Legend of the Cross section only)

1. Oxford, Bodleian Lib. Ashmole 61 (*SC* 6922) (87v–105v), late 15th c.
2. Oxford, Bodleian Lib. Rawlinson C.86 (*SC* 11951) (2r–30v), late 15th c.
3. Oxford, Bodleian Lib. Rawlinson C.655 (*SC* 15481) (1r–50r), mid-15th c.
4. Cambridge, Univ. Lib. Dd.1.1 (6r–21r), early 15th c. Partial text (see Foster, *Northern Passion: French Text,* 10–11]).
5. Cambridge, Univ. Lib. Ff.5.48 (11r–43r), 15th c.
6. Cambridge, Univ. Lib. Gg.1.1 (122r–134v), early 14th c., 1,974 lines.
7. Cambridge, Univ. Lib. Ii.4.9 (1r–42r), 15th c.
8. Cambridge, Univ. Lib. Gg.5.31 (149r–171v), later 14th c.
9. London, BL Add. 31042 (London Thornton) (33r–50r), mid-15th c.

10. London, BL Cotton Vesp. D.ix (191r–192r), mid-15th c., lines 357–470 only.

11. London, BL Harley 215 (161r), 15th c., lines 300–439 only.

The "expanded" version
IMEV 170

12. Oxford, Bodleian Lib. Rawlinson poetry f.175 (*SC* 14667) (55v–76r), mid-14th c., 3,574 lines.

13. London, BL Cotton Tiberius E.vii (165r–184r), ca. 1400. Part of the expanded version of **NHC.**

14. London, BL Harley 4196 (67r–86r), early 15th c. Part of the expanded version of **NHC.**

The poem is in couplets.

Editions: 4, 8, 9, 14—Foster, *Northern Passion: Four Parallel Texts.*
   2, 3—Foster, *Northern Passion: French Text,* 126–57 (variants only).
   5—Downing, "Critical Edition."
   6—Heuser and Foster, *Northern Passion,* 1–50.
   10, 11—Foster, *Northern Passion: French Text,* 172–76.
   12—Heuser and Foster, *Northern Passion,* 51–142.
   14—Morris, *Legends of the Holy Rood,* 62–86 (Legend of the Cross only).
Facsimile: 9—J. Thompson, *Thornton.*

NP has multiple connections with several other paraphrases and homily cycles; it is based primarily on a 1482-line French poem written ca. 1200 and extant in twenty-four manuscripts (Foster, *Northern Passion: French Text,* 49; Heuser and Foster, *Northern Passion,* vi). The English poet made his adaptation probably some one hundred years later. **NP** also appears in manuscripts of both the unexpanded and expanded versions (manuscripts 13 and 14) of **NHC.** [1]

The French poem extends from the conspiracy of the Jews to the Resurrection and was itself incorporated into the *Bible* of Herman de Valenciennes and the *Bible des sept états du monde* of Geoffrey of Paris. In the course of **NP**'s adaptation from the French and subsequent expansions in the homily cycle a number of texts appear to have been used, including the *Historia Scholastica* and **GNs.** There is clear evidence, discussed by Foster, that **NP** was in

---

1. **NP** undergoes the same expansion as the surrounding homilies. Nevanlinna, *Northern Homily Cycle,* omits the text printed in Foster, *Northern Passion: Four Parallel Texts* (i.e., manuscript 14, fols. 67r–86r).

turn used in the York, Wakefield (Towneley), and Coventry drama cycles (*Northern Passion: French Text*, 81–101).

The following outline is taken from manuscript 14 as printed in Foster, *Northern Passion: Four Parallel Texts*. Line numbers are approximate since each of the four versions, printed in parallel, are not independently numerated. The initial rubric represents the narrative as the Passion according to Mark, Matthew, Luke, and John.

Lines	Events	Bible
1–28d	Prologue; Temptation in the Desert	Matt. 4:1–4
29–43	Caiphas: "A man bus vnto dede be broght / So þat all folk peris noght" (33–34)	John 11:50
44–92	Entry into Jerusalem: "ʒowre maister of þam has nede" (70a)	Matt. 21:1–8
93–174	Anointing at Bethany; Judas objects; accepts the thirty pence	John 12:1–8; Matt. 26:14–16
175–270	Preparations for the Passover; Last Supper: "lord, es it oght I?" (258)	Luke 22:7–23; Matt. 26:20–25
271–294	John, asleep, receives vision of the Apocalypse	John 13:23
295–373	Disciples argue over precedence; Christ washes Disciples' feet	Luke 22:24–27; John 13:4–15
374–423	Peter's denials foretold; " 'twa swerdes er redy here' . . . 'Þat es inogh' " (419, 422)	Matt. 26:31–35; Luke 22:35–38
424–510	Christ prays on Mt.Olivet; comforted by the angel	Luke 22:39–46
511–602	Arrest; Malchus's ear: "he þat smites with swerd, Iwis, / Thurgh swerd he sall peris" (570–71)	Matt. 26:47–56; John 18:2–11
603–634	"John" flees, leaving his mantle	Mark 14:51–52
635–744	Christ before Caiphas: "I coniore þe thurgh god lifand / þat þou me tell to vnderstand / If þou be god sun of heuyn" (659–61); Peter's denials	Matt. 26:57–75; Luke 22:54–62
745–818	Further interrogation; Buffeting	Luke 22:63–71
819–904	Judas returns money, commits suicide: "A rightwis blude I haue bitrayd" (830)	Matt. 27:3–10; Acts 1:18–19
905–1188	Christ before Pilate and Herod: Barabbas; Dream of Pilate's wife; "Say me what es suthfastnes" (1168)	Matt. 27:11–26; Luke 23:1–25; John 18:28–40
1189–1296	Scourging; "king bot cesar haue we nane" (1268)	John 19:1–16
1297–1438	History of the Holy Rood Tree; recollection	John 5:2–7

Lines	Events	Bible
	of the pool at the Sheep Gate (lines 1391–1404)	
[independent numeration commences]		
1–684	Seth's Quest for the Oil of Mercy (Quinn, *Quest*); accounts of the Fall and of how Cain slew Abel; wonders of Moses, David, and Solomon; healing of Namaan (600); the smith who befriends Jesus	Gen. 3; 4; 4Kg. 5:1–14
[main numeration continues]		
1439–1520	Forging of the Nails	
1521–1587	Road to Calvary: "Hilles, falles doune on vs" (1547); Simon of Cyrene	Luke 23:26–32
1588–1716	Crucifixion; seamless garment; Pilate's inscription: "Als it es wreten, so sall it be" (1686); Good and Bad Thieves; vinegar and gall	John 19:17–24; Matt. 27:34–42; Luke 23:39–43
1717–1809	Mary entrusted to John; wonders at the Crucifixion; Last Words; Words of the Centurion	John 19:25–27; Lam. 1:12; Matt. 27:45–54; John 19:30; Luke 23:34, 46
1810–1842	Harrowing of Hell	
1843–1914	Joseph of Arimathea; Longinus; Deposition; Anointing; Burial	John 19:31–42
1915–2090	Precautions of the Jews; Marys at the tomb; the angel; guards bribed; final prayer	Matt. 27:62–28:15

Meditations on the Life and Passion of Christ MLP

IMEV 1034

1. London, BL Add. 11307 (7r–87v), early 15th c., 2,254 lines in octosyllabic couplets. A "Long" **ChC** and **LLB** follow.

Edition: D'Evelyn, *Meditations.*

The editor describes the poem as a "compendium of the lyric themes of Middle English religious poetry." The title reflects the principal biblical contents of the work, though the style may be more accurately characterized as a "praising" of Christ and Mary.

D'Evelyn suggests as sources (in addition to the Bible) various works by Rolle, Hugh of St. Victor's *De laude Charitatis,* and the 154-line poem *An Orison of the Passion* (*IMEV* 1761), which corresponds approximately to lines

1355–2040 (printed by D'Evelyn on pp. 60–64). However, Raby, "'Philomela,'" demonstrates that the sole source is John of Hovedon's "Philomela."

Lines	Events	Bible
1–110	Praises of Jesus and Mary with brief allusions to the Incarnation and Nativity	
111–128	Mary as a "mowe of corn" (113), a "pomegarnet" (116), "castel of kyng Dauid" (118), "Milk and hony" (121)	Cant. 7:2; 4:3, 4, 11
129–184	Magi; Slaughter of the Innocents; Simeon	Matt. 2:1–2, 11, 16; Luke 2:25–32
185–252	Miracle at Cana; Baptism; Temptation in in the Desert; raising of Lazarus; Harrowing of Hell	John 2:9; Matt. 3:13; 4:1; John 11:43
253–356	Palm Sunday; Last Supper; Jesus takes leave of his Disciples: "Þe moþer suffreþ wel to-forn / Serewe er hure child be born; / Whon it is born sho feleþ lisse, / Hure bale is tornd in-to blisse" (319–22)	Matt. 21:8; Luke 22:15–18; John 14: 2–3, 21; 13:34–35; 15:1–5, 15, 19; 16:6, 21, 22, 33; 17:20, 24; Matt. 26:31; 11:28–29
357–388	Washes Disciples' feet; sweats blood; comforted by angel on Mt. Olivet	John 13:5; Luke 22: 43–44
389–491	Betrayal; Peter's denials; Buffeting	Matt. 26:47–50, 67, 70
492–646	Christ before Pilate and Herod; Barabbas	Matt. 27:11–31
647–1172	Excurses on the thorns, the Cross, Christ's name	
1173–1272	Mary entrusted to John; the Good Thief; Christ as Adam, Joseph, Abel, Job, Judas Machabeus, David	John 19:26–27; Luke 23:43
1273–1700	Prayer that Love write the main events of the Crucifixion on poet's heart	
1701–1734	Sorrows of Job: "Curour was þere neuer non / Þat myȝte a-wey so faste gon / As don þe dayes of my lyf" (1721–23)	Job 16:13–15; 30:10; 9:25; 19:12, 13; 6:12; 7:12
1735–1938	Further meditation on the Passion: "Siþþe þei don þus in grene tre / Whan it sereþ how shal it be?" (1805–6); the Vernicle	Luke 23:31, 36
1939–2034	The Saints acclaim Christ's presence in heaven	
2035–2074	Resurrection; appearances to Mary Magdalen, Disciples, Doubting Thomas; Ascension; Pentecost	Matt. 28:1, 9; John 20:27; Acts 1:9; 2: 3–4

Lines	Events	Bible
2075–2254	Assumption of Mary; prayer for her intercession	

Versions of the *Charter of Christ* (*Testamentum Christi, Carta Dei*) ChC

IMEV/S 4182.5
Manual, 7:2343 [187]

In its various versions, **ChC** represents itself as Christ's last will and testament from the cross, whereby he deeds the bliss of heaven to those who follow His commandments, that is, pay his "rent." It is often "signed" and "notarized" by witnesses (e.g., John, Mary Magdalen, Longinus, the Evangelists). Common to the versions is the metaphor of Christ's body as a text upon which the deed was written. Cf. Col. 2:14, and see Spalding, *Charters of Christ*, xlii–li, Chaucer's "ABC" (lines 59–60), and another "ABC" poem on the Passion (196 lines) in E. Wilson, *Index*, 42–48 and Furnivall, *Political, Religious and Love Poems*, 244–50; (1903) 271–78 (*IMEV/S* 1523). Rolle's *Meditacioun of þe fyue woundes* is particularly vivid: "More зit, swete Ihesu, þi bodi is lijk a book writen wiþ reed enke: so is þi bodi al writen wiþ rede woundis. / Now, swete Ihesu, graunte me grace often to rede upon þis book."[2]

The genre of "Christ's Last Will and Testament" finds its most influential expression in Deguileville's *Pèlerinage de la vie humaine* (*Manual*, 7:2347 [192]), and in the *Poor Caitiff* tracts (*Manual*, 9:3135 [87]).

Details from the gospel Passion narratives appear throughout. Spalding provides the most complete discussion of these and related texts; all quotations are from her edition.

"Kent Charter"
IMEV 1828

1. Oxford, Bodleian Lib. Kent Charter 233 (dorso), late 14th c., forty-two lines in couplets.

Edition: Spalding, *Charters of Christ*, 97–98; Macray, "Religious Verses."

---

2. Horstmann, *Yorkshire Writers*, 1:97. Cf. lines 1531–34 of **MLP** and the description in the *Privity of the Passion:* "he was thus sprede o-brode one þe crosse more straite þan any parchemyne-skyne es sprede one þe harowe" (Horstmann, *Yorkshire Writers*, 1:206). For Rolle's other meditations on the Passion see Allen, *English Writings*, 19–36; Madigan, *Passio Domini Theme; Manual* 9:3056 [3]; and *IPMEP* 618, 800.

> "The garlond of thorn on myn hed stode,
> The schorges and the naylis long,
> And the spere my herte stong,
> The stoppe ful of eysil and galle,
> And Hely ely that I gan calle"
>   (30–34; Matt. 27:29, 46; John 19:29)

"Short Charter"
IMEV/S 4184
Approximately thirty-four lines, in couplets.

1. London, BL Sloane 3292 (2r), 16th c.
2. London, BL Stowe 620 (11v–12r), 16th c.
3. London, BL Add. Charter 5960, 16th c.
4. London, BL Add. 37049 (23r), 15th c.
5. London, BL Harley 116 (97v), 15th c.
6. London, BL Add. 24343 (6v–7r), 15th c.
7. Cambridge, Gonville and Caius College 230 (25r), 15th c.
8. Oxford, Bodleian Lib. Ashmole 61 (*SC* 6922) (106r), 16th c.
9. London, BL Harley 237 (100r–v), 15th c.
10. London, BL Add. 5465 (Fairfax) (119r–122r [rectos only]), 16th c.
11. Oxford, Bodleian Lib. Ashmole 189 (*SC* 6666) (109r–110r), 15th c.
12. Cambridge, St. John's College 37 (53r), 15th c.
13. London, BL Harley 6848 (221r–v), 18th c.
14. Cambridge, Univ. Lib. Ii.6.44 (1r).
15. Manchester, John Rylands Lib. Lat. 176 (202v), 15th c.
16. Cambridge, Univ. Lib. Add. 6686 (p. 270) (*IMEV* 1740).
17. Cambridge, Mass., Harvard Univ., Houghton Lib., W. K. Richardson 22 (71r), ca. 1400.
18. London, BL Add. 60577 (114v–115r), ca. 1500.

Editions: 1–12 — Spalding, *Charters of Christ*, 1–16.
    8 with 11 — Förster, "Texte," 195–97.
    10 — Fehr, "Fairfax MS," 69–70.
    15 — James, *Descriptive Catalogue*, 300–301.
Facsimile: 18 — Wilson and Fenlon, *Winchester Anthology*.

For descriptions of the manuscripts, see Spalding, *Charters of Christ*, xix–xxix.

> "Witnes þe erth þat þan dyd qwake
> And stones gret þat sonder brake
> Wittnes þe vayle þat þan did ryfe

And men þat rose fro ded to lyfe
Witnes þe day þat turned to nyght
And þe son þat withdrewe his light
Witnes my moder & sayn Ion
And oþer þat wer þer many one"
(manuscript 4, lines 23–28; Matt. 27:45, 51–53).

"Long Charter," in three versions:
Version A
IMEV 1718

234 lines in couplets

1. Oxford, Bodleian Lib. Eng. poet. a.1 (Vernon) (317v, col. 2–318r), ca. 1390.
2. Oxford, Bodleian Lib. Bodley 89 (*SC* 1886) (45r–49r), 15th c.
3. Oxford, Bodleian Lib. Rawlinson poetry f.175 (*SC* 14667) (94v–95v), 14th c.
4. Oxford, Bodleian Lib. Add. C.280 (*SC* 29572) (124r–125r), 15th c.
5. London, BL Harley 2346 (51r–55r), 15th c.
6. London, BL Harley 5396 (301r–305r), 1456.
7. London, BL Add. 11307 (89r–97r), 15th c.
8. Oxford, Magdalen College St. Peter in the East 18.e (62-line fragment), 15th c.

Editions: 1—Horstmann, "Nachträge" (1887), 424–32; Furnivall, *Minor Poems*, 637–57.
2–7—Spalding, *Charters of Christ*, 18–43.
8—Spalding, *Charters of Christ*, 44.
Facsimile: 1—Doyle, *Vernon Manuscript.*

Lines	Events	Bible
15–24	Conception by Mary	
25–38	Temptation in the Desert	Matt. 4:1–11
57–66	Institution of the Eucharist; Betrayal quoting Ps. 9.9a	Luke 22:14–23
67–98	Casting of lots for Christ's clothes; Crucifixion; the Scourging writes the Charter on Christ's body with 5460 wounds (89). "Abydes & lokes on me today / And redes on þis parchemyne / If any sorow be lyke to myne" (94–96)	John 19:23–24; Lam. 1:12
179–188	Lamentation of Mary; Last Words	John 19:30; Matt. 27:45

Lines	*Events*	*Bible*
189–196	Harrowing of Hell	
197–214	General references to Resurrection and Ascension	

Version B
IMEV/S 4154

414 lines in couplets. Consists of all of A, plus some two hundred lines inserted at various points (referring, e.g., to the Original Sin and Expulsion from Eden [25–32; Gen. 3]).

1. Cambridge, Univ. Lib. Ee.2.15 (90r–94r) (missing lines 1–68), ca. 1500.
2. Cambridge, Univ. Lib. Ff. 2.38 (47v–50v), 15th c.
3. Cambridge, Univ. Lib. Ii.3.26 (235r–237r), 15th c.
4. Cambridge, Univ. Lib. Ii.4.9 (42v–47r) (incomplete), 15th c.
5. London, BL Cotton Caligula A.ii (77r–79r), 15th c.
6. London, BL Harley 2382 (111v–118r), 15th. c.
7. Tokyo, Takamiya 4 (olim Phillipps 8820), Art. 3 (8)
8. Cambridge, Mass., Harvard Univ., Houghton Lib. W. K. Richardson 22 (82v–90v), ca. 1400, atelous.
9. Corning, N.Y., Museum of Glass 6 (123v–130v), 15th c.

Editions: 1–5 — Spalding, *Charters of Christ*, 46–81.
6 — Furnivall, *Minor Poems*, 637–57; Horstmann, "Nachträge" (1887), 424–32.
Facsimile: 2 — McSparran and Robinson, *Cambridge University Library MS Ff.2.38.*

Version C
IMEV 1174

1. London, BL Royal 17.C.xvii (112v–116v), early 15th c., 618 lines.

Edition: Furnivall, *Minor Poems*, 637–57.

Þe Lamentacioun þat was bytwene vre lady and seynt Bernard [of Clairvaux] LLB

Manual, 3:685 [8]

The title is from the index to the Vernon manuscript.

Version 1 (eight-line stanzas rhyming abababab)
IMEV 1869

1. Oxford, Bodleian Lib. Laud misc.463 (*SC* 1596) (160r), late 14th c.
2. Oxford, Bodleian Lib. Eng. poet. a.1 (Vernon) (287r–288v),
   ca. 1390, 736 lines
3. Oxford, Bodleian Lib. Douce 126 (*SC* 21700) (84v–91r), 15th c.
4. Oxford, Trinity College 57 (167r), ca. 1400, 548 lines, atelous.
5. Cambridge, Univ. Lib. Dd 1.1 (21r–29v), early 15th c., 764 lines.
6. London, BL Add. 11307 (97v), 15th c.

Editions: 2—Horstmann, *Minor Poems,* 297–328, with variants from 4, 5,
and 7.
2 and 5 in parallel—Kribel, "Lamentatio," 85–114.
Facsimile: 2—Doyle, *Vernon Manuscript.*

Version 2 (omits first four stanzas of Version 1)
IMEV/S 771

1. Oxford, Bodleian Lib. Rawlinson poetry f.175 (*SC* 14667) (76r–80r),
   14th c., 712 lines.
2. London, BL Cotton Tiberius E.vii (82r–85v), ca. 1400, 712 lines.
3. London, Sion College Arc. L.40.2/E.25 (39r–47v), 15th c., verses
   1–413 of manuscript 2, atelous.

Editions: 1—Fröhlich, *De lamentacione,* 63–93.
2—Horstmann, *Yorkshire Writers,* 2:274–82.

Version 3 (independent)
IMEV/S 3208

Lines 23945–24730 of **CM** in six-line stanzas, aabaab

1. Oxford, Bodleian Lib. Fairfax 14 (*SC* 3894) (102r), early 15th c.
2. London, BL Cotton Vespasian A.iii (134r), ca. 1340.
3. Edinburgh, College of Physicians (10r), early 15th c.
4. Göttingen, Niedersächsische Staats- und Universitätsbibliotek Theol.
   107r (159r), early 15th c.

Editions: 1–4—Morris, *Cursor Mundi* (vol. 68).
Study: Marx, "Middle English Verse 'Lamentation' "—how the Middle
English poet adapted the sources and how the poem functions as
popular affective piety.

The source is the Latin *Quis dabit* (*Liber de passione Christi et doloribus et planctibus matris eius*) via the Anglo-Norman *Plainte de la Vierge,* though the poet acknowledges only the Latin of St. Bernard (line 18) and "Þe gospel" (21).

The prologue expresses a strong sense of the responsibility the learned have to teach the lewed: "Þe Mon þat con, and teche nille, / He may haue drede of godes wreche" (all quotations from Horstmann, *Minor Poems,* lines 15–16). The opening lines offer his project as a substitute for the preaching that, for some unspecified reason, "wol not wonen in heore wit" (4), and he invokes the authority of John's Gospel with a minimum of reserve:

> Þe gospel nul I forsake nouȝt,
> Þauȝ hit be writen in parchemyn;
> Seynt Iones word, and hit be souȝt,
> Þer-of hit wole be witnes myn.(21–24)

"Men and wymmen" (29) are addressed as the listening audience.

The body of the poem takes the form of a dialogue almost equally divided between St. Bernard, who asks long, leading, recapitulative questions and Mary, who recounts both the events of the Passion as eyewitness and her own emotions as mother ("Þe blod out of her eȝen ron" [89]).[3]

Apart from frequent, graphic descriptions of Christ's Arrest, Trial, Buffeting, Crucifixion, Deposition, and Burial, noteworthy biblical and apocryphal matter includes:

Lines	Events	Bible
49–56	Incarnation; presentation to Simeon; Flight into Egypt (49–56)	Luke 2:25–28; Matt. 2:13–14
190	Peter severs the "Iewes ere" which Jesus restores immediately	John 18:10
270	Metaphor of Jesus as a lamb and the Jews as "Wolues"	
365–440	How the Jews mock Mary herself; commiseration between Mary and Mary Magdalen	
462	John charged to keep Mary	John 19:27
473–528	Metaphor of mankind as a stolen sheep which Jesus has saved; Mary's warning to Jesus not to	

---

3. A comparable eyewitness account appears in London, BL Add. 37787, fols. 161r–162v (ed. Baugh, *Worcestershire Miscellany,* 151–52; *IPMEP* 323), "The Vision of St John on the Sorrows of the Virgin." Mary connects each of her Five Sorrows to an event in the Life of Christ: (1) "the swerde of sorwe schal passe þrowgh þyne herte" (Luke 2:35), (2) Mary seeks Jesus in the Temple (Luke 2:48), (3) Arrest, (4) Crucifixion (Luke 23:46), (5) Deposition.

Lines	Events	Bible
	touch the sponge of gall; Jesus's assurance that "Þorw þis drynke Adam [is] bouȝt" (519); reference to the Harrowing	
529–560	Dialogue between the Thieves; Christ's promise to the Good Thief; "Heloy, heloy . . . Lamaȝabatani" (559–60)	Luke 23:43; Matt. 27:46
613–655	Spear of "Longeus" who, though blind, is not healed; angels would weep if they could feel sorrow	John 19:34

Meditations on the Supper of Our Lord MS

IMEV/S 248
Manual, 9:3106 [62]

1,142 lines in couplets

1. Oxford, Bodleian Lib. Bodley 415 (*SC* 2313) (80r–85r), early 15th c.
2. Cambridge, Trinity College 305 (150v–162r), 15th c.
3. London, BL Harley 1701 (84r–91v), earlier 15th c.
4. London, BL Add. 36983 (118r–127r), 1442.
5. London, Lambeth Palace 559 (89v–120r and 133r), 15th c.
6. Washington, Folger Shakespeare Lib. 420312 (Clopton) (84v–92v), mid-15th c.

Editions: 3—Cowper, *Meditations,* with variants from 1.
4—Horrall et al., *Southern Version,* 3:211–34 (as part of **CM** at line 14914).

IMEV 646 (missing prologue of 22 lines)

1. London, BL Harley 218 (83r–91r), 15th c.
2. London, BL Harley 2338 (1r), 15th c.

No edition.

MS has been doubtfully attributed to Robert Mannyng of Brunne; Robert's *Handlyng Synne* precedes in three of the manuscripts. The bulk of the poem is a pious meditation on Christ's Passion which, when it does not skip material from the *Meditaciones de passione Christi* (*MPC,* ed. Stallings), follows it closely. The poet adresses a "congregacyun" (line 4) to which he intends to "lere a medytacyun" (line 13). He appeals to authorities while still allowing himself considerable latitude (lines 17–20):

Take hede, for y wyl no þyng seye
But þat ys preued by crystes feye,
By holy wryt, or seyntes sermons,
Or by dyuers holy opynyons.[4]

The humanity of Christ and the emotional responses of the Disciples, especially Peter (cf. John 13:8; 18:10), are highlighted. For example, at the Last Supper Christ secretly identifies Judas as the betrayer only to John, and specifically not to Peter, since "With nayles and teþ rent hym [Judas] he [Peter] wolde" (line 116). This renders "Petro autem Dominus non dixit, quia, ut dixit Augustinus, si ipsum scivisset, dentibus proditorem illum discerpisset" (*MPC* 1.85–86). For this detail the poet refers specifically to "austyns sermoun" (line 114), and Cowper cites Augustine's Homily on the Gospel for St. John's Day (Dec. 27, John 21:19–25). But the reference in the *MPC* to Augustine's "omelia" applies to another matter—that of Peter's and John's being exemplars of the active and contemplative lives, respectively. Stallings finds Peter's implicit threat to Judas nowhere in Augustine's genuine works.[5]

The combination of piety and theology in the *MPC* and **MS** is best illustrated by their emphasis on Christ's dual nature. The Son of God genuinely fears the Crucifixion, as the verse "Pater mi, si possibile est, transeat a me calix iste" (Matt. 26:39, cf. Luke 22:42) bears witness, and as does the physical manifestation of sweating blood (Luke 22:44) which the *MPC* (3.79–80) and **MS** (line 370 ff.) underscore. In an extraordinary moment in the Latin text which was not lost on the Middle English poet, the Archangel Michael comforts Christ, saying "*Confortamini* ergo *et viriliter agite*"; "Cumforte þe weyl and do manly" (line 398).[6] The colloquial exhortation "be a man" simultaneously reinforces the theological point and the affective message.

Of the five motifs in *MPC* for which Stallings can find no source the Middle English poet reproduces three, the most interesting being that Christ's cry at the moment of death was heard by the souls in Hell, intended perhaps as a notification of the Harrowing (*MPC* 7.46–48; line 768).[7] The

---

4. All quotations from Cowper's edition. Cf. the *MPC* 2.24–26: "Non enim in hoc opusculo aliquid affirmare intendo, quod non per sacram Scripturam, vel dicta Sanctorum, vel opiniones approbatas affirmetur vel dicatur."

5. Stallings does find it in Ps.-Augustine *Sermones ad fratres in eremo*, sermo 28 (PL 40.1284–85) and in the *Legenda Aurea*, which she favors as the source here (*MPC*, 137–38; see Jacobus, *Legenda Aurea*, caput 89, p. 369). For the St. John's Day homily see Stallings's notes on p. 90.

6. *MPC* 3.99–100. Stallings calls attention to 1 Mach. 2:64: "Vos ergo filii confortamini et viriliter agite." Cf. Love's translation (**MBL**) "Beþ þen now of gude confort my lorde, & worcheþ manfully" (Sargent, *Nicholas Love's Mirror*, 166).

7. The identification of the comforting angel (Luke 22:43) as Michael is only in **MPC**

poet doubtless chose these motifs for their novelty, but at the same time he knew that they were novel and took some pains to include them in his much abridged versification. Once again, as in much other biblical literature, the poet licenses the liberal and innovative treatment of the bible story by explaining that "The euangelystys telle nat of þys doyng, / For þey myȝte nat wryte alle þyng" (lines 967–68; cf. John 20:30, 21:35). As the poet's mention of having read "Yn a story" (line 963) would suggest, several details in the *MPC* derive from the *Historia Scholastica*.[8]

Lines	Events	Bible
1–22	Prologue	
23–128	Preparations for the Last Supper; Betrayal predicted; "Long haue y desyred with ȝow, y seye, / Þys paske to ete ar þat y deye" (93–94)	Matt. 26:19–23; John 13:21–25; Luke 22:15
129–178	Washes Disciples' feet	John 13:4–8
179–218	Institutes Eucharist: "makeþ þys yn my mende" (196); how the sacrament "wundyrfully of a mayden was bore" (206)	Luke 22:17–20
219–296	Christ's "sermon" at the Supper: "ȝyf þe worlde ȝow hate now, / Weteþ þat he me hated ar ȝow" (254); enters Cedron Valley	John 13:33–35; 14:15; 15:18–19; 16:20; 17:7–12; 18:1–3
297–416	Jesus prays to the Father; the Disciples sleep; Michael comforts Christ	Luke 22:39–46; Matt. 26:36–46; Mark 14:32–37
417–474	Betrayal; Arrest; Scourging	Matt. 26:47–49, 63, 67–68; 27:40
[Hours of the Passion]		
475–538	Prime: Christ before Pilate, Herod, Caiphas: "Do scurge hym weyl, and so late hym go" (514)	Luke 23:4–16

(3.87) and **MS** (line 376), as is the cry from the Cross heard in Hell. The **MS** poet includes a third idiosyncrasy when he says how he read "Yn a story" (line 963) that Christ's beard *and* head had been cut. He cites Is. 50:6 to justify the description: "My body y ȝaue to men smytyng, / And also my chekes to men grubbyng" (lines 971–72; cf. **MPC** 10:11–12). The two unreproduced details are Christ's custom of kissing his Disciples when they return from a mission (*MPC* 3.139–41) and John's supervision of the Last Supper preparations (*MPC* 1.31–32). See Stallings, *MPC*, 24 and her commentary on these lines.

8. See Stallings, *MPC*, 22. They are the height of the cross—"quindecim pedes"—(*MPC* 5.35–36; PL 198.1634), the existence of the remains of the pillar of scourging (*MPC* 4.46–48; PL 198.1628), an explanation why Jesus cried out to the Lord on the Cross (*MPC* 3.114; PL 198.1621), and a description of the tomb of Joseph of Arimathea (not in Stallings's edited manuscript; PL 198.1634).

Lines	Events	Bible
539–604	Terce: the Road to Calvary	Matt. 27:22, 27–32, 38; Is. 53:9
605–706	Sext and None: Crucifixion (upright); the seamless garment parted; Marys at the tomb	Matt. 27:35, 40–42, 56
707–776	Seven Last Words; words of the Centurion	Luke 23:34, 43, 46–47; John 19: 26–30; Matt. 27:46
777–900	Sorrows of Mary; legs broken; spear of Longinus; "meknes of proude men ys alle dyspysed" (853)	John 19:32–34; Ecclus. 13:24
901–984	Deposition by Joseph of Arimathea and Nicodemus; Anointing	John 19:38–40; Is. 50:6
985–1120	Compline: Burial, sorrows of Mary and regrets of the Disciples	John 19:42
1121–1142	Harrowing of Hell: "Þy peple þou hast vysyted and boȝt hem to þe" (1138)	Luke 1:68

A remembraunce of the passioun of our lord Jesu Criste RP

IMEV/S 2613

1. Cambridge, Univ. Lib. Dd.11.89 (179v–185v), mid-15th c., 400 lines in quatrains rhyming abab

Edition: Bowers, *Three Religious Poems*, 33–43.

The poem is more penitential than narrative; the narrator dwells on his own and mankind's sins and highlights Christ's graphic physical suffering. The imagery is closely paralleled by Corpus Christi crucifixion plays, and there are conventional motifs and similes: Christ's nine thousand wounds (line 93); Christ as a sacrificial lamb (97), the Cross as a "baner of lyf" (169), Christ as a knight in battle with the devil (177), Mary's "Blody teres" (197).

Lines	Events	Bible
1–52	Benefits of meditating on the Passion	
53–184	The Passion; Scourging	Matt. 27:28–29, 34; Mark 15:17
185–244	Sorrows of Mary; Christ the Good Shepherd; allusion to the Harrowing	John 10:11
245–284	"In to thyn hond my spirit y be-take" (250); Longinus; recollection of Simeon's prophecy: "the swerd of sorwe ful many a sythe / Thorwȝ out here herte scholde go" (283–84)	Luke 23:46; John 19:34; Luke 2:35

Lines	Events	Bible
285–400	Deposition; Resurrection; Ascension; forgiveness of the Good Thief	John 19:38–42; Mark 16:19; Luke 23:43

Songs of Love-Longing SLL

IMEV/S 3238, a combination of *IMEV/S* 1747 and 3236

All versions are in monorhyming quatrains.

1. London, BL Harley 2253 (75r–v).
2. Oxford, Bodleian Lib. Eng. poet. a.1 (Vernon) (298r, col. 2), ca. 1390, 443 lines.
3. London, BL Royal 17.B.xvii (13v–19r), 356 lines.
4. London, BL Add. 22283 (Simeon) (89r, col. 1), ca. 1400.
5. London, BL Add. 37787 (146v–156v), 412 lines.
6. Glasgow, Univ. Lib. Hunterian 512 (33r–34r) (second poem only), 44 lines.
7. San Marino, Huntington Lib. EL.34.B.7 (85v), 124 lines.
8. Dublin, Trinity College 155 (55r), 276 lines.
9. Longleat House, Marquess of Bath 29 (53r).

Editions: 1—C. Brown, *Religious Lyrics XIVth Century,* 7–10.
  1, 2, 3—Horstmann, *Yorkshire Writers,* 2:9–24.
  2—Furnivall, *Minor Poems,* 449–62.
  5—Baugh, *Worcestershire Miscellany,* 129–142.
  6—C. Brown, *Religious Lyrics XIVth Century,* 111–12.
  7—J. Legge, *Processional,* 30–33.
Facsimiles: 1—Ker, *Harley 2253;* 2—Doyle, *Vernon Manuscript.*

The two poems which make up this text vary in the manuscripts, though they usually appear together. In manuscript 5 the first poem is sixty-four lines; the second is 348 lines and is based on the *Jesu dulcis memoria* attributed to St. Bernard.

The primary biblical portions cover the Passion.

From Baugh's edition of manuscript 5:

Lines	Events	Bible
1–2	"Swete ihesu nou wul I syng / To þe a song of loue longynge"	
77–104	Agony on Mt. Olivet: "Dere fadur I prey þe / Þis	Luke 22:

Lines	Events	Bible
	peyne passe a-wey fro me / As þou wult so mote hit be" (90–92)	39–46
153–208	Crucifixion; Last Words: "for-ȝaf hem here misdede" (179); "þe þef schulde haue blis" (183); "wummon tak her Ion" (188); "My god my god hou may þis be / Þat þu hast al for-sake me" (195–96); "In manus tuas" (198); "Consumma-tum est" (203); "Cometh & se / ȝif any serwe is like to me" (207–8)	Luke 23:34; Luke 23:43; John 19:26; Matt. 27:46; Luke 23:46; John 19:30; Lam. 1:12

William Dunbar's *Passion of Christ* PC

IMEV/S 276.5, 2161.5

Manual, 4:1046 [101], and see 6:1823 [25] (*IMEV* 2497) for another Passion narrative attributed to Dunbar

1. Cambridge, Magdalene College Pepys 2553 (pp. 203–7), ca. 1570, 144 lines.
2. Asloan, Mrs. John McCombe (290v–292v), mid-16th c., lines 1–32, 41–96 only.
3. London, BL Arundel 285 (168r–170v), 16th c., omits lines 73–80, 121–8.
4. Edinburgh, Univ. Lib. La. III.450/1, 19th c. transcript.
5. Edinburgh, Univ. Lib. La. IV.27/8, 19th c. transcript.

Editions: 1—Dunbar, *Poems,* 7–11, with variants from 2 and 3.
    2—Craigie, *Asloan,* 2:242–45.
    3—Bennett, *Devotional Pieces,* 266–69.

All versions are in ballade stanza (ababbcbc). Manuscript 1 divides at line 96 (thus the two *IMEV/S* numbers); stanzas 2–12 share the refrain "O man-kynd for the luif of the"; stanzas 13–18 comprise a prayer of contrition with various refrains.

The poem takes the form of the poet's vision in an oratory on Good Fri-day, and gives a standard treatment of the Passion: Arrest, Scourging, cloth-ing in purple (line 41, John 19:2), Crown of Thorns.

> "Betuix tuo theiffis the spreit he gaif
> On to the Fader most of micht
> The erde did trimmill, the stanis claf,
> The sone obscurit of his licht,
> The day wox dirk as ony nicht,
> Deid bodies rais in the cite."
> (81–86; Matt. 27:45, 50–52)

Kinsley's notes (Dunbar, *Poems,* 230–37) provide sources and analogues, including works in the *Meditaciones Vitae Christi* tradition and the drama. Of Dunbar's seven "Divine Poems" printed by Kinsley, only this one contains an appreciable amount of biblical paraphrase. Poem 4, "Surrexit Dominus de Sepulchro" (Edinburgh, National Lib. of Scotland 1.1.6) mentions the visit of the three Marys (Matt. 28) and goes on to describe the Harrowing (*Manual,* 4:1058 [122], 4:1047 [102]).

John Lydgate's *Cristes Passioun* (*Passionis Christi Cantus*) CP

IMEV 2081
Manual, 6:1823 [24]

1. Oxford, Bodleian Lib. Laud misc.683 (*SC* 798) (12r–14v), 15th c., 120 lines rhyming ababbcbc.
2. Cambridge, Univ. Lib. Kk.1.6 (194r–196r), 15th c.
3. Cambridge, Trinity College 601 (189v–193v), mid-15th c., 160 lines.
4. London, BL Harley 372 (54r–55r), mid-15th c.
5. London, BL Harley 7333 (147r–v), mid-15th c.
6. London, BL Add. 31042 (London Thornton) (94r, 94v–96r), mid-15th c.

Edition: 1—Lydgate, *Minor Poems,* ed. MacCracken, 216–21, with variants from 2–6.
Partial facsimile: 6—J. Thompson, *Thornton.*
Study: Pearsall, *Lydgate,* 265–68.

The poem is a penitential meditation on the Passion with an emphasis on the physical particulars:

Crown of Thorns (Matt. 27:29).
Sponge of Vinegar (Matt. 27:48).
Spear of Longinus (John 19:34).
"Consummatum est" (John 19:30).
Good Thief (Luke 23:43).
Mary Magdalen (Matt. 28:1).
Bodies rise (Matt. 27:52–53).
Pilate's inscriptions of the Greek, Hebrew, and Latin letters (John 19:20).
Prophecy of Simeon (Luke 2:35).

Lydgate wrote two other poems on the Passion: the *Dolerous Pyte of Crystes Passioun* (*Manual*, 6:1912 [188]) and the *Prayer upon the Cross* (*Manual*, 6:1919 [196]).

Scottish Passion of Christ SPC

IMEV/S 648
Manual, 2:394 [35]

Fifteenth-century, eight eight-line stanzas rhyming ababbcbc.

1. London, BL Arundel 285 (159v–161r), early 16th c.
2. Edinburgh, Univ. Lib. 205. (86v), 1477.
3. Edinburgh, National Lib. of Scotland Advocates 1.1.6 (33v–34r), 1568.

Editions: 1—Bennett, *Devotional Pieces*, 255–57; C. Brown, *Religious Lyrics XVth Century*, 131–33.
2—G. Stevenson, *Pieces*, 10–12.
3—Ritchie, *Bannatyne Manuscript*, 83–85.

In a direct and very emotional address to Christ, the poet meditates on the events of the Passion.

Lines	Events	Bible
1–16	Anointing at Bethany; Last Supper; washes Disciples' feet; Mt. Olivet	Matt. 26; John 13:5
17–32	Kiss of Judas; Christ before Caiphas and Pilate; Buffeting; Peter's denials	Matt. 26
33–48	Golgotha; "I thirst"; Mary entrusted to John	John 19
49–64	"Eli, Eli . . ."; Longinus; earthquake; words of the Centurion; Joseph of Arimathea	Matt. 27; John 19

Contemplations of the Dread and Love of God (*Fervor Amoris*) CDL

IPMEP 362
Jolliffe, *Check-List* H.15
Manual, 9:3086 [41]

16 MSS, including:

1. Maidstone, Museum 6 (1r–40v), early 15th c.

Edition: Connolly, *Contemplations.* See Horstmann, *Yorkshire Writers,*
   2:72–105, for the text from Wynkyn de Worde's 1506 printing.
Facsimile: Boenig, *Contemplations* (of the de Worde printing).

This prose work is a mystical devotional treatise mistakenly attributed to
Richard Rolle and first printed by Wynkyn de Worde in 1506. It takes the
form of a "see how" and "loke yet again" series of injunctions.
   Meditations on the Passion begin and end the piece.
   The Arrest, Trial, Scourging (with considerable amplification of the tor-
ture and suffering), and Crucifixion are treated conventionally.

Liber Aureus de Passione et Resurrectione Domini LA

1. London, BL Egerton 2658 (1r–15v), early 15th c.
2. Stonyhurst College 43 B.xliii.
3. Manchester, John Rylands Lib. English 895 (1r–125v, missing several
   leaves), 15th c.
4. Oxford, Bodleian Lib. Bodley 207 (*SC* 2021).

Edition: forthcoming by Peter Rees-Jones.

See Marx and Drennan, *Prose Complaint,* 38–39, n. 56, for this work, based
in part on the *MVC* and linked to the prose *Gospel of Nicodemus* (**GNp**) (manuscripts 1–4) and to Love's *Mirror* (**MBL**) (manuscript 4).

Versions of the Hours of the Cross (Matins of the Passion) HC

Manual, 7:2368 [227]
IMEV/S 701

1. Oxford, Bodleian Lib. Eng. poet. a.1 (Vernon) (115v–116r), ca. 1390,
   118 lines.
2. Cambridge, Gonville and Caius College 175 (pp. 118–20), 15th c.,
   eight six-line stanzas with an "O and I" refrain.
3. London, BL Royal 19.B.v (103r–v), 16th c. (with an "O and V"
   refrain).
4. London, BL Add. 37787 (12v–14r), early 15th c., ten six-line stanzas,
   aaaabb.

Editions: 1—Horstmann, *Minor Poems,* 37–43.
   2—Heuser, "O and an I," 312–14.
   3—Baugh, *Worcestershire Miscellany,* 98–100.

Facsimile: 1—Doyle, *Vernon Manuscript.*
Studies: Barratt, "Prymer and Its Influence"; Bennett, *Poetry of the Passion.*

The Hours of the Cross format was one of the most widespread modes for recounting the events of the Passion. In Vernon, six-line Latin antiphons of the *Horae Crucis* (beginning Patris sapiencia . . .) alternate with six-line English paraphrases (rhyming aaaabb) to recount the Crucifixion, followed by identical ten-line prayers for mercy (couplets). For the Latin text, see Simmons, *Lay Folks Mass Book,* 83–87. The sevenfold division of monastic time derives from Ps. 118:164.

Matins: buffeting of Christ (Matt. 26)
Prime: appearance before Pilate (Matt. 27)
Undern: Scourging; Crowning with thorns; bearing the Cross to Calvary
Sext: nailing to the Cross; administration of gall; the two Thieves; Mary
  and John (Luke 23)
None: Longinus and his spear, blindness healed; earthquake; sun dims;
  dead rise; Christ harrows Hell (John 19; Matt. 27)
Vespers: Deposition; Mary's grief; Mary foretells Resurrection (John 20)
Compline: Anointing of body; Burial; Pilate sets guards; Christ rises;
  appears to Mary Magdalen, Peter, and others.

Manuscripts 1 and 2 end, and manuscript 4 begins, with the notice that Pope John (at Avignon from 1316–34) remits a year of Purgatory for any who say these Matins.

IMEV 3230

> 1. Oxford, Bodleian Lib. Liturg. 104 (*SC* 30605) (49r–88r, on sporadic leaves), mid-14th c., 34 lines in couplets.

Editions: Morris, *Legends of the Holy Rood,* 222–24; Horstmann, *Minor Poems,*
  37–42 (printed, from Morris, below the Vernon text); C. Brown,
  Religious Lyrics XIVth Century, 50–51.

Very similar to the Vernon text (see above at *IMEV/S* 701), though the prayers are omitted, at None Christ cries "Hely," Longinus is not named, and at Compline the poem concludes with the Anointing.

One leaf (before folio 66), and perhaps one line (after line 16), are missing.

"Þe houris of oure Ladyis dollouris"
IMEV/S 3904

1. London, BL Arundel 285 (141v–42v), thirty-six lines in quatrains rhyming abab.

Editions: Bennett, *Devotional Pieces,* 234–36; Brunner, "Mittelenglische Marienstunden," 106–9; C. Brown, *Religious Lyrics XVth Century,* 138–40.

Numerous other pieces in Arundel 285 (see Bennett's edition) contain freestanding paraphrases of the Passion, Seven Last Words, and Resurrection (e.g., **PC**).

The poem is a much-condensed epigone of the *Hours of the Cross* model.

Prime: Christ before Annas and Pilate (Matt. 26)
Terce: Scourging
Sext: Crucifixion; administration of gall; earthquake (Matt. 27)
None: Christ entrusts Mary to John (John 19)
Evensong: spear pierces side; Deposition
Compline: Burial

William of Shoreham's Hours of the Cross HCS

IMEV 3681 (and see *IMEV* 1495)
Manual, 7:2368 [227] and 7:2274 [28]

1. London, BL Add. 17376 (182r–185v), mid-14th c., 178 lines in eight- and twelve-line rhyming stanzas. The first 149 leaves (out of a total of 220) contain **MPPs** with its version of **CH.**

Editions: 1—William of Shoreham, *Religious Poems,* ed. Wright, 82–89; William of Shoreham, *Poems,* ed. Konrath, 79–85.

Shoreham was vicar of Chart-Sutton in Kent from 1320. A ten-line invocation quotes (in Latin) and briefly paraphrases Ps. 50:17 and Ps. 69:2.

Matins (lines 11–50): Arrest of Christ; prayer for mercy on Doomsday; prayer to the Virgin (Matt. 26).
Prime (lines 51–70): Christ before Pilate; Buffeting; commiseration with Mary (Matt. 27)
Undern (lines 71–90): Crowning with thorns; bearing the cross to Calvary
Sext (lines 91–110): nailing to the Cross; administration of gall; taunting by the Jews to "com a-doun!" (Matt. 27:42)
None (lines 111–130): Christ cries "hely"; an anonymous "kniʒt" pierces his right side; the earth shakes and the sun dims; Mary's soul has been pierced with a sword (John 19:34; Luke 2:35)

Vespers (lines 131–50): Deposition; Christ, "Of lyf þe medicine," dies; "as a mesel (leper?) þer he lay" (Konrath [220] notes the same comparison to a "mesel" in Rolle's *Meditations on the Passion* [Horstmann, *Yorkshire Writers,* 1:85])

Compline (lines 151–70): Burial; Anointing (Matt. 27)

In lines 171–78 the author dedicates these "oures of þe canoune" to the Lord and prays that He may "graunte me þy coroune."

This poem combines the "Horae Passionis Domini" (in eight-line stanzas) with the "Horae Compassionis B. Virginis Mariae" (twelve-line apostrophes to the Virgin) to produce twenty-line sections for each Hour. Cf. a similar combination in Simmons, *Lay Folks Mass Book,* 82, 349.

John Audelay's Biblical Paraphrases on the Passion HCA

Manual, 7:2275 [29]

John Audelay, a *capellanus* at Haughmond Abbey (Augustinian; four miles northeast of Shrewsbury), included some biographical information in the collection of fifty-five (surviving) poems now attributed to him. He was deaf and blind, and wrote the first eighteen poems (including the two *Horae Crucis* poems, numbers 13 and 14) before 1426 while suffering from an illness. Audelay is neither a mystic or a theologian, and the program of the collection is penitential and lay-pietistic.

His two major biblical paraphrases are in the *Horae Crucis* tradition; biblical quotation pervades the collection.

IMEV 623

1. Oxford, Bodleian Lib. Douce 302 (*SC* 21876) (15v–16r), mid-15th c., ten nine-line stanzas rhyming aaaabcccb.

Edition: Audelay, *Poems,* ed. Whiting, 101–4.

IMEV 2764

1. Oxford, Bodleian Lib. Douce 302 (*SC* 21876) (15r–v), mid-15th c., fifteen eight-line stanzas rhyming ababbcbc with a concluding quatrain as a prayer for the "blynd Audlay, / Þat mad in Englesche þis passion" (lines 122–23). Line 9 is in Latin ("Passio Christe conforta me") and it introduces the a-rhyme for that stanza.

Edition: Audelay, *Poems,* ed. Whiting, 97–101.

Poem 13 (*IMEV* 2764) places the notice of Pope John's remission of sins at the beginning (though only thirty days, not a full year, are granted). Line 17 claims that "Þis is þe gospel of Ion truly"; the rest of the poem follows the *Horae Crucis* sequence though without quoting the Latin or citing the Hours. Since Audelay himself was blind, the healing of the "blynd k[ny]ʒt" (line 67; Longinus is named in neither poem) is a poignant moment: "He had his syʒt, þis synful mon, / Fore on Crystis passion he had pete" (lines 71–72).

Poem 14 (*IMEV* 623), after an introductory prayer for mercy in the first stanza, quotes the Latin *Horae Crucis* verses and invokes the hours. The narrative ends after the Deposition by Nicodemus and Joseph, the Burial, and the Resurrection on the third day. Whiting finds that "The phraseology of Audelay's poem is closer to that of the last-mentioned versions [in Vernon] than to that of any other" (p. 240).

Poems 4 through 7 connect the seven effusions of Christ's blood, the Seven Deadly Sins, and the Seven Last Words on the Cross. Poem 36 refers to the Slaughter of the Innocents. Poems 28–32 (the first five of twenty-five *caroles* in the collection) concentrate on the Ten Commandments and the Seven Deadly Sins. Poem 53 is an exposition of the Pater Noster.

Walter Kennedy's Passion of Christ HCK

IMEV/S 1040
Manual, 2:394 [34]

1. London, BL Arundel 285 (6r–46v), ca. 1500, 1,715 lines in 245 rhyme royal stanzas (ababbcc).

Editions: Bennett, *Devotional Pieces,* 7–63, textual notes 336–38; W. Kennedy, *Poems,* 21–94.

Kennedy died ca. 1507. This is an expanded Hours of the Cross, with a seventy-line prologue followed by an account of the Fall of Man. In line 196 the poet notes that more information concerning Christ's youth is available from "Lendulphus" (Ludolphus of Saxony; see **VC**) and "Vthiris." All quotations are from Bennett's edition.

> "now, allace, men ar mair studyus
> To reid the seige of ye toun of Tire,
> The life of Cursalem, or Hector, or Troylus,
> The vanite of Alexanderis empire." (36–39)

> "In Inglis toung I think to mak remembrance
> How God maid man, how man fell throu myschance,

Syne how greit pyne sustenit for his syne
The sone of God or he wald succour him.
In [this] proces I think als commonly,
For till exclud all curiosite,
Maist plane termes with deligence to spy,
Quhilk may be tane with small deficulte." (53–60)

Lines	Event	Bible
71–119	Creation; Fall of Man; God's charge to His Son to intercede for mankind	Gen. 1–3
120–147	Annunciation; Mary visits Elizabeth	Luke 1:26–39
148–168	Circumcision; Magi; Simeon	Luke 2:1–39; Matt. 2
169–189	Flight into Egypt; Slaughter of the Innocents	Matt. 2
190–210	Christ disputes with the Temple Doctors	Luke 2:40–52
211–217	Baptised at Jordan	Luke 3:21–23
218–224	Temptation in the Desert	Luke 4:1–13
225–238	Mention of Christ's three-year ministry	
239–252	Transfiguration	Luke 9:28–36
253–308	Judas's betrayal; Christ washes Disciples' feet	John 13
309–336	Last Supper; prophesies Peter's denials	Luke 22:19; Matt. 26:33–34
337–392	Gethsemani; Arrest; Malchus's ear	John 18:1–11

[Hours of the Cross begin]:

Lines	Event	Bible
393–469	Matins: Christ before Annas and Caiphas; Buffeting; Peter's denials	John 18:12–27
470–546	Prime: Christ before Pilate in his "tolbuth"; suicide of Judas	John 18:28–38; Matt. 27:3–10
547–644	Terce: Barabbas; Scourging; Crown of Thorns	Matt. 27:11–18, 28–31
645–973	Sext: Pilate's wife; Pilate washes hands; Simon of Cyrene; Christ rebukes Daughters of Jerusalem; two Thieves; gall; seamless garment; Pilate's inscription; "Eli, Eli"	Matt. 27:19–32; Luke 23:27–36; John 19:18–24; Matt. 27:37–50
974–1120	None: "Into your hands"; recapitulation of Crucifixion; veil of the Temple tears, earthquake	Luke 23:46; Matt. 27:51–56
1121–1190	Centurion speaks; Mary rebukes the Cross; Cross responds; Longinus	John 19:34
1191–1289	Evensong: Joseph and Nicodemus; Deposition	John 19:38–39
1290–1407	Compline: Burial; Precautions of the Jews	Matt. 27:60–66
1408–1715	Resurrection; post-Resurrection appearances to the three Marys, Peter, Cleophas, Thomas; the Ascension; Pentecost	Matt. 28; Luke 24; John 21; Acts 1–2

Meditations for Goostely Exercise in the Tyme of the Masse MTM

Manual, 7:2355 [205]

1. Oxford, Bodleian Lib. Wood empt.17 (*SC* 8605) (1r–25v), later
   15th c.
2. London, BL Harley 494 (63r–75r), ca. 1500.
3. New York, Columbia Univ. Plimpton 263 (386r–388r) (omits
   allegorizations).

Edition: 1—J. Legge, *Tracts,* 19–29.
Partial text in Simmons, *Lay Folks Mass Book,* 168.

This text is an ordinary from part of a Sarum missal. It dwells on the ceremonies and accoutrements of the Mass, whereby each action and object is connected, in a loose narrative sequence, to an event from Christ's Nativity, Passion, Resurrection, and Ascension.

Lines 12043–50 of **NHC** also connect the five turnings of the priest to the congregation during Mass to the five appearances of Christ on the day of the Resurrection (to Mary Magdalen, to the Three Marys, to the Virgin Mary [in secret], to Cleophas, and to the Disciples generally).

The following is taken from Legge's edition of manuscript 1:

Page	Event	Bible
21	Scourging; Crucifixion	Matt. 27
22	Angels appear to the shepherds	Luke 2:13–14
23	Agony in Gethsemani; Palm Sunday	Matt. 26:36; Matt. 21:7–9
24	Institution of the Eucharist	Matt. 26:26–27
25–26	Scourging; Crucifixion	Matt. 27; Luke 23:34
28	Five post-Resurrection appearances; Ascension	Luke 24

Miscellaneous New Testament Pieces

Commentary on the Benedictus (Luke 1:68–80) **CB**

IPMEP 112
Manual, 2:396 [40] and 9:3081 [36]

1. London, Lambeth Palace 472 (252v–259v), early 15th c.
2. Newcastle-upon-Tyne, Public Lib. TH.1678 (102r–104r), early 15th c.
3. Taunton, Somerset County Archives 3084 (p. 178), incipit only.

Edition: 1—Wallner, *Commentary,* with variants from 2.
Modernization: 1—Jones, *Minor Works,* 217–32.

References are to Wallner.

The commentary on the "Qui Habitat" (**QHPs**) and "Bonum Est" (**BEPs**) precede **CB** in manuscript 1, wherein other works by Walter Hilton (d. 1395–96) appear, but definite attributions remain uncertain. Manuscript 2 contains **RPs.**

CB consists of a line-by-line translation and paraphrase of each verse (quoted in Latin) from the Benedictus canticle (Luke 1:68–80) with recapitulation of preceding events (Luke 1:5–23, 57–67): how Zachary is struck dumb, regains the power of speech, and prophesies Christ's Passion and Resurrection. There are further excurses on the Harrowing of Hell, the delivery of faithful souls from the hands of enemies (quoting 1John 4:18 on p. 11), and the forgiveness of sins (quoting John 1:29 and 36 on p. 14; Matt. 3:2 on p. 15).

The metaphor of the resurrected body of Christ as a horn (Luke 1:69) is perhaps the most original and memorable passage in the commentary:

> ffor riȝt as a horne wexeth aboue þe flesche and passiþ alle þe tendirnesse of hit and torneþ into hardenesse vnfeleable, riȝt so þe body of oure lord, whanne hit was reysed be myȝt of þe godhede, wexed abouen alle þe fleschli feelyng of deedlyed and of al suffreablenesse peynful, and hit is turned in-to a blisful hardnesse. . . . ffor þis blissed horn is ful of oyle of þe god-hede, oute of þe whiche horn comeþ doun to vs, þat ere ȝit fleschli, part of þat oyle of grace, & anoynteþ oure soules and heleþ vs from alle sikenesse. (p. 5)

Ballad of the Twelfth Day BTD

(Story of the Magi and Herod from Matt. 2:1–12)
IMEV/S 4170
Manual, 2:397 [43]

> 1. Cambridge, Trinity College 323 (B.14.39) (35r–v), mid-13th c., eighty lines in stanzas rhyming abababab.

Editions: Reichl, *Religiöse Dichtung,* 388–91; Greg, "Ballad" (1913); C. Brown, *English Lyrics XIIIth Century,* 39–41.

What appears to be the final version of this ballad immediately precedes the third biblical paraphrase in Trinity 323, **TP.** C. Brown maintains (pp. 184–86) that **TP** suggested the composition of the ballad because an incomplete and partly illegible draft of the ballad appears in the lower margins of **TP** on folios 36r–38r and 41v–42r. See Greg, "Ballad" (1913 and 1914), where he identifies similar hands in this ballad and in "Judas," which appears on folio 34r (see also Reichl, pp. 375–78).

Pearl Prl

IMEV/S 2744
Manual, 2:341 [2]

> 1. London, BL Cotton Nero A.x (43r–59v), later 14th c., 1,212 lines in twelve-line stanzas rhyming ababababbcbc, with alliteration and concatenation.

Editions: Gordon, *Pearl;* Anderson, *Sir Gawain,* 1–46, and others.
Facsimile: Gollancz, *Pearl.*
Study: Fowler, *Bible in Middle English Literature,* 200–225.

This mystical, elegiac dream-vision is widely regarded as one of the finest, and most complex, poems in Middle English. *Pearl,* the first poem in the manuscript, like two of its companion pieces (**Cl** and **Pat**), contains a significant portion of biblical paraphrase. The fourth poem, *Sir Gawain and the Green Knight,* contains no biblical paraphrase. The bibliography on all of the poems in the manuscript is extensive.

The dramatic situation of the poem is the bereaved narrator's loss of his "pearl," a metaphor for his daughter, which becomes part of a sophisticated allegory concerning the afterlife and the heavenly reward.

Quotations from Gordon, *Pearl:*

Lines	Events	Bible
1–60	Narrator laments lost pearl, falls asleep; "vch gresse mot grow of grayneʒ dede; / No whete were elleʒ to woneʒ wonne" (30–31)	John 12:24
61–360	Narrator enters forest with a stream and crystal cliffs, sees and speaks with Pearl-maiden, who chides him for wishing to cross the stream	
361–480	Pearl-maiden explains that she is "sesed in alle hys herytage" (417) and that "all arn we membreʒ of Jcsu Kryst: / As hcued and arme and legg and naule" (458–59)	Rom. 8:17; Cor. 12:12
481–588	The Parable of the Vineyard: "As Mathew meleʒ in your messe / In sothfol gospel of God almyʒt, . . . 'My regne' he saytʒ, 'is lyk on hyʒt / To a lorde þat had a uyne, I wate' " (497–502); "Þe laste schal be þe fyrst þat strykeʒ, / And þe fyrst þe laste, be he neuer so swyft; / For mony ben called, þaʒ fewe be mykeʒ" (570–72)	Matt. 20:1–16
589–600	"Þou quyteʒ vchon as hys desserte" (595)	Ps. 61:13
601–732	The equality of the heavenly reward; Baptism; "Lorde, quo schal klymbe þy hyʒ hylle, Oþer rest wythinne þy holy place?" (678–79); "Koyntise onoure con aquyle; By wayeʒ ful streʒt ho con hym strayn" (690–91); "Lorde, þy seruaunt draʒ neuer to dome, for non lyuyande to þe is justyfyet" (699–700); "Do way, let chylder vnto me tyʒt. To suche is heuenryche arayed" (718–19)	Ps. 23:3–4; Wis. 10:10; Ps. 142:2; Matt. 19: 13–14, 21
733–780	The Pearl of Great Price; "Cum hyder to me my lemman swete, For mote ne spot is non in þe" (763–64)	Matt. 13:45–46; Cant. 4:7
781–840	"As a schep to þe slaʒt þer lad watʒ he"; "Lo, Godeʒ Lombe as trwe as ston, / Þat dotʒ away	Is. 53:7; John 1:28–29

Lines	Events	Bible
	þe synneʒ dryʒe / Þat alle þys worlde hatʒ wroʒt vpon' " (822–24)	
841–912	John's vision of the 144,000; "A note ful nwe I herde hem warpe" (879)	Rev. 14:1–5
913–984	Narrator asks to see the "ceté of God" or "syʒt of pes" (952)	Rev. 3:12; Heb. 12:22
985–1092	The New Jerusalem; "Of sunne ne mone had þay no nede; / Þe self God watʒ her lombe-liʒt" (1045–46)	Rev. 21:18–22:5
1093–1212	Procession ends; dreamer awakes, invokes the Eucharist	

A Disputison bitwene child Jhesu & Maistres of þe lawe of Jewus DJM

IMEV/S 1887
Manual, 3:683 [5]

1. Oxford, Bodleian Lib. Eng. poet. a.1 (Vernon) (301r, col. 3), ca. 1390, 215 verses in eight-line stanzas rhyming abababab.
2. London, BL Add. 22283 (Simeon) (91v, col. 2), ca. 1400, verses 1–104 only.
3. London, BL Harley 3954 (lines 189–325 as part of **CJ**).

Editions: 1—Horstmann, *Altenglische Legenden* (1875), 212–14; Furnivall, *Minor Poems,* 479–84.
Facsimile: 1—Doyle, *Vernon Manuscript.*

This short poem, one of several doctrinal poems which appear in the Vernon manuscript, recounts the twelve-year-old Christ's debate in the Temple with the Jewish Doctors and the exchange between Mary and Christ once his parents find him (Luke 2:41–52). It is essentially an episode from the *Long Life of Christ* in the minstrel tradition, and it may be late thirteenth century in origin.

The poet twice describes Jesus as the "best of barnes þat bar þe Belle" (lines 8, 109), and Jesus describes himself as "ful Old þeih I be ʒing" (51).

Christ expounds the doctrine of the Trinity while explicating his ABCs:

> ffor a. is lyk . þe Trinite
> Þreo partyes a haþ . of mesure
> Knet in knotte . on a. wol be
> ʒif þu wolt lerne . þou miht hure
> Hou a. is lyk . þe deite. (58–62)

The "knot" image reappears in the optical simile of Christ's conception as sunlight passing through clouds:

> hou þe sonne Beem euere is set
> Vndeparted . so is þe strem
> Of crist with God . mid knottes knet. (130–32)

Other biblical references are to Is. 7:14 ("Of a Mayden . he scholde be bore" [120]), Is. 11:1–2 (root of Jesse), and Matt. 9:34 (accusation that Jesus works through the power of the devil). Luke 2:48 is quoted in Latin ("Ego & pater tuus dolentes querebamus te" [191]).

Bodley Verse Pieces from the Gospels BVP

IMEV/S 1474, 1536, 4022, 1535
Manual, 2:396 [41]

1. Oxford, Bodleian Lib. Bodley 425 (*SC* 2325) (66v–69r; 106v–107r [repeats John passage]), mid-14th c. **SPs** precedes.
2. Cambridge, Univ. Lib. Add. 6860 (99r), John passage only.

Edition: 1—Heuser, "Eine vergessene Handschrift der Surteespsalters," 396–405.

BVP is affiliated with **RSP** and corresponding passages in **NHC.** These passages often stood at the beginning of *Horae* and Primers (see Barratt, "Prymer and Its Influence").

The order in **BVP** (John, Luke, Matthew, Mark) makes somewhat more sense than the order in **RSP** (Luke, Matthew, Mark, John) since John's opening verses logically precede the other events.

John 1:1–14, "In principio . . . ," forty four-stress lines in couplets

> In biginning worde it was,
> And þe worde at gode it vas,
> And god him selue þe worde was he,
> Þat is and euer more schal be.   (lines 1–4; John 1:1–2)

> "A Man fro god was sende, hight Iohan;
> He comes in wittnes sone on an,
> To giue witnes of þe light
> Þorou him þat alle sulde truwe it riht
> He was noght liht, bot, for to wisse,
> Þurh wittnes of þe light þat isse,
> Right light was þat lightes al
> Man come in to þis werld þat schal.
> (13–20; John 1:6–9 [exactly four verses in four couplets])

Luke 1:26–38, the Annunciation, forty-eight four-stress lines in couplets

> Haile ful of hape, god is with þe,
> In wemmen blissed þou be!
> (11–12; Luke 1:28)

Matt. 2:1–12, Visit of the Magi, fifty four-stress lines in couplets

> Giftes to him bede þei þore,
> Golde, Recles, Mirre, wel more.
> (45–46; Matt. 2:11)

Mark 16:14–20, Christ's charge to the Disciples, fifty four-stress lines in couplets.

Rawlinson Strophic Pieces from the Gospels RSP

IMEV/S 2021
Manual, 2:396 [42]

1. Oxford, Bodleian Lib. Rawlinson poetry f.175 (*SC* 14667) (132r–v), mid-14th c.
2. London, BL Add. 45896 (roll, dorso, parchment 9), mid-14th c.

Editions: 1—Heuser, "O and an I," 285–89.
2—A. H. Smith, "Lyrics in Add. Ms. 45896," 45–47 (forty-eight lines, Luke section only).

Twenty-six six-line, monorhyming stanzas, in four-stress lines with alliteration, in a northern dialect, and affiliated with **BVP** and **NHC**. The first line, "Luke in his lesson leres to me," indicates a liturgical connection. These passages often appeared in Primers (see Barratt, "Prymer and Its Influence"). On pages 290–300 Heuser prints corresponding passages from **NHC** (from London, BL Harley 4196, *IMEV* 4002), though none exist for the Mark passage. The fifth line of every stanza is an "O & I" refrain.[1] Heuser prints two other poems with this refrain: on pages 304–5 (from Oxford, Bodleian Lib. Douce 126, *IMEV* 1001) on the Passion (John 19:28–29) (also printed by C. Brown, *Religious Lyrics XVth Century,* 140–42) and, on pages 312–14, an Hours of the Cross poem (**HC; IMEV/S** 701).

From manuscript 1
Luke 1:26–38, eight six-line stanzas.

---

1. Greene, " 'O-and-I' Refrain-Phrase," argues (comparing *Inferno,* 24.100) that the refrain is a scriptorium figure of speech meaning "Indeed and without delay" (175).

Mary answerd & asked: how so suld bigyn?
I knew neuer in þis kyth kynde of mankyn.
Þan þe aungell hir warned warely iþ wyn:
Þe haly gast of þi god sall lyght þe wiþin,
Wiþ ane O & ane I, his might more & myn
Vmbeschadow þe sall wiþouten ony syn.
                        (31–36; Luke 1:29–35)

Matt. 2:1–12, eight six-line stanzas, Visit of the Magi.

Mark 16:14–20, five six-line stanzas, Christ's charge to his disciples.

All þat made er my men, my signe sall þei were,
In my name gett þei force fendes to fere,
Wiþ new tonges sall þei speke & my law lere,
And nedders & wormes oway sall þei were
Wiþ ane O and ane I, now take þe no care,
And euell venym to drynk sall do þam no dere.
                        (13–18; Mark 16:17–18)

John 1:1–14, "In principio . . . ," five six-line stanzas

John of his heghnes tyll our hereyng
Says þat þe son was in þe bigynyng . . .
                        (1–2; John 1:1)

Euangelium in Principio EP

IMEV 276
Manual, 2:407 [59]

1. Oxford, Bodleian Lib. Bodley 779 (*SC* 2567) (23v–25v), mid-15th c.,
   lacks 26-line prologue.
2. Oxford, Corpus Christi College 431 (1r–2r), mid-14th c.
3. Cambridge, Magdalene College Pepys 2344 (pp. 93–97), mid-14th c.

No edition.

With **BVP** and **RSP,** this text highlights the liturgically important passage from John (1:1–14), in this case by means of a 190-line versified paraphrase and exposition. The three manuscripts also contain the *South English Legendary.*

Joseph of Arimathea JA

IMEV 49
IMEV/S 3117.4

Manual, 1:74 [40] (for other lives of Joseph of Arimathea, see *Manual,* 2:596 [148])

  1. Oxford, Bodleian Lib. Eng. poet. a.1 (Vernon) (403r–404v),
     ca. 1390, 709 alliterative lines, acephalous.

Editions: Lawton, *Joseph of Arimathea;* Skeat, *Joseph of Arimathie,* 1–23.
Facsimile: Doyle, *Vernon Manuscript.*

The poem's main sources are the *Estoire del Saint Graal* and the Vulgate *Queste del Saint Graal;* the main themes are Joseph's experiences in obtaining and keeping the Grail. Lawton's introduction provides a thorough discussion, including appearances of the Joseph of Arimathea legend in copies of the *Gospel of Nicodemus* (Lawton, xli). The biblical setting and allusions qualify the poem as a "homiletic romance" (Lawton, xiii).

The dramatic situation is Joseph's evangelization of Evelak, King of Sarras, with an explanation of Christ's Incarnation and Passion.

Lines	Events	Bible
75–101	Annunciation: "Blessed beo þou, flour feirest of alle / Þe holigost withinne þe schal lenden and lihte / Þou schalt beren a child schal Ihesu be hoten" (80–82); Magi; Slaughter of the Innocents; Flight into Egypt	Luke 1:28–35; Matt. 2:11, 16, 14
240–312	Vision of the Crucifixion; Joseph invested as a bishop	

Versions of the Beatitudes (Matt. 5:3–16) Beat

Verse Beatitudes in John of Grimestone's Preaching Book
IMEV 526 and 2762
Manual, 7:2312 [128]

  1. Edinburgh, National Lib. of Scotland Advocates 18.7.21 (25r), 1372.
     Two versions: four lines rhyming abab; fourteen lines in couplets.
     Both cover Matt. 5:3–10, rearranging verses and omitting verse 7.

Edition: E. Wilson, *Index,* 8.

The Beatitudes in thirteen couplets
IMEV 1746

  1. London, BL Harley 1706 (208v–209r), catechetical material,
     including **TC** (205r; IMEV 3685), precedes.

No edition.

> Octo beatitudines
> Ihu seynge peplys comynge hym tylle
> He styed and sette hym on a hylle
> He opened hys mouþe wt mylde chere
> And tauȝte hys dysciples þat stode hym nere

1. Blessed be poure men in spyryte
   The kyngdome of Heuene hys her be ryȝte
2. Blessed be mylde men of mode
   ffor þei schul welde þe londe moste good
3. Blessed be men þat hungren and þristen ryȝte
   ffor þei be fylled of goddys myȝte
4. Blessed be men þat mornen for synne
   þei schul be comforted her soule wiþ ynne
5. Blessed be mercyfulle men in deede
   ffor þei schul haue mercy to meede
6. Blessed be cleene men herte ywys
   ffor þei schul see god in hys blysse
7. Blessed be pesyble men wiþ alle
   þe sones of god men schul hem calle
8. Blessed be men þat suffren for ryȝte
   þe rewme of heuene to hem ys dyȝte
9. Blessed soþely schal ye be
   Whan men schul pursewe you for me
   And curse you al yuel aȝens you swerynge
   And myseseiþ you for me liynge
   Joye ye and glad ye wiþ mylde steuene
   your mede ys moche in blys of heuene.

"A lernyng to good leuynge"
IMEV 2763
Manual, 2:398 [46]

1. Oxford, Bodleian Lib. Digby 102 (*SC* 1703)(121v–23r), early 15th c.,
   160 lines in eight-line stanzas rhyming abababab.

Edition: Kail, *"Petty Job,"* 96–101.

The manuscript includes a C-text of *Piers Plowman* and **RMPs.**

The poem's twenty stanzas cover Matt. 5:3–16, the nine Beatitudes and salt-of-the-earth exhortation which begin Christ's Sermon on the Mount. Its most striking feature is that the even stanzas (2–16) curse those guilty of the sin corresponding to the virtue blessed in the previous odd stanzas (1–15): "Blessid be man þat in herte is mylde . . . Þanne cursed be man in herte ruyde" (lines 17, 25).

The blessing of the peacemakers (stanza 11, Matt. 5:9) is transposed with the blessing on the clean of heart (stanza 13, Matt. 5:8).

The Beatitudes in a manuscript of the *South English Legendary*
IMEV 2724

　　1. Cambridge, St. John's College 28 (39r).

No edition.

Prose Version of the Beatitudes, "The Eight Blessings of God"
Manual, 7:2312 [128]

　　1. London, BL Add. 30897 (65v–66r), earlier 15th c.
　　2. Oxford, Bodleian Lib. Rawlinson C.882 (*SC* 12716) (74r), earlier 15th c.
　　3. Oxford, Trinity College 86 (36r–v), later 15th c.
　　4. London, BL Harley 2343 (86v–87v), earlier 15th c.
　　5. London, BL Lansdowne 388 (368v–369r), later 15th c.
　　6. Cambridge, Univ. Lib. Ii.6.43 (15r–16r), earlier 15th c.
　　7. London, BL Add. 60577 (156r–157r), ca. 1500.
　　8. New York, Columbia Univ. Plimpton 258 (6r–v), ca. 1400.
　　9. St. Albans, Cathedral Lib. (4v–5v).
　10. Oxford, Bodleian Lib. Bodley 788 (*SC* 2628) (246r), ca.1400.
　11. Edinburgh, Univ. Lib. 93 (22v–25v).

Editions: 3—Durkin, "Trinity College, MS 86," 2:227–36.
　　10—Wyclif, *Select Works*, 1:406–12.
　　11—C. Martin, "Edinburgh University Library Manuscript 93."
Facsimiles: 7—Wilson and Fenlon, *Winchester Anthology.*
　　8—Plimpton, *Education of Chaucer*, plate IX.11–12.

English Translations of Edmund of Abingdon's *Speculum ecclesie* (*Mirror of Holy Church, Mirror of St. Edmund*) SE

Manual, 9:3116 [72]

Verse versions:
IMEV 974

　　1. Oxford, Bodleian Lib. Eng. poet. a.1 (Vernon) (284r–286r), ca. 1390, 1,082 lines in couplets.
　　2. London, BL Add. 22283 (Simeon) (78v–80v), ca. 1400.

Edition: 1—Horstmann, *Minor Poems,* 268–97.
Facsimile: 1—Doyle, *Vernon Manuscript.*

IMEV 1512

1. Oxford, Bodleian Lib. Eng. poet. a.1 (Vernon) (227v–230r), ca. 1390.
2. London, BL Add. 22283 (Simeon) (30v–32v), ca. 1400.

Edition: 1—Horstmann, *Minor Poems,* 221–51.
Facsimile: 1—Doyle, *Vernon Manuscript.*

Prose versions:
IPMEP 706, 800, various texts, including:

1. Oxford, Bodleian Lib. Eng. poet. a.1 (Vernon) (355r–359v), ca. 1390.
2. Lincoln, Cathedral Lib. 91 (Lincoln Thornton) (197r–209r).
3. Cambridge, Univ. Lib. Ff.2.38.
4. Cambridge, Univ. Lib. Ii.6.43.
5. London, BL Royal 17.B.xvii.

Editions: for all of the prose texts, see Goymer, *"Mirror."*
1—Horstmann, *Yorkshire Writers,* 1:240–61.
2—Horstmann, *Yorkshire Writers,* 1:219–40; G. Perry, *Religious Pieces,* 16–62.
Facsimile: 1—Doyle, *Vernon Manuscript;* 2—Brewer and Owen, *Thornton Manuscript.*

Edmund, later a saint, was archbishop of Canterbury from 1234 to 1240. The Latin source, organized around the canonical hours, appears in Edmund of Abingdon, *Speculum.* See also Pantin, *English Church,* 222–24 and Allen, *Writings Ascribed,* 362–63. His works were widely read in the thirteenth and fourteenth centuries. Prominent biblical material in **SE** includes:

		Horstmann, *Yorkshire Writers*
Ten Commandments	Ex. 20:1–17	1:225–26, 247–48
Seven Works of Bodily Mercy	Matt. 25:35–40	1:228, 250
Pater Noster	Matt. 6:9–13	1:229, 251–53.
Hours of the Cross	See **HC**	1:235–37, 254–58.
Beatitudes	Matt. 5:3–16	1:246–47 (only in Vernon)

Pater Noster in English (Matt. 6:9–13) PN

Manual, 7:2279 [32]

The Pater Noster is ubiquitous in Middle English literature as are other elements of the catechism, such as the Ten Commandments, Ave Maria, and Creed, with which it often appears. The following list covers only those versions, including those in shorter expositions, that appear in print. Nevertheless, the listing is surely incomplete, and a thorough study is needed. Aarts, *Pater Noster,* provides a helpful discussion and survey. Versions which appear in other works of biblical literature are noted in their respective contexts and can be located through the Index of Biblical People, Places, and Events.

Verse Versions
Þe pater noster vndo on englissch
IMEV 206

>   1. Edinburgh, National Lib. of Scotland Advocates 19.2.1 (72r–v) (Auchinleck), 1330–40, 136 lines in couplets.

Editions: D. Laing, *Penni Worth,* 92–96; Kölbing, "Kleine Publicationen," 47–49.
Facsimile: Pearsall and Cunningham, *Auchinleck Manuscript.*

IMEV 254

>   1. Edinburgh, Univ. Lib. 205 (87r), 1477, eight lines.

Editions: G. Stevenson, *Pieces,* 117; C. Brown, *Religious Lyrics XVth Century,* 84.

IMEV/S 787

>   1. London, BL Arundel 292 (3r–v), earlier 13th c., twelve lines.

Editions: Wright and Halliwell, *Reliquiae Antiquae,* 1:235; A. Ellis, *Pronunciation,* 444; Garrett, "Religious Verses."

Pater Noster with exposition (see **CM** lines 25403–486)
IMEV 788

Jacob Ryman's religious poems
IMEV 2535

>   1. Cambridge, Univ. Lib. Ee.1.12 (61v), later 15th c., three stanzas in rhyme royal.

Edition: Zupitza, "Gedichte des Franziskaners Jakob Ryman," 247.

The Pater Noster is part of a collection of religious poems by Ryman, many of which are based on the Life of Christ: Ave Maria, Magnificat, angels' appearance to the shepherds, visit of the Magi, Slaughter of the Innocents, angel's resolution of Joseph's doubts, Crucifixion.

IMEV 2702

1. Oxford, Bodleian Lib. Rawlinson B.408 (*SC* 11755) (3v), seven stanzas in rhyme royal.

Editions: A. Clark, *Godstow Nunnery,* 5–6; Patterson, *Penitential Lyric,* 108–10.

IMEV/S 2703

1. Cambridge, Univ. Lib. Gg.4.32 (13r), eighteen lines.
2. London, BL Harley 3724 (44v), twelve lines.

Editions: 1 and 2—Wright and Halliwell, *Reliquiae Antiquae,* 1:57, 159–60.
   2—Patterson, *Penitential Lyric,* 108; A. Ellis, *Pronunciation,* 443.

IMEV/S 2704

1. Cambridge, Emmanuel College 27 (162r, col. 1), late 13th c., in five couplets.
2. Pavia, Biblioteca Universiteria 69 (41v), 13th c., six lines in couplets.

Editions: 1—Person, *Cambridge Lyrics,* 27.
   2—Thomson, *"Oure Fader,"* 236; Hussey, "Pater Noster," 10.

IMEV 2705

1. Cambridge, Univ. Lib. Hh.6.11 (70v), 13th c., eight long lines, aaabbbaa

Edition: Wright and Halliwell, *Reliquiae Antiquae,* 1:169.

IMEV 2706

1. London, BL Cotton Cleopatra B.vi (204v), five couplets.

Editions: Wright and Halliwell, *Reliquiae Antiquae,* 1:22; A. Ellis, *Pronunciation,* 442; Maskell, *Monumenta,* 3:248; C. Brown, *English Lyrics XIIIth Century,* 127.

IMEV 2708

1. Edinburgh, National Lib. of Scotland Advocates 18.7.21 (95r), 1372, three quatrains, abab.

Edition: E. Wilson, *Index,* 29.

IMEV 2709

1. London, Lambeth Palace 487 (21v), 304-line exposition.

Edition: Morris, *Old English Homilies,* 1:part 1, 55–71, and see A. Ellis, *Pronunciation,* 485.

IMEV 2710

1. Salisbury, Cathedral Lib. 82 (271v), later 13th c., ten lines.

Editions: E. Thompson, "Scraps," 215; Onions, "Pater Noster," 69.

Lydgate's paraphrase in seven eight-line stanzas
IMEV/S 2711 (cf. *IMEV* 448)
Manual, 6:1885 [138] (cf. *Manual,* 6:1885 [137])

Three MSS, including:

1. Cambridge, Trinity College 601 (R.3.21) (274r–v), later 15th c.

Edition: Lydgate, *Minor Poems,* ed. MacCracken, 18–20.
Study: Pearsall, *Lydgate,* 257–58.

Other versions, to my knowledge unprinted: *IMEV* 784, 2707, *IMEV/S* 2708.5. See also *IMEV/S* 2702.5, a 1510 printing by Wynkyn de Worde.

Prose Versions
Exposition attributed to Rolle
IPMEP 150

Six MSS, including:

1. London, Westminster School 3 (1r–67v).

Edition: Aarts, *Pater Noster,* 3–56.

Various Independent Versions
IPMEP 171

1. London, BL Arundel 57 (94r, 30r–36r), 1340. Version in the *Ayenbite of Inwyt.*
2. London, BL Cotton Vitellius A.xii (181v).
3. Cambridge, Gonville and Caius College 52/29 (43r), 13th c.

4. London, BL Royal 5.C.v (307r, final leaf), 14th c.
5. Cambridge, St John's College 142, 14th c.
6. Oxford, Bodleian Lib. Douce 246 (*SC* 21820) (15r), 15th c.
7. Salisbury, Cathedral Lib. 82 (271v).
8. Norton-on-Tees Grove House, Fairfax-Blakeborough, 1339.

Editions: 1—Wright and Halliwell, *Reliquiae Antiquae,* 1:42 (of 94r); A. Ellis, *Pronunciation,* 413 (of 94r); Morris, *Dan Michel's Ayenbite,* 99–118 (exposition on 30r–36r).
2—Wright and Halliwell, *Reliquiae Antiquae,* 1:204.
3—Wright and Halliwell, *Reliquiae Antiquae,* 1:282; Maskell, *Monumenta,* 3:248; Mätzner, *Altenglische Sprachproben,* 1:part 2, pp. 3–4.
4, 5, 6—Maskell, *Monumenta,* 3:249.
7—E. Thompson, "Scraps."
8—Fairfax-Blakeborough, "Fountains Abbey."

Exposition of the Pater Noster
IPMEP 128

1. London, BL Add. 22283 (Simeon) (101r–v), ca. 1400.

Edition: Francis, *Book of Vices and Virtues,* 334–36.

Francis prints another exposition of the Pater Noster on pages 337–39, connected to Wyclif. Versions are printed by Arnold in Wyclif, *Select Works,* 3:93–97 (from Oxford, Bodleian Bodley 789 [97r]), and by Simmons and Nolloth, *Lay Folks Catechism,* 7–11 (from London, Lambeth Palace 408 [1v–2v]). See *IPMEP* 810.

Parable of the Laborers in the Vineyard PLV

IMEV/S 2604
Manual, 2:398 [45]

1. London, BL Harley 2253 (70v col. b–71r col. b), early 14th c., sixty lines in stanzas rhyming aabaabccbccb.

Editions: Brook, *Harley Lyrics,* 42–43; C. Brown, *English Lyrics XIIIth Century,* 143–45.
Facsimile: Ker, *Harley 2253.*

One of two instances of English biblical paraphrase in this famous collection of devotional poetry and prose in English, French, and Latin (the other is **SLL**)

The paraphrase of Matt. 20:1–16 culminates in the last stanza's lament that ingratitude and greed exist in the world.

> "Why, naþ nout vch mon his?
> holdeþ nou or pees.
> A-way, thou art vnwis!
> tak al þat þin ys,
> ant fare ase foreward wees." (38–42)

The Seven Works of Bodily Mercy (Seven Corporal Works of Mercy) SWM

(Matt. 25:35–40 and Tob. 1:20)
Manual, 7:2290 [50] (see *IPMEP* 331 for a Wycliffite version)

Prose Version
1. Oxford, Trinity College 86 (32r–v).
2. New York, Columbia Univ. Lib. Plimpton 258 (2v).
3. London, BL Add. 60577 (128v), ca. 1500.
4. Oxford, Bodleian Lib. Ashmole 1286 (*SC* 8174) (211r–215v), ca. 1400.
5. Oxford, Bodleian Lib. Lyell 29 (104r–106r).
6. Leeds, Univ. Lib. Brotherton 501 (81r).
7. Ushaw, St. Cuthbert's College 28 (50v).
8. Cambridge, Univ. Lib. Nn.4.12 (37v).
9. Dublin, Trinity College 245 (218r).
10. Edinburgh, Univ. Lib. 93 (79v–80v).
11. Oxford, Bodleian Lib. Douce 246 (*SC* 21820) (107r, final leaf), 1446.
12. Cambridge, Univ. Lib. Hh.3.13 (119r), later 15th c.

Editions: 10 — C. Martin, "Edinburgh University Library Manuscript 93."
11 — Maskell, *Monumenta,* 3:255.
12 — Zupitza, "Was jedermann wissen."
Facsimiles: 2 — Plimpton, *Education of Chaucer;* 3 — Wilson and Fenlon, *Winchester Anthology.*

SWM often appears with the Seven Spiritual Works of Mercy. Matt. 25:35–40 enumerates six; the seventh (burying the dead) comes from Tob. 1:20.

Transcription from manuscript 1:

> Here sueþ þe vii werkys of mercy bodley þt crist schal reherce at þe day
> of doom. Come ȝe blessyd of my fadyr 7 take ȝe the kingdome of
> heuenes þt was ordeynyd for ȝu from the makyng of the world, ffor

wanne I hungrede ʒe fedden me. I þrustyd 7 ʒe ʒauen me drynke. I was
herborowles 7 ʒe herborowden me. I wos nakyd 7 ʒe cloþyden me. I was
in preson 7 ʒe camen to me. I was seke 7 ʒe vysytyden me. The vii werke
of mercy ys seyde in þe book of tobie byryynng of dede men þt han
nede þerto. And al þese vii werkys of mercy men doon to cryst whanne
þey doon hem to hys creaturis.

Verse version:

IMEV 645, 1959, 3459; see also IMEV/S 825.3, 1959, 4155.3

1. Oxford, Bodleian Lib., Eng. poet a.1 (Vernon) (115v), ca. 1390.
2. London, BL Add. 22283 (Simeon) (158r), ca. 1400.
3. London, BL Add. 37787 (158r–159r), early 15th c.
4. Salisbury, Cathedral Lib. 126 (5v), early 15th c.
5. San Marino, Huntington Lib. HM 127 (62v), early 15th c.
6. Oxford, Bodleian Lib. Ashmole 1286 (SC 8174) (i verso), ca. 1400.
7. Cambridge, Magdalene College Pepys 1584 (105r–106v), 15th c.

Editions: 1—Horstmann, *Minor Poems,* 34–35.
      3—Baugh, *Worcestershire Miscellany,* 146.
Facsimile: 1—Doyle, *Vernon Manuscript.*

The Woman of Samaria WomS

IMEV 3704
Manual, 2:397 [44]

1. Oxford, Jesus College 29, part 2 (178v–79v), ca. 1300, seventy-seven
   lines in couplets.

Editions: Morris, *Old English Miscellany,* 84–86; Zupitza and Schipper,
   Übungsbuch, 120–22.

WomS appears in the same manuscript as **PL;** it is a 77-line paraphrase of
Christ's meeting with the Woman at the Well (John 4:5–42). What would be
line 70 appears to be missing since line 69 forms only half of a couplet.

It is another example, like **PL, BTD,** and "Judas," of a ballad which retold
selections from the life of Christ. The opening lines are sufficiently generic:
"Þo Iesu Crist an eorþe was, mylde weren his dede: / alle heo beoþ on boke
iwryten, þat may heom rede."

These few thirteenth-century remains of biblical ballads may be the sur-
vivors of what was a substantial corpus.

The paraphrase of the dialogue is especially close (quotations from
Morris):

"Yef me drynke wymmon. he seyde myd mylde Muþe.
þeo wymmon him onswerede. al so to mon vnkuþe.
Hwat ar-tu. þat drynke me byst. þu pinchest of iudelonde.
Ne mostu drynke vnder-fo. none of myne honde.
Þo seyde ihesu crist. wymmon. if þu understóde.
Hwo it is. þat drynke bid. þu woldest beon of oþer mode.
Þu woldest bidde þat he þe yeue. drynke þat ilast euere.
þe þat ene drynkeþ þer-of. ne schal him þurste neuere."
                                      (lines 17–24; John 4:7–14)

"Go and clepe þine were. and cumeþ hider y-mene.
I nabbe heo seyde nenne were. ich am my seolf al one.
Nabbe ich of wepmonne. nones kunnes y-mone.
Wel þu seyst quaþ ihesu crist. were þat þu nauest nenne.
Fyue þu hauest ar þisse iheued. and yet þu hauest enne.
And þe þat þu nuþe hauest. and heuedest summe þrowe.
He is an oþer wyues were. more þan þin owe."
                                      (lines 30–36; John 4:16–18)

Resurrection and Apparitions RA

IMEV 3980
Manual, 2:394 [36]

1. Oxford, Bodleian Lib. Ashmole 61 (*SC* 6922) (138v–144v), late
   15th c., 605 lines rhyming aabccb.

Edition: Horstmann, "Nachträge" (1887), 441–47.

Generically, the poem is a romance, and retells the events of Christ's Resurrection and Appearances skillfully and energetically.

Lines	Events	Bible
1–65	Precautions of the Pharisees and Pilate, including the imprisonment of Joseph of Arimathea and the appointment of Sir Cosdram, Sir Emoraunte, Sir Arfax, and Sir Gemorante to guard Christ's tomb.	Matt. 27: 57–66
66–133	The knights boast in the *miles gloriosus* tradition and then fall asleep	
134–232	Christ rises, claims to have fulfilled the prophecies of Jeremias and David, appoints Gabriel and Raphael to appear to the three Marys, frees Joseph	
233–324	The angel at the tomb	Luke 24:1–9
325–358	Christ appears to Mary	John 20:15–18

Lines	Events	Bible
359–425	Appearance to Cleophas and Luke	Luke 24:13–35
426–521	Doubting Thomas	John 20:19–29
522–606	Pilate bribes the knights	Matt. 28:11–15

Story of the Resurrection SR

IMEV 2685 (London, BL Cotton Vespasian A.iii listed erroneously)

1. Cambridge, Univ. Lib. Dd.1.1 (30r–32v), ca. 1400, 268 octosyllabic lines in quatrains, rhyming abab.

Edition: Pickering, "An Unpublished Resurrection Poem."

SR is also a romantic retelling of the Resurrection, reminiscent of a ballad: Soldiers' report, Marys at the tomb, Journey to Emmaus, Harrowing of Hell, and Ascension.

The Sixteen Conditions of Charity (1 Cor. 13:1–8) SCC

Manual, 7:2292 [58]

Verse Version
IMEV 593, 2040

1. Edinburgh, National Lib. of Scotland Advocates 18.7.21 (33v), 1372, eight couplets.
2. Cambridge, Univ. Lib. Ii.6.39 (157r), earlier 15th c., fourteen eight-line stanzas.
3. London, Lambeth Palace 853 (pp. 42–47), earlier 15th c., fourteen eight-line stanzas.

Editions: 1 — E. Wilson, *Index,* 10–11.
2 — Furnivall, *Hymns to the Virgin,* 114–17.

Prose Version
Jolliffe, *Check-List,* G.4 (e)

33 MSS in seven versions, including:
1. Oxford, Trinity College 86 (35r–36r), late 15th c.
2. London, BL Harley 2343 (87v–89v), earlier 15th c.
3. Glasgow, Univ. Lib. Hunterian 512 (22v–25r).
4. Oxford, Bodleian Lib. Bodley 938 (*SC* 3054) (56r–58r), later 15th c.
5. Ushaw, St Cuthbert's College 28 (29v–34v), ca. 1450.
6. Cambridge, St John's College 257 (19r–20v).

7. Oxford, Bodleian Lib. Laud misc. 210 (*SC* 1292) (134v–136r), early 15th c.
8. Edinburgh, Univ. Lib. 93 (36v–38r), earlier 15th c.
9. New York, Columbia Univ. Lib., Plimpton 258 (5r–v), ca. 1400.
10. London, BL Add. 60577 (137r–138r), ca. 1500.

Editions: 1 through 7—Durkin, "Trinity College, MS 86," 2:144–226 (each text represents one of the seven versions).
8—C. Martin, "Edinburgh University Library Manuscript 93."
Facsimiles: 9—Plimpton, *Education of Chaucer;* 10—Wilson and Fenlon, *Winchester Anthology.*

This text is the most widely disseminated paraphrase of 1 Cor. 13:1–8. It appears in the context of other catechetical material, such as the prose Beatitudes (**Beat**), Ten Commandments (**TC**), and the Seven Works of Mercy (**SWM**).

Transcription from manuscript 2 (87v–88r)

"Iff y speke wiþ tungis of men 7 of aungels 7 y haue not charite, y am maad as bras sownyng or a symbal tynkinge, and if y han profecie 7 knowe all misteries 7 al kunnynge 7 if y haue al feiþ so þat y moue hillis fro her place 7 y haue not charite y am nouȝt 7 if y deperte all my goodis into þe metis of pore men 7 if y bitake my bodi so þat y brenne 7 y haue not charite it profitiþ to me noþing."

Sir John Clanvowe's *The Two Ways* TW

IPMEP 680
Manual, 7:2314 [133]

1. Oxford, Univ. College 97 (114r–123v), late 14th c., complete text.
2. London, BL Add. 22283 (Simeon) (116r), ca. 1400, lines 770–870 only.

Editions: 1—Scattergood, *Works of Clanvowe,* 57–80, and *Two Ways.*

Clanvowe, one of the "Lollard Knights," died in 1391. This treatise is based on the "two ways" of Matt. 7:13–14, and is composed entirely of biblical quotation (independent of the Wycliffite translation) followed by moral exhortations. Many of the verses are linked by the "way" topos.

The lineation corresponds to Scattergood, *Works of Clanvowe:*

Lines	Quotation	Bible
8–12	"The ȝaate is wyde and þe way is brood þat ledeþ to los and manye goon in þat wey, and how streit is þe ȝaate and þe weye nargh þat leedeþ to þe lyf and few fynden þat wey"	Matt. 7:13–14
25–28	"And þat blisse is so greet þat noon eye hath seyn, ne eere yherd, ne it hath not comen into mannes herte þe ioye þat God hath ordeyned for hem þat louen hym and shuln come þider"	1Cor. 2:9
53–56	"God shal teechen hem þat been meeke [in] hise weyes . . . 'Lord, shewe me þi weyes and teeche me thi styes'"	Ps. 24:4, 9
61–62	"þei leeuen hem and goon þe weyes of þe feend for lust of here flesshe or lykynge of þe world"	1John 2:16
79–80	"The wysdoom of þis world is folie byfore God"	1Cor. 3:19
85–87	"Lord, maak parfit myne outgoyngges in thi paþes so þat my steppes been not meeued"	Ps. 16:5
91–92	"Blissed been all þoo þat dreeden oure Lord and þat walken in hise weyes"	Ps. 128:1
97–100	"ȝef þu wolt entre euerelastyng lyf keepe þe commaundementz"	Matt. 19:16–17
108–109	"The dreede of God is þe bigynnyng of wisdoom"	Ps. 110:10; Prov. 1:7; 9:10
120–21	"þei been acursed þat bowen awey fro þe commaundementȝ of God"	Ps. 118:21
173–176	"we han ȝre stronge enemys . . . þat oon is þe feend; þat oother is þe world: þe ȝridde is oure flesshe"	1John 2:16
209	"God is neiȝ to hem þat dreeden hym"	Ps. 84:10
246–251	"Breþeren, beþ soobre and waaketh for ȝoure aduersaire þe deuel, rooryng as a lyon, goth aboute seechyng whom he may swolewen and distroyen, to whom withstoonde ȝe stroonge in feith"	1Pet. 5:8–9
253–254	"þe deuel is a lyere"	John 8:44
280–281	"Withstoonde ȝe þe deuel and he shal flee from ȝowe"	James 4:7
331–334	"þe flessh coueiteth aȝens spirit and þe spirit aȝens þe flessh, þise two coueiten eithere aȝens oothere. And þe werkes of the flessh been vices and þe fruyt of þe spirit is vertue"	Gal. 5:17
336–337	"þe wysdom of the flessh is deeþ and þat þe wisdom of þe spirit is lyf and pees. And þe wisdom of þe flessh is enemy to God, ne he nys, ne he ne may not bee suget to the law of God"	Rom. 8:6–7

Lines	Quotation	Bible
340–343	"ȝef we lyuen after þe flessh we shulne dyen, þat is to seye, we shuln bee dampned; and ȝef þat þoruȝ þe spirit we maken deede þe deedys of oure flessh we shuln lyue"	Rom. 8:13
351–353	"he ordeyneþ for vs ynouȝ booþe mete and drynke and clooþing"	Ecclus. 29:27
388–389	"sououre þoo thynges þat beene aboue and not þoo thynges þat been heere on eerth"	Col. 3:2
408–414	"Loue ȝe not þe world ne þoo thynges þat been in þe world, ffor he þat loueth þe world þe charitee of God is not in hym. ffor alle þing þat is in þe world it is lust of flessh, or lust of eyen, or pruyde of lyf"	1John 2:15–16
414–415	"frensshipe of this world is enemy to God"	James 4:4
446–447	"Crist seide þat it was hard for a riche man to entre into þe kyngdom of heuene"	Matt. 19:23
455–456	"þis tresour heer vpon eerthe is fals, and passyng and vnsauoury"	Matt. 6:19–20
464–465	"Thoo þat wolen bee maad riche fallen in to temptacioun"	1Tim. 6:9
524–525	"Crist suffrede for vs leeuynge vs ensaumple þat we schulden so doo folewynge hise traaces"	1Pet. 2:21
606	"alle þis world is set in euel"	1John 5:19
608–609	"we shulden not bee in wille to bee maad lich to þis world"	Rom. 12:2
629–642	Ten Commandments	Ex. 20:3–17
691–692	"hise commaundementȝ been not heuy"	1John 5:3
696–705	The greatest commandment	Matt. 22:35–40
720–774	Synopsis of Incarnation; Nativity; Christ's circumcision, preaching and miracles; Betrayal; Scourging; Crucifixion "with greete boistouse naylles" (763); "ffadir, for ȝeue hem þis gilt for þei witen not what þei doon" (766–67); vinegar and gall	John 19; Luke 23:34
775–784	Longinus; Harrowing of Hell; Resurrection and Ascension	
835–841	"Who þat loueþ me schal keepe my woordes" 23–24	John 14:21,
843–846	"And who seith þat he knoweþ God and keepeþ not hise comaundementȝ, he is a lyere and treuth is not in hym"	1John 2:3–4
846–847	"Loue we not with woord ne with toonge, but with deede and with treuth"	1John 3:18

The Quatrefoil of Love QL

IMEV 1453
Manual, 7:2334 [176]

520 alliterative lines with bob and wheel, abababababcdddc.

1. Oxford, Bodleian Lib. Add. A.106 (*SC* 29003) (6r–15v), late 15th c.
2. London, BL Add. 31042 (London Thornton) (98r–101v), ca. 1440.

Editions: 2 — Gollancz and Weale, *Quatrefoil;* Gollancz, "Quatrefoil." There
  is a 1520 printing by Wynkyn de Worde, *STC* 15345.
Partial facsimile: 2 — J. Thompson, *Thornton.*

Gollancz and Weale, in their introduction, call the poem "a medieval attempt at the sublimation of the sex instinct" (xxii–xxiii). The *chanson d'aventure* frame, within which a turtledove counsels a maiden through the allegorical associations of a four-leaf clover (Father, Son, Holy Ghost, and God
as Man), places the poem in the "love-rune" tradition, yet it is composed
primarily of biblical paraphrase.

Quotations from Gollancz and Weale:

Lines	Event	Bible
1–91	Love-counsel for the maiden by the turtledove	
92–104	Synopsis of Creation of Adam and Eve; Prohibition; Temptation; Fall: "Forbede he þam no-thynge, als I bileue, / Bot a grene appille þat grew one a tree" (94–95)	Gen. 2; 3
105–143	Annunciation to Mary; conception of Elizabeth: " 'Þou sall consayue a knaue childe comly and clere, / And all þe bale of þis werlde in þe sall be bett.' / 'Þat were a mekill meruelle þat I a childe solde bere, / Was I neuer maryede ne with man mett.' / 'Be-halde to thi Cosyn, consayuede hase to-ȝere / Elezebeth in hir elde, þat lange hase bene lett' " (118–23)	Luke 1:26–38
144–169	Nativity; ox and ass; Magi; Herod; Slaughter of the Innocents; Flight into Egypt	Matt. 2:1–16; Is. 1:3
170–195	John the Baptist; Betrayal for "thritty penys" (174); Christ before Pilate: "leue lordynges, a treuthe for to trye, / Þat semely es saklesse, say what ȝe wolde' " (185–86)	Matt. 3:1, 6; 26:15; Luke 23:14
196–221	Scourging; Crown of Thorns; gall and vinegar; Crucifixion; earthquake	Matt. 27:27–29, 48, 51
222–234	Christ entrusts John to Mary; Longinus; "Take	John 19:26, 34

Lines	Event	Bible
	John to þi son þat standis bi þi syde; John, take mary mi moder now moder to þe'" (225–26)	
235–273	Harrowing of Hell	
274–299	Resurrection; appearances to Mary Magdalen and Doubting Thomas: "He putt his hande in his syde, / And alle he blyssed in þat tyde, / Þat leuede in his wondis wyde, / And sawe þam neuer with ey" (296–99)	John 20:18, 24–29
300–324	Ascension; Assumption of Mary	Luke 24:51
325–429	Further counsel from the Turtledove on Purgatory, Last Judgment	
430–442	Seven Works of Bodily Mercy: "When þat I was hungry how haue ʒe me fedde? When I askede ʒow a drynk ʒe ne harde not my steuen" (431–32)	Matt. 25:35–36
443–520	Lament over the decadence of the times; injunction to flee sin and seek salvation	

Selected Lives from the *South English Legendary* SEL

Like the temporale narratives which preface some collections of saints lives, the sanctorale itself often contains biblical material, and any such collection can be regarded as an extension of the Acts of the Apostles.

Full coverage of all the sanctorale collections in Middle English is impossible, but the following provides a brief review of the principal biblical contents of the most important and representative collection, *The South English Legendary,* with a few related texts.[2] D'Evelyn's article in *Manual,* 2:410–29, plus her extensive bibliographic breakdown, saint by saint, on pages 561–635, provides detailed information.

The manuscript tradition of the **SEL** is very complicated (see Görlach, *Textual Tradition,* and Wells, "Structural Development"). D'Evelyn and Mill base their edition, *South English Legendary,* on the following four:

1. Cambridge, Corpus Christi College 145, early 14th c.
2. London, BL Harley 2277, ca. 1300.
3. Oxford, Bodleian Lib. Ashmole 43 (*SC* 6924), mid-14th c.
4. London, BL Cotton Julius D.ix.

---

2. See also Mirk's *Festial,* the *Speculum Sacerdotale* (ed. Weatherly), the *Scottish Legendary* (ed. Horstmann, *Barbour's*), the anonymous 1438 translation of the *Golden Legend* known as the *Gilte Legend,* and Caxton's translation of the *Golden Legend* (**CGL,** see Jacobus de Voragine, *Golden Legend*).

John the Baptist
IMEV/S 2945
Manual, 2:594 [143a]

Editions: D'Evelyn and Mill, *South English Legendary,* 1:241–46. Also in
Oxford, Bodleian Lib. Laud misc. 108 (*SC* 1486) (32v–4r), late 13th c.,
ed. Horstmann, *Early South-English Legendary*, 29–33.

Imprisonment; decollation by Herod; miracles associated with John's
head and finger (Matt. 14:1–11).

John the Evangelist
IMEV/S 2932
Manual, 2:595 [146a]

Editions: D'Evelyn and Mill, *South English Legendary,* 2:594–95. Also in
Oxford, Bodleian Lib. Laud misc. 108 (*SC* 1486), ed. Horstmann *Early
South-English Legendary,* 403.

Calling of the Disciples; John leans on Christ's breast; is charged to care
for Mary (Matt. 4:18–21, John 13:23, 19:27).

Judas
Manual, 2:596 [149]

Editions: D'Evelyn and Mill, *South English Legendary,* 2:692–97. Also in
London, BL Harley 2277 (227r–229r), ca. 1300, ed. Furnivall, *Early
English Poems,* 107.

Judas objects to the anointing, betrays Christ, hangs himself, bursts asunder (John 12:1–6, Matt. 26:15, 27:5, Acts 1:18).

Longinus
IMEV/S 2960
Manual, 2:604 [169a]

Edition: D'Evelyn and Mill, *South English Legendary,* 1:84.

Healed of blindness, witnesses earthquake (John 19:34, Matt. 27:51).

Luke
IMEV/S 2973
Manual, 2:606 [173]

Edition: D'Evelyn and Mill, *South English Legendary,* 2:440.

Sees Christ on the road to Emmaus (Luke 24:13–31).

Mary Magdalen
IMEV 3159
Manual, 2:610 [192a]

A version in some manuscripts of the *South English Legendary*

1. Oxford, Bodleian Lib. Laud misc. 108 (*SC* 1486) (190r–197r), late 13th c., 643 verses in couplets.
2. Cambridge, Trinity College 605 (R.3.25) (127v–133r), early 15th c.
3. London, Lambeth Palace 223 (137v), late 14th c.
4. Tokyo, Takamiya 54 (112v–116v), early 15th c. See Pickering and Görlach, "Newly Discovered Manuscript," 113.

Editions: 1—Horstmann, *Sammlung,* 148–62; Horstmann, *Early South-English Legendary,* 462–80.
2, 3—Horstmann, "Nachträge (Fortsetzung)" (1882).

Taken from Horstmann, *Sammlung:*
Genealogy of Mary Magdalen's family, with Martha and Lazarus; Martha's virtue and Mary's beauty and youthful folly.

The primary biblical portion is verses 78–161, which include the anointing at Simon the Leper's house (Matt. 26:6–13), Judas's objection (John 12:4–8), the Parable of the Creditor's Two Debtors (Luke 7:40–43), and Christ's expulsion of the devils from Mary (Luke 8:2).

There is no resurrection of Lazarus, and only one line mentions his sickness (146), though Martha is cured of a bleeding sickness (140–45), and Lazarus is made a bishop (537).

From this biblical base the poet launches an "Acts" of Mary, with her voyages to pagan kingdoms (with Bishop Maximus), resurrection of a Saracen queen, visits to Calvary and Rome, conversion of the pagans, Mary's life in the wilderness where she is fed by angels, and her translation to heaven.

IMEV/S 2994
Manual, 2:610 [192b]

Edition: D'Evelyn and Mill, *South English Legendary,* 1:302–15.

The episode as presented in D'Evelyn and Mill's edition of the **SEL** consists of 352 lines, and opens with the family genealogy.

Lines	Event	Bible
11–18	Betrothal of Mary to John the Evangelist (cf. lines 13424–39 of **CM** and PL 198.1559)	

Lines	Event	Bible
35–44	Anointing; expulsion of the seven demons, linked to the seven deadly sins	Matt. 26:6–13; Luke 8:2
61–278	Mission of Mary, Martha, Lazarus and other disciples to the "lond of Marcile" (69); general conversion of the population	
279–352	Mary in the wilderness; her death	

IMEV 2637
Manual, 2:610 [192c], version in **NHC**

1. London, BL Harley 4196 (157r–162r), 15th c.

Edition: Horstmann, *Altenglische Legenden*, 81–92

IMEV 12
IMEV/S 304.5
Manual, 2:610 [192d]

1. Edinburgh, National Lib. of Scotland Advocates 19.2.1 (62r–65r) (Auchinleck), early 14th c., 680 lines in octosyllabic couplets, missing twelve lines after verse 560 because of an excised intial, acephalous.

Editions: Horstmann, *Sammlung*, 163–70; Turnbull, *Legendae*, 213–57.
Facsimile: Pearsall and Cunningham, *Auchinleck Manuscript*.

Lines 1–78 conflate accounts of the Anointing at Bethany and the Raising of Lazarus from Matt. 26:6–13, Mark 14:3–9, Luke 7:36–50, 10:38–42, and John 11:1–6, 12:1–8. The passage also describes how Mary sought Christ at his grave (Mark 16:1–10, John 20:11–18) and how Christ cured Martha of a seven-year sickness (Luke 8:43–44).

As with the *IMEV* 3159 version, this biblical prologue sets the stage for Mary's missionary activity.

The poet concludes with a prayer

> Þat ʒe biseche al for him
> Þat þis stori in Inglisse rim
> Out of latin haþ ywrouʒt,
> For alle men latin no conne nouʒt.
> (Horstmann, *Sammlung*, lines 669–72)

Matthias
IMEV/S 3026
Manual, 2:613 [196]

Edition: D'Evelyn and Mill, *South English Legendary,* 1:70.

Chosen by lot (Acts 1:23–26).

Paul
IMEV/S 3041
Manual, 2:617 [221]

Edition: D'Evelyn and Mill, *South English Legendary,* 1:264–69

Conversion; healed by Ananias; rescued by Barsabas; raises Eutychus after falling from a window (Acts 9:1–28, 20:7–12).

Peter
IMEV/S 3046
Manual, 2:619 [227a]

Edition: D'Evelyn and Mill, *South English Legendary,* 1:246–47.

Calling of Peter; his question at the Last Supper; Peter cuts the Jew's ear and tries to walk on water (Matt. 4:18–19, John 13:24, 18:10, Matt. 14:28–29).

Thomas the Apostle
IMEV/S 3063
Manual, 2:628 [274a]

Editions: D'Evelyn and Mill, *South English Legendary,* 2:571–72. Also in Oxford, Bodleian Lib. Laud misc. 108, ed. Horstmann, *Early South-English Legendary,* 377.

Doubting Thomas (John 20:27–28).

❖ III.E   *Lectionaries*

Sermons and Homilies

The biblical material preserved in the various sermon and homily collections of medieval England was probably, even more so than the drama, the primary means of spreading the Word among lay folk. It is only possible to mention some of the major Middle English homily collections which continued a long Old English tradition: the Bodley Homilies (Belfour, *Twelfth-Century Homilies*); the Lambeth Homilies (12th–13th c., EETS os 29 and 34); the Kentish sermons (13th c., EETS os 49); the sermons in London, BL Royal 18.B.xxiii (14th–15th c.; Ross, *Sermons*); Mirk's *Festial* (ca. 1400). Siegfried Wenzel, "Medieval Sermons," provides a helpful guide.

Three other prose cycles, each of which contains an independent translation of the gospel lection for its respective Sundays and feast days, deserve some attention.

The first is Wyclif's own sermon cycle edited by Anne Hudson and Pamela Gradon. Its 294 sermons comprise "a complete homiliary for the ecclesiastical year" according to the readings designated by the Sarum use.[1] The amount of Latin is limited to an incipit which is translated along with the whole of the lection for that day. Exposition is interspersed throughout and is differentiated from the translation by a regimen of red underlining. Hudson favors a date very near 1400, and obviously this is a Wycliffite, if not

---

1. Hudson and Gradon, *Wycliffite Sermons*, 1:8. Of the thirty-one manuscripts, eleven have the cycle complete. See also Cigman, *Lollard Sermons*.

Wyclif's own, project, but the translations are indeed independent of either
Wycliffite version. While the debate continues concerning the use made of
the Lollard Bible by contemporaries (such as Chaucer), it is significant that
even a Wycliffite made his own translations when composing sermons.

The second cycle survives in just two manuscripts, only one of which
copies the gospel translation itself.[2] The only portion in print is in Forshall
and Madden's introduction to volume 1 of *The Holy Bible*, where Matt. 20:1–
10 is quoted.[3] The translations appear in blocks, in the "ancient" style (see
below).

The third cycle is in six manuscripts and is noteworthy because the compiler expresses his own opinions on translation (see above, p. 40). He was
perhaps prompted to do so since he models the whole collection on Robert
of Gretham's Anglo-Norman gospel lectionary, the *Miroir* or *Les Evangiles des
Domnées*, the prologue of which contrasts sacred and secular literature.

The following two entries for the *Ormulum* and the *Northern Homily Cycle*
give a representative sense of the variety and extent of biblical material
which was preached to and read by the English from the late twelfth into the
fifteenth century.

Ormulum Orm

IMEV/S 2305

1. Oxford, Bodleian Lib. Junius 1 (*SC* 5113), late 12th c., ninety leaves
   plus twenty-nine inserted leaves, some missing, many irregularly
   shaped, in double columns, atelous. Approx. twenty thousand lines,
   unalliterated, fifteen syllables per line, with caesura;
   infrequent rhyme.

Editions: Holt, *Ormulum;* White, *Ormulum.* Burchfield, "*Ormulum*
   Manuscript," 182, announces an edition in progress.
Studies: Morrison, "Orm's English Sources"; Parkes, "Presumed Date and
   Possible Origin"; Holm, *Corrections and Additions.*

---

2. They are Cambridge, Univ. Lib. Kk.6.2 and Kk.6.28, both ca. 1400. It was a common phenomenon (e.g., in later versions of **NHC**) that as these cycles were copied and
recopied the gospel paraphrases were dropped out in favor of the exposition and/or exempla which followed. Either the biblical text was considered familiar enough to bear
omission or, as the Reformation controversy heated up, copying biblical translations was
considered dangerous.

3. Forshall and Madden, *Holy Bible,* 1:xx, n. f, quoting from Cambridge, Univ. Lib.
Kk.6.28.

The *Ormulum* has little to indicate that anyone but the two scribes (one of whom was perhaps Orm himself) whose hands have been identified in the unique manuscript ever saw it. Its early date (1170–80) and size (over twenty thousand lines, one-eighth of the proposed work) and the fact that its homilies correspond to the "ancient" type make it one of the most important biblical paraphrases in Middle English. An "ancient" homily begins with a substantial preface of biblical paraphrase; a "modern" or "university" homily (the distinction begins to operate in the fourteenth century) subdivides the text into various themes and devotes the bulk of the homily to exposition (see Ross, *Sermons*, xliii–lv). Orm's expositions are lengthy and repetitious, but they dwell almost exclusively on the biblical material and its significances.

The manuscript ends in fragments, so it is unknown how much of the lectionary Orm actually completed. The extant work covers only thirty-one of the 242 lections (extending into Acts) listed between the dedication and the introduction. Line 28 of the dedication thanks Christ that the work has been brought "till ende"; given the evidence of Orm's industry, perhaps we should give him the benefit of the doubt.

Lines	Events	Bible
[vol. 1]		
1–340	Dedication (independently numbered)	
1–108	Introduction	
109–240	Zachary; Elizabeth	Luke 1:5–25
2161–2476	Annunciation: "Ne beo þu, Marʒe, nohht forrdredd" (2205)	Luke 1:26–38
2477–2512	Joseph's doubts	Matt. 1:18–25
2731–2844	Visitation: "[John the Baptist] bigann forrþrihht anan / To stirenn 7 to buttenn" (2809–10)	Luke 1:39–45
3190–3219	John the Baptist in the wilderness	Matt. 3:4–6
3270–3425	Decree of Caesar Augustus; angels appear to the shepherds	Luke 2:1–20
3426–3493	Visit of the Magi	Matt. 2:9–11
4154–4161	Circumcision	Luke 2:21
4384–4535	Ten Commandments	Ex. 20:1–17
4756–4843	Trials, patience of Job	Job 1:13–2:10
5194–5229	Eliseus inherits Elias's spirit	4Kg. 2:9–10
5632–5757	Beatitudes	Matt. 5:3–11
5800–5903	Ezekiel's vision of the Gospel Beasts	Exek. 1:10, 15
6158–6177	Seven Works of Bodily Mercy	Matt. 25:35–36
6394–6517	Herod and the Magi	Matt. 2:1–12
7571–7700	Presentation in the Temple; Simeon and	Luke 2:22–40

Lines	Events	Bible
	Anna: "læt nu þin þeoww / Ut off þiss weorelld wendenn" (7619–20)	
8001–8026	Slaughter of the Innocents	Matt. 2:16
8051–8056	"Aȝȝ whil þatt I wass litell child / Icc held o childess þæwess" (8053–54)	1Cor. 13:11
8347–8394	Flight into Egypt; death of Herod; Archelaus	Matt. 2:13–15, 19–23
8587–8610	Henoch: "Godd himm ledde aweȝȝ fra menn" (8589)	Gen. 5:24
8611–8696	Elias predicts drought; Widow of Sarephta	3Kg. 17:1, 8–16
8697–8714	Elias's rapture: "An karrte þatt wass all off fir" (8703)	4Kg. 2:11–12
8879–8982	Christ disputes with the Temple Doctors: "Ne wisste ȝe nohht tatt me birrþ / Min faderr wille forþenn?" (8951–52)	Luke 2:41–52
9123–9334	John the Baptist prepares the Way of the Lord: "Forr nuȝȝu iss bulaxe sett / Rihht to þe treowwess rote" (9281–82)	Luke 3:1–14; Matt. 3:1–6; Is. 40:3–5
[vol. 2]		
10257–10397	"Namm I nohht Godess Sune, Crist" (10281)	John 1:19–27
10478–10491	Separation of wheat from chaff	Luke 3:16–17
10648–10687	Baptism of Christ	Matt. 3:13–17
11200–11225	Genealogy of Christ (abridged)	Matt. 1:1–16
11319–11402	Temptation in the Desert	Matt. 4:1–11
12332–12375	How the Devil tempted Adam [sic]	Gen. 3:5–6
12566–12621	"Loc, here cumeþþ Godess Lamb" (12574)	John 1:29–34
12720–12831	Calling of Andrew, Peter, Philip, Nathaniel	John 1:35–51
14000–14081	Miracle at Cana: "Abid, abid, wifmann, abid, / Ne comm nohht ȝet min time" (14020–21) (six jars = six Ages of the World)	John 2:1–11
14456–14469	1st Age: Cain slays Abel	Gen. 4:8
14534–14575	2d Age: Noah's flood	Gen. 6:17–7:24
14656–14693	3d Age: Abraham and Isaac	Gen. 22:1–13
14774–14819	4th Age: Red Sea Crossing	Ex. 14:21–29
14902–14917	5th Age: proud Saul and meek David	
15008–15013	6th Age: Circumcision of Christ	Luke 2:21
15498–15519	Synopsis of healings and miracles	
15538–15635	Cleanses Temple	John 2:13–25
16048–16069	Simon Magus tries to buy the Holy Spirit	Acts 8:18–20
16132–16133	"Hat lufe towarrd Godess hus / Me freteþþ att min herrte"	Ps. 68:10

Lines	Events	Bible
16608–16755	Nicodemus and being born again: "Hu maȝȝ ald mann ben borenn efft / On elde off moderr wambe?" (16638–39)	John 3:1–21
17405–17440	Moses; the fiery and brazen serpents	Num. 21:6–9
17906–18005	John's testimony: "Bridgume iss he þatt hafeþþ brid" (17958)	John 3:22–36
18555–18556	"Þiss Word wass wiþþ þe Faderr aȝȝ; / Þe Faderr iss þatt frummþe" (18557–58)	John 1:1–4
18927–18938	"he barr wittness i þe follc / Þatt soþ lihht cumenn shollde" (18933–34)	John 1:6–8
19237–19268	Synopsis of Ministry; Transfiguration; Resurrection; Ascension.	
19551–19584	Jesus enters Galilee	John 4:1–3
19585–19614	Herod imprisons John the Baptist	Mark 6:17–18
19819–19974	Enmity of Herodias	Mark 6:19–20

The manuscript breaks off with the lection of John 4:5 ff., the Woman of Samaria.

Northern Homily Cycle **NHC**

IMEV Appendix IV (pp. 733–36) lists entries for each gospel lesson.

Original Version

16 MSS, including:
    1. Edinburgh, College of Physicians (15v–37r), ca. 1325, fragmentary.
    2. Oxford, Bodleian Lib. Ashmole 42 (*SC* 6923) (1r–257v), early 15th c.
    3. Cambridge, Univ. Lib. Dd.1.1 (39v–225v), ca. 1400.
    4. Cambridge, Univ. Lib. Gg.5.31, later 14th c.

Editions: 1 — Small, *Metrical Homilies.*
    2 — Nevanlinna, *Northern Homily Cycle,* 3:297–99 (lines 5695–770).

Expanded Version I (northern dialect)

    1. London, BL Harley 4196 (1r–132r), ca. 1400. Also contains **GN.**
    2. London, BL Cotton Tiberius E.vii (101r–240r), early 15th c. Also contains **LLB.**

Edition: 1 — Nevanlinna, *Northern Homily Cycle* (with readings from 2).

Expanded Version II (midland dialect)

    1. Oxford, Bodleian Lib. Eng. poet. a.1 (Vernon) (167r, col. 1–227v), ca. 1390.

2. London, BL Add. 22283 (Simeon) (1r–30v), ca. 1400.

Edition: 1—Horstmann, "Evangeliem-Geschichten" (selected
exempla only).
Facsimile: 1—Doyle, *Vernon Manuscript.*

Composed in its original form ca. 1300, **NHC** extends to approximately
twenty thousand lines, in octosyllabic couplets, in each of its three versions. Saara Nevanlinna has edited the "expanded" collection (ca. 1400),
which nevertheless omits parts of the "original" collection, edited by John
Small in 1862. The third version (ca. 1390), which Nevanlinna also calls "expanded," follows the original version closely where it does not add material.
In the Harley and Tiberius manuscripts "[t]hirty-four homilies, including
the *Northern Passion* [**NP**] with twenty-four tales, *exempla* or *narraciones* at-
tached to them were derived from MSS of U [the original version] in a revised or amplified form."[4] Material associated with Lives of Christ and John
the Baptist may be based on the *Historia* or the *Legenda Aurea,* and there are
some parallels to the York plays, so once again a form of biblical paraphrase,
this time a gospel lectionary, mediates between a Latin work and another
vernacular production. Nevanlinna observes that the "number of French
rhyme-words is much smaller [i.e., less than the usual 20–25 percent] in
short paraphrases of Latin Bible passages," which leads her to suggest that
the gospel texts may have been versified from an already existing vernacular
prose translation.[5]

The original version covers the readings of the ecclesiastical year and exhibits the standard medieval homiletic structure: Latin pericope, a thirty- to
seventy-line (on average) paraphrase of the biblical text, an allegorical interpretation according to Gregory, Bede, and so on, and finally an exemplum.
The transition from the paraphrase to the expository matter is often marked
by the couplet "This is the strenthe of our godspelle, / Als man on Ingelis
tung may telle." The homilies correspond to the "ancient" form of sermon
construction as opposed to the "modern" or "university" form. The amount
of biblical paraphrase in any given homily of **NHC** ranges from twenty-five
lines to over two hundred, and the percentage of paraphrase to illustrative
commentary from 10 percent to nearly 100 percent per homily. By any mea-

---

4. Nevanlinna, *Northern Homily Cycle,* 1:124. For a review of the contents of the tales,
see Gerould, *Homily Collection,* and Ward and Herbert, *Catalogue,* 3:320–36.

5. Nevanlinna, *Northern Homily Cycle,* 38:105, 126. Rising pressure against any vernacular translation may be indicated by the fact that the later manuscripts of the original version include less and less biblical material, in Latin or in English. Some manuscripts copy
only the exempla; no extant manuscript contains only the gospel paraphrases.

sure, significant amounts of the Gospels appear. None of the versions follow
the York or Sarum usage consistently, though Harley 4196 chiefly follows
York, with some exceptions.

The earliest manuscript, 1, also contains verses 18989–24968 of **CM**.[6]
At numerous points within the cycle the homilist recalls material already
preached ("And I to dai fourtenniht tald") and anticipates what is to come
("Als nethir mar man find mai / In Lenten on the first Sundai") (Small, *Metrical Homilies*, 44, 122). The use of "nethir" seems to be directed to a reader,
not a listener.

From Nevanlinna's edition of Harley 4196:

Lines	Events	Bible
[vol. 1]		
1–70	Palm Sunday: "ȝowre lord of þam has nede" (17)	Matt. 21:1–9
329–374	John prepares the Way: "With camelle hare was he cledde" (360)	Mark 1:1–18
487–692	John's teaching: "ȝe wicked folk, kind of serpentes" (505)	Luke 3:7–18
693–730	Synoptic Apocalypse	Luke 21:25–33
963–1028	John prepares the way	Mark 1:4–8; John 1:19–20
1029–1112	Proofs of Messiahship	Matt. 11:2–19
1361–1476	Annunciation	Luke 1:26–38
1605–1776	Visitation of Elizabeth; Magnificat	Luke 1:39–56
1777–1940	Archelaus; Tiberius; John preaches prophecy of Isaias	Luke 3:1–6; Is. 40:3
1941–2086	Priest and Levites interrogate John	John 1:19–28
2087–2120	"Þe law thurgh Moyses gan he gif, / To teche þe folk how þai suld lif, / Grace and pese seþin es puplist / Thurgh þe come of Jesu Crist" (2105–8).	John 1:15–18
2121–2316	Joseph's doubts concerning Mary	Matt. 1:18–22
2317–2534	Christ's genealogy	Matt. 1:1–17
2535–2834	Decree from Augustus; Nativity, ox and ass; "Ioy be euer in heuen on hight" (2795)	Luke 2:1–14; Is. 1:3
2835–2890	Visit of the shepherds	Luke 2:15–20
2891–2966	Seven Miracles at the Birth of Christ	
3071–3180	"A man to erth fra God was sent" (3107)	John 1:1–14
3181–3522	Flight into Egypt; Slaughter of the	Matt. 2:12–18

---

6. C. Brown, *Register*, 1:508–10. The homily cycle is sandwiched within this excerpt from
CM.

Lines	Events	Bible
	Innocents: "Rachel wepes for hir suns" (3493)	
3523–3608	Death of Herod	
3609–3764	Simeon and Anna: "Þe swerde of sorow sal pas thurgh þe" (3666)	Luke 2:33–40
3765–3878	Circumcision of Jesus; Covenant of Circumcision with Abraham	Luke 2:21 Gen. 17:1–12
3879–3942	Return to Israel	Matt. 2:19–23
3943–4264	Star; Magi; Scepter of Juda: "In þaire offring þare þei did / Gold, and ensens, and mir þe thrid" (4235–36)	Matt. 2:1–12; Ps. 71:10–11; Gen. 49:10; Mic. 5:2
4295–4398	Genealogy of Christ	Luke 3:21–38
4487–4596	"Þe lamb of God, mek and bowsum, Þat dose oway þe werldes syn" (4598–99); Baptism of Christ	John 1:29; Matt. 3:13–17
4625 4856	Christ disputes with the Temple Doctors: "In þe middes of þam þai saw him sitt, / Hereand þam speke of haly writ" (4723–24)	Luke 2:41–52
4857–4918	Christ preaches penance	Matt. 4:12–17; Is. 9:1–2
4919–5036	Miracle at Cana: "Wine to serue here haue þai nane" (4943)	John 2:1–11
5153–5216	Christ preaches, heals, calls Disciples	Matt. 4:23–25; 5:1; Luke 6: 13–16
5217–5296	Exorcises demon at Capharnaum: "What man es he þat chaces þe fende / Out of men þus for to wende?" (5283–84)	Luke 4:31–37
5297–5370	Jesus calms the storm: "And als þai went in waters depe, / Jesu oure Lord was laid to slepe" (5317–18)	Matt. 8:23–27
5441–5524	"lat ded men ded corses delue" (5492)	Luke 9:57–62
5525–5610	Jesus reads from the book of Isaias	Luke 4:14–22; Is. 61:1–2
[vol. 2]		
5695–5770	Parable of the Vineyard: "Þus sall sum men be last / Þat in þis werld was first rotefast" (5757–58)	Matt. 20:1–16
6087–6161	Parable of the Sower	Luke 8:4–15
6224–6273	Jesus predicts Crucifixion; heals blind man	Luke 18:31–43

Lines	Events	Bible
	in Jericho: "I bid þe þat þou se, / For þi sad trowth has saued þe"	
6456–6545	Treasure in Heaven: "'Whare þou drawes þi tresor till / þare es þi hert with all þi will'" (6520–21)	Matt. 6:16–24
6546–6689	How to pray: "þi lift hand wit noght / What es with þi right hand wroght" (6618–19); Pater Noster	Matt. 5:43–48; 6:1–15
6690–6831	Temptation in the Desert: "Wend hethin oway, wikked Sathanas" (6816)	Matt. 4:1–11
6930–7123	Rebukes searchers of signs	Matt. 12:38–50
7124–7231	Heals Canaanite Woman's daughter: "litell whelpis ettes of þe crumes / Þat fra þaire lordes burdes cumes" (7200–7201)	Matt. 15:21–28
7258–7429	Parable of the Prodigal Son	Luke 15:11–32
7444–7639	Jesus counters charges of sorcery	Luke 11:14–23
7719–7803	"Praised in his kith prophet es nane" (7739)	Luke 4:22–30
7804–7875	Christ on forgiveness	Matt. 18:15–22
7876–7981	Christ reproves the Pharisees: "Blind þai er, þat sall ȝe ken, / And also leders of blind men" (7946–47)	Matt. 15:1–20
7982–8035	"I am þe brede of lastand life" (8030)	John 6:27–35
8036–8387	Woman of Samaria: "In syn so hastou led þi liue / With oþer wiues husbandes fiue" (8170–71)	John 4:5–42
8522–8627	Woman taken in adultery	John 8:1–11
8628–8685	Feeding of the five thousand	John 6:1–14
9240–9401	Cleanses Temple	John 2:13–25
9402–9531	Jews marvel at Christ's teaching	John 7:14–31
9532–9795	Heals blind man at Siloe	John 9:1–38
9796–9887	Jesus does the work of the Father	John 5:17–29
9888–10159	Raising of Lazarus	John 11:1–45
10160–10217	"Of þis werld I am þe light"	John 8:12–20
10218–10295	Jesus called a Samaritan: "I am / Byfor þe tyme of Abraham" (10288–89)	John 8:46–59
10492–10543	"to þat place þat I am in / May ȝe noght cum by no kins gin"	John 7:32–39
10544–10617	"My tyme es noght ȝit cumen till toun, / And ȝowre tyme es ay redy boun"	John 7:1–13
10618–10709	"ȝe er noght of my schepe"	John 10:22–38
10710–10781	Disputes over Christ's Messiahship	John 7:40–53
10782–10791	Bread and blood of life: "'No man may	John 6:54–71

Lines	Events	Bible
	cum to me,' he said, / 'Bot þat my Fader has puruaid" (10856–57)	
10892–11123	Anointing at Bethany; Palm Sunday; Philip and Andrew; "A voice þan come doun fra heuyn" (11048)	John 12:1–36
11124–11263	Washes Disciples' feet	John 13:1–15

[Nevanlinna here omits the account of the Passion as edited by Foster,
Northern Passion: Four Parallel Texts]

11264–11322	Angel appears to the three Marys	Mark 16:1–7
11601–11726	Appears to Cleophas and "St Peter" on the road to Emmaus	Luke 24:13–35
11821–11900	Appears to the Disciples; eats "Rosted fissch" and "A hony camb" (11865–66)	Luke 24:36–47
11901–11990	Appears to Disciples; Doubting Thomas	John 20:19–31
12121–12174	Christ the good shepherd	John 10:11–16
12379–12416	" 'A litell while,' he said, 'sall be / In þe whilk ʒe sal noght me se' " (12381–82)	John 16:16–22
12593–12644	"þe prince of þis werld bes kast out"	John 16:5–14
12701–12734	"In prouerbes speke I þus ʒow to; Als so say, I shal it vndo" (12709–10)	John 16:23–30
12767–12786	Exemplum: the Mother of the Sons of Zebedee prays for them	Matt. 20:20–23
12831–12872	Christ commissions Disciples; ascends to heaven	Mark 16:14–20
13007–13038	Christ predicts persecution of Disciples	John 15:26–27; 16:1–4
13149–13194	Pentecost; seven gifts of the Holy Spirit	Acts 2:1–4
13195–13260	Christ promises the Holy Spirit	John 14:23–31
13363–13400	"My Fader lufed þis werld so / Þat he gaf his awin sun to slo" (13367–68)	John 3:16–21
13487–13634	Heals man lowered through roof	Luke 5:17–26
13799–13908	Heals Simon's wife's mother and others	Luke 4:38–44
13909–14091	Nicodemus and being born again	John 3:1–15
14092–14129	Exemplum: Moses and the brazen serpent	Num. 21:6–9
14178–14319	" 'Man,' he said, 'etis angell brede' " (14191); Red Sea Crossing; Manna from Heaven; Seven Works of Bodily Mercy	Ps. 77:25; Ex. 14:21–28; 16:15–20; Matt. 25:35–46
14462–14475	Institution of Eucharist	Luke 22:19
14490–14509	Damnation of unworthy communicants	1 Cor. 11:27–29
14510–14595	Bread from Heaven	John 6:53–58
14850–14927	Dives and Lazarus	Luke 16:19–31
14992–15035	Parable of the Bridal Feast	Luke 14:16–24

Lines	Events	Bible
15194–15285	Parable of the Rich Fool: "Ett now and drink and mak gude chere" (15259)	Luke 12:11–21
15286–15343	Parables of the Lost Sheep, Lost Coin	Luke 15:1–10
15390–15469	Narracio of the Fall of the Angels; Creation of Adam and Eve; Prohibition; Temptation; Fall; Expulsion	Gen. 2; 3
15470–15543	Christ preaches wise sayings: "First fra þine eghe þe balk þou take" (15514)	Luke 6:36–42
[vol. 3]		
15628–15758	Miraculous draught of fishes: "fisschers of men sall ȝe be" (15726)	Luke 5:1–11
15981–16118	Sermon on the Mount: "He þat in his hert haldes wa / And til his broþer sais 'racha,' / Ðat es noght bot a schewing kyd / Of ire þat es in þe hert hid" (16045–48)	Matt. 5:20–24
16119–16310	Gerasene swine: "Ðai prayde him pas fra þaire cuntresse / And wende to sum oþer cetesse" (16285–86)	Matt. 8:28–34; Mark 5:1–20
16311–16362	Feeding of the four thousand	Mark 8:1–9
16419–16496	Lord of the Sabbath	Matt. 12:1–9
16497–16716	Sermon on the Mount: "Whare se ȝe men on euills or morns / Gedir grapes opon þe thornes?" (16559–60)	Matt. 7:15–28
16717–16778	"if þin eghe sklander þe / Put it out, þat rede I þe" (16767–68)	Mark 9:38–48
16779–16844	Parable of the Unjust Steward	Luke 16:1–9
16899–16974	Rebukes Pharisees and Lawyers	Luke 11:37–46
16975–17037	Cleanses Temple	Luke 19:41–47
17212–17262	Parable of the Pharisee and the Publican	Luke 18:9–14
17545–17586	Heals dumb man: "Effeta" (17567)	Mark 7:31–37
17721–17789	Heals two blind men and a dumb man	Matt. 9:27–35
17790–17882	How to attain eternal life; the Good Samaritan	Luke 10:23–37
18855–18896	Heals ten lepers: "Whare er now nien of þam bicumen?" (18886)	Luke 17:11–19
18975–19063	Heals leper	Mark 1:40–45
19130–19313	Sermon on the Mount: "No man may / Serue twa lordes vnto pay" (19130–31)	Matt. 6:24–34
19314–19453	Exorcises spirit from boy	Mark 9:17–29
19454–19638	Anointing by Mary Magdalen: "And with þe hares of hir heuid / Mi fete to dri has scho noght leuid" (19605–6)	Luke 7:36–50
19771–19883	Fruitless tree; heals infirm woman	Luke 13:6–17

Lines	Events	Bible
19884–19933	Raises Widow of Nain's son	Luke 7:11–17
20105–20180	Heals dropsical man; Parable of the Bridal Feast	Luke 14:1–11
20181–20268	The Greatest Commandment; Christ the Son of David	Matt. 22:35–46
20269–20324	Parable of the Tares	Matt. 13:24–30
20325–20384	"Rise vp and þi bed with þe ta, / And hame vnto þi hows þou ga"	Matt. 9:1–8
20385–20520	Christ explains Parable of the Tares	Matt. 13:36–43
20521–20607	Parable of the Marriage Feast	Matt. 22:1–14
20696–20771	Heals nobleman's son	John 4:46–53
20842–20925	Parable of the Unforgiving Servant	Matt. 18:23–35
21020–21075	Tribute to Caesar: "Gifes Cesar his thing more and les, / And gifes vnto God þat his es"	Matt. 22:15–21
21158–21325	Heals woman with issue of blood; raises Jairus's daughter	Matt. 9:18–26
21482–21539	Feeding the five thousand	John 6:5–14

Prose Gospel Commentaries and Lives of Christ

It may seem fanciful but nevertheless is true to say that, if all the non-Wycliffite versions containing New Testament translations were assembled, virtually the entire New Testament was translated into Middle English prose before that project was undertaken by Wyclif, Hereford, Purvey, and associates ca. 1380–92. The Gospels received the most attention, but the other New Testament texts found vernacular expression. Scholarship has concentrated on the earlier and later versions of the Wycliffite Bible at the expense of these texts even though they provide evidence of widespread biblical translation independent of and in most cases earlier than the Wycliffite versions.

Identifying a text as Wycliffite or non-Wycliffite is always debatable simply because the majority of relevant manuscripts date from the fifteenth century, when Lollard influence was common, and when in fact Lollards were appropriating texts already in existence (**RPs** provides the clearest example of this kind of appropriation). There is, however, an identifiable tradition of prose translations independent of Wyclif which the following sections identify and discuss. Four obvious categories emerge: the Gospels, Acts, the Pauline and Catholic Epistles, and Revelation.

Middle English versions of the Gospels had recourse to source material well beyond that provided by the "Historia Evangelica" in the *Historia Scholastica* and beyond even what the Gospels themselves have to say. Elaborating the life and work of Christ was as widely practiced as elaborating and explaining the Old Testament narrative. While brief recapitulations of the Creation and Fall often precede gospel material, the New Testament works are not as concerned with history as are their Old Testament counterparts. They are, in general, devotional and meditative, not historical and expository.

The Gospels found their most common and consistent presentation in the various gospel harmonies and "Lives of Christ" which flourished in many forms at least as early as Tatian (2d c.). Four major Latin lives of Christ, which were extremely popular throughout the Middle Ages, were translated in their entirety into Middle English. They are the *Speculum Humanae Salvationis* (*SHS;* see above at **MMS**), Clement of Llanthony's *Unum ex Quattuor,* Ludolphus of Saxony's *Vita Christi,* and the Ps.-Bonaventuran *Meditationes Vitae Christi* (*MVC*). Excerpting and splicing these works with each other, and with other religious texts, were common practices.

The "Commentaries" on Matthew, Mark, and Luke MML

Manual, 2:395 [39], and see 2:395 [38] for the (unedited) "Glossed Gospels," connected to the Wycliffite translations.

1. Cambridge, Univ. Lib. Ii.2.12 (1r–147v), early 15th c. (Matthew). A note on 1r reads "A man of þe north cuntre drogh þis in to Englisch."
2. London, BL Egerton 842 no. 1, 14th c. (Matthew).
3. Cambridge, Corpus Christi College 32 (1r–154v), early 15th c. (Mark and Luke).

No edition.

Scholars usually consider these commentaries together, though the Matthew commentary exists independently of those on Mark and Luke. All three consist of the Latin text, an English translation, and standard patristic commentary. The absence of John would appear to be due to the commentary on that Gospel having been lost instead of omitted.[1]

Forshall and Madden identify a northern dialect of the mid-fourteenth century and print one of the prologues to Matthew which shows that translation, and not commentary, is the main purpose of the work: "sethyn the gospelle is rewle, be the whilk ich cristen man owes to lyf, and dyuers has draghen in to Latyn, the whilk tung is not knowen to ilk man but only to the leryd, and many lewd men are, that gladly wold kon the gospelle if it were

---

1. "[I]ts existence can be inferred from the fact that its prologue together with those of the other Gospels precedes the Commentary on Matthew in MS. Camb. Univ. Libr. Ii.2.12" (Paues, *English Biblical Version* [1904], xxvii, n. 1).

draghen in to Englisch tung, and so it suld do grete profete to man saule, about the whilk profete ilk man that is in the grace of God, and to whome God has sent konnyng, owes hertely to busy him."[2]

In manuscript 3 the Mark and Luke commentaries appear before a translation of the Pauline Epistles (PE).

Oon of Foure OF

IPMEP 525
Manual, 2:394 [37]

1. Oxford, Bodleian Lib. Bodley 771 (*SC* 2553) (1r–79v), ca. 1400.
2. London, BL Arundel 254 (2r–86r), late 14th c.
3. London, BL Harley 1862 (7r–77v), ca. 1400.
4. London, BL Harley 6333 (1r–138v), earlier 15th c.
5. London, BL Royal 17.C.xxxiii (2r–225r), ca. 1400.
6. London, BL Royal 17.D.viii (1r–171r), late 14th c.
7. New York, Columbia Univ. Lib. Plimpton 268 (1r–225r, missing 88, 91, 92), earlier 15th c.
8. San Marino, Huntington Lib. HM 501 (140v–145r), 15th c., partial text.
9. Oxford, Bodleian Lib. Bodley 481.
10. Oxford, Bodleian Lib. Bodley 978 (4).
11. Oxford, Christ Church Allestree F.4.1.
12. Cambridge, St. John's College 193 G.25 (68r–85r).
13. Peterborough, Cathedral Lib. 3.
14. Glasgow, Univ. Lib. 223 (13r).

Complete number of manuscripts is undetermined.

No edition.

Studies: Hudson, *Premature Reformation,* 267–68; Salter, "Ludolphus of Saxony"; Deanesly, *Lollard Bible,* 303; Forshall and Madden, *Holy Bible,* 1:x–xii.

Oon of Foure translates Clement of Llanthony's *Unum ex Quattuor* (mid-twelfth c.) in twelve books; the translation was made in the late fourteenth

---

2. Forshall and Madden, *Holy Bible,* 1:x, n. f, quoting from manuscript 1. Hudson, *Premature Reformation,* briefly reviews the very literal character of the Matthew commentary and notes that the sentiments expressed "could be conservatively Wycliffite" (414). Other discussions of these texts can be found in M. Powell, *Pauline Epistles,* ix–xvi; Ekwall, "Manuscript Collections," 27, and Deanesly, *Lollard Bible,* 279, 310.

century. Because it is very close to the earlier version of the Wycliffite Bible, Wyclif was once thought to have been responsible.

Clement's harmony was one of the largest and most complete medieval collections of New Testament material. The preface, which was also translated into Middle English, associates the work with a tradition of gospel harmonies: those by the "olde grek doctour armonyus," Theophilus bishop of Antioch, and Augustine are mentioned.[3] The translator, following Clement, continues:

> for not alle gospeleres seyn alle þingis,
> & þo þingis which þei seyn þei seyn not
> alle þingis bi kindeli ordre in her place.[4]

Manuscript 3 appends excerpts, from throughout the Bible, beyond the scope of Clement's work. They predate any Wycliffite production and are another set of English Bible translations independent of the Lollard Bible. Forshall and Madden describe these excepts as "whatever in holy Scripture was thought necessary to be learned."[5] They print these excerpts:

The Lord interrogates and curses Cain: "Vagaunt amd fliȝti thou schalt ben on erthe"	Gen. 4:10–15
The Lord's blessings on Israel	Deut. 28:1–8
The Lord's judgments	Wis. 17:1–3
"What worthi thing schal Y offren to the Lord?"	Mic. 6:6–8
"beth foleweris of God"	Eph. 5:1–5
The Incarnation	Phil. 2:5–11
The purpose of the Law	1Tim. 1:8–11
The Whore of Babylon: "a goldene cuppe in hire hond, ful of abhominacioun and vnclennesse of hire fornycacioun"	Rev. 17:1–5

Versions of Ludolphus of Saxony's *Vita Christi* (*Speculum Vitae Christi*) VC

Manual, 9:3108 [64]

---

3. Augustine's *De Consensu Evangelistarum* (CSEL 43; also PL 34.1041–1230) may have been known to the translator directly. For Theophilus (*Ad Autolycum,* ed. and trans. Robert M. Grant [Oxford, 1970]) he relies on the witness of Jerome, and for "Armonyus" (Orosius? An epithet for the "harmonizer"?) the witness of Eusebius.

4. Salter, *Myrrour,* 77, where she quotes from London, BL Harley 1862, fol. 7r, col. 1. Cf. John 20:30 and 21:25.

5. Forshall and Madden, *Holy Bible,* 1:xii, n. u. They print the selections on xi and xii.

Exceeding Clement of Llanthony's *Unum ex Quattuor* in size and popularity is Ludolphus of Saxony's *Vita Christi*.[6] It circulated widely in almost every European vernacular. Ludolphus (d. 1377) composed his work in the mid-fourteenth century and it appears in Middle English in fifteenth-century manuscripts. Because of its late date the *Vita Christi* was used primarily by fifteenth- and sixteenth-century authors such as the Scottish poet Walter Kennedy in his *Passion of Christ* (**HCK**).

The *Vita Christi* incorporates (among many other sources) parts of another major medieval life of Christ, the *Meditationes Vitae Christi* (*MVC*), though Ludolphus's work did not enjoy nearly the influence of the *MVC*. See Sargent, *Nicholas Love's Mirror*, xxv–xxvi.

The *Vita Christi* was adapted into two Middle English prose works (see Salter, "Ludolphus of Saxony"):

John Fewterer's *Myrrour or Glasse of Christes Passioun*

No edition: 1534 printing by Robert Redman (*STC* 14553).

Fewterer was confessor general of Syon Monastery in the early sixteenth century.

A translation made from Guillaume le Menand's fifteenth-century French version:

1. London, BL Add. 16609 (1r–236v), 16th c.
2. Edinburgh, Univ. Lib. 22 (1r–291v, missing 266–270), 16th c.

No edition.

Nicholas Love's *Mirrour of the Blessed Life of Jesu Christ* MBL

IPMEP 553
Manual, 9:3103 [61]

1. Cambridge, Univ. Lib. Add. 6578 (1r–124r), early 15th c.
2. Cambridge, Univ. Lib. Add. 6686 (pp. 4–216), early 15th c.
3. Oxford, Brasenose College E.ix (1r–149v), ca. 1430.

Forty-seven other complete manuscripts, seven fragments, one composite text, and nine early printings.[7] See Sargent, *Nicholas Love's Mirror* lxxii–

---

6. See Conway, *Vita Christi,* and Bodenstedt, *Vita Christi.* Ludolphus apparently made independent consultation of the *Historia Scholastica;* see Bodenstedt, 32, 46, 137.

7. The composite text is Cambridge, Trinity College 61 (B.2.18). It is a *Myrrour* manuscript which, however, begins with a narrative of the Fall and the Flood, continues with a

lxxxv. For other manuscripts of a translation of the Passion section, see below following the summary of contents.

Editions: 1 and 2—Sargent, *Nicholas Love's Mirror;* 3—L. Powell, *Mirrour. Study:* Oguro et al. *Nicholas Love.*

MBL is based on the thirteenth-century *Meditationes Vitae Christi* (*MVC*), without question the most popular devotional work dealing with Christ in medieval England.[8] Parts of its Passion section (chapters 73–85) were versified in Middle English circa 1315–1330 (**MS**), and it exists in numerous prose versions culminating in Nicholas Love's work, finished in 1409.[9]

Although the *MVC* is almost invariably ascribed to St. Bonaventure (d. 1274), it may actually be the work of friar John de Caulibus or of someone else. Scholars have also speculated that the *Meditaciones de passione Christi* (*MPC*), which forms a part of the whole *Vita*, was indeed Bonaventuran, but the most recent editor of the Passion section concludes that the whole work is Ps.-Bonaventuran.[10] Stallings claims in addition that "the *MPC*, conceived of as a work separate from the *MVC*, is English in origin."[11] The authorship debate is complicated; Sargent reviews the subject in his introduction (ix–xx). Suffice it to say that the *MVC* and Love's translation were the products of Franciscan spirituality (although Love was himself a Carthusian) and exercised widespread influence.

Love's preface provides some insight into the climate of lay devotion and Bible reading in the early fifteenth century. He explains why texts are written, who should read them, and how. Archbishop Arundel licensed this translation in 1410 "ad fidelium edificationem et hereticorum sive Lollardorum confutationem." Thus Arundel's 1408 ban must be seen as a reaction against Wyclif himself, and not against vernacular texts in general, since he obviously recognized the need for this kind of devotional text in the ver-

---

Life of the Virgin, and ends with the raising of Lazarus. Love's text then follows. Sargent (*Nicholas Love's Mirror,* cxxxiv) notes an edition in progress—*The Life of the Virgin Mary and of the Christ*—by Martha Driver.

8. Peltier, *MVC,* 12:509–630. See the translation by Ragusa and Green, *Meditations.*

9. A prose version of the *MVC,* in an Hours of the Cross format from the Agony in Gethsemani to post-Resurrection appearances, is the *Privity of the Passion* in Lincoln, Cathedral Lib. 91 (Lincoln Thornton) (179r–189r) (*IPMEP* 837; *Manual,* 9:3106 [62]; Horstmann, *Yorkshire Writers,* 1:198–218).

10. Stallings, *MPC.* The Ps.-Bede *De Meditatione Passionis Christi per septem diei horas Libellus* (PL 94.561–68) is second only to Scripture as a source. Edmund Colledge, "Source for Pseudo-Bonaventure," pursues the authorship question, and see Pickering, "Devotional Elements," 156–61 and Bestul, *Texts of the Passion,* 48.

11. Stallings, *MPC,* 36.

nacular.[12] At the same time he made official the version which, in various formats, already had been the primary source for transmitting the gospel story to lay people for over one hundred years.

Another Latin prefatory note indicates that marginal comments marked by "N" are the translator's or the compiler's; those with "B" are (or were thought to be) by Bonaventure himself. The distinction is not completely reliable, but it does demonstrate some sensitivity toward how original texts and commentary differ.[13] Love then quotes Rom. 15:4 in Latin and then in English: "þat alle thynges þat ben writen generaly in holichirche ande specialy of oure lorde Jesu crist þei bene wryten to oure lore that by pacience & conforte of holi scriptures we haue hope that is to say of the Life & Blysse that is to come in anothere worlde" (Sargent, *Nicholas Love's Mirror,* 9). The purpose of religious writing is linked directly to salvation.

Love then considers the role played by writings such as the *MVC:* "Wherfore nowe boþe men & women & euery Age and euery dignite of this worlde is stirid to hope of euery lastyng lyfe. Ande for þis hope & to þis entent with holi writte also bene wryten diuerse bokes & trettes of devoute men not onelich to clerkes in latyn, but also in Englyshe to lewde men & women & hem þat bene of symple vndirstondyng. Amonge þe whiche beþ wryten deuovte meditacions of cristes lyfe more pleyne in certeyne partyes þan is expressed in the gospell of the foure euaungelistes" (Sargent, *Nicholas Love's Mirror,* 10).

The distinction between commentary and Scripture itself is again made. Also noteworthy is the egalitarian appeal regardless of sex, age, or social status (the *MVC* is itself directed to a female) and the acceptance of English as a possible medium, even if it serves only those of "symple vndirstondyng." But most noteworthy is the statement that the commentaries are "more pleyne." Obscurities and points of theological debate are omitted: Love provides the "mylke of lyȝte doctryne, & not [the] sadde mete of grete clargye of hye contemplacion" (Sargent, *Nicholas Love's Mirror,* 10; cf. 1Cor. 3:1–3). Love essentially counsels his readers not to get stuck on the metaphors. Hence the work is a "Mirror," not just as a reflection of Christ's life so that it may be imitated but as a means to achieve some sense of the "inuisible" nature of the Kingdom of Heaven.

---

12. Hudson, *Premature Reformation,* 437–40 and Sargent, *Nicholas Love's Mirror,* xliv–lviii consider the anti-Lollard character of the prefatory materials and of the work as a whole.

13. O'Connell, *Love's Mirrour,* concludes that Love's text is quite close to the Latin he worked from (5). The scribe who attributed the "N's" and "B's" was unaware of which manuscript tradition Love was following. See also Doyle, "Reflections," and Sargent, *Nicholas Love's Mirror,* xxx.

Love adds that "seynt Jon seiþ þat alle þo þinges þat Jesus dide, bene not written in the Gospelle" (Sargent, *Nicholas Love's Mirror,* 10; cf. John 20:30 and 21:25 and the preface to **OF**). The diversity of gospel accounts licenses the diversity and idiosyncrasy of the paraphrase and commentary. The Bible is still the supreme text, but paraphrases such as these "diuerse bokes and trettes" were regarded as a superior means of transmitting the contents of "holi writte" to nonclerics. The authors of the N-town Dramatic Cycle, for example, drew from **MBL**. See Sargent, *Nicholas Love's Mirror,* lxvi–lxxi).

The work is structured as a series of meditations on the life of Christ according to the days of the week. Love inserts frequent notes that he "passes over" or "leaves this matter" in order to avoid overtaxing the attention of his "simple" audience, though he often inserts passages to confute Lollardy.

The entire work is in prose, except for Gabriel's Annunciation to Mary which, apparently, Love himself versified (capitulum 3, pp. 29–30).

Direct quotations from Scripture are rubricated in manuscripts 1 and 2 (italicized in Sargent's edition):

Capitula	Event	Bible
[Monday]		
Proem	"And þouh hit so be þat þe bigynnyng of þe matire of þis boke, þat is the blessede lif of Jesu crist, be at his Incarnacion, neuereles we mowen first deuoutly ymagine & thenk sume þinges done before, touchyng god & his angeles in heuene, & also as anentes þe blessed virgyne oure lady seynt Marie" (13)	
1	Debate of the Four Daughters of God	Ps. 84:11
2	Petitions of the Virgin Mary for virtuous living	
3	Annunciation: "How & of what maner sal þis be done, siþen I know no man fleshly" (25)	Luke 1:26–38
4	Visitation of Elizabeth	Luke 1:42–47, 57–68
5	The angel calms Joseph's doubts	Matt. 1:18–20
6	Decree of Caesar Augustus; journey to Bethlehem; the ox and ass; angels appear to the shepherds	Luke 2:1–5; Is. 1:3; Luke 6:24; 2:8–14; Heb. 1:6; Is. 9:6
7	The Circumcision; "þer is none oþere name vndur heuen in þe which we owen to be sauede" (40)	Luke 2:21; Acts 4:12; 1Tim. 6:8
8	Epiphany	Matt. 2:11–12; Ps. 44:3
9	Presentation in the Temple (Candlemass); Simeon and Anna	Luke 2:22–38; Ps. 47:10–11

Capitula	Event	Bible

[Tuesday]

10	Flight to Egypt: "þe angel of god appered to Joseph in his slepe" (51); fall of Egyptian idols	Matt. 2:13–14; Is. 19:1
11	Return to Israel; Archelaus; "I am pore & in diuerse trauailes fro my first ȝouh" (56)	Matt. 2:19–23; Ps. 87:16
12	Christ disputes with the Temple Doctors: "'Dere son, what has þou done to vs in þis maner?' . . . 'know ȝe not wele þat it behoueþ me to be occupied in þo þinges þat longen to þe wirchipe of my fadere'"? (59)	Luke 2:41–49
13	Miscellaneous verses on Christ's youth, otherwise "noȝht expressed in scripture autentike" (61): "Mannus sone came not to be seruet, but to serue" (63)	Luke 2:52; Ps. 21:7; Prov. 16:32; Luke 17:10; Gal. 6:3; Matt. 13:55; 9:34; 25:40; 20:28; 1Tim. 6:8
14	Christ's Baptism: "Lord I sholde be baptizede of þe & þou comest to me?" (66); "Lerneþ of me for I am mylde & meke in herte" (67)	Matt. 3:13–17; Luke 3:23; Matt. 11:29

[Wednesday]

15	Temptation in the Desert: "If þou be goddussone sey þat þees stones be made & turnede in to brede loues" (73); feeds five thousand; Woman of Samaria; Habacuc feeds Daniel; "Lo he þat doþe awey þe synnes of þe world" (77)	Mark 1:13; Matt. 5:8; 4:1–11; 14:19; Luke 6:1; John 4:6–8; Dan. 14:33–35; Ps. 135:25; John 1:29–32
16	Jesus reveals himself; calls Disciples: "Comeþ aftur me for I sal make ȝow fisheres of men" (79)	Luke 4:16; Is. 61:1–2; Ps. 44:3; Luke 5:3; Matt. 4:19; Luke 6:14–16
17	Miracle at Cana: "What is þat to me & to þe woman?" (82); "sitte & take þi stede in þe lowest place" (81)	John 2:1–12; Luke 14:10
18	Sermon on the Mount: "Blessed be þei þat bene pore in spirite, for hire mede is þe kyngdom of heuen" (85); Pater Noster	Matt. 5:1–3; Ps. 12:2; Matt. 6:10–13; Wis. 4:7
19	Heals Centurion's sick servant and the "king's" son	Matt. 8:5–7; John 4:46–50
20	Heals paralytic	Mark 2:3–4
21	Heals the Woman with an issue of blood (Martha, sister of Mary Magdalen)	Matt. 9:20–22

Capitula	Event	Bible
22	Anointing in Simon's house: "she kissed his fete oft & sadly wepyng & shedyng teres so þikke þat she weshe hese fete with hem . . . wipyng hees fete with hir her" (91); "If I haue not charite, soþely I am nouht" (92); Binding in earth and heaven	Luke 7:36–38, 47–50; 1Cor. 13:2; Matt. 16:19
23	Woman of Samaria: "I haue mete to ete þat ȝe knowe not" (97)	John 4:7, 8, 32
24	Plucking corn on the Sabbath: "As Dauid & hees men in nede eten þe prestes bred" (98)	Luke 6:1–5

[Thursday]

25	Feeds four thousand: "If I suffre hem go home aȝeyn in to hir owne house fasting, þei shole faile & perish by þe wey" (104)	Matt. 15:32
26	Flees those who would make him king; "He þat halt him self as ouht worþi when in soþenes he is nouht, he decyueþ foule him self" (106); "we bene vnworþi & veyn seruantes" (106)	John 6:15; Gal. 6:3; Luke 17:10
27	Parable of the Unrighteous Judge; "Askeþ & it shal be ȝiuen to ȝowe" (108); Christ walks on water: "I am he þat ȝe desiren, beþe not adrede"(110); "he beteþ euery childe þat he receyueþ to his grace" (110)	Luke 18:1–4; 11:5–9; Matt. 14:22–33; Heb. 12:6, 8
28	Objections of the Pharisees; the Bread of Life; Peter's affirmation	Matt. 15:1–3; John 6:35, 41, 66–69
29	Forsaking the world; "Lord, how grete is þe multitude of þi swetnesse þat þou hast hidde to hem þat dreden þe" (113–14)	Matt. 19:23–29; Ps. 30:20
30	Prophesies Crucifixion and Resurrection; Transfiguration: "þis is my bylouede son" (114)	Matt. 16:21, 28; 17:1–8
31	Heals the Cripple at Sheep Gate: "Go & wille þou sinne no more, lest worse wil falle to þe" (116); "What so euer befalle to þe rihtwiseman, it sal not make him sorye" (117)	John 5:2–14; Prov. 12:21
32	Cleanses Temple	Matt. 21:12–13
33	Martha and Mary: "þe best parte þat Marye chase" (119); excursus on the active and contemplative lives	Luke 10:38–42
34	Raises the ruler's daughter; the Widow of Nain's son; Lazarus; "Are þere not xij houres	Matt. 9:18–19, 23–25; Luke 7:11–15;

Capitula	Event	Bible
	of þe day?" (130); "Wille ȝe not be drunken with wyne in þe which is lechcryc" (134)	John 10:24, 25, 30; 11.3–44; Eph. 5:18
35	Jews conspire against Jesus, who retires to Ephrem	John 11:45–54
36	Anointing at Bethany; the Widow's farthing	John 12:1–6; Luke 21:1–3
37	Palm Sunday; weeps over Jerusalem; cleanses Temple	Matt. 21:1–13; Heb. 5:7
38	Tribute to Caesar; "Wo to ȝowe scribes & pharisees" (144); "mannus sone sal be betraiede fort be crucifiede" (144); Judas sells Jesus for thirty pence	Matt. 22:15–22; 23:13–33; 26:2, 14–16
39	Last Supper: "He þat with me putteþ his hande in to þe dishe" (148); washes Disciples' feet; institutes Eucharist: "þis doþ ȝe als oft os ȝe tak it in commemoracion & minde of me" (151); "how mykel is þe multitude of þi swetnes" (155); "Be not ȝour herte turblet, & drede it not. For as ȝe beleuen in god, so ȝe most beleue in me" (157, John 14:1)	Matt. 26:20–23; Luke 22:14–23; John 13:21–25, 4–8, 17; Matt. 26:26–28; Luke 22:19; Ps. 30:20; 83:3; John 13:27, 34–35; 14:1, 9, 11–12, 15, 23; 15:7, 24, 33; 16.33
[Friday]		
40	Agony in Gethsemani: "do awey fro me þis cuppe of sorowe" (164); the angel; Kiss; Arrest; Buffeting: "Prophecie nowe, & telle vs who smote þe last" (168)	Is. 53:7; Rom. 8:32; Ps. 54; 39:9; 108:5; Zach. 11:12; Luke 22:39–48; Jer. 18:20; Ps. 34:22; 21:12; Matt. 26:36–49, 67–68
41	Christ before Pilate and Herod: "I finde no cause of deþ in þis manne" (170); "Crucifye, crucifie him" (172)	Luke 23:1–16; Is. 53:2; Matt. 27:27–31; Mark 15:13
42	Road to Calvary; Simon of Cyrene; "ȝhe douhteres of Jerusalem, wepeþ not on me bot on ȝour self" (173–74); "he is now as in a parabole in alle hir mouþes" (175)	Luke 23:26; Is. 53:12; Ps. 68:12–13
43	Crucifixion (upright and recumbent); "He made oþer safe bot he may not now saue himself" (178)	Ps. 21:18; Matt. 27:38–42
44	Seven Last Words: "it is alle endete" (180); Centurion's words; "Betyde me neuer to be	Luke 23:34, 43, 46; John 19:26, 28, 30;

Capitula	Event	Bible
	ioyful bot in þe crosse of my lord Jesu Criste" (181)	Matt. 27:46, 54; Gal. 6:14
45	Thieves' legs broken; blood and water from Christ's side; "His swerde shalle perse þorh þine awne soule" (183)	John 19:32–34; Luke 2:35
46	Joseph of Arimathea and Nicodemus; Deposition; "I ȝaf my body to hem þat smyten it" (185)	John 19:38–39; Zach. 12:10; Is. 50:6
47	Burial in "a newe graue, whereinne none body was biriede before" (187)	John 19:40–42
48	Sorrows of Mary	
[Saturday]		
49	Peter recalls his denials: "he lokede on me" (192); Harrowing of Hell	Luke 22:61–62
[Sunday]		
50	Jesus appears to his mother	Ps. 117:24
51	The Marys, Peter and John at the tomb; the angel: "What seke ȝe him þat liueþ with hem þat ben dede?" (198)	Mark 16:3; Luke 24:1–5; John 20:1–15
52	"supposyng þat he hade bene a gardynere" (199); "Touche me not" (200)	John 20:15–18
53	Appears to Marys: "Goþe & seiþ to my breþerne, þat þei go in to Galile" (201)	Matt. 28:9–10
54	Appears to Peter	Luke 24:34
55	Appears to the souls newly delivered from Hell	
56	Appears on the road to Emmaus: "þi spech is gretely enflawmede as fir" (204)	Luke 24:13–33; Ps. 118:103; Luke 18:1
57	Appears to Disciples; eats honeycomb; "Pees to ȝowe" (205); "If we be felawes & perceyneres of þe passiones, we shole be perceyners of the consolaciones" (207)	Luke 24:36–43; John 20:19; 2Cor. 1:7
58	Doubting Thomas: "put in þi fingir" (208)	John 20:26–29
59	Commissions Disciples: "I am with ȝowe alle þe dayes in to þe worldes ende" (209)	Matt. 28:16–20
60	Appears to Disciples at the Sea of Tiberias; "badde him [Peter] feede his shepe" (210); appears to the Five Hundred	John 21:1, 15–17, 22; 1Cor. 15:6
61	Other appearances not specified in the Gospels	
62	Commissions Disciples; "Be not ȝour herte	Mark 16:14–16, 19;

Capitula	Event	Bible
	turblete" (213–14); the Ascension and reception in heaven: "I go vp to þe fadere" (219)	John 14:1, 28; Ps. 117:24; John 16:7; 14:28
63	Pentecost: "a wondirfull noys in brennyng tonges" (221)	Acts 2:1–4; John 16:7

A Treatise on the Sacrament follows.

Independent Prose Translation of the *Meditationes de passione Christi Manual*, 9:3106 [62]

1. Cambridge, Gonville and Caius College 669 /646 (1r–75r), 15th c.
2. Cambridge, Trinity College 322 (115v–180r), ca. 1500.
3. Oxford, Bodleian Lib. Laud misc. 23 (*SC* 655) (76r–101v), early 15th c.
4. Oxford, Bodleian Lib. Bodley 789 (*SC* 2643) (1r–51v), early 15th c.
5. Edinburgh, Univ. Lib. 91 (1r–33v), 15th c. (missing first chapter, on the Last Supper).
6. Tokyo, Takamiya 20 (the Last Supper chapter only, otherwise a manuscript of **MBL**).
7. Beeleigh Abbey, Maldon, Essex, Christina Foyle (1r–178v), early 15th c. (the Last Supper chapter only, otherwise a manuscript of **MBL**).
8. Oxford, Bodleian Lib. Laud misc. 174 (*SC* 668) (69r–76r), 15th c. (fragments).
9. Windsor, St. George's Chapel E.I.I (88r–95r), early 15th c. (fragments).
10. Cambridge, Univ. Lib. Ii.iv.9 (52r–55r) (chapter 1 only, on the Last Supper).

No edition.

The relationship of these texts to manuscripts of Love's version is very complicated, and it is unclear to what degree Love may have relied upon this translation.

See Sargent, *Nicholas Love's Mirror,* xxix–xxviii, and Reakes, "Prose Translation of *MPC* and Links with Manuscripts of Love's *Myrrour.*"

❖ III.G · *Epistles*

The Paulinc and Catholic Epistles

In *Piers Plowman,* Thought addresses the Dreamer as follows:

> And [Dobet] is ronne into religion and haþ rendred þe Bible,
> And precheþ to þe peple Seint Poules wordes,
> *Libenter suffertis insipientes cum sitis ipsi sapientes:*
> [Ye wise], suffreþ the vnwise wiþ ȝow for to libbe,
> And wiþ glad wille dooþ hem good, for so God yow hoteþ.[1]

Paul's words were rendered twice before Wyclif, in versions edited by Margaret Powell and by Anna Paues. Both versions were made sometime in the mid- to late fourteenth century, and both reflect Langland's sentiments that it is the duty of the wise to render and preach the Bible to those who are ignorant of it.

Pauline Epistles PE

IPMEP 536
Manual 2:399 [48]

1. Cambridge, Corpus Christi College 32 (155r–208v), early 15th c.

---

1. Langland, *Piers Plowman,* B.viii.90–94. This passage also appears in A.ix.82–85 (ca. 1360). The verse is 2Cor. 11:19. Cf. Gyb's comment "as euer rede I pystyll" on the shrewishness of his wife. The shepherd refers, presumably, to his reading of 1Cor. 7. *Secunda Pastorum,* in Cawley, *Wakefield Pageants,* 45.

Edition: M. Powell, *Pauline Epistles.*

The Mark and Luke commentaries (**MML**) appear before this translation of the Pauline Epistles. The connection is uncertain; although the handwriting changes, the style of illumination is the same, the vellum is of the same quality, and the arrangement and size of the columns are unchanged.[2] It may be supposed that the manuscript was meant to have some pretensions as a "New Testament."

Powell's conclusions concerning the contents may be summarized as follows. Passages of the Vulgate alternate with the sometimes ungrammatical but perfectly orthodox English translation and a few short glosses and amplifications. The frequency of the alternations varies from a verse to a whole chapter, but as a rule the passages to be translated become longer, and the amplifications become fewer, as the work progresses. Powell favors the possibility that "the translation was made for the writer's own use in giving instruction," perhaps in preaching and giving lectures, given the format of text followed by gloss, and the frequency of negative followed by positive phrasings.[3] Given also the diminishing number of glosses and the literality of the translation, she holds that it was not intended for ignorant priests or the congregation, though I do not see why someone completely ignorant of Latin could not make some use of the translation since it is syntactically complete, if sometimes inelegant.

We remain in the dark about the real use of such a manuscript; doubtless it had both public and private applications. Powell notes that the Latin text is "a fairly correct one, and is evidently based on a text of that English type . . . of the thirteenth century."[4] The apocryphal Epistle to the Laodiceans was copied but not translated, though space was left for a translation. Some manuscripts of the later Wycliffite version do translate this letter with an indication that some consider it to be noncanonical.

Pages	Bible
1–50	Rom. 1–16 ("Alle thynges þat ben writen. þat is of crist in holy bokys to oure doctrine þei ar wryten þat we thurgh pacience and comforth of holy wryttys hafe hope" [Rom. 15:4, p. 44])
51–100	1Cor. 1–16 ("ʒif I speke with aungelys tunge and mannys and hafe not forsoþe charyte. I am maad as sownande brass or as a cymballe

---

2. M. Powell, *Pauline Epistles,* xii.

3. M. Powell, *Pauline Epistles,* lix. E.g. Phil. 1:25: "I schal dwelle not lytyl while; but lenge I schal dwelle." There are frequent "that is to say" recapitulations, and some marginal notes may indicate that the work was read aloud (see xiv, xlviii, lxii).

4. M. Powell, *Pauline Epistles,* xxviii.

chymbande" [1Cor. 13:1, p. 86]; "When I was a lytyl chyld; I spac as a lytil child. and sauerd as a lytil chylde. and thoghte as a litil childe. . . . When forsoþ I am maad a man; I voydede þoo thynges þe whylke were of þe chyld. . . . Now forsoþe we seen by þe myrour in þe licnesse; þenne forsoþe we schal see; face to face" [1Cor. 13:11–12, p. 87])

101–133	2Cor. 1–13.
134–150	Gal. 1–6.
151–166	Eph. 1–6.
167–178	Philip. 1–4.
179–189	Col. 1–4.
190–191	Laodiceans (20 Latin verses, untranslated).
192–201	1Thess. 1–5.
202–207	2Thess.1–3.
208–220	1Tim. 1–6.
221–229	2Tim. 1–4.
230–235	Titus 1–3.
236–238	Philemon.
239–274	Hebrews 1–13.

Prose Version of Epistles, Acts, and Matthew PCE

IPMEP 263, 413
Manual 2:398 [47]

1. Cambridge, Selwyn College 108 L.1 (1r–139r), ca. 1400.
2. Cambridge, Corpus Christi College 434 (R.9) (1r–159r), 1425–50.
3. Oxford, Bodleian Lib. Holkham misc. 40 (132r–161r), 1400–1425.
4. Cambridge, Univ. Lib. Dd.12.39 (16r–72v), 1400–1450.
5. Oxford, Bodleian Lib. Douce 250 (*SC* 21824) (1r–80v), ca. 1400.
6. Columbia, Univ. of Missouri Lib. fragmenta manuscripta 176 (a leaf originally following fol. 35 in manuscript 5, containing Acts 16:32–38 and 17:1–6).

Editions: 1—Paues, *English Biblical Version,* (1902 and 1904).
   5—Paues, *English Biblical Version* (1902 and 1904), 209–25.[5]

---

5. The relationship of the 1902 and 1904 volumes is confusing. In 1902, Cambridge University Press printed her Uppsala thesis of that year under the title *A Fourteenth Century English Biblical Version consisting of a Prologue and Parts of the New Testament . . . together with some Introductory chapters on Middle English Biblical Versions.* The table of contents lists more chapters (without giving page numbers) than actually appear in the book. In 1904, Cambridge University Press printed the same set of Middle English texts, but with a con-

6—Hudson and Voigts, "Missing Leaf."

Manuscripts 1 and 2 contain the prologue, James, Peter, 1John, and the Pauline Epistles and form, Paues states, "the nucleus of the original composition"; Acts and the Matthew fragment (Matt. 1:1–6:13) were added later, perhaps "from some already existing version." [6] Manuscript 4 contains only the Acts of the Apostles. Manuscript 5 has parts of Matthew and Acts, and the Catholic Epistles in "an entirely different version" from the one in manuscript 1 except for 2–3John and Jude which manuscript 1 took from manuscript 5.[7] Manuscript 3 contains the Catholic and Pauline Epistles followed by the four Gospels according to the earlier Wycliffite version. As material was assembled from Genesis, Exodus, and nearly the entire New Testament, at least manuscripts 1 and 2 were intended to become some sort of "Bible." Paul's Letter to Philemon appears in none of the versions.

The prologue consists of a précis of Genesis and Exodus followed by a debate on the propriety of translation. The circumstances of the debate, wherein a learned brother debates another brother and a sister, probably indicate that the translation was made for the residents of some religious house. Unlike PF, these versions have no Latin, not even incipits. Given the importance of having the Latin present as a kind of control, its absence may account for the learned brother's unease if not for his fear of death.

The prologue abridges Gen. 1–9:17, ignoring the Creation of the World and emphasizing instead the Creation and Fall of Adam and Eve, the Fall of Lucifer, the sinful nature of mankind, and the Flood. Immediately after the covenant of the rainbow is retold, a voice interjects to begin the debate on the propriety of biblical translation.

The learned brother resumes his address at the end of Jude (the last of the Catholic Epistles) with an explanation concerning Paul's Epistles, which follow: "bote y ne may noȝt at þis tyme wryte to þe alle his pysteles as þei stondeþ; bote naþeles, ȝef it be Goddus wylle, þou schalt habbe hem heraftur." He continues with a summary of Paul's main teachings and then with what are essentially abstracts of each epistle. The compiler moves from important loci outwards. Even though he begins with Genesis, he does not move through the Bible sequentially. What in his opinion is the most impor-

---

sistent table of contents and a new introduction which left out the "chapters" on other versions, which remain in manuscript at the Lund University Library. See Ekwall, "Manuscript Collections," 23–41. All references to Paues are to the 1904 edition.

6. Paues, *English Biblical Version*, xvii.

7. See lxx. Paues prints manuscript 5 separately as Appendix I (*English Biblical Version*, 209–25).

tant material appears in condensed form, by way of abstract, paraphrase, and summary, rather than by a comprehensive and direct translation. Fuller versions are provided later when the compiler actually gets around to doing the work or when a suitable translation comes to hand. In the meantime what is essentially a subjectively compiled biblical digest substitutes for Scripture itself. Many of the manuscripts which contain biblical paraphrase show a tendency to accumulate material over time and to assume a comprehensiveness extending to both Testaments.

The paraphrase is noteworthy for its inclusion on pages 14–17 of Levitical laws and practices, and then the dismissal of their relevance on pages 47–48.

Pages	Events	Verses
1–3	Creation of Adam and Eve; Prohibition; Fall of Angels and Man; "for schame þei maden hem breches of leues" (3); "pouder þouart, & in-to pouder þou schalt be turned a-ȝeyn" (3)	Gen. 1:26–30; 2:15–17; 3
4	Cain and Abel (no mention of murder); Flood; Rainbow	Gen. 4:1–2; 6:5–8; 9:11–17
4–8	Dialogue between two brothers and a sister on the sinfulness of man and the propriety of biblical translation. Miscellaneous biblical quotations throughout	
8–9	Moses and Aaron; Pharaoh; Red Sea crossing	Ex. 1:13–14; 14
10	Mount Sinai; Ten Commandments; appointment of the Levites; Tabernacle	Ex. 19; 20; 28:41; 26
11	Golden Calf	Ex. 32
12	Moses sees God's glory	Ex. 33
13	Tables restored; horned Moses; cloud over the Tabernacle	Ex. 34; 40: 32–36
14	Service of Aaron, Levites	Ex. 28:41; Num. 3:6; 4:1–5
15	Laws on property, sodomy, theft, and thralldom	Ex. 20:3–17; 21:24–25; 22:7–9, 19
16	Laws on diet, clean and unclean beasts	Lev. 11:1–36
17	Treatment of lepers; purification of women; keeping holy days	Lev. 12; 13; 14; 15; 23

[Paues's edition marks chapter and verse numbers for the Epistles. Brief addresses by the brother to the sister introduce and conclude many of them.]

Pages	Events	Verses

18–24   1Pet. 1:3–5:11 (complete, omitting only last 3
           verses of ch. 5)

24–29   2Pet. 1:1–3:18 (complete)

29–35   James 1:1–5:20 (complete)

36–42   1John 1:1–5:21 (complete)

42–43   2John 1:1–13(complete)

43–44   3John 1:1–14 (complete)

44–47   Jude 1:1–25 (complete)

47–48   Dialogue resumes, with the sister inquiring to
           what degree faith in Christ obviates the need to
           follow the Old Law, especially since "we beþ noȝt
           of þe chyldren of Israel, for oure auncestres weren
           heþen men þat weren y-turned to byleuen in Crist
           by Poul þe apostel" (47). The brother answers that
           Paul teaches that the Old Law "ne was but a
           schadewe" (48)

48–54   Rom. 5:19–8:39

54–56   Rom. 12:1–13:14 ("Þe nyȝt is passed, & þe day
           wole neyȝlyche: & þerfore þrowe we a-wey werkes
           of derknesse, & be we cloþed wiþ armer of lyȝt. &
           walke we honestlyche as in day-tyme, noȝt in
           etynge out of mesure, ne in dronkenesse, ne in
           kouchynges abedde, ne in vnclannesse, ne in
           hatynge" [Rom. 13:12–13; cf. Augustine's
           Confessions 8.12, the famous "tolle, lege" passage])

56–59   1Cor. 1:10–3:23

59–64   1Cor. 5:1–7:40

64–68   1Cor. 11:1–13:13

68–69   2Cor. 6:1–18

69–71   Gal. 5:2–6:17

71–76   Eph. 4:1–6:24

76–77   Phil. 1:27–2:18

77–79   Phil. 3:1–4:9

79–83   Col. 1:9–4:8

84–88   1Thess. 1:2–5:25

88–91   2Thess. 1:3–3:16

91–109   Heb. 1:1–13:21 (complete except for 13:22–25)

109–116   1Tim. 1:1–6:21 (complete)

116–120   2Tim. 1:1–4:5 (complete except for 4:6–22)

120–122   Titus 1:5–3:11 (complete except for 1:1–4;
           3:12–15)

123–199   Acts 1:1–28:31 (complete)

199–208   Matt. 1:1–6:13 (ends with the Pater Noster)

Pages   *Events*   *Verses*

[Appendix I, texts from MS 5]
209–213   James
213–217   1Pet. (including 5:12–14)
217–221   2Pet.
221–225   1John

[Appendix II]
226–229   Variants from MS 3

Versions of Revelation

Apocalips of Jesu Crist, with commentary AJC

IPMEP 584
Manual 2:400 [49]

The Book of Revelation exists in two complete Middle English translations. They are independent of and prior to the Wycliffite translation, though several manuscripts attest to Wycliffite appropriation. Versions A and B contain virtually the same commentary.

Version A

1. London, BL Harley 874 (2r–31r), mid-14th c.
2. London, BL Harley 3913 (113v–203v), early 15th c.
3. London, BL Royal 17.A.xxvi (37r–106v), early 15th c.
4. Cambridge, Magdalene College Pepys 2498 (pp. 226–63), ca. 1400.
5. Cambridge, St. John's College 193 (G.25) (17r–67r), 15th c.
6. Cambridge, Gonville and Caius College 231/117 (1r–86v), 14th c., acephalous.
7. Oxford, Bodleian Lib. Laud misc.33 (*SC* 661) (96v–144v), 15th c.
8. Oxford, Bodleian Lib. Laud misc.235 (*SC* 1580) (265r–300r), later 14th c.
9. Oxford, Bodleian Lib. Rawlinson C.750 (fifty-one folios), 14th c.
10. Manchester, John Rylands Lib. 92 (forty-six folios), ca. 1400.
11. Dublin, Trinity College 69 (55v–64v, 72r–77r), 14th c.
12. New York, Columbia Univ. Plimpton Add. 3 (203r–237v), ca. 1400.

13. Cambridge, Trinity College 50 (B.2.7) (146 leaves in two volumes), 16th c.
14. Cambridge, Fitzwilliam Museum McClean 133 (227r–252r), 16th c.
15. London, BL Add. 5901 (248r), 18th c.

Edition: 1—Fridner, *Apocalypse Version*, with variants from 2–11, and with the French source text in parallel from Delisle and Meyer, *L'Apocalypse*.[1]

Version B

1. London, BL Harley 171 (2r–109r), late 14th c.
2. London, BL Harley 1203 (1r–63v), ca. 1400.
3. Cambridge, Magdalene College 5 (F.4.5) (40r–65r), 15th c. [an illustrated Latin text of the Apocalypse with commentary precedes, itself prefaced (fol. 1r) by two Middle English poems, *IMEV* 1793 and 4096, printed by Robbins, *Secular Lyrics*, 93–94].

Edition: 1—Sauer, *Übersetzung der Apokalypse.*

There are only minor omissions of verses in some manuscripts, the most notable being the omission of Rev. 1:1–8 in manuscript 1 and all three manuscripts of Version B. These verses appear in most of the other manuscripts, however.

The prologue translates and adapts the Latin of Gilbert de la Porée (d. 1154); it quotes Luke 12:13, Matt. 28:20, and John 16:33 in Version A (pp. 1–5 of Fridner); 2Tim. 3:12, Matt. 28:10, 20, and John 16:33 in Version B. This is the same prologue as in the *Glossa Ordinaria.*

Both translations are taken from the "Norman" Apocalypse, which survives in some of the earliest fragments from the Ile de France region; there are twenty-four manuscripts of this translation, the earliest being mid-thirteenth century.[2] Many are illustrated; perhaps half were produced in England. The same version appears in those copies of the *Bible Historiale* which include an Apocalypse. The French commentary is demonstrably Franciscan and thus post-1210, though the exact source is unknown.

In its original (pre-Wycliffite) form these Middle English translations may represent, after the Psalter, the first complete post-Conquest translation of

---

1. Fridner had access to unpublished materials deposited at the Lund University Library by Anna C. Paues, who was one of the first (around the turn of the century) to identify and work with these and many other Middle English biblical manuscripts. Unfortunately, much of her work remains in rough form. See Ekwall, "Manuscript Collections."
2. Delisle and Meyer, *L'Apocalypse.* See Brieger, *Trinity Apocalypse,* for discussion and facsimile of Cambridge, Trinity College R.16.2. The Anglo-Norman commentary is, however, in a separate tradition.

a biblical book. Four manuscripts, including manuscript 1, are "earlier than the Lollard Bibles, or at least uninfluenced by them," though manuscript 1 is erroneously attributed to Wyclif on an inserted leaf. Later manuscripts do show influence from Wyclif's later version, not vice versa, as Forshall and Madden demonstrate.[3]

The translations contain some phrases which appear neither in the French nor in the Vulgate. For example, Fridner notes that the translation of "je vos commencerei a vomir de ma bouche" is "þou makest me to wlaþþen. I schal bigynne to cast þe out of my mouthe by the fore feete."[4] The *Ancrene Riwle* quotes the same verse from Revelation as "þu makest me uorto wlatien. and ich chulle speouwen ðe ut. bute ȝif þu iwurðe hattre."[5] The added phrase ("you cause me to feel disgust") common to both the *Ancrene Riwle* and **AJC** suggests a coincidental use of an idiom, a common source, or a direct dependence. The phrase "by the fore feete" also has no counterpart, and one might speculate that it is a response to an illustration in one of the French manuscripts of a lukewarm Laodicean being vomited out.[6] Given the popularity and importance of the Apocalypse, especially in works like *Pearl, Piers Plowman,* and the lapidaries, closer investigations may well turn up more correspondences and signs of influence. The eschatological tenor of the later Middle Ages, which has received extensive critical attention, also enhances the significance of these Apocalypse translations.[7]

The apparatus in Fridner and Sauer make finding any given verse in either version a simple matter.

---

3. Forshall and Madden, *Holy Bible* 1:viii.

4. Fridner, *Apocalypse Version*, xxxvii. Version B is "for þou are neiþir hoote neiþir coold; but for þou art lewe, I schal bigynne to caste þee out of my mouþ" (Sauer, *Übersetzung der Apokalypse*). The Vulgate reads "sed quia tepidus es, et nec frigidus, nec calidus: incipiam te evomere ex ore meo" (Rev. 3:16).

5. Day, *Ancrene Riwle*, 183, lines 2–4.

6. Fridner suggests corruption of a phrase such as "by way of forfeit" (note to 3/16, p. 217), but the line is descriptive and meaningful enough as it stands. Another manuscript reads "be-fore her fet," but it is unclear who "they" are before whose feet the tepid believer is cast.

7. Gordon, *Pearl*, esp. line 781 ff.; Evans and Serjeantson, *Lapidaries*. See also Bloomfield, *Fourteenth-century Apocalypse*, and Emmerson, *Antichrist*, esp. chap. 5, which discusses **CM,** the *Pricke of Conscience*, the Chester Cycle, *Piers Plowman*, and other relevant texts.

Bibliography

Aarts, Florent G. A. M. *Þe Pater Noster of Richard Ermyte: A Late Middle English Exposition of the Lord's Prayer.* Nijmegen: Gebr. Janssen, 1967.

Adler, M., and M. Kaluza. "Studien zu Richard Rolle de Hampole. III. Ueber die Richard Rolle de Hampole zugeschriebene paraphrase der sieben busspsalmen." *Englische Studien* 10 (1887): 215–55.

Aelred of Rievaulx. *Aelred of Rievaulx's De Institutione Inclusarum: Two English Versions.* Edited by John Ayto and Alexandra Barratt. EETS os 287. London, 1984.

Alain de Lille. *Anticlaudianus or The Good and Perfect Man.* Translated by James J. Sheridan. Toronto: Pontifical Institute of Mediaeval Studies, 1973.

Alford, John A. "Biblical *Imitatio* in the Writings of Richard Rolle." *Journal of English Literary History* 40 (1973): 1–23.

———. "The Role of the Quotations in *Piers Plowman.*" *Speculum* 52 (1977): 80–99.

———. "Rolle's English Psalter and the Lectio Divina." *BJRL* 77 (1995): 47–59.

Allen, Hope Emily. *Writings Ascribed to Richard Rolle, Hermit of Hampole, and Materials for His Biography.* Modern Language Association of America Monograph Series, vol. 3. New York: D. C. Heath; London: Oxford University Press, 1927.

———, ed. *English Writings of Richard Rolle, Hermit of Hampole.* Oxford: Clarendon Press, 1931, 1963. Reprint. Gloucester, Mass.: Allen Sutton, 1988.

Anderson, J. J., ed. *Cleanness.* Manchester: Manchester University Press, 1977.

———, ed. *Patience.* Manchester: Manchester University Press, 1969.

———, ed. *Sir Gawain and the Green Knight, Pearl, Cleanness, Patience.* Everyman. London: J. M. Dent; Rutland, Vt.: Charles E. Tuttle, 1996.

Andersson-Schmitt, Margarete. "Die Verwendung der *Historia scholastica* in einigen volkssprachigen Bibelwerken des Mittelalters." *Kungl. Humanistiska Vetenskaps-Samfundet i Uppsala, Årsbok* (1985): 5–31.

Arngart, Olof. "St. Avitus and the *Genesis and Exodus* Poet." *English Studies* 50 (1969): 487–95.

———, ed. *The Middle English Genesis and Exodus.* Lund Studies in English, vol. 36. Lund: Gleerup, 1968.

Aston, Margaret. *Thomas Arundel: A Study of Church Life in the Reign of Richard II.* Oxford: Clarendon Press, 1967.

Audelay, John. *The Poems of John Audelay.* Edited by Ella Keats Whiting. EETS os 184. London, 1931. Reprint, 1971.

Augustine. *On Christian Doctrine.* Translated by D. W. Robertson, Jr. Indianapolis, Ind.: Bobbs-Merrill, 1958.

Baldwin, John W. "Masters at Paris from 1179 to 1215: A Social Perspective." In *Renaissance and Renewal in the Twelfth Century,* edited by Robert L. Benson and Giles Constable with Carol D. Lanham, 138–72. Cambridge, Mass.: Harvard University Press, 1982.

Barnum, Priscilla Heath, ed. *Dives and Pauper.* EETS os 275, 280. London, 1976–80.

Barratt, Alexandra. "The Prymer and Its Influence on Fifteenth Century English Passion Lyrics." *MÆ* 44 (1975): 264–79.

———, ed. *The Seven Psalms: A Commentary on the Penitential Psalms Translated from French into English by Dame Eleanor Hull.* EETS os 307. London, 1995.

Bately, Janet M. "Lexical Evidence for the Authorship of the Prose Psalms in the Paris Psalter." *Anglo-Saxon England* 10 (1982): 69–95.

Baugh, Nita Scudder. *A Worcestershire Miscellany Compiled by John Northwood, c. 1400. Edited from British Museum MS. Add. 37,787.* Philadelphia, 1956.

Bäuml, Franz H. "Varieties and Consequences of Medieval Literacy and Illiteracy." *Speculum* 55 (1980): 237–65.

Bazire, Joyce, and Eric Colledge, eds. *The Chastising of God's Children and the Treatise of Perfection of the Sons of God.* Oxford: Basil Blackwell, 1957.

Beadle, Richard. "The Origins of Abraham's Preamble in the York Play of *Abraham and Isaac.*" *Yearbook of English Studies* 11 (1981): 178–87.

Bede. *A History of the English Church and People.* Translated by Leo Sherley-Price. Revised by R. E. Latham. Harmondsworth: Penguin, 1968.

Belfour, A. O., ed. *Twelfth-Century Homilies in MS. Bodley 343 with an English Translation.* EETS os 137. London, 1909, 1962.

Bennett, J. A. W., ed. *Devotional Pieces in Verse and Prose from MS. Arundel 285 and MS. Harleian 6919.* Scottish Text Society, 3d series, vol. 23. Edinburgh: William Blackwood & Sons, 1955.

———. *Poetry of the Passion: Studies in Twelve Centuries of English Verse.* Oxford: Clarendon Press, 1982.

Berger, Samuel. *La Bible française au moyen âge: Étude sur les plus anciennes Versions de la Bible écrites en prose de Langue d'Oïl.* Paris: Imprimerie Nationale, 1884. Reprint. Geneva: Slatkine, 1967.

Berkhout, Carl T., and Jeffrey B. Russell. *Medieval Heresies: A Bibliography, 1960–79.* Toronto: Pontifical Institute of Mediaeval Studies, 1981.

Besserman, Lawrence L. *Chaucer's Biblical Poetics.* Norman: University of Oklahoma Press, 1998.

———. *The Legend of Job in the Middle Ages.* Cambridge, Mass.: Harvard University Press, 1979.

Besserman, Lawrence L., Gail Gilman, and Victor Weinblatt. "Three Unpublished Middle English Poems from the Commonplace-Book of John Colyns (B.M. MS Harley 2252)." *Neuphilologische Mitteilungen* 71 (1970): 212–38.

Bestul, Thomas H. *Texts of the Passion: Latin Devotional Literature and Medieval Society.* Philadelphia: University of Pennsylvania Press, 1996.

Biblia Pauperum. Facsimile ed. Edited by Avril Henry. Ithaca, N.Y.: Cornell University Press, 1987.

Biblia Sacra iuxta Vulgatam Clementinam. Ed. Alberto Colunga and Laurentio Turrado. 4th ed. Madrid: Biblioteca de Autores Cristianos, 1965.

Bishop, Edmund. *The Prymer or Lay Folks Prayer Book.* EETS os 109. London, 1897. Reprint, 1975. Vol. 2, introduction to EETS os 105, text ed. Henry Littlehales.

Black, William Henry, ed. *A Paraphrase on the Seven Penitential Psalms in English Verse, supposed to have been written by Thomas Brampton, S.T.P. in the year 1414, together with a Legendary Psalter of Saint Bernard, in Latin and in English Verse.* Publications of the Percy Society, vol. 7. London, 1842. Reprint. New York: Johnson Reprints, 1965.

Blake, N. F. "The Biblical Additions in Caxton's 'Golden Legend.' " *Traditio* 25 (1969): 231–47.

———, ed. *Middle English Religious Prose.* Evanston, Ill.: Northwestern University Press, 1972.

Bloomfield, Morton W. *Piers Plowman as a Fourteenth-century Apocalypse.* New Brunswick, N.J.: Rutgers University Press, 1961.

Blunt, John Henry, ed. *Myroure of oure Ladye.* EETS es 19. London, 1873. Reprint, 1973.

Bodenstedt, Mary Immaculate. *The Vita Christi of Ludolphus the Carthusian.* Studies in Medieval and Renaissance Latin Language and Literature, vol. 16. Washington, D.C.: Catholic University of America Press, 1944.

Boenig, Robert, ed. *Contemplations of the Dread and Love of God (1506).* Delmar, N.Y.: Scholars' Facsimiles and Reprints, 1990.

Boffey, Julia, and John J. Thompson. "Anthologies and Miscellanies: Production and Choice of Texts." In *Book Production and Publishing in Britain: 1375–1475,* edited by Jeremy Griffiths and Derek Pearsall, 279–315. Cambridge: Cambridge University Press, 1989.

Bolton, Brenda. "Innocent III's Treatment of the *Humiliati.*" In *Popular Belief and Practice,* edited by G. J. Cuming and Derek Baker, 73–82. SCH 8. Cambridge: Cambridge University Press, 1972.

Bonnard, Jean. *Les Traductions de la Bible en vers français au moyen âge.* Paris: Imprimerie Nationale, 1884. Reprint. Geneva: Slatkine, 1967.

Bosworth, Joseph, and T. Northcote Toller. *An Anglo-Saxon Dictionary.* Oxford: Clarendon Press, 1882–98. *Supplement* by T. Northcote Toller. Oxford: Oxford University Press, 1921. Enlarged Addenda and Corrigenda by Alistair Campbell. Oxford: Clarendon Press, 1972.

Bottigheimer, Ruth B. *The Bible for Children: From the Age of Gutenberg to the Present.* New Haven: Yale University Press, 1996.

Bowers, R. H., ed. *Three Middle English Religious Poems.* University of Florida Monographs in the Humanities, vol. 12. Gainesville: University of Florida Press, 1963.

Boyle, Leonard E. "The Fourth Lateran Council and Manuals of Popular Theology." In *The Popular Literature of Medieval England,* edited by Thomas J. Heffernan, 30–43. Tennessee Studies in Literature, vol. 28. Knoxville: University of Tennessee Press, 1985.

———. "Innocent III and Vernacular Versions of Scripture." In *The Bible in the Medieval World: Essays in Memory of Beryl Smalley,* edited by Katherine Walsh and Diana Wood, 97–107. SCH subsidia 4. Oxford: Basil Blackwell, 1985.

Brewer, D. S., and A. E. B. Owen, eds. *The Thornton Manuscript (Lincoln Cathedral MS. 91).* 2d facsimile ed. London: Scolar Press, 1977.

Brieger, Peter H. *The Trinity College Apocalypse.* 2 vols. Facsimile edition. London: Eugrammia Press, 1967.

Brink, Bernhard ten. *Geschichte der englischen Litteratur.* 2 vols. Berlin, 1877–93.

Brook, G. L., ed. *The Harley Lyrics: The Middle English Lyrics of MS. Harley 2253.* 2d ed. Manchester: Manchester University Press, 1956.

Brown, Beatrice Daw, ed. *The Southern Passion: Edited from Pepysian MS. 2344 in the Library of Magdalene College, Cambridge.* EETS os 169. London, 1927. Reprint, 1971.

Brown, Carleton. "The *Cursor Mundi* and the 'Southern Passion.'" *MLN* 26 (1911): 15–18.

———. "An Early Mention of a St. Nicholas Play in England." *SP* 28 (1931): 594–601. [pp. 62–69 of Royster Memorial Studies].

———. *A Register of Middle English Religious and Didactic Verse.* 2 vols. Oxford: Oxford University Press, 1916–20. Vol. 1, list of manuscripts; vol. 2, index of first lines and index of subjects and titles.

———. "The Towneley *Play of the Doctors* and the *Speculum Christiani.*" *MLN* 31 (1916): 223–26.

———, ed. *English Lyrics of the XIIIth Century.* Oxford: Clarendon Press, 1932.

———, ed. *Religious Lyrics of the XVth Century.* Oxford: Clarendon Press, 1939.

———, ed. *Religious Lyrics of the XIVth Century.* 2d ed. Edited by G. V. Smithers. Oxford: Clarendon Press, 1952.

Brown, Carleton, and Rossell Hope Robbins. *The Index of Middle English Verse.* New York: Columbia University Press, 1943.

Brunner, Karl, ed. "Mittelenglische Marienstunden." *Englische Studien* 70 (1935–36): 106–9.

———, ed. *Der mittelenglische Versroman über Richard Löwenherz.* Wiener Beiträge zur Englischen Philologie, vol. 42. Vienna: W. Braumüller, 1913.

———, ed. "Zwei Gedichte aus der Handschrift Trinity College, Cambridge 323 (B.14.39)." *Englische Studien* 70 (1935–36): 221–43.

Buchthal, Hugo. *Miniature Painting in the Latin Kingdom of Jerusalem.* Oxford: Clarendon Press, 1957.

Buehler, Philip. *The Middle English Genesis and Exodus: A Running Commentary on the Text of the Poem.* De Proprietatibus Litterarum: Series Practica, vol. 74. The Hague: Mouton, 1974.

Bühler, Curt F. "A Lollard Tract: On Translating the Bible into English." *MÆ* 7 (1938): 167–83.

———. "The Middle English Texts of Morgan MS. 861." *PMLA* 69 (1954): 686–92. Reprinted in *Early Books and Manuscripts: Forty Years of Research,* 498–502. New York: Grolier Club and Pierpont Morgan Library, 1973.

Bülbring, Karl D. *The Earliest Complete English Prose Psalter, together with Eleven Canticles and a Translation of the Athanasian Creed.* EETS os 97. London, 1891. Reprint, 1975.

Burchfield, Robert. "Line-End Hyphens in the *Ormulum* Manuscript (MS Junius I)." In *From Anglo-Saxon to Early Middle English: Studies Presented to E. G. Stanley,* edited by Malcolm Godden, Douglas Gray, and Terry Hoad, 182–87. Oxford: Clarendon Press, 1994.

Butterworth, Charles C. *The English Primers (1529–1545): Their Publication and Con-*

nection with the English Bible and the Reformation in England. Philadelphia: University of Pennsylvania Press, 1953. Reprint. New York: Octagon, 1971.

Campbell, Gertrude H., ed. "The Middle English *Evangelie.*" *PMLA* 30 (1915): 529–613, 851–53.

Caviness, Madeline H. "Biblical Stories in Windows: Were They Bibles for the Poor?" In *The Bible in the Middle Ages: Its Influence on Literature and Art,* edited by Bernard S. Levy, 103–47. Medieval and Renaissance Texts and Studies, vol. 89. Binghamton, N.Y.: 1992.

Cawley, A. C., ed. *The Wakefield Pageants in the Towneley Cycle.* Manchester: Manchester University Press, 1958, 1971.

Charland, Th.-M. *Artes praedicandi: Contribution à l'histoire de la rhétorique au moyen âge.* Publications de l'Institut d'études médiévales d'Ottawa, vol. 7. Paris: J. Vrin; Ottawa: Institut d'études médiévales, 1936.

Charlesworth, James H., ed. *The Old Testament Pseudepigrapha.* 2 vols. Garden City, N.Y.: Doubleday, 1983–85.

Chaucer, Geoffrey. *The Riverside Chaucer.* General editor Larry D. Benson. 3d ed. Boston: Houghton Mifflin, 1987.

Chaytor, H. J. *From Script to Print: An Introduction to Medieval Vernacular Literature.* Cambridge: W. Heffner, 1945.

Christopher, Georgia. *Milton and the Science of the Saints.* Princeton: Princeton University Press, 1982.

Cigman, Gloria, ed. *Lollard Sermons.* (BL Add. 41321, Bodleian Lib. Rawlinson C.751, John Rylands Lib. Eng 412.) Description of the manuscripts by Jeremy Griffiths; analysis of the language by Jeremy Smith. EETS os 294. London, 1989.

Clanchy, M. T. *From Memory to Written Record: England, 1066–1307.* 2d ed. Oxford: Blackwell, 1993.

Clark, Andrew, ed. *The English Register of Godstow Nunnery near Oxford, written about 1450.* EETS os 129. London, 1905. Reprint, 1971.

Clark, Cecily. "People and Languages in Post-Conquest Canterbury." *Journal of Medieval History* 2 (1976): 1–34.

———, ed. *The Peterborough Chronicle 1070–1154.* 2d ed. Oxford: Clarendon, 1970.

Coleman, Janet. *Medieval Readers and Writers: 1350–1400.* New York: Columbia University Press, 1981.

Colledge, Edmund. " 'Dominus cuidam devotae suae': A Source for Pseudo-Bonaventure." *Franciscan Studies* 36 (1976): 105–7.

Collier, J. Payne, ed. *Illustrations of Early English Popular Literature.* 2 vols. London, 1863. Reprint. New York: Benjamin Blom, 1966.

Collier, Wendy E. J. " 'Englishness' and the Worcester Tremulous Hand." *Leeds Studies in English* 26 (1995): 35–47.

Connolly, Margaret, ed. *Contemplations of the Dread and Love of God.* EETS os 303. London, 1993.

Conway, Charles Abbott, Jr. *The Vita Christi of Ludolph of Saxony and Late Medieval Devotion Centered on the Incarnation: A Descriptive Analysis.* Analecta Cartusiana, vol. 34. Salzburg, 1976.

Copeland, Rita. "The Fortunes of 'non verbo pro verbo': or, Why Jerome Is Not a Ciceronian." In *The Medieval Translator: The Theory and Practice of Translation in the Middle Ages,* edited by Roger Ellis, 15–35. Cambridge: D. S. Brewer, 1989.

Cornelius, Roberta D. "The Figurative Castle: A Study in the Mediaeval Allegory of the Edifice with Especial Reference to Religious Writings." Diss., Bryn Mawr College, 1930.

Cowper, J. Meadows, ed. *Meditations on the Supper of Our Lord, and the Hours of the Passion.* EETS os 60. Pages 51–54 appended in 1878. London, 1875. Reprint, 1973.

Craigie, W. A., ed. *The Asloan Manuscript: A Miscellany in Prose and Verse.* Scottish Text Society, ns 14, 16. Edinburgh: William Blackwood & Sons, 1923–25.

Crawford, S. J. "The Late Old English Notes of MS. (British Museum) Cotton Claudius B.iv." *Anglia* 47 (1923): 124–35.

———, ed. *The Old English Version of the Heptateuch, Aelfric's Treatise on the Old and New Testament and His Preface to Genesis.* EETS os 160. London, 1922. Reprinted with the texts of two additional manuscripts transcribed by N. R. Ker. London, 1969.

Crotch, W. J. B., ed. *The Prologues and Epilogues of William Caxton.* EETS os 176. London, 1928. Reprint, 1971.

Daly, Saralyn Ruth. "The Historye of the Patriarks." Diss., Ohio State University, 1950.

Day, Mabel, ed. *The English Text of the Ancrene Riwle: Edited from Cotton MS. Nero A.XIV.* EETS os 225. London, 1952, 1957.

———, ed. *The Wheatley Manuscript: A Collection of Middle English Verse and Prose Contained in a MS Now in the British Museum Add. MSS. 39574.* EETS os 155. London, 1921. Reprint, 1971.

Deanesly, Margaret. *The Lollard Bible and Other Medieval Biblical Versions.* Cambridge Studies in Medieval Life and Thought. Cambridge: Cambridge University Press, 1920. Reprinted with new prefatory note and errata list, 1966.

Delisle, L., and P. Meyer, eds. *L'Apocalypse en français au XIIIe siècle.* Societé des anciens textes français. Paris: Firmin Didot et Cie, 1901. Reprint. New York: Johnson, 1965.

Deusen, Nancy van. *The Place of the Psalms in the Intellectual Culture of the Middle Ages.* Albany: State University of New York Press, 1999.

D'Evelyn, Charlotte. "The Middle-English Metrical Version of the *Revelations* of Methodius; with a Study of the Influence of Methodius in Middle-English Writings." *PMLA* 33 (1918): 135–203. Corrections *PMLA* 34 (1919): 112–13.

———, ed. *Meditations on the Life and Passion of Christ.* EETS os 158. London, 1921. Reprint, 1971.

D'Evelyn, Charlotte, and Anna J. Mill, eds. *The South English Legendary.* 3 vols. EETS os 235, 236, 244. London, 1956–59, 1967.

Dickins, Bruce, and R. M. Wilson, eds. *Early Middle English Texts.* Cambridge: Bowes & Bowes, 1951.

Dodwell, C. R., and Peter Clemoes, eds. *The Old English Illustrated Hexateuch: British Museum Cotton Claudius B.IV.* Early English Manuscripts in Facsimile, vol. 18. Copenhagen: Rosenkilde and Bagger, 1974.

Downing, Janay Young, ed. "A Critical Edition of Cambridge University MS Ff.5.48." Diss., University of Washington, 1969.

Doyle, A. I. "Reflections on Some Manuscripts of Nicholas Love's *Myrrour of the Blessed Lyf of Jesu Christ.*" *Leeds Studies in English* ns 14 (1983): 82–93.

———, ed. *The Vernon Manuscript: A Facsimile of Bodleian Library, Oxford, MS. Eng. Poet. a.1.* Cambridge: D. S. Brewer, 1987.

Duffy, Eamon. *The Stripping of the Altars: Traditional Religion in England c. 1400–c. 1580.* New Haven: Yale University Press, 1992.

Dunbar, William. *The Poems of William Dunbar.* Edited by James Kinsley. Oxford: Clarendon Press, 1979.

Duncan, T. G. "The Middle English *Mirror* and Its Manuscripts." In *Middle English Studies Presented to Norman Davis,* edited by Douglas Gray and E. G. Stanley, 115–26. Oxford: Oxford University Press, 1983.

Dunstan, A. C. "The Middle English *Canticum de Creatione* and the Latin *Vita Adae et Evae.*" *Anglia* 55 (1931): 431–42.

Durkin, Philip N. R. "A Study of Oxford, Trinity College, MS 86, with Editions of Selected Texts, and with Special Reference to Late Middle English Prose Forms of Confession." 2 vols. D. Phil. Thesis, Oxford, 1994.

Eco, Umberto. *Art and Beauty in the Middle Ages.* Translated by Hugh Bredin. New Haven: Yale University Press, 1986.

Edden, Valerie. "Richard Maidstone's *Penitential Psalms.*" *Leeds Studies in English* 17 (1986): 77–94.

Edmund of Abingdon. *Speculum religiosorum; and Speculum ecclesie.* Edited by Helen P. Forshaw. Auctores Britannici Medii Aevi, vol. 3. London: Oxford University Press, 1973.

Ekwall, Eilert. "The Manuscript Collections of the Late Professor Anna Paues." *Studia Neophilologica* 21 (1948–49): 23–41.

Elliott, J. K. *The Apocryphal New Testament: A Collection of Apocryphal Christian Literature in an English Translation.* Oxford: Clarendon Press, 1993.

Ellis, Alexander J. *On Early English Pronunciation.* Parts 1 and 2. EETS es 2, 7. London, 1869.

Ellis, F[rederick] S[tartridge], ed. *Psalmi Penitentiales.* Kelmscott Press Publications, vol. 30. Hammersmith: William Morris, 1894.

Emmerson, Richard Kenneth. *Antichrist in the Middle Ages: A Study of Medieval Apocalypticism, Art, and Literature.* Seattle: University of Washington Press, 1981.

Evans, J. M. *Paradise Lost and the Genesis Tradition.* Oxford: Clarendon Press, 1968.

Evans, Joan, and Mary S. Serjeantson, eds. *English Mediaeval Lapidaries.* EETS os 190. London, 1933, 1960.

Everett, Dorothy. "The Middle English Prose Psalter of Richard Rolle of Hampole." *MLR* 17 (1922): 217–27, 337–50; 18 (1923): 381–93.

Fairfax-Blakeborough, J. "Fountains Abbey Parchments." *N&Q,* 12th ser., 10 (1922): 128.

Faverty, Frederic E. "Joseph in Old and Middle English." *PMLA* 43 (1928): 79–104.

Fehr, Bernhard, ed. "Die Lieder des Fairfax Ms." *Archiv* 106 (1901): 48–70.

Fein, Susanna Greer. "*Haue Mercy of Me* (Psalm 51): An Unedited Alliterative Poem from the London Thornton Manuscript." *MP* 86 (1989): 223–41.

———, ed. *Moral Love Songs and Laments.* Middle English Texts. Kalamazoo, Mich.: Medieval Institute Publications, 1998.

Fischer, Rudolf, ed. "Vindicta Salvatoris." *Archiv* 111 (1903): 285–98 and 112 (1904): 25–45.

Forshall, Josiah, and Frederic Madden, eds. *The Holy Bible containing the Old and New Testaments with the Apocryphal Books in the Earliest English Versions made from the Latin Vulgate by John Wycliffe and his Followers.* 4 vols. in folio. [Vol. 1: Preface,

Prologue, Jerome's Epistles, Gen.–Ruth; Vol. 2: 1 Kings–Psalms; Vol. 3: Prov.–2Mach.; Vol. 4: Matt.–Rev., Tables, Glossary.] Oxford, 1850. Reprint. New York: AMS, 1982.

Förster, Max, ed. "Kleine Mitteilungen zur mittelenglische Lehrdichtung." *Archiv* 104 (1900): 293–309.

——, ed. "Kleinere mittelenglische Texte." *Anglia* 42 (1918): 145–224.

Foster, Frances A., ed. *The Northern Passion: Four Parallel Texts and the French Original with Specimens of Additional Manuscripts.* EETS os 145. London, 1913. Reprint, 1971.

——, ed. *The Northern Passion: French Text, Variants and Fragments, etc.* EETS os 147. London, 1916. Reprint, 1971.

——, ed. *A Stanzaic Life of Christ: Compiled from Higden's Polychronicon and the Legenda Aurea, Edited from MS. Harley 3909.* EETS os 166. London, 1926. Reprint, 1971.

Fowler, David C. *The Bible in Early English Literature.* Seattle: University of Washington Press, 1976.

——. *The Bible in Middle English Literature.* Seattle: University of Washington Press, 1984.

Francis, W. Nelson, ed. *The Book of Vices and Virtues: A Fourteenth Century English Translation of the Somme Le Roi of Lorens D'Orléans.* EETS os 217. London, 1942.

Franzen, Christine. *The Tremulous Hand of Worcester: A Study of Old English in the Thirteenth Century.* Oxford: Clarendon Press, 1991.

Fridner, Elis. *An English Fourteenth Century Apocalypse Version with a Prose Commentary: Edited from MS Harley 874 and Ten Other MSS.* Lund Studies in English, vol. 29. Lund: Gleerup, 1961.

Friedman, John B., and Jessica M. Wegmann. *Medieval Iconography: A Research Guide.* Garland Medieval Bibliographies, vol. 20. New York: Garland, 1998.

Fritzsche, A. "Ist die altenglische 'Story of Genesis and Exodus' das Werk eines Verfassers?" *Anglia* 5 (1882): 43–90.

Frölich, Walter, ed. *De lamentacione sancte Marie: Eine englische Dichtung des 14. Jahrhunderts.* Leipzig, 1902.

Furnivall, Frederick J., ed. *Adam Davy's 5 Dreams about Edward II. The Life of St. Alexius. Solomon's Book of Wisdom. St. Jerome's 15 Tokens Before Doomsday. The Lamentation of Souls.* EETS os 69. London, 1878. Reprint, 1973.

——, ed. *Early English Poems and Lives of Saints, (with those of the wicked Birds Pilate and Judas).* Berlin: A. Asher & Co., 1862. Reprint. New York: AMS, 1974.

——, ed. *Hymns to the Virgin and Christ, The Parliament of Devils, and other Religious Poems, Chiefly from . . . Lambeth MS. No. 853.* EETS os 24. London, 1867.

——, ed. *The Minor Poems of the Vernon MS.* Vol. 2. EETS os 117. London, 1901. Reprint, 1973. Vol. 1 EETS os 98, edited by Carl Horstmann.

——, ed. *Political, Religious, and Love Poems.* EETS os 15. London, 1866. 2d ed., 1903. Reprint, 1962.

Garmonsway, G. N., and R. R. Raymo. "A Middle English Metrical Life of Job." In *Early English and Norse Studies Presented to Hugh Smith in Honour of His Sixtieth Birthday,* edited by Arthur Brown and Peter Foote, 77–98. London: Methuen, 1963.

Garrett, Robert Max. "Religious Verses from MS. Arundel 292." *Archiv* 128 (1912): 367–68.

Gerould, G. H. *The North English Homily Collection.* Diss., Oxford. Lancaster, Pa.: privately printed, 1902.

Gillespie, Vincent. "*Doctrina* and *Predicacio:* The Design and Function of Some Pastoral Manuals." *Leeds Studies in English* 11 (1980): 36–50.

Girvan, R., ed. *Ratis Raving and Other Early Scots Poems on Morals.* Scottish Text Society, 3d series, vol. 11. Edinburgh: William Blackwood & Sons, 1939.

Goates, Margery, ed. *The Pepysian Gospel Harmony.* EETS os 157. London, 1922. Reprint, 1971.

Gollancz, Israel. "The Quatrefoil of Love: An Alliterative Religious Lyric." In *An English Miscellany Presented to Doctor Furnivall.* Oxford: Clarendon Press, 1901. 112–32.

———, ed. *Pearl, Cleanness, Patience and Sir Gawain.* Facsimile ed. EETS os 162. London, 1923.

Gollancz, Israel, and Magdalene M. Weale, eds. *The Quatrefoil of Love.* EETS os 195. London, 1935. Reprint, 1987.

Gordon, E. V., ed. *Pearl.* Oxford: Clarendon Press, 1953.

Görlach, Manfred. *The Textual Tradition of the South English Legendary.* Leeds Texts and Monographs, ns 6. Leeds: University of Leeds School of English, 1974.

Goymer, C. R. "A Parallel Text Edition of the Middle English Prose Versions of the *Mirror of St. Edmund* Based on the Known Complete Manuscripts." M.A. Thesis, London University, 1962.

Grabmann, Martin. *Die Geschichte der scholastischen Methode.* 2 vols. Freiburg im Bresgau: Herdersche, 1909–11. Reprint. Basel: Benno Schwabe, 1961.

Gradon, Pamela. "Langland and the Ideology of Dissent." *Proceedings of the British Academy* 66 (1980): 179–205.

Gransden, Antonia. *Historical Writing in England c. 550 to c. 1307.* Ithaca, N.Y.: Cornell University Press, 1974.

———. *Historical Writing in England c. 1307 to the Early Sixteenth Century.* Ithaca, N.Y.: Cornell University Press, 1982.

Gray, Douglas. *Themes and Images in the Medieval English Religious Lyric.* London: Routledge & Kegan Paul, 1972.

Greene, Richard Leighton. "A Middle English Love Poem and the 'O-and-I' Refrain-Phrase." *MÆ* 30 (1961): 170–75.

———, ed. *The Early English Carols.* 2d ed. Oxford: Clarendon Press, 1977.

Greg, W. W. "A Ballad of Twelfth Day." *MLR* 8 (1913): 64–67.

———. "A Ballad of Twelfth Day." *MLR* 9 (1914): 235–36.

Hageneder, Othmar, Werner Maleczek, and Alfred A. Strnad, eds. *Die Register Innocenz' III. 2: Pontifikatsjahr, 1199/1200.* Rome: Austrian Academy of Sciences, 1979.

Hamer, Richard. *A Manuscript Index to the Index of Middle English Verse.* London: British Library, 1995.

Hanna, Ralph III. *The Index of Middle English Prose, Handlist XII: Smaller Bodleian Collections.* Woodbridge, Suffolk: D. S. Brewer, 1997.

———. "Sir Thomas Berkeley and His Patronage." *Speculum* 64 (1989): 878–916.

Hargreaves, Henry. "*The Mirror of Our Lady:* Aberdeen University Library MS. 134." *Aberdeen University Review* 42 (1968): 267–80.

———. "The Wycliffite Versions." In *The Cambridge History of the Bible.* Vol. 2. Ed. G. W. H. Lampe. Cambridge University Press, 1969. 387–415.

Harsley, Fred. *Eadwine's Canterbury Psalter.* EETS os 92. Vol. 2, text and notes; vol. 1 never published. London, 1889. Reprint, 1973.

Hassall, W. O. *The Holkham Bible Picture Book*. Facsimile with introduction and commentary. London: Dropmore Press, 1954.

Hefele, Charles Joseph, ed. *Histoire des Conciles*. Translated from the German. 2d ed. with critical and bibliographical notes by H. Leclercq. 11 vols. in 21. Paris: Letouzey et Ané, 1907–52.

Heffernan, Thomas J. "Sermon Literature." In *The Popular Literature of Medieval England*, edited by Thomas J. Heffernan, 177–207. Tennessee Studies in Literature, vol. 28. Knoxville: University of Tennessee Press, 1985.

———, ed. *The Popular Literature of Medieval England*. Tennessee Studies in Literature, vol. 28. Knoxville: University of Tennessee Press, 1985.

Heist, William W. *The Fifteen Signs before Doomsday*. East Lansing: Michigan State University Press, 1952.

Herbert, J. A., ed. *Titus and Vespasian, or The Destruction of Jerusalem, in rhymed couplets*. London: Roxburghe Club, 1905.

Herrtage, Sidney J. H., and Henry B. Wheatley, eds. *Catholicon Anglicum: an English Latin Wordbook dated 1483*. EETS os 75. London, 1881. Reprint, 1973.

Heuser, W[ilhelm]. "Die alttestamentlichen dichtungen des ms. Seld. Supra 52 der Bodleiana." *Anglia* 31 (1908): 1–24.

———. "Eine vergessene Handschrift der Surteespsalters und die dort eingeschalteten mittelenglischen Gedichte." *Anglia* 29 (1906): 385–412.

———. "With an O and an I." *Anglia* 27 (1904): 283–319.

———, ed. "Das frühmittelenglische Josephlied." *Bonner Beiträge zur Anglistik* 17 (1905): 83–121.

———, ed. *Die Kildare-Gedichte: Die ältesten mittelenglischen Denkmäler in anglo-irischer Überlieferung*. Bonner Beiträge zur Anglistik, vol. 14. Bonn: P. Hanstein, 1904. Reprint. Darmstadt: Wissenschaftliche Buchgesellschaft, 1965.

Heuser, W[ilhelm], and Frances A. Foster, eds. *The Northern Passion (Supplement): Cambridge University MS. Gg.1.1, Oxford MS. Rawlinson Poetry 175*. EETS os 183. London, 1930. Reprint, 1971.

Higden, Ranulph. *Polychronicon Ranulphi Higden Monachi Cestrensis: together with the English translations of John Trevisa and of an Unknown Writer of the Fifteenth Century*. 9 vols. Vols. 1–2 edited by Churchill Babington; vols. 3–9 edited by Joseph Rawson Lumby. Rolls Series, vol. 41. London, 1865–86.

Hill, Betty. "The Middle English Prose Version of the *Gospel of Nicodemus* from Washington, Library of Congress pre-Ac 4." *N&Q*, ns 34, 232 (1987): 156–75.

Holden, Alan Walter. "The *Gospel of Nicodemus* in Middle English Prose: From British Museum MS Egerton 2658, John Rylands English MS. 895, Bodleian Library MS Bodley 207, Stonyhurst MS. XLIII." Thesis, University of London, 1951.

Holm, Sigurd. *Corrections and Additions in the Ormulum Manuscript*. Uppsala: Almqvist & Wicksells, 1922.

Holmstedt, Gustaf, ed. *Speculum Christiani: A Middle English Religious Treatise of the 14th Century*. EETS os 182. London, 1933.

Holt, Robert, ed. *The Ormulum: With the Notes and Glossary of Dr. R. M. White*. 2 vols. Oxford: Clarendon Press, 1878. Reprint. New York: AMS, 1974.

Holthausen, Ferdinand. *Altenglisches etymologisches Wörterbuch*. Germanische Bibliothek, vol. 1. Sämmlung germanischer Elementar- und Handbücher. IV Reihe: Wörterbücher, siebter Band. Heidelberg: Carl Winter, 1934.

————. "Zum mittelenglischen Gedicht, 'Kindheit Jesu.'" *Archiv* 127 (1911): 318–22.

Horrall, Sarah M. "'For the Commun at Understand': *Cursor Mundi* and Its Background." In *De Cella in Seculum: Religious and Secular Life and Devotion in Late Medieval England,* edited by Michael G. Sargent, 97–107. Cambridge: Brewer, 1989.

————. "'Man Yhernes Rimes for to Here': A Biblical History from the Middle Ages." In *Art into Life: Collected Papers from the Kresge Art Museum Medieval Symposia,* edited by Carol Garrett Fisher and Kathleen L. Scott, 73–93. East Lansing: Michigan State University Press, 1995.

————. "The Manuscripts of *Cursor Mundi.*" *Text: Transactions of the Society for Textual Scholarship* 2 (1985): 69–82.

————. "William Caxton's Biblical Translation." *MÆ* 53 (1984): 91–98.

Horrall, Sarah M., Roger R. Fowler, Henry J. Stauffenberg, and Peter H. J. Mous, eds. *The Southern Version of Cursor Mundi.* Vols. 1 (lines 1–9228), 2 (lines 9229–12712), 3 (lines 12713–17082), 4 (lines 17289–21346) published to date. [Vol. 5, lines 21347–23898, with general introduction, forthcoming.] Ottawa Mediaeval Texts and Studies, nos. 5, 13, 14, 16. Ottawa: University of Ottawa Press, 1978–90.

Horstmann, Carl, ed. *Altenglische Legenden: Kindheit Jesu, Geburt Jesu, Barlaam und Josaphat, St. Patrik's Fegefeuer.* Paderborn: Ferdinand Schöningh, 1875.

————, ed. *Altenglische Legenden Neue Folge.* Heilbronn: Gebr. Henninger, 1881.

————, ed. *Barbour's des Schottischen Nationaldichters Legendensammlung.* 2 vols. Heilbronn, 1881–82. Reprint. Wiesbaden: M. Sandig, 1967.

————, ed. "Canticum de Creatione. Aus Ms. Trin. coll. Oxf. 57." *Anglia* 1 (1878): 287–331. Reprinted as pp. 124–38 of the *Sammlung.*

————, ed. *The Early South-English Legendary or Lives of Saints I. MS. Laud, 108, In the Bodleian Library.* EETS os 87. London, 1887. Reprint, 1973.

————, ed. "Die Evangeliem-Geschichten der Homiliensammlung des Ms. Vernon." *Archiv* 57 (1877): 241–316.

————, ed. "Evangelium Nicodemi in der altschottischer Mundart aus Ms. Harl. 4196 fol. 206 (14. Jhdt)." *Archiv* 53 (1874): 389–424.

————, ed. "Informacio Alredi Abbatis Monastterij de Rieualle ad Sororem suam inclusam." *Englische Studien* 7 (1884): 304–44.

————, ed. *Leben Jesu.* (Published as Part 1; Part 2 [though not so-called], *Kindheit Jesu,* appeared in 1875 in *Altenglische Legenden*). Münster: Friedrich Regensburg, 1873.

————, ed. "Die Legenden von Celestin und Susanna." *Anglia* 1 (1878): 55–101.

————, ed. *The Minor Poems of the Vernon MS.* Vol. 1. EETS os 98. London, 1892. Reprint, 1973. (Vol. 2 EETS os 117, edited by F. J. Furnivall).

————, ed. "Mittheilungen aus MS. Vernon." *Englische Studien* 8 (1885): 254–77.

————, ed. "Nachträge zu den Legenden." *Archiv* 62 (1879): 406–13.

————, ed. "Nachträge zu den Legenden." *Archiv* 74 (1885): 327–65. Four items: 1. Kindheit Jesu, aus MS. Addit. 31,042 [327–39]; 2. Susanna, aus MS. Cheltenham 8252 [339–44]; 3. The lyfe of Adam 1) aus MS Bodl 596 (c. 1430) [345–53]; 2) The Life of Adam and Eue, aus MS. Harl. 4775 [353–65].

————, ed. "Nachträge zu den Legenden." *Archiv* 79 (1887): 411–70. Ten items, of which four are relevant: 4. Testamentum Christi [424–32]; 7. Romanze von Christi Auferstehung [441–47]; 8. De Matre et VII pueris [447–54]; 9. Lamentacion of oure lady [454–59].

————, ed. "Nachträge zu den Legenden (Fortsetzung)." *Archiv* 68 (1882): 52–73. Parallel editions of Life of Mary Magdalen from Cambridge, Trinity College 605, and London, Lambeth Palace 223.

————, ed. "Nachträge zu den Legenden (Schluss.): Evangelium Nicodemi, aus Ms. Sion, fol. 13–39." *Archiv* 68 (1882): 207–24.

————, ed. *Sammlung Altenglischer Legenden.* Heilbronn: Gebr. Henninger, 1878. Reprint. Hildesheim: Georg Olms, 1969.

————, ed. *The Three Kings of Cologne.* EETS os 85. London, 1886. Reprint, 1972.

————, ed. *Yorkshire Writers: Richard Rolle of Hampole, an English Father of the Church and His Followers.* 2 vols. London, 1895–96.

Hudson, Anne. "The Debate on Bible Translation, Oxford 1401." *English Historical Review* 90 (1975): 1–18. Reprinted in *Lollards and Their Books,* 67–84. London: Hambledon Press, 1985.

————. *The Premature Reformation: Wycliffite Texts and Lollard History.* Oxford: Clarendon Press, 1988.

————. "Some Aspects of Lollard Book Production." In *Schism, Heresy, and Religious Protest,* edited by Derek Baker, 147–57. SCH 9. Cambridge: Cambridge University Press, 1972.

Hudson, Anne, and Pamela Gradon, eds. *English Wycliffite Sermons.* 5 vols. Oxford: Clarendon Press, 1983–96.

Hudson, Anne, and Linda Ehrsam Voigts. "A Missing Leaf from MS. Douce 250." *Bodleian Library Record* 10 (1981): 221–24.

Hugh of St. Victor. *The Didascalicon: A Medieval Guide to the Arts.* Translated by Jerome Taylor. Records of Civilization Sources and Studies, vol. 64. New York: Columbia University Press, 1961.

Hughes, Jonathan. *Pastors and Visionaries: Religion and Secular Life in Late Medieval Yorkshire.* Woodbridge, Suffolk: Boydell Press, 1988.

Hulme, William Henry, ed. *The Middle English Harrowing of Hell and Gospel of Nicodemus.* EETS es 100. London, 1907, 1961, 1976.

Hupe, H., ed. "Robert Grosseteste's *Chasteau d'Amour* (Castel of Love)." *Anglia* 14 (1892): 415–55.

Hussey, Maurice. "The Petitions of the Pater Noster in Mediaeval English Literature." *MÆ* 27 (1958): 8–16.

Illich, Ivan. *In the Vineyard of the Text: A Commentary to Hugh's Didascalicon.* Chicago: University of Chicago Press, 1993.

Jacobus de Voragine. *The Golden Legend or Lives of the Saints as Englished by William Caxton.* Edited by F[rederick] S[tartridge] Ellis. 7 vols. Temple Classics. London: J. M. Dent, 1900. A deluxe 3 vol. version of this edition was published in 1892 by Kelmscott Press.

————. *Legenda Aurea Jacobi a Voragine.* Edited by Th. Graesse. 3d ed. [Leipzig], 1890. Reprint. Osnabrück: Otto Zeller, 1969.

James, Montague Rhodes. *A Descriptive Catalogue of the Latin Manuscripts in the John Rylands Library at Manchester.* Vol. 1. Manchester: Manchester University Press, 1921.

————, ed. *The Canterbury Psalter.* Facsimile ed. with introduction. London: Friends of Canterbury Cathedral, 1935.

————, ed. and trans. *De Nugis Curialium: Courtiers' Trifles.* (Walter Map). Revised by C. N. L. Brooke and R. A. B. Mynors. Oxford: Clarendon Press, 1983.

————, ed. *Illustrations of the Book of Genesis.* Facsimile ed. Oxford: Roxburghe Club, 1921.

Jenkinson, Francis. *The abbaye of the holy ghost: Printed at Westminster by Wynkyn de Worde about the Year 1496.* Facsimile ed. Cambridge: Cambridge University Press, 1907.

Jocelin de Brakelond. *The Chronicle of Jocelin of Brakelond, concerning the Acts of Samson, Abbot of the Monastery of St. Edmund.* Edited and translated by H. E. Butler. New York: Oxford University Press, 1949. Reprint. New York: Thomas Nelson, 1951.

Jolliffe, P. S. *A Check-List of Middle English Prose Writings of Spiritual Guidance.* Toronto: Pontifical Institute of Mediaeval Studies, 1974.

Jones, Dorothy, ed. *Minor Works of Walter Hilton.* Orchard Books, vol. 17. New York: Benzinger Brothers, 1929.

Kail, J., ed. *Twenty-six Political and Other Poems (including "Petty Job") from the Oxford MSS. Digby 102 and Douce 322.* EETS os 124. London, 1904. Reprint, 1973. Only vol. 1 appeared.

Kalén, Herbert, ed. *A Middle English Metrical Paraphrase of the Old Testament.* Stanzas 1–500. Göteborgs Högskolas Årsskrift 28, vol. 5. Gothenburg: Elanders, 1923.

Kartschoke, Dieter. *Bibeldichtung: Studien zur Geschichte der epischen Bibelparaphrase von Juvencus bis Otfrid von Weissenburg.* Munich: Wilhelm Fink, 1975.

Kellogg, A. L., and Ernest W. Talbert. "The Wyclifite *Pater Noster* and Ten Command-ments, with Special Reference to English MSS. 85 and 90 in the John Rylands Library." *BJRL* 42 (1959–60): 345–77.

Kelly, T. D., and John Irwin. "The Meaning of *Cleanness:* Parable as Effective Sign." *Mediaeval Studies* 35 (1973): 232–60.

Kennedy, Edward Donald. Review of *The Popular Literature of Medieval England,* edited by Thomas J. Heffernan. *Anglia* 107 (1989): 180–83.

Kennedy, Walter. *The Poems of Walter Kennedy.* Edited by J. Schipper. Denkschriften der kaiserlichen Akademie der Wissenschaften, philosophisch-historische Classe, 48:1–94. Vienna, 1902.

Ker, N. R. *Catalogue of Manuscripts Containing Anglo-Saxon.* Oxford: Clarendon Press, 1957. Reissued with supplement, 1990.

————. *Facsimile of British Museum MS. Harley 2253.* EETS os 255. London, 1965.

————. "A Middle-English Summary of the Bible." *MÆ* 29 (1960): 115–18.

Kingdon, H. T. "An Early Vernacular Service." *Wiltshire Archaeological and Natural History Magazine* 18 (1879): 62–70.

Kock, A., ed. *Three Middle English Versions of the Rule of St. Benet.* EETS os 120. London, 1902. Reprint, 1972.

Kölbing, Eugen, ed. "Kleine Publicationen aus der Auchinleck-HS." *Englische Studien* 9 (1886): 42–50.

————, ed. "Zwei mittelenglische Bearbeitungen der Sage von St. Patriks Purgato-rium." *Englische Studien* 1 (1877): 57–121.

Kolve, V. A. *The Play Called Corpus Christi.* Stanford: Stanford University Press, 1966.

Kreuzer, James R. "Richard Maidstone's Version of the Fifty-First Psalm." *MLR* 66 (1951): 224–31.

————. "Thomas Brampton's Metrical Paraphrase of the Seven Penitential Psalms:

A Diplomatic Edition of the Version in MS Pepys 1584 and MS Cambridge University Ff 2.38 with Variant Readings from All Known Manuscripts." *Traditio* 7 (1949–51): 359–403.

Kribel, G. "Studien zu Richard Rolle de Hampole. II. Lamentatio St. Bernardi de compassione Mariae." *Englische Studien* 8 (1885): 67–114.

Kuczynski, Michael P. *Prophetic Song: The Psalms as Moral Discourse in Late Medieval England.* Philadelphia: University of Pennsylvania Press, 1995.

Laing, D., ed. *A Penni Worth of Witte.* N.p.: Abbotsford Club, 1857.

Laing, Margaret. *Catalogue of Sources for a Linguistic Atlas of Early Middle English.* Cambridge: D. S. Brewer, 1993.

Langland, William. *Piers Plowman: A Parallel-Text Edition of the A, B, C and Z Versions.* Edited by A. V. C. Schmidt. Vol. 1, text; vol. 2, notes and glossary (forthcoming). London: Longman, 1995.

Lawton, David A., ed. *Joseph of Arimathea: A Critical Edition.* Garland Medieval Texts, vol. 5. New York: Garland, 1983.

Laȝamon. *Laȝamon: Brut, Edited from British Museum MS. Cotton Caligula A.ix and British Museum MS. Cotton Otho C.xiii.* Edited by G. L. Brook and R. F. Leslie. 2 vols. EETS os 250, 277. London, 1963–78.

Legge, J. Wickham, ed. *The Processional of the Nuns of Chester.* Henry Bradshaw Society, vol. 18. London, 1899.

———, ed. *Tracts on the Mass.* Henry Bradshaw Society, vol. 27. London, 1904.

Legge, M. Dominica. *Anglo-Norman Literature and Its Background.* Oxford: Oxford University Press, 1963. Corrected rpt. 1971.

Lewis, R. E., N. F. Blake, and A. S. G. Edwards. *Index of Printed Middle English Prose.* Garland Reference Library of the Humanities, vol. 537. New York: Garland, 1985.

Liljegren, S. B. Review of *A Middle English Metrical Paraphrase of the Old Testament,* edited by Herbert Kalén. *Anglia Beiblatt* 34 (1923): 227–28.

Lindström, Bengt, ed. *A Late Middle English Version of the Gospel of Nicodemus.* Acta Universitatis Upsaliensis, Studia Anglistica, vol. 18. Uppsala: Almqvist & Wiksell, 1974.

Little, A. G. *Studies in English Franciscan History: Being the Ford Lectures Delivered in the University of Oxford in 1916.* Manchester: Manchester University Press, 1917.

Littlehales, Henry, ed. *Pages in Facsimile from a Layman's Prayer-Book in English about 1400 A.D.* London: Rivingtons, 1890.

———, ed. *The Prymer or Lay Folks Prayer Book.* Vol. 1, text. EETS os 105. London, 1895. Reprint, 1975. Vol. 2, introduction by Edmund Bishop.

———, ed. *The Prymer or Prayer-Book of the Lay People in the Middle Ages.* 2 vols. Vol. 1, text. Vol. 2, collation of manuscripts. London: Longmans, Green & Co., 1891–92.

Liuzza, Roy Michael. "The Yale Fragments of the West Saxon Gospels." *Anglo-Saxon England* 17 (1988): 67–82.

———, ed. *The Old English Version of the Gospels.* Vol. 1 (text). EETS os 304. London, 1994. Vol. 2 (notes) forthcoming.

Lortsch, D. *Histoire de la Bible en France: Suivie de fragments relatifs à l'histoire générale de la Bible.* Paris: Agence de la Société Biblique Britannique et Étrangère; Geneva: M. Jeheber, 1910.

Lotspeich, C. M. "Old English Etymologies." *JEGP* 40 (1941): 1–4.

Lumby, J. Rawson, ed. *Ratis Raving, and Other Moral and Religious Pieces, in Prose and Verse*. EETS os 43. London, 1870. Reprint, 1973.

Lydgate, John. *The Minor Poems of John Lydgate*. Edited by Henry Noble MacCracken. Part 1. EETS es 107. London, 1911. Part 2 in EETS os 192.

Lyte, H. C. Maxwell, and G. J. Morris, eds. *Calendar of the Patent Rolls Preserved in the Public Record Office: Richard II. A.D. 1381–1385*. London: Eyre and Spottiswoode, 1897.

———, eds. *Calendar of the Patent Rolls Preserved in the Public Record Office: Richard II. A.D. 1385–1389*. London: Norfolk Chronicle Company, 1900.

MacCracken, Henry Noble, ed. "Lydgatiana I: The Life of Holy Job." *Archiv* 126 (1911): 365–70.

———, ed. "Lydgatiana III: The Three Kings of Cologne." *Archiv* 129 (1912): 50–68.

———, ed. "The Storie of Asneth: An Unknown Middle English Translation of a Lost Latin Version." *JEGP* 9 (1910): 224–64.

Macrae-Gibson, O. D., ed. *Of Arthour and of Merlin*. 2 vols. Vol. 1, text. Vol. 2, intro., notes, glossary. EETS os 268, 279. London, 1973–79.

Macray, W. D., ed. "Fifteenth-Century Religious Verses." *N&Q*, 9th series, 8 (1901): 240.

Madan, Falconer, et al. *A Summary Catalogue of Western Manuscripts in the Bodleian Library at Oxford*. 7 vols. in 8. Oxford: Clarendon Press, 1895–1953. Reprint. Munich: Millwood, N.Y.: Kraus-Thomson, 1980.

Madigan, Mary Felicitas. *The Passio Domini Theme in the Works of Richard Rolle: His Personal Contribution in Its Religious, Cultural, and Literary Context*. Salzburg Studies in English Literature: Elizabethan and Renaissance Studies, vol. 79. Salzburg: Institut für englische Sprache und Literatur, 1978.

Maidstone, Richard. *Richard Maidstone's Penitential Psalms: Edited from Bodl. MS Rawlinson A 389*. Edited by Valerie Edden. Middle English Texts, vol. 22. Heidelberg: Carl Winter, 1990.

Mannyng, Robert. *Handlyng Synne*. Edited by Idelle Sullens. Medieval and Renaissance Texts and Studies, vol. 14. Binghamton, N.Y.: Medieval and Renaissance Texts and Studies, 1983.

Mansi, Joannes, ed. *Sacrorum Conciliorum Nova et Amplissima Collectio*. 53 vols. in 58. 1759–98. Reprint. Paris, 1901–27.

Marsden, Richard. *The Text of the Old Testament in Anglo-Saxon England*. Cambridge Studies in Anglo-Saxon England, vol. 15. Cambridge: Cambridge University Press, 1995.

Martin, Anthony. "The Middle English Versions of the Ten Commandments, with Special Reference to Rylands English MS 85." *BJRL* 64 (1981): 191–217.

Martin, Clarence Anthony, ed. "Edinburgh University Library Manuscript 93: An Annotated Edition of Selected Devotional Treatises with a Survey of Parallel Versions." 2 vols. Diss., University of Edinburgh, 1977.

Marx, C. William. *The Devil's Rights and the Redemption in the Literature of Medieval England*. Woodbridge, Suffolk: Boydell and Brewer, 1995.

———. "The Middle English Verse 'Lamentation of Mary to St. Bernard' and the 'Quis dabit.'" In *Studies in the Vernon Manuscript*, edited by Derek Pearsall, 137–57. Cambridge: D. S. Brewer, 1990.

————, ed. *The Devil's Parlament and The Harrowing of Hell and Destruction of Jerusalem.* Middle English Texts, vol. 25. Heidelberg: Carl Winter, 1993.

Marx, C. William, and Jeanne F. Drennan, eds. *The Middle English Prose Complaint of Our Lady and Gospel of Nicodemus.* Middle English Texts, vol. 19. Heidelberg: Carl Winter, 1987.

Maskell, William. *Monumenta Ritualia Ecclesiae Anglicanae: The Occasional Offices of the Church of England according to the Old Use of the Salisbury, the Prymer in English, and Other Prayers and Forms.* 3 vols. 2d. ed. Oxford: Clarendon Press, 1882. Reprint. Farnborough, Hants.: Gregg, 1970.

Mätzner, Eduard, ed. *Altenglische Sprachproben.* Vol. 1 (Part 1, poetry; part 2, prose). Berlin: Weidmannsche, 1867–69.

McCarthy, Adrian James, ed. *Book to a Mother: An Edition with Commentary.* Elizabethan and Renaissance Studies, vol. 92. Salzburg: Institut für Anglistik und Amerikanistik, 1981.

McGerr, Rosemarie Potz. "Guyart Desmoulins, the Vernacular Master of Histories, and His *Bible historiale.*" *Viator* 14 (1983): 211–44.

McIntosh, Angus. "The Middle English *Estoire del Euangelie:* The Dialect of the Original Version." *Neuphilologische Mitteilungen* 88 (1987): 186–91.

McSparran, Frances, and P. R. Robinson, eds. *Cambridge University Library MS Ff.2.38.* London: Scolar Press, 1979.

Mehl, Dieter. *Die mittelenglischen Romanzen des 13. und 14. Jahrhunderts.* Anglistische Forschungen, vol. 93. Heidelberg: Carl Winter, 1967. English trans. London, 1968.

Menner, Robert J., ed. *Purity: A Middle English Poem.* Yale Studies in English, vol. 61. New Haven, Conn.: Yale University Press, 1920. Reprint. Archon Books, 1970.

Meyer, Paul. "Les Manuscrits Français de Cambridge." *Romania* 8 (1879): 305–42; 15 (1886): 236–357.

Middle English Dictionary. Edited by Hans Kurath, Sherman M. Kuhn, John Reidy, Robert E. Lewis, et al. Ann Arbor: University of Michigan Press, 1954– .

Middleton, Anne. "The Idea of Public Poetry in the Reign of Richard II." *Speculum* 53 (1978): 94–114.

Migne, J.-P. *Patrologiae cursus completus . . . Series [Latina].* 221 vols. Paris, 1844–64.

Millward, Celia, ed. *La Estorie del Euangelie: A Parallel Text Edition.* Middle English Texts, vol. 30. Heidelberg: Carl Winter, 1998.

Minnis, A. J. *Medieval Theory of Authorship.* 2d ed. Philadelphia: University of Pennsylvania Press, 1988.

————. "Medium and Message: Henry of Ghent on Scriptural Style." In *Literature and Religion in the Later Middle Ages: Philological Studies in Honor of Siegfried Wenzel,* edited by Richard G. Newhauser and John A. Alford, 209–35. Binghamton: Medieval and Renaissance Texts and Studies, 1995.

Mirk, John. *Instructions for Parish Priests.* Edited by Gillis Kristensson. Lund Studies in English, vol. 49. Lund: Gleerup, 1974.

————. *Mirk's Festial: A Collection of Homilies.* Edited by Theodor Erbe. EETS es 96. London, 1905. Reprint, 1973.

The Mirour of Mans Saluacioune: A Middle English Translation of Speculum Humanae Salvationis. Edited by Avril Henry. Philadelphia: University of Pennsylvania Press, 1987.

Miskimin, Alice, ed. *Susannah: An Alliterative Poem of the Fourteenth Century.* Yale Studies in English, vol. 170. New Haven: Yale University Press, 1969.

Moe, Phyllis, ed. *The ME Prose Translation of Roger D'Argenteuil's Bible en François: Edited from Cleveland Public Library, MS W q 091.92-C 468.* Middle English Texts, vol. 6. Heidelberg: Carl Winter, 1977.

Moore, R. I. *The Birth of Popular Heresy.* Documents of Medieval History, vol. 1. New York: St. Martin's Press, 1975.

Morey, James H. Entry on the *Gospel of Nicodemus.* In *Sources of Anglo-Saxon Literary Culture: A Trial Version,* edited by Frederick M. Biggs, Thomas D. Hill, and Paul E. Szarmach, 45–48. Binghamton, N.Y.: Medieval and Renaissance Texts and Studies, 1990.

———. "The Fall in Particulate." *Yearbook of Langland Studies* 5 (1991): 91–97.

———. "Legal and Spiritual Sanctuary in the *Northern Homily Cycle* and *Piers Plowman* B, XVII, 1–126." *JEGP* 93 (1994): 326–35.

———. "Peter Comestor, Biblical Paraphrase, and the Medieval Popular Bible." *Speculum* 68 (1993): 6–35.

Morgan, Nigel. "Old Testament Illustration in Thirteenth-Century England." In *The Bible in the Middle Ages: Its Influence on Literature and Art,* edited by Bernard S. Levy, 149–98. Medieval and Renaissance Texts and Studies, vol. 89. Binghamton, N.Y.: 1992.

Morrell, Minnie Cate. *A Manual of Old English Biblical Materials.* Knoxville: University of Tennessee Press, 1965.

Morrill, Georgianna Lea, ed. *Speculum Gy de Warewyke: An Early English Poem.* EETS es 75. London, 1898. Reprint, 1973.

Morris, Richard, ed. *Cursor Mundi: (The Cursur o the World) a Northumbrian Poem of the XIVth Century in Four Versions.* EETS os 57, 59, 62, 66, 68, 99, 101. London, 1874–93. Reprint, 1961–66.

———, ed. *Dan Michel's Ayenbite of Inwyt, or, Remorse of Conscience.* EETS os 23. London, 1866. Corrected reprint, 1965. Intro., notes, and glossary by Pamela Gradon in EETS os 278. London, 1979.

———, ed. *Legends of the Holy Rood: Symbols of the Passion and Cross Poems.* EETS os 46. London, 1871.

———, ed. *Old English Homilies and Homiletic Treatises (Sawles Warde, and Þe Wohunge of Ure Lauerd: Ureisuns of Ure Louerd and of Ure Lefdi, &c.) of the Twelfth and Thirteenth Centuries.* Vol. 1 in 2 parts. EETS os 29, 34. London, 1867–68. Vol. 2. EETS os 53, edited by Morris.

———, ed. *An Old English Miscellany: Containing a Bestiary, Kentish Sermons, Proverbs of Alfred, Religious Poems of the Thirteenth Century.* EETS os 49. London, 1872.

———, ed. *The Pricke of Conscience (Stimulus Conscientiae).* Berlin: Asher, 1863. Reprint, 1973.

———, ed. *The Story of Genesis and Exodus: An Early English Song, about A.D. 1250.* 2d ed. EETS os 7. London, 1873. Reprint, 1973.

Morrison, Stephen. "Orm's English Sources." *Archiv* 221 (1984): 54–64.

Mundy, John Hine. *The Repression of Catharism at Toulouse.* Studies and Texts, vol. 74. Toronto: Pontifical Institute of Mediaeval Studies, 1985.

Napier, Arthur S., ed. *Iacob and Iosep: A Middle English Poem of the Thirteenth Century.* Oxford: Oxford University Press, 1916.

Nevanlinna, Saara, ed. *The Northern Homily Cycle: The Expanded Version in MSS Harley 4196 and Cotton Tiberius E vii.* Mémoires de la Société Néophilologique de Helsinki 38 (1972), 41 (1973), 43 (1984). [Vol. 1, lines 1–5695; vol. 2, lines 5696–15627; vol. 3, lines 15628–21612].

O'Connell, Patrick F. *Love's Mirrour and the Meditationes Vitae Christi.* Analecta Cartusiana, vol. 82, part 2, pp. 3–44, edited by James Hogg. Salzburg: Institut für Anglistik und Amerikanistik, Universität Salzburg, 1980.

Ogilvie-Thomson, S. J. *The Index of Middle English Prose, Handlist VIII: Oxford College Libraries.* Cambridge: D. S. Brewer, 1991.

Oguro, Shoichi, Richard Beadle, and Michael G. Sargent, eds. *Nicholas Love at Waseda.* Cambridge: D. S. Brewer, 1997.

Ohlander, Urban. "Old French Parallels to a Middle English Metrical Paraphrase of the Old Testament." In *Contributions to English Syntax and Philology,* edited by Frank Behre, 203–24. Gothenburg Studies in English, vol. 14. Stockholm: Almqvist and Wiksell, 1962.

———, ed. *A Middle English Metrical Paraphrase of the Old Testament II.* Stanzas 501–802. Göteborgs Universitets Årsskrift 61, no. 2. Also Gothenburg Studies in English, vol. 5. Stockholm: Almqvist and Wiksell, 1955.

———, ed. *A Middle English Metrical Paraphrase of the Old Testament III.* Stanzas 803–1174. Göteborgs Universitets Årsskrift 66, no. 7. Also Gothenburg Studies in English, vol. 11. Stockholm: Almqvist and Wiksell, 1960.

———, ed. *A Middle English Metrical Paraphrase of the Old Testament IV.* Stanzas 1175–1531. Gothenburg Studies in English, vol. 16. Stockholm: Almqvist and Wiksell, 1963.

———, ed. *A Middle English Metrical Paraphrase of the Old Testament V: Glossary.* Gothenburg Studies in English, vol. 24. Stockholm: Almqvist and Wiksell, 1972.

O'Neill, Patrick P. "Another Fragment of the Metrical Psalms in the Eadwine Psalter." *N&Q* 35 (1988): 434–36.

———. "The English Version." In *The Eadwine Psalter: Text, Image, and Monastic Culture in Twelfth-Century Canterbury,* edited by Margaret Gibson, T. A. Heslop, and Richard W. Pfaff, 123–38. London & University Park: MHRA with the Pennsylvania State University Press, 1992.

Onions, C. Talbut. "A Thirteenth-Century Pater Noster by an Anglo-French Scribe." *MLR* 3 (1907): 69–71.

Orme, Nicholas. *Education and Society in Medieval and Renaissance England.* London: Hambledon Press, 1989.

Ovide moralisé: Poème du commencement du quatorzième siècle. Edited by C. de Boer. Verhandelingen der Koninklijke Akademie van Wetenschappen te Amsterdam, Afdeeling Letterkunde, N. R. 15, 21, 30, nos. 3, 37, 43. 5 vols. Amsterdam, 1915–38. Reprint. Weisbaden: Sändig, 1966–68.

Owst, G. R. *Literature and Pulpit in Medieval England: A Neglected Chapter in the History of English Letters and of the English People.* 2d ed. Oxford: Oxford University Press, 1961. Reprint. 1966.

———. *Preaching in Medieval England: An Introduction to Sermon Manuscripts of the Period.* Cambridge: Cambridge University Press, 1926. Reprint. New York: Russell & Russell, 1965.

Pantin, William Abel. *Documents Illustrating the Activities of the General and Provincial Chapters of the English Black Monks, 1215–1540.* 3 vols. Camden Society 3d Series, vols. 45, 47, 54. London, 1931–37.

———. *The English Church in the Fourteenth Century.* Cambridge: Cambridge University Press, 1955. Reprint. Toronto: University of Toronto Press, 1980.

Parkes, M. B. "The Literacy of the Laity." In *Literature and Western Civilization: The Medieval World.* Vol. 2 of *Literature and Western Civilization,* edited by David Daiches and Anthony Thorlby, 555–77. London: Aldus, 1973.

———. "On the Presumed Date and Possible Origin of the Manuscript of the *Ormulum:* Oxford, Bodleian Library, MS Junius 1." In *Five Hundred Years of Words and Sounds: A Festschrift for Eric Dobson,* edited by E. G. Stanley and Douglas Gray, 115–27. Cambridge: D. S. Brewer, 1983.

Patschovsky, Alexander. "The Literacy of Waldensianism from Valdes to *c.* 1400." In *Heresy and Literacy, 1000–1530,* edited by Peter Biller and Anne Hudson, 112–36. Cambridge Studies in Medieval Literature, vol. 23. Cambridge: Cambridge University Press, 1994.

Patterson, Frank Allen. *The Middle English Penitential Lyric: A Study and Collection of Early Religious Verse.* New York: Columbia University Press, 1911.

Paues, Anna C., ed. *A Fourteenth Century English Biblical Version Consisting of a Prologue and Parts of the New Testament Edited from the Manuscripts together with Some Introductory Chapters on Middle English Biblical Versions (Prose Translations).* Cambridge: Cambridge University Press, 1902.

———, ed. *A Fourteenth Century English Biblical Version.* Cambridge: Cambridge University Press, 1904. Reprint. New York: AMS, 1974.

Pearsall, Derek. *John Lydgate.* London: Routledge & Kegan Paul, 1970.

———. "The Origins of the Alliterative Revival." In *The Alliterative Tradition in the Fourteenth Century,* edited by Bernard S. Levy and Paul E. Szarmach, 1–24. Kent, Ohio: Kent State University Press, 1981.

———, ed. *Studies in the Vernon Manuscript.* Cambridge: D. S. Brewer, 1990.

Pearsall, Derek, and I. C. Cunningham, eds. *The Auchinleck Manuscript, National Library of Scotland Advocates' MS. 19.2.1.* Facsimile ed. with intro. London: Scolar Press, 1977. Reprint. 1979.

Peck, Russell A., ed. *Heroic Women from the Old Testament in Middle English Verse.* Middle English Texts. Kalamazoo, Mich.: Medieval Institute Publications, 1991.

Peltier, A. C., ed. *Meditationes Vitae Christi S. Bonaventurae Opera Omnia.* 15 vols. Paris, 1864–71. 12:509–630.

Pépin, J. "A propos de l'histoire de l'exégèse allégorique: l'absurdité, signe de l'allégorie." In *Studia Patristica: Papers Presented to the Second International Conference on Patristic Studies Held at Christ Church, Oxford, 1955,* edited by Kurt Aland and F. L. Cross, 1:395–413. 2 vols. Texte und Untersuchungen zur Geschichte der altchristlichen Literatur, 5th series, vols. 8, 9. Berlin: Akademie, 1957.

Perry, George G., ed. *Religious Pieces in Prose and Verse: Edited from Robert Thornton's MS. (Cir. 1440) in the Lincoln Cathedral Library.* Rev. ed. EETS os 26. London, 1914.

Person, Henry A. *Cambridge Middle English Lyrics.* Rev. ed. Seattle: University of Washington Press, 1962.

Peter the Chanter. *Verbum Abbreviatum.* PL 205.21–370.

Peter Comestor. *Historia Scholastica.* PL 198.1049–1722.

Peters, Edward. *Heresy and Authority in Medieval Europe.* Philadelphia: University of Pennsylvania Press, 1980.

Pickering, O. S. "The 'Defence of Women' from the *Southern Passion:* A New Edition." In *The South English Legendary: A Critical Assessment,* edited by Klaus P. Jankofsky, 154–76. Tübingen: Francke, 1992.

———. "Devotional Elements in Two Early Middle English Lives of Christ." *Leeds Studies in English* ns 14 (1983): 152–66.

———. "*A Newe Lessoun off Crystys Ressurrectoun:* A Second Manuscript and Its Use of *La Estoire del Evangelie.*" *English Philological Studies* 13 (1972): 43–48.

———. "The Outspoken South English Legendary Poet." In *Late Medieval Religious Texts and Their Transmission: Essays in Honour of A. I. Doyle,* edited by A. J. Minnis, 21–37. Cambridge: D. S. Brewer, 1994.

———, ed. *The South English Ministry and Passion: Edited from St. John's College, Cambridge, MS B.6.* Middle English Texts, vol. 16. Heidelberg: Carl Winter, 1984.

———, ed. *The South English Nativity of Mary and Christ: Edited from MS BM Stowe 949.* Middle English Texts, vol. 1. Heidelberg: Carl Winter, 1975.

———. "The *Southern Passion* and the *Ministry and Passion:* The Work of a Middle English Reviser." *Leeds Studies in English* ns 15 (1984): 33–56.

———. "The *Temporale* Narratives of the *South English Legendary.*" *Anglia* 91 (1973): 425–55.

———. "Three South English Legendary Nativity Poems." *Leeds Studies in English* 8 (1975): 105–19.

———. "An Unpublished Middle English Resurrection Poem." *Neuphilologische Mitteilungen* 74 (1973): 269–82.

Pickering, O. S., and Manfred Görlach. "A Newly Discovered Manuscript of the *South English Legendary.*" *Anglia* 100 (1982): 109–23.

Plimpton, George A. *The Education of Chaucer: Illustrated from the Schoolbooks in Use in His Time.* London: Oxford University Press, 1935.

Pollard, A. W., and G. R. Redgrave. *A Short Title Catalogue of Books Printed in England, Scotland, and Ireland and of English Books Printed Abroad 1475–1640.* London, 1926. 2d ed. by W. A Jackson, F. S. Ferguson, and K. F. Pantzer. London, 1976–86.

Powell, Lawrence F., ed. *The Mirrour of the Blessed Lyf of Jesu Christ, A Translation of the Latin Work Entitled Meditationes Vitae Christi, Attributed to Cardinal Bonaventura, Made before the Year 1410 by Nicholas Love, Prior of the Carthusian Monastery of Mount Grace.* Oxford: Clarendon Press; London: Henry Frowde, 1908. 2 vols. Reprint, edited by James Hogg. Analecta Cartusiana, vol. 91. Salzburg: Institut für Anglistik und Amerikanistik, Universität Salzburg, 1989.

Powell, Margaret Joyce, ed. *The Pauline Epistles Contained in MS. Parker 32 Corpus Christi College, Cambridge.* EETS es 116. London, 1916. Reprint, 1973.

Powell, Sue. "The Transmission and Circulation of *The Lay Folks' Catechism.*" In *Late Medieval Religious Texts and Their Transmission: Essays in Honour of A. I. Doyle,* edited by A. J. Minnis, 67–84. Woodbridge, Suffolk: D. S. Brewer, 1994.

Procter, Francis, and Christopher Wordsworth, eds. *Breviarium ad Usum Insignis Ecclesiae Sarum.* 3 vols. Cambridge, 1879–86. Reprint. Farnborough, 1970.

Quinn, E. C. *The Quest of Seth for the Oil of Life.* Chicago: University of Chicago Press, 1962.

Raby, F. J. E. "A Middle English Paraphrase of John of Hoveden's 'Philomela' and the Text of His 'Viola.'" *MLR* 30 (1935): 339–43.

Ragusa, Isa, trans. and ed., and Rosalie B. Green, ed. *Meditations on the Life of Christ.* Princeton: Princeton University Press, 1961.

Reakes, Jason. "The Middle English Prose Translation of the *Meditationes Passione Christi* and Its Links with Manuscripts of Love's *Myrrour.*" *N&Q* ns 27 (1980): 199–202.

Reichl, Karl, ed. *Religiöse Dichtung in Englischen Hochmittelalter: Untersuchung und Edition der Handschrift B.14.39 des Trinity College in Cambridge.* Texte und Untersuchungen zur Englischen Philologie, vol. 1. Munich: Wilhelm Fink, 1973.

Reilly, Robert. "A Middle English Summary of the Bible: An Edition of Trinity College (Oxon) MS 93." Diss., University of Washington, 1966.

Remley, Paul G. *Old English Biblical Verse: Studies in Genesis, Exodus and Daniel.* Cambridge: Cambridge University Press, 1996.

Rhetorica ad Herennium: De ratione dicendi. Translated by Harry Caplan. Loeb Classical Library. Cambridge, Mass.: Harvard University Press; London, Heinemann, 1954.

Richter, Michael. "Latina Lingua—Sacra seu Vulgaris?" In *The Bible and Medieval Culture,* edited by W. Lourdaux and D. Verhelst, 16–34. Mediaevalia Lovaniensia Series, vol. 1 / Studia VII. Louvain: Leuven University Press, 1979.

———. "A Socio-linguistic Approach to the Latin Middle Ages." In *The Materials, Sources and Methods of Ecclesiastical History,* edited by Derek Baker, 69–82. SCH 11. Oxford: Basil Blackwell, 1975.

Riley, Henry T., trans. *Ingulph's Chronicle of the Abbey of Croyland.* Bohn's Antiquarian Library. London, 1854.

Ritchie, W. Tod, ed. *The Bannatyne Manuscript, Writtin in Tyme of Pest 1568.* Vol. 2. Scottish Text Society, 2d series, no. 22. Edinburgh: William Blackwood & Sons, 1928.

Robbins, Rossell Hope, ed. *Secular Lyrics of the XIVth and XVth Centuries.* Oxford: Clarendon Press, 1952.

Robbins, Rossell Hope, and John L. Cutler. *Supplement to the Index of Middle English Verse.* Lexington: University of Kentucky Press, 1965.

Robert of Gretham. *Miroir ou Les Evangiles des Domnées.* Edited by Saverio Panunzio. 2d ed. Biblioteca di Filologia Romanza, vol. 26. Bari: Adriatica Editrice, 1974.

Roberts, Michael. *Biblical Epic and Rhetorical Paraphrase in Late Antiquity.* ARCA Classical and Medieval Texts, Papers and Monographs, vol. 16. Liverpool: Francis Cairns, 1985.

Robertson, D. W., Jr. *A Preface to Chaucer: Studies in Medieval Perspectives.* Princeton: Princeton University Press, 1962. Reprint, 1969, 1973.

Robertson, D. W., Jr., and Bernard F. Huppé. *Piers Plowman and Scriptural Tradition.* Princeton Studies in English, vol. 31. Princeton: Princeton University Press, 1951. Reprint. New York: Octagon Books, 1969.

Rogers, William Elford. "Richard Maidstone's Version of the Fifty-First Psalm." In *Image and Abstraction: Six Middle English Lyrics.* Anglistica 18 (1972): 107–24.

Rolle, Richard. *English Prose Treatises of Richard Rolle de Hampole: Edited from Robert Thornton's MS. (Cir. 1440 A.D.) in the Library of Lincoln Cathedral.* Edited by George G. Perry. Rev. ed. EETS os 20. London, 1921.

———. *The Psalter or Psalms of David and Certain Canticles, with a Translation and Ex-*

position in English by Richard Rolle of Hampole. Edited by H. R. Bramley. Glossary revised and completed by W. W. Skeat. Oxford: Clarendon Press, 1884.

———. *Richard Rolle's Version of the Penitential Psalms.* Edited by Geraldine Hodgson. London: Faith Press, 1928.

Rollins, Hyder E., ed. *Old English Ballads, 1553–1625, Chiefly from Manuscripts.* Cambridge: Cambridge University Press, 1920.

Ross, Woodburn O., ed. *Middle English Sermons Edited from British Museum MS. Royal 18 B.xxiii.* EETS os 209. London, 1940. Reprint, 1981.

Rost, Hans. *Die Bibel im Mittelalter: Beiträge zur Geschichte und Bibliographie der Bibel.* Augsburg: M. Seitz, 1939.

Rouse, Richard H., and Mary A. Rouse. *Preachers, Florilegia and Sermons: Studies on the Manipulus Florum of Thomas of Ireland.* Toronto: Pontifical Institute of Mediaeval Studies, 1979.

Royster, James Finch. "A Middle English Treatise on the Ten Commandments." Part 1, text and notes, *SP* 6 (1910): 3–39. Part 2, intro., *SP* 8 (1911): iii–xxiii.

Sajavaara, Kari, ed. *The Middle English Translations of Robert Grosseteste's Chateau d'Amour.* Mémoires de la Société Néophilologique de Helsinki, vol. 32. 1967.

Salter, Elizabeth. "Ludolphus of Saxony and His English Translators." *MÆ* 33 (1964): 26–35.

———. *Nicholas Love's Myrrour of the Blessed Lyf of Jesu Christ.* M.A. thesis, University of London. Edited and revised by James Hogg. Analecta Cartusiana, vol. 10. Salzburg: Institut für Englische Sprache und Literatur, 1974.

Samson, Annie. "The *South English Legendary:* Constructing a Context." In *Thirteenth Century England I,* edited by P. R. Coss and S. D. Lloyd, 185–95. Proceedings of the Newcastle upon Tyne Conference, 1985. Woodbridge, Suffolk: Boydell & Brewer, 1985.

Sargent, Michael G. "The McGill University Fragment of the 'Southern Assumption.'" *Mediaeval Studies* 36 (1974): 186–98.

———, ed. *Nicholas Love's Mirror of the Blessed Life of Jesus Christ: A Critical Edition Based on Cambridge University Library Additional MSS 6578 and 6686.* Garland Medieval Texts, vol. 18. New York: Garland, 1992.

Sauer, Walter, ed. *The Metrical Life of Christ, Edited from MS BM Add. 39996.* Middle English Texts, vol. 5. Heidelberg: Carl Winter, 1977.

———, ed. *Die mittelenglische Übersetzung der Apokalypse mit Kommentar (Version B).* Diss., University of Heidelberg, 1971.

Scattergood, V. J., ed. "*The Two Ways:* An Unpublished Religious Treatise by Sir John Clanvowe." *English Philological Studies* 10 (1967): 33–56.

———, ed. *The Works of Sir John Clanvowe.* Cambridge: D. S. Brewer; Totawa, N. J.: Rowman & Littlefield, 1975.

Scheffer-Boichorst, Paul, ed. *Chronica Albrici Monachi Trium Fontium.* Monumenta Germaniae Historica: Scriptores, 23:631–950. Hanover, 1874.

Schutzner, Svato. *Medieval and Renaissance Books in the Library of Congress: A Descriptive Catalog.* Vol. 1. Washington, D.C.: Library of Congress, 1989.

Schwarz, Werner. *Principles and Problems of Biblical Translation: Some Reformation Controversies and Their Background.* Cambridge: Cambridge University Press, 1955.

Selma Jónsdóttir. *Illumination in a Manuscript of Stjórn.* Translated by Peter G. Foote. Reykjavík: Almenna bókafélagið, 1971.

Severs, J. Burke, and Albert E. Hartung, gen. eds. *Manual of the Writings in Middle English: 1050–1500*. 10 vols. to date. New Haven: Connecticut Academy of Arts and Sciences, 1967–98. Based on John Edwin Wells, *A Manual of the Writings in Middle English: 1050–1400* and *Supplements* 1–9. New Haven: Connecticut Academy of Arts and Sciences, 1916–51.

Seymour, St. John D. *Anglo-Irish Literature: 1200–1582*. Cambridge: Cambridge University Press, 1929. Reprint. Folcroft, Penn.: Folcroft Press, 1969; New York: Octagon, 1970.

Shepherd, Geoffrey. "English Versions of the Scriptures before Wyclif." In *The Cambridge History of the Bible*, vol. 2, edited by G. W. H. Lampe, 362–87. Cambridge: Cambridge University Press, 1969.

Simmons, Thomas Frederick, ed. *The Lay Folks Mass Book, or the Manner of Hearing Mass with Rubrics and Devotions for the People in Four Texts, and Offices in English according to the Use of York, from Manuscripts of the Xth to the XVth Century*. EETS os 71. London, 1879. Reprint, 1968.

Simmons, Thomas Frederick, and Henry Frederick Nolloth, eds. *The Lay Folks Catechism or the English and Latin Versions of Archbishop Thoresby's Instruction for the People*. EETS os 118. London, 1901.

Sisam, Celia, and Kenneth Sisam, eds. *The Salisbury Psalter*. EETS os 242. London, 1959. Reprint, 1969.

Skeat, Walter W., ed. *The Four Gospels in Anglo-Saxon, Northumbrian, and Old Mercian Versions*. 4 vols. Cambridge: Cambridge University Press, 1871–87.

———, ed. *Joseph of Arimathie: Otherwise Called the Romance of the Seint Graal, or Holy Grail*. EETS os 44. London, 1871.

Small, John, ed. *English Metrical Homilies from Manuscripts of the Fourteenth Century*. Edinburgh: William Paterson, 1862. Reprint. New York: AMS, 1973.

Smalley, Beryl. *The Study of the Bible in the Middle Ages*. 3d ed. Oxford: Basil Blackwell, 1983.

Smeets, Jean Robert. "Les traductions, adaptations, et paraphrases de la Bible en vers." In *La Littérature Didactique, Allégorique et Satirique*. Vol. 6 of Grundriss der romanischen Literaturen des Mittelalters. Gen. ed. Hans Robert Jauss. Heidelberg: Carl Winter, 1968–70. 6:part 1, 48–57 (text); part 2, 81–96 (documentation).

Smetana, Cyril L. "Paul the Deacon's Patristic Anthology." In *The Old English Homily and Its Backgrounds*, edited by Paul E. Szarmach and Bernard F. Huppé, 75–97. Albany: State University of New York Press, 1978.

Smith, A. H. "The Middle English Lyrics in Additional Ms. 45896." *London Mediaeval Studies* 2 (1951): 33–49.

Smith, Toulmin, and Lucy Toulmin Smith. *English Gilds: The Original Ordinances of More Than One Hundred Early English Gilds*. EETS os 40. London, 1870. Reprinted with additional notes, 1892. Reprint, 1924, 1963. Intro. by Lujo Brentano.

Smyth, Mary W. *Biblical Quotations in Middle English Literature before 1350*. Yale Studies in English, vol. 41 (1911). Reprint. Folcroft, Penn.: Folcroft Library Editions, 1974.

Spalding, Mary Caroline. *The Middle English Charters of Christ*. Bryn Mawr College Monographs, vol. 15. Bryn Mawr, Penn., 1914.

Spearing, A. C. *Criticism and Medieval Poetry*. 2d ed. New York: Barnes & Noble, 1972.

Speculum Humanae Salvationis: Kritische Ausgabe, Übersetztung von Jean Mielot (1408).

Edited by J. Lutz and P. Perdrizet. 2 vols. Vol. 1, text and commentary; vol. 2, plates. Leipzig: Karl W. Hiersemann, 1907–9.

Speculum Spiritualium. Paris, 1510.

Spencer, H. Leith. *English Preaching in the Late Middle Ages.* Oxford: Clarendon Press, 1993.

Stallings, M. Jordan, ed. *Meditaciones de passione Christi olim Sancto Bonaventurae Attributae.* Studies in Medieval and Renaissance Latin Language and Literature, vol. 25. Washington, D.C.: Catholic University of America Press, 1965.

Stevenson, George, ed. *Pieces from the Makculloch and the Gray MSS.* Scottish Text Society, 1st series, no. 65. Edinburgh: William Blackwood & Sons, 1918.

Stevenson, Joseph. *Anglo-Saxon and Early English Psalter.* 2 vols. Surtees Society Publications, vols. 16 and 19. London, 1843–47.

Stillingfleet, Edward. *The Council of Trent Examin'd and Disprov'd by Catholick Tradition.* London, 1688.

Stock, Brian. *The Implications of Literacy: Written Language and Models of Interpretation in the Eleventh and Twelfth Centuries.* Princeton: Princeton University Press, 1983.

Tanner, Norman P., ed. *Decrees of the Ecumenical Councils.* 2 vols. London: Sheed & Ward; Washington, D.C.: Georgetown University Press, 1990.

Thompson, Edward Maunde. "Scraps from Middle-English MSS." *Englische Studien* 1 (1877): 214–15.

———, ed. *Customary of the Benedictine Monasteries of Saint Augustine, Canterbury, and Saint Peter, Westminster.* 2 vols. Henry Bradshaw Society, vols. 23, 28. London: Harrison and Sons, 1902–4.

Thompson, John J. *The Cursor Mundi: Poem, Texts and Contexts.* Medium Ævum Monographs, ns 19. Oxford: Society for the Study of Medieval Languages and Literature, 1998.

———. "The *Cursor Mundi,* the 'Inglis tong,' and 'Romance.' " In *Readings in Middle English Romance,* edited by Carol M. Meale, 99–120. Woodbridge, Suffolk: D. S. Brewer, 1994.

———. "Literary Associations of an Anonymous Middle English Paraphrase of Vulgate Psalm L." *MÆ* 57 (1988): 38–55.

———. "Popular Reading Tastes in Middle English Religious and Didactic Literature." In *From Medieval to Medievalism,* edited by John Simons, 82–100. London: Macmillan, 1992.

———. Review of *The Southern Version of Cursor Mundi,* edited by Sarah M. Horrall et al. *MÆ* 57 (1988): 118–21.

———. *Robert Thornton and the London Thornton Manuscript: British Library MS Additional 31042.* Manuscript Studies, vol. 2. Partial facsimile. Woodbridge, Suffolk: D. S. Brewer, 1987.

———. "Textual Instability and the Late Medieval Reputation of Some Middle English Religious Literature." *Text: Transactions of the Society for Textual Scholarship* 5 (1991): 175–94.

———. "Textual Interpolations in the Cotton Manuscript of the Cursor Mundi." *Neuphilologische Mitteilungen* 92 (1991): 15–28.

Thomson, S. Harrison. "A XIIIth Century *Oure Fader* in a Pavia MS." *MLN* 49 (1934): 235–37.

Thouzellier, Christine. *Catharisme et valdéisme en Languedoc à la fin du XIIe et au début du*

XIIIe siècle. 2d ed. Publications de la Faculté des Lettres et Sciences Humaines de Paris: Série "Recherches," vol. 27. Paris: Presses Universitaires de France, 1969.

Tomlins, T. E., et al., eds. *The Statutes of the Realm Printed by Command of His Majesty King George the Third.* 11 vols. London: Dawsons of Pall Mall, 1810–28. Reprint. Dobbs-Ferry, N.Y.: Trans-Media Microfilms, 1972.

Tschann, Judith, and Malcolm Parkes, eds. *Facsimile of Oxford, Bodleian Library, MS Digby 86.* EETS ss 16. London, 1996.

Tubach, Frederic C. *Index Exemplorum: A Handbook of Medieval Religious Tales.* Folklore Fellows Communications, vol. 86, no. 204. Helsinki: Suomalainen Tiedeakatemia, Akademia Scientiarum Fennica, 1969.

Turnbull, W. B. D. D. *Legendae Catholicae: A Lytle Boke of Seyntlie Gestes.* Edinburgh, 1840 [forty copies printed]. Reprint, 1860. Five stories, all from the Auchinleck MS: Pope Gregory (pp. 1–67), St. Margaret (pp. 71–122), Joachim and Anne (pp. 125–64), St. Katherine (pp. 167–209), Mary Magdalen (pp. 213–57).

Turner, Ralph V. *"Descendit ad Inferos:* Medieval Views on Christ's Descent into Hell and the Salvation of the Ancient Just." *Journal of the History of Ideas* 27 (1966): 173–94.

Turville-Petre, Thorlac. *England the Nation: Language, Literature, and National Identity, 1290–1340.* Oxford: Clarendon Press, 1996.

———. "The Relationship of the Vernon and Clopton Manuscripts." In *Studies in the Vernon Manuscript,* edited by Derek Pearsall, 29–44. Cambridge: D. S. Brewer, 1990.

Waldron, Ronald. "Trevisa's Original Prefaces on Translation: a Critical Edition." In *Medieval English Studies Presented to George Kane,* edited by Edward Donald Kennedy, Ronald Waldron, and Joseph S. Wittig, 285–99. Woodbridge, Suffolk; Wolfeboro, NH: D. S. Brewer, 1988.

Wallner, Björn, ed. *A Commentary on the Benedictus.* Lund Universitets Årsskrift, N.F, Avd.1, vol. 53, no. 1. Lund, 1957.

———, ed. *An Exposition of Qui Habitat and Bonum Est in English.* Lund Studies in English, vol. 23. Lund: C. W. K. Gleerup; Copenhagen: Einar Munksgaard, 1954.

Walsh, James, and Eric Colledge, eds. *Of the Knowledge of Ourselves and of God: A Fifteenth-Century Spiritual Florilegium.* London: A. R. Mowbray, 1961.

Ward, H. L. D., and J. A. Herbert, eds. *Catalogue of Romances in the Department of Manuscripts in the British Museum.* 3 vols. London, 1883–1910.

Watson, Nicholas. "Censorship and Cultural Change in Late-Medieval England: Vernacular Theology, the Oxford Translation Debate, and Arundel's Constitutions of 1409." *Speculum* 70 (1995): 822–64.

Weatherly, Edward H., ed. *Speculum Sacerdotale: Edited from British Museum MS. Additional 36791.* EETS os 200. London, 1936.

Wells, Minnie E. "The Structural Development of the *South English Legendary." JEGP* 41 (1942): 320–44.

Wenzel, Siegfried. *Macaronic Sermons: Bilingualism and Preaching in Late-Medieval England.* Ann Arbor: University of Michigan Press, 1994.

———. "Medieval Sermons." In *A Companion to* Piers Plowman, edited by John A. Alford, 155–72. Berkeley and Los Angeles: University of California Press, 1988.

———. *Preachers, Poets, and the Early English Lyric.* Princeton: Princeton University Press, 1986.

————. *Verses in Sermons: Fasciculus Morum and Its Middle English Poems.* Cambridge, Mass.: Medieval Academy of America, 1978.

White, Robert Meadows. *The Ormulum.* 2 vols. Oxford: Oxford University Press, 1852.

Whiteford, Peter, ed. *The Myracles of Oure Lady.* Middle English Texts, vol. 23. Heidelberg: Carl Winter, 1990.

Whitelock, D[orothy], M. Brett, C. N. L. Brooke, F. M. Powicke, and C. R. Cheney, eds. *Councils and Synods: With Other Documents Relating to the English Church.* 2 vols. in 4. Oxford: Clarendon Press, 1964–81.

Wilkins, David, ed. *Concilia Magnae Britanniae et Hiberniae.* 4 vols. London, 1737. Reprint. Brussels, 1964.

William of Malmesbury. *Gesta Regum Anglorum: The History of the English Kings.* Vol. 1. Edited and translated by R. A. B. Mynors, R. M. Thomson, and M. Winterbottom. Oxford: Clarendon Press, 1998.

William of Shoreham. *The Poems of William of Shoreham, AB. 1320 Vicar of Chart-Sutton.* Edited by M. Konrath. EETS es 86. London, 1902. Part 1: Preface, Introduction, Text, and Notes. [Part 2: Dialect, Meter, and Glossary, never appeared.]

————. *The Religious Poems of William de Shoreham, Vicar of Chart-Sutton, in Kent, in the Reign of Edward II.* Edited by Thomas Wright. Percy Society, vol. 28. London, 1849.

Wilson, Adrian, and Joyce Lancaster Wilson. *A Medieval Mirror: Speculum humanae salvationis, 1324–1500.* Berkeley and Los Angeles: University of California Press, 1984.

Wilson, Edward, ed. *A Descriptive Index of the English Lyrics in John of Grimestone's Preaching Book.* Medium Ævum Monographs, ns 2. 1973. Reprint, 1977.

Wilson, Edward, and Iain Fenlon, eds. *The Winchester Anthology: A Facsimile of British Library Additional Manuscript 60577.* Woodbridge, Suffolk: D. S. Brewer, 1981.

Wilson, J. M. "Worcester Cathedral Library Report." *Library: Transactions of the Bibliographical Society,* 4th ser., 2 (1922): 257–65.

Wilson, R. M. "English and French in England, 1100–1300." *History* ns 28 (1943): 37–60.

Wilson, Robert H. "*The Stanzaic Life of Christ* and the Chester Plays." *SP* 28 (1931): 413–32.

Woolf, Rosemary. *The English Mystery Plays.* Berkeley and Los Angeles: University of California Press, 1972.

————. *The English Religious Lyric in the Middle Ages.* Oxford: Clarendon Press, 1968.

Wordsworth, Christopher, ed. *Horae Eboracensis: The Prymer or Hours of the Blessed Virgin Mary.* Surtees Society, vol. 132. London, 1920.

Wordsworth, Christopher, and Henry Littlehales. *The Old Service-Books of the English Church.* 2d ed. London: Methuen, 1910.

Wormald, Francis. "Bible Illustration in Medieval Manuscripts." In *The Cambridge History of the Bible,* vol. 2, edited by G. W. H. Lampe, 309–37. Cambridge: Cambridge University Press, 1969.

Wright, Thomas. *The Chester Plays: A Collection of Mysteries Founded upon Scriptural Subjects.* 2 vols. London: Shakespeare Society, 1843–47. Reprint, 1966.

Wright, Thomas, and James Orchard Halliwell, eds. *Reliquiae Antiquae: Scraps from Ancient Manuscripts, Illustrating Chiefly Early English Literature and the English Language.* 2 vols. London, 1841–43. Reprint. New York: AMS, 1966.

Wyclif, John. *Johannis Wyclif Opera Minora.* Edited by Johann Loserth. Vol. 21 of

Wyclif's Latin Works. 22 vols. London: Wyclif Society, 1883–1922. Reprint. New York: Johnson, 1966.

———. *Select English Works of John Wyclif.* Edited by Thomas Arnold. 3 vols. Oxford: Clarendon Press, 1869–71.

Zim, Rivkah. *English Metrical Psalms: Poetry as Praise and Prayer 1535–1601.* Cambridge: Cambridge University Press, 1987.

Zupitza, Julius, ed. "Die Gedichte des Franziskaners Jakob Ryman." *Archiv* 89 (1892): 167–338.

———, ed. "The Prouerbis of Wysdom." *Archiv* 90 (1893): 241–68.

———, ed. "Was jedermann wissen und andere lehren muss." *Archiv* 90 (1893): 297–98.

———, ed. "Zwei Umschreibungen der Zehn Gebote in mittelenglischen Versen." *Archiv* 85 (1890): 44–48.

Zupitza, Julius, and [J.] Schipper, eds. *Alt- und mittelenglisches Übungsbuch mit einem Wörterbuch.* 14th rev. ed., Albert Eichler. Vienna: Wilhelm Braumüller, 1931.

Index of Biblical Chapters

Portions of the following biblical chapters are cited either in the text or under the entry for the Middle English work (perhaps at more than one point in that work, and not necessarily in canonical order):

GENESIS (*see also* MES, HP)

1   3, 137; FP, TP, CA, CHG, CM, Poly, MMS, BRA, LAE, CC, TCE, GE, OTH, POT, CGL, HCK, PCE
2   FP, TP, CA, CM, Poly, MMS, BRA, LAE, CC, TCE, GE, OTH, POT, CGL, HCK, QL, NHC, PCE
3   FP, TP, CA, CHG, CM, Poly, MMS, BRA, LAE, CC, TCE, GE, OTH, POT, CGL, Cl, BM, NP, ChC, HCK, QL, Orm, NHC, PCE
4   10; TP, CM, Poly, MMS, BRA, LAE, CC, GE, OTH, POT, CGL, SLC, NP, Orm, OF, PCE
5   TP, CM, Poly, GE, OTH, POT, CGL, Cl, Orm
6   CM, Poly, BRA, GE, OTH, POT, CGL, JJ, Cl, Orm, PCE
7   Poly, GE, OTH, POT, CGL, JJ, Cl, Orm
8   Poly, GE, OTH, POT, CGL, Cl, SLC
9   CM, Poly, MMS, GE, OTH, POT, CGL, Cl, PCE
10 CM, Poly
11 CM, Poly, MMS, GE, OTH, POT, CGL

12 CM, Poly, GE, OTH, POT, CGL
13 CM, Poly, GE, CGL
14 CM, Poly, MMS, BRA, GE, POT, CGL, SLC
15 CM, MMS, GE, POT, CGL
16 CM, Poly, GE, OTH, POT, CGL
17 CM, Poly, GE, OTH, POT, CGL, SLC, NHC
18 138; CM, GE, OTH, POT, CGL, Cl
19 CM, Poly, MMS, BRA, GE, OTH, POT, CGL, Cl
20 CM, GE, CGL
21 CM, Poly, GE, OTH, POT, CGL
22 CM, MMS, HP, GE, OTH, POT, CGL, SLC, Orm
23 CM, Poly, GE, OTH, POT, CGL
24 CM, Poly, MMS, GE, OTH, POT, CGL
25 CM, GE, OTH, POT, CGL, SLC
26 CM, GE, POT
27 CM, GE, OTH, POT, CGL, SLC
28 CM, MMS, GE, OTH, POT, CGL
29 CM, GE, OTH, POT, CGL, JJ
30 CM, Poly, GE, POT, CGL, JJ
31 CM, GE, OTH, CGL
32 CM, HP, GE, OTH, POT, CGL
33 CM, GE, OTH, CGL

GENESIS (*continued*)

34 GE, CGL
35 GE, OTH, CGL
36 GE
37 CM, Poly, MMS, GE, OTH, POT, CGL, JJ
38 MMS, POT
39 CM, GE, OTH, POT, CGL, JJ, SA, SLC
40 CM, MMS, GE, OTH, POT, CGL, JJ, SA
41 9, 159; CM, Poly, GE, OTH, POT, CGL, JJ, SA, SLC
42 CM, GE, OTH, POT, CGL, JJ, SA, SLC
43 CM, GE, OTH, POT, CGL, JJ
44 CM, GE, OTH, POT, CGL, JJ
45 CM, GE, OTH, POT, CGL, JJ
46 CM, Poly, CGL, JJ
47 CM, GE, OTH, CGL, JJ
48 CM, CGL
49 CM, Poly, OTH, CGL, SA, TK, SLC, NHC
50 CM, Poly, HP, GE, OTH, POT, CGL

EXODUS (*see also* MES)

1   CM, Poly, GE, OTH, POT, CGL, PCE
2   9; CM, Poly, MMS, GE, OTH, POT, CGL
3   CM, MMS, GE, OTH, POT, CGL
4   9; CM, Poly, GE, OTH, POT, CGL
5   CM, GE, POT, CGL
6   CM, GE, CGL
7   CM, GE, OTH, POT, CGL, GNs
8   CM, GE, OTH, POT, CGL, KP
9   CM, GE, OTH, POT, CGL, KP
10 CM, GE, OTH, POT, CGL, KP
11 CM, GE, POT, CGL
12 CM, MMS, GE, OTH, CGL, KP
13 CM, Poly, GE
14 CM, Poly, MMS, GE, OTH, POT, CGL, GNp, SLC, Orm, NHC, PCE
15 CM, GE, POT, CGL, CH, SLC
16 CM, Poly, MMS, GE, OTH, POT, CGL, SLC, NHC
17 18; CM, Poly, GE, OTH, POT, CGL
18 CM, GE, POT, CGL
19 33; CA, CM, Poly, GE, OTH, CGL, SLC, PCE

20 CA, CM, MMS, BRA, GE, OTH, CGL, TC, PPs, BM, SE, TW, Orm, PCE
21 CM, [MMS], OTH, PCE
22 47; CM, OTH, PCE
23 47; CM, OTS
24 18; OTH, CGL
25 MMS, GNp
26 PCE
28 PCE
31 GE
32 18; CM, MMS, GE, OTH, POT, CGL, PCE
33 CM, PCE
34 CM, OTH, PCE
35 CM
36 CM
37 CM, POT
40 POT, PCE

LEVITICUS (*see also* MES, GE)

8   GE
11 OTH, PCE
12 OTH, PCE
13 PCE
14 PCE
15 PCE
18 OTH
19 OTS, OTH
23 PCE
24 Cl
27 OTH

NUMBERS (*see also* MES)

1   POT
3   PCE
4   PCE
10 GE, CGL
11 GE
12 MMS, GE, POT, CGL
13 Poly, MMS, GE, POT, CGL
14 Poly, GE, POT, CGL
16 MMS, GE, POT
17 MMS, GE, POT, CGL, SLC
20 GE, POT, CGL
21 GE, POT, CGL, Orm, NHC
22 GE, OTH, POT, SLC
23 GE, POT, SLC
24 TP, MMS, OTH, POT, TK, NMC, SLC
25 GE, POT
26 GE, POT

27 GE
31 POT
32 POT

DEUTERONOMY (*see also* MES)

 5 TC
 6 79; BM
 7 OTH
25 BM
27 BM
28 BM, OF
32 CH, BM
33 GE
34 CM, Poly, GE, OTH, POT, CGL

JOSUE (*see also* MES)

 1 CM, Poly
 2 CM, POT
 3 CM, Poly, MMS, POT
 4 MMS, POT
 5 Poly, POT
 6 POT
 7 POT
 8 POT
 9 POT
10 POT, CGL
11 POT
12 POT
13 POT
14 POT
15 POT
16 POT
17 POT
18 POT
19 POT
20 POT
21 POT
22 POT
23 POT
24 POT

JUDGES (*see also* MES)

 3 CM, Poly, MMS, POT
 4 CM, Poly, MMS, POT
 6 CM, Poly, MMS, OTH, POT
 7 POT
 8 MMS
 9 Poly, MMS, POT
10 CM, Poly
11 CM, Poly, MMS, POT
12 CM, Poly, POT
13 CM, POT

14 CM, MMS, OTH, POT
15 CM, MMS, OTH, POT
16 CM, Poly, MMS, OTH, POT
19 POT
20 POT

RUTH (*see also* MES)

 1 MMS, POT
 2 POT
 3 POT
 4 POT

1 KINGS [1Samuel] (*see also* MES)

 1 MMS, POT, CGL
 2 POT, CGL, CH
 3 POT, CGL
 4 CM, Poly, POT, CGL
 5 POT, CGL
 6 POT, CGL
 7 POT
 8 CM, POT, CGL
 9 CM, POT
10 CM, Poly, POT, CGL
11 CM, POT
12 CM, POT
13 CM, POT
14 CM, POT
15 CM, POT, CGL
16 CM, OTH, POT, CGL, BM
17 CM, MMS, OTH, POT, CGL
18 CM, MMS, OTH, POT, CGL
19 CM, MMS, OTH, POT, CGL
20 CM, POT
21 CM, POT
22 CM, POT
23 CM, POT
24 CM, POT, CGL
25 CM, MMS, POT, CGL
26 CM, POT, CGL
27 CM, POT, CGL
28 CM, POT, CGL
29 CM, POT
30 CM, POT, CGL
31 CM, OTH, POT, CGL

2 KINGS [2Samuel] (*see also* MES)

 1 CM, OTH, POT
 2 OTH, POT
 3 MMS, POT
 4 POT
 5 POT, CGL
 6 MMS, POT, CGL, BM

2 KINGS (*continued*)

  7 POT
  9 POT
10 MMS, POT
11 CM, OTH, POT, CGL
12 CM, MMS, OTH, POT, CGL
13 MMS, OTH, POT, CGL
14 MMS, POT, CGL
15 POT, CGL
16 MMS, POT, CGL
17 POT
18 MMS, OTH, POT, CGL
19 OTH, POT, CGL
20 MMS, POT, CGL
21 POT
22 POT
23 MMS
24 OTH, POT, CGL

3 KINGS (*see also* MES)

  1 CM, OTH, POT, CGL
  2 MMS, OTH, POT, CGL, GNp
  3 CM, Poly, OTH, POT, CGL
  4 OTH, POT, CGL
  5 CM, POT, CGL
  6 Poly, MMS, POT
  7 MMS, POT
  8 POT
  9 POT, CGL
10 Poly, MMS, POT, CGL
11 CM, OTH, POT, CGL
12 Poly, OTH, POT, CGL
13 POT
14 CM, Poly, POT
15 CM, POT
16 Poly, OTH, POT
17 75, 82; OTH, POT, Orm
18 CM, POT
19 OTH, POT
20 POT
21 POT
22 POT, CM

4 KINGS (*see also* MES)

  1 OTH, POT
  2 75; CM, Poly, MMS, OTH, POT,
     Orm
  3 MMS, POT
  4 MMS, OTH, POT
  5 68; MMS, POT, NP
  6 POT
  7 POT

  8 POT
  9 Poly, POT
10 POT
11 Poly, POT
12 POT
13 POT
14 Poly, POT
15 CM, Poly, POT
16 CM
18 CM
19 CM, Poly, MMS
20 CM, Poly
21 CM, Poly
22 CM, Poly
23 Poly
24 CM
25 CM, Poly

1 PARALIPOMENON [1 Chronicles]
(*see* MES)

2 PARALIPOMENON [2 Chronicles]
(*see also* MES)

10 POT
11 POT
12 POT
13 POT
14 POT
15 POT
16 POT
17 POT
18 POT
20 POT
21 POT
22 POT
23 POT
24 POT
25 POT
26 POT
33 MMS
36 Cl

1 ESDRAS [Ezra] (*see also* MES)

  1 MMS, SLC
  4 Poly, MMS
  5 Poly
  7 Poly

2 ESDRAS [Nehemiah] (*see also* MES)

  2 Poly
  4 Poly
  8 Poly

3 ESDRAS (*see* MES)

4 ESDRAS (*see* MES)

TOBIAS (*see also* MES)

1 POT, CGL, BM, SWM
2 POT, CGL, BM
3 181; POT, CGL, BM
4 MMS, OTS, POT, CGL
5 MMS, POT, CGL
6 MMS, POT, CGL, BM
7 POT, CGL
8 POT, CGL, BM
9 POT, CGL
10 MMS, POT, CGL
11 POT, CGL
12 POT, CGL, BM
13 BM
14 POT, CGL, BM

JUDITH (*see also* MES)

1 POT, CGL
2 POT, CGL
3 POT, CGL
4 POT, CGL
5 3
6 MMS, CGL
7 POT, CGL
8 POT, CGL
9 POT, CGL
10 POT, CGL
11 POT, CGL
12 MMS, POT, CGL
13 Poly, POT, CGL
14 POT, CGL
15 POT, CGL
16 POT, CGL

ESTHER (*see also* MES)

1 MMS, POT
2 POT
3 POT
4 POT
5 POT, BM
6 POT
7 MMS, POT, BM
8 POT
13 BM

JOB (*see also* MES)

1 MMS, POT, CGL, MLJ, Orm
2 MMS, POT, CGL, MLJ, Orm

3 POT
4 POT
5 POT
6 POT, SLC, MLP
7 POT, PJ, PPs, MLP
8 POT
9 POT, MLP
10 POT, PJ, PPs
11 POT
12 POT
13 POT, PJ, PPs
14 POT, PJ, PPs
15 POT
16 POT, MLP
17 POT, PJ, PPs
18 WA, POT
19 169; POT, PJ, PPs, SLC, MLP
20 POT
21 POT
22 POT
23 POT
24 POT
25 POT
26 POT
27 POT
28 POT
29 POT
30 POT, MLP
31 POT
32 POT
38 POT
39 POT
40 POT
41 POT, SLC
42 POT, CGL, MLJ

PSALMS (*see also* MES, SPs, MPPs, RPs)

5 PPs, JPs, BM
6 RMPs, TBPs, PPs, JPs
7 PPs
8 PPs
9 CC
12 PPs, JPs, BPs, MBL
13 TCE
16 JPs, TW
17 176
18 PPs, JPs
21 263; MMS, JPs, MBL
22 MMS, PPs
23 PPs, Prl
24 PPs, JPs, TW
25 23; JPs

PSALMS (*continued*)

26 PPs, JPs
27 JPs
29 PPs
30 WA, JPs, BPs, MBL
31 RMPs, TBPs, PPs
32 JPs
34 82; JPs, MBL
35 JPs
36 WA
37 RMPs, TBPs, PPs
38 WA, JPs, BPs
39 PPs, JPs, MBL
40 PPs, JPs
41 PPs
42 PPs, LPs
43 JPs
44 MBL
47 TK, NMC, SLC, MBL
48 SLC
50 82; RMPs, TBPs, PPs, JPs, MPs,
    HCS
52 TCE
53 PPs, JPs, LPs
54 JPs, MBL
58 JPs
61 Prl
62 PPs
63 33
64 PPs
66 PPs
68 CHG, JPs, MBL, Orm
69 MMS, JPs, HCS
70 JPs
71 TK, NHC
73 JPs
75 WA, TBPs
77 BM, NHC
78 JPs
79 JPs, EE
83 MBL
84 CA, CHG, TBPs, JPs, DP, TW, MBL
85 181; JPs, BPs
87 JPs, MBL
88 JPs, LPs
89 JPs
90 78, 79; MMS, QHPs
91 BEPs
92 PPs
93 Cl, Pat
94 PPs

99 PPs
101 RMPs, TBPs, PPs, JPs
102 LPs
103 SLC
104 PPs
108 JPs, MBL
110 WS, TW
113 WA
114 PPs
115 BPs
116 PPs
117 RMPs, PPs, MBL
118 285; WA, OTS, PPs, JPs, MBL, TW
119 PPs
120 PPs
121 PPs
122 PPs, JPs
123 PPs
124 PPs, JPs
125 PPs, JPs
126 PPs
127 PPs
128 PPs, TW
129 RMPs, TBPs, PPs, JPs, DPPs
130 PPs
131 PPs
132 30; PPs
133 PPs
135 MBL
137 PPs, JPs
138 PPs
140 JPs
141 JPs, BPs
142 RMPs, TBPs, PPs, JPs, Prl
143 CHG, MMS
145 PPs
148 PPs, CJ, NMC
149 PPs
150 PPs

PROVERBS (*see also* MES)

1 WS, TW
4 WA
9 WS, TW
10 OTS
11 OTS
12 44; MBL
14 OTS
15 OTS
16 MBL
17 OTS
18 OTS

21 44; OTS
22 OTS
23 OTS
24 TBPs
26 OTS
28 OTS
29 OTS
31 ES

ECCLESIASTES (*see also* MES, WS)

2 OTS
5 WA

CANTICLE OF CANTICLES
[Song of Solomon] (*see also* MES)

1 MMS, BM
2 BM, SLC
3 CHG, BM
4 CHG, MMS, MLP, Prl
5 CHG, MMS
6 CHG
7 MLP

WISDOM (*see also* MES)

1 OTS
4 BM, MBL
5 BM
9 CHG, SLC
10 WA, Prl
17 OF

ECCLESIASTICUS [Jesus Sirach]
(*see also* MES)

1 OTH
3 OTS
4 OTS, OTH
6 OTH
7 264; OTS, OTH
8 OTH
9 OTH
11 OTS
12 OTH
13 MS
14 OTS, OTH
16 OTS, OTH, BM
19 OTH
20 OTH
21 OTH
22 OTH
23 WA, OTS
28 OTS
29 TW

30 OTS, OTH
36 MMS
37 OTH

ISAIAS (*see also* MES)

1 9, 263; CM, Cl, CJ, EE, PGH, NHC,
   LLC, EN, SLC, QL, NHC, MBL
5 OTS
6 16
7 CM, MMS, EE, TK, SLC, DJM
9 217; CA, CM, RFL, GNs, MP, SLC,
   NHC, MBL
10 OTS
11 248; TP, CM, MMS, CJ, NMC,
   ConM, DJM
12 CH
14 9, 92; FP, TCE, GE, Cl, DP
16 MMS
19 MMS, CJ, EE, GNp, NMC, EN,
   MBL
24 OTS
30 97; CM
38 PPs, CH
40 Orm, NHC
45 Poly
47 OTS
50 263, 278; MBL
53 263; MBL, MS, Prl
58 18
59 SLC
60 TK
61 MBL, NHC
63 263
64 CHG
65 NMC

JEREMIAS (*see also* MES)

1 Poly
4 SLC
9 CHG, OTS
17 OTS
18 MBL
43 Poly
45 CHG
46 WA
48 OTS
52 Cl

LAMENTATIONS (*see also* MES)

1 263; CHG, MMS, NP, ChC, SLL
2 CHG
5 CHG

BARUCH (*see also* MES)

3　BM
4　BM

EZEKIEL (*see also* MES)

1　Orm
2　BM
3　BM
44　MMS, SLC

DANIEL (*see also* MES)

1　Cl
2　MMS
3　Poly, MMS, PPs, CH
4　Poly, MMS, Cl
5　Poly, MMS, Cl
6　Poly, OTH
7　Poly
9　Poly
10　Poly
12　OTS
13　Poly, PSS
14　MMS, OTH, TK, MBL

OSEE [Hosea] (*see* MES)

JOEL (*see also* MES)

2　MMS
3　CM, TBPs

AMOS (*see* MES)

ABDIAS [Obadiah] (*see also* MES)

JONAS (*see also* MES)

1　MMS, POT, Pat
2　Pat
3　POT, Pat
4　POT, Pat

MICHEAS [Micah] (*see also* MES)

4　263
5　NHC
6　OF

NAHUM (*see* MES)

HABACUC (*see also* MES)

3　CH

SOPHONIAS [Zephaniah] (*see* MES)

AGGEUS [Haggai] (*see* MES)

ZACHARIAS (*see also* MES)

11　MBL
12　MBL
13　263

MALACHIAS (*see* MES)

1 MACHABEES (*see also* MES)

1　Poly
2　277
6　MMS
10　Poly
11　Poly
12　Poly
13　Poly
14　Poly
15　Poly
16　Poly

2 MACHABEES

2　Poly
3　Poly, MMS
5　Poly
6　Poly, POT
7　Poly, POT
8　Poly, OTS
9　Poly, POT
10　Poly
14　Poly
15　Poly

MATTHEW (*see also* MES, MML, OF, VC, *MPC*)

1　TP, CM, Poly, MMS, BRA, EE, PGH, GNs, NMC, LLC, EN, SLC, Orm, NHC, MBL, PCE
2　75; TP, CM, Poly, MMS, BRA, CGL, CJ, EE, PGH, RFL, GNp, DP, TK, BM, NMC, EN, MLC, SLC, MLP, LLB, HCK, BTD, BVP, RSP, JA, QL, Orm, NHC, MBL, PCE
3　TP, CM, MMS, BRA, EE, PGH, RFL, TK, BM, MP, ALC, MLC, SLC, PL, MLP, CB, QL, Orm, NHC, MBL, PCE
4　78, 217; CA, CHG, CM, MMS, WA, EE, PGH, RFL, DP, BM, MP, ALC, MLC, SLC, PL, NP, MLP, ChC, SEL, Orm, NHC, MBL, PCE
5　Cl, Pat, EE, PGH, TV, BM, MP, Beat, SE, Orm, NHC, MBL, PCE

6 CM, WA, PPs, BM, MP, SE, PN,
  NHC, MBL, PCE
7 17, 30, 31, 32; OTS, TBPs, SLC, TW,
  NHC
8 68; MMS, PGH, GNp, MP, MLC,
  NHC
9 PGH, GNp, TV, BM, MP, MLC,
  DJM, NHC, MBL
10 PGH, MP, MLC, SLC
11 68; CA, DP, BM, MLP, NHC, MBL
12 231; PGH, GNp, TV, MP, SLC, NHC
13 16, 32; Cl, PGH, BM, MP, SP, PL,
  Prl, NHC, MBL
14 CA, CM, Poly, BRA, PGH, DP, MP,
  ALC, MLC, SLC, SEL, MBL
15 BRA, PGH, LLC, MLC, NHC,
  MBL
16 OTS, PGH, MP, LLC, MLC, MBL
17 PGH, DP, MP, LLC, MLC, SLC,
  MBL
18 MMS, PGH, MP, NHC
19 CHG, PGH, MP, Prl, TW, MBL
20 320; PGH, PCL, MP, Prl, PLV,
  NHC, MBL
21 CM, MMS, BRA, RMPs, EE, PGH,
  RFL, GNp, PCL, MP, SP, LLC,
  MLC, SLC, PL, NP, MLP, MTM,
  NHC, MBL
22 16; CHG, BRA, Cl, PGH, TV, BM,
  MP, SP, LLC, TW, NHC, MBL
23 PGH TV, BM, MP, LLC, MBL
24 TV, BM, MP, SP, LLC
25 47; CA, MMS, EE, CR, PGH, BM,
  MP, SP, LLC, SE, SWM, QL, Orm,
  NHC, MBL
26 23, 277; FP, TP, CHG, CM, MMS,
  BRA, CGL, RMPs, EE, PGH, RFL,
  GNs, GNp, PCL, TV, BM, MP, SP,
  MLC, SLC, PL, NP, MLP, MS, PC,
  SPC, CDL, HC, HCS, HCA, HCK,
  MTM, QL, SEL, MBL
27 7, 8, 9, 263; FP, TP, CA, CHG, CM,
  Poly, MMS, BRA, POT, CGL, EE,
  PGH, RFL, GNs, GNp, PCL, DP,
  HH, TK, TV, BM, MP, SP, MLC,
  SLC, PL, NP, MLP, ChC, LLB,
  MS, RP, SLL, PC, CP, SPC, CDL,
  LA, HC, HCS, HCA, HCK, MTM,
  RA, QL, SEL, MBL
28 352; TP, CM, MMS, BRA, CGL, EE,
  PGH, GNs, GNp, PCL, HH, TV,

MP, SP, MLC, SLC, PL, MLP, PC,
  CP, LA, HCA, HCK, RA, MBL

MARK (*see also* MES, MML, OF, VC,
MPC)
1 PGH, BM, NHC, MBL
2 PGH, RFL, MBL
3 PGH, BM, SLC
5 PGH, BM, NHC
6 PGH, BM, Orm
7 PGH, MP, LLC, NHC
8 PGH, GNs, MP, LLC, NHC
9 PGH, MP, LLC, MLC, NHC
10 BM
11 OTS
12 PGH, MP
14 MMS, PGH, MP, SP, PL, NP, MS,
  SEL
15 RP, MBL
16 34; FP, CA, MMS, BRA, CGL, CR,
  PGH, GNp, PCL, DP, TV, MP, SP,
  SLC, RP, BVP, RSP, SEL, NHC,
  MBL

LUKE (*see also* MES, MML, OF, VC,
MPC)
1 72; FP, TP, CM, Poly, MMS, BRA,
  PPs, CH, EE, PGH, RFL, DP,
  HH, BM, NMC, LLC, EN, SLC,
  MS, HCK, CB, BVP, RSP, JA, QL,
  Orm, NHC, MBL
2 217, 275; CA, CHG, CM, Poly,
  MMS, BRA, CGL, RMPs, PPs,
  CH, CJ, EE, PGH, RFL, GNs, DP,
  TK, BM, NMC, ConM, EN, ALC,
  MLC, SLC, MLP, LLB, RP, CP,
  HCS, HCK, MTM, DJM, Orm,
  NHC, MBL
3 73; Poly, CGL, SLC, HCK, Orm,
  NHC, MBL
4 Poly, PGH, MP, HCK, NHC, MBL
5 MMS, PGH, MLC, NHC, MBL
6 MMS, WA, PGH, MP, NHC, MBL
7 10; PGH, BM, MP, MLC, SEL,
  NHC, MBL
8 10, 32; MMS, CR, DP, MP, SEL,
  NHC
9 PGH, DP, MP, HCK, NHC
10 9; MMS, PGH, RFL, BM, MP, SEL,
  NHC, MBL
11 WA, OTS, PGH, MP, NHC, MBL

LUKE (*continued*)

12   352, WA, PGH, MP, SLC, NHC
13   PGH, MP, LLC, NHC
14   Cl, PGH, MP, LLC, NHC, MBL
15   MMS, PGH, BM, MP, LLC, NHC
16   146; POT, PGH, BM, MP, LLC, NHC
17   PGH, GNs, NHC, MBL
18   PGH, MP, LLC, MLC, SLC, NHC, MBL
19   MMS, PGH, TV, MP, SP, LLC, SLC, NHC
20   SP
21   LLC, SP, NHC, MBL
22   277; CM, MMS, EE, PGH, PCL, MP, SP, LLC, MLC, PL, NP, MLP, ChC, SLL, MS, HCK, NHC, MBL
23   146, 222, 275; MMS, BRA, POT, RMPs, EE, PGH, RFL, GNs, GNp, PCL, HH, NMC, MP, SP, EN, MLC, SLC, PL, NP, MLP, LLB, MS, SLL, RP, CP, HC, HCK, MTM, TW, QL, MBL
24   263; BRA, CGL, CR, PGH, GNs, GNp, PCL, HH, MP, SP, MLC, SLC, PL, HCK, MTM, RA, QL, SEL, NHC, MBL

JOHN (*see also* MES, OF, VC, *MPC*)

1   83, 137; PGH, MP, MLC, SLC, EP, CB, Prl, BVP, RSP, Orm, NHC, MBL
2   CA, CM, Poly, MMS, CJ, PGH, DP, TV, BM, MP, LLC, ALC, MLC, SLC, MLP, Orm, NHC, MBL
3   217; PGH, DP, MP, LLC, SLC, Orm, NHC
4   PGH, BM, MP, LLC, WomS, Orm, NHC, MBL
5   CM, PGH, GNs, MP, MLC, NP, NHC, MBL
6   CM, OTS, PGH, MP, MLC, NHC, MBL
7   217; PGH, MP, SLC, NHC
8   CHG, CM, WA, PGH, RFL, TV, BM, MP, LLC, MLC, TW, NHC
9   CM, PGH, GNs, SLC, NHC
10   BRA, PGH, MP, LLC, RP, NHC, MBL
11   146; CA, CM, BRA, POT, RMPs, PGH, GNp, PCL, DP, TV, BM, MP, LLC, MLC, NP, MLP, SEL, NHC, MBL
12   CM, PGH, RFL, TV, BM, MP, SP, LLC, SLC, PL, NP, Prl, SEL, NHC, MBL
13   277; CHG, CM, MMS, BRA, PGH, RFL, PCL, DP, BM, MP, SP, LLC, MLC, NP, MLP, MS, SPC, HCK, SEL, NHC, MBL
14   MMS, OTS, PGH, BM, MP, SP, LLC, SLC, MLP, MS, TW, NHC, MBL
15   68; MMS, OTS, PGH, BM, MP, LLC, MLP, MS, NHC, MBL
16   352; MMS, PGH, BM, MP, SP, LLC, MLP, MS, NHC, MBL
17   TBPs, PGH, BM, SP, MLP, MS
18   277; MMS, BRA, EE, PGH, RFL, GNp, PCL, TV, MP, SP, MLC, SLC, PL, NP, LLB, MS, HCK, SEL
19   217; FP, CHG, CM, MMS, BRA, CGL, EE, PGH, RFL, GNs, GNp, PCL, TV, MP, SP, MLC, SLC, PL, NP, MLP, ChC, LLB, MS, RP, SLL, PC, CP, SPC, HC, HCK, TW, QL, SEL, MBL
20   278, 334, 338; FP, TP, CA, CM, BRA, CGL, EE, CR, PGH, RFL, DP, MP, SP, MLC, SLC, PL, MLP, HC, RA, QL, SEL, NHC, MBL
21   277, 334, 338; CM, PGH, MP, SP, MLC, SLC, HCK, MBL

ACTS (*see also* MES)

1   264; CM, Poly, MMS, EE, CR, PGH, TV, MP, SP, MLC, PL, NP, MLP, HCK, SEL, PCE
2   CA, CM, MMS, BRA, CGL, EE, CR, PGH, DP, MP, SP, MLC, SLC, PL, MLP, HCK, NHC, MBL, PCE
3   CM, MP, SP, PCE
4   CM, MP, SP, SLC, MBL, PCE
5   PCE
6   CM, PCE
7   3; CM, Poly, PCE
8   CM, SP, Orm, PCE
9   CM, Poly, SEL, PCE
10   CM, PCE
13   3; PCE
12   PCE
13   PCE

14   PCE
15   PCE
16   346; PCE
17   346; SP, PCE
18   PCE
19   PCE
20   SEL, PCE
21–28 PCE

ROMANS (*see also* MES)

1   PE
2   PE
3   PE
4   SLC, PE
5   PE, PCE
6   SLC, PE, PCE
7   PE, PCE
8   SLC, Prl, TW, MBL, PE, PCE,
9   MMS, PE
10   PE
11   PE
12   TW, PE, PCE
13   PE, PCE
14   PE
15   14, 15, 83, 146, 151, 337, 345; PE
16   PE

1 CORINTHIANS (*see also* MES)

1   PE, PCE
2   TW, PE, PCE
3   32, 337; BM, TW, PE, PCE
4   BM, PE
5   BM, PE, PCE
6   BM, PE, PCE
7   344; PE, PCE
8   PE
9   PE
10   PE
11   NHC, PE, PCE
12   BM, SLC, Prl, PE, PCE
13   346; BM, SLC, SCC, Orm, MBL,
      PE, PCE
14   OTS, PE
15   PGH, DP, MP, SLC, MBL, PE
16   PE

2 CORINTHIANS (*see also* MES)

1   MBL, PE
2   PE
3   SLC, PE
4   OTS, BM, PE

5   PE
6   BM, PE, PCE
7   PE
8   PE
9   WA, PE
10   PE
11   344; PE
12   PE
13   PE

GALATIANS (*see also* MES)

1   PE
2   PE
3   PE
4   BM, PE
5   TW, PE, PCE
6   MBL, PE, PCE

EPHESIANS (*see also* MES)

1   PE
2   PE
3   PE
4   PE, PCE
5   SLC, OF, MBL, PE, PCE
6   PE, PCE

PHILIPPIANS (*see also* MES)

1   PE, PCE
2   MMS, SLC, OF, PE, PCE
3   PE, PCE
4   PE, PCE

COLOSSIANS (*see also* MES)

1   PE, PCE
2   270; PE, PCE
3   TW, PE, PCE
4   PE, PCE

1 THESSALONIANS (*see also* MES)

1   PE, PCE
2   BM, PE, PCE
3   PE, PCE
4–5 BM, PE, PCE

2 THESSALONIANS (*see also* MES)

1–3 BM, PE, PCE

1 TIMOTHY (*see also* MES)

1   21; OF, PE, PCE
2   BM, PE, PCE
3   PE, PCE

1 TIMOTHY (*continued*)

4   21; PE, PCE
5   BM, PE, PCE
6   BM, TW, MBL, PE, PCE

2 TIMOTHY (*see also* MES)

1–2   PE, PCE
3   22, 352; BM, PE, PCE
4   21; CGL, BM, SLC, PE, PCE

TITUS (*see* MES)

1–3   PE, PCE

PHILEMON (*see* MES, PE)

HEBREWS (*see also* MES)

1   MBL, PE, PCE
2   PE, PCE
3   PE, PCE
4   SLC, PE, PCE
5   MBL, PE, PCE
6   BM, PE, PCE
7   SLC, PE, PCE
8   PE, PCE
9   PE, PCE
10   BM, PE, PCE
11   3; PE, PCE
12   33; Prl, MBL, PE, PCE
13   PE, PCE

JAMES

1   BM, PCE
2   BM, PCE
3   44; BM, SLC, PCE
4   BM, TW, PCE
5   BM, PCE

1 PETER

1   BM, SLC, PCE

2   BM, TW, PCE
3   9; BM, PCE
4   BM, PCE
5   BM, TW, PCE

2 PETER

1   PCE
2   9; BM, PCE
3   BM, PCE

1 JOHN

1   BM, PCE
2   RMPs, BM, SLC, TW, PCE
3   BM, TW, PCE
4   BM, CB, PCE
5   BM, TW, PCE

2 JOHN

1   BM, PCE

3 JOHN

1   PCE

JUDE

1   9; BM, PCE

REVELATION (*see* AJC for complete text)

3   Prl
5   BM
8   CM
12   9; MMS, BM
14   Prl
17   OF
19   SLC
20   CM
21   OTS, Prl
22   BM, Prl

Index of Biblical People, Places, and Events

Biblical citations in parentheses are for identification and reference purposes only, and do not necessarily mean that the person or place in question appears only in that chapter. Spellings follow the usage in a modern-spelling Douay Rheims Bible.

Aaron: 18, 30; Poly, GE, OTH, POT, CGL, PCE. *See also* Golden Calf
—flowering rod of: MMS, GE, POT, CGL, SLC
Abdias, minor prophet: CM
Abdias (3Kg. 18): POT
Abdon, judge of Israel (Judg. 12): CM, Poly, POT
Abednego. *See* Azarias (Dan. 1)
Abel. *See* Cain and Abel
Abela, woman of, type of Mary (2Kg. 20): MMS
Abesan, judge of Israel (Judg. 12): CM, Poly, POT
Abia, son of Samuel (1Kg. 8): CGL
Abiam, son of Roboam (3Kg. 14): CM, Poly, POT
Abigail, wife of Nabal (1Kg. 25): MMS, POT, CGL
Abimelech, king of Gerara (Gen. 20): CM, GE, CGL
Abimelech, son of Gedeon (Judg. 9): POT, Poly, MMS
Abiron (Num. 16): MMS, GE, POT
Abisag (3Kg. 1): POT
Abisai (1Kg. 26): POT

Abner, Saul's commander-in-chief (2Kg. 3): MMS, POT, CGL
Abraham: TP, CM, Poly, MMS, BRA, GE, OTH, POT, CGL, DPPs, Cl, CJ, CR, NMC, MP, SLC, Orm, NHC. *See also* Isaac
—angel appears to (Gen. 18): GE, OTH, POT, CGL, Cl
—call of/covenant with (Gen. 15): HP, GE, OTH, POT
—circumcision of: GE, SLC, NHC
Absalom, son of David (2Kg. 18): MMS, OTH, POT, CGL
Abygee, childhood friend of Mary: NMC, LLC
Achab, king of Israel (3Kg. 16): Poly, OTH, POT
Achan (Josh. 7): POT
Achaz (4Kg. 16): CM
Achimelech (1Kg. 21, 22): POT
Achior (Judith 5): MMS, CGL
Achis (1Kg. 27): POT, CGL
Achitophel (2Kg. 17): POT
Acre, siege of: TV
Acts, Book of: 4, 8, 60, 62, 346, 352, 362, 377

Ada, wife of Lamech (Gen. 4): MMS, GE
Adam: 3, 69; TP, CA, CHG, CM, Poly,
     MMS, TCE, Cl, GNs, MLP, LLB, Orm,
     NHC
—genealogy of: CM, GE, Cl
—origin of Adam's apple: BRA
—origin of his name: 72; LAE
—repents in River Jordan: LAE, CC
Adam and Eve, chastity of: CC
—creation of: 2, 3, 50, 331, 347; FP, TP,
     CA, CM, Poly, MMS, BRA, LAE, CC,
     TCE, GE, OTH, POT, CGL, HCK, QL,
     NHC, PCE
—cursed by God: TP, CHG, CM, Poly,
     BRA, LAE, CC, TCE, GE, OTH, CGL
—expelled from Eden: CA, CM, Poly,
     MMS, BRA, LAE, CC, GE, OTH, CGL,
     BM, ChC, NHC
—fall of: 2, 3, 50, 121, 288, 331, 335,
     347; FP, TP, CA, CM, Poly, MMS, BRA,
     LAE, CC, TCE, GE, OTH, POT, CGL,
     Cl, DP, LLC, NP, HCK, QL, NHC, PCE
—granted lordship over the earth: CHG
—prohibition given to: FP, CA, CHG,
     CM, BRA, LAE, CC, TCE, GE, OTH,
     POT, CGL, Cl, QL, NHC, PCE
—sons and daughters of: LAE, CC, GE
—temptation of: FP, CA, CHG, CM, Poly,
     MMS, BRA, LAE, CC, TCE, GE, OTH,
     POT, CGL, Cl, QL, Orm, NHC
Adonias, son of David (3Kg. 1): OTH,
     POT, CGL
Agag (1Kg. 15): POT, CGL
Agar, wife of Abraham: CM, Poly, GE,
     OTH, POT, CGL
—angel appears to (Gen. 16): OTH
Aggeus (1Esdras 5): Poly
Ahialon, judge of Israel (Judg. 12): CM,
     Poly, POT
Ahias (3Kg.11): POT
Alexander Bales (1Mach. 10): Poly
Alexander the Great: 288
Amalec (Ex. 17): GE, POT, CGL
Amalecites: POT
Aman (Est.): MMS, POT, BM
Amasa: (2Kg. 20): MMS, POT
Amasias, king of Israel (4Kg. 14): Poly,
     POT
Ammon, son of Lot (Gen. 19): GE, CGL
Ammonites (2Kg. 10): POT
Amnon (2Kg.13): POT, OTH, CGL

Amon, son of Manasses (4Kg. 21): Poly
Amos, minor prophet: CM
Amri (3Kg. 16): POT
Ananias (Hebrew name of Shadrach,
     Dan. 1): Cl. See also Three Children
Ananias (Acts 5, 9): CM, Poly, SEL
Andrew, one of the Twelve: 154, 158;
     CHG, EE, PGH, BM, MP, MLC, Orm,
     NHC
Angel(s): MBL. See also Gabriel; Michael;
     Raphael; various appearances to
     Abraham, Agar, Aseneth, Balaam,
     Christ, David, Gedeon, Jacob, John (of
     Patmos), Joseph (husband of Mary),
     Lot, Marys at the Tomb, Shepherds,
     Zachary
—creation of: CM, LAE, OTH
—at the crucifixion: LLB
—fall of: 2, 3, 9, 121, 347; FP, TP, CA,
     CM, MMS, LAE, CC, TCE, GE, Cl,
     PGH, DP, BM, NHC, PCE
—guardian angels: LAE, CC
—takes tree to Paradise: CJ
Anna, daughter of Phanuel (Luke 2):
     CM, Poly, MMS, EE, PGH, TK, BM,
     EN, SLC, Orm, NHC, MBL
Anna, mother of Samuel (1Kg. 1, 2):
     POT, CGL
—song of: LPs, CH
Anna, wife of Tobias senior: MMS, POT,
     CGL
Annas, high priest: MMS, PGH, PCL,
     MP, SP, SLC, HC, HCK
Anne, mother of Mary: 235; CM, NMC,
     LLC, ConM
Annunciation to Mary. See Mary, mother
     of Christ, annunciation to
Annunciation to the shepherds. See
     Shepherds, annunciation to
Anointing of Christ. See Christ, anoint-
     ing of
Antichrist: 12; CM, GE
Antiochus (2Mach.): 147; Poly, POT
Aod (Judg. 3): CM, Poly, MMS, POT
Apame (3Esdras 4): MMS
Apocalypse: 20, 92, 352; NP, AJC. See also
     Doomsday
—synoptic: PGH, TV, MP, SP, NHC
Apostles: 3, 32, 75; RMPs, MP, MLC. See
     also Disciples
—acts of: 107; TP, CM, PL

—arrested/freed: CM, SP
—Creed. *See* Creed in General Index
—fates of: TP, CM, MP
Aran, father of Lot (Gen. 11): GE
Ararat, Mount: Cl
Archelaus (Matt. 2): TP, EE, EN, MLC,
    Orm, NHC, MBL
Archetriclin, wedding of: CJ
Arfax, Sir (knight at Christ's tomb): RA
Ark of Noah. *See* Noah
Ark of the Tabernacle/Covenant. *See*
    Tabernacle
Arphaxad, son of Sem (Gen. 11): GE
Arrest of Christ. *See* Christ, arrest of
Artaxerxes, king of the Persians (1Esdras
    7): Poly
Asa (3Kg. 15): CM
Asael, nephew of David (2Kg. 2): POT
Ascension of Christ. *See* Christ, ascen-
    sion of
Aseneth, Egyptian wife of Joseph (Gen.
    41): CGL, SA
—angel appears to: SA
Aser (Gen. 30, son of Zelpha): GE
Asmodeus (Tob.): MMS, POT, CGL
Assuerus (Est.): MMS, POT
Assyrians (Judith): POT
Astiages (Dan. 14), dream of: MMS
Attropa, alternate name for Baltas-
    sar: CM
Ave Maria: 64, 168, 173, 182, 302, 303;
    PPs, BM, PN. *See also* Mary, mother of
    Christ, annunciation to
Azarias (4Kg. 14): CM, Poly, POT
Azarias (Dan. 1): Cl. *See also* Three
    Children
Azarias, alias of Raphael (Tob. 5): POT

Baal: GE, POT
Baana (2Kg. 4): POT, CGL
Babel, tower of: CM, Poly, MMS, GE,
    OTH, POT, CGL
Babylonian captivity: Poly, BRA, Cl, TV,
    SLC
Baker of Pharaoh (Gen. 40): JJ
Bala, handmaid to Rachel (Gen. 30): GE
Balaam (and his ass, the angel) (Num.
    22): GE, OTH, POT, SLC
—his prophecies: TP, MMS, OTH, TK,
    NMC, SLC
Balac (Num. 22): GE, POT, SLC

Baldad, one of Job's comforters: POT,
    CGL
Baltassar (Dan. 5): Poly, MMS, Cl
Baltassar, one of the Magi: CM, NMC, EN
Banaias (2Kg. 23): MMS
Barabbas: FP, CM, MMS, BRA, CJ, EE,
    PGH, GNs, GNp, PCL, MP, MLC, PL,
    NP, MLP, HCK
Barac (Judg. 4): CM, Poly, POT
Barsabas (Acts 1, 9): MLC, SEL
Bartholomew, one of the Twelve: MLC
Basa (3Kg. 14, 15): POT
Basan (Num. 21): GE
Beatitudes (Matt. 5): Pat, EE, PGH, BM,
    MP, Beat, SE, SCC, Orm
Bel (Dan. 14): MMS
Benadad (3Kg.20): POT
Benedicite, Song of the Three Children
    (Dan. 3:57–90): MMS, PPs, CH
Benedictus (Luke 1:68–79): 25; PPs, CH,
    EE, ConM, CB. *See also* Zachary
Benjamin, brother of Joseph: CM, GE,
    OTH, POT, CGL, JJ, SA
Benjaminites (Judg. 19, 20): POT
Bethany: TV, MP, SP, LLC, NP, SPC, NHC,
    MBL. *See also* Christ, anointing of
Bethel (Gen. 28, 35): GE, CGL
Bethlehem: LAE, FE, EN, MBL. *See also*
    Christ, nativity of
Bethsabee (2Kg. 11): TP, CM, OTH,
    POT, CGL
Bethsaida, Christ heals at (Mark 8, John
    5): MP
Bethulia, siege of (Judith): CGL
Boanerges (James and John, sons of
    Zebedee): PGH
Booz (Ruth): POT
Buffeting of Christ. *See* Christ, buffet-
    ing of
Butler of Pharaoh (Gen. 40): MMS, JJ
Burning bush. *See* Moses, burning bush

Cades, water from a rock at (Num. 20):
    GE, POT
Caesar. *See also* Claudius; Dacian; Nero;
    Theodosius; Tiberius; Titus; Vespasian
—Augustus (Octavian), decree of (Luke
    2): TK, Poly, EE, NMC, MLC, SLC,
    Orm, NHC, MBL
—tribute to: CHG, PGH, TV, MP, LLC,
    NHC, MBL

Cain and Abel: 10; TP, CM, Poly, MMS, BRA, LAE, CC, GE, OTH, POT, CGL, NMC, LLC, SLC, NP, MLP, Orm, OF, PCE

Caiphas, high priest: 18; CHG, BRA, CJ, EE, PGH, PCL, TV, MP, SP, MLC, PL, NP, MS, SPC, HCK

—death of: BRA

Caleb (Num. 14): CM, GE, POT, CGL

Calvary: POT, EE, NP, MS, HC, HCS, SEL, MBL. See also Christ, crucifixion of

Cana, miracle at. See Christ, miracles of

Canaan

—twelve spies sent to (Num. 13, 14): Poly, GE, POT

—woman of (Matt. 15, Mark 7): PGH, MP, NHC

Candlemass (Purification of Mary): BM, EN, MLC, SLC, MBL. See also Christ, presentation in the Temple

Capharnaum, Christ heals at (Mark 1, Luke 4, John 4): PGH, NHC

Carius, witness to the Harrowing of Hell: CM, GNs, GNp, PCL, HH, TV, MLC

Carmel, Mount, contest on (3Kg. 18): POT

Carpus, his vision of Christ (cf. 2Tim. 4:13): CGL, SLC

Cedron Valley (John 18): MS

Ceila (1Kg. 23): POT

Cenez (Judg. 3): POT

Centurion (Matt. 27): PGH, GNs, GNp, PCL, TV, MP, MLC, NP, MS, SPC, HCK, MBL

Centurion (Luke 23): RMPs, PGH,

Centurion's servant (Matt. 8, Luke 7): MMS, PGH, MLC, MP, MBL

Cetura, wife of Abraham (Gen. 25): CM, GE, POT

Chaldeans (Gen. 15, Dan. 4): MMS, Cl

Cham, son of Noah: CM, MES, MMS, GE, POT, CGL, Cl

Chanaan, son of Cham (Gen. 9): MES

Christ: TBPs, Cl, PGH, NMC

—angel appears to on Mt. Olivet (Luke 22): SP, NP, MLP, SLL

—anointing of (Matt. 26, Mark 14, Luke 7, John 12): 10; PGH, RFL, TV, BM, MP, SP, LLC, MLC, NP, SPC, SEL, NHC, MBL

—appearances of: TP, BRA, CGL, EE, CR, PGH, GNs, PCL, DP, MP, SP, MLC, SLC, PL, NP, MLP, HC, HCK, MTM, RA, NHC, MBL. See also Marys at the tomb; Thomas, doubts of; Tiberias, sea of

—arrest of: CHG, MMS, BRA, EE, RFL, BM, MP, SP, MLC, NP, LLB, MS, PC, CDL, HCS, HCK, MBL

—ascension of: 2, 3; FP, TP, MMS, BRA, CGL, EE, CR, PGH, GNs, GNp, PCL, DP, TV, MP, SP, ALC, MLC, SLC, PL, MLP, ChC, RP, HCK, MTM, SR, TW, QL, Orm, NHC, MBL

—baptism of: TP, CM, Poly, MMS, BRA, CGL, EE, PGH, RFL, TK, BM, MP, ALC, MLC, SLC, PL, MLP, HCK, Orm, NHC, MBL. See also John the Baptist

—before Annas: MMS, PGH, PCL, MP, SP, SLC, HC, HCK

—before Caiphas: CHG, MMS, BRA, EE, PGH, BM, PCL, MP, SP, MLC, PL, NP, MS, SPC, HCK

—before Herod: CM, MMS, EE, PGH, GNp, PCL, MP, SP, MLC, NP, MLP, MS, MBL

—before Pilate: 62; FP, CM, MMS, BRA, EE, PGH, RFL, GNs, GNp, PCL, MP, SP, MLC, SLC, PL, NP, MLP, MS, SPC, HC, HCS, HCK, QL, MBL

—betrayal of: FP, TP, CM, MMS, BRA, RMPs, CJ, EE, DP, MP, LLC, MLC, SLC, MLP, ChC, MS, HCK, TW, QL, SEL, MBL. See also Judas Iscariot, kiss of

—buffeting of: 23; CM, MMS, PGH, PCL, MP, MLC, NP, MLP, LLB, SPC, HC, HCS, HCK, MBL

—burial of: FP, MMS, PGH, GNs, GNp, PCL, MP, MLC, PL, NP, LLB, MS, HC, HCS, HCA, HCK, MBL

—calls disciples: TP, CHG, Poly, BRA, EE, PGH, BM, MP, MLC, SLC, SEL, Orm, NHC, MBL

—charges John and Mary: CM, BRA, MP, SP, NP, MLP, LLB, SPC, QL, SEL

—circumcision of: CA, Poly, CGL, EE, PGH, NMC, EN, MLC, SLC, HCK, TW, Orm, NHC, MBL. See also Sodomites, death of

—cleanses Temple: CM, Poly, MMS, PGH, TV, MP, LLC, MLC, SLC, PL, Orm, NHC, MBL

—commissions disciples: FP, TP, CA, BRA, PGH, GNp, PCL, DP, MP, SP, MLC, PL, BVP, RSP, NHC, MBL

—coronation of: MMS

—crucifixion of (and associated implements and signs): 3, 47, 78, 263, 303; FP, TP, CHG, CM, Poly, MMS, BRA, EE, PGH, RFL, GNs, GNp, PCL, DP, TV, BM, NMC, MP, SP, MLC, SLC, PL, NP, MLP, ChC, LLB, MS, SLL, PC, CP, SPC, CDL, HC, HCS, HCA, HCK, MTM, JA, TW, QL, NHC, MBL. See also Crown of thorns; Passion of Christ

—deposition of: FP, MMS, RFL, GNs, GNp, PCL, HH, MP, SP, MLC, NP, LLB, MS, RP, HC, HCS, HCA, HCK, MBL. See also Joseph of Arimathea; Nicodemus

—disputes with Temple doctors (Luke 2): CHG, CM, Poly, MMS, BRA, PGH, RFL, DP, BM, NMC, EN, MLC, SLC, LLB, HCK, DJM, Orm, NHC, MBL

—enters Jerusalem. See Palm Sunday

—flies into Egypt. See Egypt, flight into

—genealogy of: POT, PGH, NMC, ConM, Orm, NHC

—harrows Hell. See Hell, Harrowing of

—incarnation of: 3, 257, 295; FP, CA, CHG, GE, RMPs, PGH, RFL, SLC, MLP, LLB, JA, TW, OF. See also Mary, mother of Christ, conception of Christ

—infancy and youth: CM, CJ, MBL

—Last Supper of: 343; CHG, CM, MMS, PGH, PCL, MP, PL, NP, MLP, MS, SPC, HCK, SEL, MBL. See also Eucharist; Passover

—last words of: 8; CHG, MMS, BRA, EE, PGH, RFL, GNs, GNp, MP, SP, NP, ChC, LLB, MS, RP, SLL, CP, SPC, HC, HCS, HCA, HCK, TW, MBL. See also Christ, crucifixion of

—leaps of: CGL, CJ, SLC

—lives of: 2, 5, 6, 18, 112, 116, 118, 179, 216, 275, 303, 307, 324, 331, 332, 338

—ministry of: CM, MP, ALC, HCK, Orm

—miracles of: TP, CA, PGH, DP, TV, NMC, TW, Orm

    —Cana, wedding at: CA, CM, Poly, CJ,

PGH, DP, BM, MP, ALC, MLC, SLC, MLP, Orm, NHC, MBL

    —draught of fishes (Luke 5, John 21): PGH, MLC, SLC, NHC

    —exorcising demons: CR, PGH, GNp, DP, BM, MP, MLC, NHC. See also Canaan, woman of; Gerasene swine; Mary Magdalen, exorcism of

    —healing: 68, 264; CM, BRA, EE, PGH, GNs, GNp, DP, MP, LLC, MLC, SLC, PL, Orm, NHC, MBL. See also Capharnaum; Centurion's servant; Jericho, blind men of; Sabbath, healing/working on; Siloe, blind man of; Simon's wife's mother; woman with issue of blood

    —feeding of the five thousand (four thousand): CA, CM, Poly, BRA, PGH, DP, MP, LLC, MLC, SLC, NHC, MBL

    —raising Jairus's daughter (Matt. 9, Mark 5): PGH, MP, NHC

    —raising Lazarus: 336; CA, CM, BRA, POT, RMPs, PGH, GNp, PCL, DP, TV, BM, MP, LLC, MLC, MLP, SEL, NHC, MBL

    —raising ruler's daughter (Matt. 9): BM, MLC, MBL

    —raising widow of Nain's son (Luke 7): PGH, BM, MP, MLC, NHC, MBL

    —walking on water (Matt. 14, John 6): PGH, MP, MLC, MBL

—name(s) of: 72; CGL, SLC, MLP

—nativity of: 3, 8, 9; CHG, CM, MMS, CGL, CJ, EE, PGH, RFL, DP, TK, NMC, EN, ALC, MLC, SLC, MLP, MTM, TW, QL, MBL. See also Magi

    —Ox and Ass at (cf. Is. 1:3): 9; CJ, CJ, EE, PGH, NMC, EN, SLC, QL, NHC, MBL

—"New Man": CM

—preaches: 62, 264; TP, BRA, EE, PGH, TV, PL, TW, NHC. See also Beatitudes; Parables

    —Sermon on the Mount (Matt. 5–7): 237, 253, 299; MP, Beat, NHC, MBL

    —Sermon on the Plain (Luke 6): PGH, MP

—presentation in the Temple: MMS, EE, CJ, NMC, SLC, Orm, MBL. See also Candlemass; Simeon (Luke 2)

Christ: (*continued*)
—prince of peace: CA, NHC
—resurrection of: 2, 3, 127, 169, 266; FP, CM, MMS, CGL, EE, PGH, GNp, PCL, DP, HH, TV, MP, LLC, ALC, MLC, SLC, PL, MLP, ChC, RP, PC, LA, HC, HCA, MTM, CB, RA, SR, TW, QL, Orm, MBL
—scourging of: 8; FP, TP, CHG, CM, MMS, BRA, PGH, RFL, GNs, GNp, TV, BM, MP, SP, SLC, PL, NP, ChC, MS, RP, PC, CDL, HC, HCK, MTM, TW, QL
—temptation of: 78, 264; CA, CHG, CM, Poly, MMS, EE, PGH, RFL, DP, BM, MP, ALC, SLC, PL, NP, MLP, ChC, HCK, Orm, NHC, MBL
—transfiguration of (Matt. 17, Mark 9, Luke 9): PGH, DP, MP, LLC, MLC, SLC, HCK, Orm, MBL
—travels in Egypt: CM, Poly, MMS, CJ, EE
—washes disciples' feet: 62; CHG, CM, MMS, BRA, PGH, RFL, PCL, BM, MP, SP, MLC, NP, MLP, MS, SPC, HCK, NHC, MBL
Chusai (2Kg. 17): POT
Chusan, king of Mesopotamia (Judg. 3): Poly
Cilicia, burning of the ships at: EE
Circumcision, covenant of: OTH, CGL, SLC, NHC. *See also* Abraham, circumcision of; Christ, circumcision of
Cis, father of Saul (1Kg. 9): POT
Claudius, Emperor: GNs
Cleophas (Luke 24): CR, PGH, MP, MLC, SLC, HCK, MTM, RA, NHC
Codrus, king of Greece: MMS
Core, schism of (Num. 16): GE, POT
Cornelius (Acts 10): CM
Cosdram, Sir (knight at Christ's tomb): RA
Creation of heavens, earth: 3, 5, 20, 47, 101, 107, 121, 234; TP, CA, CM, Poly, LAE, CC, TCE, HP, GE, OTH, POT, CGL, RMPs, TBPs, HCK
Creation of man. *See* Adam and Eve, creation of
Cross. *See also* Christ, crucifixion of; Christ, deposition of; *Hours of the Cross* (in general index); Passion of Christ

—history/legends of: 105, 118, 121, 265, 266, 278, 279; CM, LAE, NP
—inscription above. *See* Pilate, inscription above cross
—rebuked by Mary: HCK
—wood of: BRA, MLP
Crown of thorns: MMS, GNs, SLC, MLP, ChC, PC, CP, HC, HCS, HCK, QL. *See also* Crucifixion
Crucifixion. *See* Christ, crucifixion of
Cyrus of Persia (Is. 45, 1Esdras 1): Poly, MMS

Dacian, Emperor: 265
Dagon (1Kg. 5): CGL
Dalila (Judg. 16): TP, CM, OTH, POT
Dan (Gen. 30, 49): GE, SA
Daniel: CA, MMS, BRA, DPPs, PSS, Cl, MBL
—interprets dreams: Poly, Cl
—in lions' den: Poly, MMS, OTH
—visions of: Poly
Darius (Dan. 5): Cl
Darius, king of Persia (1Esdras 4, 5; 3Esdras 4): Poly, MMS
Dathan (Num. 16): MMS, GE, POT
Daughters of God. *See* God, four daughters of
David: 19, 79, 172; TP, CA, CHG, CM, MMS, BRA, OTH, POT, CGL, TBPs, EE, BM, NP, MLP, RA, Orm, NHC, MBL
—angel appears to (2Kg. 24): OTH
—and Goliath (1Kg. 17): CM, MMS, OTH, POT, CGL, LPs
—the musician: Poly, POT, CGL
—the psalmist: CC, CGL
—slays bear and lion (1Kg. 17): MMS
Dead Sea: Cl
Debbora (Judg. 4): CM, Poly, POT, LPs
Demetrius (1Mach. 10, 2Mach. 14): Poly
Deposition of Christ. *See* Christ, deposition of
Devil(s). *See* Satan
Dina (Gen. 34): MMS, GE, CGL
Dionysius the Areopagite (St. Denis) (Acts 17): MP, SP
Dirige (Office of the Dead from the Book of Job): 168, 169, 182; PPs
Disciples: PGH, GNs, SP, NP, MLP, MS, MTM, NHC. *See also* Christ, calls dis-

ciples; Christ, commissions disciples; Christ, washes disciples' feet; names of individual disciples
— commissioning of the seventy-two (Luke 10): PGH
Dismas, the good thief: CM, POT, CJ, EE, PGH, RFL, GNs, GNp, PCL, HH, MP, SP, MLC, SLC, PL, NP, MLP, LLB, RP, PC, CP, HC, HCK, MBL. See also Christ, crucifixion of
Dives (Luke 16): POT, PGH, BM, MP, LLC, NHC
Doeg (1Kg. 22): POT
Doomsday: 3, 5, 17, 20, 41, 42, 75, 101, 131, 172, 177, 209, 234, 244; PJ, RMPs, TBPs, CR, HCS, QL. See also Apocalypse
— fifteen signs before: 86, 102, 105, 252; CM, ALC
Dorcas (Acts 9): CM

Easter. See also Christ, resurrection of; Passover
— date of: 34, 93
Eden: CM, LAE, CJ. See also Adam and Eve, creation of; Adam and Eve, expelled from Eden; Creation of heavens, earth
— honeycomb of: SA
Edom, Esau in: GE
Eglon, king of Moab (Judg. 3): Poly, POT
Egypt. See also Christ, travels in Egypt; Joseph, son of Jacob, in Egypt; Moses, Red Sea crossing of; Pharaoh; Plagues
— Abraham and Sarah in: GE
— fall of the idols (cf. Is. 19:1): MMS, CJ, EE, NMC, EN, MBL
— flight into by Holy Family: TP, CM, Poly, MMS, CJ, EE, PGH, RFL, GNs, GNp, TK, BM, NMC, EN, MLC, SLC, LLB, HCK, JA, QL, Orm, NHC, MBL
Ehud. See Aod
Ela (3Kg. 16): POT
Elcana (1Kg. 1): POT, CGL
Eli. See Heli
Elias (Elijah): 68, 69, 75, 82; CA, CM, Poly, MMS, OTH, POT, GNp, HH, SLC, Orm
Eliazar, son of Abinadab (1Kg. 7): POT
Eliazar (1 and 2Mach.): MMS, POT

Eliezer, Abraham's servant (Gen. 24): MMS, GE
Eliezer, son of Moses (Ex. 2, Num. 20): GE, POT
Eliphaz, one of Job's comforters: POT, CGL
Eliseus (Elisha): CA, CM, OTH, POT, Orm
— and the widow's jar of oil (4Kg. 4): MMS, OTH, POT
Elizabeth, mother of John the Baptist: CM, Poly, EE, PGH, NMC, ConM, QL, Orm
— visitation of (Luke 1): MMS, EE, PGH, RFL, BM, SLC, HCK, Orm, NHC, MBL
Elon. See Ahialon
Emmanuel (Is. 7:14): SLC
Emmaus: NHC, MLC, SR, MBL
Emorante, Sir (knight at Christ's tomb): RA
Endor, witch of (1Kg. 28): POT, CGL
Eneas (Acts 9): CM
Engedi: MMS, POT
Enoch. See Henoch
Enos, son of Seth (Gen. 4): GE
Ephraim, son of Joseph (Gen. 41): GE, OTH, CGL, SA
Ephrem, city (John 11): TV, MBL
Epiphany: 8, 235; Poly, MMS, CGL, NMC, SLC, MBL. See also Magi; Star in the East
Esau: 158; TP, CM, GE, OTH, POT, CGL, SLC
Esdras, scribe (1Esdras 7): Poly
Esther, Book of: 173
Ethiopians, war with: GE. See also Tharbis
Eucharist: 34, 35, 62, 204; CGL, CJ, MP, SP, MLC, ChC, MS, MTM, Prl, NHC, MBL. See also Christ, Last Supper of
Eutychus (Acts 20): SEL
Eve: 3; CA, CHG, CM, MMS, TCE, GE, Cl, NHC. See also Adam and Eve
— charter with the Devil: SLC
— green flesh of: LAE, CC
— repents in River Tigris: LAE, CC
Evilmerodach (4Kg. 25): Poly, MMS
Ezechias (4Kg. 19): CM, Poly
— song of (Is. 38): LPs, CH
Ezekiel: BRA, TBPs
— song of: PPs
— visions of: MMS, SLC, Orm

Fall of the Angels. *See* Angels, fall of
Fall of Man. *See* Adam and Eve, fall of
Feast of Tents (Ex. 16): SLC
Feeding of the five thousand (four thousand). *See* Christ, miracles, feeding of the five thousand
Flight into Egypt. *See* Egypt, flight into
Flood. *See* Noah, flood
Four Daughters of God. *See* God, four daughters of

Gabaonites (Josh. 9): POT
Gabelus (Tob. 1): POT, CGL
Gabriel, archangel: 93, 160; Poly, MMS, LLC, RA. *See also* Mary, mother of Christ, annunciation to
Gad (Gen. 30, 49): GE, SA
—city of (Num. 32): POT
Gad (2Kg. 24, prophet of David): CGL
Galileans (Luke 13): PGH
Galilee: EE, PGH, MP, Orm, MBL
Gaza, gates of: MMS
Gedeon, judge of Israel: CM, Poly, MMS
—angel appears to, the fleece (Judg. 6): MMS, OTH, POT
Gemorante, Sir (knight at Christ's tomb): RA
Genesar (Matt. 14): PGH
Gerasene swine (Matt. 8, Mark 5): PGH, BM, MP, NHC
Gersam (Ex. 2, son of Moses): GE
Gestas (bad thief): RMPs, GNs, GNp, PCL, MP, MLC, SLC, NP, LLB, PC, HC, HCK, MBL
Gethsemani, agony in: 336; CHG, CM, EE, PGH, RFL, PCL, MP, MLC, PL, MS, HCK, MTM, MBL
Gideon. *See* Gedeon
Giezi (4Kg. 5): 68, 69; POT
God. *See also* under separate headings for actions in connection with Adam and Eve, Abraham, Moses, and so on
—four daughters of: CA, CHG, CM, MBL
—judgments of (Wisd. 17): OF
—names of: CM, GE
—throne of: BM
—wrath of (Deut.): BM
Godolias (4Kg. 25): Poly
Golden calf (Ex. 32): 18; CM, MMS, GE, OTH, POT, CGL, PCE. *See also* Aaron; Levites, wrath of

Golgotha: SPC
Goliath. *See* David and Goliath
Gomorrha: CM, OTH, CGL, Cl

Habacuc (Dan. 14): MMS, OTH, TK, MBL
Habacuc (minor prophet): CA
—prayer of: LPs, CH
Hagar. *See* Agar
Hai, sack of (Josh. 8): POT
Ham. *See* Cham
Hannah. *See* Anna
Hanon (2Kg. 10): MMS, POT
Harrowing of Hell. *See* Hell, Harrowing of
Hazael, king of the Syrians (4Kg. 8): POT
Heaven: MP. *See also* Manna
—bread from (John 6): NHC
—creation of. *See* Creation of heavens, earth
—joys of: 3; CM, MMS, CR, MLP
—treasures in (Matt. 6): MP, NHC
—voice from (John 12): MP, SP, NHC
Heber (Gen. 11): GE
Hebrews, oppressed by Pharaoh: Poly, CGL
Hebron, Vale of: CA, LAE
Heli, judge of Israel (1Kg. 2, 4): CM, Poly, POT, CGL
Heliodorus (2Mach. 3): Poly, MMS
Hell
—Harrowing of: 9, 68, 75, 78, 102, 169, 216, 217, 253, 264, 277, 282, 291; FP, TP, CA, CHG, MMS, LAE, GE, CGL, GNs, GNp, PCL, DP, HH, MLC, SLC, PL, NP, MLP, ChC, LLB, MS, RP, HC, CB, SR, TW, QL, MBL. *See also* Carius; Lucius
—nine pains of: 3, 106
Henoch (Gen. 5): TP, Poly, GE, OTH, CGL, HH, SLC, Orm
Her (Gen. 38): MMS
Herod: TP, CM, MMS, CJ, EE, PGH, GNp, TK, BM, NMC, MP, SP, LLC, EN, MLC, SLC, NP, MLP, MS, BTD, QL, Orm, NHC, MBL. *See also* Christ, before Herod; Slaughter of the innocents
Herodias (Mark 6): Orm
Hezekiah. *See* Ezechias
Hiram (3Kg. 9): CGL

Holofernes (Judith): Poly, POT, CGL, LPs

Holy Spirit: 3, 262. *See also* Trinity
—dove: SLC. *See also* Christ, baptism of
—gifts of: NHC

Hophni. *See* Ophni

Hosea. *See* Osee

Hur, associate of Moses and Aaron (Ex. 32): 23, 18, MMS

Hus, land of (Job 1): POT, CGL, MLJ

Iannes, magician of Pharaoh (Ex. 7): GE, GNs

Ibzan. *See* Abesan

Incarnation. *See* Christ, incarnation of

Irad (Gen. 4): GE

Isaac: 158; TP, Poly, BRA, GE, POT, CGL, CR
—offered as a sacrifice: CM, GE, OTH, POT, CGL, NMC, LLC, SLC, Orm
—type of Christ: MMS

Isachar, father of Anne, mother of Mary: Poly, NMC, LLC, ConM

Isaias: CHG, CM, MMS, BRA, NHC
—prophecies of Christ: 73; CA, CM, GNs, TK, MP, SLC, NHC
  prophecy concerning Cyrus: Poly
—song of (Is. 12): LPs, CH

Isboseth (2Kg. 4): POT, CGL

Ismael, son of Agar (Gen. 16): CM, Poly, GE, OTH, POT, CGL

Ismerye, mother of Elizabeth: NMC, LLC

Israel (the Nation) blessed by God: OF
—division of (Josh. 13–21, 3Kg. 12): OTH, POT
—enters Egypt: Poly, OTH, JJ
—numbering, naming, census: OTH, POT, CGL
—tribes of: GE, POT

Jabes-Galaad (1Kg. 11): POT

Jabin (Josh. 11, Judg. 4): POT

Jacob: 158; TP, CM, Poly, MMS, BRA, GE, OTH, POT, CGL, JJ, SA, SLC
—death of: CM, Poly, HP, GE, OTH, POT, CGL
—enters Egypt: Poly, OTH, JJ
—ladder of (Gen. 28): MMS, GE, OTH, POT, CGL
—wrestles with angel (Gen. 32): HP, GE, OTH, POT, CGL

Jaffa, siege of: TV

Jahal (Judg. 4): MMS

Jair (Judg. 10): CM, Poly

Jairus's daughter. *See* Christ, miracles of, raising Jairus's daughter

James, the Greater: 226; CHG, EE, PGH, BM, MP, MLC, SLC. *See also* Boanerges
—mother of (Matt. 20): MP

James, the Less, brother of Christ: DJ, TV, MLC

Japheth, son of Noah: CM, GE, POT, CGL, Cl

Jason (2Mach. 5): Poly

Jasper (one of the Magi): CM, NMC, EN

Jebusites (2 Kg. 5): POT

Jehu, king of Israel (4Kg. 10): Poly, POT

Jephte, judge of Israel: CM, Poly
—sacrifices daughter (Judg. 11): MMS, POT

Jeremias: CA, CHG, BRA, RA
—in captivity (Jer. 43): Poly
—lament of (Lam. 1): MMS
—visions of (Jer. 1): Poly

Jericho: POT, MLC
—blind men of (Luke 18, Matt. 20): PGH, MLC, NHC

Jeroboam I: OTH, POT
—idolatry of (3Kg. 12): Poly, CGL

Jeroboam II (4Kg. 14): Poly

Jerusalem: TBPs, WS, PGH, Prl
—Christ enters. *See* Palm Sunday
—Christ laments over: MMS, PGH, TV, MP, SP, SLC, MBL,
—daughters of (Luke 23): EE, PCL, HCK, MBL
—destruction of: BRA, Cl, DJ, TV, MP, SP, LLC, MLC
—walls of: Poly, RMPs

Jesse: CM, DJM
—rod of (Is. 11:10): TP, MMS

Jesus Christ. *See* Christ

Jethro, kinsman of Moses (Ex. 18): GE, CGL. *See also* Raguel

Jews: GNs, GNp, TV, ALC, MLC, SLC, PL, LLB, HCS, MBL
—precautions at Christ's tomb: MMS, BRA, EE, PGH, GNs, GNp, PCL, HH, MP, MLC, PL, NP, HCK, RA
—unbelief of: 16; CM, NHC

Jezabel (4Kg. 9): Poly, POT

Joab, David's general: MMS, OTH, POT, CGL

Joachim, father of Mary: 235; CM, Poly, NMC, LLC, ConM
Joachin (4Kg. 24, 25): CM, Poly
Joas, son of Ahaziah (4Kg. 11): Poly, POT
Joatham (4Kg. 15): CM
Job: MMS, POT, CGL, PJ, MLJ, MLP, Orm
—comforters of: POT, CGL, MLJ. *See also* Eliphaz; Sophar
—feast of: MMS
—God speaks to: POT, PJ, MLJ
—wife of: MMS, CGL, MLJ
Jochabed, mother of Moses (Ex. 2): GE
Joel, minor prophet: CM, MMS
Joel, son of Samuel (1Kg. 8): CGL
John the Baptist: 68, 71; TP, CM, Poly, MMS, CGL, CJ, EE, CR, PGH, GNs, NMC, MP, ConM, SLC, BVP, QL, SEL, Orm, NHC
—arrested/imprisoned: EE, PGH, BM, SLC, SEL, Orm
—death/decollation of: CM, Poly, PGH, DP, BM, NMC, MP, LLC, ALC, SLC, SEL
—naming of: EE, PGH, ConM
John the Evangelist (of Patmos): 3, 92, 267, 270, 277; CHG, RMPs, EE, PGH, RFL, BM, MP, SP, MLC, SLC, PL, NP, ChC, SEL, MBL
—angel appears to (Rev. 19): SLC
—entrusted to Mary at the Cross: CM, BRA, PGH, RFL, GNp, GNp, PCL, MP, SP, NP, MLP, LLB, SPC, HC, QL, SEL
—mother of (Matt. 20): MP
—visions of: 275; Prl, NP
John Hyrcanus (1Mach. 16): Poly
Jonas: CA, MMS, POT, DPPs, Pat, PGH
—minor prophet: CM
—raised by Elias (3Kg. 17): OTH
Jonathan Apphus (1Mach. 10): Poly
Jonathan, son of Saul: CM, OTH, POT, CGL
Joram, son of Achab (4Kg. 9): Poly, POT
Joram, son of Josaphat (3Kg. 22): CM
Jordan (river): MMS, CJ, HCK
—Adam repents in: LAE
—stops flowing: LAE, CC, POT
Josaphat (son of Asa, 3Kg. 15, 2Para. 17–20): CM, POT
Josaphat, Vale of: CM, TBPs
Joseph (husband of Mary): 5
—as carpenter: CJ

—doubts concerning Mary reassured by angel (Matt. 1): 8, 303; TP, CM, Poly, MMS, EE, PGH, NMC, LLC, EN, SLC, Orm, NHC, MBL
—flies into Egypt. *See* Egypt, flight into
—flowering rod of: CM, NMC, LLC, ConM
—genealogy of: CM
Joseph (son of Jacob): 8, 158; TP, Poly, MMS, GE, CGL, JJ, SA, DPPs, CJ, SLC, MLP
—bones of: Poly, GE
—and brothers: CM, Poly, GE, JJ
—death of (Gen. 50): Poly, GE, OTH, POT, CGL, JJ
—dreams of (Gen. 37): CM, Poly, GE, OTH, POT, CGL, JJ
—in Egypt: CM, Poly, GE, OTH, POT, CGL, JJ, SA, SLC
Joseph of Arimathea: 278; FP, CM, BRA, EE, PGH, RFL, GNs, GNp, PCL, HH, DJ, TV, MLC, PL, NP, SPC, HCA, HCK, JA, RA, MBL
Josias: CM
—book of the law (4Kg. 22): Poly
—death in battle (4Kg. 23): Poly
Josue, servant of Moses: CM, Poly, GE, OTH, POT, CGL, SLC
Jubal (Gen. 4): MMS, GE, POT, CGL
Juda (Gen. 29, 38): GE, POT
—scepter of (Gen. 49): TK, NHC, SLC
Judas Iscariot: 264, 277; MMS, POT, RMPs, EE, CJ, PGH, RFL, GNp, PCL, DP, TV, MP, SP, LLC, MLC, PL, NP, MS, HCK, SEL, MBL. *See also* Satan, enters Judas
—bursts (Acts 1): CM, EE, TV, MP, NP, SEL
—kiss of: MMS, PGH, PCL, MP, PL, SPC, MBL. *See also* Christ, betrayal of
—life of: Poly, TV, SP, SLC
—objects to anointing: PGH, RFL, LLC, SLC, NP, SEL
—repents: CM, GNp, SP
—suicide of (Matt. 27): CM, PGH, TK, TV, MP, MLC, SLC, NP, HCK, SEL
—thirty pence of: TV, MP, SP, MLC, SLC, PL, NP, QL, MBL
—history of: TK
—as type of Saul: MMS
Judas Machabeus: Poly, MLP
Jude, one of the Twelve: MLC

Judges of Israel: CM
Judith: Poly, MMS, POT, CGL, LPs
—type of Mary: MMS

Keturah. See Cetura

Laban (Gen. 29): 158; CM, Poly, GE,
    OTH, POT, CGL
Lamech, father of Noah (Gen. 5): 10, TP,
    Poly, MMS, GE, CGL
Laodiceans: 353
Last Judgment. See Doomsday
Last Supper. See Christ, Last Supper of
Last Words. See Christ, last words of
Law(s). See Ten Commandments
—miscellaneous: OTH, OF, PCE
—Mosaic: 33, 47, 263; CA, CM, BRA,
    OTH, POT, SLC, NHC, PCE
—natural: CA, CM
—positive: CA, CM
—tables of: GE, PCE
Lazarus (raised from dead). See Christ,
    miracles of, raising Lazarus
Lazarus (Luke 16): POT, PGH, BM, MP,
    LLC, SEL, NHC
Leah. See Lia
Levi (Gen. 29, 34): GE, CGL, SA
Levites: 30, 77; GE, NHC, PCE
—wrath of (Ex. 32): GE, OTH, POT,
    CGL. See also Golden calf
Lia, wife of Jacob (Gen. 29): 184; CM,
    GE, POT, CGL
Longinus, the blind centurion (John 19):
    270, 288; BRA, EE, RFL, GNs, GNp,
    PCL, TV, MP, SP, MLC, PL, NP, LLB,
    MS, RP, CP, SPC, HC, HCS, HCK, TW,
    QL, SEL
Lord's Prayer. See Pater Noster
Lot: CM, MMS, GE, POT, CGL, Cl
—angel appears to (Gen. 19): GE, OTH,
    POT, CGL, Cl
—wife and daughters of (Gen. 19): CM,
    Poly, MMS, GE, OTH, POT, CGL, Cl
Lucius (witness to the Harrowing of
    Hell): CM, GNs, GNp, PCL, HH, TV,
    MLC
Luke, one of the Twelve: 267; CR, PGH,
    MP, RA, SEL

Madianites (Judg. 7): POT
Magi (Matt. 2): 77, 227, 303; TP, CM,
    BRA, CJ, EE, PGH, RFL, GNs, GNp,
DP, TK, BM, NMC, EN, MLC, SLC,
    MLP, HCK, BTD, BVP, RSP, JA, QL,
    Orm, NHC. See also Christ, nativity of;
    Epiphany; Star in the East
Magnificat (Luke 1): 303; MMS, PPs, LPs,
    CH, EE, ConM, SLC, NHC
Malchus, servant of the High Priest
    (Matt. 26, Luke 22): CHG, MMS, PGH,
    RFL, PCL, MP, SP, MLC, PL, NP, LLB,
    HCK, SEL
Mambre, Abraham and Lot in (Gen.
    13): GE
Mambres, magician of Pharaoh (Ex. 7):
    GE, GNs
Manahem (4Kg. 15): Poly
Manasses, son of Hezekiah (4Kg. 21):
    CM, Poly, MMS
—prayer of (2Par. 33): MMS
Manasses, son of Joseph (Gen. 41): GE,
    OTH, CGL, SA
Manna (Ex. 16): Poly, MMS, GE, OTH,
    POT, CGL, SLC, NHC. See also Sinai,
    wandering in
Manue and his wife (Judg. 13): POT
Mara, waters of (Ex. 15): GE, POT, CGL.
    See also Sinai, wandering in
Marcile, land of (site of Mary Magdalen's
    mission): SEL
Mardochai (Est.): POT, BM
Mark, one of the Twelve: 267
Martha (Luke 10): CM, RMPs, ES, PGH,
    RFL, BM, MP, SEL, MBL
Martyrs, fates of: MMS
—first: CM, Poly, CC. See also Maximille;
    Stephen
Mary of Bethany (Luke 10): ES, PGH,
    RFL, BM, MP, MBL
Mary Magdalen: 10, 249, 270; TP, MMS,
    CGL, EE, CR, PGH, RFL, GNs, MP,
    SP, MLC, SLC, PL, MLP, LLB, MS, CP,
    HC, HCK, MTM, RA, QL, SEL, NHC
—exorcism of (Luke 8): CR, SEL
Mary, mother of Christ: 3, 187; TP, CA,
    CM, Poly, RMPs, TBPs, ES, CJ, PGH,
    RFL, PCL, SLC, ChC, LLB, HCK,
    MTM, NHC, MBL
—annunciation to (Luke 1): 8, 127, 160;
    FP, TP, CM, Poly, MMS, BRA, EE,
    PGH, RFL, DP, NMC, LLC, ConM,
    HCK, BVP, RSP, JA, QL, Orm, NHC,
    MBL
—as ark of the covenant: MMS, RA

Mary, mother of Christ: (*continued*)
—assumption of: 81; CM, MMS, MLC, MLP, QL
—childhood of: CM, MMS, NMC, LLC, ConM
—conception of Christ: 295; CM, Poly, MMS, OTH, TBPs, CJ, ConM, ChC, DJM. *See also* Christ, incarnation of
—conception of, immaculate: 101, 145; MMS, CM, TBPs
—coronation of: DP
—doubted by Joseph. *See* Joseph, husband of Mary, doubts
—as enclosed garden: MMS
—entrusted to John at the Cross: CM, BRA, PGH, RFL, GNp, GNp, PCL, MP, SP, NP, MLP, LLB, SPC, HC, QL, SEL
—flies into Egypt. *See* Egypt, flight into
—genealogy of: CM, Poly, NMC
—joys of: 112; CM, MMS
—lamentation of: CM, MMS, ChC, LLB
—life of: 336
—marriage of: CM, MMS
—as mediator, intercessor: MMS, CR
—miracles of: 49, 69; SLC
—presentation at the Temple: MMS
—purification in the Temple. *See* Candlemass
—represented allegorically: MMS, MLP
—sorrows of: 112, 222, 275; FP, MMS, MS, RP, HC, HCS, MBL
—visitation of Elizabeth. *See* Elizabeth, visitation of
Mary, mother of James (Matt. 27): GNs, PCL, MP, MLC, SLC, MS, HCK, MTM, RA, NHC, MBL
Mary, sister of Moses (Num. 12, 20): GE, POT, CGL
Marys at the tomb of Christ: BRA, CR, PGH, RFL, GNs, GNp, HH, PCL, TV, MP, SP, MLC, SLC, NP, PC, HCK, MTM, RA, SR, NHC, MBL
Mathusala (Gen. 5): GE, POT
Matthew, one of the Twelve: 267; PGH, MP, MLC
Matthias (Acts 1): Poly, EE, CR, TV, MP, SP, MLC, SEL
Maviael (Gen. 4): GE
Maximille, "first" Christian martyr: CC
Maximus, bishop (voyages with Mary Magdalen): SEL

Melchior, one of the Magi: CM, NMC, EN
Melchisedech (Gen. 14): CM, Poly, MMS, GE, POT, CGL, SLC
Melchy, would-be father-in-law of Christ: CJ
Melsha, wife of Nachor (Gen. 11): GE
Menorah: MMS
Meschach. *See* Misael
Michael, archangel: 93, 277; LAE, CC, MS
Micheas, minor prophet: CM
Micheas (3Kg. 22): POT
Michol, wife of David (1Kg. 19): MMS, OTH, POT, CGL
Miphiboseth (2Kg. 9): POT
Miriam. *See* Mary, sister of Moses
Misael (Dan. 1): Cl. *See also* Three Children
Moab, son of Lot (Gen. 19): GE, OTH, POT, CGL
Moab, king of (4Kg. 3): MMS
Moabites (Num. 25, 4Kg. 3, 2Para. 20): POT
Moses: 9, 45; FP, TP, CA, CM, BRA, DPPs, GNp, SLC, NP, PCE. *See also* Law, Mosaic; Ten Commandments
—and brazen serpent (Num. 21): GE, CGL, POT, Orm, NHC
—Burning Bush (Ex. 3): CM, MMS, GE, OTH, POT, CGL
—death of (Deut. 34): CM, Poly, GE, OTH, POT, CGL
—horned (Ex. 34:29): CM, OTH, PCE
—marries Sephora (Ex. 2): Poly
—on Mount Sinai (Ex. 19, 20): Poly, GE, OTH, CGL
—murders Egyptian (Ex. 2): 9; Poly, GE, OTH, POT, CGL
—Red Sea crossing of (Ex. 14): CM, Poly, MMS, GE, OTH, POT, CGL, TV, SLC, Orm, NHC, PCE
—rescued by Teremuth (Ex. 2): Poly, MMS, GE, OTH, POT, CGL
—rods of (Ex. 4): CC, GE, OTH, POT
—song(s) of (Ex. 15, Deut. 32): POT, LPs, CH
—spurns Pharaoh's crown (apocryphal): Poly, MMS, GE, OTH, POT

Naaman, cured of leprosy (4Kg. 5): 68, 69; MMS, POT, PGH, NP

Naas (1Kg. 11): POT
Nabal (1Kg. 25): POT, CGL
Naboth, vineyard of (3Kg. 21): POT
Nabuchodonosor: CM, Poly, BRA, POT, CGL, Cl
—dreams of (Dan. 4): Poly, MMS
Nabuzardan (Jer. 52): Cl
Nachor (Gen. 11): GE
Nain, widow's son of. See Christ, miracles of, raising widow of Nain's son
Naomi. See Noemi
Nathan, prophet (2Kg. 12): CM, MMS, OTH, POT, CGL
Nathan, Jewish ambassador to Rome: TV
Nathanael, one of the Twelve (John 1): PGH, Orm
Nativity. See Christ, nativity of
Nazareth: PGH, TK, NMC, MP, EN
Nebuchadnezzar. See Nabuchodonosor
Nehemias (2Esdras 2, 4): Poly
Nemrod (Gen. 10): CM, Poly, GE
Nephtali (Gen. 30, son of Bala): GE
Nero, Emperor: 265
Nicanor (2Mach. 14): Poly
Nicodemus: CM, BRA, EE, PGH, GNs, GNp, PCL, TV, SLC, MS, HCA, HCK
—born again (John 3): PGH, MP, LLC, Orm, NHC
—deposes Christ (John 19): CM, BRA, EE, MLC, MBL
Nimrod. See Nemrod
Ninive, city (Jonah): POT, CGL, Pat
Noah: TP, CM, Poly, MES, BRA, GE, OTH, POT, Cl, SLC, Orm·
—drunkenness of (Gen. 9): CM, MES, MMS, POT, CGL, CH
—Flood (Gen. 6, 7, 8): 41, 335, 347; TP, CA, CM, Poly, BRA, GE, OTH, POT, CGL, JJ, Cl, Orm, PCE
　　—Ark: Poly, GE, OTH, Cl
　　—rainbow: 347; CM, Poly, MES, GE, OTH, CGL, PCE
　　—raven and dove: GE, OTH, CGL, Cl
—sons of: CA, CM, Poly, MES, MMS, GE, POT, CGL, Cl. See also Cham; Japheth; Sem
—wife of: CA, Cl
Noemi (Ruth): MMS, POT
Numbers, Book of: 3, 8, 71, 160
Nunc dimittis (Luke 2:29–32): PPs, CH, EE, PGH, NMC, Orm. See also Simeon

Obadiah. See Abdias
Ochozias (4Kg. 1): POT
Octavian. See Caesar, Augustus
Og (Num. 21): POT
Old Testament
—history of translations of: Poly
—summary of: 111; TP, TV
Olivet, Mount: CM, GNs, PCL, SP, MLC, SLC, NP, MLP, SLL, SPC. See also Christ, angel appears to
Omri. See Amri
Onan (Gen. 38): MMS, POT
Ophni, son of Heli (1Kg. 2, 4): CM, POT, CGL
Osee (minor prophet): CM
Othoniel (Judg. 3): CM, Poly
Ozias, son of Micah (Judg. 7): POT

Palm Sunday: 244; CM, MMS, BRA, EE, PGH, RFL, GNp, PCL, MP, SP, LLC, MLC, PL, NP, MLP, MTM, NHC, MBL
Parables
—bridal feast (Great Supper; Luke 14): PGH, MP, LLC, NHC
—cornerstone (Matt. 21): MMS, PGH
—creditor's two debtors (Luke 7): SEL
—evil husbandmen (Matt. 21, Luke 20): PGH, MP, SP, LLC,
—fig tree (Luke 13): PGH
—Good Samaritan (Luke 10): MMS, PGH, MP, NHC
—leaven (Matt. 13): PGH
—lost coin (Luke 15): MMS, PGH, NHC
—lost sheep (Luke 15, Matt. 18): MMS, PGH, MP, NHC
—marriage feast (Matt. 22): PGH, BM, Cl, MP, SP, NHC
—mustard seed: (Matt. 13): PGH
—pearl of great price (Matt. 13): PGH, BM, SP, Prl
—Pharisee and the Publican (Luke 18): PGH, MP, LLC, NHC
—Prodigal Son (Luke 15): MMS, PGH, BM, MP, LLC, NHC
—rich fool (Luke 12): NHC
—sons (Matt. 21): PGH
—sower (Matt. 13, Luke 8): PGH, MP, NHC
—talents (Matt. 25): 47; MMS, PGH, MP, SP, LLC
—tares (Matt. 13): NHC

Parables (*continued*)
—ten pounds (Luke 19): PGH
—ten virgins (Matt. 25): PGH
—unforgiving servant (Matt. 18): MP, NHC
—unjust steward (Luke 16): PGH, NHC
—unrighteous judge (Luke 18): PGH, MBL
—vineyard (Matt. 20): MMS, PGH, Prl, PLV, NHC
—watchful servant (Matt. 24): MP
—wise and foolish virgins (Matt. 25): MMS, MP, SP, LLC
Paradise. *See* Eden
Passion of Christ: 2, 3, 5, 8, 18, 62, 68, 100, 118, 177, 179, 194, 206, 210, 243, 263–90, 328, 336; CA, CM, MMS, CGL, RMPs, DPPs, PGH, ALC, SLC, MLP, MS, RP, SLL, PC, CP, SPC, CDL, LA, HC, HCS, HCA, MTM, CB, JA. *See also* Christ, crucifixion of
Passover: MMS, GE, OTH, CGL, SLC, NP. *See also* Last Supper
Pater Noster (Matt. 6, Luke 11) **PN**: 19, 34, 45, 50, 61, 64, 166, 168, 173, 182, 237, 302–5; WA, PPs, PGH, BM, MP, SE, NHC, MBL, PCE
—exposition of: 305; CM, HCA
Patriarchs: Poly, MMS, GNp. *See also* Abraham, Moses, etc.
Paul (Saul): 151, 344, 347; SEL, PCE
—conversion of (Acts 9): CM, Poly, SEL
Pearl of great price. *See* Parables
Pentapolis (Gen. 14, War of the Five Kings): Poly, BRA, GE, POT, CGL
Pentecost (Acts 2): 2, 3, 34, 264; TP, CA, CM, MMS, BRA, CGL, EE, CR, PGH, DP, TV, MP, SP, MLC, SLC, PL, MLP, HCK, NHC, MBL
Perez. *See* Phares
Persia, queen of, hanging garden of: MMS
Peter (Simon-Peter): 277; CHG, MMS, CGL, EE, CR, PGH, BM, MP, SP, LLC, MLC, SLC, MS, HC, HCK, SEL, Orm, NHC, MBL
—arrested (Acts 4): MP
—heals Aeneas and Dorcas (Acts 9): CM
—heals a cripple at the Beautiful Gate (Acts 3): CM, MP, SP
—keys of the kingdom: 254

—threefold denial of Christ (Matt. 26): CM, BRA, EE, PGH, RFL, PCL, MP, SP, MLC, PL, NP, MLP, SPC, HCK, MBL
—vision of (Acts 10): CM
Peter's wife's mother: 238
Phaleg (Gen. 11): GE
Phaltiel (2Kg. 3, second husband of Michol): MMS
Pharaoh: SA, KP, CJ, PCE. *See also* Joseph; Moses
—dreams of (Gen. 41): Poly, GE, JJ
—oppresses Hebrews (Ex. 5): Poly, GE, OTH, POT, CGL. *See also* Plagues
—son of: SA
—wiles of: KP
Phares (Gen. 38): POT
Pharisee(s): 78; PGH, MP, LLC, RA, NHC, MBL. *See also* Jews, precautions at Christ's tomb; Parables, Pharisee and the Publican; Simon the Pharisee
Phasga (Deut. 34): GE, CGL
Phenenna (1Kg. 1): CGL
Philip, one of the Twelve: CM, PGH, MP, SP, MLC, Orm, NHC
Philistines (Judg. 15, 1Kg. 13, 2Kg. 5): OTH, POT
Phinees, son of Eleazar (Josh. 22): POT
—zeal of: (Num. 25): GE, POT
Phinees, son of Heli (1Kg. 2, 4): CM, POT, CGL
Pilate: 62; FP, CM, MMS, BRA, EE, PGH, RFL, GNs, GNp, DJ, EN, MLC, SLC, PL, MLP,MS, SPC, HC, HCS, HCK, RA, QL, MBL. *See also* Christ, before Pilate
—enmity with Herod (Luke 23:12): NMC, EN
—inscription above Cross (John 19): BRA, PGH, GNs, GNp, PCL, MLC, PL, NP, CP, HCK
—letter to Rome: CM, GNs
—life of: CGL, TV, SLC
—washes hands (Matt. 27): MMS, BRA, EE, PGH, GNs, GNp, PCL, MP, SP, MLC, HCK
—wife of (Procula, Matt. 27): 78; MMS, BRA, EE, PGH, GNs, GNp, DP, HH, TV, MP, SP, MLC, NP, HCK
Pillars of fire and cloud (Ex. 13): GE
Pisgah. *See* Phasga

"Placebo" (Ps. 114:9): 168, 182
Plagues (Ex. 7–12): CM, Poly, GE, OTH, POT, CGL, SLC
Procula. See Pilate, wife of
Prohibition of fruit/tree. See Adam and Eve, prohibition given to
Promised Land, grape cluster from (Num. 13): MMS
Prophets: TP, CA, GNp, SLC
—coming of: FP
—minor: CM
—summary of: BRA
Proverbs, Book of: 6, 222
Psalms: SPs, MPPs, RPs, RMPs, TBPs, PPs, JPs, BPs, LPs, MPs, QHPs, BEPs, DPPs. See also Psalter in General Index
—of commendation: 206; PPs
—gradual: 194, 206, 219; PPs, DPPs
—penitential: 194, 201, 204, 206, 216, 219; PPs, MPs, DPPs
—primer version of: 206
Putiphar (Gen. 39): Poly, GE, JJ, SA
—wife of (Gen. 39): CM, OTH, POT, CGL, JJ

Rabbath, city (2Kg. 12): MMS
Rachel, wife of Jacob (Gen. 29, 30): 158; CM, GE, OTH, POT, CGL, NHC
Raguel, father-in-law of Moses (Ex. 2): POT. See also Jethro
Rahab (Josh. 2): POT
Rainbow. See Noah, Flood
Raphael, archangel: POT, CGL, RA
Rebecca (Gen. 24): 158; TP, CM, Poly, MMS, GE, OTH, POT, CGL
Rebecca, childhood friend of Mary: NMC, LLC
Rechab (2Kg. 4): POT, CGL
Red Sea. See Moses, Red Sea crossing of
Rehoboam. See Roboam
Resurrection of Christ. See Christ, resurrection of
Resurrection, general: 117; MMS
Reu (Gen. 11): GE
Reuben, brother of Joseph: GE, JJ
—city of (Num. 32): POT
Revelation, Book of: 4, 362, 381
Roboam, son of Solomon: CM, Poly, OTH, POT, CGL
Rome: CM, EE, SEL
Ruth: POT

Saba
—gifts from (Is. 60:6): TK
—queen of (3Kg. 10, Matt. 12:42): Poly, MMS, CGL, PGH
—revolt of (2Kg. 20): POT, CGL
Sabbath
—institution of: CA, GE. See also Creation of heavens, earth
—healing/working on: CM, PGH, TV, MP, LLC, NHC, MBL
Sael, childhood friend of Mary: NMC, LLC
Sale (Gen. 11): GE
Salome, daughter of Herodias (Matt. 14, Mark 6): PGH, MP
Salome, midwife to Mary: NMC, EN, MLC, SLC
Samaria, woman of (woman at the well; John 4): PGH, BM, MP, LLC, WomS, Orm, NHC, MBL
Samaria, women of (4Kg. 6): POT
Samaritan(s) (Luke 9, John 8): MP, NHC
—Good (Luke 10): MMS, PGH, MP, NHC
Samgar, judge of Israel (Judg. 3): CM, Poly, MMS, POT
Samson (Judg. 14, 15, 16): TP, MMS, OTH, POT
—judge of Israel: CM, Poly
—type of Christ: MMS
Samuel: CA, CM, Poly, MMS, POT, CGL, DPPs
—anoints David (1Kg. 16): OTH, CM, POT, CGL
Sanhedrin: PCL
Saphira (Acts 5): CM
Sara, wife of Abraham: TP, CM, MMS, GE, OTH, POT, CGL, Cl
—death of (Gen. 23): Poly, GE, OTH, POT, CGL
Sara, wife of Tobias: MMS, POT, CGL
Sarephta, widow of (3Kg. 17): 75, 82; OTH, POT, PGH, Orm
Sarug (Gen. 11): GE
Satan: 68, 78, 80, 168, 171, 206, 279, 295, 311, 322. See also Adam and Eve, temptation of; Angels, fall of; Christ, temptation of; Hell, Harrowing of
—bound for one thousand years: CM
—debates with Christ/other devils: DP, HH

Satan: (*continued*)
—enters Judas (John 13): PGH, PCL,
  LLC
—reasons for envy of mankind: LAE,CC
—recites psalter: 83, 189; BPs
—scourges Job: MMS, CGL, PJ, MLJ
Saul: CM, Poly, OTH, POT, CGL, BM
—jealousy of David (1Kg. 19): CM, OTH,
  POT, CGL, Orm
—reports of his death (1Kg. 31, 2Kg. 1):
  CM, OTH, POT, CGL
—as type of Judas: MMS
Second Coming (Luke 17:20–22): PGH
Sedecias, king of Juda (4Kg. 24, Jer. 52):
  CM, Cl
Sehon (Num. 21): POT
Sella, wife of Lamech (Gen. 4): MMS, GE
Sellum (4Kg. 15): Poly
Sem, son of Noah: CM, MES, GE, POT,
  CGL, Cl, SLC
Semei (2Kg. 16, 3Kg. 2): MMS, POT
Sennacherib (4Kg. 19): Poly, MMS
Sephar, childhood friend of Mary: NMC,
  LLC
Sephora, wife of Moses (Ex. 2): Poly, GE,
  POT, CGL
Sermon on the Mount. *See* Christ,
  preaches
Sermon on the Plain. *See* Christ, preaches
Sesac, king of Egypt (2Par. 11, 12): POT
Seth (Gen. 4): TP, CM, Poly, LAE, CC,
  GE, OTH, POT, CGL, SLC
—makes tablets of Solomon: LAE,
—quest for oil of mercy: 101; LAE, CC,
  CGL, GNs, HH, NP
Seven works of bodily mercy (Matt. 25):
  CA, MMS, EE, CR, BM, SE, SWM,
  SCC, QL, Orm, NHC·
Seven works of spiritual mercy: SWM
Seventy, appointment of (Num. 11): GE
Shadrach. *See* Ananias
Shamgar. *See* Samgar
Sheba. *See* Saba
Shelah (Gen. 38): POT
Shem. *See* Sem
Shepherds, annunciation to (Luke 2): 21,
  303; BRA, CGL, EE, PGH, RFL, DP,
  TK, BM, NMC, EN, MLC, SLC, MTM,
  Orm, NHC, MBL
Siba (2Kg. 9): POT
Siceleg, sack of (1Kg. 30): POT
Sichem (Gen. 34): GE, CGL

Siloe, blind man of (John 9): PGH, NHC
Siloe, tower of (Luke 13): PGH
Simeon (Gen. 29, 34): GE, CGL, SA
Simeon (Luke 2): CM, MMS, CJ, EE,
  PGH, GNs, GNp, PCL, TK, BM, NMC,
  ConM, EN, MLC, SLC, MLP, LLB, RP,
  CP, HCS, HCK, Orm, NHC, MBL. *See
  also* Nunc dimittis
Simon of Cyrene (Matt. 27, Luke 23):
  MMS, PGH, GNp, PCL, MP, SP, MLC,
  NP, HCK, MBL
Simon the Leper (Matt. 26): SEL
Simon Magus (Acts 8): CM, Orm
Simon the Pharisee (Luke 7): CM, PGH,
  BM, MP, MBL
Simon Thassi (1Mach. 13): Poly
Simon the Zealot, one of the Twelve:
  MLC
Simon's wife's mother (Mark 1, Luke 4):
  PGH, NHC
Sinai
—Mount: CA, Poly, GE, OTH, CGL, PCE
—wandering in: CM, MMS, CGL, GNs,
  GNp, TV, SLC. *See also* Manna; Mara;
  Moses; Pillars of fire and cloud
Sisara (Judg. 4): MMS
Sixteen conditions of charity (1Cor.
  13:1–8): SCC
Slaughter of the Innocents (Matt. 2):
  303; TP, CM, Poly, MMS, BRA, POT,
  CJ, EE, PGH, GNs, GNp, DP, BM,
  NMC, EN, MLC, SLC, MLP, HCA,
  HCK, JA, QL, Orm, NHC. *See also*
  Herod
Soccoth (Judg. 8): MMS
Socoth (Gen. 33): GE
Sodom (Gen. 19): CM, MMS, GE, OTH,
  POT, CGL, Cl
Sodomites, death of: NMC, EN
Solomon: TP, CHG, BRA, OTH, POT,
  CGL
—accession to throne (3Kg. 1): CM
—authorship of biblical books: CM, POT
—builds Temple (3Kg. 5, 6): CM, Poly,
  OTH, POT, CGL
—death of (3Kg. 11): CM, OTH, POT,
  CGL
—God appears to (3Kg. 9): CGL
—judgment of (3Kg. 3): Poly, OTH,
  POT, CGL
—successors of: CM
—tablets of: LAE, CC

—throne of: MMS
—wisdom of (3Kg. 3): CM, OTH, POT, CGL, WS, SLC,
—wonders of: CM, NP
Sophar, one of Job's comforters: POT, CGL
Sorrows of Mary. See Mary, mother of Christ, sorrows of
Star in the East (Matt. 2): MMS, EE, TK, MLC, SLC, NHC. See also Epiphany; Magi
Star out of Jacob (Num. 24:17): OTH, TK, NMC, SLC. See also Balaam, his prophecies
Stephen, stoning of (Acts 7): CM, Poly, MP, SP
Sunamite woman (4Kg. 4): MMS
Susanna (Dan. 13): Poly, PSS
Susanne, childhood friend of Mary: NMC, LLC,
Sydrake (would-be father-in-law of Christ): CJ
Symond, St. (companion of Cleophas, Luke 24): MLC
Syrians (4Kg. 6, 7, 8): POT
Syrophoenicia, woman of. See Canaan, woman of

Tabernacle: GE, OTH, POT, LPs, PCE. See also Temple
—ark of: 77; CM, Poly, MMS, POT, CGL, GNp, BM. See also Mary, as ark of the covenant
—feast of: PGH
Tebel, midwife to Mary: NMC, EN, MLC, SLC
Temple (Jerusalem): 78; POT, EE, LLC, SLC, DJM, Orm, MBL. See also Candlemass; Christ, cleanses Temple; Christ, disputes with Temple doctors; Christ, presentation in the Temple; Solomon, builds Temple; Tabernacle
—beams of: CC
—dedication of, feast of the: SLC
—defiled by Antiochus, later purified (2Mach. 5): Poly
—destroyed by Nabuchodonosor (4Kg. 25): Poly
—destroyed by Romans. See Titus; Vespasian
—destroying and raising in three days: FP, CM, DP, TV, MP, LLC

—rebuilt after Babylonian Captivity (1Esdras 5): Poly
—sea of brass in (3Kg. 7:23–25): MMS
—vessels, veil of: CGL, Cl, NMC, LLC
Temptation of Christ. See Christ, temptation of
Temptation of man. See Adam and Eve, temptation of
Ten Commandments (Ex. 20, Deut. 5) TC: 5, 34, 162–67, 182, 210, 298, 302, 310; CA, CM, MMS, BRA, GE, OTH, CGL, PPs, BM, HCA, SE, SCC, TW, Orm, PCE
—expositions of: TC, PGH
Teremuth. See Moses, rescued by Teremuth
Thabor, Mount (Matt. 28): SP, SLC
Thamar (Gen. 38): MMS, POT
Thamar (2Kg. 13): OTH, POT, CGL
Tharbis (Num. 12): MMS, GE
Thare (Gen. 11): GE
Tharsis, ships of (Ps. 47:8): TK, NMC, EN, SLC
—king of (Ps. 71:10): TK
Thecua, woman of (type of Mary, 2Kg. 14): MMS
Theodosius, Emperor: GNs
Thirty pence. See Judas, thirty pence of
Thola, judge of Israel (Judg. 10): CM, Poly
Thomas of India: SP, MLC
his doubts (John 20): TP, CA, CM, EE, CR, PGH, DP, TK, MP, SP, MLC, SLC, MLP, HCK, RA, QL, SEL, NHC, MBL
Three Children (Dan. 3): MMS, LPs. See also Benedicite
Tiberias, Sea of (John 21): PGH, MP, SP, MBL
Tiberius, Emperor: TV, MLC, NHC
Tigris (river): LAE
Titus, Emperor: DJ, TV, MP, SP, LLC
Tobias junior: MMS, POT, CGL
—dog of: (Tob. 6:1): POT, CGL
Tobias senior: MMS, POT, CGL, BM
Transfiguration. See Christ, transfiguration of
Trinity: 15, 18, 69, 125, 137, 294, 313; CM, TCE, GE, DJM, QL
Tryphon (1Mach. 12): Poly
Tubalcain (Tubal) (Gen. 4): MMS, GE, POT
Tyre: 288

Urias (2Kg. 11): TP, CM, OTH, POT, CGL
Uz. See Hus
Uzziah. See Azarias; Ozias

Vasthi (Esth. 1): POT
Vernicle, the: MLC, MLP
Veronica: BRA, CGL, GNp, PCL, TV, SLC
Vespasian, Emperor: BRA, DJ, TV, MP, SP, LLC, MLC

Whore of Babylon (Rev. 17): OF, AJC
Widow's farthing (Mark 12, Luke 21): PGH, MP, SP, LLC, MBL
Woman with issue of blood (Matt. 9): PGH, MP, NHC, MBL
Woman of Samaria. See Samaria, woman of
Woman taken in adultery (John 8): CHG, CM, PGH, RFL, DP, TV, MP, LLC, MLC, NHC

Zabulon (Gen. 30): GE
Zacharias, son of Addo (priest in 1 Esdras 5): Poly

Zacharias, son of Jeroboam (4Kg. 15): Poly
Zacharias, son of Joiada (2Para. 24): POT
Zachary, schoolmaster of Jesus: CJ
Zachary and the angel (Luke 1): CM, EE, PGH, HH, NMC, LLC, ConM, CB, Orm. See also Benedictus
Zacheus (Luke 19): CM, PGH, MP, LLC
Zambri (3Kg. 16): Poly, POT
Zara (Gen. 38): POT
Zebedee, sons of: CHG, PGH, NHC. See also James the Greater; John the Evangelist
Zedekiah. See Sedecias
Zelpha, handmaid to Lia (Gen. 30): GE
Ziba. See Siba
Ziklag. See Siceleg
Zillah. See Sella
Zion: RMPs, TBPs, LPs
Ziph, wastes of (1Kg. 23): POT
Zipporah. See Sephora
Zophar. See Sophar
Zorobabel (1Esdras 4): Poly

Index of Manuscripts

The index lists only those manuscripts mentioned in the text or listed in the entries, and it should not be construed as a complete list of manuscripts containing Middle English biblical literature. Some—by no means exhaustive—effort has been made to indicate (in parentheses) former, and other, shelf mark designations, since these manuscripts are cited variously, especially in older editions. As far as is possible, the index follows the usage in Hamer, *Manuscript Index*, and *IPMEP*. More information on most of these manuscripts can be found in the catalogues conveniently listed by Friedman and Wegmann, *Iconography*, 20–30.

Asloan, Mrs. John McCombe (National
    Library of Scotland Acc. 4233):
    PC

Beeleigh Abbey, Maldon, Essex
    Christina Foyle: MBL
    Christina Foyle (Huth): MMS

Cambridge
    Corpus Christi College
        32: MML, PE
        145: SEL
        278: SPs
        434: PCE
        444: GE
    Emmanuel College 27 (I.2.6): TC, PN
    Fitzwilliam Museum McLean 133: AJC
    Gonville and Caius College
        52/29: PN
        175: HC
        230: ChC
        231/117: AJC
        669*/646: MBL

Jesus College 56: LPs
King's College 13, Part II: SP
Magdalene College
    5 (F.4.5): AJC
    Pepys 1584: TC, PJ, TBPs, SWM
    Pepys 2014: TV
    Pepys 2030: TBPs
    Pepys 2344: SP, ConM, EP
    Pepys 2498: MPPs, CH, PGH, PCL,
        AJC
    Pepys 2553 (Maitland Folio): PC
Selwyn College 108 L.1: PCE
Sidney Sussex College
    55: 45; TC
    89 (δ.5.3): RPs, CH
St. John's College
    28 (B.6): 154; OTH, HH, DJ,
        NMC, MP, LLC, Beat
    37 (B.15): ChC
    142 (F.5): PN
    192 (G.24): PPs
    193 (G.25): OF, AJC
    198 (G.31): HP

Cambridge / St. John's (*continued*)
204 (H.1): Poly
257 (S.25): SCC
Trinity College
43 (B.1.45): TC
50 (B.2.7): AJC
61 (B.2.18): MBL
305 (B.14.19): 45; MS
322 (B.14.38): MBL
323 (B.14.39): TP, WA, TC, BTD
588 (R.3.8): CM
600 (R.3.20): TBPs, LPs
601 (R.3.21): LAE, PJ, LPs, CP, PN
605 (R.3.25): OTH, NMC, MP,
LLC, ConM, EN, ALC, SEL
950 (R.16.2): 352
987 (R.17.1): 50
University Library
Add. 6578: MBL
Add. 6686 (Ashburnham 140):
ChC, MBL
Add. 6860 (Gurney): BVP
Dd.1.1: RMPs, QHPs, BEPs, NP,
LLB, SR, NHC
Dd.11.82: PPs
Dd.11.89: RP
Dd.12.39: PCE
Ee.1.12: PN
Ee.2.15: ChC
Ee.4.32: TK
Ff.2.38: TC, PJ, TBPs, ChC, SE
Ff.5.48: SP, NP
Ff.6.15: TC
Ff.6.33: KP
Gg.1.1: NP
Gg.4.32: PN
Gg.5.31: 83; NP, NHC
Gg.6.26: KP
Hh.1.11: QHPs, BEPs
Hh.3.13: TC, SWM
Hh.6.11: PN
Ii.2.11: 217
Ii.2.12: MML
Ii.3.26: ChC
Ii.4.9: NP, ChC, MBL
Ii.6.39: SCC
Ii.6.43: Beat, SE
Ii.6.44: ChC
Kk.1.5: WS
Kk.1.6: 177; CP
Kk.6.2: 47, 320

Kk.6.28: 47, 320
Mm.1.29: GNp
Nn.4.12: SWM
Cambridge, Mass., Harvard Univer-
sity, Houghton Library, W. K.
Richardson 22: ChC
Cleveland, Ohio, Public Library
W q091.92-C468: BRA
Columbia, University of Missouri Library
fragmenta manuscripta 176: PCE
Corning, N.Y., Museum of Glass 6: ChC

Dublin
Trinity College
69 (A.4.4): MPPs, CH, AJC
155 (C.5.7): SLL
245 (C.5.6): SWM
423 (D.4.3): 98

Edinburgh
College of Physicians: 69; CM, LLB,
NHC
National Library of Scotland Advocates
1.1.6 (Bannatyne): PC, SPC
18.7.21: TC, Beat, PN, SCC
19.2.1 (Auchinleck): 65, 82, 217,
235; LAE, MPs, GNs, NMC, LLC,
PN, SEL
University Library
22 (D.b.I.14): VC
91 (Laing 65): MBL
93 (Laing 140): TC, Beat, SWM,
SCC
205 (Laing 149) (Makculloch):
SPC, PN
La.III.450/1: PC
La.IV.27/8: PC

Glasgow
University Library
223: OF
Hunterian 270: TC
Hunterian 496 (V.7.23): JPs
Hunterian 512 (V.8.15): SLL, SCC
Hunterian V.7.23: JPs
Göttingen, Niedersächsische Staats- und
Universitätsbibibilotek Theol.
107r: CM, LLB

Leeds, University Library Brotherton
501: PCL, SWM

Lincoln, Cathedral Library 91 (A.5.2)
    (Lincoln Thornton): 45, 49, 336;
    TC, JPs, SE
London
  Arundel College of Arms LVII: CM
  British Library
    Add. 5465 (Fairfax): ChC
    Add. 5901: AJC
    Add. 10036: RMPs, TV
    Add. 10626: NMC, LLC
    Add. 11307: MLP, ChC, LLB
    Add. 15225: DP
    Add. 16165: GNp
    Add. 16609: VC
    Add. 17010: PPs
    Add. 17376: TCE, TC, MPPs, CH,
     HCS
    Add. 22283 (Simeon): 15; CA, TC,
     PSS, SLL, DJM, SE, PN, SWM,
     TW, NHC
    Add. 24343: ChC
    Add. 27592: PPs
    Add. 30897: BM, Beat
    Add. 31042 (London Thornton):
     CM, LPs, MPs, AIC, TK, NP, CP,
     QL
    Add. 32427: MPs
    Add. 32578: GNs
    Add. 33381: BPs
    Add. 34360: LPs
    Add. 35290: 147
    Add. 35298: LAE, KP
    Add. 36523: TV
    Add. 36983 (Bedford): CM, TK,
     TV, MS
    Add. 37049: ChC
    Add. 37492: DP
    Add. 37787: 275; TC, BPs, SLL,
     HC, SWM
    Add. 38666: SLC
    Add. 39574 (Wheatley): LAE, PJ,
     RMPs
    Add. 39996 (Phillips 9803): GNs,
     MLC
    Add. 45896: RSP
    Add. 60577 (Winchester An-
     thology): OTS, ChC, Beat, SWM,
     SCC
    Add. Charter 5960: ChC
    Arundel 57: TC, PN
    Arundel 254: OF
    Arundel 285: PC, SPC, HC, HCK

Arundel 292: PN
Cotton Appendix VII: CA
Cotton Caligula A.ii: LPs, PSS,
  ChC
Cotton Cleopatra B.vi: PN
Cotton Galba E.ix: GNs
Cotton Julius D.ix: SEL
Cotton Nero A.x: 12; Cl, Pat, Prl
Cotton Nero A.xiv: 82
Cotton Tiberius E.vii: NP, LLB,
  NHC
Cotton Vespasian A.iii: 80, 309;
  CM, SP, LLB
Cotton Vespasian A.25: 82
Cotton Vespasian B.xvi: OTH
Cotton Vespasian D.vii: SPs
Cotton Vespasian D.ix: NP
Cotton Vitellius A.xii: PN
Egerton 614: SPs
Egerton 826: BM
Egerton 842: MML
Egerton 876: LAE, KP
Egerton 927: CA
Egerton 1894: 13
Egerton 1993: OTH, ConM, EN,
  ALC
Egerton 2658: GNp, LA
Egerton 2710: 147
Egerton 2891: SP
Harley 78: TC
Harley 116: LPs, ChC
Harley 149: GNp
Harley 171: AJC
Harley 215: NP
Harley 218: MS
Harley 237: ChC
Harley 372: CP
Harley 494: MTM
Harley 665: TC
Harley 874: AJC
Harley 913: FP, TC
Harley 1197: KP
Harley 1203: AJC
Harley 1701: MS
Harley 1704: LAE, TC, TBPs, TK
Harley 1706: TC, PJ, Beat
Harley 1770: SPs
Harley 1845: BPs
Harley 1862: OF
Harley 2250: SLC
Harley 2251: LPs
Harley 2252: DPPs

London / British Library (*continued*)
   Harley 2253: GNs, SLL, PLV
   Harley 2255: LPs
   Harley 2261: Poly
   Harley 2277: SP, SEL
   Harley 2338: MS
   Harley 2343: CH, Beat, SCC
   Harley 2346: ChC
   Harley 2382: ChC
   Harley 2388: LAE, KP
   Harley 2391: TC
   Harley 2397: QHPs, BEPs
   Harley 2399: AIC
   Harley 3724: PN
   Harley 3909: SLC
   Harley 3913: AJC
   Harley 3954: AIC, DJM
   Harley 4196: 296; GNs, NP, SEL,
     NHC
   Harley 4733: TV
   Harley 4775: LAE, KP
   Harley 5085: 47
   Harley 5396: ChC
   Harley 6333: OF
   Harley 6580: TC
   Harley 6848: ChC
   Harley 7333: CP
   Lansdowne 344: TC
   Lansdowne 388: OTS, EE, Beat
   Royal 1.A.xiv: 51
   Royal 5.C.v: PN
   Royal 8.F.viii: TC
   Royal 17.A.xxvi: AJC
   Royal 17.A.xxvii: BPs
   Royal 17.B.xvii: 82; SLL, SE
   Royal 17.C.xvii: EE, CR, ChC
   Royal 17.C.xxxiii: OF
   Royal 17.D.viii: OF
   Royal 18.A.x: TK
   Royal 18.B.xxiii: 319
   Royal 19.B.v: HC
   Royal 20.B.v: PCL
   Sloane 1853: TBPs
   Sloane 3292: ChC
   Stowe 620: ChC
   Stowe 949: OTH, NMC, LLC
Dulwich College XXII: 40; EE
Gray's Inn 15: TC
Lambeth Palace
   72: LAE, KP
   223: OTH, NMC, LLC, ALC, SEL
   408: 45, 305

   472: QHPs, BEPs, CB
   487: PN
   559: MS
   853: TC, DP, SCC
Sion College: QHPs, BEPs
   Arc.L.40.2/E.25: GNs, LLB
University Library V.17 (Clopton): EE
Westminster Abbey Treasury 4: QHPs,
   BEPs
Westminster School 3: PN
Longleat, Wiltshire
   Marquess of Bath 29: SLL
   Marquess of Bath 257: POT

Maidstone, Kent, Museum 6: CHG, CDL
Manchester
   John Rylands Library
     Eng. 85: TC
     Eng. 92: AJC
     Eng. 895: GNp, LA
     Lat. 176: ChC
Montreal, McGill University Library 142:
   CM

Newcastle-upon-Tyne, Public Library
   TH.1678: CB
New Haven, Conn.
   Yale University Beinecke Library
     360: JPs
     Osborn a11: TV
New York
   Columbia University Library
     Plimpton 258: Beat, SWM, SCC
     Plimpton 263: MTM
     Plimpton 268 (Phillipps 7157): OF
     Plimpton Add. 3: AJC
   Pierpont Morgan Library
     M99: RMPs
     M818 (Ingilby): PSS
     M861: TC
     M898: TV
Norton-on-Tees Grove House, Fairfax-
   Blakeborough: PN

Oxford
   Bodleian Library
     Add. A.106 (*SC* 29003): QL
     Add. B.107 (*SC* 29560): CA
     Add. C.38 (*SC* 30236): 40; EE, SP
     Add. C.220 (*SC* 29430): OTH,
       NMC, LLC
     Add. C.280 (*SC* 29572): ChC

Ashmole 42 (*SC* 6923): NHC
Ashmole 43 (*SC* 6924): ConM, SEL
Ashmole 59 (*SC* 6943): LPs, ES
Ashmole 61 (*SC* 6922): CA, TC, NP, ChC, RA
Ashmole 189 (*SC* 6666): ChC
Ashmole 244 (*SC* 7419): LAE
Ashmole 802 (*SC* 6909): LAE
Ashmole 1286 (*SC* 8174): SWM
Bodley 89 (*SC* 1886): TC, ChC
Bodley 207 (*SC* 2021): GNp, LA
Bodley 288 (*SC* 2438): CH
Bodley 410 (*SC* 2305): TC
Bodley 415 (*SC* 2313): MS
Bodley 416 (*SC* 2315): JPs, BM
Bodley 423 (*SC* 2322): RFL
Bodley 425 (*SC* 2325): SPs, BVP
Bodley 481 (*SC* 2045): OF
Bodley 596 (*SC* 2376): LAE
Bodley 649 (*SC* 2293): 45
Bodley 652 (*SC* 2306): JJ
Bodley 771 (*SC* 2553): OF
Bodley 779 (*SC* 2567): NMC, SP, LLC, ConM, EN, EP
Bodley 788 (*SC* 2628): Beat
Bodley 789 (*SC* 2643): 45, 305; MBL
Bodley 841 (*SC* 8714): TC
Bodley 921 (*SC* 3027): SPs
Bodley 938 (*SC* 3054): SCC
Bodley 978: OF
Digby 18 (*SC* 1619): RMPs
Digby 86 (*SC* 1687): GNs
Digby 102 (*SC* 1703): PJ, RMPs, Beat
Digby 230 (*SC* 1831): TV
Douce 15 (*SC* 21589): LAE, KP
Douce 78 (*SC* 21652): TV
Douce 126 (*SC* 21700): 296; TV, LLB
Douce 141 (*SC* 21715): RMPs
Douce 246 (*SC* 21820): CH, PN, SWM
Douce 250 (*SC* 21824): PCE
Douce 275 (*SC* 21849): CH
Douce 302 (*SC* 21876): TC, HCA
Douce 322 (*SC* 21896): PJ
Douce 372 (*SC* 21947): LAE, KP
English poet. a.1 (*SC* 3938, Vernon): 13, 15, 42; CA, CHG, LAE, OTH, TC, RMPs, QHPs, BEPs,

PSS, EE, RFL, SP, ChC, LLB, SLL, HC, DJM, JA, SE, SWM, NHC
Fairfax 14 (*SC* 3894): CM, LLB
Hatton 12 (*SC* 4127): TC
Hatton 38 (*SC* 4090): 51
Hatton 111 (*SC* 4050): OTS, JPs
Holkham misc. 40 (Holkham Hall, Earl of Leicester 672): 47, PCE
Junius 1 (*SC* 5113): Orm
Junius 11 (*SC* 5123): 7
Kent Charter 233: ChC
Laud misc. 22 (*SC* 655): MBL
Laud misc. 33 (*SC* 661): AJC
Laud misc. 108 (*SC* 1486): CJ, MP, LLC, SEL
Laud misc. 174 (*SC* 668): MBL
Laud misc. 210 (*SC* 1292): CHG, BM, SCC
Laud misc. 235 (*SC* 1580): AJC
Laud misc. 286 (*SC* 1151): RPs, CH
Laud misc. 416 (*SC* 1479): CM
Laud misc. 463 (*SC* 1596): SP, LLB
Laud misc. 509 (*SC* 942): 54
Laud misc. 622 (*SC* 1414): OTH, TV, ConM, EN, ALC
Laud misc. 636 (*SC* 1003): 54
Laud misc. 683 (*SC* 798): CP
Liturg. 104 (*SC* 30605): HC
Lyell 29: SWM
Rawlinson A.389 (*SC* 11272): RMPs
Rawlinson B.408 (*SC* 11755): PN
Rawlinson C.86 (*SC* 11951): NP
Rawlinson C.655 (*SC* 15481): EE, NP
Rawlinson C.670 (*SC* 12514): TC
Rawlinson C.750 (*SC* 12593): AJC
Rawlinson C.882 (*SC* 12716): Beat
Rawlinson Liturg. e.7 (*SC* 15839): TC
Rawlinson poetry f.32 (*SC* 14526): TC
Rawlinson poetry f.175 (*SC* 14667): NP, ChC, LLB, RSP
Rawlinson poetry f.225 (*SC* 14716): NMC, LLC, ConM, EN
Selden Supra 52 (*SC* 3440): POT
Tanner 17 (*SC* 9837): SP
Wood empt.17 (*SC* 8605): MTM
Brasenose College E.ix: MBL
Christ Church Allestree F.4.1: OF
Corpus Christi College 431: EP

Oxford / Bodleian Library (*continued*)
    Jesus College 29: PL, WomS
    Magdalen St. Peter in the East 18.e:
        ChC
    New College 88: TC
    St. John's College 94: TC
    Trinity College
        29: Poly
        57: CC, SP, LLB
        86: OTS, Beat, SWM, SCC
        93: MES
    University College
        64: RPs, CH
        96: TC
        97: TW
        179: JPs

Paris
    Bibliothèque de l'Arsenal
        5211: 13
        2083: 44
    Bibliothèque Nationale Fonds Latin
        8824: 50
Pavia, Biblioteca Universitaria 69: PN
Peterborough, Cathedral Library 3: OF

Saint Albans, Hertfordshire, Cathedral
        Library: Beat
Salisbury
    Cathedral Library
        39: GNp
        82: PN
        126: TC, SWM
        152: MPs
San Marino, Calif.
    Huntington Library

EL.26.A.13: SA
EL.34.B.7: SLL
HM 114 (Phillips 8252): PSS
HM 127: SWM
HM 140: PJ
HM 144: PCL
HM 147: TC
HM 501: JPs, OF
Stonyhurst College B.xliii: GNp, LA

Taunton, Somerset County Archives
        3084 (Heneage): CB
Tokyo
    Takamiya 4 (Phillips 8820): ChC
    Takamiya 15: QHPs, BEPs
    Takamiya 20: MBL
    Takamiya 32 (Penrose 10; Delamere):
        JJ
    Takamiya 54: NMC, SP, ALC, SEL

Ushaw, St. Cuthbert's College 28: SWM,
        SCC

Washington, D.C.
    Folger Shakespeare Library 420312
        (V.b.236): (Clopton): MS
    Library of Congress pre-AC 4: GNp
Winchester College 33: OTH, GNp
Windsor, St. George's Chapel E.I.I: TC,
        MBL
Worcester
    Cathedral Library
        F.19: TC
        F.172: GNp

York Minster XVI.L.12: TC

General Index

Abbey of the Holy Ghost: 98
"ABC": 204, 270, 294
Abelard: 68
Abridged Life of Christ **ALC:** 236–38, 252
"Acta Pilati": 217
Acts, Book of: 3, 5, 42, 314, 321, 331, 347
Ad Autolycum (Theophilus of Antioch): 334
Adso Dervensis: 105
Advent: 8, 68
Ælfric: 7, 52, 54, 55, 71
Aelred of Rievaulx: 215
Aeneas (of Troy): 31
Ages of the World: 20, 101, 108, 256, 322
Alain de Lille: 17, 22
Alberic (monk): 35
Albigensians: 22
Alcock, John: 181
Alexander, archbishop of York: 38
Alexander III, pope: 28, 31
Alford, John: 129, 130
Alfred, king: 28, 47, 50, 60, 81
Allde, John (printer): 158
Ambrose: 17, 181
Ancrene Riwle: 63–65, 210, 215, 231, 353
Anglo-Saxon Chronicle: 51
Anne of Bohemia: 42
Anticlaudianus (Alain de Lille): 17, 22
Antiquities (Josephus): 134
Apocalips of Jesu Crist **AJC:** 210, 221, 351–53
Apocrypha: 6, 9, 11, 13, 86, 88, 92, 101,
112, 124, 143, 159, 170, 199, 200, 203,
210, 235, 238, 243, 250, 261, 275; PSS,
Cl, CJ, EE, PGH, PCL, LLB
Aquinas, Thomas: 112
Aristotle: 17
"Armonyus": 334
Arsenal Bible: 13
Arundel, Thomas, archbishop: 19, 42, 43,
47, 336
—ban on translation: 19, 25, 38, 39, 336
aspersio: 192
Atalanta: 159
Audelay, John: 162, 287, 288
Augustine of Hippo: 17, 18, 72, 181, 193,
209, 223, 249, 257, 277, 334, 349
Augustine of Kent: 50
Avignon: 285
Avitus, Alcimus: 134
Ayenbite of Inwyt: 162, 166, 304

Balbus, John: 152
Bale, John: 181
Ballad of the Twelfth Day **BTD:** 92, 127, 292,
307
ballads: 5, 127, 158, 264, 292, 307, 309
Baptism: 126, 248
Beatitudes **Beat:** 131, 298, 310
Bede: 2, 3, 7, 28, 51, 59, 79, 81, 324
Beghards: 45
Benedictine Reform: 50
Benedictine Rule: 63, 172

Bennett, J. A. W.: 263
Bernard of Clairvaux: 83, 189, 193, 209, 222, 244, 275, 280
Bestiary (Middle English): 133, 206
Bestul, Thomas H.: 18, 263
Béziers (France): 36
Bible
—Authorized Version (King James): 85, 173
—Gutenberg: 9
—Massoretic: 173
—in Old English: 2, 7, 10, 85
—Septuagint: 34, 54, 173
—*Vetus Latina* (Old Latin): 34, 54, 173, 176
—Vulgate: 1, 3, 5, 7, 20, 34, 50, 54, 86, 88, 112, 118, 129, 132, 134, 173, 224, 243, 244, 345, 353
—Wycliffite (Lollard): 1, 2, 8, 11, 19, 38, 43, 47, 83, 85, 111, 122, 167–69, 198, 306, 310, 319, 320, 331, 332, 334, 347, 351, 353
Bible de Herman de Valenciennes: 101, 158, 266
"Bible des Pauvres": 27
Bible des septs etats du monde (Geoffrey of Paris): 158, 266
Bible Historiale (Guyart Desmoulins): 132, 168, 352
Bible moralisée: 21
Bible of Roger D'Argenteuil **BRA:** 118, 229
"Bible of the Poor": 12
Biblia Pauperum: 21
Boccaccio: 22
Bodley Homilies: 319
Bodley Verse Pieces from the Gospels **BVP:** 174, 295–97
Boethius: 55
Bologna: 36
Bonaventure (pseudo-): 98, 332, 336
"Bonum est" **BEPs:** 193, 291
Book of Vices and Virtues: 166
Book to a Mother **BM:** 231
Boyle, Leonard E.: 33, 35
Boys, Lady Sibille: 197
Brampton, Thomas: 177, 181
—Brampton's Penitential Psalms **TBPs:** 173, 180, 181
Breviaries: 36, 180
—Hereford: 129
—Sarum: 129, 169, 187, 199, 290, 319, 325

—York: 129, 187, 325
Brigittines: 28, 39
Brown, Beatrice Daw: 244
Brut (Laȝamon): 81
Brut (prose): 83
Bury St. Edmunds: 48

Cædmon: 1, 3, 28, 63, 81
Caesar, Julius: 31
Canterbury, archbishop of: 38
Canticle of Canticles: 103, 231
Canticles: 5, 182, 195, 196, 291
Canticum de Creatione **CC:** 121, 124
Capons, Sir John (friend of Caxton): 157
cardinal virtues: 97
carols: 5, 8, 288
Carta Dei: 270
Castle of Love and Grace: 95, 103
Cathars: 36
Catholicon (John Balbus): 152
Cato's *Morals:* 107
Caviness, Madeline H.: 21
Caxton, William: 2, 15, 22, 154, 157, 166, 314
chanson d'aventure: 160, 313
chanson de geste: 147
Charlemagne: 31, 264
Charter of the Abbey of the Holy Ghost **CHG:** 98
Charter of Christ **ChC:** 98, 231, 268, 270–73
Chart-Sutton, Kent: 125, 286
Chastising of God's Children: 52, 215
Chateau d'Amour **CA:** 95, 101, 103
Chaucer, Alice (de la Pole, countess of Suffolk): 190
Chaucer, Geoffrey: 14, 15, 18, 25, 57, 86, 270, 320
—"ABC": 270
—*Boece:* 57
—*Canterbury Tales:* 83; *Man of Law's:* 45; *Nun's Priest's:* 14; *Parson's Prologue:* 21; *Prioress's:* 182; "Retraction": 15
—*House of Fame:* 61
—*Parliament of Fowls:* 57
—*Romaunt of the Rose:* 57
Chaucer, Thomas: 190
Chester: 256, 257
Childhood of Jesus **CJ:** 99, 104, 203–5, 247, 294
Christ Church Canterbury: 54
Christopher, Georgia: 22
Chronicle of Nicholas Trevet: 47

Chronicles: 107
Church, Catholic: 1, 2, 19, 24, 27, 28, 31, 34, 37, 38, 41, 44, 53, 63, 86, 173
Clanchy, M. T.: 25
Clanvowe, Sir John: 310
Cleanness **Cl:** 12, 16, 199–202, 293
Clement of Llanthony: 206, 332–35
Cloud of Unknowing: 193
Codex Fuldensis (Victor of Capua): 207
Colledge, Eric: 63
Cologne: 227
"Commentaries of Nicodemus": 217
Commentaries on Matthew, Mark and Luke **MML:** 42, 332, 333, 345
Commentary on the Benedictus **CB:** 25, 291
commonplace book: 5, 8
Compline: 182
Concepcio Marie **ConM:** 143, 236, 249, 250
"Confession of Breaking the Ten Commandments": 165
Confessions (Augustine): 349
Constitutions of Arundel (1408): 19, 20, 25, 38, 43
Contemplations of the Dread and Love of God **CDL:** 283, 284
Contra Johannem Hierosolymitanum: 169
conversi: 65, 70
courtly love: 263
Creed, Apostles': 45, 62, 106, 166, 209, 256, 302
—Athanasian: 125, 196
—Nicene: 173, 182
Cristes Passioun **CP** (Lydgate): 99, 177, 282
Croyland Abbey: 52
Cursor Mundi **CM:** 3, 14, 22, 58–60, 71, 81, 95, 99–102, 121, 158, 205, 243, 274, 276, 302, 316, 325, 353
Customary of St. Augustine's, Canterbury: 63

Daniel, Book of: 108, 199
Deanesly, Margaret: 11, 33, 37
De Anthioco: 147, 153
De Consensu Evangelistarum (Augustine): 334
Decretals (of Pope Innocent III): 45
De Doctrina Christiana (Augustine): 18, 83
"Defense of Women": 246
De Fide Catholica contra Haereticos: 22
Deguileville, Guiliaume: 270
De haeretico comburendo (1401): 38

De Institutione Inclusarum (Aelred of Rievaulx): 215
De laude Charitatis (Hugh of St. Victor): 268
De matre cum vii filiis: 146, 153
De Meditatione Passionis Christi per septem diei horas Libellus (Ps.-Bede): 336
Denmark, king of: 106, 145
De Nugis Curialium (Walter Map): 28, 31
Deor: 93
De ortu et tempore antichristi (Adso Dervensis): 105
"De profundis" **DPs:** 194
"Descensus Christi ad Inferos": 217
Deschamps, Eustache: 57
Destruction of Jerusalem **DJ:** 226
Deuteronomy, Book of: 52, 231
D'Evelyn, Charlotte: 268
Devil's Parliament **DP:** 224
Dialogue between Christ and Man: 105
Dialogus inter Dominum et Clericum: 27, 81
"Dicta Salomonis": 197
Dionysius the Areopagite, Pseudo-: 193
Disputison bitwene child Jhesu & Maistres of þe lawe of Jewus **DJM:** 104, 204, 294, 295
Dives et Pauper: 166
Dolerous Pyte of Crystes Passioun (Lydgate) 283
drama: 5, 6, 121, 129, 147, 244, 282, 319
—Chester Cycle: 147, 257, 353
—Corpus Christi Plays: 279
—Coventry (N-town) Cycle: 147, 267, 338
—Saint Nicholas, Play of: 127, 129
—Wakefield (Towneley) Cycle: 147, 267, 344
—York Cycle: 147, 217, 267, 324
Dream of the Rood: 263
Drennan, Jeanne F.: 221, 222
Duffy, Eamon: 25, 26
Dunbar, William: 281, 282

Ecclesiastes, Book of: 4, 103, 198
Ecclesiasticus, Book of: 143
Echo: 159
Eco, Umberto: 19
Edmund of Abingdon: 19, 81, 83, 300, 301
Edward I, king of England: 77
Egerton Genesis 13
"Eight Blessings of God": 300
Elsey, story of: 106

Elucidarium (Honorius Augustodunensis): 105

Ember days: 155

Epistles, Catholic: 41, 42, 110, 231, 331, 344–50

Epistles, Pauline: 2, 27, 31, 32, 41, 42, 231, 261, 331, 333, 344–50

Epistle to Sibille (Lydgate): 197

Erasmus: 1

Esdras, Books of: 3, 111

Esther, Book of: 146, 260

Estienne, Robert ("Stephanus"): 21, 174

Estoire del Saint Graal: 298

Estorie del Evangelie **EE**: 13, 15, 25, 40, 130, 178, 205–7, 209

Eusebian Canons: 21

Eusebius: 334

Evangélaire des laïques de Metz: 27

Evangelium in Principio **EP**: 297

Evangiles de l'Enfance: 203

Evangiles des Domnées (Robert of Gretham) 40, 320

Evelak, king of Sarras: 298

Evensong: 174, 182, 214

exempla: 5, 6, 8, 20, 40, 46, 47, 68, 69, 73, 130, 202, 320, 324

Exodus, Book of: 2, 3, 41, 42, 52, 347

Expanded Nativity **EN**: 236, 249, 250

Expositio in Canticis Canticorum (Gregory I) 45

Ezekiel, Book of: 47

Fairford, Gloucestershire: 21

Fall and Passion **FP**: 7, 91

Fasciculus Morum: 165

felix culpa: 126

Fervor Amoris: 283

Festial (Mirk): 314, 319

Fête de la conception Notre Dame: 104, 106

Fewterer, John: 335

Foster, Frances A.: 257

Frangipani, Romain, cardinal: 36

Frederick Barbarossa: 227

Friars: 11, 12, 21, 27, 34

Fyve Wyles of King Pharao **KP**: 161

Gaytryge, John: 34

Genesis, Book of: 2, 3, 13, 41, 42, 50, 52, 132, 137, 146, 231, 347

Genesis (Ælfric): 7, 52

Genesis and Exodus **GE**: 14, 69, 133–38, 146

Geoffrey of Paris: 266

"Gesta Pilati": 217

Gesta Regum Anglorum (William of Malmesbury): 54

Gilbert de la Porée: 352

Gilte Legend (1438): 122, 154, 161, 314

Glossa Ordinaria: 50, 352

Godard, John: 38

Golden Legend (Caxton) **CGL**: 3, 154, 314

Gospel Harmony (Tatian): 257

Gospel of Nicodemus **GNs** & **GNp**: 216–22, 224, 226, 229, 266, 284, 298

Gospel of Ps. Matthew: 104, 203, 210, 235

Gospels: 2, 18, 27, 31, 32, 40, 42, 62, 66, 68, 71, 76, 89, 217, 229, 245, 247, 263, 264, 275, 325, 331

Gower, John: 57

Grabmann, Martin: 17

Grail: 298

Gregory I, pope: 17, 32, 45, 79, 157, 257, 324

Gregory, VII, pope: 46

Gregory IX, pope: 36, 45

Gregory of Nyssa: 68

Grosseteste, Robert: 95, 97, 101

Guild of St. Katherine, Norwich: 168

Guillaume le Menand: 335

Guyart Desmoulins: 132, 168, 169

Habacuc, Book of: 196

Handlyng Synne (Robert Mannyng): 42, 83, 162, 276

Harrowing of Hell **HH**: 226

Haughmond Abbey: 287

Hector (of Troy): 288

Heffernan, Thomas J.: 56

Hegesippus: 229

Helen, Saint: 228, 251

Henry V, king of England: 60

Henry of Ghent: 82

Heptateuch (Old English): 7

Hercules: 102

Hereford. *See* Nicholas of Hereford

Herman de Valenciennes: 101, 158, 266

Hexateuch (Old English): 54

Higden, Ranulph: 22, 28, 107, 147, 256

Hilton, Walter: 193, 291

Historia Ecclesiastica: 79

"Historia Evangelica": 331

Historia Scholastica (Peter Comestor): 6, 7, 13–17, 20, 37, 70, 71, 101, 112, 132–35,

137, 143, 146, 147, 152, 168, 206, 207, 224, 244, 253, 257, 266, 278, 324, 331
Historia Trium Regium: 227
Historye of the Patriarks **HP**: 132
"History of Jacob and his Twelue Sonnes": 158
Holkham Bible Picture Book: 21
Holm Hale, Norfolk: 197
Holthausen, Ferdinand: 60
homilies: 5, 6, 8, 28, 40, 51, 71, 121, 202, 231, 298, 319–25
—ancient and modern: 72, 320, 321, 324
"Homily on the Ten Commandments": 164
Honorius Augustodunensis: 105
"Horae Compassionis B. Virginis Mariae": 287
Horae Crucis: 284
"Horae Passionis Domini": 287
Hothom, John: 38
"Houris of oure Ladyis dollouris": 285
hours, canonical: 64, 210, 253, 285
Hours of the Cross (Passion) **HC**: 112, 175, 278, 284–89, 296, 301, 336, 312–18, 325, 367; CM, MMS, CGL, MPPs, PPs, PGH, MLC, MS, HCS, HCA, HCK, SE
Hours (Matins) of the Virgin: 36, 52, 182, 187, 295
Hudson, Anne: 25, 43, 319, 333
Hugh of St. Victor: 17, 23, 244, 268
Hull, Dame Eleanor: 177
Humiliati: 31
Hymns: 195

Iacob and Iosep **JJ**: 158
Ile de France: 352
Inclina, Domine, aurem tuam: 194
Infancy Gospel of St. Thomas: 203
Ingulph's Chronicle: 52
Innocent III, pope: 22, 31, 33–36, 45, 46
Instructions for Parish Priests (Mirk): 172, 205
Insufflation: 262
Interpretacio Misse (Lydgate): 190
Isaias, Book of: 326
Isidore of Seville: 22, 257

Jacob van Maerlant: 37, 42
Jacobus de Voragine: 154, 314
Jehan de Vignai: 154, 161
Jehan Malkaraume: 158

Jeremias, Book of: 47
Jerome: 17, 28, 38, 50, 54, 55, 169, 173, 257, 334
Jesu dulcis memoria (Bernard of Clairvaux): 280
Jewish War (Josephus): 229
Jews: 16, 77, 78, 204, 229, 231, 246, 252, 260, 265, 266, 275
Job, Book of: 3, 47, 146, 168
—moralization of (Gregory's *Moralia*): 32
Jocelin of Brakelond: 48
John, Gospel of: 51, 81, 89, 137, 247, 264, 275, 288, 332
John, pope: 285, 288
John de Caulibus: 336
John de Marry (monk): 49
John of Gaunt: 59, 178
John of Grimestone: 298
John of Hildesheim: 227
John of Hovedon: 269
Jonas, Book of: 152, 202
Joseph of Arimathea **JA**: 297, 298
Josephus: 71, 108, 110, 134, 229, 230, 257
"Judas" (ballad): 292, 307
Judges, Book of: 3
Judith, Book of: 3, 146, 153

Kennedy, Walter: 288, 335
"Kentish Sermons": 319
Ker, Neil: 111
Kildare-Gedichte: 91
Kindheit Jesu: 203
Kings, Books of: 3, 146
Kirkby, Margaret: 176
Kyng Alisaunder: 82
Kyrie Eleison: 194

Lacy, John: 167
Laȝamon: 81, 133
Lambeth *Constitutions* (1281): 34
Lambeth Homilies: 319
Lamentacioun þat was bytwene vre lady and seynt Bernard **LLB**: 42, 106, 268, 273–75
Land of Cockaygne: 91
Lanfranc: 50
Langland, William: 57, 60, 83, 86, 130, 344
Langton, Stephen: 21, 174
Languedoc: 36
Laodiceans, Epistle to: 345, 346
Lapidaries: 353

Lateran Council, Third (1179): 28
Lateran Council, Fourth (1215): 2,
    33–36, 44, 129
Lay Folks Catechism: 34, 66, 162, 167
Lay Folks Mass Book: 61, 62, 66, 81, 83
—omission of biblical material: 47, 81, 82
Legenda Aurea (Jacobus de Voragine):
    112, 122, 154, 224, 226, 229, 231, 235,
    253, 256, 257, 277, 324
Legende dorée (Jehan de Vignai): 154, 161
Legend of Veronica: 118
Lent: 199, 224, 325
Lernyng to good leuynge: 299
Leviticus, Book of: 41, 42, 52, 133, 141,
    146, 257, 348
lewed, appeal to: 57, 58, 65–67, 70, 76, 77,
    80, 127, 134, 153, 258, 275, 332, 337
—etymology of: 60, 81
*Liber Aureus de Passione et Resurrectione
    Domini* LA: 284
*Liber de passione Christi et doloribus et
    planctibus matris eius:* 222, 275
Life of Adam and Eve LAE: 102, 121–24, 161
Life of the Virgin Mary and Christ: 98, 336
Lincoln: 27
Lindisfarne Gospels: 7
Litany: 63, 93, 180, 182, 261
Liturgy (terminology, parts of): 2, 5, 6,
    20, 93, 129, 154, 182, 192, 196, 244,
    245, 296, 297
Liuzza, Roy: 51
Lollards: 1, 2, 19, 25, 28, 38, 41, 42, 44,
    45, 47, 53, 59, 85, 176, 310, 331, 336,
    338
Lombardy: 31
Long Life of Christ LLC: 203, 235–37,
    247–49, 294
Lotspeich, C. M.: 60
Love, Nicholas: 5, 43, 57, 277, 284,
    335–38, 343
"love-rune" tradition: 313
Lucan: 31
Ludolphus of Saxony: 288, 332, 334, 335
Luke, Gospel of: 88, 332
Luther, Martin: 22
Lutterworth: 43
Lydgate, John: 60, 146, 160, 177, 190,
    194, 197, 227, 282
—paraphrase of Pater Noster: 304
—psalms versified by: 173, 189–91
Lyrics: 5

Machabees, Books of: 3, 13, 110, 146
Macheronnte: 71
Magna Glossatura (Peter Lombard): 176,
    193
Maidstone, Richard: 177, 178
—Maidstone's Penitential Psalms RMPs:
    173, 177, 205, 299
Malory, Sir Thomas: 15
Mannyng, Robert: 42, 83, 276
Map, Walter: 22, 28, 30, 31, 33, 35, 44
Mark, Gospel of: 88, 332
Marx, C. William: 221, 222, 224
Matins of the Passion. *See* Hours of the
    Cross
Matthew, Gospel of: 42, 88, 202, 332, 347
Meditaciones de passione Christi (MPC): 62,
    244, 276–78, 336, 343
Meditacioun of þe fyue woundes (Rolle): 270
Meditationes Vitae Christi (MVC): 18, 98,
    231, 243, 244, 282, 284, 332, 335–37
*Meditations for Goostely Exercise in the Tyme
    of the Masse* MTM: 190, 290
Meditations on the Life and Passion of Christ
    MLP: 7, 268, 270
Meditations on the Passion (Rolle): 287
Meditations on the Supper of Our Lord MS:
    62, 99, 244, 276–78, 336
Merlin's Prophecies (Anglo-Norman): 59
Methodius: 134
Metrical Life of Christ MLC: 23, 252, 253
Metrical Life of Job MLJ: 170, 171
Metz, archbishop of: 31, 32
Metz, city of: 35
Michael of Kildare (friar): 91
*Middle English Metrical Paraphrase of the
    Old Testament* POT: 3, 14, 22, 69–71, 76,
    146, 147
Middle English Prose Complaint of Our Lady
    PCL: 210, 221, 222
Middle English Summary of the Bible MES:
    110, 111, 210
Middleton, Anne: 57
Midrash: 6, 124, 158
Milan: 227
miles gloriosus: 308
Milton, John: 22, 97
Minnis, A. J.: 14, 82
Mirk, John: 172, 205, 314, 319
Miroir (Robert of Gretham): 14, 40, 210,
    320
Mirour of Mans Saluacioune MMS: 23, 25,
    112, 332

Mirror of Holy Church: 300
Mirror of St. Edmund: 300
Mirror of the Blessed Life of Jesus Christ **MBL:**
 5, 42, 43, 57, 277, 284, 335–38, 343
"Miserere" **MPs:** 99, 173, 191, 192
Moralia siue expositio in Iob (Gregory I): 32,
 45, 157
Muir, Lawrence: 4
Myroure of Oure Lady: 28, 39, 44
Myrour of Lewed Men: 96
Myrrour or Glasse of Christes Passioun
 (Fewterer): 335

Nevanlinna, Saara: 324
Newe lessoun Off Crystys ressurectoun **CR:**
 205, 208, 209
Nicholas, Saint, play of: 127, 129
Nicholas of Hereford: 11, 38, 331
Nicholas of Lyra: 111
Nicholas Trevet: 47
Nile: 158
nocturns: 174
Norfolk: 48
Norman Conquest: 2, 24, 25, 51, 52, 59,
 80, 352
Northern Homily Cycle **NHC:** 5, 15, 21, 23,
 40, 66, 68, 81, 83, 86, 99, 218, 266,
 290, 295, 296, 317, 320, 323–25
Northern Passion **NP:** 99, 147, 205, 210,
 243, 253, 257, 265–67, 324, 328
Norwich: 49, 168
Numbers, Book of: 3, 5, 52, 133

O & I refrain: 296
Of Arthour and of Merlin: 65, 66
Old Testament History **OTH:** 15, 142, 143,
 207, 226
Old Testament Sentences **OTS:** 4, 130
Olympus, Mount. 258
O'Neill, Patrick P.: 51, 54
On the Trinity, Creation, the Existence of
 Devils, Adam and Eve, etc. **TCE:** 125
Oon of Foure **OF:** 333, 334, 338
Origen: 54
original sin: 69, 97, 126, 273
Orison of the Passion: 268
Orm: 14, 27, 71–80, 133, 321
Ormulum **Orm:** 5, 6, 23, 27, 71–80, 206,
 320, 321
Orosius: 334
Our Lady's Psalter: 173, 187

Ovide Moralisée: 15, 22
Oxford translation debate: 46

"Palmer's Determination": 55
Pantin, W. A.: 18
Parable of the Laborers in the Vineyard **PLV:**
 305, 306
Paradise Lost: 10, 83, 91, 121
Paradise Regained: 91
Paraphrase, definition: 4, 5, 7, 12
 —earlier traditions: 21
 —motives for: 19, 21
Paris, University of: 6
Paris Psalter (Old English): 7, 51
Parliament: 59
Passionis Christi Cantus (Lydgate): 282
Passion of Christ **PC** (Dunbar): 281, 282,
 286
Passion of Our Lord **PL:** 7, 264, 307
Passioun of Christ **HCK** (Kennedy): 288,
 335
"pastoralia": 6, 34, 71
Patience **Pat:** 12, 200–202, 293
"Patris sapiencia": 285
Patschovsky, Alexander: 33
Pauline Epistles **PE:** 25, 333, 344–45, 347
Pearl **Prl:** 12, 57, 170, 192, 200, 292, 293,
 353
Pearl-poet: 57
Pearsall, Derek: 234
Pecham, Archbishop: 34, 39
Pèlerinage de la vie humaine: 270
penance, three means of: 106
penitentials: 172, 209, 279, 282, 287, 326
Pepin: 31
Pepysian Gospel Harmony **PGH:** 22, 208–10,
 221
Peterborough: 51
Peter Comestor ("Master of Stories"): 6,
 13, 15–18, 20, 70, 108, 123, 132, 134,
 138, 147, 160, 168, 206, 238, 244, 257
Peter Lombard: 176, 193
Peter the Chanter: 22, 27, 28
Pety Job **PJ:** 46, 168–70
Philemon, Epistle to: 347
"Philomela": 269
pia fraus: 78
Pickering, Oliver: 234, 235, 238, 243–45,
 250, 252
Piers Plowman: 15, 16, 60, 83, 93, 129, 130,
 182, 210, 265, 299, 344, 353

Pistel of Swete Susan **PSS:** 15, 198, 199
"Placebo" (Ps. 114:9): 168, 182
Plainte de la Vierge: 275
Planctus Mariae: 244
Plato: 6
*Poematum de Mosaice historiae gestis libri
    quinque* (Avitus): 134
Polychronicon **Poly:** 3, 20, 28, 81, 107, 108,
    147, 256, 257
Poor Caitiff: 270
Powell, Margaret Joyce: 344, 345
Prayer upon the Cross (Lydgate): 283
preaching: 18, 20, 33–35, 38, 44, 49, 50,
    62, 77, 86, 129, 275, 298, 319–25, 344,
    345
Prester John: 228,
Pricke of Conscience: 66, 99, 181, 353
Priests, office of: 106
— unclean: 200
Primers: 162, 168, 173, 182, 183, 195, 196,
    295, 296
Privity of the Passion: 270, 336
Prose Version of Epistles, Acts, & Matthew
    PCE: 7, 22, 41, 44, 47, 111, 118, 346–48
Protoevangelium of James: 248
Proverbs, Book of: 4, 103, 197
Proverbs of Solomon: 99
"Proverbs of Wisdom": 162
Psalms
— Gradual: 173, 182, 194, PPs, DPPs
— in primers: 173, 182–83, PPs
— of commendation: 182, PPs
— Penitential: 173, 177–82, 191, 194, PPs,
    MPs, DPPs
Psalter: 4, 10, 25, 29, 32, 34, 36, 50, 51,
    54, 64, 81, 83, 130, 172–95, 263, 352
— Brampton's Penitential Psalms **TBPs:**
    173, 180, 181
— "De profundis" **DPPs:** 194
— Eadwine (Canterbury): 50, 52
— Gallican: 173, 176
— Hebraicum: 173
— Jerome's Abbreviated **JPs:** 173, 186,
    187, 189
— Maidstone's Penitential Psalms **RMPs:**
    173, 177, 205, 299
— Midland **MPPs:** 173, 175, 176, 196, 210,
    221, 286
— "Miserere" **MPs:** 99, 173, 191, 192
— Old English: 50, 51, 176
— *Our Lady's:* 173, 187

— Rolle's **RPs:** 47, 51, 172, 173, 175–77,
    195, 291, 331
— Roman: 173
— Saint Bernard's **BPs:** 83, 173, 189
— Surtees **SPs:** 51, 173, 174, 176, 295
— Utrecht: 50
Purgatory: 194, 285, 314
Purvey, John: 11, 21, 47, 331

Quatrefoil of Love **QL:** 313
Queste del Saint Graal: 298
"Qui habitat" **QHPs:** 193, 291
Quis Dabit: 222, 275

Rainerius (monk): 45
Rawlinson Strophic Pieces **RSP:** 295–97
Raymo, Robert R.: 4
Redman, Robert (printer): 335
Reformation: 1, 7, 36, 51, 82, 85, 320
*Remembraunce of the passioun of our lord Jesu
    Criste* **RP:** 279
Resurrection and Apparitions **RA:** 308, 309
Revelation, Book of: 3, 110, 231, 331,
    351–53
Revelations (Methodius): 134
Rhetorica ad Herennium: 83
Richard II, king of England: 42, 168
Richard the Lionheart: 65
Robert of Gretham: 14, 40, 210, 320
Roger D'Argenteuil: 118
Rolle, Richard: 46, 86, 167, 172, 175, 176,
    178, 193, 196, 268, 270, 284, 287, 304
— Rolle's Psalter and Commentary **RPs:**
    58, 69, 195–99, 220, 319, 362
Romance: 56, 65, 66, 71, 77, 97, 134, 235
Roman de la Rose: 201
Romsey, abbot of: 145
Royal Book (Caxton): 166
Rushworth Gospels: 7
Ruth, Book of: 111
Ryman, Jacob: 302

Saint Augustine's, Canterbury: 49, 63
Saint John's Day Homily: 277
St. Patrick's Purgatory: 93
Saints: 225, 269
Saints, lives of (and see sanctorale): 3,
    94, 147, 314–18,
Samson, abbot of Bury St. Edmund's:
    48, 49
Samson, Annie: 234

sanctorale: 3, 93, 154, 158, 234, 245, 314.
  See also Saints, lives of
Sauer, Walter: 253
Sayings of the Four Philosophers: 82
Schedula Diversarum Artium: 19
Scottish Legendary: 234, 314
Scottish Passion of Christ **SPC:** 283
Secunda Pastorum: 344
Septuagint. *See* Bible
Sermones ad fratres in eremo (Ps.-Augustine): 277
sermons: 6, 8, 20, 24, 28, 40, 49, 62, 129, 130, 224, 319–25
seven deadly sins: 106, 166, 182, 209, 288, 317
seven gifts of the Holy Spirit: 328
"Seven Werkys of Mercy Gostly": 11
Seven Works of Bodily Mercy **SWM:** 131, 306, 307, 310, 314, 321, 328
Seven Works of Spiritual Mercy: 306
Seymour, St. John D.: 91
Shepherd, Geoffrey: 10
Shrewsbury: 49, 287
Sibyl, the: 113, 125, 236
Siege of Jerusalem: 118, 229
Siege of Thebes: 146
Sir Gawain and the Green Knight: 12, 293
Sixteen Conditions of Charity **SCC:** 309, 310
Skeat, Walter W.: 51
Smalley, Beryl: 17, 77
Somme le Roi: 166
"Song of the Decalogue" (Audelay): 162
Songs of Love Longing **SLL:** 280, 305
South English Legendary (*SEL*): 15, 100, 121, 123, 143, 203, 205, 226, 234, 235, 238, 243, 245, 247, 249, 297, 300, 314–18
South English Ministry and Passion **MP:** 226, 235–38, 243, 244, 255
South English Nativity of Mary and Christ **NMC:** 82, 226, 235–38, 243, 244, 247, 250, 252
Southern Assumption: 100
Southern Passion **SP:** 5, 99, 238, 242–45, 247, 253
Southern Resurrection: 205
Speculum Christiani: 163
Speculum Ecclesie **SE** (Edmund of Abingdon): 19, 83, 300, 301
Speculum Gy de Warewyke: 82
Speculum Historiale (Vincent of Beauvais): 37, 118, 160, 226

Speculum Humanae Salvationis (*SHS*): 21, 23, 112, 114, 332
Speculum Sacerdotale: 314
Speculum Spiritualium: 189
Speculum Vitae Christi: 334
Spencer, H. Leith: 25, 26, 28
Stallings, M. Jordan: 277, 336
Stanzaic Life of Christ **SLC:** 5, 121, 147, 256–58
Stillingfleet, Edward: 36, 46
Stjórn: 22
Stock, Brian: 25
Storie of Asneth **SA:** 9, 159, 160
Story of the Resurrection **SR:** 309
Summa Theologica (Aquinas): 112
"Surrexit Dominus de Sepulchro" (Dunbar): 282
Syon: 28, 39, 335

Tarragona (Spain): 36
Tatian: 257, 332
Te Deum: 181, 196
temporale: 3, 121, 143, 154, 226, 234, 235, 238, 245, 247, 253, 314
Testamentum Christi: 270
Theophilus, bishop of Antioch: 334
Thomas of Berkeley, Lord: 28
Thompson, John J.: 58, 100, 101
Thoresby of York, archbishop: 34
Three Kings of Cologne **TK:** 226, 227
Thurgarton, Nottinghamshire: 193
Titus and Vespasian **TV:** 228, 229
Tobias, Book of: 3, 146, 152, 231
"To Mary, Queen of Heaven" (Lydgate): 160
Toulouse, Council of (1229): 36, 37, 46
Traduction anonyme de la Bible entière: 101
Translation: 1, 2, 28, 31–47, 53, 59, 347
Tremulous Hand (of Worcester): 51, 52, 54
Trent, Council of (1545–63): 37
Tretys of Adam and Eve: 121
Tretys That Is a Rule and a Forme of Lyvynge Perteynyng to a Recluse **RFL:** 215, 216
Trevet, Nicholas: 47
Trevisa, John: 27, 28, 81, 107
Trinity Poem on Biblical History **TP:** 92, 127, 292
Troilus: 159, 288
Troy: 58, 60, 102
Troy Book (Lydgate): 81
Turville-Petre, Thorlac: 58, 91, 206

Two Ways **TW**: 310
Tyndale, William: 85
typology: 3, 14, 19, 21, 68, 77–79, 112, 172

Ullerston, Richard: 47
Unum ex Quattuor: 332, 333, 335

La Venjance de Nostre Seigneur: 229
Verbum abbreviatum (Peter the Chanter): 44
Victorines: 17, 18, 129
Victor of Capua: 206
Vincent of Beauvais: 37, 118, 160
Vindicta Salvatoris: 118, 229
Virgil (Maro): 31
Virgilius: 44, 86
Virtues of the Mass (Lydgate): 190
"Vision of St. John on the Sorrows of the Virgin": 275
Vita Adae et Evae: 121
Vita Christi (Ludolphus of Saxony): 288, 332, 334, 335
Vulgate. *See* Bible

Wace: 104, 106

Waldensians: 22, 27–30, 34–36, 42, 44, 45
Waldo, Peter (Pierre Valdus): 27, 33
Walter (dedicatee of *Ormulum*): 74, 75
Watson, Nicholas: 25, 26, 39, 43, 57
Wenzel, Siegfried: 24–26
Westminster: 154
West Saxon Gospels: 7, 51
William de Risseby: 38
William of Malmesbury: 50
William of Shoreham: 125, 165, 175, 286
William the Bastard (the Conqueror): 106, 145
Wise Admonitions: Biblical Texts Paraphrased **WA**: 25, 92, 127–30
Wisdom of Solomon **WS**: 197, 198
Woman of Samaria **WomS**: 307, 308
Worcester: 49, 51, 52, 54,
Wyclif, John: 1, 2, 4, 11, 12, 19, 20, 25, 38, 39, 43, 85, 305, 319, 320, 331, 334, 336, 344, 353
—sermon cycle: 319, 320
Wynkyn de Worde: 98, 158, 284, 304, 313
Wyring: 59, 81

Ypokrephum: 203

JAMES H. MOREY is an associate professor of English at Emory University. He teaches Old and Middle English and is currently editing several works of Middle English biblical literature.

Illinois Medieval Studies

Book and Verse: A Guide to Middle English
    Biblical Literature *James H. Morey*
Medieval Lyric: Genres in Historical Context
    Edited by William D. Paden

ILLINOIS MEDIEVAL STUDIES IS A CONTINUATION

OF THE SERIES ILLINOIS MEDIEVAL MONOGRAPHS,

WHICH INCLUDED:

Celestina: Tragicomedia de Calisto y Melibea
    Fernando de Rojas, ed. Miguel Marciales
The *Nibelungenlied:* History and Interpretation
    Edward R. Haymes
The *Bugarštica:* A Bilingual Anthology of the Earliest Extant
    South Slavic Folk Narrative Song   *John S. Miletich*

Typeset in 10/13 New Baskerville
Designed by Copenhaver Cumpston
Composed by Tseng Information Systems, Inc.
for the University of Illinois Press
Manufactured by Thomson-Shore, Inc.

University of Illinois Press
1325 South Oak Street
Champaign, IL 61820-6903
www.press.uillinois.edu

Morey, James H., 1961-
Book and verse : a guide to
Middle English Biblical
literature